A
DICTIONARY
OF
PSYCHOTHERAPY

A
DICTIONARY
OF
PSYCHOTHERAPY

Sue Walrond-Skinner

ROUTLEDGE & KEGAN PAUL
London and New York

FOR DOROTHY LANGDALE-SMITH
who knows a lot about all this

Part of the proceeds from the sale of this book are
dedicated to those many people of the developing
world for whom daily living is a battle for physical
survival and for whom psychotherapy of any kind is
an irrelevant luxury.

First published in 1986
by Routledge & Kegan Paul plc
11 New Fetter Lane, London EC4P 4EE

Published in the USA by
Routledge & Kegan Paul Inc.
in association with Methuen Inc.
29 West 35th Street, New York, NY 10001

Set in Ehrhardt
by Columns, Reading
and printed in Great Britain
by T J Press (Padstow) Ltd
Padstow, Cornwall

Library of Congress Cataloging in Publication Data
Walrond-Skinner, Sue.
A dictionary of psychotherapy.
Includes bibliographies.
1. Psychotherapy – Dictionaries.   I. Title.
[DNLM: 1. Psychotherapy – encyclopedias.   WM 13 W221d]
RC475.7.W35   1986   616.89'14'0321   85-28267
British Library CIP data also available
ISBN 0-7100-9978-9

Contents

Preface

S. Lesse's (1981) editorial to the 35th edition of the *American Journal of Psychotherapy* (no. 4) produced some interesting figures regarding the information explosion of the twentieth century. He remarked that there are now more than 62,000 scientific journals in existence so that anyone who attempts research into even a highly limited field of enquiry – one aspect of psychotherapy for example – must scan hundreds of thousands of articles to obtain a reliable overview of the given field. In terms of human resources – time, effort and endurance – the task becomes one of mind-boggling proportions. We are faced with the relentless fact that the total volume of available printed information in the world now doubles every ten years and by the year 2000 it is likely to double *in just one year.*

In the field of psychotherapy there are now literally thousands of journals in existence, each producing articles several times a year, whilst the number of books produced in each sub-specialty of the field every year runs into many hundred. This dictionary can therefore only be classed as a modest offering within an already burgeoning growth area of encyclopaedia, compendia and word books, all attempting to bring some order to the field and offer some maps to guide the serious student of psychotherapy over a rough and uneven terrain. Its *raison d'être* stems from the rapidity with which our field has developed within the last ten years, making many excellent word books and dictionaries already out of date. Not only have a bewildering array of new therapies come on to the scene (since, for example, H.J. Eysenck's *Dictionary of Psychology* was published in 1972), but the usage of terms shifts subtly in the older psychotherapies as they are influenced by and seek to influence, in an implicit two-way dialectic, the changing social, political and intellectual context in which they are embedded. The private, specialised language of our profession grows and develops with a life of its own and new entrants need to be acquainted with the current usage of its terminology as well as the vertical connections with history and the lateral connections with terms currently used across the different areas of psychotherapy. It is mainly for these that this dictionary has been prepared but I hope too that experienced practitioners who specialise in one or two forms of treatment will be intrigued and enlightened, as I have been, with the different understanding that can be gained from considering how the same technique or concept is used by theorists and practitioners from a range of different approaches.

Many problems surround the compilation of this sort of book. Selection is the obvious first and I have no doubt been biased unconsciously in what I have chosen to include and what I have left out. Consciously I have wanted to ensure the inclusion of many new ideas, forms and interventions that do not figure in older dictionaries. This means that less space has been devoted to classical concepts from the behavioural and psychoanalytic approaches. In any case, I would expect there to be less need to be comprehensive in these areas although I have tried to be representative. I have wanted to include the most important aspects of behavioural and psychoanalytic theory and practice and whilst relying heavily on secondary material, I have returned as often as possible to the original sources and to the classic texts, new and old, in order to gain as accurate a picture as possible of the current use of the term. I have tried to refer to journal articles on each subject area published during the last five years as well as to primary source material, beginning in most cases with the original writer's early work.

This brings me to another problem. Terms are used differently and often polemically by different theorists and practitioners. Many definitions may be held of the same term – so how does one arrive at a statement which embodies its crucial meaning, without boiling down areas of difference into a false consensus? Commenting in 1958 on this problem in the preface to his *Comprehensive Dictionary of Psychological and Psychoanalytical Terms*, Horace English wrote: 'A particular art is required to phrase a definition that will represent, not just a single author's meaning, but the "centre of gravity" of a whole cluster' of individual meanings. I have sought to deal with this problem by treating the work more as an encyclopedia and less as a dictionary in the strict sense. Thus, although I do in the main attempt a definition for each term, I have tried to elaborate, in an article of varying length, on the *different* usages made of the concept. I have provided a short bibliography for most items, to guide the reader towards the most recent specialist texts which will help him or her to study the concept more fully. Where a topic is discussed by many different writers from widely different perspectives, I have used just a few examples from the method literature with which I have been most familiar or which has been most easily accessible to me.

Any book is a temptation to fly one's own idiosyncratic kites; to shape and bend the ideas of others to conform to one's own predilections. I have tried to avoid these pitfalls – though undoubtedly not altogether successfully. I have, I admit, 'censored' some types of interventions which I have stumbled across during the course of my researches, if they have seemed very short on supporting authorities other than their 'inventor's' enthusiasm, but I have included a range of ideas which practitioners from the more orthodox and long-established areas of the field are likely to find bizarre, distasteful or 'unprofessional'. Here I fall back on a lexicographical rationalisation and claim that it is the dictionary compiler's duty to include what *is* in existence rather than only what *ought* to be!

I considered calling the book a *Dictionary of the Psychotherapies* in the hope of bypassing the many wrangles about what does and what does not constitute psychotherapy. But 'mixedness and muddle' is part of the core identity of psychotherapy in the mid-1980s and psychotherapy should be regarded and rejoiced in as a plural noun rather than excused and tidied up. No doubt many will take issue with me as to what I have included and what I have left out. Purists would probably feel that this is a word book about *psychotherapeutic* interventions rather than psychotherapy proper, and even then they might quarrel with some of the inclusions!

I have made a particular point of studying the many previous compilations of psychotherapeutic terms, and to these and to the many major handbooks, reference books and glossaries that have already been produced, I bear a great debt. In the field of psychoanalysis I have drawn particularly from the following: English and English (1958), *Comprehensive Dictionary of Psychological and Psychoanalytic Terms*; Rycroft (1968), *A Critical Dictionary of Psychoanalysis*; and LaPlanche and Pontalis (1980), *The Language of Psychoanalysis*. In the behavioural field I have consulted in particular Eysenck, Arnold and Meili (1972), *Encyclopaedia of Psychology* and Wolman (1973), *Dictionary of Behavioral Science*. For many entries in the dictionary I have consulted an outstanding work of great importance to the whole field of psychotherapy, Wolman's 12-volume *International Encyclopaedia of Psychiatry, Psychology, Psychoanalysis and Neurology* (1977). I would commend this massive work to the reader along with the recently published English *Encyclopedic Dictionary of Psychology* (1983) edited by Harré and Lamb. For many ideas and comparisons I have relied upon some of the major handbooks in the field, in particular, the *Handbook of Psychotherapy and Behavior Change* edited by Garfield and Bergin (1978), and Gurman and Razin's *Effective Psychotherapy* (1977). Many other invaluable reference and source books are far too numerous to pay tribute to here. Zusne's (1975) source book of biographies, *Names in the History of Psychology*, was helpful in filling gaps in the short biographical entries on outstanding contributors to psychotherapy. I have followed usual practice and only included those who are dead.

My thanks are due to innumerable people who have helped me in many different ways during eighteen months of intensive work, to handle a vast amount of material in a short space of time. First, I am tremendously grateful for the opportunities afforded by the University of Bristol library and, latterly by the Bodleian Library, Oxford, and the library of the Tavistock Clinic, London. In particular I should like to thank the staff of the Inter-Library Loans Service at Bristol University, who have tracked down obscure items for me from libraries all over Britain. Without them it would have been impossible to obtain essential resources. My second debt is to all those experts I have consulted, both formally and informally, regarding different subject areas. Especially I would like to thank Dr Christopher Dare, Consultant Psychiatrist, the Bethlem Hospital and the Maudsley Hospital, London, who gave extensive advice on the psychoanalytic entries; Miss Sally Box, Principal Social Worker in the Adolescent Department of the Tavistock Clinic, London, who advised on the Kleinian entries; Dr Glin Bennet, Consultant Senior Lecturer in the Department of Mental Health, University of Bristol, who advised on the terms relating to Jungian psychotherapy; Dr Dougal McKay, Director of Psychological Services to the Bristol & Western Health Authority, who advised on behaviour therapy, the cognitive therapies and social learning approaches; Dr Andrew Treacher, Lecturer in Mental Health at the University of Bristol, who advised on personal construct theory, social influence theory, outcome studies and many of the entries relating to general psychology; and Mr Philip Kingston, Lecturer in the Department of Applied Social Studies, University of Bristol, who advised on the entries relating to family, marital and systems therapy. Two colleagues have made particular contributions to the specialist areas of psychological tests and philosophical concepts. Mr Peter Gardner, Principal Psychologist for the County of Avon, has contributed the entry under personality tests and assessment and many of the entries on psychological tests; and Mr David Watson, Lecturer in the Department of Social Administration, University of Bristol, has contributed much of the opening descriptions of the following entries: epistemology, causality, phenomenology, Cartesian and the theory of types. I am particularly grateful to Dr R.D. Hinshelwood for his comments on the manuscript as a whole and for his expert help with the psychoanalytic entries, to Dr Malcolm Pines for his help with entries relating to group psychotherapy and to Mr Andrew Samuels for his assistance with entries relating to analytical psychology. Any errors that remain in the text are of course my own.

I would also like to thank all the many friends and colleagues who have loaned, advised about or given me books and articles from their own libraries. Next, I would like to thank Mrs Sheila Salisbury for typing and word-processing the manuscript with exceptional care and for taking such an interest in it, Philippa Brewster, editor at Routledge & Kegan Paul, for keeping me sane in the early days with regular doses of encouragement, and Elizabeth Taylor for her detailed work on the typescript. And finally, all my friends whom I mainly deserted for a whole year and especially Di, who put up with it all and only complained when *every* room in the house was covered with papers and books.

A

A-historical

Approaches to psychotherapy which de-emphasise the use of the patient's history in either *diagnosis* or treatment or both. Most therapies which are described as a-historical use the term relatively, since some form of *history taking* is often found helpful even though perhaps not at the beginning of contact with the patient. The term is used to distinguish those psychotherapies (*psychoanalysis* and the *depth psychologies*) which connect the patient's psychopathology with the past and especially with his early experiences of infancy; and those therapies which focus on the *presenting problem* (*behaviour therapy*) and on the here and now events of current interaction with the therapist and with his significant others.

The distinction is quite hard to maintain since *analysts* would argue that the analysis of the *transference* and the focus on the patient's *free associations* are both here and now emphases; and Jungians would want to claim a future-directed, teleological aspect to their therapy which supersedes in importance the historical exploration. However, these cannot be described as a-historical in the same way since the purpose of both is to link the present with the patient's past and to enable him to gain *insight* into the way he is impeded by its influence. *Systemic therapies* such as *family therapy* tend to be a-historical as they afford opportunities for exploring the 'horizontal' network of current relationships *in vivo* which tends to reduce the need to examine 'vertical' networks of past relationships. This would not, however, be true of transgenerational family therapy or *psychoanalytic family therapy*. Some forms of *strategic therapy*, *brief therapy* and *crisis intervention* are almost entirely a-historical, the best example being brief symptom-focused therapy. Cooklin (1982) discusses some of the issues involved in comparing historical with a-historical approaches to the treatment of *systems*. Any discussion of the two is inevitably value-laden, as those who advocate an a-historical approach are often concerned to move away from what they perceive as the deterministic framework of history, whilst those who underline the need for using the patient's historical context are anxious to establish the logical and scientific status of a deductively derived theory of change.

COOKLIN, A. (1982) Change in 'here and now' systems vs systems over time (in Bentovim, A., Gorell-Barnes, G. and Cookling, A. (eds), *Family Therapy: Complementary Frameworks of Theory and Practice*, Academic Press, London.)

See also *Behavioural analysis, Phenotype*.

A-symptomatic

Having no *symptoms*.

Abraham, Karl (1877-1925)

One of Freud's earliest and most senior collaborators, Abraham holds a foremost place in the history of *psychoanalysis*. Born in Bremen of Jewish parents, he studied medicine at Freiburg and later joined the Vienna Psychoanalytic Circle along with Jung, Adler, Ferenczi and others. In 1910, he founded the Berlin Institute which became one of the foremost psychoanalytic training institutes. Abraham was one of Freud's most stalwart supporters and the two men engaged in regular correspondence over theoretical and technical issues. He took an active part in trying to keep Freud's circle free of 'dissent', although Freud expressed concern at Abraham's zeal, pointing out that it was easier for Abraham than for Jung, 'because of racial kinship', to remain consistent in his acceptance of Freud's work. Abraham made important contributions to the theory of psycho-sexual development, subdividing the *oral stage* into oral-dependent and oral-aggressive; and the *anal stage* into anal-eliminative and anal-retentive. He had a considerable influence on many psychoanalysts whom he analysed himself at the Berlin Institute, including Hélène Deutsch, Karen Horney and Melanie Klein. He died in

Berlin of a lung complaint in 1925, leaving his major works to be collected together in 1948 and published as 'Selected papers on psychoanalysis'. His daughter, Hilde, became a well-known analyst in London.

Abreaction

The release of emotional energy which occurs either spontaneously or during the course of psychotherapy and which produces *catharsis*. Spontaneous abreaction usually occurs soon after a traumatic event and this has the effect of mobilising the individual's *coping behaviour* and hastening his re-adaptation to the new situation. If spontaneous abreaction does not occur, the affect attached to the memory of the loss is *repressed* and is likely to produce *symptoms* of depression, withdrawal or other neurotic presentations. The term was introduced by Breuer and Freud (1893) to describe the release of emotion attached to a previously repressed experience, and abreaction is still considered to be an important element in the therapeutic process not only within psychoanalytic therapies but also among many forms of *group psychotherapy*, *encounter groups*, *Gestalt therapy* and those therapies that make use of *psychodrama* and re-enactment to help the patient integrate repressed material.

Not all abreaction leads to catharsis however, and sometimes the patient may be left worse off than before following an abreaction. The therapeutic inducement of abreaction needs to take place in a protected setting with the safeguards that the therapeutic relationships can afford. Barber (1969) has discussed its use in hypnosis, and Wolpe (1973), in *behaviour therapy*. Wolpe suggests that the therapeutic effects obtained during abreaction might be a special case of the *non-specific factors* that operate in a proportion of cases receiving any form of psychotherapy.

BARBER, T. X. (1969), *Hypnosis: A Scientific Approach* (Van Nostrand, Reinhold & Company, New York).
BREUER, J. and FREUD, S. (1893), 'On the psychical mechanism of hysterical phenomena: preliminary communication' (in Studies on Hysteria, *Standard Edition of the Complete Psychological Works of Sigmund Freud*, vol. 2, Hogarth Press, London).
JUNG, C. G. (1928), 'The therapeutic value of abreaction' (*Collected Works*, vol. 16, Routledge & Kegan Paul, London).
WOLPE, J. (1973), *The Practice of Behaviour Therapy* (Pergamon Press, New York).

See also *Trauma*.

Absent member manoeuvre

A form of *resistance* identified by Sonne *et al.* (1962) in the context of *family therapy*. A key member of the family absents himself either from the first session so that treatment cannot begin or during a critical phase later on in the treatment process. Family therapists vary in their response. Some refuse to see the family if the key member is absent; others prefer to work with the resistance, using it as a means of understanding the roles taken by individuals and the way in which *coalitions* and *alliances* are formed.

SONNE, J. *et al.* (1962), 'The absent member manoeuvres as a resistance in family therapy of schizophrenia' (*Family Process*, vol. 1, pp. 44-672).

See also *Folie à deux*.

Acceptance

A quality believed to be necessary for a therapist to display in relation to the client, in order to promote effective psychotherapy. Van der Veen (1970) defines acceptance as 'valuing or prizing all aspects of the client including the parts that are hateful to himself or appear wrong in the eyes of society'. Used interchangeably with *unconditional positive regard* by *client-centred therapists*, the concept of acceptance enables the therapist to distinguish between the client's self and his behaviour – a distinction which other schools of therapy, for example *behaviour therapy*, would find difficult to sustain. Acceptance involves the recognition by the therapist of the client's worth without necessarily implying either approval of his behaviour, or an emotional attachment on the part of the therapist.

VAN DER VEEN, F. (1970), 'Client perception of therapist conditions as a factor in psychotherapy' (in Hart, J. T. and Tomlinson, T. M. (eds), *New Dimensions in Client Centred Therapy*, Houghton Mifflin, Boston).

See also *Accommodation, Core conditions, Empathy, Joining, Non-specific factors, Relationship factors*.

Accommodation

Term used to describe the need for the therapist to adapt and harmonise his *style* and techniques with each particular family or client. The term is used mainly in the context of *family therapy* but the process is relevant to all modalities and is fundamental to the creation of a *therapeutic alliance*. The therapist responds to this need by developing *joining* techniques and creating the *core conditions* of the treatment process. Both these enable him to move from a position of accommodation to a position of challenge, promoting change, *insight* and the acquisition of new skills for *problem solving interventions*. In the context of family therapy, accommodation lays the groundwork and makes possible the restructuring interventions by which the family system begins to change.

MINUCHIN, S. (1974), *Families and Family Therapy* (Tavistock, London).

Accreditation

See *Regulation (of psychotherapists)*.

Ackerman, Nathan Ward (1908-1971)

Pioneer of *family therapy*, Ackerman was born into a Jewish family in Bessarabia. He was one of five children that survived infancy, the family emigrating to the United States in 1912. He studied medicine at Columbia University, New York, and later psychiatry. Between 1937 and 1942 he was a candidate at the New York Psychoanalytic Institute, working simultaneously as a psychiatrist for the Jewish Board of Guardians. In 1937 he married Gwendolyn Hill and they had two daughters. He became a member of the American Psychoanalytic Association in 1943, but in 1955 he helped found the American Academy of Psychoanalysis which became a principal alternative organisation for those who refused to confine *psychoanalysis* to being a medical speciality. His approach to psychoanalysis was unorthodox and creative and although he retained his links with, and use of, psychoanalytic theory throughout his life, his appreciation of the wider social and cultural determinants of psychological disturbance began to lead him towards the treatment of the family as a group. In 1960 he founded the Family Institute, New York, and from then on he specialised in the practice and teaching of family therapy. In the same year, he co-founded, with Don Jackson, the journal *Family Process*, which remains the foremost family therapy journal in the world. He left behind a huge legacy of books and articles and also film material of his clinical work. His best-known books are *The Psychodynamics of Family Life* (1958) and *Treating the Troubled Family* (1966).

Acting in

Term sometimes used as a contrast to *acting out* to denote an intermediate form of expression, which lies midway between acting out on the one hand and verbalisation on the other. Body postures, facial expressions and the patient's whole repertoire of *non-verbal communication*, adopted during the therapeutic session, is thus described as acting in. The term is also used to describe *any* behaviour that occurs *within* the therapeutic session (as a substitute for the work of verbalising *repressed* material), as contrasted with that which occurs *outside* the session.

DEUTSCH, F. (1947), 'Analysis of postural behaviour' (*Psychoanalytic Quarterly*, vol. 16, pp. 195-213).
MAHL, G. F. (1967), 'Some clinical observations on non-verbal behaviour in interviews' (*J. of Nervous and Mental Diseases*, vol. 144, pp. 492-505).

Acting out

The making *conscious* of *unconscious* impulses and conflicts through action. Freud

3

(1940) used the term in the context of psycho-analytic treatment and in relation to the *transference*, suggesting that the patient 'acts it before us, as it were, instead of reporting it to us'. Freud (1914) had already used the term in contrast to remembering, to mean the compelling urge to repeat the forgotten past and then relive it in the analytic situation. In *psychoanalysis* the term is used to refer to all those actions which take place, both within the therapeutic session or outside, which relate to the breaking through into behaviour of repressed material from the past. Acting out may be manifested by aggressive or sexual responses, directed either towards the therapist or to others. In psychoanalytic treatments, acting out is viewed as a hindrance and a *resistance* since it acts as a substitute for words and prevents the patient from gaining *insight* into his feelings and behaviour. Techniques for its management include *containment*, *interpretation*, prohibition and efforts to increase the patient's *ego strengths*. Sandler *et al.* (1970) point out that the term is now used in two main ways: first, in Freud's original sense, and second, to describe habitual modes of behaviour which flow from the patient's personality structure rather than from the treatment process. The term is also used in contrast to *acting in*.

Many therapeutic approaches encourage modified forms of acting out through the medium of *action techniques*, and in these methods, insight is believed to be gained through engaging the body in symbolic behavioural acts which can afterwards be expressed in words.

ABT, L. E. and WEISMAN, S. L. (1965), *Acting out – Theoretical and Clinical Aspects* (Grune & Stratton, New York).
FREUD, S. (1914), 'Remembering, repeating and working through' (*Standard Edition*, vol. 12, Hogarth Press, London).
FREUD, S. (1940), 'An outline of psycho-analysis' (*Standard Edition*, vol. 23, Hogarth Press, London).
GADDINI, E. (1982), 'Acting out in the psychoanalytic session' (*Int. J. of Psychoanalysis*, vol. 63, pp. 57–64).

JOHNSON, A. M. and SZUREK, S. A. (1952), 'The genesis of anti-social acting out in children and adolescents' (*Psychoanalytic Quarterly*, vol. 21, p. 323).
NETS, B. B. (1973), 'Acting out in psycho-therapeutic groups' (*Group Analysis*, vol. 6, pp. 12-17).
SANDLER, J. *et al.* (1970), 'Basic psychoanalytic concepts: acting out' (*Brit. J. of Psychiatry*, vol. 117, p. 329).
SCHWARTZ, L. and SCHWARTZ, R. (1971), 'Therapeutic acting out' (*Psychotherapy: Theory, Research and Practice*, vol. 8, pp. 205-7).

Action techniques
All those techniques which rely primarily on movement, bodily expression or *non-verbal communication*. They may also make use of words alongside the action, but their potency resides in their non-verbal aspect. Examples are *play therapy, psychodrama, family sculpting, role play, music therapy, art therapy, dance therapy*, etc. Many techniques which rely primarily on a verbal interchange with the client nevertheless often use action techniques in addition drawn from a variety of sources. For example, the use of charts, drawings and *diagrams* such as the *genogram, sociogram, lifespace* drawing, and the use of *relaxation* exercises in *systematic desensitisation*. The efficacy of action techniques stems from their use of *analogic communication* and their recognition of the importance of the analogic mode in describing and understanding relationships.

Active analysis
A technique introduced by Stekel to reduce *resistance* and shorten the duration of *psychoanalysis*. Stekel believed that Freud had exaggerated the importance of the *unconscious*. He suggested that many of the patient's conflicts lie instead within the realm of consciousness, and that the patient chooses not to deal with them. Resistance is therefore seen as a defence against the treatment, which the analyst must overcome by 'attacking the patient's system by storm'. Stekel advocated giving *advice*, treating *symptoms*, using frequent *confrontation* and *interpretations* and suggesting lines along which the patient might profitably develop *free association*. Originally a devoted

pupil of Freud, Stekel later broke away and developed his own theories through a prodigious literary output.

STEKEL, W. (1950), *The Autiobiography of Wilhelm Stekel: The Life History of a Pioneer Psychoanalyst* (Liveright Publishing Company, New York).
STEKEL, W. (1950), *Technique of Analytical Psychotherapy* (Liveright Publishing Company, New York).

Active technique

An approach to *psychoanalysis* introduced by Ferenczi. It took two contrasting forms. Originally Ferenczi suggested privation, whereby the patient was encouraged to reduce all sources of gratification outside the analytic experience, so as to make all libidinal energy available to the therapeutic process and hasten the overcoming of *resistance*. Later, however, he suggested that the *analyst* should offer love to the patient and that the 'indispensable healing power [lying in] the therapeutic gift of love' (De Forest, 1954) should be the chief tool of treatment. In other words, far from adopting *neutrality* and using *interpretations* as the main form of therapeutic activity, the analyst's task is to provide the patient with a form of *corrective emotional experience* with the analyst. The first approach arose out of Freud's concept of abstinence but the second was directly opposed to many of the basic assumptions of Freudian psychoanalytic method and Freud made his disapproval clear. A break between Freud and Ferenczi was avoided, however, probably because of Ferenczi's early death in 1933.

DE FOREST, I. (1954), *The Haven of Love* (London).
FERENCZI, S. (1920), 'Further development of an active technique in psychoanalysis' (in *Further Contributions to the Therapy and Technique of Psychoanalysis*, Hogarth Press, London).
FERENCZI, S. (1955), *Final Contributions to the Problems and Methods of Psychoanalysis* (Hogarth Press, London).

Actualising therapy

A form of humanistic therapy designed to help an individual become aware of his core conflicts, engage with them and use the energy which is thus released for creative living. It developed as a synthesis of ideas derived from Maslow's (1954) *self-actualisation* and the writings of other *humanistic psychologists* such as Carl Rogers, Rollo May, Alexander Lowen and Victor Frankl. Like *client-centred therapy*, this approach relies heavily on the belief that human beings possess an innate tendency towards self-realisation or self-actualisation. This approach is therefore subject to the same criticisms, because of its underlying assumptions, as client-centred therapy and other humanistic therapies.

Like other humanistic approaches, actualising therapy emphasises the need to help the *client* to develop his full potential by overcoming core conflicts, developing an awareness of feelings and the ability to express them, accepting one's weaknesses and limitations, and discovering meaning and purpose in life. The polarities of anger-love and strength-weakness are viewed as basic to developing a fully actualised personality. The approach is concerned with the growth and development of the whole personality, not with the cure of a disease or the solution to an immediate *presenting problem*. The subject of the therapy is called the client.

Actualising therapy can be used in the one-to-one relationship or in a group and the two are often combined. Techniques used in therapy include the *reflection* of the client's experience and feeling back to him; the therapist's *self-disclosure*; *interpretation*; exercises to get in touch with feelings through body work; and the *clarification* of values. *Action techniques* are used such as *role play* and *role reversal*; breathing exercises; the release of aggression and the experience of love and care through touch. Actualising therapy is useful mainly with mildly disturbed, neurotic clients or individuals who feel the need to develop different aspects of their personality. Actualising tendencies are measurable using the *Personal Orientation Inventory* (Shostrom,

1963) developed by Maslow and Shostrom, and the Actualising Assessment Battery (Shostrom, 1976).

BRAMMER, L. M. and SHOSTROM, E. L. (1977), *Therapeutic Psychology: Fundamentals of Actualising Counseling and Therapy* (3rd edn, Prentice-Hall, Englewood Cliffs, New Jersey).
MASLOW, A. H. (1954), *Motivation and Personality* (Harper & Row, New York).
SHOSTROM, E. L. (1963), *Personal Orientation Inventory* (Edits, San Diego).
SHOSTROM, E. L. (1976), *Actualising Assessment Battery* (Edits, San Diego).
SHOSTROM, E. L. (1976), *Actualising Therapy: Foundations for a Scientific Ethic* (Edits, San Diego).

Adaptability
See *Morphogenesis*.

Adler, Alfred (1870-1937)

Founder of *individual psychology*, Adler was born in Vienna and was one of six children of Hungarian-Jewish parents. He studied at the Viennese College of Medicine and in 1902 joined the Vienna Psychoanalytic Circle founded by Freud. He broke with Freud in 1911, to develop his own approach to *psychoanalysis*. In 1897, he married Raissa, the politically sophisticated daughter of a Russian merchant, and out of his relationship with her grew his interest in socialism and in Marxist ideas. He was also influenced by her in his views on the importance of sexual equality. In 1913 Adler founded the Society of Individual Psychology, a name which, considering the social and relational emphasis of Adler's thinking, seems somewhat inappropriate. He founded several child guidance clinics and took a great interest in the education of children, lecturing once a fortnight to parents and teachers in different schools for many years. Adler held a variety of teaching appointments in Europe and the United States and continued his analytic practice and interest in the education and treatment of children alongside his teaching and writing. His own experiences of feeling inferior and of having to carve out his own identity in a large family when a child contributed to the formation of his view that the experience of powerlessness, not sexuality, was at the root of neurotic disturbance. Adler died whilst on a lecture tour in Scotland in 1937, leaving behind a considerable literary output. His most important books include *The Practice and Theory of Individual Psychology* (1924), *Understanding Human Nature* (1927), and *Social Interest: A Challenge to Mankind* (1933). Although Adler remained committed to the treatment of individuals, many of his ideas foreshadowed the development of social and interpersonal approaches to psychotherapy.

Adlerian therapy
See *Individual psychology*.

Advice

Opinion offered by the therapist to the client as to the action or direction he should take. Advice is considered to be inappropriate in the *psychoanalytic* and *non-directive* therapies. Freud (1917), for example, was clear that 'advice and guidance in the affairs of life plays no part in psychoanalysis' except in the case of the very young or with particularly disturbed or helpless individuals. Generally speaking, the humanistic approaches and all those methods which are concerned with the 'whole' person and thus with growth in all areas of the client's life try to avoid advice giving. By contrast, the directive therapies, such as *behaviour therapy*, *cognitive therapy*, *strategic therapy*, *crisis intervention* and *brief therapy*, rely heavily on advice giving of a particular kind, though it is clearly different from the lay meaning of the term. In these methods, which are all focused on specific and restricted aspects of the client's life, the advice offered relates to the problems being examined in therapy. Moreover, it is directed more to the means of achieving the therapeutic *goals* than to the goals themselves. For example, instructions will be given regarding practice exercises, *homework assignments* and other *tasks* to be accomplished inside or between sessions but not about major decisions such as the choice of a job, a partner, children, etc. An exception to this is to be found in crisis intervention and some of the brief therapies, when the worker may take over the management of the client's life for a brief period while the client is not capable of doing so for himself or herself. Thus a further distinction can be made between advice about how the client's life should be lived and instructions concerning the client's therapy.

FREUD, S. (1917), 'Mourning and melancholia' (*Standard Edition*, vol. 14, Hogarth Press, London).

Affiliation

Literally from the Latin 'affiare' meaning 'to adopt a son'. The process whereby an *alliance* is created between one or more members of a family or group which may or may not include the therapist. Affiliative behaviour stems from early attachment behaviour between the infant and its mother (see *Attachment theory*). Affiliation may have the effect of both increasing *cohesion* between those members included in the alliance and encouraging a *coalition* against those who are not. Referring to *stranger groups*, Kellerman (1981) points out that 'affiliation in the group implies that a set of expectations on that affiliation has been met' and that members who make an affiliation have concurred with basic group attitudes. Thus, as Yalom (1970) comments, group cohesion and affiliation are very closely intertwined.

The effect of an affiliation is determined by its *context* and by the roles taken by those who are making the affiliation. For example, the pairing affiliation in a group may have the effect of mobilising *basic assumption behaviour* and stultifying the performance of the group task. Affiliations that take place across generations in a family are usually *dysfunctional* if they create a coalition against other members, though an exception to this would usually be an affiliation made between a single parent and *parental child*. On the other hand, affiliations made within natural *sub-systems* in the family strengthen the cohesion of the family group. The family and group therapist can use affilia-

tion as an *unbalancing* technique in his work with *systems*. Affiliation is always an essential part of the *joining* process.

KELLERMAN, H. (1981), 'The deep structures of group cohesion' (in *Group Cohesion*, Grune & Stratton, New York).
MINUCHIN, S. and FISHMAN, H. C. (1981), *Family Therapy Techniques* (Harvard University Press, Cambridge, Mass.).
SCHACHTER, S. (1959), *The Psychology of Affiliation* (Stanford University Press, Stanford, Calif.).
YALOM. I. D. (1970), *The Theory and Practice of Group Psychotherapy* (Basic Books, New York).

See also *Triangulation*.

After education

Term used by Freud (1940) to describe the way in which the *analyst* helps the patient to move from his underlying childish attitudes towards the analyst to more mature ones. Freud suggests that the whole healing process of *psychoanalysis* involves the patient putting the analyst in the place of his father or mother and thus giving him the power which his *superego* exercises over his *ego*. 'The new superego now has an opportunity for a sort of after education of the neurotic; it can correct blunders for which his parental education was to blame.' The process enables the patient to gain a less distorted view of others and a more realistic, mature view of the self.

FREUD, S. (1940), 'An outline of psychoanalysis' (*Standard Edition*, vol. 23, Hogarth Press, London).

See also *Corrective emotional experience, Transference*.

Agency

The term is used in two ways. First, in psychoanalytic terminology, it is used to describe the three structures of the *psyche* – the *ego*, the *id* and the *superego*. Second, it refers to the setting in which psychotherapeutic work is carried out, for example, hospital, clinic, residential home, school, social work department, or general practice. The setting surrounds the psychotherapeutic treatment with particular opportunities and limitations.

Alexander, Franz Gabriel (1891-1964)

An important figure in the field of *psychoanalysis*, Alexander was born in Budapest, the youngest child following three sisters. Following his father, he studied first philosophy and then later medicine at the University of Budapest. In 1913 he was appointed to the Hygiene Institute of Budapest and after the outbreak of the First World War he became a military physician. In 1919 he went to study psychoanalysis at the new Berlin Psychoanalytic Institute, receiving his personal analysis from Hans Sachs. He became an assistant at the Institute and began a series of important contributions to the literature. In 1929 he was appointed the first ever professor of psychoanalysis at the University of Chicago's new Department of Medicine. In 1931 he founded the Chicago Psychoanalytic Society and became its first director, remaining there for the next twenty-four years. By then he had produced important studies of the personality and applications of psychoanalytic theory to criminality. He had a major interest in psychosomatic medicines and founded a journal by the same name. In 1946 his most important work was published, *Psychoanalytic Therapy*, in which he developed his ideas regarding the importance of the *corrective emotional experience* within analytic therapy and the possibility of using briefer approaches to psychoanalysis. It was greeted by a storm of protest and he left Chicago for California, taking a professorship at the University of Southern California. His last published work was *The Scope of Psychoanalysis*.

Alexander technique

A physical and psychological approach to developing improved body/mind integration. The technique was introduced by an Australian, Frederick Mathias Alexander. It focuses on the reduction of stress and rigidity in the muscles and aims at breaking down the blocks that originate in emotional and psychological problems and get expressed in bodily rigidity, tension and pain. *Relaxation* guidance on posture and use of the body are the basic techniques used. Barlow (1973) suggests that the Alexander technique is a useful adjunct to psychotherapy with depressed and narcissistic patients since better control and use of the body increases self-confidence and self-esteem and lessens the need to manipulate others or to turn aggression against the self.

ALEXANDER, F. M. (1932), *The Use of The Self* (Dutton, New York).
BARLOW, W. (1973), *The Alexander Technique* (Knopf, New York).
JONES, S. P. (1976), *Body Awareness in Action* (Schocken Books, New York).

See also *Autogenic training, Body therapies, Character armour, Meditation, Reichian therapy.*

Algorithm

A problem solving device that enables a sequence of operations to be undertaken in a step-by-step progression, the next step in the sequence being made dependent on the result of the previous one. Algorithms are a relatively new introduction within the therapeutic field. They enable clinical material to be processed in a systematic way by breaking down complex procedures into their component parts; placing these units in their appropriate sequence; expressing the units in the form of questions and/or statements and linking the units by using yes/no answers to the questions to indicate how to proceed with the material. Algorithms are being used more frequently for matching *diagnosis* and treatment approach; and in *training*. Orsolitis and Murray (1982) discuss the use of an algorithm in a psychiatric emergency unit for the treatment of depression and Blechman (1981) presents an algorithm for matching families and behavioural child-related interventions.

BLECHMAN, E. A. (1981), 'Toward comprehensive behavioral family intervention: an algorithm for matching families and interventions' (*Behavior Modification*, vol. 5, pp. 221-37).
ORSOLITIS, M. and MURRAY, M. (1982), 'A depression algorithm for psychiatric emergen-

cies' (*J. of Psychiatric Treatment and Evaluation*, vol. 4, pp. 137-42).

Alienation

Alienation is an important theme in Fromm's writings. Deriving the concept from Marx, Fromm contrasts alienation with the ability to relate to others and to the natural world and hence to find meaning. The term is also used by Erikson and by *existential psychotherapists* to signify the patient's core problem of meaninglessness which has to be overcome.

FROMM, E. (1974), *The Art of Loving* (Harper & Row, New York).

FROMM, E. (1978), *Anatomy of Human Destructiveness* (Fawcett, New York).

Alignment

See *Pseudohostility, Pseudomutuality*.

Alliance

The product of an *affiliation* between two or more members of a family or *stranger group* which may or may not include the therapist. Alternatively, an alliance may be created by the therapist with one or more members of the family or group. An alliance is made for the positive purpose of engaging in a mutual task or sharing common interests and in this sense should be distinguished from a *coalition*. Examining the alliances that exist in a family group or other natural *network* is an essential part of the *diagnosis* in systems therapy; and the strengthening or weakening of *functional* or *dysfunctional* alliances is an important part of the treatment process. Since alliances build up *cohesion* they are usually functional, except when they create a coalition against outsiders to the alliance; or when they lead to fusion or *symbiosis* so that growth and change between members of the alliance is stultified. Both sorts of pathological alliance occur as a defence against threat from the outside or the inside, through, for example, a developmental *crisis*. The therapist's task is to strengthen functional alliances within *sub-systems* (between marital partners or siblings) and to weaken those that create coalitions against others or lead to symbiosis.

See also *Collusion, Therapeutic alliance*.

Allport, Gordon (1897-1967)

Founder of a humanistic approach to therapy, Allport was one of the '*third force*' psychologists, along with Rogers, Maslow and Goldstein. He was born in Indiana and studied psychology at Harvard University. His personality theory emphasised the place of traits and the part played by both physiological and psychological processes in the development of personality. He described the unifying core of the personality as the proprium, equivalent to the *ego* or self, and he viewed propriate striving as all those forms of behaviour by which the individual tries to gain *self-actualisation*. After his studies at Harvard, he travelled in Europe and was greatly influenced by the German psychologist, William Stern. In 1925, he married Ada, and had one son. After teaching social psychology and personality theory at Dartmouth, he returned to Harvard in 1930 and remained there until his death in 1967. Allport was interested in social issues and he retained a strong interest in social psychology, editing the *Journal of Abnormal and Social Psychology* for many years. In 1939 he became president of the American Psychological Association. His literary output was not great, but his major theoretical ideas were set out in *Personality: A Psychological Interpretation* (1937), *The Nature of Personality: Selected Papers* (1950), *Becoming* (1955), and *Personality and Social Encounter* (1960).

Alter ego

See *Doubling*.

Ambience

The setting in which psychotherapy takes place. Winnicott (1958) suggests that the therapist should provide a 'holding environment', free from interruption, which allows the therapist to concentrate on what the patient is saying and the patient to relax and think about himself. Frank (1978) describes ambience as the provision of 'the aura of a healing temple'. Privacy, structure, consistency and appropriate material circumstances all contribute to the provision of a setting which is conducive to

9

the execution of the therapeutic task. Specific forms of therapy have additional requirements, for example, sufficient comfortable chairs and space for family or group treatments; access to play material if children are involved; and to audio visual equipment if this is part of the therapeutic method. The need to create the right ambience also affects the choice of whether therapy should take place in the therapist's office or in the patient's/family's home.

CARPELAN, H. (1981), 'On the importance of the setting in the psychoanalytic situation' (*Scandinavian Psychoanalytic Review*, vol. 14, pp. 151-60).
FRANK, J. (1978), *Psychotherapy and the Human Predicament* (Schocken Books, New York).
WINNICOTT, D. W. (1958), *Collected Works* (Hogarth Press, London).

Ambivalence

The co-existence of opposing feelings or attitudes towards a person or situation. Freud (1905), in his discussion of infantile sexuality, attributed the term to Bleuler and used it to describe the way in which 'opposing pairs of instincts are developed to an approximately equal extent'. Freud, and the psychoanalytic tradition generally, uses the term to describe the holding of opposite *feelings* towards the same *object*, usually the feelings of love and hate (Suttie, 1935). It is used to describe the opposing experience of negative and positive *transference* towards the *analyst* and also the way in which the individual handles conflict engendered by other people, notably by the parents during infancy. For the *Kleinian school*, the concept is central. First experienced acutely during the *paranoid-schizoid position*, the infant splits the two feelings by projecting them on to 'good' and 'bad' objects. During the integrative phase of the *depressive* position he 'realises more clearly that it is the same person – himself – who loves and hates the same person – his mother' (Segal, 1973). It is generally agreed amongst psychotherapists that strongly experienced positive emotion contains within it an opposing negative.

Bleuler seems to have used the term orginally in a much less restrictive sense to describe ambivalence of the will and intellectual ambivalence as well as the current psychoanalytic meaning of ambivalence of impulses and emotions. This broader definition foreshadows some behavioural concepts such as the *approach-avoidance conflict* and *cognitive dissonance*. Thus the broader definition of ambivalence, to mean a conflict of the affective, behavioural or cognitive experience of the individual or group, is a useful extension within the broad range of psychotherapies.

FREUD, S. (1905), 'Three essays on the theories of sexuality' (*Standard Edition*, vol. 7, Hogarth Press, London).
HOLDER, A. (1975), 'Theoretical and clinical aspects of ambivalence' (*Psychoanalytic Study of the Child*, vol. 30, pp. 197-220).
SEGAL, H. (1973), *Introduction to the Work of Melanie Klein* (Hogarth Press, London).
SUTTIE, I. (1935), *The Origins of Love and Hate* (Penguin Books, Harmondsworth).

See also *Repression, Resistance*.

Anal stage

The second psychosexual stage of human development occurring between the ages of about 2 and 4 years and lying between the *oral stage* and the *phallic stage*. Freud (1905) first described the anal stage, whereby the anus acts as an *erogenous zone* by which sensual pleasure can be experienced and a relationship with the outside world conducted. Freud suggested that polarisaton of activity and passivity are marked features of this stage, shown by the instinct of mastery and acceptance. Abraham (1924) subdivided the anal stage into anal-eliminative, characterised by destructive and sadistic feelings, and anal-retentive, characterised by the desire to possess and control. Because of the importance attached to *object relations* by Melanie Klein in the very earliest years, she followed Freud in seeing these two subdivisions as important prototypes for the *ambivalence* which the child and adult expresses towards *objects* in later life. This, in Klein's view, increases the pre-existing oral tendency to split them into 'good' and 'bad'. Klein adds the urethral impulses, characterised by burning or drowning attacks.

In his analysis of the eight developmental stages of man, Erikson (1950) suggests that the anal stage is characterised by the growth of autonomy leading to the will to be oneself. If this stage is not satisfactorily accomplished, the child experiences shame and self-doubt. Erikson views the establishment of law and order as the societal concomitant of the anal stage. Developmentally, the infant is concerned with the mastery of his own body sphincters and the socialisation of the impulses connected with them. Freud (1908) suggested that orderliness, parsimony and obstinacy were the noteworthy characteristics of a person *fixated* at the anal stage, and these comprised the obsessional character. He further suggested (1917) that symbolic meanings of giving and withholding are developed at the anal stage so that faeces are viewed as a gift to the mother which in later life is equated with the giving and receiving of money. Farrell (1981) and others have criticised Freud's understanding of the erotic nature of the anal stage and also the cultural and social extrapolations made by Erikson.

ABRAHAM, K. (1924), 'A short study of the development of libido as viewed in the light of mental disorders' (in *Selected Papers*, Hogarth Press, London).
ERIKSON, E. H. (1950), *Childhood and Society* (Penguin Books, Harmondsworth).
FARRELL, B. A. (1981), *The Standing of Psychoanalysis* (Oxford University Press, Oxford).
FREUD, S. (1905), 'Three essays on the theory of sexuality' (*Standard Edition*, vol. 7, Hogarth Press, London).
FREUD, S. (1908), 'Character and oral eroticism' (*Standard Edition*, vol. 9, Hogarth Press, London).
FREUD, S. (1917), 'On the transformation of instinct as exemplified in anal eroticism' (*Standard Edition*, vol. 17, Hogarth Press, London).

See also *Stages of development*.

Analogic

A form of *communication* which depends on the use of analogues to describe what is to be represented. The analogue means that which is represented (for example, a picture of a horse), unlike the *digital* mode where the word horse acts as a symbol to express what is meant. Used in contrast to digital communication, the concept is derived from two models: first, the biological model of the humoral system, whereby discrete quantities of specific substances are released into the body; and second, the cybernetic model of the analogue computer, whereby data is manipulated in the form of discrete positive magnitudes. Analogic communication is the non-verbal accompaniment of speech, and takes the form of gestures, facial expression, non-verbal phonations, body posture, voice inflection and the rhythm and tone of the words themselves.

Analogic communication is considered by communication theorists to convey the 'relational aspect' of communication as distinct from the 'content' that is conveyed by the digital mode. It provides the rich, primitive means of conveying the emotional, affective and contextual aspects of the relationship in which verbal communications are embedded. It suffers from a lack of exactitude and is often ambiguous and illogical, with one sign being used to express several different meanings. Its characteristics therefore reflect the qualities of the *primary process* of the *id* and the *unconscious* both in terms of its lack of order and refinement and its potential for rich expressiveness and creativity. Communication problems arise between individuals because human beings make use of both communication modes simultaneously and therefore the need for translation between the two modes has to be addressed. Problems of compatibility between digital and analogue communication are discussed under *Communication*.

BATESON, G. (1955), 'A theory of play and fantasy' (*Psychiatric Research Reports*, vol. 2, pp. 39-51, reprinted in *Steps to an Ecology of Mind*, Paladin, New York, 1972).
BATESON, G. (1966), 'Problems in cetacean

and other mammalian communication' (reprinted in *Steps to an Ecology of Mind*, Paladin, New York, 1972).

WATZLAWICK, P. *et al.* (1967), *Pragmatics of Human Communication* (W. W. Norton, New York).

See also *Causality, Non-verbal communication*.

Analysand

A patient or trainee who is undergoing *psycho-analysis*.

Analysis

See *Psychoanalysis*.

Analyst (or psychoanalyst)

The name given to a therapist who is qualified to practice psychoanalysis, *analytical psychology* or *child analysis*.

Analytic pact

See *Therapeutic alliance*.

Analytic therapy

See *Psychoanalysis*.

Analytical psychology

The approach to personality and to psychotherapy developed by Carl Gustav Jung (1875-1961). Jung (1929) himself defined analytical psychology as 'a general concept embracing both psychoanalysis and individual psychology as well as other endeavours in the field of "complex psychology"'. Although he showed considerable awareness of the wider problems of the outside world and of other cultures, Jung believed that change interventions should focus on the individual.

Jung's work was greatly influenced by that of Freud. Many of the same problems were discussed by both and they shared ideas through meetings and correspondence between 1906 and 1913. However, analytical psychology is distinctively different from Freudian psychoanalysis and Jung arrives at different conclusions regarding the *unconscious*, the meaning of *dreams*, *transference*, the origins of psychic disturbance and the psycho-

therapeutic approach to the disturbed individual. Jung disagreed fundamentally with Freud's exclusive emphasis on the sexual origins of psychopathology and this disagreement caused a lifelong rift between them. In analytical psychology, the therapeutic process involves four stages: confession, elucidation, education and transformation. The goal of therapy is to help the individual gain *insight* and journey towards *individuation*. The therapist's primary task, however, is to help the patient experience himself differently by facilitating a greater integration of his *conscious* and *unconscious* components. Jung was interested in the transformation of the whole person and, like Freud, he believed that psychic disturbance often manifested itself in physical *symptoms*. Dreams, however, are a more important means by which the individual reveals the contents of his or her unconscious mind and *dream interpretation* was used by Jung to understand the individual's current problems and aspirations as well as to uncover past conflicts. Jung, like Freud, used *free association* and *interpretation* in his therapeutic approach but he also favoured a more active form of analysis with more use of the real relationship between patient and *analyst*. He introduced some original concepts such as the various *archetypes* (notably the *shadow*, the *persona*, and the *animus* and *anima*, the *collective unconscious*, and a bi-polar understanding of the personality, described in his work on *psychological types*.

Although Jung (1963) described analytical psychology as 'fundamentally a natural science', his theories are greatly influenced by his interest in religion and a lifelong study of mysticism and *parapsychology*. Analytical psychology has not achieved the popularity of the Freudian approach to psychoanalysis, chiefly because it places less emphasis on scientific credibility and allows for the existence of the individual's spiritual aspirations. Even so, Jung's ideas have become increasingly influential in the general field of psychotherapy, particularly at the interface between religion and psychology. Although Jung himself was sceptical about its value, a recent development and application of his ideas has been to the group work setting (Whitmont 1964). Analytical psychology as a discipline has developed greatly since Jung's death in 1961. Many of Jung's ideas have been developed or challenged, and unofficial though persuasive new schools have grown up (Samuels 1984). In many centres, a rapprochement with psychoanalysis is under way.

BENNET, E. A. (1961), *C. G. Jung* (Barrie & Rockliff, London).
EVANS, R. (1964), *Conversations with Carl Jung* (Van Nostrand, New York).
FORDHAM, F. (1953), *Introduction to Jung's Psychology* (Penguin Books, Harmondsworth).
FORDHAM, M. (1978), *Jungian Psychotherapy* (Wiley, London).
FORDHAM, M. *et al.* (1980a), *Technique in Jungian Analysis* (Academic Press, London).
FORDHAM, M. *et al.* (1980b), *Analytical Psychology* (Academic Press, London).
HANNAH, B. (1976), *Jung: His Life and Work* (Putnam, New York).
HOMANS, P. (1979), *Jung in Context* (University of Chicago Press, Chicago).
JUNG, C. G., *Collected Works* (18 volumes plus general index plus bibliography, Routledge & Kegan Paul, London).
JUNG, C. G. (1929), 'Problems of modern psychotherapy' (*Collected Works*, vol. 16, Routledge & Kegan Paul, London).
JUNG, C. G. (1953), *Psychological Reflections* (ed. Jolande Jacobi, Routledge & Kegan Paul, London).
JUNG, C. G. (1963), *Memories, Dreams, Reflections* (Fontana, London).
JUNG, C. G. (1963), *Analytical Psychology: Its Theory and Practice* (Routledge & Kegan Paul, London).
JUNG, C. G. (1964), *Man and His Symbols* (Aldus, London).
MCGUIRE, W. (ed.) (1974), *The Freud-Jung Letters* (Routledge & Kegan Paul/Hogarth Press, London).
PAPADOPOULOS, R. K. and SAAYMAN, G. S. (1984), *Jung in Modern Perspective* (Wildwood House, London).
SAMUELS, A. (1984), *Jung and the Post-Jungians* (Routledge & Kegan Paul, London).
STORR, A. (1976), *C. G. Jung* (Viking Press, New York).
STORR, A. (1983), *Jung: Selected Writings* (Fontana, London).
VAN DER POST, L. (1976), *Jung and the Story of our Time* (Hogarth Press, London).
WHITMONT, E. C. (1964), 'Group therapy and analytical psychology' (*J. of Analytical Psychology*, vol. 9, no. 1).

Anamnesis
Literal Greek meaning 'not forgetting'. The active process whereby the patient is helped to recall past events and the feelings associated with them. The term is used more specifically to describe the fairly lengthy, retrospective investigation into the patient's past conducted prior to diagnosis in long-term treatments.

See also *History taking, Medical model.*

Aneclectic
Literal Greek meaning 'not eclectic'. Practising a specialist method of psychotherapy.

Angyal, Andras (1902-1960)
A psychologist and psychiatrist who espoused a holistic view of man and was an adherent of *humanistic psychology*. Angyal was born in Hungary and studied at the Universities of Vienna and Turin where he gained a PhD and MD respectively. In 1932 he emigrated to the United States and for twelve years he worked at the State Hospital in Worcester, Massachusetts. His early research was conducted into theories of cognition and later into schizophrenia. He noted that disturbance in his patients arose from their inability to define their relationship with the environment appropriately. He developed a theoretical view of life as a total biological process and of human beings as *open systems*. His systemic (see *Systemic therapies*) view of human functioning led him to view the exploration of *causality* as being multi-faceted, rather than linear, although it did not lead him into the treatment of *systems* in his practice. Angyal died in Boston, Massachusetts, in 1960, leaving his ideas contained in his books, *Foundations for a Science of Personality* (1941) and *Neurosis and Treatment: A Holistic Theory* (1965).

13

Anima

The latent feminine principle which, according to Jung, exists in every man and which forms one of the major *archetypes* in the *collective unconscious* in a similar manner to that of the *animus* in women. The anima both influences and is derived from the parental *imago*, the man's relationship with his mother which is internalised when the *Oedipus complex* is resolved. The anima often manifests itself in *dreams* in which female figures may serve as guides, or perform other helpful functions. In so doing, they act as 'gatekeepers' for the *unconscious*. The anima unconsciously influences the man in his attitudes, choices, and relationships with women. It has the potential to be either negative and disruptive or to contribute to the *psyche*'s wholeness and well-being. According to Jung, the repression of feminine traits causes these contrasexual demands to accumulate in the unconscious and an important part of the psychotherapeutic process lies in helping the man to recognise and integrate the feminine aspect of himself.

JUNG, C. G. (1951), 'Aion' (*Collected Works*, vol. 9, part 2, Routledge & Kegan Paul, London).
JUNG, C. G. (1953), 'Two essays on analytical psychology' (*Collected Works* vol. 7, Routledge & Kegan Paul, London).
JUNG, C. G. (1957) *Animus and Anima* (Spring Publications, New York).

See also *Analytical psychology*.

Animus

The latent masculine principle which, according to Jung, exists in every woman and which forms one of the major *archetypes* in the *collective unconscious* in a similar manner to the *anima* in men. The animus both influences and is derived from the parental *imago*, internalised at the resolution of the *Oedipus complex*. It is often said that, unlike the anima, the animus is usually represented in *dreams* by a plurality of figures. Emma Jung (1957) explained this by reference to the predominantly personal attitude of the woman's conscious mind, to which her animus forms a contrast. The animus colours a woman's relationship with men and it can be negative and destructive unless she is able to recognise and integrate the masculine aspects of herself – the latter being a major task of the therapeutic process.

JUNG, C. G. (1951), 'Aion' (*Collected Works*, vol. 9, part 2, Routledge & Kegan Paul, London).
JUNG, C. G. (1953), 'Two essays on analytical psychology' (*Collected Works*, vol. 7, Routledge & Kegan Paul, London).
JUNG, E. (1957), *Animus and Anima* (Spring Publications, New York).

See also *Analytical psychology*.

Annihilation

A particular anxiety that would seem to have its origin in very early stages of development. Winnicott (1960) postulates that the original infantile state is omnipotent in that the infant does not recognise his dependence on his mother, but if the environment impinges on him in such a way that his dependence is felt by him, it is experienced as annihilation and leads to the development of a *false self* to cover over the sense that 'the continuity of being is interrupted'. Such impingement is, according to Winnicott, the underlying problem in the generation of schizophrenia.

WINNICOTT, D. W. (1960), 'The theory of the parent-infant relationship', in *Maturational Processes and the Facilitating Environment* (Hogarth Press, London).

See also *Death anxiety, Modes of relatedness, Transitional object*.

Anxiety management training

An approach to *coping skills interventions* developed by Suinn and Richardson (1971). As with the coping skills approach developed by Goldfried (1971), *relaxation training* is used as an active ingredient of the programme. *Covert modelling* is then introduced and the client is trained in coping responses to a variety of anxiety-inducing events. The approach is based on *counter conditioning* principles.

GOLDFRIED, M. R. (1971), 'Systematic desensitisation as training in self control' (*J. of Consulting and Clinical Psychology*, vol. 37, pp. 228-34).
SUINN, R. and RICHARDSON, F. (1971), 'Anxiety management training: a non-specific behavior therapy program for anxiety control' (*Behavior Therapy*, vol. 2, pp. 498-510).

See also *Problem solving interventions, Self instructional training, Stress inoculation.*

Approach-avoidance conflict
A concept introduced originally by Kurt Lewin and developed by Miller (1944, 1959) to explain the roots of neurotic conflict. Miller suggests that conflict arises when two *drives* compete. The conflict can be exemplified in three different ways: approach-approach conflict, when the individual has to choose between two desirable alternatives; avoidance-avoidance conflict, when he has to choose between undesirable alternatives; and approach-avoidance conflict, when he has to choose between something that is both desirable but painful or awkward, such as entering therapy, engaging in a course of study, etc. The pain or hard work of engaging in the enterprise conflicts with the attraction of the hoped-for rewards at the end. Miller suggests that there are four assumptions about the way in which a goal is approached or avoided: the closer one gets to a goal, the more strongly the individual pursues it; the nearer he comes to a feared event, the stronger the tendency to avoid it; the avoidance tendency is stronger than the approach tendency; and the strength of the drives govern the strength of the tendency to approach or avoid. Moreover, in an approach-avoidance situation, the further the individual is from his goals, the stronger the tendency to approach; but the nearer he comes to it, the greater the tendency to draw back. Thus, he becomes stuck between two competing drives. An effort to resolve this impasse may motivate the individual to enter therapy. Miller's work in this area is an attempt to provide a learning theory

explanation for the psychoanalytic concept of conflicting drives.

MILLER, N. (1944), 'Experimental studies of conflict' (in Hunt, J. (ed.), *Personality and the Behavior Disorders*, Rolland, New York).
MILLER, N. (1959), 'Liberalisation of basic SR concepts' (in Koch, S. (ed.), *Psychology – A Study of a Science*, McGraw-Hill, New York).

Archetype
A term adopted by Jung (1959) to describe 'patterns of instinctual behaviour', the potential for which, in Jung's view, is inherited in the same way that instinctual behaviour is inherited in animals. It is important to distinguish between the archetypical *structure*, a purely skeletal concept which is essentially unknowable, and archetypal images, themes and patterns (see *Imagery*) which are based on the structure. For example, the potential for a powerful bond between mother and child exists in both, so that the mother archetype (which could also be called the 'mother-child archetypal structure') becomes activated in the form of images during the early days of their relationship. When a man falls in love, images deriving from the archetype of the *anima* are activated. Aggression may be the expression of the archetype of the *shadow*, and Jung has maintained that the rise of Nazism in Germany in the 1930s was an example of the shadow being activated at a collective level. Other manifestations of archetypes are the *animus*, the hero and the self, and these manifest themselves in *dreams*, *myths* and religious symbolism. It was the discovery that these symbols exist in widely disparate cultures which led Jung to formulate his concept of the *collective unconscious*.

Archetypes are 'pre-existent forms of experience' (Jung, 1959) and are constituted out of the basic human experiences of life which have remained the same down the ages. These include the knowledge of night and day; birth and death; the search for food and shelter; the flight from danger; the daily rhythm of work and sleep; the search for a mate and sexual intercourse. The archetype constitutes the *unconscious* component of *conscious* acts and relationships and so gives them their power and numinosity. Archetypes can function creatively but they can also exert a negative influence if they remain inaccessible to consciousness. The shadow, for example, represents the individual's potential for evil. If this potential is made conscious, then due allowance can be made for it. If it is denied, Jung suggests that it may then take over and dominate the individual because the archetype which is suppressed is liable to work destructively below the level of consciousness. Jung's work on archetypes as innate and predetermined forms of inherited behaviour patterning is open to criticism but Stevens (1982) offers a careful critique which reveals the usefulness as well as the difficulties of Jung's theory.

JUNG, C. G. (1959), 'The archetypes and the collective unconscious' (*Collected Works*, vol. 9, part 1, Routledge & Kegan Paul, London).
NEUMANN, E. (1955), *The Great Mother: An Analysis of the Archetype* (Routledge & Kegan Paul, London).
STEVENS, A. (1982), *Archetype – A Natural History of the Self* (Routledge & Kegan Paul, London).

Arica training
See *Psychocalisthenics*.

Art therapy
The use of art forms to enable the expression of conflicts, problems and aspirations, first as a substitute for neurotic *symptoms* and later as a way of developing latent creative energy. The term art therapy was introduced by Adrian Hill in Britain during the 1940s and developed out of his work with TB patients. Art therapy has both diagnostic and treatment potential. It is used either as an adjunct to other forms of psychotherapy or, more fully, as a therapy in its own right. Children's drawings made during *play therapy* or in a *family therapy* session fall into the first category. Many individual therapies encourage the patient to express himself through art and Jung, for example, viewed drawing and painting as important adjuncts to

analytical psychology, which it still is.

When used as a therapy in its own right, the value of the artistic production itself is the focus, with opportunities given to develop the picture or model over a longer period of time. The art therapist may subsequently discuss the latent meaning and *symbolism* of the picture with the patient and use a sequence of pictures painted over some months to examine emergent themes and changes in the patient's feelings, fantasies, self-concept and his perceptions of the external world. Art therapists who use a psychoanalytic approach (e.g. Naumberg 1966) stress the need to interpret the artistic production alongside the patient's associations to it, if *unconscious* themes and phenomena such as *transference* are to be fully understood. Other therapists put more emphasis on the healing processes of *catharsis* and *sublimation*. Art therapy may be conducted on a one-to-one basis, in groups or with families, and Rhyne (1973) has shown how art therapy and *Gestalt therapy* can be combined.

GANTT, L. and SCHMAL, M. S. (1974), *Art Therapy – A Bibliography: January 1940 to June 1973* (National Institute of Mental Health, Rockville, Maryland).
KWIATKOWSKA, H. (1967), 'Family art therapy' (*Family Process*, vol. 6, pp. 37-55).
LEVICK, M. F. (1975), 'Art in psychotherapy' (in Masserman, J., *Current Psychotherapies*, Grune & Stratton, New York).
NAUMBERG, M. (1966), *Dynamically Oriented Art Therapy: Its Principles and Practice* (Grune & Stratton, New York).
NEUMANN, E. (1959), *Art and the Creative Unconscious* (Routledge & Kegan Paul, London).
RHYNE, J. (1973), *The Gestalt Art Experience* (Brooks/Cole, Monterey, California).
ULMAN, E. and DACKINGER, P. (eds) (1975), *Art Therapy in Theory and Practice* (Schocken Books, New York).

Assagioli, Roberto (1888-1974)
Assagioli, the founder of *psychosynthesis*, was born in Venice in 1888. He studied medicine at the University of Florence and became an early student of *psychoanalysis*, introducing his

professors to Freud's thinking while he was still a medical student. He was considered by Freud to be the representative and hope for the development of psychoanalysis in Italy. However, almost from the beginning, he was laying the groundwork for a critique of psychoanalysis, anticipating the insights and emphases of *humanistic psychology* on the whole person by many years. He saw the need for a theory that would encompass the spiritual and creative aspects of the individual as well as his *drives* and instinctual life. He was thus one of the early exponents of a *transpersonal psychology*. He corresponded widely with clinicians of different schools including Jung and Maslow, and in 1926 he founded the Instituto di Psicosintesi in Rome. This became the centre for his teaching and practice until the hostility of the Fascist regime forced the Institute to close. After the war, Assagioli began writing and teaching again and encouraged the growth of new psychosynthesis centres throughout the world.

Assertiveness training

A procedure introduced by Salter (1949) for increasing the social skills and lowering the anxiety level of unassertive individuals. Assertiveness is defined as a strong appropriate response to another human being that is neither submissive nor aggressive. Assertiveness is viewed as a way of participating in interpersonal relationships which reflects a healthy self-concept and high self-esteem without infringing the rights of others. In particular, the training, which often takes place in groups, makes use of *social skills training, modelling* and *behavioural rehearsal* (which originated in assertiveness training programmes). *Simulation* of feared situations, *role play* and other *structured exercises* are used to increase the individual's repertoire of skills; and *systematic desensitisation* and *relaxation training* may be used to decrease anxiety. The therapist may also try to change the patient's cognitive view of his social skills competency by *self-instructional* and *anxiety management training*.

ALBERTI, R. E. (1977), *Assertiveness: Innovations, Applications and Issues* (Impact Publishers, San Louis, Obispo).
BOWER, S. A. and BOWER, G. H. (1976), *Asserting Yourself* (Addision-Wesley, Reading, Mass.).
MCFALL, R. M. and TWENTYMAN, C. T. (1973), 'Four experiments on the relative contributions of rehearsal, modeling and coaching to assertion training' (*J. of Abnormal Psychology*, vol. 81, pp. 199-218).
RICH, A. R. and SCHROEDER, H. E. (1976), 'Research issues in assertiveness training' (*Psychological Bulletin*, vol. 83, pp. 1081-96).
SALTER, A. (1949), *Conditional Reflex Therapy*, Capricorn Books, New York).

See also *Coping skills interventions, Feminist therapy, Problem solving interventions, Role reversal.*

Attachment theory

A theory of the relationship between the infant and his primary caregiver developed by Bowlby (1969, 1973, 1980) at the Tavistock Clinic, London. Using insights from *psychoanalysis*, developmental psychology and ethology, Bowlby revealed how the earliest relationship between the child and his chief caretaker forms the starting point for all later relationships. Attachment behaviour is defined by Bowlby (1975) as 'any form of behaviour that results in a person attaining or retaining proximity to some other differentiated and preferred individual, usually conceived as stronger and/or wiser. It is developing during the second trimester of life and is evident from six months onward when an infant shows by his behaviour that he discriminates sharply between his mother-figure, a few other familiar people and everyone else.' Bowlby and his research collaborators, Ainsworth, the Robertsons, Parkes and others, have shown that attachment behaviour persists as an important part of the person's behavioural equipment not only during later childhood but during adolescence and adult life as well. In adults it is especially evident when a person is distressed, ill or afraid. Ainsworth *et al.* (1978) have developed the 'strange-situation' test for measuring the degree of attachment to the mother figure in early childhood. The test measures the difference in the child's behaviour when mother is present, when mother is away and when she returns.

Bowlby has shown how, by the second half of the first year of life, the infant is capable of organising his behaviour in terms of goal setting and goal correction designed to maintain the proximity of the caregiver. The primary attachment figure is associated with feelings of security and he or she is especially needed when the infant experiences threat. When attachment is interrupted, separation anxiety is experienced and Robertson and Bowlby (1952) have shown that in these circumstances, the child typically passes through stages of protest, despair and detachment. When mother returns, the child engages in avoidance/resistance as well as attachment behaviour. Further studies of responses to major separations are summarised by Bowlby (1973).

The quality of the attachment experience is of crucial importance and Bowlby makes it clear that although there may be a hierarchy of attachment figures for the young child, there still needs to be one principal figure with which bonding, of a warm and intimate quality, can occur. This principal figure is normally, though not necessarily, the mother – a mother substitute can be satisfactory so long as the quality of the relationship facilitates bonding and reduces as far as possible the experience of separation anxiety.

In his third volume, Bowlby (1980) shows how the processes of readjustment after the loss of significant figures in adulthood and the success with which new intimacies are forged are related to the degree of security/anxiety present in the person's early attachment relationship. However, as other researchers have pointed out (see Parkes and Stevenson-Hinde 1978), this does not mean that the early relationship is such that later benign experiences cannot effectively ameliorate earlier separation traumata.

Bowlby's work has been criticised by psychoanalysts because of the introduction of work from other knowledge bases into his theoretical framework; by feminists because of the apparent exclusive emphasis on the mother-infant tie; and by others who have felt that his theory implies that the effects of early maternal deprivation cannot be reversed (Rutter, 1972; Clarke and Clarke, 1976; Schaffer, 1977). Later reworkings and modifications of the theory have however taken note of these criticisms. The literature on attachment theory is now vast and the area remains a fertile one for new developments. Many different aspects have been considered. For example, Herbert *et al* (1982) have pointed to the growing interest in the process of mother-to-infant bonding as being a complementary process to attachment behaviour in the infant. They suggest that, as in the case of infant attachment behaviour, what we currently know regarding the bonding process 'suggests that a pessimistic view of the irreversibility of early events or a nihilistic therapeutic stance with regard to mother-to-infant attitudes and behaviour are both misplaced'. Other researchers have directed increased attention to the role of the father and other attachment figures (Lamb, 1977; Lamb, 1982). Attachment theory has had important practical consequences for the organisation of children's hospitals and other institutions and on child rearing practices; and in the way it has increased understanding of the *grief* and mourning processes, of loneliness and detachment in later life and of the cycle of emotional deprivation which results in the continuation of maternal deprivation in the next generation (Fraiberg 1980). Sroufe and Waters (1977) have described attachment theory as an organisational construct which links individual difference to the different development needs of individuals in different environments.

AINSWORTH, M. D. S. *et al.* (1978), *Patterns of Attachment* (John Wiley, Chichester).
ATKINS, F. R. *et al.* (1981), *Parent-Child Separation: An Abstracted Bibliography* (Plenum Press, New York).

BOWLBY, J. (1969), *Attachment and Loss*, vol. 1, 'Attachment' (Penguin, Harmondsworth).

BOWLBY, J. (1973), *Attachment and Loss*, vol. 2, 'Separation' (Penguin, Harmondsworth).

BOWLBY, J. (1975), 'Attachment theory, separation anxiety and mourning' (in Hamburg, D. A. and Brodie, H., *American Handbook of Psychiatry*, vol. 6, Basic Books, New York).

BOWLBY, J. (1977), 'The making and breaking of affectional bonds' (*Brit. J. of Psychiatry*, vol. 130, pp. 201-10).

BOWLBY, J. (1980), *Attachment and Loss*, vol. 3, 'Loss' (Penguin, Harmonsworth).

CLARKE, A. M. and CLARKE, A. D. B. (1976), *Early Experience: Myth and Evidence* (Open Books, London).

FRAIBERG, S. (ed.) (1980), *Clinical Studies in Infant Mental Health* (Tavistock, London).

HERBERT, M. *et al.* (1982), 'Mother-to-infant "bonding" ' (*J. of Child Psychol. and Psychiatry*, vol. 23, pp. 205-21).

HERD, D. H. (1978), 'From object relations to attachment theory: a basis for family therapy' (*Brit. J. of Med. Psychology*, vol. 51, pp. 67-76).

HINDE, R. A. (1979), *Towards Understanding Relationships* (Academic Press, London).

LAMB, M. E. (ed.) (1977), *The Role of the Father in Child Development* (Wiley, New York).

LAMB, M. E. (1982), 'Paternal influences on early socio-emotional development' (*J. of Child Psychol. and Psychiatry*, vol. 23, pp. 185-90).

PARKES, C. M. and STEVENSON-HINDE, J. (eds) (1982), *The Place of Attachment in Human Behavior* (Tavistock, London).

ROBERTSON, J. and BOWLBY, H. (1952), 'Responses of young children to separation from their mothers' (*Courrier du Centre Internationale de L'Enfant*, vol. 2, pp. 131-42).

ROBERTSON, J. and ROBERTSON, J. (1971), 'Young children in brief separations' (in Eissler, R. K. *et al.*, *The Psychoanalytic Study of the Child*, vol. 26, Yale University Press, New Haven, Connecticut).

RUTTER, M. (1972), *Maternal Deprivation Reassessed* (Penguin, Harmondsworth).

SCHAFFER, H. R. (1977), *Studies in Mother-Infant Interaction* (Academic Press, London).

SROUFE, L. A. and WATERS, E. (1977), 'Attachment as an organisational construct' (*Child Development*, vol. 48, pp. 1184-99).

Attempted solution

The means which the prospective client has already tried in order to gain relief from his problem, prior to coming to a therapist. Neighbours, friends and family members may have already given advice and the client is likely to have tried out the 'common sense' solutions to his difficulties. Failure to identify these will involve the therapist in repetitious and unproductive work with the client. The *presenting problem* or *symptom* itself may represent one of the client's attempted solutions. Fisch *et al.* (1982) describe five basic attempted solutions commonly found when clients present themselves to a therapist: attempting to force something to happen which can only occur spontaneously (this usually relates to the client's own performance, e.g. sexual performance, insomnia, memory blocks, stuttering, addictions, etc.); attempting to master a feared event by postponing it (e.g. a variety of phobias, anxiety states, shyness, public performance blocks, examination nerves); attempting to produce compliance in another by force (e.g. marital conflicts, behaviour problems in children, etc.); attempting to produce a voluntary agreement to a repudiated action or behaviour (e.g. suggesting that person A should *want* to do what person B requires); and confirming an accuser's suspicions by defending oneself from his accusation (e.g. denying or explaining away behaviour which has provoked another's accusations). Therapists working within *strategic therapy* or *focused problem resolution* regard the client's attempted solution to his problem as a major problem to be addressed in therapy. They view the attempted solution as being the problem and a real solution may likewise reside in the acceptance of the 'problem' which the client has ineffectively tried to solve.

FISCH, R. *et al.* (1982), *Tactics of Change: Doing Therapy Briefly* (Jossey-Bass, San Francisco).

Attending

The process whereby the therapist listens, takes in and receives the verbal and non-verbal responses of the patient. Attending is a basic interviewing skill, and an essential therapist activity in all psychotherapeutic methods. As Ivey and Authier (1978) point out, 'without the ability to attend, the helping interview – regardless of theoretical orientation – becomes an empty sham'. It involves the therapist in being open to incoming stimuli from the patient and it is an essential ingredient in the creation of an effective relationship with him. Focused attending requires the use of a kind of free-floating attention to allow as much of the patient's responses as possible to penetrate the therapist's consciousness. It involves too, a relative freedom from those conflicts which might lead the therapist to block off the patient's material and an ability to manage his or her own anxieties so that he or she avoids anticipating or assuming the contents of the patient's communication. Disturbed attentiveness may arise from the therapist's own physical or psychological crises or from his *counter transference* reactions to the patient. Bion (1970) suggests that the therapist should enter each session without desire, memory or understanding. Following such advice greatly enhances the therapist's capacity to listen productively, but it clearly conflicts to some extent with other imperatives such as the need to maintain a clear focus on treatment *goals*, devise *tasks*, develop *hypotheses*, etc., in an ongoing way from session to session. The type of listening described by Bion (1970) and Langs (1978) is primarily directed towards the psychoanalytic therapies but in a modified form, active and creating attending or listening by the therapist is the essential prerequisite in all therapeutic approaches. It enables him to experience *empathy* and *acceptance*; to engage in *reflection* and to offer *containment* for the patient's disturbing phantasies. Langs (1978) proposes that the patient has an urgent need to cure the therapist and that a person becomes a therapist out of his own need to place his pathology into the patient. The listening process involves this mutual interaction between patient and therapist. Chessick (1982) offers a critique of Langs's views. Because of its importance in creating empathy, effective listening is particularly emphasised in the *humanistic* approaches. But it is also essential in task-focused directive therapies. It allows the therapist to formulate effective working hypthoses, develop an appropriate treatment plan and provide a model for effective *communication*.

The complexity of the listening process is greatly increased in the *systemic therapies* and in *group* work, and *co-therapy* is often used to enable the listening process to be more effective. Ivey and Authier (1978) identify six skills which they regard as the behavioural indicators of effective attending: closed questioning; *open-ended questioning*; minimal encouraging (see *Tracking*); paraphrasing (see *Clarification*); *reflection* and summarisation. The therapist needs to *convey* the fact that he is listening and the therapist's ability to convey this to the patient acts as a reinforcer for further *self-disclosure* by the patient.

BION, W. R. (1970), 'Attention and interpretation' (in *Seven Servants*, Jason Aronson, New York).

CHESSICK, R. D. (1982), 'Psychoanalytic listening with special reference to the views of Langs' (*Contemporary Psychoanalysis*, vol. 18, pp. 613-34).

IVEY, A. E. and AUTHIER, J. (1978), *Micro Counseling* (2nd edn, Charles C. Thomas, Springfield, Ill.).

LANGS, R. (1978), *The Listening Process* (Jason Aronson, New York).

Attraction

The personal quality which draws a person to want to associate with and/or be influenced by another. A considerable amount of social psychological research has examined the determinants and consequences of interpersonal attraction and its meaning in terms of *social influence*. These studies suggest that cooperativeness, physical appearance, liking, similarity, perceived *expertness*, warmth and familiarity are important determinants of attractiveness. Goldstein (1971) examined the determinants of client attraction to the therapist in the early stages of therapy, suggesting that the more attracted the client is to the therapist, the more likely he is to return and to co-operate with the treatment. No correlations have been found to exist between therapist attractiveness and positive therapeutic *outcome*, except indirectly through its beneficial effect on maintaining the client in treatment, increasing the therapist's influence over him and enhancing his level of *self-disclosure*. However, some studies suggest that *perceived* counsellor expertness and trustworthiness contribute to the client's attraction to the therapist and hence to his satisafction with therapy.

BERSCHEID, E. and WALSTER, E. H. (1978), *Interpersonal Attraction* (Addison-Wesley, Reading, Mass.).
GOLDSTEIN, A. P. (1971), *Psychotherapeutic Attraction* (Pergamon Press, New York).
HEPPNER, P. P. and HEESACKER, M. (1982), 'The interpersonal influence process in real-life counseling' (*J. of Counseling Psychology* vol. 29, pp. 215-23).
HEPPNER, P. P. and HEESACKER, M. (1983), 'Perceived counselor characteristics: client expectations and client satisfaction with counseling' (*J. of Counseling Psychology* vol. 30, pp. 31-9).
HUSTON, T. (ed.) (1974), *Foundations of Interpersonal Attraction* (Academic Press, New York).

See also *Affiliation, Alliance, Cohesion, Therapeutic alliance.*

Attribution theory

A social psychological theory concerned with the origins, nature and consequences of the individual's perception of *causality*. Interest in this area stems mainly from the work of Heider (1958) who examined the way in which individuals made cause and effect analyses in everyday situations. Interest in the subject was extended by Jones and Davis (1965); by Kelley (1967) and by Laing (1961). Jones *et al.* (1971) suggest three fundamental propositions of attribution theory: people assign causes for important instances of behaviour and seek causally relevant information to support their hypothesis; the attribution of causes follows systematic rules; and causal attributions have important affective and behavioural consequences, since an important component of the meaning attached to an event, behaviour, feeling or problem is the cause to which it is attributed.

A common distinction that is made both by patients and therapists is whether the cause of a problem should be located *inside* the patient (intrapsychic causation) or *outside* the patient (interpersonal or environmental causation). A variety of studies have shown that manipulating the patient's attribution from internal to external causes can be beneficial, a fact that is made use of by therapists who use *reframing* as a technique. Others (e.g. *reality therapists* and *logotherapists*) suggest that it is more helpful if the patient can own responsibility for his situation rather than projecting responsibility on to others. Johnson and Matross (1977) suggest that 'instead of focussing upon the "truth" of an explanatory definition of the client's problems, attribution theory focusses the therapist upon providing explanatory systems which facilitate the client's acceptance of responsibility for positive change'. Laing (1961) points out how the attributions placed on an individual by others helps him form his sense of identity. Attributions which are experienced as incongruent with self-perception invalidate the sense of self. Much of Laing's work has been devoted to showing how the individual can be 'driven crazy' by the contradictory attributions of others.

HEIDER, F. (1958), *The Psychology of Interpersonal Relations*, Wiley, New York.
HEWSTONE, M. (ed.) (1983), *Attribution Theory* (Blackwell, Oxford).
JOHNSON, D. W. and MATROSS, R. (1977), 'Interpersonal influence in psychotherapy: a social psychological view' (in Gurman, A. S. and Razin, A. E., *Effective Psychotherapy*, Pergamon Press, New York).

JONES, E. E. and DAVIS, K. E. (1965), 'From acts to dispositions: the attribution process in person perception' (in Berkowitz, L. (ed.), *Advances in Experimental Social Psychology*, vol. 2, Academic Press, New York).

JONES, E. E. *et al.* (1971), *Attribution: Perceiving the Causes of Behaviour* (General Learning Press, Morristown, New Jersey).

KELLEY, H. H. (1967), 'Attribution theory in social psychology' (*Nebraska Symposium on Motivation*, vol. 15, pp. 192-210).

LAING, R. D. (1961), *The Self and Others* (Penguin Books, Harmondsworth).

See also *Communication, Diagnosis, Doublebind, Labelling, Mystification, Scapegoat.*

Audio tape
See *Audio visual equipment.*

Audio visual equipment
A wide range of audio visual equipment is currently used in the practice and teaching of psychotherapy. Predictably, the newer methods of psychotherapy have been more enthusiastic in their use of these techniques, but many traditional approaches have been increasingly prepared to exploit their potential, particularly as training tools. Audio visual equipment for present purposes is defined as including films, video tapes, audio tapes, *telephones* and the 'bug in ear' device. As training tools, the major use of audio-visual equipment is as follows:

Films Modelling (both positive and negative) of experienced practitioners at work, illustrating *microskills*, treatment techniques, the general approach adopted by a particular method of psychotherapy, the salient features of a particular clinical syndrome, etc. The impact of film material can be enhanced by combining it with *role play*, so that identification with the characters on the film is increased. The film may be interrupted at crucial points by the trainer to emphasise particular learning aspects, or it may be edited with a suitable commentary added to maximise its learning value.

Video tapes In addition to their use in the above ways, video recordings can be made of the trainee's own work, enabling him to play it back to himself, to a group of colleagues, or to a supervisor afterwards. The accuracy of the material presented greatly exceeds a verbal or written case record. *Process, behavioural sequences, non-verbal communication* and the *congruence* of the therapist with the patient can all be noted. Selection of material for presentation to colleagues or to a supervisor may focus on particular themes, problem areas, etc. Films and video material do have limitations, however. Images are distorted and affect is considerably toned down. Moreover, when video (or audio) is used in supervision, it cannot convey any but the outward manifestations of the therapist's thoughts and feelings. A further problem surrounding video films for hire is that there is no universally compatible standard of equipment for playing tapes and cassettes made on other equipment.

Audio tapes These can be used routinely to record all interviews where video equipment may be too cumbersome (on *home visits* for example). The data which is retrievable from an audio tape is more limited but nevertheless greatly exceeds that of a verbal or written case record. The therapist's unconscious blocks can be checked by writing a record of the *interview* first and playing back the audio tape afterwards, checking what has been omitted or distorted.

The telephone This is used in conjunction with the *one-way screen* enabling the therapist to receive observations, instructions, etc., from a supervisor or *team* who sit in an observation room. The telephone, and often the instructions given by the supervisor, are audible to the patient or family group. It also allows the therapist to discuss the supervisor's comments, indicating his understanding, agreement, etc.

The bug in ear Described by Birchler (1975), this is also used in conjunction with a one-way screen. It is a small electronic device inserted into the therapist's ear and enables the supervisor or team member to speak directly to the therapist during the session. Unlike the telephone, messages are inaudible to the patient and he has no indication if and when a message is being received by the therapist. Alternatively, the supervisor can speak to family members direct if they are also fitted with bugs in ears, and considerably modify and manipulate the course of treatment. The bug in ear is the most efficient way of enabling the supervisor to intervene in the treatment while it is occurring. Both the telephone and the bug in ear are important aids in live supervision and enable concurrent *feedback* and *knowledge of results* to be gained by the trainee.

Audio and video taped material can be effectively used in treatment. Alger (1973) and others have shown how video tape play back can be used in marital and family therapy to overcome *resistance* and to enable family members to gain *insight*. Behaviour therapists use video tape play back in *modelling* and *coping behaviour*, and audio taped material is routinely used in *relaxation training, assertiveness training* and in a variety of *self-help* procedures. Paul (1976) has developed a technique which he describes as *cross confrontation* which makes use of video taped play back as a stimulus stresser.

ALGER, I. (1973), 'Audio visual techniques in family therapy' (in Bloch, D., *Techniques of Family Psychotherapy*, Grune & Stratton, New York).

ALGER, I. (1976), 'Integrating immediate video playback in family therapy' (in Guerin, P., *Family Therapy: Theory and Practice*, Gardner Press, New York).

BERGER, M. M. (ed.) (1970), *Video Tape Technique in Psychiatric Training and Treatment* (Brunner/Mazel, New York).

BIRCHLER, G. (1975), 'Live supervision and instant feed back in marriage and family therapy' (*J. of Marriage and Family Counseling*, vol. 1, pp. 331-42).

PAUL, N. L. (1976), 'Cross confrontation' (in Guerin, P., *Family Therapy: Theory and Practice*, Gardner Press, New York).

Authenticity
See *Genuineness*.

Autogenic training
A psychophysiologic form of psychotherapy that works with the body and mind simultaneously. Originating in Germany in the early twentieth century, many of its practitioners are of German origin. The patient is taught to alter his bodily states through the voluntary control of his autonomic nervous system and thereby to relieve and reduce stress. The patient is then taught how to enter an altered state of consciousness similar to a self-induced hypnotic trance, or a meditative state. He is encouraged to explore his unconscious mind with or without the help of a therapist. Schulz and Luthe (1959) encourage the patient to adopt an 'interrogatory attitude' and to expect to receive answers to problems from the unconscious. The therapist works directly with the patient's unconscious to clarify problem areas, encourage new solutions to problems and to help establish new behaviour and thought patterns. A variety of breathing and relaxation exercises are practised, and six standard autogenic exercises are used to induce the trance-like state. Patients are asked to visualise their problem and its possible solution. Sessions end with the affirmation of well-being and progress towards the desired direction. Patients are advised to practise the six standard exercises three times a day for between five and twenty minutes per session.

Autogenic training is primarily a *self-help* tool though it can be used routinely as a direct therapeutic procedure. Its proponents claim its usefulness for a range of psychosomatic illnesses, stress conditions and also for some apparently organic illnesses such as cancer. The six standard exercises, inducing *relaxation* and reduction of stress, are likely to be useful for anyone and assist problem solving in the same way as *meditation*. Its advocates see psychotic states and heart diseases as contraindicated for autogenic training.

BRENNEKE, H. (1981), 'Autogenic training' (in Corsini, R., *Handbook of Innovative Psychotherapies*, Wiley, New York).

LINDERMANN, H. (1973), *Relieve Tensions the Autogenic Way* (Wyden, New York).

LUTHE, W. (1969), *Autogenic Therapy* (Grune & Stratton, New York).

SCHULZ, J. and LUTHE, W. (1959). *Autogenic Training: A Psychophysiologic Approach to Psychotherapy* (Grune & Stratton, New York).

See also *Body therapies*.

Auxiliary ego

Term used in *psychodrama* to describe any member of the group or a professional person (other than the therapist) who takes part in a psychodramatic *enactment* to help the *protagonist* work on his problems. The effect of the auxiliary ego is the *intensification* of the protagonist's involvement in the enactment. Roles played by the auxiliary ego can include important significant people in the protagonist's psycho-social *context*, both dead and alive; inanimate objects such as the housework, the government, etc.; or abstract concepts or fantasy figures such as conscience, the devil, an idealised self-concept, etc. The protagonist briefs the auxiliary ego on how to play the role and the auxiliary ego mirrors the protagonist's perceptions as closely as possible as well as bringing his own spontaneous reactions to bear upon the part. The auxiliary ego may engage in *role reversal* with the protagonist so that the latter can experience both sides of the situation that is being enacted.

A major difference between psychodrama and *Gestalt therapy* is the former's use of auxiliary egos. Fritz Perls believed that the patient or subject should play *all* the roles himself but when group members are used as auxiliary egos, there is often added learning accruing to them in dealing with their own difficulties. Choice of a group member to play a particular auxiliary ego should therefore take into account the special *empathy* which he may feel for a particular role. After an enactment, the participants, who have played auxiliary egos, are asked to share their own perceptions and experiences of the role and to offer suggestions to the protagonist from their own special *participant-observer* position. A particular variety of auxiliary ego is called the alter ego or double (see *Doubling*). Auxiliary egos can be used in any group work situation even when other psychodramatic techniques are not being employed.

BLATNER, H. A. (1973), *Acting-In: Practical Applications of Psychodramatic Methods* (Springer, New York).

Aversion therapy

Administration of an aversive *stimulus* to inhibit an unwanted emotional response and the behaviour associated with it. Aversion therapy is a special application of *reciprocal inhibition*, and it makes use of the principle of *avoidance learning*. Although there are cases where aversion treatment and *punishment* occur together in therapy, they are quite different procedures. With punishment, the aversive stimulus follows the response that it is designed to modify; with aversive therapy the aversive stimulus should occur simultaneously, whenever the undesired behaviour is practised.

Aversion therapy has been used in the treatment of obsessions, homosexuality, sexual perversions, compulsions, drug addiction and alcoholism. It was first used as a treatment for alcoholism in the Soviet Union in the 1920s and during the 1930s and 1940s it was similarly used in the United States (Lemere and Voegtlin, 1950). The aversive stimulus used was the injection of an emetic which produced vomiting when the patient drank alcohol. Electric shock is frequently used as an aversive stimulus with other dysfunctional symptoms. Wolpe (1974) summarises guidelines for the administration of aversion therapy. He suggests that the aversive stimulus must be introduced at a high level of intensity and not gradually; it must be administered simultaneously with the pleasurable stimulus; it should ideally be administered at every evocation of the pleasurable response; and an alternative emotional target should be provided and responses to it reinforced. Wolpe points out that 'aversion therapy should not be administered before seeking out the possible anxiety bases of the unadaptive behaviour and treating them if found'.

Aversion therapy is based on the principles of *classical conditioning*, a strong aversive stimulus being paired with the stimulus which produces the undesired response. In the treatment of male homosexuality, for example, electric shocks are administered simultaneously with the projection of pictures of attractive male figures. Any stimulus that is experienced as being unpleasant by the patient can be used as a source of aversive conditioning, for example the presentation of a highly unpleasant smell simultaneously with food in cases of obesity. Various ethical objections can be raised against the use of aversive stimuli. Bengelman (1975), for example, discusses the use of aversion treatment in cases of homosexuality, which, whether effective or not, reinforces society's stigmatisation of a group of people who merely have a different sexual orientation and who are neither deviant nor ill. Even though treatment is only likely to be administered on their request, the objection still holds good. Other objections surround the fact of administering painful or distressing stimuli within a therapeutic context.

BENGELMAN, D. A. (1975), 'Ethical and legal issues of behavior modification' (in Hersen, M. *et al.* (eds), *Progress in Behavior Modification* (vol. 1, Academic Press, New York).

LEMERE, F. and VOEGTLIN, W. L. (1950), 'An evaluation of the aversion treatment of alcoholism' (*Quarterly Journal of Studies in Alcoholism*, vol. 11, pp. 199-204).

MATESANZ, A. (1982), 'Auditory stimuli in aversion therapy: a new technique' (*Behavior Therapist*, vol. 5, pp. 25-6).

RACHMAN, S. and TEESDALE, J. (1969), *Aversion Therapy and Behaviour Disorders* (Routledge & Kegan Paul, London).

WOLPE, J. (1974), *The Practice of Behavior Therapy* (2nd edn, Pergamon, New York).

aversive event until the individual responds to the signal alone and engages in avoidance behaviour whether the aversive event occurs or not. Thus, the behaviour is maintained by negative *reinforcement*. Avoidance responses also produce fear reduction which acts as a *reinforcer* of the avoidance learning. Mowrer (1939) took a major part in developing these ideas and his view of avoidance learning is still widely held. Solomon and Wynne (1954) showed how avoidance responses can continue for long after the feared event has ceased to occur. Avoidance learning contributes to the development and maintenance of a wide range of problem behaviours but its principles can also be utilised in their treatment. Feldman and MacCulloch (1965) have used avoidance learning in helping to change the sexual orientation of homosexuals. Bolles (1972) holds that although avoidance behaviour is motivated by fear, it is reinforced by the presence of a *new* stimulus which indicates that relief has now been achieved.

BOLLES, R. C. (1972), 'The avoidance learning problem' (in Bower, G. H. (ed.), *The Psychology of Learning and Motivation*, vol. 6, Academic Press, New York).

FELDMAN, M. P. and MACCULLOCH, M. J. (1965), 'The application of anticipatory avoidance learning to the treatment of homosexuality' (*Behavior, Research and Therapy*, vol. 2, pp. 165-183).

MOWRER, O. H. (1939), 'A stimulus-response analysis of anxiety and its role as a reinforcing agent' (*Psychological Review*, vol. 46, pp. 553-65).

SOLOMON, R. L. and WYNNE, L. C. (1954), 'Traumatic avoidance learning: the principles of anxiety conservation and partial irreversibility' (*Psychological Review*, vol. 61, pp. 353-85).

See also *Aversion therapy, Neurotic paradox.*

Avoidance learning

An *operant conditioning* procedure which consists in pairing a warning signal with an

B

Balint, Michael (1896-1970)

Balint was born in Budapest, the son of a general practitioner. After serving in the First World War, he completed his medical studies in 1920 and graduated from the University of Budapest. He married his first wife, Alice, in 1921. They immediately moved to Berlin where they both trained as psychoanalysts. Balint undertook his training analysis with Hans Sachs and, returning to Budapest, finished his training with Ferenczi. After Ferenczi's death in 1933, Balint became director of the Budapest Psychoanalytic Clinic, where he also began to develop his interest in working with general practitioners. The Balints left Hungary for England to escape persecution and settled in Manchester in 1939. There he obtained British medical qualifications together with a postgraduate degree in psychology, but after the sudden death of Alice, he moved to London where he became a training analyst for the British Psychoanalytic Society. In 1948 he joined the staff of the Tavistock Clinic, London, and remained there until 1961. Between 1948 and 1953, he worked at the Family Discussion Bureau (now renamed the Institute of Marital Studies) at the Tavistock Clinic, where he met and married Enid, a member of the Bureau. With her he wrote extensively on psycho-therapeutic training, and together they refined the training groups for general practitioners, described in his best-known book, *The Doctor, His Patient and the Illness*. After leaving the Tavistock Clinic, the Balints travelled abroad, teaching and developing training groups in many countries. Michael Balint made valuable contributions to psychoanalytic theory, one of the most important being the emphasis he placed on the early relationship in the mother-infant dyad and the resulting experience of *basic fault* if this relationship goes wrong. Theoretically, he is usually placed in the *British school* of *psychoanalysis*. His views about the basic fault and techniques of psycho-therapy were influenced by Ferenczi's *active analysis*.

Barrier

Term used by Lewin in *field theory* to denote any object or event which inhibits the individual's movement within his *lifespace*. The barrier produces *forces* which counteract the forces that are already operating within lifespace and acts as an obstacle to them.

Base line

A period which follows the *behavioural analysis* of the client's problems and precedes the initiation of treatment, during which the nature and frequency of the problems are established. Time sampling, behavioural counts, observer rating scales and self-report inventories are among the techniques used for recording the pre-treatment situation so as to enable both client and therapist to assess the changes that may occur as a result of treatment.

See also *Behaviour therapy*.

Basic assumption behaviour

A term introduced by Bion to describe the shared unconscious behaviour of a small group by which the task or *work group* activity is obstructed or diverted. Basic assumption behaviour is regressive and constitutes *resistance* to the task of the work group. It parallels the function of the *pleasure principle* and the operation of *primary process* in the individual. Bion suggests that there are three varieties of basic assumption behaviour: dependency, pairing and fight/flight, only one of which interacts at any one time with the work group activity. Dependency develops around the *phantasy* that the group leader is infallible and omnipotent and that he can therefore be relied upon to solve the group's problems, to save it from external threats and to accomplish its tasks for it. Pairing involves the group's reliance on the power and fertility that may be produced by two members of the group in their interaction. Fight/flight involves the group's defensive escape into activity for its own sake and the preservation of the group is seen as linked with the attack on an outsider, on another group, or on one of its own *scapegoated* members; or in diversion and flight from its work group activity. Basic assumption activities are essentially the shared phantasies and *defence mechanisms* of the whole group. Three characteristics of basic assumption behaviour are that emotions such as anxiety, love, hate, fear, etc., take on different forms according to which of the three basic assumptions is being mobilised; time plays no part; and there is no process of development, either from one basic assumption to another or in terms of work group activity. Basic assumption behaviour operates in all groups in varying degrees, whether these be formally structured groups such as committees, unstructured groups or therapeutic groups.

BION, W. R. (1955), 'Group dynamics: a review' (in Klein, M. *et al.*, *New Contributions to Psychoanalysis*, Maresfield Reprints, Karnac, London).
BION, W. R. (1961), *Experiences in Groups* (Tavistock, London).
PINES, M. (ed.) (1984), *Bion and Group Psychotherapy* (Routledge & Kegan Paul, London).

Basic fault

A concept introduced by Balint (1968) to describe the individual's experience of missing something very fundamental inside. Balint arrived at the concept through his work with deeply regressed patients whose experience seemed to differ from the experience of having *libido* or repressed material blocked off and needing release. However, Balint came to believe that the 'experience of something missing' was, in some degree, a universal experience and that it derived from a failure of fit between the infant's needs and the mother's response. Balint's concept thus has similarities with Winnicott's idea of the *good enough mother*. If the mother fails, this leads to a split in the infant between a *true* and *false self*. The basic fault arises from the dyadic relationship between mother and infant and it thus occurs prior to the more complex triangular relation-

ship which has to be negotiated during the Oedipal phase (Balint, 1958). If the basic fault period is not successfully dealt with, the developing child and adult remains dependent and clinging in his relationship with *objects*. The concept has similarities with Lacan's concept of dehiscence, occurring in the pre-Imaginary stage of human development (see *French school of psychoanalysis*).

BALINT, M. (1958), 'The three areas of the mind' (*Int. J. of Psychoanalysis*, vol. 39, pp. 328-40).
BALINT, M. (1968), *The Basic Fault: Therapeutic Aspects of Regression* (Tavistock, London).

Basic id

See *Multi modal therapy*.

Bateson, Gregory (1904-1980)

Gregory Bateson, anthropologist, *communication* theorist and *systems* thinker, was born in Grantchester, near Cambridge, in 1904. He was the son of William and Beatrix Bateson, William being the leading biologist and geneticist of his time and profoundly involved with the rediscovery of Mendel's work in genetics. Gregory (named after Gregor Mendel) was the youngest of three brothers, and grew up in the intellectual atmosphere of his father's devotion to the natural sciences. From 1917 to 1921 he was a student at Charterhouse and in 1922 he went to St John's College, Cambridge, where he gained first class honours in the natural history tripos and an MA in anthropology. In 1925 he published his first paper in collaboration with his father, on the pattern and symmetry of colours in the feathers of red-legged partridges. From 1927 to 1929 Bateson began his career in anthropology by doing field work in New Britain and New Guinea. In 1931 he was made a fellow of St John's College and continued his field studies in New Guinea. In 1936 he married Margaret Mead, working with her in Bali and New Guinea. (Their marriage was dissolved in 1950, their daughter, Mary Catherine, becoming herself an anthropologist and linguist of distinction.) In 1940, Bateson entered the United States as a resident and after visiting professorships in New York and Cambridge, Massachusetts, he spent a year (1948-9) working with Jürgen Ruesch in California. Their book on *Communication: The Social Matrix of Psychiatry* was published in 1951 and pointed the way towards Bateson's major interest in communication paradox and schizophrenia. From 1954 to 1959 he was director of the research project on schizophrenic communication and along with Don Jackson, Jay Haley and John Weakland he published the seminal work *Toward a Theory of Schizophrenia* in 1956. This was destined to provide the basis for the development of the *systemic therapies* during the late 1950s. For some years he continued work on communication and family psychotherapy and remained an inspiration to the *family therapy* field and to its efforts in developing a truly systemic *epistomology*. He spent his last years at the Esalen Institute, California, where he died in 1980.

Behaviour modification

Like *behaviour therapy*, the term is used both to describe all those methods and techniques which derive from the principles of *learning theory*, and second, in a narrower sense, to describe only those techniques which are derived from Watsonian and Skinnerian principles. Here, the term is used in its narrow sense, to describe treatment techniques based on *operant conditioning* principles and, to a lesser extent, on the principles of imitation learning and *modelling* developed by Bandura (1969). Behaviour modification techniques also embrace those procedures used in in-patient settings, such as *contingency management* and the development of a *token economy*. Behaviour modification has even been suggested as a way of running whole societies (Skinner, 1948). *Bio-feedback* techniques are also frequently used for an assessment of the patient's problems. The cognitive and affective levels of the patient are usually not addressed directly and the patient-therapist relationship is not considered to be an important treatment variable.

Although considerable successes have been

claimed for its use with some extremely intractable problems, behaviour modification has been severely criticised on ethical grounds. Criticisms focus on its manipulative use of techniques on patients who may not be in a position to give informed consent. The *contract* for the treatment is often made between the therapist and a third party, such as a nurse or parent, rather than with the patient him or herself. The patient may therefore be in a very unfavourable position to influence the *goals* or the course of treatment. Moreover, serious abuses of patient groups may occur when staff are so enthusiastic about achieving specific goals that they override all other considerations (Bengelman, 1975). A specialised journal is published, *Behavior Modification*, over and above the other journals published for behaviour therapy. (See *Behaviour therapy* for further discussion of issues which are generic to both approaches.)

BANDURA, A. (1969), *Principles of Behavior Modification* (Holt, Rinehart & Winston, New York).

BENGELMAN, D. A. (1975), 'Ethical and legal issues of behavior modification' (in Hersen, M. *et al.* (eds), *Progress in Behavior Modification*, vol. 1, Academic Press, New York).

HERSEN, M. *et al.* (1981), *Progress in Behavior Modification* (Academic Press, New York).

KALISH, H. (1981), *From Behavior Science to Behaviour Modification* (McGraw-Hill, New York).

KAZDIN, A. E. (1978), *History of Behavior Modification* (University Park, Baltimore).

KRASNER, L. and ULLMAN, L. P. (1966), *Research in Behavior Modification* (Holt, Rinehart & Winston, New York).

SKINNER, B. F. (1948), *Walden II* (Macmillan, London).

SKINNER, B. F. (1953), *Science and Human Behavior* (Macmillan, New York).

SKINNER, B. F. (1971), *Beyond Freedom and Dignity* (Knopf, New York).

WATSON, J. B. (1930), *Behaviorism* (revised edn, Harpers, New York).

Behaviour therapy

The term is used both in a broad sense and in a narrower, less inclusive way. Broadly, it is used to describe one of the three major therapeutic orientations to the treatment of psychological disorders. As with the other major orientations to psychotherapy (*psychoanalysis* and the *humanistic* approach), the term behaviour therapy covers a group of related methods and techniques, rather than a homogenous approach.

Grounded in experimental psychological research, behaviour therapy is derived from the principles and constructs of *learning theory* and the developments of this by Wolpe and Skinner. Thus, maladaptive behaviour results from either a deficiency of functional learning or from an acquisition of dysfunctional learning. Treatment interventions are therefore directed towards enabling new learning to take place or towards helping the client unlearn maladaptive habits. Behaviour therapists reject the idea that the *presenting problem* is symptomatic of an underlying disorder and treatment approaches are therefore geared to eliminating or reducing the intensity or frequency of the problem behaviour as presented.

The most widely used methods are those based on *classical conditioning* principles such as *systematic desensitisation*, used for phobias and anxiety states. Other methods of behaviour therapy include *anxiety management training, flooding, social skills training* and *assertiveness training.*

Looking at the term as an umbrella for a wide variety of approaches, several distinct groups can be discerned. Those workers who follow Skinner represent the far end of objective behaviourism (*behaviour modification*) where only what can be described as the observable and measurable behaviours of the individual are treated as data relevant to treatment and change. At the other end of the spectrum, *cognitive behaviour therapists* view cognitions and mental imagery as important to the assessment and treatment of problems. Currently the debate between behaviour therapists and cognitive behaviour therapists is lively and there is a considerable effort to try and determine whether the conditioning of behaviour or the changing of cognitions is the more effective primary strategy. Some of the issues are discussed by Tryon (1981). Valerio and Stone (1982) found no differential treatment effects between the two approaches. But the challenge from cognitive behaviour therapy is very strong, partly because it provides a more acceptable approach to those who criticise behaviour therapy for its *reductionism. Cognitive therapy* also has links and a position within the behavioural field as a whole and further challenges the more reductionist approaches by its greater interest in the client as a 'whole person'.

Features held in common by all varieties of behaviour therapy are a primary focus on the presenting problem; a *phenotypic* approach to behavioural assessment; the use of behavioural *contract*; and an emphasis on *outcome* evaluation, linked as far as possible to the methodology of the experimental laboratory. In contrast to behaviour modification, the therapist-client relationship has become a growing area of interest to behaviour therapists and several groups of clinicians have pointed to its importance (Wilson and Evans, 1977).

Behaviour therapy is used for some of the most complex therapeutic challenges, including chronic schizophrenia and mental handicap. Social workers, psychologists, psychiatrists, nurses and teachers have all made use of behavioural techniques with a range of client populations and behavioural principles have been used in *family, marital* and *group therapy.*

Similar criticisms have been made of behaviour therapy as of behaviour modification, although with perhaps less justification. They are concerned with its reductionism; its focus on *symptoms* with the danger of *symptom substitution* and *symptom transfer;* and with the ethics of applying treatment, however effective, sometimes without the full consent of the patient. The latter objection applies in particular to the use of behavioural techniques with children and with psychotic patients, especially when those techniques may involve the administration of painful stimuli. Wolpe (1973) and others reply that there is a good deal of experimental evidence to suggest that behavioural techniques are effective, and the first ethical duty of the clinician is to be effective. (See *Ethics* for a further discussion.)

Compared with other treatment methods and modalities, there is a large body of outcome research into behavioural methods. Rachman and Wilson's (1980) important review confirms the efficacy and enduring positive effect of behaviour therapy. Several professional associations exist, the most prominent of which is the Association for the Advancement of Behaviour Therapy in the United States. A variety of specialised journals are published including *Behaviour Research and Therapy*, *Behavior Therapy*, and the *Journal of Behavior Therapy and Experimental Psychiatry*.

BELLACK, A. *et al.* (1982), *International Handbook of Behavior Modification and Therapy* (Plenum Press, New York).

FOA, E. B. and EMMELKAMP, P. (1983), *Failures in Behavior Therapy* (Wiley, New York).

FRANKS, C. M. (1969), *Behavior Therapy: Appraisal and Status* (McGraw-Hill, New York).

KANFER, F. H. and PHILLIPS, J. S. (1970), *Learning Foundations of Behavior Therapy* (Wiley, New York).

RACHMAN, S. J. and WILSON, G. T. (1980), *The Effects of Psychological Therapy* (Pergamon, Oxford).

RIMM, D. C. and MASTERS, J. C. (1979), *Behaviour Therapy: Techniques and Empirical Findings* (Academic Press, London).

TRYON, W. W. (1981), 'The practice of clinical behaviorism: an overview' (*J. of Behavior Therapy and Experimental Psychiatry*, vol. 12, pp. 197-202).

VALERIO, H. P. and STONE, G. L. (1982), 'Effects of behavioral, cognitive and combined treatments for assertion as a function of differential deficits' (*J. of Counseling Psychology*, vol. 29, pp. 158-68).

WILSON, G. T. and EVANS, I. (1977), 'The

therapist-client relationship in behavior therapy' (in Gurman, A. S. and Razin, A. M., *Effective Psychotherapy*, Pergamon, New York).

WOLPE, J. (1973), *The Practice of Behavior Therapy* (2nd edn, Pergamon, New York).

WOLPE, J. and LAZARUS, A. (1966), *Behavior Therapy Techniques* (Pergamon, New York).

YATES, A. (1970), *Behavior Therapy* (Wiley, New York).

Behavioural analysis

The systematic study and recording of the relationship of problem behaviours and their consequences in order to establish a *base line* prior to and alongside the introduction of treatment. Behavioural analysis is the first step taken in the *behavioural therapies* and involves a thorough assessment of the behaviour to be changed, the situations in which it occurs and the consequences that follow. Part of the behavioural analysis may be undertaken by the client (*self-monitoring*); by a parent or spouse or by some other third party such as a nurse. The therapist will usually combine the information he collects from the client, with an investigation of his history. Behavioural analysis is, however, essentially *phenotypic* and is not concerned to classify *symptoms* or patients according to psychiatric taxonomies so much as examine the interaction between *stimulus* and *response*, and between *reinforcer* and *symptom* from which a programme of behaviour therapy can be tailored to the individual client's needs.

Mackay (1976) suggests a six-stage approach to behavioural analysis as follows: obtain a precise description of the maladaptive behaviour (using direct observation, *simulation* of anxiety-provoking situations, self-monitoring, etc.); define the controlling stimuli; determine the reinforcers; test out the *hypotheses* using *homework assignments*; administer treatment techniques and evaluate results. Mackay emphasises that behavioural analysis needs to be an ongoing process which is only terminated when the treatment *goals* have been achieved.

KANFER, F. H. and SASLOW, G. (1969), 'Behavioral diagnosis' (in Franks, C. M. (ed.),

Behavior Therapy: Appraisal and Status, McGraw-Hill, New York).

MACKAY, D. (1976), *Clinical Psychology: Theory and Therapy*, Methuen, London).

See also *Diagnosis*.

Behavioural family therapy

An approach to *family therapy* which emphasises some of the theoretical and technical aspects of *behaviour therapy*, adapting these to work with the family *system*. Behaviour therapy is a relatively new influence on family therapy but it is growing rapidly. Therapy consists in changing the contingencies by which the *identified patient* and other family members receive concern and attention from one other. Liberman (1972) summarises the task of the therapist in conjunction with the family as being 'to 1. Specify the maladaptive behaviour. 2. Choose reasonable goals which are alternative, adaptive behaviours. 3. Direct and guide the family to change the contingencies of their social reinforcement patterns from maladaptive to adaptive target behaviours'.

Essential to behavioural family therapy is the use by the therapist of himself as a social reinforcer for adaptive behaviours; the assessment of family problems in behavioural terms using a *behavioural analysis*; and the use of behavioural techniques such as *reinforcement, modelling, tasks, extinction* and *behavioural rehearsal*. Treatment proceeds on the basis of a *contract* between family and therapist. Although Liberman's approach is clearly directed towards the family as a whole, there is a tendency amongst behavioural family therapists to work with *sub-systems* and, for example, to teach parents how to modify the behaviour of children (Hawkins *et al.* 1966) or couples to modify the behaviour of the other spouse. One of the theoretical difficulties encountered in behavioural family therapy is how to integrate the essentially linear causal S-R model into a systems framework. Barton and Alexander (1981) have broken important ground in this respect in their model of functional family therapy which attempts to integrate *systems theory* with *behaviour therapy* and apply the result in family treatment. Some aspects of behavioural family therapy are closely related to *structural family therapy*. The outcome of behavioural family therapy has been researched by Patterson and Fleishman (1979).

ALEXANDER, J. F. and BARTON, C. (1976), 'Behavioural systems therapy for families' (in Olson, D. H. (ed.), *Treating Relationships*, Graphic Press, Lake Mills, Iowa).

BARTON, C. and ALEXANDER, J. F. (1981), 'Functional family therapy' (in Gurman, A. S. and Kniskern, D. P., *Handbook of Family Therapy*, Brunner/Mazel, New York).

HAWKINS, R. P. *et al.* (1966), 'Behaviour therapy in the home' (*J. of Experimental Child Psychology*, vol. 4, pp. 99-107).

LIBERMAN, R. P. (1972), 'Behavioural approaches to family and couple therapy' (in Sager, C. and Kaplan, H. S. (eds), *Progress in Group and Family Therapy*, Brunner/Mazel, New York).

PATTERSON, G. R. and FLEISHMAN, M. (1979), 'Maintenance of treatment effects: some considerations concerning family systems and follow-up data' (*Behaviour Therapy*, vol. 10, pp. 168-73).

STUART, R. B. (1971), 'Behavioural contracting within the families of delinquents' (*J. of Behavioural Therapy and Experimental Psychiatry*, vol. 2, pp. 1-11).

Behavioural interactional model (BIM)

An instrument devised by Lickorish for use as a basis for the *behavioural analysis* of couples or family groups. A dyadic system of analysis is used, with the behaviour of each member of the pair in the group being examined separately. The analysis is usually confined to the verbal behaviour of the dyad, which is carried out in three stages, the results of each stage being entered on an analysis sheet. The information is coded using *constructs* and *elements* and is processed using computer programmes devised for data cast in the form of *repertory grids*. The BIM forms a useful basis for organising and analysing data about the family and it is capable of being extended to large family groups and *networks*.

LICKORISH, J. R. (1975), 'A behavioural interactional model for assessing family relationships' (reprinted in Walrond-Skinner, S., *Developments in Family Therapy*, Routledge & Kegan Paul, London, 1981).

Behavioural marital therapy

A form of marital treatment based on the principles of *behaviour therapy* and *cognitive therapy*. As in the case of *family therapy* behavioural techniques were applied to marital therapy only rather recently, although as O'Leary and Turkewitz (1978) point out, behavioural marital therapy is now one of the three main approaches to *conjoint marital therapy*. Most behavioural marital therapy is conducted in *conjoint* sessions with husband and wife seen simultaneously. Liberman (1970) shows how each spouse can be helped to *shape* the behaviours of the other more satisfactorily, using techniques of positive *reinforcement* and *extinction*. Such intervention on the part of the therapist presupposes that a *behavioural analysis* has been undertaken and a *contract* has been worked out clarifying the behaviours which each spouse wishes changed in the other. Jacobson (1981) lists a complex pre-treatment assessment format which takes three weeks to complete. *Operant conditioning* and behaviour exchange procedures based on *contingency management* form an important part of therapy using a *quid pro quo* format. *Behavioural rehearsal* and *feedback* are included as part of the teaching of communication and problem solving skills. Various criticisms have been levied against behavioural marital therapy from the systems perspective, which are summarised by Gurman and Kniskern (1978) and Knudson *et al.* (1979). They include the fact that this method tends to concentrate on overt behaviours; it assumes an over-optimistic amount of co-operation; and it de-emphasises relationship skills on the part of the therapist. Jacobson and Weiss (1978) defend the position of behavioural marital therapy. Leadbeater and Farber (1983)

suggest a means of integrating different models of marital therapy, based on a differential assessment of need.

BANCROFT, J. (1975), 'The behavioural approach to marital problems' (*Brit. J. of Med. Psych.*, vol. 48, pp. 147-52).

FILSINGER, E. E. and LEWIS, R. A. (1980), *Assessing Marriage: New Behavioral Approaches* (Sage, Beverly Hills).

GURMAN, A. S. and KNISKERN, D. P. (1978), 'Behavioral marriage therapy: II and IV' (*Family Process*, vol. 17, pp. 139-48; and pp. 165-80).

JACOBSON, N. S. (1981), 'Behavioral marital therapy' (in Gurman, A. S. and Kniskern, D. P., *Handbook of Family Therapy*, Brunner/Mazel, New York).

JACOBSON, N. S. and MARGOLIN, G. (1979), *Marital Therapy* (Brunner/Mazel, New York).

JACOBSON, N. S. and WEISS, R. L. (1978), 'Behavioral marriage therapy: III (*Family Process*, vol. 17. pp. 149-64).

KNUDSON, R. M. *et al.* (1979), 'Behavioral marital therapy: a treatment in transition' (in Franks, C. and Wilson, G., *Annual Review of Behavior Therapy and Practice*, Brunner/Mazel, New York).

LEADBEATER, B. and FARBER, B. (1983), 'The limits of reciprocity in behavioral marriage therapy' (*Family Process*, vol. 22, pp. 229-37).

LIBERMAN, R. (1970), 'Behavioral approaches to family and couple therapy' (*Am. J. of Orthopscyh.*, vol. 40, pp. 106-18).

O'LEARY, K. D. and TURKEWITZ, H. (1978), 'Marital therapy from a behavioral perspective' (in Paolino, T. J. and McCrady, B. S. (eds), *Marriage and Marital Therapy*, Brunner/Mazel, New York).

STUART, R. B. (1980), *Helping Couples Change* (Guilford Press, New York).

Behavioural rehearsal

The practice of a new behaviour in an artificial setting until it has become comfortably part of the client's repertoire of responses and he has become able to use it appropriately in his real-life situation. The technique has been used most frequently in *assertiveness training* but is appropriate in other situations where there is a deficit of social skills or where dysfunctional behaviour is being replaced by a more adaptive response. According to Wolpe (1973) the technique was originally called 'behavioristic psychodrama'. It is usually preceded by instructions on the execution of the behaviour to be learned and by the *modelling* of this behaviour by the therapist. As the client attempts to perform the behaviour himself, the therapist may use *reinforcement*, *shaping* and *coaching* to encourage the client to move towards *successive approximations* of the desired behaviour. The theme of, for example, assertiveness may be practised using several different situations. The client may *role play* the behaviour of an employee approaching his employer, a husband talking to his wife, a customer complaining to a shopkeeper, or whatever the situations may be in which the client finds assertive behaviour difficult. The therapist is able to give the client immediate *feedback* and *knowledge of the results* of his performance, and suggest new ideas, thus maximising the learning potential of the situation. Wolpe and Lazarus (1966) describe the use of this technique. McFall and Marston (1970) have shown the efficacy of behavioural rehearsal with unassertive college students and McFall and Twentyman (1973) showed that rehearsal was an important ingredient in a comparative study of assertiveness treatments. As Wolpe (1973) points out, behavioural rehearsal also acts as a deconditioner of anxiety. Behavioural rehearsal forms an important element in a number of treatment approaches including *self-instructional training*, *coping skills interventions*, *social skills training* and *problem solving* approaches. Most researchers conclude that behavioural rehearsal improves *outcome* when combined with other strategies. In most situations it is a more effective technique than *covert modelling*.

McFALL, R. and MARSTON, A. (1970), 'An experimental investigation of behavior rehearsal in assertive training' (*J. of Abnormal Psychology*, vol. 76, pp. 295-303).

McFALL, R. and TWENTYMAN, C. (1973), 'Four experiments on the relative contributions of rehearsal, modeling and coaching to assertion training' (*J. of Abnormal Psychology*, vol. 81, pp. 199-218).

WOLPE, J. (1973), *The Practice of Behavior Therapy* (Pergamon, New York).

WOLPE, J. and LAZARUS, A. (1966), *Behavior Therapy Techniques* (Pergamon, New York).

See also *Fixed role therapy, Task.*

Behavioural sequence

The chain of *responses* together with their antecedent *stimuli*. Each unit of behaviour, viewed from the *learning theory* perspective, acts as a stimulus in relation to the responses that follow it and as a response to the stimulus that precedes it. The behavioural sequence engendered by the functional relationship between stimuli and responses (S-R theory) is the fundamental premise from which learning theory and *behaviour therapy* is developed. Thus, behaviour is conceived of as resulting from a *linear* though complex causal relationship between behavioural units. This dual function of behavioural occurrences is the basis of the 'vicious circle' phenomenon.

Behaviourism

The proposition that the subject matter of psychology is the study of observable behaviour and not the inner mental life of the individual. The term is used in two main ways: first, in a broad sense to describe an emphasis on behaviour and communication, which does not necessarily exclude what cannot be observed but may be inferred, and second, in a narrow sense, as intended by its originator, J. B. Watson (and developed further by Skinner) to mean only those external events of behaviour which can be observed. These two somewhat different meanings are reflected in their closest therapeutic derivatives, *behaviour therapy* and *behaviour modification* respectively.

The proposition was first stated in its pure or narrow form by Watson (1913): 'Psychology as the behaviorist views it is a purely objective branch of natural science. Its theoretical goal is the prediction and control of behavior. Introspection forms no essential part of its methods. . . . The behaviorist, in his efforts to get a unitary scheme of animal response, recognises no dividing line between man and brute. The behavior of man, with all its refinement and complexity, forms only a part of the behaviorist's total scheme of investigation.' Watson gave *conditioning* a prominent place and central to his views were his *stimulus-response* (S-R) concept. Behaviour always involves a response of the organism to a stimulus. Behaviourism is strongly marked by *reductionism* whereby human behaviour is seen as being ultimately explainable in terms of physiology. It stands in strong contrast to *psychoanalysis, humanistic psychology* and *systems theory* as a major explanatory principle of human functioning.

COHEN, D. (1979), *J. B. Watson: The Founder of Behaviorism* (Routledge & Kegan Paul, London).
SKINNER, B. F. (1953), *Science and Human Behavior* (Macmillan, New York).
WATSON, J. B. (1913), 'Psychology as the behaviorist views it' (*Psychological Review*, vol. 20, pp. 158-77).
WATSON, J. B. (1930), *Behaviorism* (revised edn, Harpers, New York).

Bereavement

The experience of loss which is precipitated by the death of a significant *object* or relationship. Some writers, by contrast, define bereavement as a process which includes *grief* and *mourning* in addition to the experience of the loss itself (Averill 1975). The loss experience may relate to material objects, pets, people, parts of the self, role, occupation, etc. The typical reaction to and result of bereavement is the experience of grief followed by a period of mourning. Smith (1982) states that bereavement imposes a disruption in 'taken-for-granted' reality – an attenuation of meaning and a threat to identity. The experience of bereavement is affected by the nature of the bereavement and the life cycle position of the bereaved.

AVERILL, J. R. (1975), 'Grief, its nature and significance' (in Carr, A. C., *Grief: Selected Readings*, Sciences Publishing, New York).
PARKS, C. M. (1972), *Bereavement: Studies of Grief in Adult Life* (Tavistock, London).
SCHOENBERG, B. *et al.* (1975), *Bereavement – Its Psychosocial Aspects* (Columbia University Press, New York).
SMITH, C. (1982), *Social Work with the Dying and Bereaved* (Macmillan, London).

Bereavement counselling

Therapeutic help offered to those who have experienced *bereavement*. Ideally, the therapist will have become involved before the loss or separation and can then offer help as part of the ongoing process involved in anticipatory *grief* and *mourning*. Elements of counselling the bereaved may be summarised as follows:

(1) Support the bereaved in making immediate decisions – in the case of death, attending the funeral, seeing the dead body, etc., any of which may help the bereaved later in doing his grief work.

(2) Facilitate the *catharsis* of feelings, recognising the need for defences against these feelings, while the person is in the early stages of grief.

(3) Tolerate the feelings when they are expressed.

(4) Reassure the bereaved that their intense feelings are normal (Glick *et al.* 1974).

(5) Enable the continuous repetition of expressions of loss, anger, sadness and guilt, as repetition is necessary for the mastery of loss (Simos, 1979).

(6) Encourage a developing acceptance of the finality of the loss, using techniques such as re-grief therapy (Wolkan, 1975).

(7) Facilitate disengagement from the deceased by helping gradually to sever the patient's identification with him or her.

(8) Help the bereaved regain a realistic memory of the deceased through repeated reflective discussion and help him replace this for the idealised or disillusioned picture he may be holding.

(9) Help the bereaved come to terms with the changes in role, social situation and

self-image involved in becoming a widow, fatherless, childless, no longer pregnant, handicapped, etc.

(10) Encourage the bereaved to consider and begin to make new relationships and link him or her with relevant *self-help* organisations where appropriate (for example, Cruse for widows, and Compassionate Friends for parents who have lost a child).

COOPER, J. (1980), 'Parental reaction to still-birth' (*Brit. J. of Social Work*, vol. 10, pp. 55-69).

GLICK, I. *et al.* (1974), *The First Year of Bereavement* (Wiley, New York).

PRITCHARD, E. *et al.* (eds) (1977), *Social Work with the Dying Patient and his Family* (Columbia, New York).

SCHOENBERG, B. (ed.) (1980), *Bereavement Counselling* (Greenwood Press, London).

SIMOS, B. G. (1979), *A Time to Grieve* (Family Service Association of America, New York).

WEINSTEIN, S. (1978), 'Sudden infant death syndrome' (*Am. J. of Psychiatry*, vol. 135, pp. 831-4).

WILKENFELD, L. (ed.) (1977), *When Children Die* (Kendall/Hunt, Dubuque, Iowa).

WOLKAN, V. D. (1975), 'Re-grief therapy' (in Schoenberg, B. *et al.*, *Bereavement – Its Psychosocial Aspects*, Columbia, New York).

See also *Crisis intervention.*

Berne, Eric (1910-1970)

Founder of *transactional analysis*, Eric Berne gained his MD at McGill University in 1935 and undertook his psychiatric residency at Yale from 1936 to 1941. He began his psychoanalytic training in New York, with an interruption of three years for army service during the war. During this period he started working with groups, gaining new insights into the opportunities afforded by moving beyond the one-to-one therapeutic situation. After the war he moved to Carmel, California, and continued his psychoanalytic studies with Paul Federn and with Erik Erikson as his training analyst. Berne was greatly influenced by *ego psychology* from which his own work on *ego*

states emerged. However, he had already begun to move beyond *psychoanalysis* and in 1958 he published his first paper on transactional analyisis. This was the outcome of work he had been doing during the 1950s on the nature of intuition with the support of a small seminar of interested professionals. By 1964 an International Association of Transactional Analysis had been formed. Other influences on Berne during the 1950s were the development by Bateson and his associates of *communication* theory and Perls's work on *Gestalt therapy*. Drawing on these developments, which were also taking place in California during this period, Berne's attention was turned to the nature of *transactions* and he began to classify the variety of *games* that individuals play in their effort to communicate with one another. This work led him finally to develop his ideas on the *scripts* which get used to map out adult actions based upon childhood decisions. Berne was a prolific writer up until his sudden death in 1970. His best-known books include *Games People Play* (1964) and *What Do You Say After You Say Hello?* (1972). His main theoretical ideas were set out in *Transactional Analysis in Psychotherapy* (1961) and *Principles of Group Treatment* (1966).

Bibliotherapy

Literal Greek meaning 'book healing'. The therapeutic use of literature and of other audio visual materials to promote the growth, development or psychological healing of the individual. Shrodes (1950) defines bibliotherapy as 'a process of dynamic interaction between the personality of the reader and the literature as a psychological field which may be utilized for personality assessment, adjustment and growth'. Additionally, bibliotherapy is often seen as an adjunct to other kinds of psychotherapy.

Bibliotherapy may be conducted in a one-to-one relationship with a therapist or in a group work setting. Rubin (1978) has suggested a three-fold classification of bibliotherapy according to the setting, goals and type of participants involved: institutional, where the patients are often hospitalised, psychiatric patients, and the objective is the dissemination of information; clinical, where the patients may have emotional or behavioural problems, and the objective is therefore the development of *insight* or behaviour change, through the use of *catharsis* and empathy-inducing imaginative literature; and third, developmental, where the patients are normal individuals, though they may be experiencing a *crisis*, and the goal is therefore growth and *self-actualisation* through the use of both imaginative and didactic literature.

Sweeney (1976) outlines four principles of bibliotherapy: it is *biophilous*; its aim is to overcome moralisation; it must actively involve the participants; and it must foster competence. Part of the rationale behind biblio-therapy lies in the notion that the patient can be helped to approach his own threatening emotions and behaviour by having them *displaced* on to a neutral situation of a story or action involving others rather than the self. The psychological distance created allows the individual to identify gradually with a situation that can help him to change. Howie (1983) describes a bibliotherapy group run in a psycho-geriatric day hospital where she and her co-leader encouraged group members to explore themes such as loneliness, death, relationships and change by bringing news-paper cuttings, memorabilia, photos and pictures, and using songs and taped music. Bibliotherapy may be used to give didactic information regarding particular problems, e.g. *sex therapy*, child rearing and stress; or to help children cope with special difficulties such as learning about their adoption, the birth of a new baby or visiting the doctor or dentist for the first time. Where young children are coping with similar problems, the therapist may read a suitable story to a group of children as part of a *play therapy* session.

HOWIE, M. (1983), 'Bibliotherapy in social work' (*Brit. J. of Social Work*, vol. 13, pp. 287-319).

RUBIN, R. (1978), *Using Bibliotherapy: A Guide to Theory and Practice* (Oryx Press, Phoenix).

SHRODES, B. (1950), 'Bibliotherapy: a theor-etical and clinical experimental study' (unpublished dissertation, University of California).

SWEENEY, D. (1976), 'Bibliotherapy and the elderly' (in Rubin, R. (ed.), *Bibliotherapy Source Book*, Oryx Press, Phoenix).

Binswanger, Ludwig (1881-1966)
Binswanger was born in Kreuzlingen, Switzerland, in 1881. He gained his MD from the University of Zurich in 1907 and became a physician at the Burgholzli Mental Hospital in Zurich. During this period he came under the influence of C. G. Jung who was chief physician at the hospital and in 1907, he accompanied Jung on a visit to Vienna to meet Freud. After undertaking training in *psycho-analysis*, Binswanger took a post under his father at the Sanatorium Bellevue at Kreuzlingen, becoming chief medical director in 1917 and remaining there until 1956. Whilst remaining closely affiliated with psychoanalysis, Binswanger became strongly influenced by the existential philosophers Husserl and Heidegger, and later by Buber. His major contribution to psychotherapy was the integration of existential thought with psychoanalytic practice in his *existential psycho-therapy*. Binswanger died at Kreuzlingen in 1966. His main work in English translation is *Being in the World* (1967).

Biodynamic psychology
A term introduced by Masserman (1980) to describe an approach to psychotherapy which is directed towards an integration of the individual's physical, social and meta-psychological needs. These three needs are termed by Masserman 'ur' needs, indicating their ultimate and universal quality. Masserman advocates a *holistic* therapy, with a unified and non-compartmentalised approach to the patient's mind, body and spirit, through proper psychological, organic and spiritual methods.

From work on animal studies, Masserman has elaborated five biodynamic principles which link animal and human needs and behaviour: motivational development – all behaviour originates in emergent physiological needs; individual – each organism evolves patterns of adaptation resulting from its innate potential, its maturational development and its individual and social experiences; adaptability – most frustrations are met by re-adjusting the approach to the problem or substituting new goals; conflictual uncertainty – deviations in conduct result from subjecting an organism to conflicts and uncertainties; and therapeutics – problems can be alleviated by a mixed psychosocial/physical approach. First, the patient's physical handicaps should be alleviated or eliminated as far as possible; second, through his *interpersonal* influence, the therapist tries to open up other approaches to his problems which include less reliance on defensive or self-destructive behaviour; and third, he helps the patient to find a belief system and a practical philosophy of life from which to gain comfort and serenity.

Masserman advocates using an eclectic range of techniques derived from a variety of sources and their application to the three-fold aspect of the 'ur' needs of all. Finally, he views the essential ingredients of therapy as resting not on any one approach but on a set of factors analogous to Frank's (1971) *non-specific factors*. For Masserman, these are 'the 7 Pil-R's' of therapeutic wisdom: reputation (of the therapist), rapport, relief, review, re-orientation, rehabilitation and resocialisation.

FRANK, J. D. (1971), 'Therapeutic factors in psychotherapy' (*Am. J. of Psychotherapy*, vol. 25, pp. 350-61).
MASSERMAN, J. H. (1980), *Principles and Practice of Biodynamic Psychotherapy: An Integration* (Thieme/Stratton, New York).

Bio-energetics

A derivative of Reichian therapy developed by Alexander Lowen. Lowen dropped Reich's emphasis on the development of orgastic potency as a primary goal of treatment and introduced instead the concept of grounding the self in the body and its relationship to the earth. He uses *structured exercises* for iden-

tifying stress positions in the body and for releasing the flow of energy. Exercises are designed to uncover restrictions and blockages in breathing and in the musculature. Much bio-energetic therapy is, like *Reichian therapy*, aimed at loosening the *character armour*. Lowen (1975) comments, 'energy, tension and character are inter-related since the total tension pattern controls the amount and use of the body energy. Therefore, bio-energetic analysis is basically a character analytic method of seeing people.' Other exercises resemble those employed by *Gestalt* therapists for releasing emotion and pent-up frustration. Massage and various forms of touch are used by the therapist. Although verbal and non-verbal phonations are encouraged whilst tension is being released, bio-energetic therapists focus almost entirely on physical rather than verbal means of expressing emotions, conflicts and repressed problems. In this sense, bio-energetics is rather one-sidedly directed towards the body in the same way as the verbal therapies are directed towards the mind. Bio-energetic therapy can be conducted in a group as well as in a one-to-one situation. No controlled studies have been reported of the *outcome* of bio-energetic therapy.

LOWEN, A. (1958), *The Language of the Body* (Collier Macmillan, London).
LOWEN, A. (1969), *The Betrayal of the Body* (Collier Macmillan, London).
LOWEN, A. (1975), *Bio-energetics* (Penguin, Harmondsworth).

See also *Autogenic training, Bio-feedback, Body therapies, Emotional flooding approaches, Primal therapy*.

Bio-feedback

The electrical *feedback* and monitoring of psycho-physiological events that occur within the individual, to provide a basis for the self-regulation of these processes. Bio-feedback is used in three main ways as a tool in different therapeutic approaches. First, to provide a diagnostic *base line* by establishing the exact physiological reactions to stressful events;

second, to enable the therapist to correlate this information with the patient's verbal reports, reducing the gaps and distortions in the patient's information; and third, as a means of treatment, relaxation being brought about in that part of the body to which the bio-feedback apparatus is applied.

Various kinds of apparatus are used to measure and treat different physiological processes. The patient is attached to the apparatus and the therapist gives instructions and help during the early sessions, after which the patient is able to monitor his responses by himself. *Relaxation training* or *meditation* is often suggested to help the patient control his stress reactions. Bio-feedback introduces a new *feedback loop* between the body and the brain which can aid self-regulation and, although it is used mainly by *behaviour therapists*, viewed in this broad way it is a relevant tool for a wide variety of approaches.

BASMAJIAN, J. V. (ed.) (1979), *Bio-feedback – Principles and Practice for Clinicians* (Williams & Wilkins, Baltimore).

FORGIONE, A. G. and HOLMBERG, R. (1981), 'Bio-feedback therapy' (in Corsini, R. (ed.), *Handbook of Innovative Psychotherapies*, Wiley, New York).

OLTON, D. S. and NOONBERG, A. B. (1980), *Bio-feedback: Clinical Applications in Behavioral Medicine* (Prentice-Hall, Englewood Cliffs, New Jersey).

ROMANO, J. L. (1982), 'Biofeedback training and therapeutic gains: clinical impressions' (*Personnel and Guidance Journal*, vol. 60, pp. 473-6).

SCHWARTZ, G. E. (1978), 'Psychobiological foundations of psychotherapy and behavior change' (in Garfield, S. and Bergin, A. E., *Handbook of Psychotherapy and Behavior Change*, Wiley, New York).

See also *Body therapies, Psychobiology*.

Bion, Wilfred, R. (1897-1979)
Bion, a member of the *British School* of psychoanalysis and an original thinker of great stature in the psychoanalytic field was born in India, the son of a British Government officer.

He was educated in Britain from the age of eight and, as a young man, joined the Royal Tank Corps soon after the outbreak of the First World War. He entered Queen's College, Oxford in 1919 where he read Modern History. In 1924 he went to study medicine at London University and later entered psychoanalytic training, taking a post at the Tavistock Clinic, London, from 1933 to 1948. Again, his work was interrupted, this time by the Second World War. He was profoundly affected by his experiences during both wars, and during the second he was able to gain valuable experience in the use of group work methods and their application to the selection and training of army officers. In 1945 he became Chairman of the Medical Committee at the Tavistock Clinic and he entered analysis with Melanie Klein, whose work profoundly affected his own. In 1961 he published in book form a collection of papers entitled *Experiences in Groups*, and although the remainder of his professional life was devoted mainly to *psychoanalysis* his contribution to the understanding of *group process* was seminal. During the 1950s and early 1960s, Bion was a prominent member of the British Psychoanalytic Society and along with his private psychoanalytic practice, he produced a series of important books on theory and practice: *Learning from Experience* (1962); *Elements of Psychoanalysis* (1963), *Transformations* (1965); *Attention and Interpretation* (1970); and *Second Thoughts* (1978). In 1968 he left Britain and spent the last years of his life practising and teaching in California. Here he wrote his three-volume autobiographical novel, *A Memoir of the Future*, and a volume of autobiography describing his childhood and First World War experiences, *The Long Weekend*. He returned to die in Oxford in 1979.

Biophilous
See *Modes of relatedness*.

Birth order
See *Family constellation*.

Birth trauma

A concept defined by Otto Rank (1929) in which he suggests that the anxiety experienced by the infant at birth is the prototype of all later anxiety and that psychic life in its totality has at its roots this original traumatic event. Freud had suggested that the birth experience may account for the origins of some neurotic anxiety and Moxon (1926) considered Rank's ideas as an anticipation of Freud's concept of the *death instinct*. But Rank's extension of the concept was rejected by Freud and by Freudian psychoanalysts. Rank suggested that the healing factors in *psychoanalysis* were the representation of birth symbols, the re-enactment of the oneness with mother through the *transference* and the separation from mother's womb acted out through the separation from the analyst at the end of treatment. The universal neurotic wish was a desire to return to the womb and only when this is overcome is the analysis complete. Recently, new interest has been shown in the psychological effects of the birth process by advocates of natural childbirth and Leboyer (1975) suggests that the quiet, calm and loving separating of the baby from the uterus enhances the baby's mental health and facilitates the bonding process with mother.

LEBOYER, F. (1975), *Birth without Violence* (Knopf, New York).
MOXON, C. (1926), 'Freud's death instinct and Rank's libido theory' (*Psychoanalytic Review*, vol. 13, pp. 294-303).
RANK, O. (1929), *The Trauma of Birth* (Harcourt Brace & Company, New York).

See also *Attachment theory*, *Primal therapy*, *Rebirthing*, *Will therapy*.

Bleuler, Eugene (1857-1939)

Eugene Bleuler was born at Zollikon near Zurich in 1857. After gaining his MD from the University of Zurich, he began work at a psychiatric hospital at Rheinau in 1886. In 1898, he was appointed professor of psychiatry at the University of Zurich and director of the Burgholzli Clinic. He was instrumental in applying Freud's ideas to psychiatry and in 1911 he published his major work on dementia praecox, for which he coined and substituted the term schizophrenia. He took a more optimistic view of schizophrenia than was usual at the time and suggested that it was a group of disorders not all of which resulted in inevitable deterioration. He wrote extensively on schizophrenia, autism and related areas and he coined the term *ambivalent* to describe the experience of conflicting emotions and impulses at an unconscious level, often at the root of neurotic disorder.

Body language

See *Non-verbal communication*.

Body therapies

Term used to describe a group of therapies which emphasise the part played by the body in the genesis and resolution of psychological conflict. They include *autogenic training*, *relaxation training*, *Reichian therapy*, the *Alexander technique*, *bio-energetics*, *bio-feedback*, *rebirthing*, *primal therapy*, *structural integration* and *dance therapy*. The general rationale underlying the body therapies has been the closure of what their founders perceived to be a mind/body split and the development of a more *holistic* approach to treatment.

See also *Psychobiology*.

Breuer, Josef (1842-1925)

Breuer was born in Vienna in 1842 and gained his MD from the University of Vienna in 1867. His contribution to psychotherapy took the form of close co-operation with the early development of Freud's ideas and his influence is partly seen in his reinforcement of Freud's biological emphases. His own therapeutic work with Anna O. provided an early breakthrough into understanding *unconscious* processes, and particularly the operation of *transference*. Freud took over the treatment of Anna O. from Breuer (who had treated her from 1880 to 1882 by hypnosis) and began to experiment with the use of *free association* as a substitute for hypnosis. In 1895 Breuer and Freud published their seminal book, *Studies on*

Hysteria, in which they describe the beginnings of *psychoanalysis*. Soon after publication, however, the friendship between the two men deteriorated due to their disagreement about the existence of infantile sexuality, and their professional collaboration ceased. Breuer continued conducting a private practice in Vienna and died in Vienna in 1925.

Brief focal family therapy
An approach to *family therapy* derived from *focal psychotherapy* and other brief psychoanalytic approaches to individual treatment developed at the Tavistock Clinic, London by Malan and others. Brief focal family therapy has been developed by a group of workers at the Hospital for Sick Children's Department of Psychological Medicine, Great Ormond Street, London. The approach emphasises a focus on the family or couple as a whole; the gathering of information to test a *focal formulation* and the generation of dynamic hypotheses which are condensed into a *focal hypothesis* which serves as a guide to the therapist throughout his contact with the family. The treatment plan which is summarised in the focal hypothesis is adapted and modified as treatment progresses, with the help of an ongoing record kept on a *focal therapy record sheet*. The sequence of sessions varies from once- to six-weekly and the period of contact with the family is from three to nine months. A variety of tools is being developed to assess the *outcome* of this approach and to evaluate its results.

KINSTON, W. and BENTOVIM, A. (1981), 'Creating a focus for brief marital or family therapy' (in Budman, S., *Forms of Brief Therapy*, Guilford Press, New York).

Brief psychoanalytic psychotherapy
A group of approaches which have their roots in the earliest development of *psychoanalysis*. Many of Freud's own treatments were relatively short-term, but as psychoanalysis became established and the length of treatment increased, other members of the original group, Ferenczi, Stekel and Rank, and later

Alexander, began to introduce modifications, tending towards briefer treatments. However, it was not until much later that there was an increase in interest in these, and during the 1960s and 1970s several different models were developed including Malan's *focal psychotherapy*, Mann's *time-limited psychotherapy*, Sifneos's *short-term anxiety-provoking psychotherapy*, and Bloom's *single session therapy*. Although each of these methods has its own particular emphasis, they are all characterised by the setting of a fixed time limit for treatment, their focus on a specific problem, their expectation of a high level of motivation, and a higher level of activity on the part of the therapist than is usual in psychoanalytic work. Favourable results have been reported by Wolberg (1965) and others.

BELLACK, L. (1981), 'Brief psychoanalytic psychotherapy of non-psychotic depression' (*Am. J. of Psychotherapy*, vol. 35, pp. 160-72).
DAVANLOO, H. (1978), *Basic Principles and Techniques in Short Term Dynamic Psychotherapy* (Spectrum, New York).
GILLIERON, E. (1981), 'Psychoanalysis and brief psychotherapy' (*Psychotherapy and Psychosomatics*, vol. 351, pp. 244-56).
MARMOR, J. (1979), 'Short term dynamic psychotherapy' (*Am. J. of Psychiatry*, vol. 136, pp. 149-55).
STONE, L. (1951), 'Psychoanalysis and brief psychotherapy' (*Psychoanalytic Quarterly*, vol. 20, pp. 215-36).
WOLBERG, L. R. (ed.) (1965), *Short Term Psychotherapy* (Grune & Stratton, New York).

See also *Active analysis, Active technique, Brief therapy, Corrective emotional experience, Crisis intervention, Will therapy*.

Brief therapy
A term used to describe a range of therapies, deliberately structured to be of short duration. Varied in their theoretical approaches, they are linked by their common focus on relative brevity.

It is important to distinguish between planned short-term therapy and unplanned premature termination. Brief therapy, as defined here, refers to planned short-term work. Some of the earliest psychoanalytic treatments were rendered in a very short time period by Freud himself, and each new orientation and approach to therapy has produced a model of brief work suitably adapted from its parent orientation. Thus, brief behavioural therapy, short-term family therapy, etc., have been developed. Butcher and Koss (1978) list nine elements which they call 'common technical characteristics of crisis oriented and brief psychotherapy'. These can be summarised as follows: time limits – these range from *single session therapy* to treatments lasting up to about twenty-five sessions, the average number of sessions falling between about six to ten; limited goals – a focus is sought on specific symptoms, problems or areas of disturbance; present centredness – a focus is kept on the current problems and their immediate context; directiveness and activity on the part of the therapist; rapid early assessment and interwoven treatment; need for flexibility on the part of the therapist; need to allow the patient opportunity for ventilation; speed in forming a *therapeutic alliance*; correct selection of patients – the weight of evidence suggests that brief therapy is more suitable with less disturbed patients (exceptions to this being the work of Balint *et al.* (1973)).

The need to offer psychotherapeutic treatment to a wider range of the population, debarred from long-term therapies by the investment of time required (and money where this is relevant), acted as a spur for the development of briefer models. Some writers sharply distinguish *crisis intervention* from brief therapy. Specifically, brief therapy is thought to be best suited to those in whom the behavioural problem is of acute onset (though advocates of *focal psychotherapy* would disagree with this); those whose previous adjustment has been good; those with a good ability to relate; and those with high initial motivation. Brief therapy is considered to be particularly suitable for individuals from a low socioeconomic situation because of the concrete nature of the *goals* established and the more directive nature of the therapist's intervention (although both factors would also hold good for a variety of other directive therapies).

Rapid ability to form a *therapeutic alliance* and to assess the patient's problems are essential therapist skills. Factors thought to be associated with successful *outcome* include expectancy effects; the high level of emotional arousal present if the patient comes into therapy in a state of crisis; the pressure to change induced by the knowledge that therapy is time-limited (where this is relevant); the activity level of the therapist in sessions, though Rush and Gerner (1972) suggest that low activity at the beginning and high activity in the last part of the session is the important factor for a positive outcome to occur; high levels of encouragement by the therapist and the enhancement of the patient's sense of mastery (Frank 1974). The outcome literature has sought to answer three questions regarding brief therapy: Does brief psychotherapy result in patient improvement? How do the results of short-term and long-term therapies compare? Is one short-term approach superior to another? Most studies suggest that, as well as being more efficient in terms of the use made of the therapist's time, brief therapies can claim results comparable with equivalent long-term approaches. Budman (1981) suggests that the use of brief therapy could help alter the expectation of psychotherapeutic services from the continuous, relatively long-term model to the intermittent approach offered by other professions such as general practitioners, solicitors, etc. Brief therapy models have been developed over the past thirty years to counteract the criticism often levied against long-term treatments that they are self-perpetuating, indulgent, dependence-inducing and can be abused by therapists who cannot or will not separate from their patients. Criticisms of brief therapies include their encouragement of a desire for instant solutions to problems and a preparedness to take short cuts which, while bringing about immediate symptom relief, may not produce long-term change. Research efforts have sought to answer these criticisms but they are not easily addressed even when positive long-term follow-up results are produced, since questions are raised as to the overall purpose and goals of the psychotherapeutic process which cannot easily be resolved.

BALINT, M. *et al.* (1973), *Focal Psychotherapy* (Tavistock, London).
BARTEN, H. H. (1971), *Brief Therapies* (Behavioural Publications, New York).
BUDMAN, S. (ed.) (1981), *Forms of Brief Therapy* (Guilford Press, New York).
BUTCHER, J. N. and KOSS, M. P. (1978), 'Research on brief and crisis oriented therapies' (in Bergin, A. E. and Garfield, S. L., *Handbook of Psychotherapy and Behavior Change*, Wiley, New York).
FRANK, J. D. (1974), 'Therapeutic components of psychotherapy – a twentyfive year progress report of research' (*J. of Nervous and Mental Diseases*, vol. 159, pp. 325-42).
RUSH, T. N. and GERNER, R. H. (1972), 'A study of the process of emergency psychotherapy' (*Am. J. of Psychiatry*, vol. 128, pp. 882-5).
SMALL, L. (1971), *The Briefer Psychotherapies* (Brunner/Mazel, New York).

British school (of psychoanalysis)

The term is used in a broad sense to distinguish the British contribution to psychoanalysis from American and other contributions. It originated with Ernest *Jones* and Edward *Glover*, but more specifically it is used by Sutherland (1980) to describe one group of British psychoanalysts whose work was fundamentally concerned with *object relations* and with the development of object relations theory. The group includes primarily W. R. D. Fairbairn, Harry Guntrip, Donald Winnicott, Michael Balint and John Bowlby. Although this group did not produce any joint work, their individual contributions embody a common development. The term 'British' is used to distinguish them from the English *Kleinian school* whose work nevertheless greatly influenced them. In contrast with the Kleinian school and with most other psychoanalytic schools, the British school emphasises the relationship of the individual to his environment, and some of Winnicott's (1965) statements, for example, 'there is no such thing as a baby – only babies with mothers', laid the groundwork for *conjoint* psychotherapeutic work. Bowlby's *attachment theory* is likewise embedded in the relationship of the individual to his environment. Sutherland summarises some of the common themes to be found amongst this group: all placed the therapeutic task as paramount, because all remained rooted in clinical work; all believed that the seeds of future psychopathology are sown in the early failure of the mother-baby relationship; and all saw the environment as integral to the understanding of *intrapsychic* processes. Sutherland (1980) comments that the 'British group does not presume to have made anything like an adequate conceptual map of the development of the *psyche*. The theoretical problems are far too complex for that. They have however shown a fruitful direction and have influenced many areas of contemporary psychoanalytic thought.'

BALINT, M. (1952), *Primary Love and Psychoanalytic Technique* (Hogarth Press, London).
BOWLBY, J. (1969, 1973, 1980), *Attachment and Loss* (3 vols, Penguin, Harmondsworth).
FAIRBAIRN, W. R. D. (1952), *Psychoanalytic Studies of the Personality* (Tavistock, London).
GUNTRIP, H. (1961), *Personality Structure and Human Interaction* (Hogarth Press, London).
SUTHERLAND, J. D. (1980), 'The British object relations theorists' (*J. of Am. Psychoan. Assoc.*, vol. 28, pp. 829-58).
WINNICOTT, D. W. (1965), *Collected Papers* (Hogarth Press, London).

Bug in ear

See *Audio visual equipment.*

Burn out

An expression used to describe the deleterious effects of psychotherapy upon the therapist resulting in his physical or psychological withdrawal. Cherniss (1980), in his study of stress in the helping professions generally, describes burn out as 'a process in which a service provider psychologically disengages from the work in response to job-related stress'. Burn out is characterised by chronic low energy, defensiveness and *distancing* manoeuvres. Despite the prevalence of this experience in therapists, the effects of psychotherapy on the therapist have not received very much attention. Orlinsky and Howard (1977) offer several reasons for the paucity of research into the therapist's experience of the therapeutic process, but they conclude from their own studies that therapists look forward to sessions with patients whom they judge are doing well and dread those which are not. The *reinforcement* gained from 'good' sessions is the polar opposite to the experience of sessions with patients who are doing badly and which, it can be assumed, have an aversive and debilitating effect on the therapist.

Faber and Heifetz (1982) have corroborated this assumption, suggesting that therapist satisfaction and withdrawal from therapy stems primarily from lack of therapeutic success. They also suggest that burn out relates to the particular character of the therapeutic relationship: 'burn out is primarily a consequence of the non-reciprocated attentiveness, giving and responsibility demanded of the therapist'. In addition, they found (1981) that overt expression of severe psychopathological symptoms in sessions and prolonged *resistance* on the part of the patient makes the therapist feel personally depleted and disengage from the therapeutic process. The reduction in anxiety gained from *experience, credibility* and perceived *competence* may all militate against burn out.

CHERNISS, C. (1980), *Staff Burn Out: Job Stress in the Human Services* (Sage, London).
COOPER, C. L. and PAYNE, R. (1978), *Stress at Work* (Wiley, Chichester).
FABER, B. and HEIFETZ, L. J. (1981), 'The satisfactions and stresses of psychotherapeutic work: a factor analytic study' (*Professional Psychology*, vol. 12, pp. 621-30).
FABER, B. and HEIFETZ, L. J. (1982), 'Process and dimensions of burn out in psychotherapists' (*Professional Psychology*, vol. 13, pp. 293-301).

ORLINSKY, D. E. and HOWARD, K. I. (1977), 'The therapist's experience of psychotherapy' (in Gurman, A. S. and Razin, A. M., *Effective Psychotherapy* (Pergamon, New York).
PARRY, G. and GOWLER, D. (1983), 'Career stresses on psychological therapists' (in Pilgrim, D., *Psychology and Psychotherapy*, Routledge & Kegan Paul, London).
PINES, A. M. and ARUNSEN, E. (1981), *Burn Out* (The Free Press, New York).

See also *Therapist variable.*

C

Calibration

A term used by Bateson (1961) to describe the fixed range or 'setting' within which a *system* operates. An example is the setting of the thermostat on a central heating system. When the room temperature drops below the calibration, the system will be activated and the room temperature returns to within the calibrated range. The process whereby the temperature of the room is increased while the calibration remains the same is called *negative feedback*. A change in the calibration of the central heating system is described as a *step function*. The term is useful in understanding the difference in their tolerance of change shown by families and other *systems*. Those which are calibrated at one level will adapt and adjust to stresses coming from the environment; those calibrated at a different level will find a much lower level of stress difficult to cope with. In the second group, tension may escalate into *runaway* or crystallise into an over-rigid *homeostasis*.

BATESON, G. (1961), 'The bio-social integration of the schizophrenic family' (in Ackerman, N. W. *et al.* (eds), *Exploring the Base for Family Therapy*, Family Service Association of America, New York).
WATZLAWICK, P. *et al.* (1967), *Pragmatics of*

Human Communication (W. W. Norton & Company, New York).

See also *Schismogenesis*.

Cartesian

Of or relating to René Descartes (1596-1650), French philosopher and mathematician. The term 'Cartesian' may also be used to refer to the theoretical products of his contemporaries and immediate successors in attempting to supply what they found lacking in his remarkable attempt to reconstitute the whole of human knowledge.

According to Descartes's 'method of doubt', nothing should be accepted as true if there can be any occasion to doubt it. This meant that for Descartes, only scientific knowledge is certain, evident knowledge, and this view continues to be reflected in the idea that the only valid way of understanding human beings and their environment is the scientific method. Although, according to Descartes, knowledge is restricted to what can be known without doubt, one thing at least he cannot doubt: his own existence as a thinking being. Doubting, indeed, having any thought at all, presupposes existence as a thinking thing, summarised in his most famous formulation, *cogito ergo sum*.

Descartes argues for a general dualism: the theory that there are just two fundamental categories into which all things fall. The method of doubt, and the discovery of the indubitability of his own existence as a thinking thing in particular, led Descartes to a dualistic concept of the person. If I can be certain of my existence as a thinking thing while in doubt that I have a body, then I and my body, if I have one, must be really distinct. It is not necessarily the case that, existing as a mind, I must also exist as a body. A person, once grounds have been developed to believe that such exists, is made up of only two distinct 'substances', a mind (*res cogitans*) and a body (*res extensa*). Whilst the latter is extended in space and time, the former is not.

Descartes's method is essentially analytic and consists in breaking down problems or units of study into their constituent parts, understanding them as parts and arranging them in their logical order. This method has been extremely important and influential in modern scientific thought. There are, however, a variety of problems attached to Cartesian thinking in its application to psychosocial problems. First, we are left with the problem as to how the two radically different 'substances' defined by Descartes might interact to constitute the life of the person. The way in which cognitions, emotions and bodily events seem interwoven is inexplicable within Cartesian theory. Second, its *reductionism* disallows the complexity experienced in interactions between the parts of a person and between a person and his environment. Third, it encourages a reification of the person and a mechanistic understanding of therapeutic intervention.

CAPRA, F. (1982), *The Turning Point: Science, Society and the Rising Culture* (Wildwood House, London).
HALDANE, E. S. and ROSS, G. T. R. (translators) (1934), *The Philosophical Works of Descartes* (2 vols, Cambridge University Press).
KENNY, A. (1968), *Descartes* (Random House, New York).
STRAWSON, P. F. (1959), *Individuals* (Methuen, London).
VROOMAN, J. R. (1970), *René Descartes* (Putnam, New York).
WILLIAMS, B. (1978), *Descartes: The Project of Pure Enquiry* (Penguin, Harmondsworth).

See also *Holism, Systems theory*.

Castration complex

Term introduced by Freud (1908, 1909) to describe the anxiety engendered in children when they perceive the difference between the sexes. Freud suggested that, when boys realise that girls have no penis, they experience a parental threat of castration which they believe to be a punishment for their incestuous desire for a sexual relationship with their mother. Girls experience the castration complex as a punishment that has already been carried out for their desire for a sexual relationship with their father. For boys, the castration complex arises *out of* the *Oedipus complex*, whilst for a girl, the discovery that she does not have a penis and the resulting castration complex moves her *towards* the Oedipus complex.

The resolution of the Oedipus complex and the formation of the *super ego* leads to the repression of the castration complex, leaving girls with a residual *penis envy*. Freud (1912) linked the castration complex with the *incest taboo* for which it serves as a major prohibitor. Some psychoanalytic writers have suggested that the origins of the castration complex lie instead in the baby's experience of separation from mother at birth and the ensuing *birth trauma*; and others that it stems from the baby's experience of the mother's nipple being removed at the end of each feed.

The concept is a controversial one, especially outside *psychoanalysis*. Hare (1962) has shown that there were good reasons for children fearing castration in the nineteenth century, since it was used as a routine threat to prevent masturbation. Moreover, as Schatzman (1976) has pointed out, Freud's (1909) account of 'Little Hans's' phobia about horses and the links Freud made with the little boy's castration complex, omits to take note of Hans's parents' frequent overt castration threats as being obvious explanatory material for Hans's 'complex'.

FREUD, S. (1908), 'On the sexual theories of children' (*Standard Edition*, vol. 9, Hogarth Press, London).
FREUD, S. (1909), 'Analysis of a phobia in a five-year old boy' (*Standard Edition*, vol. 10, Hogarth Press, London).
FREUD, S. (1912), 'Totem and taboo' (*Standard Edition*, vol. 13, Hogarth Press, London).
HARE, E. H. (1962), 'Masturbatory insanity: the history of an idea' (*J. of Mental Science*, vol. 108, pp. 1-25).
SCHATZMAN, M. (1976), *Soul Murder* (Penguin, Harmondsworth).

Catharsis

Literal Greek meaning 'cleansing'. The emotional release achieved by *abreaction*. Catharsis occurs either after spontaneous abreaction or as a result of psychotherapy. It produces release from repressed emotion and a subsequent feeling of relief and well-being. The term was used by Aristotle in his *Poetics* to describe the emotional release experienced by an audience after witnessing and emotionally participating in a tragic play. Freud and Breuer (1893-5) adopted the term to describe an essential effect of the therapeutic process in terms of their blocked-affect model. With the development of the theory of *transference* and the importance placed on *interpretations* and *working through* the importance of catharsis in psychoanalytic therapies diminishes. However, catharsis is an important part of the patient's therapeutic experience and it remains a treatment *goal* in a wide variety of group and individual psychotherapies. For example, in *primal therapy*, *rebirthing*, *Z-process attachment therapy* and many other of the newer therapies, catharsis is the primary treatment tool.

FREUD, S. and BREUER, J. (1893-5), 'Studies on hysteria' (*Standard Edition*, vol. 2, Hogarth Press, London).

Cathexis

The magnetic power of an idea, memory, image or *object* for the individual. The degree to which an object, etc., is cathected is the degree to which it possesses a 'quota of affect' for the individual. The term denotes both *the action* of cathecting an object, idea, etc., with attractive power for the *psyche* and *the energy* with which it is cathected. The term can be translated into the word 'investment' without loss of meaning. The concept derives from Freud's original use of neurophysiology as a basis for his psychological theories. It is thus fraught with ambiguities and problems and attracts criticism from those who find Freud's biological metaphors unhelpful and unnecessary. Berne (1961) adopted the term and suggested that cathexis occurs in three forms: bound (latent cathexis held in an inactive *ego state*; unbound (indigenous cathexis held in an active ego state); and free (active cathexis that can move across ego boundaries). Whichever ego state is currently cathected holds the executive power in the psychic system.

BERNE, E. (1961), *Transactional Analysis in Psychotherapy* (Grove, New York).
FREUD, S. (1900), 'The interpretation of dreams' (*Standard Edition*, vols 4 and 5, Hogarth Press, London).

See also *Economic model*.

Causality

The classical view of causality rests on the notion that a causal relation exists between two events or states of affairs which are designated 'cause' and 'effect' respectively, the cause being antecedent to the effect. According to quantum theory in atomic physics, however, some events at the atomic level do not have causes but occur at random or spontaneously, which brings into question the classical view of causality.

The manner in which one event necessitates another is by no means clear, and the Scottish philosopher, David Hume, took the view that what are identified as causal relations are simply experienced regularities of non-necessary constant conjunction. Events which are human actions raise special problems. If causes necessitate effects, then either our reasons for action are its 'compelling' causes, or our action is not in fact determined by the reasons we give in explanation of it. In either case we seem less free than we supposed, and in the latter case, seriously confused. Again the Humean account provides only temporary relief: the motives, desires and beliefs usually mentioned in giving reasons for intentional action may be sufficiently constant to be called 'causes' on Hume's account, but no necessitating connection is thereby alleged.

Causality is treated in different ways in the various approaches to psychotherapy. Classical science is dependent upon *Cartesian* thinking with the result that the world is analysed into parts according to a linear arrangement of causal laws. Thus, psychotherapeutic approaches which stress their scientific basis tend to rely on the explanatory

principles of linear causality. *Psychoanalysis*, *learning theory* and *behaviour therapy*, for example, make considerable, although not exclusive, use of linear causality. By contrast, the *systemic therapies* emphasise the non-linear interconnectedness of the whole *system*, whether individual or group, and make use of multi- or circular causality as an explanatory principle. The danger of linear causal thinking is that it may lead to *reductionism* and determinism; the danger of multi-causal thinking is that its complexity, although more appropriately reflecting the complexity of living organisms, may lead to conceptual confusion and stasis.

See also *First order change*, *Second order change*, *Teleology*, *Theory of types*.

Censorship

A mechanism of the *ego* which prevents memories and wishes passing from the *unconscious* to the *preconscious* (primary censorship) and from either into the conscious mind (secondary censorship). In his Introductory Lectures, Freud describes the mechanism as being like a sort of doorkeeper standing at the entrance to the conscious mind, protecting it from painful memories and from prohibited wishes. It is synonymous with *repression*. In his later writing, he equated censorship with one of the functions of the *superego*. Freud also used the term to discuss the way in which dream material is distorted and disguised, a point with which Jung (1954) disagreed.

FREUD, S. (1915), 'The unconscious' (*Standard Edition*, vol. 14, Hogarth Press, London).
FREUD, S. (1916), 'Introductory lectures on psychoanalysis' (*Standard Edition*, vols 15 and 16, Hogarth Press, London).
JUNG, C. G. (1954), 'Some aspects of modern psychotherapy' (in *The Practice of Psychotherapy*, Collected Works, vol. 16, Routledge & Kegan Paul, London).

Chain phenomena

Term used in *group psychotherapy* and *group analysis* to describe the way in which freefloating discussion can produce effects parallel to those of *free association* in the individual psychoanalytic situation. A chain phenomenon, according to Foulkes and Anthony (1957), makes its appearance at moments of tension within the group when some theme which produces *resonance* with several group members makes its appearance. Foulkes described the chain phenomenon as one of several group-specific factors.

FOULKES, S. H. and ANTHONY, E. J. (1957), *Group Psychotherapy* (Penguin, Harmondsworth).

See also *Condenser phenomena, Mirror phenomena.*

Character analysis
A term introduced by Reich (1945) to describe the therapist's task in helping to liberate the patient's repressed *orgone energy*. Reich suggests that the patient has an inbuilt pathological character structure which is evidenced in his physical *character armour* and which serves to maintain the *repression* of his sexual and social freedom of expression. Reich identified six character structures that most typically confront the therapist: the phallic-narcissistic male; the passive-feminine male; the masculine-aggressive female; the hysterical female; the compulsive character; and the masochistic character. Because the whole character structure is involved, the patient is typically highly *resistant* to the therapist's efforts to produce change.

REICH, W. (1945), *Character Analysis* (Orgone Institute, New York).

See also *Reichian therapy.*

Character armour
A term introduced by Reich (1945) to describe the rigid character structures that produce *fixation* of the *orgone energy* or *libido*, preventing the release of emotions and the liberation of the personality. Reich believed that the repression of this energy was brought about by an oppressive, authoritarian society; a repressive family group which instils into the child taboos and guilt about his sexuality; and the

individual's own repressive style of life. The effect of this repression is visible in the patient's muscular spasms, cramps and tensions and his inability to attain full orgastic potency. Reich (1951) suggests that there are seven rings of muscular armour, moving from the ring of muscles around the neck and head down to the ring around the pelvis and genitals. Therapy consists in releasing each in turn and liberating the energy that has become locked in.

REICH, W. (1945), *Character Analysis* (Orgone Institute, New York).
REICH, W. (1951), *Selected Writings* (Farrar, Strauss & Giroux, New York).

See also *Reichian therapy.*

Character training approaches
Approaches which share a moral view of the aetiology and treatment of psychological disturbance. Basically this involves helping the client to recognise the part he plays in the formation of *symptoms* and owning his responsibility for bringing about change. The alteration of the client's attitudes and lifestyle is the focus of treatment. Therapeutic approaches include *Morita therapy, Naikan therapy, meditation, integrity groups, psychosynthesis* and *will therapy.*

Charcot, Jean Martin (1825-1893)
Jean Martin Charcot was born in Paris in 1825. He gained his MD from the University of Paris in 1853 and took up an appointment as physician at the Central Hospital Bureau in 1856. In 1860 he took the chair of pathological anatomy at the University of Paris and two years later he became director of the Salpetrière Hospital in Paris. Here he established the most famous neurological clinic of the nineteenth century and he was recognised as outstanding both as a clinician and teacher, particularly because of his ability to relate symptoms to the anatomy of the nervous system. His major clinical researches were conducted into the neuroses and he classified hysteria into a complex series of stages. He made an intensive study of hypnotism and

demonstrated its use with hysterics. Freud went to Paris to study hypnosis under Charcot and with Charcot's help he began to develop hypotheses concerning the connection between sexuality and neurotic disorders. Janet also studied under Charcot, as well as many others who attended his regular clinical demonstrations. In 1889 he was made honorary president of the first International Congress of Psychology.

Child analysis

The psychoanalytic treatment of children. Although Freud's work was confined to the analysis of adults, one of his most famous cases, that of Little Hans, involved the treatment of a five-year-old boy (Freud 1909). The treatment however, was carried out indirectly through the child's father, and it was left to Freud's daughter Anna, and to Melanie Klein, to pioneer the use of analytic techniques with children.

From the beginning, the methods of Anna Freud and Melanie Klein differed significantly (see Klein 1927 and Freud 1946 for discussions of the debate). These differences resulted in two distinct strands of child analysis being adopted by their followers. The main differences between them revolve around the use of the *transference*; the age at which a child can appropriately be analysed; the range of application of child analysis; the use of *play therapy*; and whether or not educational measures, in addition to pure analytic techniques, should be used. Melanie Klein believed that play could appropriately be substituted for the *free association* required of adults, and that free play would give the therapist direct access to the child's *unconscious*. The *symbolism* of the child's play could then be subjected to direct, in-depth *interpretations*, including interpretations of the transference and *transference neurosis*.

Anna Freud, on the other hand, believed that play was not a direct substitute for free association and its main purpose was to help create a positive relationship with the analyst. Other derivatives of the child's unconscious, such as day and night dreams, capable of expression in words, were required. Transference and transference neurosis did not develop in children in the same way as in adults, because of the continuing dependence of the child on the real relationship with its parents. Thus, educative support through nursery school education, etc., was an important adjunct of child analysis. Because verbal ability was not considered important, Melanie Klein was prepared to analyse children as young as two-and-three-quarter years, but Anna Freud's work was mainly directed to older children, from four or five years and older. Whereas Klein believed that early analysis was needed to safeguard against the effects of the *paranoid-schizoid* and *depressive positions*, Anna Freud felt that it should be reserved for only the most severe cases of infantile neurosis. Both writers concur, however, in the particular advantage inherent in child analysis – namely the proximity of the child's current and past experiences.

Child analysis is practised and taught at the Hampstead Clinic and the Tavistock Clinic, London. It is practised by child psychotherapists trained at these centres in either the Kleinian or Freudian approach or in an eclectic synthesis of both. Treatment in child guidance clinics involves seeing the child individually for from one to five sessions per week, although some *group psychotherapy* sessions may also be included. Child analysts work mainly in child guidance clinics, special schools, departments of psychological medicine attached to hospitals and in young people's units.

EISSLER, R. *et al.* (eds) (1970), *Psychoanalytic Study of the Child* (rev. edn, International University Press, New York).

FREUD, A. (1929), 'Introduction to the technique of child analysis' (*Nervous and Mental Diseases Monograph*, no. 48).

FREUD, A. (1946), *The Psychoanalytic Treatment of Children* (Hogarth Press, London).

FREUD, A. (1965), *Normality and Pathology in Childhood* (Hogarth Press, London).

FREUD, S. (1909), 'Analysis of phobia in a five year old boy' (*Standard Edition*, vol. 10, Hogarth Press, London).

GELEERD, E. R. (1967), *The Child Analyst at Work* (International University Press, New York).

HUG-MELLUTH, H. V. (1921), 'On the technique of child analysis' (*Int. J. of Psychoan.*, vol. 2, pp. 287-305).

JOKIPALTIO, L.-M. (1982), 'Dreams in child psychoanalysis' (*Scandinavian Psychoan. Review*, vol. 5, pp. 31-47).

JURKOVIC, G. and ULRICI, D. (1982), 'The nature of insight in child psychotherapy' (*J. of Clinical Child Psychology*, vol. 11, pp. 209-15).

KLEIN, M. (1923), 'Infant analysis' (in *Contributions to Psychoanalysis*, Hogarth Press, London).

KLEIN, M. (1927), 'Symposium on child analysis' (in *Contributions to Psychoanalysis*, Hogarth Press, London).

KLEIN, M. (1932), *The Psychoanalysis of Children* (Hogarth Press, London).

MAHLER, M. *et al.* (1975), *The Psychological Birth of the Human Infant* (Hutchinson, London).

WINNICOTT, D. W. (1971), *Therapeutic Consultations in Child Psychiatry* (Hogarth Press, London).

WINNICOTT, D. W. (1978), *The Piggle: An Account of the Psychoanalytic Treatment of a Little Girl* (Hogarth Press, London).

Child psychotherapy

The psychotherapeutic treatment of children as individuals, in family sessions or in groups. Several theoretical approaches to child psychotherapy have been developed, the most influential being the psychoanalytic approach (see *Child analysis*), the behavioural approaches, the family approach and the client-centred approach.

Childhood disorders can be grouped into anti-social behaviour (temper tantrums, stealing, fire raising, aggression and destructiveness); psychosis (schizophrenia, autism); neurosis (night terrors, obsessive-compulsive behaviour, depression, self-injury and phobias); habit disorders (tics, anorexia, eneuresis, encopresis, glue sniffing, drug taking, sleep disorders and hyperkinesis); and psychosomatic disorders and relationship problems with peers and/or family. The way in which the aetiology and treatment of the problem is regarded depends, as in the case of adult disturbances, upon the theory of psychopathology adopted and the 'school' of psychotherapy to which the therapist subscribes. However, as Schaefer and Millman (1977) point out, child therapists have become keen to adopt an eclectic or pluralist position and to try to tailor a specific therapeutic approach to the individual needs of each child: 'Combining methods often increases therapeutic impact by tapping the child's capacity to participate in the experience in a more intense, holistic manner.' Recent trends include the effort to increase the success of *generalisation* to the child's living situation by using his or her caretakers as therapists – for example, in *filial therapy* and *parenting skills training*; involving father and other family members through concurrent or *conjoint* methods of treatment and emphasising prevention, through education and other *psychoprophylactic* measures.

The practice of *behaviour therapy* with children has increased enormously and techniques of *operant conditioning, systematic desensitisation, flooding* and *implosion* have been used with success, particularly with phobias. Varieties of *group psychotherapy* described by Slavson and Schiffer (1975) and Schaefer *et al.* (1982) include *psychodrama, transactional analysis, group analysis* and *social skills training*. Specialised groups have been run for foster children, children coping with divorce, and the physically disabled. Paradoxical interventions, *symptom prescription* and *time out* procedures have been successfully used with temper tantrums and other conduct disorders. *Family therapy* has been particularly successful with anorexic, school phobic and *scapegoated* children. As a method, family therapy is by definition directed towards the treatment of the child's problem within the context of his family system and even when the child is not the *identified patient* his or her inclusion in the therapeutic programme acts as a preventative strategy.

BARKER, P. (1979), *Basic Child Psychiatry* (Granada, London).

CAREK, D. J. (1972), *Principles of Child Psychotherapy* (Charles C. Thomas, Springfield, Ill.).

DARE, C. and LINDSEY, C. (1979), 'Children in family therapy' (*J. of Family Therapy*, vol. 1, pp. 253-69).

EVANS, J. (1982), *Adolescent and Pre-adolescent Psychiatry* (Academic Press, London).

GRACIANO, A. M. (ed.) (1971, 1975), *Behavior Therapy with Children* (2 vols, Aldine Publishing, Chicago).

GROUP FOR THE ADVANCEMENT OF PSYCHIATRY (1982), *The Process of Child Therapy* (Brunner/Mazel, New York).

GUTTMANN, H. A. (1975), 'The child's participation in conjoint family therapy' (*J. of the Am. Academy of Child Psychiatry*, vol. 14, pp. 490-9).

LEVITT, E. (1971), 'Research on psychotherapy with children' (in Bergin, A. E. and Garfield, S. L. (eds), *Handbook of Psychotherapy and Behavior Change*, Wiley, New York).

NOSHPITZ, J. D. (1981), 'Psychotherapy with children: basic principles (in Masserman, J. H., *Current Psychiatric Therapies*, vol. 20, Grune & Stratton, New York).

ROSS, A. O. (1981), *Child Behavior Therapy* (Wiley, New York).

RUTTER, M. (1975), *Helping Troubled Children* (Penguin, Harmondsworth).

RUTTER, M. (1982), 'Psychological therapies in child psychiatry: issues and prospects' (*Psychological Medicine*, vol. 12, pp. 723-40).

SCHAEFER, C. E. and MILLMAN, H. L. (1977), *Therapies for Children* (Jossey-Bass, San Francisco).

SCHAEFER, C. E. *et al.* (eds) (1982), *Group Therapies for Children and Youth* (Jossey-Bass, San Francisco).

SCHAEFER, C. E. *et al.* (eds) (1984), *Family Therapy Techniques for Problem Behaviors of Children and Teenagers* (Jossey-Bass, San Francisco).

SLAVSON, S. R. and SCHIFFER, M. (1975), *Group Psychotherapies for Children* (International University Press, New York).

Childhood amnesia

The period of infantile sexuality from birth till the *phallic stage* is more or less totally repressed, according to psychoanalytic theory. Therefore there is subsequently a total amnesia for the first three to four years of life.

Chronogram

See *Group therapy interaction chronogram.*

Circular causality

See *Causality.*

Circular questioning

Term used by Palazzoli *et al.* (1980) to describe an interviewing technique which rests upon the logic of circular *causality* in *systems*. The technique is further predicated upon the belief that new information creates difference and that the introduction of difference into a relationship creates change. The basic method involves inviting every member of the family to comment upon the relationship between two other members – in other words it focuses upon the investigation of a series of dyadic relationships as seen by a third person. Because the third party is also a member of a set of dyadic relationships and thus also gets 'investigated', and because there is in general a complex overlap in the triadic relationships, the usual limitations imposed by the linear quality of the therapist interaction with family members is bypassed and the non-summative reality of the family system begins to unfold. 'The model is triadic – a member of the family is invited to describe in what manner another member reacts to the symptom and in what way yet another family member reacts to that reaction' (Palazzoli *et al.*, 1980).

Palazzoli *et al.* make five further suggestions regarding circular questioning: focus on concrete behaviour; elucidate which family member does more or less of the behaviour under discussion; get each member to rank the others in order of their display of the behaviour; investigate the changes in behaviour of family members before and after a precise event, such as the complained-about behaviour of the *identified patient*; investigate hypothetical possibilities ('who do you think would be most upset if your sister left home?'). Apart from its major efficiency in revealing the systemic nature of family interaction, circular questioning is a powerful method of putting the therapist in charge of the therapeutic process. It forms a complete contrast to the technique of *open-ended questioning* employed in the *humanistic* approaches. Penn (1982) has identified nine categories of circular questioning.

PALAZZOLI, M. S. *et al.* (1980), 'Hypothesising – circularity – neutrality; three guidelines for the conductor of the session' (*Family Process* vol. 19,. pp. 3-12).

PENN, P. (1982), 'Circular questioning' (*Family Process*, vol. 21, pp. 267-80).

Circumflex model

A diagnostic tool developed by Olson *et al.* (1979) for use in formulating treatment *goals* and guidelines with marital pairs and families. Family *cohesion*, adaptability (see *morphogenesis*) and *communication* are taken as the three dimensions of *systems* functioning which are of primary importance. Family cohesion, which is defined as the emotional bonding of family members, is divided into four levels: *disengaged*, separated, connected, and *enmeshed*. It is hypothesised that the two central levels make for optimal functioning and the two outer levels for poor functioning. Family adaptability, which is defined as the ability of the system to change its power structure, role relationships and rules in response to stress, is also divided into four levels: rigid (very low), structured, flexible, chaotic (very high). As with cohesion, it is hypothesised that the two central levels are functional and the two outer levels are not. Whilst it is vital for optimal family functioning, family communication is seen as a facilitating dimension and is not therefore included in the graphic representation of the model. The 4 × 4 matrix so formed yields 16 cells, each of which identifies one family type.

OLSON, D. H. *et al.* (1979), 'Circumflex model of marital and family systems' (*Family Process*, vol. 18, pp. 3-15).

OLSON, D. H. *et al.* (1983), 'Circumflex model of marital and family systems: theoretical update' (*Family Process*, vol. 22, pp. 69-83).

Circumspection-pre-emption-control (CPC) cycle

A cyclical process described by G. A. Kelly, in which the individual develops a *personal construct* system enabling him to interpret the world and anticipate future events. Kelly suggested that when faced with a novel situation or new material to be learned, the individual typically approaches it first by loosening his constructs (circumspection) then by tightening them (pre-emption), and finally, when the situation or material has been integrated, by developing a new elaboration (control).

KELLY, G. A. (1955), *A Psychology of Personal Constructs* (W. W. Norton, New York).

See also *Personal construct theory*.

Clarification

The process whereby the therapist gains an accurate understanding of the client's problems, personality and aspirations. The therapist tests his understanding of the cognitive content of the client's communications by asking *open-ended questions*, offering non-interpretive summaries of his understanding of the client or the therapeutic process so far and inviting *feedback* from the client to correct the errors in his understanding. An important means of clarifying what the client is trying to communicate is by paraphrasing his communication and feeding it back in a restated form.

Clarification is an interviewing skill which is required for the effective operation of most therapeutic approaches. It is used particularly by non-directive therapists as a means of developing accurate *empathy*. Since clarification is a necessary part of functional communication, its use by the therapist provides the client with a model from which he can learn.

See also *Interview, Microskill*.

Classical conditioning
The process whereby a neutral *stimulus* is paired repeatedly with an *unconditioned stimulus* until it elicits a *response* in the absence of the unconditioned stimulus. This learning procedure was made famous by Pavlov (1927) after experiments in which a bell (neutral stimulus) was paired with food (unconditional stimulus) until the sound of the bell alone produced salivation in the dog. Pavlov called the elicitation of salivation by food the unconditioned response and unconditioned stimulus respectively since salivation on the sight of food is not dependent on learning. The bell and the salivation response were called the conditioned stimulus and conditioned response respectively, since the salivation response in this instance was conditional upon learning.

Watson and Rayner (1920) applied the same principles to an experiment with an eleven-month-old baby, Albert, in which a loud noise (unconditional response) of which the baby was afraid was paired with a white rat (neutral stimulus) until the sight of the rat alone produced fear in the baby. His fear was generalised to other animals and other similar objects. Bootzin (1975) summarised the difference between classical and *operant* (instrumental) *conditioning* as follows: 'classical conditioning changes the stimulus value of the neutral stimulus while instrumental conditioning focuses on changing the response pattern.' Lazarus, Wolpe and others have made use of classical conditioning concepts to develop a number of *counter-conditioning* techniques, such as *systematic desensitisation, extinction, flooding* and *implosion*. Wolpe (1981) points out that an accurate behavioural analysis is essential for determining the correct source of the neurotic behaviour prior to the institution of treatment.

BOOTZIN, R. R. (1975), *Behavior Modification and Therapy: An Introduction* (Winthrop,

Cambridge, Mass.).
PAVLOV, I. P. (1927), *Conditioned Reflexes* (Oxford University Press, Oxford).
WATSON, J. B. and RAYNER, R. (1920), 'Conditional emotional reactions' (*Journal of Experimental Psychology*, vol. 3, pp. 1-14).
WOLPE, J. and LAZARUS, A. (1966), *Behaviour Therapy Techniques* (Pergamon, Oxford).
WOLPE, J. (1981), 'The dichotomy between classical conditioned and cognitively learned anxiety' (*J. of Behavior Therapy and Experimental Psychiatry*, vol. 12, pp. 35-42).

Classical psychoanalysis
Term used to denote a particular stream of development of psychoanalytic ideas including the various reformulations that Freud himself made, and including the present *ego psychology* school in America. It can be contrasted with the *object relations* school and its contemporary variations.

Client
Term used by some workers to denote the subject of the therapeutic process. The term is used by some to suggest that the therapeutic work is directed primarily to the *conscious* rather than to the *unconscious* portion of the *psyche*. Non-medical therapists have traditionally used this term to distinguish their work from that of a medical therapist, although professional discipline has not been shown to influence or alter the nature of the interventions used in therapy. Rogerian therapists and many others use the term to indicate the active and voluntary nature of the part played by the subject. The term implies that the subject of therapy has a 'problem' rather than an 'illness' which, in turn conveys a greater prospect of movement and change. Some workers have suggested that the term in its original meaning has legal connotations and that it therefore should be used to imply agreement to and acceptance of a *contract* of work with the therapist. The voluntary nature of the relationship implied by the term client is problematic in some forms of coercive *behaviour modification* when, as in *aversion therapy*, some constraints must be imposed if treatment is to

succeed and when arrangements for treatment have sometimes been made between the therapist and a third party rather than with the client himself. In practice, the terms client and patient are used interchangeably in most forms of psychotherapy. The client variable has been studied as a factor in *outcome* research (Garfield 1978) and the client's original personality make-up, age, socio-economic status, social class, type of problem and motivation for therapy have all been studied. Results are inconclusive but Garfield suggests that more attention must be paid to client variables if treatments are to be effectively tailored to the particular needs of different client groups.

GARFIELD, S. L. (1978), 'Research on client variables in psychotherapy' (in Garfield, S. L. and Bergin, A. E., *Handbook of Psychotherapy and Behavior Change*, Wiley, New York).

Client-centred therapy

A method of *non-directive* counselling or therapy originated by Carl Rogers in the early 1940s. The subject of the therapeutic process is called the *client* and the approach emphasises the capacity and strengths of the client in directing the course of therapy. Chen (1981), for example, has analysed the speech characteristics of three different forms of psychotherapy and found that interviews conducted by Rogers are client-dominated to a significant degree. Although client-centred therapy is primarily directed towards the individual, some of its techniques have been extended to work with groups.

It represents a major break from both *psychoanalysis* and the *behaviour therapies*, yet it is indebted both to Freudian insights into unconscious processes on the one hand (Rogers 1965) and also to the research emphasis of *learning theory*. It is embedded in the *humanistic* approach to psychotherapy and is influenced also by existentialism (see *existential analysis* and *existential psychotherapy*) and *phenomenology*. Rogers's theoretical formulations and his work on the *relationship factors* of therapy have been derived from the

observable behaviour that occurs between client and therapist. He was the first therapist to publish complete verbatim case records from *audio tapes* (Rogers 1942) and client-centred therapy has, from the beginning, been concerned with the development of research tools for conducting evaluation and *outcome* studies.

Great emphasis is placed on the role of the therapist's attitudes and presentation of self. These attitudes, which must be genuinely part of the therapist's self, are described by Rogers as the *core conditions* of therapy. Rogers is strongly anti-technical and he prefers to talk about the therapist's skill in 'implementing his attitudes' rather than describing the therapist's interventions as techniques. Client-centred therapy is part of the humanistic tradition, viewing human beings as intrinsically good, capable of directing their own destiny and bringing about their own *self-actualisation*. It focuses upon the wholeness of the individual, discernible beneath the fragments of *symptoms*, neuroses and fears which the client presents to the therapist. Respect and *acceptance* of the individual as he is allows the therapist to be non-directive and to avoid trying to interpret, evaluate or guide the client's experience or behaviour. Such an attitude does not, however, mean that the therapist is passive; it involves a continual struggle to lay aside preconceptions and to adopt the client's frame of reference.

The core conditions which the therapist must offer, according to Rogers, are variously described in client-centred therapy as *empathy*; *non-possessive warmth*; *genuineness*; *congruence*; and *unconditional positive regard*. These are believed to be both the necessary and the sufficient conditions for a positive therapeutic outcome to occur. Raskin (1974) has shown that the outstanding characteristic of the client-centred therapist is his empathy and studies of empathy are suggestive of its high correlation with positive therapeutic outcome. (See below, and see also *Core conditions*, for a further discussion of this point.)

The process of therapy involves the client's experience of the therapist's acceptance and understanding. This enables him to feel safe enough to explore his problems, feelings and attitudes, and to experience the less acceptable parts of himself, including those parts which lie beyond the masks he usually wears. For Rogers, therapy is a learning process. Having experienced himself differently, the client can then learn new ways of relating to others and new ways of behaving. The goal of client-centred therapy is self-discovery. The therapist's chief objective is to help clients 'become what they are'. Rogers (1967) believes that the client's problems are always reducible to two major existential questions: 'Who am I? and 'How can I become myself?'

The client population is wide for which client-centred therapy is deemed to be useful. Rogers (1965) claims its applicability to marital problems, vocational problems, speech difficulties, psychosomatic conditions, a wide range of neurotic problems, behaviour problems in children, and some psychotic problems in adults. Much of Rogers's work has been undertaken amongst graduate and undergraduate populations, giving rise to the criticism that client-centred therapy is unsuitable for less intelligent clients. Rogers, however, illustrates his work with case material drawn from a wide socio-economic spectrum. A more pertinent criticism may be that the approach is not very effective with severely disturbed psychotic clients, but this criticism can also be levied at many other therapeutic models. Beyond the psycho-therapeutic situation, the principles of client-centred therapy have been widely applied in the classroom; in colleges; and to a smaller extent, in organisations and in a variety of groups.

Criticisms which have been made of client-centred therapy are as follows. First, it is naive in its disregard of harsh environmental realities which may get in the way of the client learning to 'become what he is'. Second, Rogers proposes a sort of therapeutic 'trickle down' theory (Rogers 1977) and argues that the many power imbalances in the world can best be changed through a summation of changed individuals rather than through

changing the structures and *systems* themselves. Third, research suggests that Rogers's claim that the core conditions are sufficient for therapeutic change to occur is difficult to substantiate unequivocally, although the evidence is controversial. (See *Core conditions*.)

CHEN, C. L. (1981), 'Speech rhythm characteristics of client centred, Gestalt and rational emotive therapy interviews' (*J. of Communication Disorders*, vol. 14, pp. 311-20).

HART, J. T. and TOMLINSON, T. M. (eds) (1970), *New Directions in Client Centred Therapy* (Houghton Mifflin, New York).

MITCHELL, K. *et al.* (1977), 'A re-appraisal of the therapeutic effectiveness of accurate empathy, non-possessive warmth and genuineness' (in Gurman, A. and Razin, A. (eds), *Effective Psychotherapy*, Pergamon, New York).

RASKIN, N. J. (1974), *Studies of Psychotherapeutic Orientation: Ideology and Practice* (Research Monograph 1, American Academy of Psychotherapists, Florida).

ROGERS, C. R. (1942), *Counselling and Psychotherapy* (Constable, London).

ROGERS, C. R. (1965), *Client Centred Therapy* (Constable, London).

ROGERS C. R. (1967), *On Becoming a Person* (Constable, London).

ROGERS, C. R. (1977), *Personal Power 'Inner Strength and its Revolutionary Impact'* (Constable, London).

ROGERS, C. R. (1980), *A Way of Being* (Houghton Mifflin, Boston).

ROGERS, C. R. and DYMOND, R. (eds) (1954), *Psychotherapy and Personality Change* (University of Chicago, Chicago).

WEXLER, D. A. and RICE, L. N. (eds) (1974), *Innovations in Client Centred Therapy* (Wiley, New York).

Closed system

A *system* which is characterised by a rigid boundary and is closed to inputs from the environment. All biological and social systems have to be open to some degree in order to survive but a *relatively* closed psycho-social system is incapable of increasing its variety through the process of *morphogenesis*. A family or other social group that is closed reduces its potential resources from the environment, increases the burden on its members and its vulnerability to stress.

See also *Feedback loop, Homeostasis, Open system*.

Coaching

Term used in *behaviour therapy* to describe the way in which the therapist teaches the patient to move through *successive approximations* to the treatment *goal* by *shaping* his behaviour. In *psychodrama* the term refers to the way in which the *auxiliary egos* are helped to reflect aspects of the *protagonist* and his situation. Bowen (1978) uses it to describe the therapist's function in helping the patient to develop new behaviours in relation to members of his family. Coaching is a method employed by *transgenerational family therapists* to help individual family members achieve greater *differentiation* from their family of origin. The work consists of identifying the patterns and especially the *triangles* that have developed in previous generations and helping the client develop definite strategies for behaving differently within current triangular relationships. The family member who is coached is usually an adult son or daughter being helped to differentiate from his or her family of origin.

BOWEN, M. (1978), *Family Therapy and Clinical Practice* (Jason Aronson, New York). CARTER, E. and ORFANIDIS, M. M. (1976) 'Family therapy with one person' (in Guerin, P., *Family Therapy: Theory and Practice*, Gardner Press, New York).

Coalition

A combination of two or more members of a group, family, or other natural *network*, the effect of which is to create an *alliance* against those others who do not belong. Minuchin *et al.* (1978) use the term 'stable coalition' to describe one of three strategies used by families to create a rigid triad, the others being *triangulation* and *detouring*. The original group of researchers into *communication* theory and

the *double bind* had viewed the central pathological relationship as being dyadic. The shift in their understanding to the importance of the triad marks their recognition of the part played by coalitions of two against one, whereby the essential discomfort of the excluded/excluding experience creates what Bateson (1972) calls 'the infinite dance of shifting coalitions'. Haley (1967) develops this idea by showing that coalitions that occur across generations (or status levels) but which are denied at the *metacommunicative* level are always pathological and result in symptomatic behaviour and/or the dissolution of the system. Haley's observations refer primarily to the formation of the coalitions in family groups.

Caplow (1968) describes a similar process that occurs in organisations whereby an 'improper coalition' can be defined as any three-person coalition that increases the power of one superior while undermining the legitimate authority of another. The functional situation in both families and organisations is for peers to be in coalition with each other. The greatest problems arise both for the individual and the system when the individual is called upon to join two warring coalitions simultaneously.

The excluded member of a coalition may take various options depending on his relationship with those who are in coalition with each other. If, for example, *individual* members of the coalition invite his loyalty, he may act in order to split the coalition or to relate to each part separately so as deliberately to *avoid* splitting it. Alternatively he may, by becoming a *scapegoat* or adopting the *sick role*, reinforce the coalition to which he is an outsider, but dispel its discomfort by making it overt and therefore apparently 'rational'.

Minuchin and Fishman (1981) discuss the participation of the therapist as a member of a coalition against one or more family members and they describe the way in which the therapist can use this kind of coalition in *family therapy* as an *unbalancing* technique.

BATESON, G. (1972), *Steps to an Ecology of*

55

Mind (Granada, London).

CAPLOW, T. (1968), *Two Against One: Coalitions in Triads* (Prentice-Hall, Englewood Cliffs, New Jersey).
HALEY, J. (1967), 'Toward a theory of pathological systems' (in Watzlawick, P. and Weakland, J. (eds) (1977). *The International View*, W. W. Norton, New York).
MINUCHIN, S. *et al.* (1978), *Psychosomatic Families* (Harvard University Press, Cambridge, Mass.).
MINUCHIN, S. and FISHMAN, H. C. (1981), *Family Therapy Techniques* (Harvard University Press, Cambridge, Mass.).

Co-counselling
See *Re-evaluation counselling.*

Cognitive behaviour therapy
A set of principles and procedures developed chiefly by Meichenbaum (1977) and his colleagues. Meichenbaum's model is one of stimulus-response-reinforcement and is essentially an *operant conditioning* approach, with the patient's self statements being regarded as discriminative stimuli. Approaches to cognitive behaviour therapy include *self-instructional training, stress inoculation* and *coping skills interventions*. Although cognitive behaviour therapy has some areas in common with Beck's *cognitive therapy*, notably its recognition of the importance of cognitive processes, it is also closely related to behavioural techniques and ideas.

FOREYT, J. P. and RATHJEN, D. R. (1978), *Cognitive Behavior Therapy* (Plenum Press, New York).
MCMULLIN, R. and GILES, T. (1981), *Cognitive Behavior Therapy* (Grune & Stratton, New York).
MEICHENBAUM, D. (1977), *Cognitive-Behavior Modification: An Integrative Approach* (Plenum Press, New York).

See also *Cognitive restructuring approaches, Cognitive structure.*

Cognitive complexity
A term introduced by Bieri (1955) and defined by him as the capacity to construe social behaviour in a multi-dimensional way. The more cognitively complex individual uses a more differentiated system for perceiving the behaviour of others than does the less cognitively complex individual. Cognitive complexity can be measured using a *repertory grid*; the lower the correlations between *constructs* the higher the degree of cognitive complexity. In order to indicate cognitive complexity, however, the low correlations must occur in a non-random, consistent manner when a subject is tested repeatedly. If low correlations between constructs occur in a random and inconsistent way, this merely indicates thought disorder. Bannister and Fransella (1965) have clarified the way in which schizophrenics produce random correlations between constructs and that this is *not* a measure of cognitive complexity. The concept, which has caused immense methodological problems, has been further discussed by Adams-Webber (1969) and Epting (1972).

ADAMS-WEBBER, J. (1969), 'Cognitive complexity and sociality' (*Brit. J. of Social and Clinical Psychology*, vol. 8, pp. 211-16).
BANNISTER, D. and FRANSELLA, F. (1965), 'A repertory grid test of schizophrenic thought disorder' (*Brit. J. of Social and Clinical Psychology*, vol. 2, pp. 92-102).
BIERI, J. (1955), 'Cognitive complexity-simplicity and predictive behaviour' (*Journal of Abnormal and Social Psychology*, vol. 51, pp. 263-8).
CROCKETT, W. H. (1965), 'Cognitive complexity and impression formation' (in Maher, B. A. (ed.), *Progress in Experimental Personality Research*, vol. 2, Academic Press, London).
EPTING, F. R. (1972), 'The stability of cognitive complexity in construing social issues' (*Brit. J. of Social and Clinical Psychology*, vol. 11, pp. 122-5).

Cognitive dissonance
A concept introduced by Festinger (1957) which postulates that the individual experiences discomfort and tension when holding two dissonant beliefs simultaneously.

Festinger suggests that there are three possible types of relationship between an individual's cognitive elements or beliefs: the relationship will be either consonant, dissonant or unconnected. If experienced as dissonant, he will try to reduce the tension by changing, abandoning or introducing new cognitions into his *cognitive structure*. Although the concept has been criticised by psychologists for its vagueness (Chapanis and Chapanis 1964), it has useful features for the psychotherapist in helping him to guard against introducing interventions that are inappropriately challenging to the patient's belief system and which will therefore be resisted.

CHAPANIS, N. and CHAPANIS, A. (1964), 'Cognitive dissonance: five years later' (*Psychological Bulletin*, vol. 61, pp. 1-22).

FESTINGER, L. (1957), *A Theory of Cognitive Dissonance* (Stanford University Press, Stanford, Calif.).

WICKLAND, J. W. and BREHM, J. W. (1976), *Perspectives in Cognitive Dissonance* (Wiley, New York).

See also *Ego alien, Resistance*.

Cognitive restructuring approaches
A group of therapeutic approaches which have, as their overall goal, the alteration of the client's cognitions, thought sequences and imagery which determine his problem or undesirable behaviour. Mahoney and Arnkoff (1978) list the three main approaches as *rational emotive therapy, self-instructional training* and *cognitive behaviour therapy*, but *cognitive therapy* and *personal construct therapy* should clearly also be included. They hold in common the belief that if behaviour is to change, the cognitions and *cognitive structure* which determine behaviour must first be altered. Cognitive restructuring approaches are closely related to *coping skills interventions* and *problem solving interventions* and like these approaches, they have developed during the last ten years out of the concepts of *behaviour therapy*. Referring to the group as a whole, Mahoney and Arnkoff (1978) suggest that their distin-

guishing feature is 'their simultaneous endorsement of the importance of cognitive *processes* and the functional promise of experimentally developed (and often behaviouristic) *procedures*'.

MAHONEY, M. J. and ARNKOFF, D. B. (1978), 'Cognitive and self control therapies' (in Garfield, S. and Bergin, A. E. (eds), *Handbook of Psychotherapy and Behaviour Change*, Wiley, New York).

Cognitive structure
A concept used in *cognitive therapy* and *cognitive behaviour therapy* to indicate the consistent framework in which thought patterns, inner speech and imagery develop and are held, and which in turn determines behaviour. The concept pre-dates cognitive behaviour therapy, having been used by Lewin in the development of *field theory*. Meichenbaum (1977) defines cognitive structure as the 'organising aspect of thinking that seems to monitor and direct the strategy, root and choice of thoughts'.

MEICHENBAUM, D. (1977), *Cognitive-Behavior Modification* (Plenum Press, New York).

Cognitive therapy
A therapeutic approach developed by Beck *et al.* (1979) for use with depressed patients in particular. Beck emphasises that cognitive processes affect behaviour and that behaviour can be changed through cognitive techniques. The therapeutic approach has some ideas in common with *behaviour therapy*, but although its overall goal is to help the patient alter his dysfunctional behaviour, it contrasts with behaviour therapy in rejecting *conditioning* as a sufficient principle for behaviour change to occur. Instead, it emphasises the importance of the patient's thoughts, feelings, imagery, attitudes and hopes. Beck maintains that overt behavioural *and* emotional responses result from cognitive processes.

Cognitive therapy aims at altering the underlying assumptions that dictate the patient's perceptual view, leading to his negative automatic thoughts upon which his behaviour is based. The patient's *cognitive structure* is developed around a triad of negative thoughts: in relation to the self, his experience of the world and his perception of the future. Beck describes cognitive therapy as 'an active, directive, time-limited, structural approach . . . based on an underlying therapeutic rationale that an individual's affect and behaviour are largely determined by the way in which he structures the world' (Beck *et al.* 1979).

The therapist first engages the patient in a *behavioural analysis*, in which he tries to gain an understanding of the underlying assumptions and automatic thoughts which dictate his behaviour. The therapist then tries to define target *symptoms*. The patient is often asked to keep a daily record of *dysfunctional* thoughts. Beck *et al.* (1979) suggest that the patient's dysfunctional cognitions typically include the drawing of arbitrary conclusions from minimal evidence, selective abstraction of a few of the facts, over-generalisation, magnification and minimisation, personalising events inappropriately, and dichotomised thinking, which allows for no 'shades of grey' in drawing conclusions about events.

The therapist engages the patient as a collaborator in rational discussion of his faulty cognitions and how they might be altered. He challenges the patient's negative assumptions about himself and his perceptions of others and suggests ways in which he might engage in appropriate *reality testing. Tasks* designed to increase the patient's self-esteem are suggested, and therapeutic interventions also draw upon the related methods of *cognitive behaviour therapy, fixed role therapy* and *rational emotive therapy.*

Cognitive therapy has been criticised by behaviour therapists such as Eysenck (1979) and Wolpe (1978). Eysenck comments that although currently fashionable, 'cognitive theory per contra does not even exist as a "theory" that could meaningfully be criticised or tested.' On the other hand, the inclusion of the affective and symbolic mental processes renders the approach more accessible to non-

behavioural therapists. Cognitive therapy has gained a well-established position as an effective treatment method, particularly for depression. The *Journal of Cognitive Therapy and Research* exists for publishing research and clinical papers.

BECK, A. T. (1976), *Cognitive Therapy and the Emotional Disorders* (International Universities Press, New York).
BECK, A. T., RUSH, A. J., SHAW, B. F., EMERY, G. (1979), *Cognitive Therapy of Depression* (Wiley, New York).
EYSENCK, H. J. (1979), 'Behaviour therapy and the philosophies' (*Behaviour, Research and Therapy*, vol. 17, pp. 511-14).
KENDALL, P. C. and HOLTON, S. D. (eds) (1979), *Cognitive-behavioural Interventions: Theory, Research and Procedures* (Academic Press, New York).
MAHONEY, M. J. (1974), *Cognition and Behaviour Modification* (Ballinger, Cambridge, Mass.).
MAHONEY, M. J. (1977), 'Reflections on the cognitive-learning trend in psychotherapy' (*American Psychologist*, vol. 32, pp. 5-13).
MAHONEY, M. J. (ed.) (1980), *Psychotherapy Process: Current Issues and Future Directions* (Plenum Press, New York).
WOLPE, J. (1978), 'Cognition and causation in human behaviour and its therapy' (*American Psychologist*, vol. 33, pp. 437-46).

Coherence
See *Homeostasis.*

Cohesion
Cohesion has been studied as a variable within the context of both *family therapy* and *group psychotherapy*. Miller (1977) defines cohesiveness as 'the tendency of systems to maintain sufficient closeness in space-time among subsystems and components – or between them and the channels in physical space which convey information among them – to enable them to interact, resisting forces which would disrupt such relationships'. According to Miller cohesion is maintained by common memories, messages signalling the interlocking relation-

ship between units, common purposes and goals, common rewards and by common punishments for actions leading to the dissolution of the system. Family cohesion is defined by Olson *et al.* (1979) as the emotional bonding that family members develop with each other. The theme of family cohesion is most highly developed in the work of Minuchin and his colleagues and they view the axes of 'belonging' and 'separateness' as crucial. Within these variables, they characterise families as being either *enmeshed, disengaged* or at some point on a continuum between these two poles, an in-between position characterising a functional family system. Ravich (1981) discusses cohesion in marital pairs and family groups in terms of the structuring of the 'space between' in relationships, a concept analogous to the synaptic gap in the nervous system of higher organisms. Within the range of normality, cohesion is contrasted with *differentiation*; the interplay between the two constantly changes but within a pattern that recurs over time.

Cohesion can be viewed as the manifestation of group or family members' capacity for belonging, so that functioning occurs at the optimal point on the continuum, producing bonding without fusion. However, the degree to which cohesion is functional either for the family, group or its members, has always got to be weighed against its needs for separateness at any particular point in its development. Lewis *et al.* (1976), studying a group of 'healthy' families, confirm the view that high cohesiveness is a characteristic of well-functioning families. Abel (1981), in her review of different cultural contexts, suggests that although the *nature* of cohesion is altered by cultural difference, the *value* of cohesiveness within family structure remains.

Cohesiveness can however be achieved dysfunctionally by the production of *symptoms*, by *detouring* conflict through a third party, by *projecting* and *displacing* it on to an outsider or by *scapegoating* an insider. Therapeutic strategies therefore involve the reduction of these dysfunctional efforts at cohesion maintenance and the modulation of an appropriate balance between cohesion and differentiation.

Kellerman (1981) defines group cohesion as the crystallisation of the group's values and attitudes. The effect of cohesion is to 'generate motivation in individuals to be part of the group, keep the group stable, maintain the group's course toward the achievement of . . . its goals and . . . regulate and generate the expression of group attitudes in a consistent way'. Behr (1979) points out that the degree to which the group's boundaries are well-defined without being over-rigid, determines the degree to which it is cohesive. The need of individuals to *affiliate* with others produces the motivation for joining a group. The promotion of group cohesion is an important aspect of any type of *group psychotherapy*. If the group is to remain in being to accomplish the therapeutic task, *basic assumption behaviour*, whilst highly cohesive in its effects, acts as a powerful form of *resistance*, and a barrier to the work of the group. Kellerman links cohesion with style of *leadership*. He discusses the conflict between the individual's need to be autonomous and the group's need for cohesion, and thus for conformity. A task of the therapy group is to enable members to experiment with affiliative and autonomous behaviour, building up a moderate group cohesion but resisting a highly conforming cohesive structure.

Kellerman (1981) points out how the concept of cohesion is considered an important though often latent variable in many scientific fields, including physics, biology and ethology, and the inter-disciplinary study of the concept is potentially of great value to psychotherapeutic work with groups.

ABEL, T. M. (1981), 'Family structure in cultural contexts' (in Kellerman, op. cit.).

BEHR, H. L. (1979), 'Cohesiveness in families and therapy groups' (*Group Analysis*, vol. 12, pp. 9-12).

KELLERMAN, H. (ed.) (1981), *Group Cohesion: Theoretical and Clinical Perspectives* (Grune & Stratton, New York).

LEWIS, J., BEAVEN, W. R., GOSSETT, J. T. and PHILLIPS, V. A. (1976), *No Single Thread: Psychological Health in Family Systems*

(Brunner/Mazel, New York).
MILLER, V. G. (1977), *Living Systems* (McGraw-Hill, New York).
MINUCHIN, S. (1974), *Families and Family Therapy* (Tavistock, London).
OLSON, D. H. *et al.* (1979), 'Circumplex models of marital and family systems I: cohesion and adaptability dimensions, family types and clinical applications' (*Family Process*, vol. 18, pp. 3-28).
RAVICH, R. A. (1981), 'On the nature of cohesion in intimate relationships and family structures' (in Kellerman, op. cit.).
THIBAUT, J. W. and KELLEY, H. H. (1959), *The Social Psychology of Groups* (Wiley, New York).

See also *Homeostasis*.

Collaborative marital therapy

The use of two therapists, each of whom acts as therapist to one of the spouses separately. The therapists then meet together regularly to discuss their two patients. The method has been reported by Bannister and Pincus (1965) and Dicks (1967), all of whom use it within a psychoanalytic framework. Martin and Bird (1953) describe the process as a 'stereoscopic technique'. Through a careful reconstruction of the material produced by the spouses in the meeting of the two therapists, the complementary pathology of the marital pair can be understood. In addition, by examining the *transference* relationship that develops between each therapist and each patient, the early traumata of infancy can be understood using the routine techniques of *psychoanalysis*. The method also introduces a third element, the relationship between the two therapists, which can enrich the understanding that each gains of his own patient, his colleague's patient and the relationship between them. The approach combines some of the advantages of the individual approach with an interpersonal perspective. It is, however, somewhat complex and time-consuming and may miss out on the full advantages of a *conjoint* approach whilst retaining too few of the advantages of the individual orientation. Dicks (1967) suggests

that conjoint marital therapy can usually usefully supersede this kind of collaborative work between four people.

BANNISTER, K. and PINCUS, L. (1965), *Shared Phantasy in Marital Problems: Therapy in a Four Person Relationship* (Codicote Press, London).
DICKS, H. B. (1967), *Marital Tensions* (Routledge & Kegan Paul, London).
MARTIN, P. A. and BIRD, H. W. (1953), 'An approach to the psychotherapy of marriage partners – the stereoscopic technique' (*Psychiatry*, vol. 16, pp. 123-7).
MARTIN, P. (1976), *A Marital Therapy Manual* (Brunner/Mazel, New York).
PAOLINO, T. J. and McCRADY, B. S. (eds) (1978), *Marriage and Marital Therapy* (Brunner/Mazel, New York).

See also *Combined marital therapy, Concurrent marital therapy, Conjoint marital therapy, Co-therapy*.

Collective unconscious

Term introduced by Jung (1933) to describe those aspects of the *psyche* which are common to all humankind, and which are transmitted genetically in the same way as physical attributes. The collective unconscious forms a common psychic substratum, present within each individual as part of his *unconscious*. It consists of *archetypes* i.e. universal structures expressing themselves via a series of fundamental, primordial images, accumulated down the ages and across cultures. Jung suggests that the archetype is to the collective unconscious what the *complex* is to the *personal unconscious*. The material in the collective unconscious is transpersonal and, although its influence on emotional life may be extensive, it has never existed in the *conscious*. It has not therefore been repressed, in the way that material in the personal unconscious is formed, according to Jung, out of material repressed by the conscious mind.

Topographically, the collective unconscious represents a deeper level of unconsciousness than the personal unconscious. Jung found verification for this shared level of unconscious mental life from the dream images, religious symbolism, *myths*, folk stories and *symbols* that are universally shared by humanity. Thus, Jung maintained that the unconscious 'contains all the patterns of life and behaviour inherited from . . . ancestors, so that every human child, prior to consciousness, is possessed of a potential system of adapted psychic functioning'. From this theoretical construct, Jung went on to assert that the task of psychotherapy is to help the individual realise the potential that already exists within him.

His biographer, Bennet (1961), describes how Jung's dream of a house, containing several levels and going back through time, finally clarified the concept of the collective unconscious in Jung's mind and it remained central to his theoretical framework. From the start, however, it attracted criticism from Freud and other major figures in the psychoanalytic field and it has remained one of the more contentious psychoanalytic concepts, used only by Jung's own followers within the school of *analytical psychology*. However, parallels have been drawn between the concept of the collective unconscious and the *Kleinian* idea of unconscious *phantasy* (Samuels 1985, pp. 42-4).

BENNET, E. A. (1961), *C. G. Jung* (Barrie & Rockliff, London).
JUNG, C. G. (1933), *Modern Man in Search of a Soul* (Routledge & Kegan Paul, London).
JUNG, C. G. (1959), 'The archetypes and the collective unconscious' (*Collected Works*, vol. 9, part 1, Routledge & Kegan Paul, London).
SAMUELS, A. (1985), *Jung and the Post-Jungians* (Routledge & Kegan Paul, London).

Collusion

An unconscious process whereby two or more individuals create an *alliance* based upon a shared defensive need. For example, a parent who fails to support his or her partner in disciplining their child colludes with the child's disruptive behaviour and in so doing forms an alliance with the child against the other parent. He or she is then able to attack the partner through an alliance with the child. Particularly clear examples of collusive processes in families can be seen operating in the *folie à deux*, marital *fit* and *family myth*. Collusion between therapist and patient occurs when the therapist unconsciously allies with dysfunctional, defensive aspects of the patient's self in order to avoid dealing with areas that would be threatening to either the patient or the therapist. Collusion within therapeutic and other small groups is described by Bion, where group members collude in supporting *basic assumption behaviour* and thus avoiding the group's task. Laing and Esterson (1958) also noted the effects of 'collusive pairing' among members of a psychotherapeutic group.

BION, W. R. (1961), *Experiences in Groups* (Tavistock, London).
LAING, R. D. and ESTERSON, A. (1958), 'The collusive function of pairing in analytic groups' (*Brit. J. of Med. Psychol.*, vol. 31, pp. 117-23).

See also *Induction*.

Combined marital therapy

The use of a combination of individual, *concurrent*, *collaborative* and *conjoint marital therapy* sessions in a flexible way, at the discretion of the therapist(s). The approach has been described systematically by Greene *et al.* (1965) and Greene (1970). It is, however, an approach that is frequently used in clinical practice on a pragmatic basis, to meet particular crises or needs which either the patients or the therapists experience at any particular time. Combined therapy tends to be a treatment of last resort, when other types of marital therapy have reached an impasse. Hollender (1971) suggests that unless the therapeutic *contract* is worked out very clearly with all concerned, a great deal of confusion can result. It also renders the therapist highly susceptible to *collusion* with the *resistance* of one or both marital partners.

GREENE, B. L. (1970), *A Clinical Approach to Marital Problems* (Charles C. Thomas, Springfield, Ill.).

GREENE, B. L. *et al.* (1965), 'Treatment of marital disharmony: the use of individual, concurrent and conjoint sessions as a "combined approach" ' (in Greene, B. (ed.), *Psychotherapies of Marital Disharmony*, Free Press, New York).

HOLLENDER, M. H. (1971), 'Selection of therapy for marital problems' (in Masserman, J. H., *Current Psychotherapies*, Grune & Stratton, New York).

PAOLINO, T. J. and McCRADY, B. S. (eds) (1978), *Marriage and Marital Therapy* (Brunner/Mazel, New York).

Communication

Because of its centrality in understanding human interaction, psychological disturbance and the therapeutic process, communication has been studied from a range of different points of view. Communication study is now a huge and complex research area, the main subdivisions of which can only be touched upon here.

The first approach to communication study is the psychoanalytic approach. *Psychoanalysis* is much concerned with communication. Although Freud's interest was in the *intrapsychic*, his framework postulates the continuous battle of control of communication between the *id* and the *censorship* of the *ego*. Mechanisms such as *conversion*, *condensation* and *paraprayes* can be viewed simultaneously as attempts by the contents of the id to communicate with the *conscious* and the effort of the ego to disguise such communication. Freud varied in the emphasis he placed on the communicational value of these processes; and he both denied and affirmed at different times the communicational function of the *dream*, for example. Second, Sullivan's interest in interpersonal processes led him to investigate human communication and to describe a developmental sequence of *referential processes*. Third, Lacan, perhaps more than most psychoanalysts, has highlighted the communicational function of psychic processes. He has described the *unconscious* as being structured like a language and the task of psychoanalysis as the restoration of full communication to the patient. (See *French school of psychoanalysis*.)

The second major approach to communication is the informational approach. This is a linear approach to the sending, receiving and decoding of messages which assumes that the content of communication can be arrived at relatively independently of its *context*. Shannon and Weaver (1949) proposed an early model consisting of five elements: an information source; a transmitter; a transmission channel; a receiver; and a destination. The message is encoded by the sender or information source and is decoded by the receiver. Important later additions to this model are the notion of *feedback*, enabling future messages to be modified; and the notion of 'noise' or the recognition that there may be interference in the message as sent before it gets to the receiver. These concepts provide a useful framework for locating problems which may occur at different stages of the communication process, preventing the message received being the same as the message sent. The model can be applied to any form of dyadic communication, including communication between patient and therapist. It is, however, a relatively simple linear model of what is essentially a complex non-linear process.

Third, the interactional approach, which has studied the organisation of behaviour between the communication parties. Several groups of workers have developed this approach, in particular, Argyle and his associates (1969, 1972). This group stresses the effect that the interactional context has upon the nature of the communication process and the interactional approach moves beyond the simple linear conception of informational communication. Argyle has contributed fundamental work on the importance of *nonverbal communication* and Argyle and Kendon (1967) have suggested that interpersonal transactions are developed via a series of small, goal-oriented, yet tentative steps in much the same way as other social skills are acquired. Argyle and Dean (1965) suggest that a balance is maintained in the interaction between the two parties who are communicating, so that each compensates for changes made by the other in the type, quantity and degree of the behaviour being used. Dowling (1979) has shown that a similar type of compensation occurs within a *co-therapy* team.

Fourth, the transactional approach to communication has been developed from kinesics, cybernetics and *systems theory* by several groups of workers. Birdwhistell (1959) stresses the difference between this approach to communication and others: the individual 'does not originate communication, he participates in it. Communication as a system is not to be understood on a simple model of action and reaction, however complexly stated. As a system it is to be comprehended on the transactional level.' For these workers, communication and behaviour are synonymous and it becomes impossible not to communicate. The most influential work carried out in this area has been by Bateson and his associates (Bateson 1972; Bateson, 1979; Bateson *et al.* 1956) and by subsequent workers at the Mental Research Institute (Watzlawick *et al.* 1967; Watzlawick *et al.* 1974). In formulating the theory of the *double bind*, Bateson *et al.* laid the groundwork for an immensely rich reconstruction of the interrelationship between communicators, their interpersonal relationship and their context. Watzlawick *et al.* have thus elaborated a transactional model of communication theory and have incorporated concepts of symmetry, complementarity, *punctuation, metacommunication* and *paradox* into an overall framework of pathology and therapeutic intervention. Their work has been applied in the *systemic therapies* and in *strategic therapy*. They present five axioms of communication as being: one cannot not communicate; every communication has both a detonative or content aspect and a relationship or metacommunicative aspect such that the latter classifies the former; the nature of the relationship is contingent upon the punctuation of the communicational sequences; human communication involves both *digital* and *analogic* communication and all human communication is either *symmetrical*

or *complementary* depending upon whether it is based on similarity or difference.

Grinder and Bandler (1976) have further extended these concepts from the transactional approach. They postulate the idea of a representational field through which the individual perceives experiences and information. The representational field is the person's individual representation of the world developed by input from the five senses – vision, audition, kinesics (body sensations), smell and taste. Although information is received via all five senses in each person, one sense will usually predominate. Further, the language which people use to describe their experiences replicates their favoured sensory input channel. Thus, if a person 'sees' the situation and tries to 'show' his picture to a spouse who 'feels' the same situation, some bridge is needed to 'overlap' their different experiences. The task of the therapist is to broaden their experience of the event into more than one representational field. This dramatically extends the choices available in relation to the external world and makes possible functional communication about it with others.

ARGYLE, M. (1969), *Social Interaction* (Methuen, London).

ARGYLE, M. (1972), *The Psychology of Interpersonal Behaviour* (2nd edn, Penguin, Harmondsworth).

ARGYLE, M. and DEAN, J. (1965), 'Eye contact, distance and affiliation' (*Sociometry*, vol. 28, pp. 289-304).

ARGYLE, M. and KENDON, A. (1967), 'The experimental analysis of social performance' (in Berkowitz, L. (ed.), *Advances in Experimental Social Psychology*, Academic Press, London).

BANDLER, R. and GRINDER, J. (1975), *The Structure of Magic* (vol. 1, Science and Behavior Books, Palo Alto, Calif.).

BATESON, G. (1972), *Steps to an Ecology of Mind* (Granada, New York).

BATESON, G. (1979), *Mind and Nature: A Necessary Unity* (Dutton, New York).

BATESON, G. *et al.* (1956), 'Toward a theory of

schizophrenia' (*Behavioral Science*, vol. 1, pp. 251-64).

BIRDWHISTELL, R. L. (1959), 'Contribution of linguistic-kinesic studies to the understanding of schizophrenia' (in Auerbach, A. (ed.), *Schizophrenia: An Integrated Approach*, Ronald Press, New York).

BODIN, A. M. (1981), 'The interactional view: family therapy approaches at the MRI' (in Gurman, A. S. and Kniskern, D. P., *Handbook of Family Therapy*, Brunner/Mazel, New York).

DOWLING, E. (1979), 'Co-therapy: a clinical researcher's view' (in Walrond-Skinner, S. (ed.), *Family and Marital Psychotherapy*, Routledge & Kegan Paul, London).

GRINDER, J. and BANDLER, R. (1976), *The Structure of Magic* (vol. 2, Science and Behavior Books, Palo Alto, Calif.).

JACKSON, D. D. (ed.) (1968), *Human Communication* (vols 1 and 2, Science and Behavior Books, New York).

SHANNON, C. E. and WEAVER, W. (1949), *A Mathematical Theory of Communication* (University of Illinois Press, Urbana).

WATZLAWICK, P. *et al.* (1967), *Pragmatics of Human Communication* (W. W. Norton, New York).

WATZLAWICK, P. *et al.* (1974), *Change: Principles of Problem Formation and Problem Resolution* (W. W. Norton, New York).

See also *Neuro-linguistic programming, Psycholinguistics, Theory of types.*

Compensation

A term used by Adler to describe the process whereby the individual reacts to and disguises from himself his inferiority complex. Substitutory or symptomatic behaviour is engaged in to make up for feelings of frustration and perceived lack of ability.

See also *Decompensation, Individual psychology.*

Competence

Adequate and appropriate practice on the part of the therapist as measured by some external standard, which enables him to help his patients to move towards an approximate achievement of their *goals*. Hogan (1979) discusses the complex issues involved in establishing a definition of minimal competence; of defining the criteria by which it may be judged; and developing means of effective *regulation* within the psychotherapy profession to ensure that at least minimal competence is achieved in practice. Hogan discusses competence under several distinct headings: personal qualities and characteristics; technical skills; theoretical knowledge; diagnostic ability; work experience; academic qualifications; type of training and personal therapy. Personal qualities and characteristics have been discussed by Frank (1973) and by Holt and Luborsky (1958) who suggest that the primary factors for competent practice are an introspective orientation which allows *empathy* to develop; an intellectual predisposition that encourages self-examination and the development of *insight*; and a relativistic perspective which values individual and cultural differences. Research subsumed under work on the *core conditions* of therapy is also primarily concerned with the therapist's personal characteristics.

With regard to technical skills and theory, considerable research evidence exists to suggest that the differences between schools and approaches are unimportant and that competence does not reside in the practice of any one particular method. Fiedler's (1950) research into this aspect has been replicated and substantiated by most subsequent findings. Most practitioners believe, however, that some theoretical and technical knowledge (of whatever kind) *is* important, although Rogers (1957) and Whitaker (1976) are amongst those who would see both as either irrelevant or a hindrance to competence. Even if, however, it is hard to demonstrate any relationship between theoretical/technical knowledge and competence (a fact underlined by research into *outcome* achieved by *paraprofessionals* with low-level achievements in these areas) other subtle effects of such knowledge may increase competence – for example, the patient's conception of therapist credibility, *attraction* and *expertness*, perceptions which in turn may have the reciprocal effect of promoting the therapist's best efforts on the part of the patient. Although apparently not relevant to minimal competence, high levels of ability in theory and technique may nevertheless be relevant to high levels of competence. Likewise, although academic qualifications have not been found to be good predictors of competence, they produce some of the same positive side effects. Diagnostic ability is also problematic as a measure of competence, since *diagnosis* itself, in the psychological field, is notoriously lacking in validity and reliability, making it hard to measure skills in it at all. Evidence regarding the relation of experience to competence is equivocal and there are no correlations between competence and personal therapy. Hogan (1979) concludes that 'the ability of the therapist to create the impression of expertise and to instil confidence, rather than actual possession of particular technical skills, may be the critical factor'. Moreover as he goes on to say, the evidence 'suggests that formal training, theoretical knowledge and technical abilities are far less important than specific personality characteristics and interpersonal skills'.

FIEDLER, F. E. (1950), 'A comparison of therapeutic relationships in psycho-analytic, non-directive and Adlerian therapy' (*Journal of Consulting Psychology*, vol. 14, pp. 436-45).
FRANK, J. D. (1973), *Persuasion and Healing: A Comparative Study of Psychotherapy*, revised edn (Johns Hopkins Press, Baltimore).
HOGAN, D. B. (1979), *The Regulation of Psychotherapists*, vol. 1 (Ballinger, Cambridge, Mass.).
HOLT, R. R. and LUBORSKY, L. (1958), *Personality Patterns of Psychiatrists* (Basic Books, New York).
PARLOFF, M. B. *et al.* (1978), 'Research on therapist variables in relation to process and outcome' (in Garfield, S. L. and Bergin, A. E., *Handbook of Psychotherapy and Behavior Change*, Wiley, New York).
ROGERS, C. R. (1957), 'The necessary and sufficient conditions of therapeutic personality change' (*Journal of Consulting Psychology*, vol. 21, pp. 95-103).

WHITAKER, C. (1976), 'The hindrance of theory in clinical work', in Guerin, P., *Family Therapy: Theory and Practice* (Gardner Press, New York).

Complementary

Term used to describe a type of interaction which is characterised by difference between the parties. The parties complement each other's behaviour and difference between them is maximised. Typically, one person occupies the primary and the other the secondary position in terms of power and executive functions. This may be dictated by the formal role relationship which exists, for example, patient-therapist, tutor-student, or it may arise from the characteristics of the individuals themselves. Since each person retains his definition of self by having his partner play an opposite or complementary role, the relationship becomes dysfunctional at the point when this need for complementarity becomes rigid and refuses to yield to changes in circumstances, for example, a new developmental stage in the life cycle (see *Stages of development*). Thus, the dovetailing of an authoritative husband and a dependent wife may work well for both until the wife develops new awareness of the possibilities for women and ceases to be so dependent. Whilst dysfunctional *symmetrical* relationships lead to open fights and the disintegration of the relationship, dysfunctional complementary relationships are more likely to lead to *symptom* formation and a vicious circle of interlocking but covert pathology. Jackson (1959) classified *relationships* rather than *interactions* as being either symmetrical or complementary, but Hinde (1976) makes a plea for making the interaction the object of description on the grounds that describing a whole relationship in this way leads to too global a use of the descriptive terminology.

HINDE, R. A. (1976), 'On describing relationships' (*J. of Child Psychology and Psychiatry*, vol. 17, pp. 1-19).
JACKSON, D. (1959), 'Family interaction, family homeostasis and some implications for

conjoint family psychotherapy' (in Masserman, J. (ed.) *Individual and Family Dynamics*, Grune & Stratton, New York).

WATZLAWICK, P. *et al.* (1967), *Pragmatics of Human Communication* (W. W. Norton, New York).

See also *Collusion, Folie à deux, Marital fit, Skew.*

Complex

Term introduced by Jung to describe a cluster of associated ideas, themes and memories, holding special significance for the individual, and originating in early experience of interpersonal relationships with the parents and possessing an *archetypal* core. This complex has a magnetic quality, by which other congruent ideas and memories are attracted to it. The complex is determined not only by the individual's experiences but also by his way of responding to those experiences. Experientially, a complex functions as a kind of expectation or a filter through which life is perceived. It is made up of repressed material and is therefore an unconscious phenomenon. So far as Jung is concerned, it can arise from either the individual's *personal unconscious* or from the *collective unconscious* or both. For example, the 'mother complex' is held to exist in both the personal and the collective unconscious. A complex is autonomous. According to Jung (1934), 'it forces itself tyrannically upon the conscious mind.'

The term remains central in Jung's schema but Freud expressed misgivings about its usefulness, partly because of its pathological connotations, and apart from particular usages such as the *castration complex* and the *Oedipus complex* it has largely been abandoned amongst Freudian therapists. Adler used the term in a specific sense to describe two particular kinds of complexes relating to character types, the *inferiority complex* and the *superiority complex.* Murray (1938) distinguishes several infantile complexes relating to the *erogenous zones*, and he added to Freud's list a claustral complex, stemming from the *birth trauma*, and a urethral complex, manifested in bed wetting and

exhibitionism. Jung's original formulations in this area owed much to his *word association* experiments.

JUNG, C. G. (1934), 'A review of the complex theory' (in *The Structure and Dynamics of the Psyche, Collected Works*, vol. 8, Routledge & Kegan Paul, London).

MURRAY, H. A. (1938), *Explorations in Personality: A Clinical and Experimental Study of Fifty College Age Men* (Oxford University Press, Oxford).

Component instincts

Freud's theory of neurosis derived from conflict between instincts. On the one hand there were the sexual instincts (collectively called *libido* and aimed biologically at the preservation of the species), and on the other the ego instincts used for self-preservation. The sexual instincts have components that derive from each of the phases of development (oral, anal and phallic), and these can be either loving or sadistic. All children have a full set of all these sexual impulses towards both sexes and have a fundamental polymorphous perversion.

Conciliation

A legal/therapeutic process whereby a counsellor or therapist mediates between a husband and wife at the point when they have begun, or are considering beginning, the legal process to end their marriage. In 1974 the Finer Report drew attention to the fragmented, costly and adversarial facilities which existed for ending marriages and proposed procedures for encouraging the settlement of differences by negotiation and conciliation.

Conciliation requires close liaison with solicitors and extensive knowledge of divorce law and court procedures as well as therapeutic skills appropriate to working with couples in conflict. The aim of conciliation is to help the parties to negotiate with each other with the help of a therapist or *co-therapy* pair over matters that are in dispute. These may include the divorce itself (where one party's decision to end the marriage is opposed by the other); child custody and access issues; and financial and property arrangements. As well as the considerable amount of practical and legal *advice* that is required, therapeutic work focuses on clarifying the areas that require resolution; helping the couple to move towards a 'co-operative win' rather than prolonged and destructive litigation; separating their parental from their marital roles so that whilst the latter can be dissolved, each agrees to help the other to continue their parenting responsibilities effectively, with children having the right to free access to both parents; beginning the *mourning* process for the relationship; identifying as many good memories and productive areas from the past as possible and working out a *ritual* for ending the relationship.

As well as seeing the couple together and each partner separately, some workers use *multiple couples therapy* in the early stages, to help couples who are uncertain as to whether they wish to proceed with the divorce or not. The group may help them clarify their aims and also give them support in carrying these through. Other approaches may include re-engaging each party with his/her family of origin; providing *group psychotherapy* for children of divorcing parents and encouraging the couple to make links with *self-help* groups in the community, such as Gingerbread, Families Need Fathers, and Mothers Apart from their Children. The extent to which children are included directly in the individual couples' meetings varies considerably. The conciliator may see the children on her own and they may also be included in some of the sessions with their parents. At the end of the conciliation process, the agreements reached are normally recorded in writing and sent to both parties.

Most conciliation work is short-term and *crisis*-oriented. However, longer-term *goals* when working with the single divorced person, include supporting them through their initial anxiety and depression; helping the process of *grief* and mourning to continue to a healthy resolution; enabling the client to understand what went wrong in the previous relationship and to gain *insight* into the negative features of

the marital *fit*; helping the client gain in self-esteem and self-confidence and helping him or her to move either towards a new and more functional relationship or into a period of independence and autonomy on their own.

A considerable number of independent conciliation services, specialising entirely in this work, now exist in Britain. The Bristol Courts Family Conciliation Service which opened in Bristol in 1979 was the first. Other services exist in Cleveland, Leicester, Bromley, Telford, Barnet, Dorking, Coventry, Swindon, Liverpool and Leeds. Conciliation is also undertaken by some probation services and by the court welfare services.

AMBROSE, P. *et al.* (1983), *Surviving Divorce: Men Beyond Marriage* (Harvester Press, Hassocks, Sussex).

BLOCH, D. (1980), 'Divorcing: clinical notes' (in Andolfi, M., *Dimensions of Family Therapy*, Guilford Press, New York).

DUCK, S. (ed.) (1982), *Dissolving Personal Relationships* (Academic Press, New York).

GADDIS, S. (1978), 'Divorce decision making: alternatives to litigation' (*Conciliation Courts Review*, vol. 16, pp. 43-5).

HAYNES, J. N. (1980), 'Managing conflict: the role of the mediator' (*Conciliation Courts Review*, vol. 18, pp. 9-13).

IRVING, H. (1981), *Divorce Mediation: A Rational Alternative to the Adversarial System* (Universe Books, New York).

LAZARUS, A. (1981), 'Divorce counseling or marriage therapy? A therapeutic option' (*J. of Marital and Family Therapy*, vol. 7, pp. 15-22).

LITTLE, M. (1982), *Family Break-up* (Jossey-Bass, San Francisco).

MURCH, M. (1980), *Justice and Welfare in Divorce* (Sweet & Maxwell, London).

PARKINSON. L. (1983), 'Conciliation: a new approach to family conflict resolution' (*Brit. J. of Social Work*, vol. 13, pp. 19-37).

TAYLOR, A. Y. (1981), 'Toward a comprehensive theory of mediation' (*Conciliation Courts Review*, vol. 19, pp. 1-12).

WALLERSTEIN, J. and KELLY, J. (1980), *Surviving the Break-up* (Grant McIntyre, London).

CONCRETENESS

WINNANS, A. (1983), *Divorce and Separation: Every Woman's Guide* (Sheldon Press, London).

Concreteness

The therapist's specificity of expression towards the client. Truax and Carkhall (1964) found that concreteness of expression correlates highly with emotional proximity between client and therapist, accuracy of the therapist's responses, and reciprocal specificity on the part of the client. Ivey and Gluckstern (1976) stress the importance of concreteness in the giving of *direction* and stress the need for concreteness, regardless of the theoretical model of therapy being used. An exception to this is when an *interview* has become highly charged with emotion and the use of more vague or abstract interventions by the therapist serves to reduce the affective temperature temporarily. Bandler and Grinder (1975) discuss the need for a parallel quality of completeness of expression, which contains both the surface and the deep structure of meaning. The task of the therapist is to help the client realise the full deep structure of his communications, by engaging in completeness and concreteness himself.

BANDLER, J. and GRINDER, R. (1975), *The Structure of Magic*, vol. 1 (Science and Behavior Books, Palo Alto, Calif.).
IVEY, A. and GLUCKSTERN, N. (1976), *Basic Influencing Skills: Leader and Participant Manuals* (North Amherst, Mass., Microtraining).
TRUAX, C. B. and CARKHALL, R. (1964), 'Concreteness: a neglected variable in research in psychotherapy' (*J. of Clinical Psychology*, vol. 20, pp. 264-7).

Concurrent marital therapy

The concurrent but separate treatment of the two spouses by the same therapist. Although Oberndorf (1938) first reported this procedure, Mittleman (1948) was responsible for expanding the understanding and practice of concurrent treatment, originally as a specialised technique in *psychoanalysis*. It was viewed initially with disfavour, as potentially contaminating the analyst's understanding of the individual's *internal world* and interfering with the *transference*. But as Rodgers (1965) points out, 'complementary neurotic interactions play a large role in marital discord and have an autonomy of their own over and above the individual pathology of the partners.' Such an understanding has been utilised most fully by the *conjoint* or *systemic* therapies, so that concurrent treatments tend to be disfavoured both by those who feel that the individual should be seen alone and by those who believe that the marital *system* should be treated *in vivo*. Dicks (1967), for example, calls it the 'worst of both worlds. One is treating interaction, but keeps the interacting persons separate.' However, concurrent marital therapy is still quite widely practised in marriage guidance clinics. Contra-indications suggested by Martin (1976) for concurrent treatment, in addition to the reservations expressed above, are given as: the inability of either spouse to share a therapist; the presence of severe psychosis or character disorders in one or both spouses; and the fragility of *defence mechanisms* in one or both partners.

DICKS, H. V. (1967), *Marital Tensions* (Routledge & Kegan Paul, London).
GREENE, B. and SOLOMON, A. (1963), 'Marital disharmony. concurrent psychoanalytic therapy of husband and wife by the same psychiatrist' (*Am. J. of Psychiatry*, vol. 17, pp. 443-50).
MARTIN, P. (1976), *A Marital Therapy Manual* (Brunner/Mazel, New York).
MITTLEMAN, B. (1948), 'The concurrent analysis of married couples' (*Psychoanalytic Quarterly*, vol. 17, pp. 182-97).
MITTLEMAN, B. (1952), 'Simultaneous treatment of both parents and their child' (in Bychowski, G. and Despert, J. L. (eds) *Specialised Techniques in Psychotherapy*, Basic Books, New York).
OBERNDORF, P. (1938), 'Psychoanalysis of married couples' (*Psychoanalytic Review*, vol. 25, pp. 453-75).
PAOLINO, T. J. and McCRADY, B. S. (eds)

(1978), *Marriage and Marital Therapy* (Brunner/Mazel, New York).

RODGERS, T. C. (1965), 'A specific parameter: concurrent psychotherapy of the spouse of an analysand by the same analyst' (*Int. J. of Psychoan.*, vol. 46, pp. 237-43).

See also *Collaborative marital therapy, Combined marital therapy, Conjoint marital therapy, Folie à deux.*

Condensation

The reductive process whereby a cluster of ideas or feelings are represented through a single image as in a *dream* or through a piece of behaviour, as in a *symptom*. In the case of dreams, the *manifest content* represents a condensation of the *latent content*. Freud (1916-17) suggested that it was simultaneously both the means by which the *unconscious* evaded the *censorship* of the *ego* and also the means by which that censorship operated.

FREUD, S. (1916-17), 'Introductory lectures on psychoanalysis' (*Standard Edition*, vol. 15, Hogarth Press, London).

Condenser phenomena

Term used in *group psychotherapy* and *group analysis* to describe the way in which emotional charges can be stored up within a group and discharged under the stimulus of some shared group event. The discharge may take the form of a *dream* or a *phantasy*. These symbols can often be more readily understood in the group situation because the group, through what it holds in common, creates a condensing effect upon the *unconscious* phenomena within each individual member. Thus unconscious material can often be expressed more readily and more fully in the group situation because of the loosening effects on individual members' *resistance* produced by the group interaction. Foulkes and Anthony (1957) described condenser phenomena as group-specific factors.

FOULKES, S. H. and ANTHONY, E. J. (1957), *Group Psychotherapy* (Penguin, Harmondsworth).

See also *Chain phenomena, Mirror phenomena, Resonance.*

Conditioned response

A behavioural event which follows from a *conditioned stimulus* as a result of learning or conditioning. In *classical conditioning* theory, the response is brought about as a result of the pairing of a neutral with an *unconditioned stimulus*. Thus, the salivation response that occurred in Pavlov's dogs when it followed the ringing of a bell (conditioned stimulus) is the conditioned response that they have learned.

Conditioned stimulus

A cue which provokes a *response* as a result of learning or *conditioning*. In *classical conditioning*, the pairing of a neutral *stimulus* with an *unconditioned stimulus* produces a conditioned stimulus. The conditioned stimulus is capable of producing the same response as the unconditioned stimulus. Watson and Rayner (1920) showed that a young child's fear of loud noises could be *generalised* by conditioning to a white rat. In this example, the white rat is the conditioned stimulus since the fear associated with the loud noise has been transferred to the rat.

WATSON, J. B. and RAYNER, R. (1920), 'Conditional emotional reactions' (*Journal of Experimental Psychology*, vol. 3, pp. 1-14).

Conditioning

According to *learning theory*, the means by which behaviour is changed. Conditioning, which may take the form of either *classical* or *operant conditioning*, involves establishing new stimulus-response sequences through a form of environmental manipulation. Conditioning is the basic principle behind the techniques of *behaviour therapy* but is challenged by the propositions of *cognitive therapy* and *cognitive behaviour therapy*.

Confidentiality

See *Ethics.*

Confrontation

Challenging the client's incongruencies in relation to his perceptions of his relationship with others. Ivey and Gluckstern (1976) define confrontation as 'the pointing out of discrepancies between or among attitudes, thoughts or behaviours'. This may involve pointing out the discrepancies between the detonative and *metacommunicative* levels of the client's *communication*, between his self-concept and *ego ideal*, or between the shifting perceptions of group or family members. Confronting the client may be done by offering him *feedback*, by making complex *interpretations* or by attacking his *defence mechanisms* as, for example, in *primal therapy*, *Reichian therapy*, *provocative therapy*, etc.

BERENSON, B. and MITCHELL, K. (1974), *Confrontation* (Human Resource Development, Amherst, Mass.).
IVEY, A. E. and GLUCKSTERN, N. (1976), *Basic Influencing Skills: Leader and Participant Manuals* (North Amherst, Mass., Microtraining).

See also *Interview, Microskill.*

Congruence

The therapist's ability to match his words and actions to the way he feels. Rogers (1967) uses the term to describe both a *core condition* of therapy and the means by which a core condition, *genuineness*, is achieved. The terms genuineness and congruence are often used interchangeably. Congruence implies the therapist's ability to be *integrated* both within the therapeutic encounter and in terms of the integrity of his personal and professional values and lifestyle. Helping the client to achieve congruence is also an important *goal* in the *humanistic* approaches to psychotherapy.

ROGERS, C. R. (1967), *On Becoming a Person* (Constable, London).

Conjoint

The simultaneous treatment of a couple, family or other natural *system* by one or more therapists. The term is sometimes erroneously used instead of *co-therapy* to describe simultaneous treatment by two or more therapists. The term conjoint is used as a prefix to marital therapy and *family therapy* to distinguish either from non-conjoint approaches such as *concurrent* or *collaborative* treatments.

Conjoint family therapy

See *Family therapy.*

Conjoint marital therapy

Term coined by Jackson (1959) to describe the meeting of the therapist with a husband and wife simultaneously. The term is used to distinguish this form of treatment from *concurrent, collaborative* and *combined marital therapy* and from the practice of working with the marriage by treating one of the partners alone. Conjoint marital therapy is treated in the literature both as a sub-specialty of *family therapy* and as a method in its own right, having its own separate historical development. Olson (1970) has described the way in which conjoint marital therapy emerged out of marital counselling and alongside the development of conjoint family therapy. Having been the less favoured form of marital psychotherapy, it is now the treatment of choice for most problems of marital dysfunction where both spouses are prepared to attend. In addition, it may be the most appropriate treatment for much individually located symptomatology presented by one spouse.

The growth in popularity of the conjoint approach is partly due to systematic research produced in favour of the involvement of both spouses by Gurman and his associates. Gurman and Kniskern (1978) showed that when both spouses are involved in therapy, there is a much higher improvement rate (65 per cent) than when only one partner is treated (48 per cent). As Gurman (1978) points out, this does not necessarily mean that conjoint treatment is superior to concurrent or collaborative forms, since these also involve both spouses in treatment. But as he goes on to say, theorists of 'practically every theoretical persuasion recommend conjoint or conjoint group therapy over concurrent.'

Conjoint marital therapy is practised within a psychoanalytic, behavioural or communicational framework. Gurman (1978) offers a comparative analysis of these three models and examines four specific dimensions of the treatment process: the role of the past and the *unconscious*; the nature and meaning of the presenting problem; the relative importance of mediating versus ultimate treatment goals; and the nature of the therapist's roles and functions. He concludes that behavioural approaches are no more effective than non-behavioural ones and that therapist *relationship factors* have a major impact on *outcome* regardless of theoretical orientation. Ables and Brandsma (1977) suggest a model based on teaching the couple negotiation, communication and re-education. A heterosexual *co-therapy* team is often used in conjoint marital therapy which reduces the risk of *triangulation* and provides opportunities for *modelling* functional behaviour and conflict resolution.

Conjoint marital therapy frequently forms a part of the treatment process within conjoint family therapy, with marital sessions being offered after abatement of the *identified patient*'s *symptoms* and prior to sessions with the parents' families of origin. Conjoint marital therapy may also be offered within the context of a group setting, as *multiple couples therapy*.

ABLES, B. S. and BRANDSMA, J. (1977), *Therapy for Couples* (Jossey-Bass, San Francisco).

GURMAN, A. S. (1978), 'Contemporary marital therapies' (in Paolino, T. J. and McCrady, B. S., *Marriage and Marital Therapy*, Brunner/Mazel, New York).

GURMAN, A. S. and KNISKERN, D. P. (1978), 'Research in marital and family therapy' (in Garfield, S. L. and Bergin, A. E. (eds), *Handbook of Psychotherapy and Behavior Change*, Wiley, New York).

GURMAN, A. S. and RICE, D. G. (1975), *Couples in Conflict* (Jason Aronson, New York), JACKSON, D. D. (1959), 'Family interaction, family homeostasis and some implications for

conjoint family psychotherapy' (in Masserman, J., *Individual and Family Dynamics*, Grune & Stratton, New York).

OLSON, D. H. (1970), 'Marital and family therapy: integrative review and critique' (*Journal of Marriage and the Family*, vol. 32, pp. 501-38).

Conscious

The region of the mind described by Freud as the perceptual conscious or part of the *psyche* which is open to immediate awareness, in contrast to both the *preconscious* and the *unconscious*. Prior to Freud, the conscious level of the mind had been studied as being equivalent to the whole psyche; its analysis and description was the primary focus of study for nineteenth-century psychologists. With the advent of psychoanalytic researches, however, interest in the conscious was temporarily eclipsed in favour of the unconscious. As with the other levels of the psyche, the conscious is seen by psychoanalytic writers as both a region of the mind and a mode in which the psychic *agencies* function. Consciousness is the primary mode of operation for the *ego* and also for some of the functions of the superego. Thus, the ego functions of reality testing, perception, observation and evaluation are all conscious activities and only the ego's *defence mechanisms* and its *censorship* lie outside the realm of consciousness. The superego's functions of criticism and conscience are also mainly conscious. Later Freud (1926) described the conscious as 'the sense organ of the ego' giving warning of dangerous situations (especially internally). Jung (1934) criticised what he felt to be Freud's loss of perspective regarding the balance between the conscious and the unconscious aspects of the psyche, as well as noting the opposite error that had occurred before Freud: 'It is true that the conscious mind has been over valued by the rationalists. Hence it was a healthy sign to give the unconscious its due share of value. But this should not exceed the value accorded to consciousness.' Freud himself redressed this balance to some extent in his later writings.

The study of consciousness increases in interest for non-psychoanalytic theorists in inverse proportion to their disinterest in the unconscious. Thus, behaviour therapists, humanistic practitioners and phenomenologists all focus on the conscious experience of the individual, but from different points of view. Behaviour therapists who adopt a radical perspective eliminate the need to *explain* the conscious as having a role in the causation of behaviour (Watson 1925), but as Taylor (1970) describes, the behaviourist is still interested in examining and trying to understand the *mechanisms* by which consciousness operates. Therapists who aspire to phenomenological approaches to psychotherapy have done more than any other school to describe and analyse the functions of consciousness. Gurwitsch (1957, 1966) has studied the intentionality of consciousness and the relationship between consciousness and what he calls its 'objectivating function'. Following phenomenological philosophers such as Husserl, Gurwitsch refuses to make a distinction between phenomena and noumena – that is, between the conscious experience of things and things in their objective sense. For Gurwitsch, the object is only real in so far as it is experienced in the consciousness of the individual. The emphasis of other phenomenologists to such as Minowski (1933) and Straus (1966) is on the present and future and the importance of experience. This means that their attention is naturally focused on the activities of the conscious. Gurwitsch suggests that consciousness is inconceivable without an awareness of time passing and he identifies the ego's experience with that of the context or *stream of consciousness*. Thus, the past and present are linked and together form the individual's identity within present conscious awareness.

FREUD, S. (1926), 'Inhibitions, symptoms and anxiety' (*Standard Edition*, vol. 20, Hogarth Press, London).

FREUD, S. (1940), 'An outline of psychoanalysis' (*Standard Edition*, vol. 23, Hogarth Press, London).

GURWITSCH, A. (1957), *The Field of Consciousness* (Duquesne University Press, Pittsburg).

GURWITSCH, A. (1966), *Studies in Phenomenology and Psychology* (North Western University Press, Evanstown, Ill.).

JUNG, C. G. (1930), 'Some aspects of modern psychotherapy' (in *The Practice of Psychotherapy, Collected Works*, vol. 16, Routledge & Kegan Paul, London).

JUNG, C. G. (1934), 'The practical use of dream analysis' (in *The Practice of Psychotherapy, Collected Works*, vol. 16, Routledge & Kegan Paul, London).

MINOWSKI, E. (1933), *Lived Time* (Northwestern University Press, Evanston, Ill.).

STRAUS, E. (1966), *Phenomenological Psychology* (Basic Books, New York).

TAYLOR, J. G. (1970), 'Consciousness: theory versus non-theory' (*Bull. Brit. Psycholog. Soc.*, vol. 23, pp. 43-6).

WATSON, J. B. (1925), *Behaviourism* (Routledge & Kegan Paul, London).

See also *Topographical model.*

Consciousness raising

The process whereby an exploited and underprivileged individual or group develops awareness of the origins of its powerlessness and seeks to remedy it. Consciousness raising usually takes place in groups and it has been particularly associated with the women's movement. For this reason, consciousness raising groups, combining *self-help* with therapy, are an important ingredient of *feminist therapy*. Within the women's movement, consciousness raising groups usually meet regularly; are composed of six to twelve women; are leaderless; and provide opportunities for women to talk about their experiences of frustration, pain and violence in an empathic and accepting atmosphere. They also build confidence through mutual association and develop political and personal awareness.

Constriction

A term used by Kelly to describe the way in which a person narrows his perceptual field in order to minimise apparent incompatibilities.

The concept is implied in Kelly's choice *corollary*.

KELLY, G. A. (1955), *The Psychology of Personal Constructs* (W. W. Norton, New York).
KELLY, G. A. (1963), *A Theory of Personality* (W. W. Norton, New York).

See also *Cognitive dissonance, Personal construct theory*.

Construct
According to G. A. Kelly, a construct is an individual's interpretation of external reality. Kelly (1963) suggested that the term bore a close resemblance to the term 'concept' but felt that the latter was too limited in its scope. The act of construct formation or construing enables the individual to judge similarities and differences between people and events or *elements* as they are called in Kelly's *personal construct theory*. In his construction *corollary* Kelly asserts that the individual can anticipate or predict events in the future by construing their replications or similarities with the past. Each construct is bi-polar in nature, for example, happy-sad, happy and sad being the two *poles* of the construct. The construct can be said to have a limited range and *focus of convenience*. Some constructs are so central to the individual's identity that they can be described as core constructs; if these are shaken, the individual may experience anxiety and fear. Others are more peripheral and can be altered without serious modification to the core structure. A superordinate construct is one which includes other subordinate constructs as elements in its own range of convenience. A construct is described as permeable if it is capable of admitting newly discovered elements into its *context*. Kelly described three ways in which constructs can encompass their elements: pre-emptive constructs, which pre-empt the elements for membership into their own realm exclusively; constellatory constructs, which fix the realm membership of their elements, for example *stereotypes*; and propositional constructs which do not disturb the other realm memberships of the elements. A construct can either be tight,

leading to unvarying predictions, or loose, leading to varying predictions whilst still retaining its identity.

KELLY, G. A. (1955), *The Psychology of Personal Constructs* (W. W. Norton, New York).
KELLY, G. A. (1963), *A Theory of Personality* (W. W. Norton, New York).

Constructive alternativism
The basic premise which underlies Kelly's theory of personal constructs and therefore of his *personal construct therapy*. Kelly asserted that a person is by nature a scientist and that his approach to the world is the scientist's approach whereby a *hypothesis* is selected and tested out against the empirical evidence. People use *constructs* as hypotheses to help them predict and hence control the world around them. Since, like any other hypothesis, a construct can be abandoned or modified to the extent to which it is confirmed or not by the evidence of living, Kelly's use of the term constructive alternativism indicates the essential premise underlying his theory. Thus, unlike psychoanalytic theory with its emphasis on the primary influence of the remote past in the formation of personality and the aetiology of psychological disorder, Kelly emphasises the alternatives that are always open for the individual to consider, should he fail to validate one construct or construct system. Moreover Kelly (1963) asserted that since no absolute construction of the universe is feasible, 'we assume that all of our present interpretations of the universe are subject to revision or replacement.' Kelly's theory asserts that a person's most appropriate response to his or her world is a flexible construction of external reality which remains open to alternative constructions. 'We take the stand that there are always some alternative constructions available to choose among in dealing with the world . . . no-one needs to be the victim of his biography.'

KELLY, G. A. (1955), *The Psychology of Personal Constructs* (W. W. Norton, New York).
KELLY, G. A. (1963), *A Theory of Personality* (W. W. Norton, New York).

Consultant

A senior practitioner of any professional mental health discipline or psychotherapeutic approach, who offers specialised help and advice to therapists or to a *team*. Although the term is often used interchangeably with supervisor, it implies a relationship between peers and that the therapist seeking help with his patient is himself a fully qualified practitioner. In a more specialised sense, the term is used for the leader of a study group in *Tavistock group training*. Consultation is a growing area of interest and expertise in the helping professions and several writers have recently attempted to analyse the specific skills and knowledge base required of a consultant.

GALLESSICK, J. (1982), *The Profession and Practice of Consultation* (Jossey-Bass, San Francisco).

KADUSHIN, A. (1977), *Consultation in Social Work* (Columbia University Press, New York).

KASLOW, F. W. (1977), *Supervision, Consultation and Staff Training in the Helping Professions* (Jossey-Bass, San Francisco).

PARSONS, R. D. and MEYERS, J. (1984), *Developing Consultation Skills* (Jossey-Bass, San Francisco).

Containment

The therapist's ability to receive and hold the patient's projections without absorbing them or acting them out, enabling him to mediate them back to the patient in a more digestible form. This in turn allows the patient to become aware of and integrate parts of himself that he has not formerly been able to tolerate. The term was introduced by Bion (1962) whose metaphor 'container' is derived from the bodily containment of the penis by the vagina and of the breast by the baby's mouth. The baby projects into mother those feelings that threaten to overwhelm his immature *ego*. Ideally, mother is able to accept and hold these unacceptable feelings for the baby, in what Bion calls 'a state of reverie'. The infant's development depends on *introjecting* his mother, who has dealt with his anxiety, and then, through identifying with her on the basis of this introjection, he can begin to feel able to

deal with his own anxiety himself. *Object relations* psychoanalysts view this process as a model for the therapeutic effect of analysis and the therapist is seen as doing the same for the patient as the mother for her infant. The image of the therapist as a container is a more dynamic one than the therapist as a passive recipient of the patient's *projections*, since it involves him in actively receiving, tolerating and digesting the unwanted feelings and re-introducing them to the patient at an appropriate moment and in a suitable form. The therapist's containment of the multiple projections of a family group is discussed by Box (1982) and Waddell (1982).

Winnicott uses the term 'holding' to describe a similar maternal function for the infant. The mother reflects, as in a mirror, the infant's emotional states. This idea in turn is related to Lacan's concept of the mirror phase in the infant's development.

BION, W. R. (1962), *Learning from Experience* (Heinemann, London).

BOX, S. (1982), 'Working with the dynamics of the session' (in *Psychotherapy with Families: An Analytic Approach*, Routledge & Kegan Paul, London).

WADDELL, M. (1982), 'The family and its dynamics' (in Box, S., *Psychotherapy with Families: An Analytic Approach*, Routledge & Kegan Paul, London).

WINNICOTT, D. W. (1965), 'Theory of the parent-infant relationship' (in *Maturational Processes and the Facilitating Environment*, Hogarth Press, London).

See also *Acting out, French school (of psychoanalysis), Projective identification.*

Context

A term used in several different ways within psychotherapy. (a) The psychosocial environment of the individual which becomes, in *conjoint* therapies, the *unit of treatment*. The psychosocial environment or context is composed of the emotional *network*, comprising family members and significant others; the professional network which may be involved with the individual or family; and the therapist's own emotional, professional and *agency* network. (b) The situation in which a behaviour is embedded and which gives it its meaning. The same behaviour may be labelled deviant, sick, normal or creative depending upon the circumstances in which it takes place. Used in this sense, the context of behaviour includes the characteristics of the behaving person (e.g. sex, social class, age, race), the characteristics of the person making a judgment upon that behaviour, and the interpersonal relationship in which the behaviour occurs. (See also *Communication, Diagnosis, Identified patient, Labelling, Scapegoat*.) (c) The ambient conditions of therapy. (See *Ambience, Non-specific factors*.) (d) In *personal construct theory*, Kelly asserts that the context of a *construct* is made up of those *elements* from which the individual discriminates by means of a construct. The term is more restricted than that implied by the construct's *range of convenience* but more extensive than that implied by its *focus of convenience*. (e) In *field theory* Lewin's special contribution to psychotherapy was the new emphasis he placed on the context of personality development.

Contextual family therapy
See *Transgenerational family therapy*.

Continental school (of psychoanalysis)
Name given to the school of *psychoanalysis* which formed around Anna Freud in England after the Second World War. It was used to distinguish the group of primarily European psychoanalysts who fled to England before the war, from other analysts working in Britain. (See *British school* and *Kleinian school*.)

Anna Freud made two major contributions to psychoanalysis. First, in her work on the individual *ego* and its *defence mechanisms* she paved the way for the development of *ego psychology* and a new direction in psychoanalysis. Second, through her work at the Hampstead Clinic, London, she pioneered new developments in *child psychotherapy*. The Hampstead Clinic became the centre of the

continental school's therapeutic work, training and research. Anna Freud's theoretical extension of Freud's work was set out in her book, *The Ego and the Mechanisms of Defence*, published in Britain in 1937. It was designed to redress the imbalance that she perceived in psychoanalytic theory and practice brought about by the almost exclusive priority given to the analysis of the *id*. But as Anna Freud (1937) pointed out, 'Anything which comes into analysis from the side of the ego is just as good material as an id derivative. We have no right to regard it as simply an interruption to the analysis of the id.' She expanded the earlier work done on defence mechanisms and added five more: denial in fantasy; denial in word and act; restriction of the ego; identification with the aggressor; and altruistic surrender. Sigmund Freud (1937), in one of his last books, showed how the defence mechanisms, as elaborated by his daughter, may become 'fixated in the ego' as 'regular modes of reaction', a situation which he described as the 'alteration of the ego'.

Anna Freud's work was developed over the forty years she lived in England and it parallels some of the work undertaken by the *Kleinian school*. During the 1940s the points of difference between the two groups were hammered out in what came to be known as the Controversial Discussions (see *Kleinian school*).

FREUD, A. (1937), *The Ego and the Mechanisms of Defence* (Hogarth Press, London).
FREUD, S. (1937), 'Analysis terminable and interminable' (*Standard Edition*, vol. 23, Hogarth Press, London).
PETERS, V. H. (1985), *Anna Freud* (Weidenfield & Nicolson, London).

Contingency management
The process of changing the probability and frequency of a *response* by controlling the consequences (or contingencies) of that response. Contingency management is based on the principles of *operant conditioning*. There are five main types of contingency management: positive reinforcement and

negative reinforcement (both are described under *Reinforcement); punishment; response cost*; and *extinction*. Contingency management is preceded by a *behavioural analysis* and the establishment of a *base line*; the selection of appropriate *reinforces* or punishments; and the drawing up of a *contract*. It is the principles behind the operation of a *token economy*.

Contract

A formal agreement between patient and therapist regarding the *goals* of therapy, the means by which they may be achieved and the terms of the therapeutic relationship. A contract implies an explicit agreement between all the parties involved. In the case of individual treatment, the contract is made between the individual and the therapist. In *family therapy*, the therapist needs to consider at what age children can appropriately be included in its terms. In group treatments, the terms of the contract may include the reciprocal responsibilities of group members to each other as well as the relationship between the therapist and the group. Likewise, in family and *marital therapy* the contract often includes the *quid pro quo*, 'give to get' arrangements worked out between family members with the help of the therapist.

Contracts are used most often in the behavioural approaches. Contracting is in some respects an extension of *contingency management* where the patient agrees to perform certain *tasks* or *homework assignments* or to engage in certain behaviours in exchange for rewards or (if the behaviour is not performed) *punishment*. The contract may be written down and signed by both therapist and patient(s).

In a broader sense, a less formal contract is usually made at the outset of treatment in most approaches, in which the ground rules of therapy are agreed, including the venue, frequency of sessions, boundaries of confidentiality, time limits (if used in the approach), the persons to be included in the *unit of treatment* (in the *systemic therapies*), fees (if relevant), the broad requirements of the treatment approach (for example, that the patient will talk about whatever comes into his mind, report his

dreams, etc.), the duties and responsibilities of each party, the goals of treatment (in broad outline or in specific detail, depending upon the approach) and the way in which *outcome* will be evaluated. Using a contract to formulate the relationship between patient and therapist helps to ensure the professional nature of the relationship, reduces the likelihood of the exploitation of severely depressed patients, minors and the mentally handicapped, and protects the therapist from the consequences of the patient's unrealistic expectations. Contracts can also be used to regulate the relationship between a supervisor and trainee in *training* or between a *consultant* and *team* at the commencement of their work together.

SAGER, C. J. (1976), *Marriage Contracts and Couple Therapy* (Brunner/Mazel, New York).

See also *Reciprocity, Token economy*.

Control group

A group of subjects who receive no formal psychotherapeutic treatment and are used as a comparison for measuring the *outcome* of treatment on a similar matched group. Frank (1959) discussed the use of controls in psychotherapy research. Numerous technical and ethical problems surround their use. To reduce the ethical difficulty of administering no treatment to disturbed patients, 'minimal treatment' rather than 'no treatment' controls are sometimes used, but the random assignment of patients to these groups as well as the random assignment of therapists to different treatment approaches remains a very difficult task. Bergin and Lambert (1978) have discussed the technical difficulties involved – namely that there is no way of telling how much informal therapeutic input a control group receives from friends and other non-professional therapists. The efficacy of non-professional input is unknown but it might be as effective as professional input, and *non-specific factors* such as hope, expectancy and the belief that treatment *is* being administered when it isn't may all act as potent agents of change.

BERGIN, A. E. and LAMBERT, M. (1978), 'The evaluation of therapeutic outcome' (in Bergin, A. E. and Garfield, S. L., *Handbook of Psychotherapy and Behavior Change*, Wiley, New York).

FRANK, J. D. (1959), 'Problems of controls in psychotherapy' (in Rubenstein, E. A. and Parloff, M. B. (eds), *Research in Psychotherapy*, American Psychological Association, New York).

Conversion

The mechanism whereby psychic conflict is transformed into a *symptom*, with a specific symbolic content. The symptom thus operates as a form of condensed communication between the *unconscious*, where the conflict has been repressed, and the client's *conscious*. Freud (1895) introduced the term to describe the specific case of the conversion of conflict in cases of hysteria into somatic presentations. The term is now used more generally. The fact that the physical symptom symbolises the original conflict can lead the therapist towards an understanding of that conflict: for example, writer's cramp may express the unconscious wish to abandon a writing project.

FREUD, S. (1894) 'The neuro-psychoses of defence' (*Standard Edition*, vol. 3, Hogarth Press, London).
FREUD, S. and BREUER, J. (1895), 'Studies in hysteria' (*Standard Edition*, vol. 2, Hogarth Press, London).
FREUD, S. (1909), 'Some general remarks on hysterical attacks' (*Standard Edition*, vol. 9, Hogarth Press, London).

See also *Condensation*.

Coping behaviour

Purposeful actions undertaken by the individual in order to accomplish a goal in relation to the environment. Lazarus (1966), who developed the concept, describes four types of coping behaviour, the first three of which are unproductive: *regression*, when the individual resorts to behaviour learned at an earlier developmental stage, or to a role, such as the *sick role* which has, as its aim, the unconscious avoidance of the problem; *denial*, when the problem confronting the individual is made to 'disappear'; inertia, when the individual withdraws from attempting to solve the problem into a state of *helplessness*; and problem solving behaviour, when the individual realistically defines the problem, identifies alternative methods of coping, tries out (mentally or in reality) these alternatives, selects one of them and takes appropriate steps to put it into effect. The ability to exhibit coping behaviour in a *crisis* does not appear to depend on previous psychiatric history, but on the severity of the hazardous event and the presence or absence of interlocking developmental crises.

LAZARUS, R. S. (1966), *Psychological Stress and the Coping Process* (McGraw-Hill, New York).

See also *Coping skills interventions, Crisis theory, Defence mechanisms, Problem solving interventions.*

Coping skills interventions

A variety of techniques designed to help the client develop a repertoire of effective *coping behaviours* which can be *generalised* to a variety of stress situations. These include *self-help* procedures which may initially be taught by a therapist; *covert modelling*; a modified form of *systematic desensitisation* introduced by Goldfried (1971), whereby clients are taught to cope with, rather than avoid, anxiety-inducing imagery, by *relaxation training*, *anxiety management training*; and *stress inoculation*. Coping skills interventions draw from the theoretical and technical ideas of both *cognitive behaviour therapy* and the *problem solving interventions*. Their distinguishing feature is their emphasis on teaching ways of *coping* with stress rather than extinguishing, reducing or avoiding it. Features that are common to the various coping skills interventions are: teaching the client the role of cognitions in the development of the problem; training the client to monitor his own self-statements; training the client in the fundamentals of problem solving; *modelling* for the client adaptive self-statements; *behavioural rehearsal* of adaptive self-statements; and the application of these and problem solving skills to increasingly difficult tasks.

GOLDFRIED, M. R. (1971), 'Systematic desensitisation as training in self control' (*J. of Consulting and Clinical Psychology*, vol. 37, pp. 228-34).
GOLDFRIED, M. R. and DAVISON, G. C. (1976), *Clinical Behavior Therapy* (Holt, Rinehart & Winston, New York).
MEICHENBAUM, D. *et al.* (1975), 'The nature of coping with stress' (in Saracen, I. and Spielberger, C. (eds), *Stress and Anxiety*, vol. 2, Wiley, New York).

See also *Crisis intervention, Helplessness.*

Core conditions

Term used to describe the relationship skills employed in varying degrees by most therapists alongside technical interventions. *Client-centred therapists* define these conditions as *empathy*, *non-possessive warmth* and *genuineness* or *congruence*, and claim that, when they are not only present in the therapist, but appropriately expressed to the client, they are sufficient for achieving a positive therapeutic outcome.

The subject has attracted an immense body of research. Truax and Mitchell (1971) summarised the literature up until 1971 and found that a considerable body of evidence suggested that the core conditions were effective. Mitchell *et al.* (1977), however, show that high levels of the core conditions are only partially related to therapeutic outcome. They suggest that earlier work had been directed to gross outcome studies and that the core conditions 'might be used differentially dependent on client diagnosis'. Criticism in fact centres around their 'sufficiency' rather than their 'necessity' in the therapeutic relationship.

Egan (1975) and others suggest that there are distinct developmental phases in the therapeutic process and that while Rogers's core conditions are very important in the early phase, other inventions are required later on, such as *confrontation*, immediacy and therapist *self-disclosure*. Moreover, Troemel-ploetz (1980) has shown that when subjected to linguistic analysis, empathic interventions, for example, can carry implicit messages at deeper levels of meaning. These interventions have properties which are also found in *interpreting*, restructuring, and *paradoxical* interventions. If this is so, the notion of the sufficiency of the core conditions is called into question. Further problems arise concerning the degree to which the core conditions can be separated into conceptually discrete and therefore measurable entities.

Some workers have attempted to integrate behavioural techniques with client-centred therapy (see *Learning-based client-centred therapy*) believing that both the core conditions and technical interventions are important. Others have shown that these core conditions are necessary ingredients in the therapeutic relationship even when the emphasis is on the importance of highly technical interventions or even physical treatments.

Both psychoanalytic and behavioural therapists have attempted to separate the two major elements in the therapeutic transaction, namely technique from *relationship factors*. Psychoanalytic therapists attempt to control relationship factors in particular ways, whilst behavioural therapists view technique as being of much greater or even of sole importance. However, a considerable body of opinion supports the view that relationship factors, and in particular the ability of the therapist to provide the core conditions, is perhaps the most fundamental element in achieving a positive therapeutic outcome, though used on their own they are probably insufficient. Mitchell *et al.* (1977) suggest that 'the recent evidence, although equivocal, does seem to suggest that empathy, warmth and genuineness are related in some way to client change but that their potency and generalizability are not as great as once thought'. They summarise the present position by saying that the relationship between these variables and outcome is much more complex than had been understood earlier and their work shows that greater account must be taken of therapist orientation, type of client and the type of therapy being used.

EGAN, G. (1975), *The Skilled Helper: A Model for Systematic Helping and Interpersonal Relating* (Brooks-Cole, Monterey, Calif.).

GURMAN, A. S. and RAZIN, A. M. (1977), *Effective Psychotherapy* (Pergamon, New York).

MITCHELL, K. M. *et al.* (1977), 'A reappraisal of accurate empathy, non-possessive warmth and genuineness' (in Gurman and Razin, op. cit.).

TROEMEL-PLOETZ, S. (1980), ' "I'd come to you for therapy": interpretation, redefinition and paradox in Rogerian therapy' (*Psychotherapy: Theory, Research and Practice*, vol. 17, pp. 246-57).

TRUAX, C. B. and MITCHELL, K. M. (1971), 'Research on certain therapist interpersonal skills in relation to process and outcome' (in Bergin, A. E. and Garfield, S. L. (eds), *Handbook of Psychotherapy and Behavior Change*, Wiley, New York).

Corollary

The inferred propositions which follow from Kelly's *fundamental postulate* in *personal construct theory*. Kelly described eleven corollaries which he suggests follow from the fundamental postulate and which elaborate it in greater detail. These are as follows:

(i) construction corollary: a person anticipates events by construing their replications;

(ii) individuality corollary: persons differ from each other in their construction of events;

(iii) organisation corollary: each person characteristically evolves, for his convenience in anticipating events, a construction system embracing ordinal

relationships between constructs;

(iv) dichotomy corollary: a person's construction system is composed of a finite number of dichotomous constructs;

(v) choice corollary: a person chooses for himself that alternative in a dichotomised construct through which he anticipates the greater possibility for extension and definition of his system;

(vi) range corollary: a construct is convenient for the anticipation of a finite range of events only;

(vii) experience corollary: a person's construction system varies as he successively construes the replication of events;

(viii) modulation corollary: the variation in a person's construction system is limited by the permeability of the constructs within whose *ranges of convenience* the variants lie;

(ix) fragmentation corollary: a person may successively employ a variety of construction *sub-systems* which are inferentially incompatible with each other;

(x) commonality corollary: to the extent that one person employs a construction of experience which is similar to that employed by another, his psychological processes are similar to those of the other person;

(xi) sociality corollary: to the extent that one person construes the construction processes of another he may play a role in a social process involving the other person.

KELLY, G. A. (1955), *The Construction of Personal Constructs* (W. W. Norton, New York).
KELLY, G. A. (1963), *A Theory of Personality* (W. W. Norton, New York).

Corrective emotional experience

A term coined by Alexander (Alexander and French 1946) to describe the way in which the therapist should manage the *transference* in order to provide the patient with a relationship that is markedly different and more beneficial than an early relationship with a significant other. The corrective emotional experience acts as a deconditioner to the early negative experience which has damaged the patient. By interaction with the therapist, the patient's *ego* develops in maturity and both the traumatic influence of early experiences and the patient's current difficulties become more manageable. The essence of the curative factor is the *reality testing* which accompanies it. The patient gradually becomes aware that his reactions to the therapist are not 'suited to the analyst's reactions, not only because he, the analyst, is objective, but also because he is what he is, a person in his own right' (Alexander and French 1946).

Alexander's work in this area indicates a development away from a more passive view of the therapist's role towards the acceptance of a more engaged relationship with the patient; and from a preoccupation with the origins of psychic disturbance towards a greater interest in the patient's current predicaments. Balint, who trained with Ferenczi (himself influential on Alexander's work), also believed that the patient needed his relationship with the analyst to help make good the *basic fault* which had occurred in infancy. Winnicott (1963), amongst others, however, points out that a corrective emotional experience is not enough, and no analyst 'should set out to provide a corrective experience in the transference because this is a contradiction in terms'. He agrees, however, that the analytic relationship may possess various emotionally corrective features such as attentiveness, objectivity, etc. Outside *psychoanalysis*, proponents of many forms of psychotherapy and counselling would view the therapist's relationship with the patient as therapeutic because of its potential for being emotionally corrective. Frank and Ascher (1951) have applied the concept to the group work setting.

ALEXANDER, F. and FRENCH, T. (1946), *Psychoanalytic Therapy: Principles and Applications* (Ronald Press, New York).
FRANK, J. and ASCHER, E. (1951), 'The corrective emotional experience in group therapy' (*Am. J. of Psychiatry*, vol. 108, pp. 126-31).
WINNICOTT, D. W. (1963), 'Dependence in infant-care, in child-care and in the psycho-analytic setting' (*Int. J. of Psychoanalysis*, vol. 44, pp. 339-44).

See also *Active technique.*

Co-therapy

The treatment of an individual, couple, family or group by two or more therapists. The practice, which was first introduced by Adler for the treatment of children at the Vienna Child Guidance Clinic, is sometimes called multiple therapy. It is mainly used as a technique in *family*, *marital* and *group psychotherapy* and the term co-therapy is usually reserved for two therapists working in the room together with the patient, family or group. The two therapists may be of different sexes, professional disciplines and levels of therapeutic experience. A co-therapy relationship allows for a division of labour between the therapists, with each *modelling* different roles and functions. For example, one therapist can be much more confronting if he knows that his partner will support and nurture the family or group member. Whitaker (1967) describes how he feels able to regress alongside the seriously disturbed *identified patient* or other vulnerable family members, knowing that his co-therapist will maintain the therapist's boundary keeping function for the total group. In group psychotherapy one therapist may take on the instrumental and the other the expressive role in the group, although in all these examples it is usually important for the co-therapists to be able to exchange roles and therapeutic tasks flexibly. As a pair, the co-therapists can model a functional relationship for the family or group. This is especially useful in marital therapy, when, to maximise the potential of the modelling, the co-therapists should be of different sexes. Some therapists have experimented with the use of married co-therapists in marital work (Skynner 1976).

Sonne and Lincoln (1965) describe a subtle use of co-therapy, using the therapist's relationship to mirror and internalise the dysfunctional aspects of the couple or family group and then to work them through and ultimately to resolve them through 'a period of symbolic gestation in the [therapeutic] "marriage" '. Rice, Fey and Kepecs (1972) have shown that an equality of experience between co-therapists produces a better *outcome* for the family. Dowling (1979) describes the way in which co-therapists, paired with different partners, compensate for differing levels of input of essential therapeutic functions. The importance for the co-therapists to have time to discuss their relationship, deal with competitiveness and misunderstandings and clarify *transference* and *counter transference* phenomena coming from the patient or family group cannot be over-estimated. Russell and Russell (1979) suggest that co-therapy is misapplied when it is used to lessen the insecurity of individual therapists; when it leads to gross competitiveness and the resulting bizarre behaviour of one or both therapists or when the patients are unclear as to its purpose. Bowers and Gauron (1981) point out some of the hazards that may be involved for patients, spouses, significant others and therapists themselves.

BOWERS, W. A. and GAURON, E. F. (1981), 'Potential hazards of the co-therapy relationship' (*Psychotherapy: Theory, Research and Practice*, vol. 18, pp. 225-8).
DOWLING, E. (1979), 'Co-therapy: a clinical researcher's view' (in Walrond-Skinner, S. (ed.), *Family and Marital Psychotherapy*, Routledge & Kegan Paul, London).
HOLT, M. and GREINER, D. (1976), 'Co-therapy in the treatment of families' (in Guerin, P. (ed.), *Family Therapy: Theory and Practice*, Gardner Press, New York).
MACLENNAN, B. W. (1965), 'Co-therapy' (*Int. J. of Group Psychotherapy*, vol. 15, pp. 154-65).
RICE, D. G., FEY, W. F. and KEPECS, J. C. (1972), 'Therapist experience and "style" as factors in co-therapy' (*Family Process*, vol. 11,

pp. 1-12).
RUBENSTEIN, D. and WEINER, O. R. (1967), 'Co-therapy teamwork relationships in family therapy' (in Zuk, G. H. and Borszormenyi-nagy, I., *Family Therapy and Disturbed Families*, Science and Behavior Books, Palo Alto, Calif.).
RUSSELL, A. and RUSSELL, L. (1979), 'The uses and abuses of co-therapy' (*J. of Marital and Family Therapy*, vol. 5, pp. 39-46).
SKYNNER, A. C. R. (1976), *One Flesh: Separate Persons* (Constable, London).
SONNE, J. and LINCOLN, G. (1965), 'Heterosexual co-therapy relationships and their significance in family therapy' (in *Psychotherapy for the Whole Family*, Springer, New York).
TREPPA, J. A. (1971), 'Multiple therapy: its growth and importance' (*Am. J. of Psychotherapy*, vol. 25, pp. 447-57).
WHITAKER, C. (1967), 'The growing edge' (in Haley, J. and Hoffman, L. (eds), *Family Therapy Techniques*, Basic Books, New York).
YALOM, I. D. (1970), *The Theory and Practice of Group Psychotherapy* (Basic Books, New York).

See also *Collaborative marital therapy, Greek chorus, Live supervision, Multiple impact therapy, Team.*

Counter conditioning

Techniques derived from the learning principles of *classical conditioning*, whereby responses that are incompatible with the undesirable behaviour are repeatedly paired with the stimuli which evoke that behaviour. Wolpe (1958) is primarily responsible for the introduction of a variety of methods which make use of counter conditioning techniques, including *systematic desensitisation* and *aversion therapy. Flooding* and *implosion* are other counter conditioning techniques. In these, anxiety is inhibited as a protective reaction to its own strong and sustained evocation. One of the earliest recorded uses of counter conditioning was Jones's (1924) treatment of a young child, Peter, who had a strong fear of rabbits. The rabbit was repeatedly paired with food so that the pleasure of eating overcame

Peter's fear of the rabbit, by the process of reciprocal inhibition. *Modelling* has also been described as a counter conditioning technique. Phobias and social skills deficits such as unassertiveness are particularly responsive. Counter conditioning techniques are based on the principle that anxiety, not conflict, generates symptoms.

JONES, M. C. (1924), 'The elimination of children's fears' (*J. of Experimental Psychology*, vol. 7, pp. 382-90).
WOLPE, J. (1958), *Psychotherapy by Reciprocal Inhibition* (Stanford University Press, Stanford, Calif.).

See also *Assertiveness training*.

Counter paradox
See *Therapeutic double bind*.

Counter phobic
A preventative action taken or attitude adopted as protection from a feared situation. An individual may adopt an angry posture for example, if he or she fears that the other person is about to be angry himself. The purpose of a counter phobic response is to distract the other person from acting in the way which is dreaded. The result, however, may be to provoke hostility where none originally existed. It is a form of manic defence whereby fear is mastered by acting omnipotently.

Counter transference
Two broad understandings of this term appear in the psychoanalytic literature. The first is given by Freud (1910) who used it to describe the unconscious response of the analyst to the patient's *transference*. Freud made it clear that he believed counter transference to have an adverse effect on the treatment and that the therapist should strive to recognise and overcome it. Reich (1951) elaborated this classical view, stating that it 'comprises the effects of the analyst's own unconscious needs and conflicts on his understanding or technique'. This description views counter transference as the therapist's own transference projected on to the patient and which, like the patient's, may

get expressed through sexual or aggressive feelings. Reich (1951) distinguishes between acute and chronic counter transference, the former occurring under special circumstances and with specific patients, the latter representing some habitual need of the therapist and occurring with all patients.

The second view holds that counter transference is not pathological, but is an inevitable process and like transference is an integral and vital part of the therapy. Counter transference is seen as including the whole of the therapist's feelings and his *conscious* and *unconscious* reactions to the patient (Heimann 1950, 1960). Heimann and others support the value of the therapist's use of his feelings and reactions as a tool in helping him to understand the patient. This second, broader view is the one more commonly adopted amongst psychoanalytic therapists and the one used, often more loosely, by adherents of other approaches, to describe the therapist's feelings and attitudes to the patient. The broader view is, however, open to criticism by the 'classicists' because it is overinclusive and makes exact definition difficult; and it appears to undervalue the therapist's *neutrality*. All writers, however, stress the importance of having counter transference reactions under conscious control and the therapist's need to develop emotional maturity and to find satisfaction for his own needs outside the therapy situation. For a discussion of the two different views, see Kernberg (1965). Kernberg also suggests guidelines to safeguard the therapist from the potential dangers of the counter transference. Sandler *et al.* (1970) reviewed the literature on counter transference and advocate the 'broad' definition of the term. Baum (1969-70) outlines the areas of consensus and differences between the two views. He also discusses the way in which counter transference responses can help or hinder the therapist's *empathy* with the patient. Segal (1977), offering a Kleinian view, suggests that the therapist's capacity to contain rather than discharge the feelings aroused in him helps the patient deal with the reactions evidenced by his own feelings.

Some quantitative research has been attempted on counter transference phenomena, despite the obvious difficulties. Bandura (1956) found that therapists who were able to express their own anger directly and had low needs for approval were more able to allow patients to express hostility. All therapists in this study found it easier to allow and encourage patients' expressions of hostility when they were directed towards someone else other than the therapist. Cutler (1958), in a similar study, showed that material which the therapist found threatening affected the accuracy of his perceptions. Moreover, the therapist's interventions were judged to be less effective when the material related to his own conflicts. Fiedler (1951) showed that therapists judged as competent by other therapists show fewer signs of counter transference and Strupp (1958) drew the same conclusion from his study of experienced therapists. One of the conclusions drawn from their review of the research by Singer and Luborsky (1977) is that the patient influences the therapist to a much more marked degree than the clinical literature would suggest. The notion of counter transference, feelings or attitudes causing a block in the psychoanalyst's ability to understand and help his patient led to Freud advocating a *training analysis* for psychoanalysts in training. This view is completely accepted by all major schools of dynamic psychotherapy.

BANDURA, A. (1956), 'Psychotherapists' anxiety level, self insight and psychotherapeutic competence' (*J. of Abnormal and Social Psychology*, vol. 52, pp. 333-7).

BAUM, O. E. (1969-70), 'Counter transference' (*Psychoanalytic Review*, vol. 56, pp. 621-37).

CUTLER, R. L. (1958), 'Counter transference effects in psychotherapy' (*J. of Consulting Psychology*, vol. 22, pp. 349-56).

FIEDLER, F. E. (1951), 'A method of objective quantification of certain counter transference attitudes' (*J. of Clinical Psychology*, vol. 7, pp. 101-7).

FREUD, S. (1910), 'The future prospects of psychoanalytic therapy' (*Standard Edition*, vol. 11, Hogarth Press, London).

HEIMANN, P. (1950), 'On counter transference' (*Int. J. of Psychoanalysis*, vol. 31, pp. 81-4).

HEIMANN, P. (1960), 'Counter transference' (*Brit. J. of Medical Psychology*, vol. 33, p. 9-15).

KERNBERG, O. (1965), 'Notes on counter transference' (*J. of the American Psychoanalytic Assoc.*, vol. 13, pp. 38-56).

REICH, A. (1951), 'On counter transference' (*Int. J. of Psychoanalysis*, vol. 32, pp. 25-31).

SANDLER, J. *et al.* (1970), 'Basic psychoanalytic concepts: counter transference' (*Brit. J. of Psychiatry*, vol. 117, pp. 83-8).

SEGAL, H. (1977), 'Counter transference' (*Int. J. of Psychoan. Psychotherapy*, vol. 6, pp. 31-7).

SINGER, B. A. and LUBORSKY, L. (1977), 'Counter transference: the status of clinical versus quantitative research' (in Gurman, A. S. and Razin, A. M., *Effective Psychotherapy*, Pergamon, New York).

STRUPP, H. H. (1958), 'The psychotherapist's contribution to the treatment process' (*Behavioral Science* vol. 3, pp. 34-67).

Coverant control

A procedure introduced by Homme (1965) in which undesirable thought sequences are interrupted by the *reinforcement* of alternative appropriate cognitions. The word 'coverant' is an ellipsis of part of the words 'covert' and 'operant'. An individual is asked to use first a negative coverant (for example, 'excess fat predisposes one to a coronary') followed by a positive coverant (for example, 'if I lose weight I can wear my new dress') and then reward the use of both by a pleasant activity. A very meagre success rate has been reported for this procedure.

HOMME, L. E. (1965), 'Perspectives in psychology: XXIV Control of coverants, the operants of the mind' (*Psychological Record*, vol. 15, pp. 501-11).

Covert modelling

Cognitive rehearsal strategies designed to

develop *coping behaviour*. Unlike *behavioural rehearsal*, covert modelling (or covert conditioning, as it is also called) is a form of *mental* rehearsal of the real-life situation that is causing the problem and is useful when actual practice is for some reason impractical. However, covert modelling may be followed by behavioural rehearsal as a step-by-step progression towards tackling the real-life situation. Thase and Mose (1976) have compared the relative effectiveness of covert modelling and behavioural rehearsal. Preliminary research by Kazdin (1977) and others has supported the efficacy of covert modelling in the treatment of phobias and unassertiveness.

CAUTELA, J. R. (1971), 'Covert conditioning' (in Jacobs, A. and Sacks, L. B. (eds), *The Psychology of Private Events: Perspectives on Covert Response Systems*, Academic Press, New York).

CAUTELA, J. R. *et al.* (1974), 'Covert modeling: an experimental test' (*Behavior Therapy*, vol. 5, pp. 494-502).

KAZDIN, A. E. (1977), 'Research issues in covert conditioning' (*Cognitive Therapy and Research*, vol. 1, pp. 45-58).

THASE, M. E. and MOSE, M. K. (1976), 'The relative efficacy of covert modeling procedures and guided participant modeling on the reduction of avoidance behavior' (*J. of Behavior Therapy and Experimental Psychiatry*, vol. 7, pp. 7-12).

See also *Assertiveness training, Covert sensitisation, Modelling*.

Covert sensitisation

The imaginary association of an undesired behaviour with unpleasant consequences as a means of suppressing the behaviour. The technique has been used with obesity, alcoholism, smoking, nail biting and sexual disorders. For example, an obese person might be asked to imagine a detailed chain of events from the moment a meal has been eaten to the moment vomiting occurs. As yet, very meagre positive results have been reported for this technique, even though several variations have been tried.

It does not seem to affect the outcome, for example, whether the aversive event precedes or follows the undesirable behaviour in the imagined scene.

CAUTELA, J. R. (1967), 'Covert sensitisation' (*Psychological Reports*, vol. 20, pp. 459-68).

Creativity cycle

A concept developed by Kelly to describe the creativity process. He postulated that the individual begins the process by loosening his system of *constructs* and ends it with a tightening and validation of his construct system.

KELLY, G. A. (1955), *The Psychology of Personal Constructs* (W. W. Norton, New York).

See also *Personal construct theory*.

Credibility

The perceived ability of the therapist to possess the skill and knowledge required by the patient together with a preparedness to use these on the patient's behalf. Griffin (1967) and Johnson (1973) have identified several constituents of therapists' credibility: objective indicators of *expertness* such as professional qualifications and *experience*; perceived reliability; perceived trustworthiness; the person's expression of warmth and friendliness; his dynamism as measured by his confidence and activity as a communicator; and his reputation amongst others whose opinion is trusted. Other researchers have sought to determine how far these factors are relevant to the therapist-patient relationship. In analogue studies using college students, Bergin (1962) and other researchers have shown that the attitudes of students to the interviewer can be altered by the credibility factor, but only when the differences in perceived credibility are extreme. Johnson and Matross (1977) conclude that these findings suggest that the ability to exert *social influence* and therefore to conduct effective therapy depends more upon the relationship between interviewer and subject than on the personal qualities of the interviewer or therapist.

BERGIN, A. E. (1962), 'The effects of dissonant persuasive communications upon changes in a self-referring attitude' (*J. of Personality*, vol. 30, pp. 423-38).

GRIFFIN, K. (1967), 'The contribution of studies of source credibility to a theory of interpersonal trust in the communication process' (*Psychological Bulletin*, vol. 68, pp. 104-21).

JOHNSON, D. W. (1973), *Contemporary Social Psychology* (Lippincott, Philadelphia).

JOHNSON, D. W. and MATROSS, R. (1977), 'Interpersonal influence in psychotherapy: a social psychological view' (in Gurman, A. S. and Razin, A. M., *Effective Psychotherapy*, Pergamon Press, New York).

PARLOFF, M. B. *et al.* (1978), 'Research on therapist variables in relation to process and outcome' (in Garfield, S. L. and Bergin, A. E., *Handbook of Psychotherapy and Behavior Change*, Wiley, New York).

Crisis

Literal Greek meaning 'turning point' or 'time of decision'. A limited period of acute psychological and emotional disorganisation, precipitated by a challenging or hazardous event occurring in the environment. Caplan (1961) defines a crisis as occurring when 'a person faces an obstacle to important life goals that is, for the time, insurmountable through the utilisation of his customary methods of problem solving'. Crisis has also been defined as an upset in a steady state of being – a movement from *equilibrium* to disequilibrium.

CAPLAN, G. (1961), *An Approach to Community Mental Health* (Grune & Stratton, New York).

Crisis induction

The deliberate stimulation by the therapist of emotional *crisis* in an individual or family, for the purpose of disrupting an entrenched pathological *equilibrium*. The process of therapy itself may be experienced by the client as a crisis, enabling him to respond to the particular interventions of the therapist with a low level of *resistance*. Minuchin and Barcai (1969) discuss the use of therapeutically induced crisis in *family therapy*. Turner and

Gross (1976) describe the way in which the therapist must serve both to activate the crisis and to promote its resolution. Sifneos (1972) describes a similar process using the acceleration of anxiety in the client in individual psychotherapy. Some behaviour modification techniques also act in this way: for example, *flooding* and *implosion* serve to heighten the individual's anxiety regarding his problem prior to developing his coping skills. Some types of group therapy explicitly seek to induce stress in members to the point where they become open to suggestion by the leader or other group members.

MINUCHIN, S. and BARCAI, A. (1969), 'Therapeutically induced family crisis (in Masserman, J. (ed.), *Science and Psychoanalysis*, Grune & Stratton, New York).

SIFNEOS, P. E. (1972), *Short-term Psychotherapy and Emotional Crisis* (Harvard University Press, Cambridge, Mass.).

TURNER, M. B. and GROSS, S. J. (1976) 'An approach to family therapy – an effective rule altering model' (*J. of Family Counseling*, pp. 50-6).

Crisis intervention

Psycho-social procedures offered to individuals, families or groups experiencing a state of *crisis*. Jacobson *et al.* (1968) describe four types of crisis intervention. The first involves the provision of social and material assistance of various kinds, appropriate to the particular nature of the crisis. This service provision may be carried out by neighbours or paraprofessionals and/or be mobilised by a professional worker as additional to his psychotherapeutic intervention with the client. The second type of intervention consists of 'emotional first aid' whereby the worker's intervention is limited to *supportive psychotherapy*, containment and care, especially during the early days of a crisis. Such an approach is particularly suitable for highly psychologically disturbed individuals. The third type consists of the generic approach, associated with the originators of *crisis theory*. Using large-scale studies of groups in crisis, they showed how an individual's abnormal behaviour in a crisis related to his experience of the crisis itself and not to the existence of a pre-morbid personality. Advocates of this approach argue that particular crises such as *bereavement* have a similar meaning and effect upon individuals regardless of their personalities; that they will pass through certain normal stages and that therefore they can be approached in similar ways. Fourth, there is the individual approach developed by Ewing (1978) and others, whereby the worker uses the crisis situation to help the client understand the antecedents of his present perceptions of 'crisis' in his past personality dynamics. Assessment of the client's unique intrapsychic reality is undertaken and the treatment focuses on why and how the pre-crisis equilibrium was disturbed and on how a new integration of the personality may be achieved.

The minimum objective of all approaches to crisis intervention is 'the psychological resolution of the immediate crisis and restoration to at least the level of functioning that existed prior to the crisis' (Aquilea and Messick 1974). Because the client may be in a state of shock, be exhausted or extremely distressed, the therapist is typically more active and directive when using crisis intervention compared with other forms of treatment. During the stage of acute crisis, psychotropic drugs may be required and also expert advice and guidance. Intensive care may be needed for a short period and the client's responsibilities may have to be taken over. After the initial period of acute crisis has passed, therapeutic work should include the promotion of *catharsis* and the ventilation of feelings; facilitation of communication; identification of the problem and its various aspects; bolstering of the client's self-esteem and the facilitation of problem-solving behaviour. Crisis intervention embraces a variety of methods and arose in the USA out of a need to develop immediate, inexpensive, relevant and often non-medical sources of help. Social work theorists have been particularly attracted to it as it provides a useful body of theory appropriate for the non-medical mental health professional (Golan 1978). Langsley (1981) comments that there is pitifully little research on crisis intervention even now and that attention needs to be given to examining when crisis intervention is an appropriate method as compared with other forms of short-term treatment.

AQUILEA, D. C. and MESSICK, J. M. (1974), *Crisis Intervention: Theory and Methodology* (C. V. Mosby, St Louis).
EVERSTINE, D. S. and EVERSTINE, L. (1983), *People in Crisis* (Brunner/Mazel, New York).
EWING, C. P. (1978), *Crisis Intervention as Psychotherapy* (Oxford University Press, Oxford).
GOLAN, N. (1978), *Treatment in Crisis Situations* (Free Press, New York).
JACOBSEN, G. F. *et al.* (1968), 'Generic and individual approaches to crisis intervention' (*Am. J. of Public Health*, vol. 58, pp. 338-43).
LANGSLEY, D. G. (1981), 'Crisis Intervention: an update' (in Masserman, J. H., *Current Psychiatric Therapies*, vol. 20, Grune & Stratton, New York).

See also *Bereavement counselling, Brief therapy, Family crisis intervention.*

Crisis theory

A framework for describing and understanding the effect of a *crisis* upon an individual, family or group. There are five components of a crisis situation: the hazardous event; the vulnerable state; the precipitating factor; the state of active crisis; and the stage of reintegration or crisis resolution. The hazardous event may involve a sudden or unexpected event or series of events which induce stress in the individual. These stressful events produce three broad types of crisis. First, accidental crises: these include unanticipated events which happen to the individual, such as physical illness, death of a significant other, an unwanted pregnancy, rape, premature birth, burglary, loss of home; or major disasters such as earthquake, flood, nuclear attack, train disasters, etc. In the latter case, whole groups or communities may become disequilibrated and dysfunctional and while this may produce additional threat to the individuals involved, it may also offer a supportive experience of 'shared fate'. Second, developmental or maturational crises: internally generated crises brought about by normal progress through the life cycle. They affect both the individual and the family as a whole and include the move from each stage in the life cycle to the next. Erikson (1968) is particularly associated with developing this idea of maturational crisis. Third, role transitional crises, including such events as divorce, retirement, a move to a new neighbourhood or country, promotion at work, or redundancy, all involving a change in role and usually involving a status passage.

The hazardous event creates a vulnerable state of distress during which the individual tries to use his customary coping mechanisms and fails, thereby increasing his distress. This state of rising tension peaks when some precipitating factor (maybe insignificant in its own right) finally pushes the individual into a state of acute crisis. This state produces a series of predictable reactions including physiological disturbances to body functions (insomnia, diarrhoea, vomiting, sweating, weeping, faintness, etc.), and psychological disturbance (aimless activity, immobilisation, preoccupation with events leading up to the crisis, depression, agitation). The crisis is perceived as either a threat, a loss or a challenge, and depending on how it is perceived, it may be greeted with anxiety, depression or fear respectively. Resolution occurs either naturally, with the informal help of others, or by *crisis intervention* undertaken by a professional worker. The individual's ability to resolve a crisis without recourse to professional help depends on his psychological capacity to adjust to stress; the availability of informal outside resources in the form of key significant others, and the degree of intensity of the crisis. A crisis is neither an illness nor a pathological condition, although the behaviour of individuals in crisis may resemble pathological states.

The state of active crisis is time-limited, often lasting from a few hours to about six weeks (though this limit, often quoted in the early literature on crisis theory, has now been challenged). A crisis can occur in an individual, a family, a group or community, and although the process will be differently manifested depending on which of these is affected, there will be common features visible in each situation. Crisis as an opportunity for growth and psychological development has always been stressed in crisis theory and the greater preparedness of an individual to accept outside help when in crisis makes it possible for a help giver to intervene more rapidly and effectively.

As the period of active crisis subsides, some form of resolution takes place. If the resolution is to be adaptive, three phases need to occur: correct cognitive perception of the problem and the processes that have taken place; acceptance of and release of feelings associated with the event; the development of new coping behaviours adapted to the new situation. If these phases of resolution do not occur, maladaptive responses may take place instead, including the *projection* or *introjection* of anger; *denial* of what has occurred; increasing hostility towards others and life in general, which in turn produces a hostile response from the individual's environment, creating a further lowering in his or her self-esteem.

Holmes and Rahne (1967) developed a scale for evaluating the stress potential of a number of common life events. The scale helps to show how apparently minor events taken together can be sufficient to precipitate a crisis. Lindermann (1944) is rightly seen as the pioneer of crisis theory. His classic study of work with the bereaved families of the Coconut Grove Nightclub disaster in 1943 set the stage for the development of crisis theory and the generic form of *crisis intervention*. With his colleague, Caplan, the theory was refined and Caplan (1961) produced a detailed description of its application within a community health programme. Rapoport (1962) and Parad (1965) developed the theory particularly in relation to social work. Rapoport (1970) links the development of crisis intervention during the 1950s to four factors: the need to serve more people; the gap between needs and resources; research which questioned the effectiveness of traditional methods; the development of new methods of intervention. She also points out that in the early stages, crisis intervention developed hand in hand with *brief therapy* and in response to the same pressures. More recently, however, crisis intervention has developed an identity which is separate from the brief therapy models and more obviously adapted to situations for which it is especially appropriate: for example, emergency hospitalisation, suicide prevention and major disasters. Mobile crisis units and psychiatric teams able to respond immediately to family crises are extensions of the application of the theory (for example Scott 1973).

CAPLAN, G. (1961), *An Approach to Community Mental Health* (Tavistock, London).

CAPLAN, G. (1964), *Principles of Preventive Psychiatry* (Tavistock, London).

ERIKSON, E. (1968), *Identity: Youth and Crisis* (W. W. Norton, New York).

HOLMES, T. H. and RAHNE, R. H. (1967), 'The social re-adjustment rating scale' (*J. of Psychosomatic Research*, vol. 11, pp. 213-18).

LINDERMANN, E. (1944), 'Symptomatology and management of acute grief' (*Am. J. of Psychiatry*, vol. 101, pp. 141-8).

PARAD, H. J. (ed.) (1965), *Crisis Intervention: Selected Readings* (Family Service Asssociation of America, New York).

RAPOPORT, L. (1962), 'The state of crisis: some theoretical considerations' (*Social Service Review*, no. 6, pp. 211-17).

RAPOPORT, L. (1970), 'Crisis intervention as a form of brief treatment' (in Roberts, R. W. and Nee, R. H. (eds), *Theories of Social Casework*, University of Chicago Press, Chicago).

SCOTT, R. D. (1973), 'The treatment barrier' (*Brit. J. of Medical Psychology*, vol. 46, pp. 45-67).

Cross confrontation
A technique introduced by Paul (1976), and Paul and Paul (1975) whereby emotionally charged material, derived from one patient or couple, is used as a stimulus stressor for another patient or couple. Originally (Paul 1966), the material came from earlier sessions with the same family. The stimulus material is usually in the form of audio or video tapes but can also include poems, letters and pieces of literature. The purpose is to encourage patients to empathise with the material so that they can then empathise with themselves. It also helps normalise a range of emotions and behaviours so that they can be more easily accepted and therefore discussed. The technique can be used with individuals, couples and families.

PAUL, N. L. (1966), 'Effects of playback on the family members of their own previously recorded conjoint material' (*Psychiatric Res. Rep.*, American Psychiatric Association, vol. 20, pp. 175-85).

PAUL, N. L. and PAUL, B. B. (1975), *A Marital Puzzle* (W. W. Norton, New York).

PAUL, N. L. (1976), 'Cross confrontation' (in Guerin, P., *Family Therapy: Theory and Practice*, Gardner Press, New York).

See also *Audio visual equipment.*

Customer
The person who is actively seeking professional help, either for himself or for another. The term is used in *strategic therapy* and in *focused problem resolution*. The customer is not necessarily the person who is experiencing the *presenting problem* or *symptom*. It implies a relationship with the helper based on a *contract*. The customer is the person in the psycho-social situation who is motivated to work with the therapist.

FISCH, R. *et al.* (1982), *Tactics of Change: Doing Therapy Briefly* (Jossey-Bass, San Francisco).

D

Daily record of dysfunctional thoughts
A *homework assignment* used in *cognitive behaviour therapy*, whereby the patient records his cognitions and responses each day in such

a way that he can evaluate the changes that are occurring. Standard record sheets are of various sizes but the fullest sheet is divided into five columns, headed situation; emotion; automatic thought; rational response; and outcome. The therapist teaches the patient to rate the degree of his emotional experiences; the degree to which he believes the automatic thought, and to record both as a percentage in the column marked 'outcome'. The therapist's goal is to increase the patient's objectivity about his cognition; to differentiate between realistic and distorted interpretations of events; and to gain an understanding of the link between unpleasant affect, negative automatic thoughts and unproductive behaviour.

BECK, A. T. *et al.* (1979), *Cognitive Therapy of Depression* (Wiley, New York).

See also *Self-monitoring*.

Dance therapy

Dance therapy is defined by the American Dance Therapy Association as the psychotherapeutic use of movement to further the emotional and physical integration of the individual. Movement is the medium used by the therapist for diagnosing the patient's difficulties, producing a therapeutic experience and bringing about change. Its modern development has stemmed from several different influences but particularly from the work of Marion Chace. She used dance to work with highly disturbed, nonverbal, psychotic patients, enabling them to express some of their conflict through movement and using dance to form a relationship with them.

Bernstein (1979) has identified eight different theoretical approaches to dance therapy. The most widely practised are Chace dance therapy, using Marion Chace's techniques of empathising, mirroring and interacting with the patient in terms of his energy level and range of emotion; Jungian dance therapy, developed by Mary Whitehouse, again in the United States, where the therapist interprets the patient's move-

ment in Jungian terms; developmental dance, in which the therapist assesses the developmental level of the patient through his movement and relates to him at this level in turn through carefully designed reciprocal movement; and Gestalt movement therapy, in which the therapist extends the patient's focus on the *figure* of his body movements into a connected expression of his conflicts. The American Dance Therapy Association publishes the *American Journal of Dance Therapy*.

BERNSTEIN, P. L. (ed.) (1979), *Eight Theoretical Approaches in Dance/Movement Therapy* (Kendall/Hunt, Dubuque, Iowa).
CHAIKLIN, H. (ed.) (1975), *Marion Chace: Her Papers* (American Dance Therapy Association, Columbia, New York).

Dasein

Literal German meaning 'being there'. The term, used originally by Heidegger, is used in *existential* approaches to psychotherapy to describe the different aspects of an individual's experience of 'being-in-the-world'. This includes his awareness of self, others and his environment and the choices which he makes in deciding how to act upon his environment. The concept stresses unity of the individual as viewed existentially, without a split between subject and object, and the inescapability of a person's *context* in defining and understanding his individuality. To help define the person as Dasein, Binswanger used the terms *Umwelt*, *Mitwelt* and *Eigenwelt*, all of which are inhabited simultaneously by the individual. In the healthy individual these three worlds are in harmony; in psychological disturbances they are in conflict. Although Dasein involves choice and freedom it also entails being determined by the limitations of history and culture. The individual struggles between freedom and limitation. Binswanger (1949) suggests that psychological disturbance consists of 'a process in which the Dasein is abandoning itself in its actual, free potentiality of being-itself and giving itself over to a specific world-design'. Boss (1971) also uses the term Dasein, translating it as 'being-the-there'. He describes the Da as 'that open realm of perception and responsiveness to the presence of beings' and sees the goal of Dasein as becoming progressively more open, responsible and authentic, especially within social relationships. His existential approach to psychotherapy is known as *Daseinanalysis*.

BINSWANGER, L. (1949), 'The case of Lola Voss' (in *Being-in-the-World*, Harper & Row, New York).

BOSS, M. (1971), *Existential Foundations of Medicine and Psychology* (Jason Aronson, New York).

Daseinanalysis

A form of *existential psychotherapy* which makes use of classical psychoanalytic technique, and is associated particularly with the work of Medard Boss (1957). When functioning healthily, Boss views *Dasein* as being open to the world, authentic, autonomous and able to share and pariticipate with others through being fully aware of and responsible for self and the self's existence. Boss acknowledges the role of both the past and the future in influencing the individual's current behaviour. He views Daseinanalysis as the process of bringing about knowledge for the patient in which phenomena disclose themselves to Dasein. Since psychological disturbance stems from disturbed interpersonal relationships and the consequent sense of alienation and loneliness which occurs, therapy involves helping the individual to engage in the existential task of commitment to a responsive relationship. The relationship with the therapist is an important means of achieving this goal. Like *humanistic* therapists and other existential therapists, Boss looks upon the therapeutic relationship as requiring the full participation of both parties in a real relationship rather than only within the *transference*; and he replaces the concept of *counter transference* with that of 'psychotherapeutic eros'. As in *client-centred therapy*, Boss (1971) stresses the curative power of 'enduring, unshakable, benevolent and tactful devotion that a patient

regularly receives from an analyst' and feels that this, rather than *interpretations* or other techniques, produces the beneficial effects of *psychoanalysis* and similar therapies. Like Jung, Boss incorporates a spiritual dimension to his work and he opposes *reductionism* and everything that fragments the indivisibility of the individual's existence.

BOSS, M. (1957), *Psychoanalysis and Dasein-analysis* (Basic Books, New York).

BOSS, M. (1971), *Existential Foundations of Medicine and Psychology* (Jason Aronson, New York).

Death anxiety

The fear of death and/or the process of dying. The basis of the anxiety is reported by Kastenbaum and Aisenberg (1972) as 'the fear of extinction, annihilation, obliteration, or ceasing to be'. This involves both the fear of extinction, and the prospect of the loss of things that are enjoyed in this life. It is thus closely akin to *separation anxiety*. In psychoanalytic theory, death anxiety is distinguished from the *death instinct*. Originally, psychoanalytic theory excluded the possibility of a basic fear of death and Freud argued that one cannot fear what one cannot conceive of and it was impossible to conceive of anything as negative as being nothing. Although the literature about death often uses the terms 'fear of death' and 'death anxiety' interchangeably, the two ideas need to be distinguished: death anxiety may be present when no objective reason for it may be apparent. Death anxiety in professionals has been studied by Kastenbaum (1967) who reports five categories of responses to the dying, the first four of which stem from the professional's own death anxiety: false reassurance, denial, changing the subject, fatalism, and discussion. Feifel (1959) has explored the way in which physicians' own death anxiety may incapacitate them from relating to the dying patient. Glaser and Strauss (1965) invoke the term 'awareness context' to discuss the degree to which knowledge of the death can be tolerated amongst relatives, patient and professionals. They describe four typical awareness contexts: closed, suspected, mutual pretence, and open. In contrast to Freud, Melanie Klein asserted that death anxiety is at the root of all anxiety. Her contributions to this topic have been discussed by Money-Kyrle (1955).

FEIFEL, H. (1959), 'Attitudes toward death in some normal and mentally ill populations' (in Feifel, H. (ed.), *The Meaning of Death*, McGraw-Hill, New York).
GLASER, B. G. and STRAUSS, A. L. (1965), *Awareness of Dying* (Aldine, Chicago).
KASTENBAUM, R. (1967), 'Multiple perspectives on a geriatric "death valley" ' (*Community Mental Health Journal*, vol. 3, pp. 21-9).
KASTENBAUM, R. and AISENBERG, R. (1972), *The Psychology of Death* (Springer, New York).
MONEY-KYRLE, R. E. (1955), 'An inconclusive contribution to the theory of the death instinct' (in Klein, M. *et al.*, *New Directions in Psychoanalysis*, Maresfield Reprints, Karnac, London).

See also *Annihilation*.

Death instinct

The destructive impulses (sometimes referred to as thanatos) that are opposed to the life instincts and the life energy of *libido*. Freud (1920) introduced the term but although it has remained a part of psychoanalytic theory it is usually regarded as a more speculative and controversial part compared with most other aspects of the theory. Freud introduced the concept to explain the existence of certain phenomena in psychoanalytic treatment, including a peculiar reluctance to accept correct interpretations (see *negative therapeutic reaction*), as well as hate, destructiveness and other aggressive impulses directed both towards the self and to others, which were incompatible with his theory of sexuality as the root of instinctual life. It is in keeping with his tendency to seek for dualistic explanations of psychic phenomena. Melanie Klein is one of the few psychoanalysts to have developed and augmented the concept and the *Kleinian school* of psychoanalysis suggests that there is strong clinical evidence in the analyses of small children for the existence of a death instinct. The concept has not been developed in other varieties of psychotherapy to any degree and it attracts particular criticism from the opponents of psychoanalytic theory.

FREUD, S. (1920), 'Beyond the pleasure principle' (*Standard Edition*, vol. 18, Hogarth Press, London).
KLEIN, M. (1932), *The Psychoanalysis of Children* (Hogarth Press, London).
MONEY-KYRLE, R. E. (1955), 'An inconclusive contribution to the theory of the death instinct' (in Klein, M. *et al.*, *New Directions In Psychoanalysis*, Maresfield Reprints, Karnac, London).
MYKEL, S. J. (1980), 'Psychoanalytical theory and the role of the death instinct' (*Issues in Ego Psychology*, vol. 3, pp. 13-23).
ROSENFELD, H. A. (1971), 'A clinical approach to the psychoanalytic theory of the life and death instincts' (*International Journal of Psychoanalysis*, vol. 52, pp. 169-78).

Decompensation

The return to a symptomatic state or state of *compensation*. Decompensation occurs as a setback in the individual's effort to move towards being symptom-free and *functional*. Thus, it occurs during treatment, as a temporary *regression*.

Defence mechanisms

The means by which the *ego* protects itself from the instinctual demands of the *id* and from the threat perceived in the external world. Although explicit as a self-protective activity in his early writings, it was not until 1926 that Freud argued the case for a hypothetical construct to describe the ego's protective functions. Psychoanalytic writers vary in their lists of defence mechanisms. Anna Freud (1937), who devoted a major treatise to this topic, lists ten. The following are generally considered to be defence mechanisms by most writers: *introjection, projection, regression, reaction formation, sublimation, denial, idealisation, intellectualisa-*

tion, fixation, rationalisation, displacement, splitting and *projective identification.*

Because of its importance in other areas of psychoanalytic theory, *repression* was considered by Freud and early psychoanalytic theorists to be in a category on its own, although it obviously has a vital defensive function. Freud (1926), commenting on this point, said that the term defence mechanism should be used 'provided we employ it explicitly as a general designation for all the techniques which the ego makes use of in conflicts which may lead to a neurosis, while we retain the word "repression" for the special method of defence which the line of approach taken by our investigations made us better acquainted with'.

Defence mechanisms are employed as a normal part of the functioning of the *psyche*. As part of their protective function, defence mechanisms play their part in the production of *symptoms*. Certain defence mechanisms (for example, denial, projection, splitting) can, if intense enough, cause loss of contact with the external world. Massive denial or repression blocks off much of the potential richness of the id and personality development is then impaired. There is always a price to pay for these defensive manoeuvres even though they are necessary for the ego's survival.

A goal of most forms of psychotherapy is the modification of the ego's defences without allowing the anxiety thus aroused to become intolerable. Expansion of the individual's problem-solving skills and his ability to accept, understand and integrate the phantasy life of his *internal world* reduces the need for the ego to use its defences.

Klein distinguishes primitive (or psychotic) mechanisms as a sub-group of defence mechanisms which are employed against the very early infantile anxieties derived from conflicts between love and hate. They appear to underlie the 'neurotic' defences which are employed against the later conflicts between *libido* and the *superego*. These primitive defence mechanisms are splitting, denial, projection, introjection, identification (projective and introjective) and idealisation.

Primitive mechanisms are particularly helpful in understanding group processes, especially in the large group (Main, 1975).

FREUD, A. (1937), *The Ego and the Mechanism of Defence* (Hogarth Press, London).
FREUD, S. (1896), 'Further remarks on the neuro-psychoses of defence' (*Standard Edition*, vol. 3, Hogarth Press, London).
FREUD, S. (1926), 'Inhibitions, symptoms and anxiety' (*Standard Edition*, vol. 20, Hogarth Press, London).
LAUGHLIN, H. P. (1970), *The Ego and its Defences* (Appleton-Century-Crofts, New York).
MAIN, T. F. (1975), 'Some psychodynamics of large groups' (in *The Large Group*, ed. L. Kreeger, Constable, London).

Demoralisation

The condition defined by Frank (1974) as fundamental to all forms of psychic disturbance. Frank views *symptoms* both as the means of expressing the state of demoralisation and the attempt to cope with it. He suggests five categories through which demoralisation is manifested: the psychotic, the neurotic, the shaken, the unruly and the discontented. Whatever its manifestation, demoralisation is characterised by a sense of *alienation*, resentment, guilt, loss of control, depression and anxiety arising from the individual's loss of belief in his own significance, in the purpose of his life and in his ability to love and be loved. Frank suggests that the effectiveness of all forms of psychotherapy, regardless of school and regardless of symptoms, depends upon its ability to combat the patient's demoralisation.

FRANK, J. D. (1971), 'Therapeutic factors in psychotherapy' (*Am. J. of Psychotherapy*, vol. 25, pp. 350-61).
FRANK, J. D. (1974), 'Psychotherapy: the restoration of morale' (*Am. J. of Psychiatry*, vol. 131, pp. 271-4).

Denial

A *defence mechanism* whereby the individual refuses to recognise the existence of a painful or anxiety-provoking external reality or internal demand. Freud (1940) regarded the lack of a penis in women and the consequent anxiety produced by this realisation in both sexes as being a frequent source of the denial mechanism. The denial of this fact is seen by Freud as a prototype of other denials of reality. It is commonly associated with *splitting* and is therefore to be included amongst the primitive *defence mechanisms*. It is typical of the manic patient who characteristically denies his whole internal world. The mechanism is also commonly employed in situations of external threat such as *crisis* and serves an important protective function for the *ego*.

FREUD, S. (1940), 'An outline of psycho-analysis' (*Standard Edition*, vol. 23, Hogarth Press, London).

Dependency
See *Basic assumption behaviour*.

Depressive position
A term introduced by Melanie Klein to des-cribe a normal developmental process occurring during the second half of the first year of life (Klein, 1935). It is characterised by greater integration, and by a beginning capacity to recognise that the other has *both* good and bad aspects and to feel guilt and concern in relation to him. The mother can now be perceived as a whole *object* and the infant begins to tolerate the *ambivalence* of his feelings towards her without having to split them to such an extent (or without having to engage to such an extent in the use of *projective identification*). In other words, he begins to tolerate conflict between love and hate, to feel guilt about his destructive impulses and con-cern about the object of them. At the same time, there is an awareness of the possibility of making some reparation for them and of restoring the damaged object in *phantasy* (and possibly also its representation in the external world).

The experience of the mother as a whole object also parallels a growing recognition of the separateness from her and sadness at her absence (rather than rage and persecution). The infant is more able, at some level, to differentiate between internal and external reality and to recognise the destructive feel-ings that arise from within himself.

Negotiation of the depressive position depends on the *introjection* of the mother so that she becomes a securely held *internal* loved object and the expansion of the ego's activities into the formation of other whole object relations. New possibilities are further opened to the infant with the entry into his world of others such as his father. Successful negotia-tion of the depressive position entails the capacity to mourn and experience *grief* and *bereavement* over loss; and it is this capacity to face and integrate experiences of disappoint-ment and loss which is seen as such a crucial determinant of the individual's later qualities of relating and healthy psychic functioning.

KLEIN, M. (1935), 'A contribution to the psychogenesis of manic-depressive states' (in *The Writings of Melanie Klein*, vol. 1, Hogarth Press, London).
KLEIN, M. (1952), 'Some theoretical con-clusions regarding the emotional life of the infant' (in *The Writings of Melanie Klein*, vol. 3, Hogarth Press, London).
SEGAL, H. (1973), *Introduction to the Work of Melanie Klein* (Hogarth Press, London).

See also *Kleinian school, Paranoid-schizoid position, Position*.

Depth psychology
Psychodynamic approaches to psychotherapy, so described because of their primary focus on the *unconscious* which, according to Freud's typology, is the 'deepest' level of the psyche. Unconscious processes are viewed as explan-atory in the aetiology of psychological disturbance and treatment interventions are directed towards these unconscious processes and not to the *presenting problem* or *symptom*. The acquisition of *insight* in the psychoanalytic sense is seen as being the primary curative factor. Which theorists are included in the term depth psychology and which are left out varies: for example, Wyss (1966), in his study

of depth psychology, includes neo-Freudian and *existential* therapists such as Fromm and Binswanger as well as the strictly psychoanalytic schools.

WYSS, D. (1966), *Depth Psychology: A Critical History* (Allen & Unwin, London).

Dereflection

A technique used in *logotherapy* whereby the individual is encouraged to divert his attention from the anxiety provoked by his *symptom* or *crisis*. As a result, the symptom may either abate (if, as in sexual problems, it has been exacerbated by the individual's concern about it) or he may become able to live a more fulfilling life *despite* the symptom, now that his attention has been refocused on to other things.

See also *Paradox, Symptom prescription*.

Desensitisation

See *Systematic desensitisation*.

Deterioration

The possibility that psychotherapy may do some patients harm has engaged the concern of clinicians from the early days of *psychoanalysis* and Freud (1937) discussed the possibility of psychotherapy having negative consequences as well as beneficial ones. Frank *et al.* (1959) discussed the reasons why some patients leave psychotherapy prematurely and in 1966 Bergin introduced the term 'deterioration effect' to describe the general finding that a certain proportion of patients get worse after psychotherapy. The negative effects of therapy include the worsening of the patient's *symptoms*; the development of new symptoms (*symptom substitution*); sustained dependency on the therapist or on the therapy; and the development of unrealistic expectations of the self or others leading to disillusionment or despair.

Deterioration seems to occur amongst a wide variety of patient populations across all the major treatment approaches and within the different modalities. Client variables (such as poor quality of interpersonal relationships,

severity and durability of symptoms and low motivation) and therapist variables (such as exploitation of patient dependency, inexperience, premature confrontation, aggressive or intrusive *leadership* in group treatments, punitive and rejecting attitudes and poor ability to convey facilitative or *core conditions*) have been found to correlate with deterioration. Some therapists also appear to possess personal qualities which render them *psychonoxious* with at least some patients. (See *Pathogenesis*.) Neither race, sex nor class differences between patient and therapist appear to be contributory factors to deterioration, although some studies suggest that *similarities* between therapist and patient within these variables may facilitate communication and therefore increase the likelihood of a *positive* therapeutic outcome. The likelihood that some therapists and some patients will interact deleteriously has been studied by Berzins (1977) and Parloff *et al.* (1978), and more understanding about appropriate therapist-patient matching appears to be an important area to pursue.

Patient variables, therapist variables and types and severity of disorder have been studied as potential factors in producing negative effects. Bergin (1971) concluded that for patients in individual treatment, 10 per cent deteriorated compared with 5 per cent for those in *control groups*. In family and marital therapy, Gurman and Kniskern (1978) have showed that both behavioural and non-behavioural approaches produce deterioration but that deterioration is significantly less than when one of the individuals involved in a relationship problem is treated alone. Some factors negatively influencing *outcome* were found to be therapists' inexperience; difference in experience within a *co-therapy* pair; and therapists' inability to convey *empathy*, *unconditional positive regard* and *genuineness*. Gurman and Kniskern conclude that *relationship factors* are far more important than technical skills in both preventing deterioration and yielding a positive therapeutic outcome.

The negative effects of group treatment have received a lot of attention. Hartley *et al.*

(1976) examined the deterioration effects of *encounter groups* and found the median casualty rate to be 6 per cent but the variation across studies was from 1 per cent to 50 per cent. Lieberman *et al.* (1973) identified some *group process* variables which related to negative effects. These included the encouragement of *confrontation*; expression of anger; rejection by the group or by the leader; and *feedback* overload. Negative effects produced by various types of *brief therapy* are discussed by Butcher and Koss (1978). Therapist inexperience appears to be highly related to deterioration effects in brief therapy and *crisis intervention*. Haley (1969) provides a short, amusing and thought-provoking comment on one way of explaining failure.

BECVAR, R. J. *et al.* (1982), 'Let us first do no harm' (*J. of Marriage and Family Therapy*, vol. 8, pp. 385-91).

BERGIN, A. E. (1966), 'Some implications of psychotherapy for therapeutic practise' (*J. of Abnormal Psychology*, vol. 71, pp. 235-46).

BERGIN, A. E. (1971), 'The evaluation of therapeutic outcomes' (in Garfield, S. and Bergin, A. E., *Handbook of Psychotherapy and Behavior Change*, Wiley, New York).

BERGIN, A. E. and LAMBERT, M. J. (1978), 'The evaluation of therapeutic outcomes' (in Garfield, S. and Bergin, A. E., *Handbook of Psychotherapy and Behavior Change*, Wiley, New York).

BERZINS, J. I. (1977), 'Therapist-patient matching' (in Gurman, A. S. and Razin, A. M. (eds), *Effective Psychotherapy*, Pergamon Press, New York).

BUTCHER, J. N. and KOSS, M. P. (1978), 'Research on brief and crisis-orientated psychotherapies' (in Garfield, S. L. and Bergin, A. E. (eds), *Handbook of Psychotherapy and Behavior Change*, Wiley, New York).

FRANK, J. D. *et al.* (1959), 'Why patients leave psychotherapy' (*Archives of Neurological Psychiatry*, vol. 77, pp. 283-99).

FREUD, S. (1937), 'Analysis terminable and interminable' (*Standard Edition*, vol. 23, Hogarth Press, London).

GURMAN, A. S. and KNISKERN, D. P. (1978),

'Deterioration in marital and family therapy – empirical, clinical and conceptual issues' (*Family Process*, vol. 17, pp. 3-20).

HALEY, J. (1969), 'The art of being a failure as a therapist' (*Am. J. of Orthopsychiatry*, vol. 39, pp. 691-5).

HARTLEY, D. *et al.* (1976) 'Deterioration effects in encounter groups' (*American Psychologist*, vol. 31, pp. 247-55).

LAMBERT, M. J. *et al.* (1977), 'Therapist-induced deterioration in psychotherapy' (in Gurman, A. S. and Razin, A. M., *Effective Psychotherapy*, Pergamon Press, New York).

LIEBERMAN, M. A. *et al.* (1973), *Encounter Groups: First Facts* (Basic Books, New York).

PARLOFF, M. B. *et al.* (1978), 'Research on therapist variables in relation to process and outcome' (in Garfield, S. and Bergin, A. E., *Handbook of Psychotherapy and Behavior Change*, Wiley, New York).

Detonative level
See *Metacommunication*.

Detouring
One of the processes whereby a rigid pathological triad is created and maintained. The term is used by Minuchin (1974) and Minuchin *et al.* (1978) in relation to parent-child triads but the same process could operate in other triadic relationships. The stress and tension between the parental pair is deflected through the child and, by a process that is analogous to *displacement* in the individual, the couple use the child to detour the conflict away from the parental/marital *sub-system*. Minuchin *et al.* (1978) describe two types of detouring strategies. First, detouring-attacking, when the child is defined as the source of the family's problems and through the *scapegoating* that results, the parents are able to retain the myth of an illusory harmony within their relationship. Second, detouring-supportive, when the child is defined as sick or weak and the parents are drawn to unite in order to protect and support him. The first type of detouring most typically produces deviance and other *acting out* behaviour in the child; the second produces psychosomatic and

other *acting in* types of behaviour.

MINUCHIN, S. (1974), *Families and Family Therapy* (Tavistock, London).
MINUCHIN, S. *et al.* (1978), *Psychosomatic Families* (Harvard University Press, Cambridge, Mass.).

See also *Coalition, Detriangulation, Mirror-image disagreement, Triangulation.*

De-triangulation

The process whereby the therapist unlocks the *triangulation* strategy of a family system. The triangulated person may be a family member or the therapist himself. Strategies for de-triangulating family members include strengthening alliances between other family members, particularly within generational groupings; fostering relationships with peers outside the family group; and excluding the triangulated member from treatment and, if a child, working with the parental pair alone. *Unbalancing* techniques and *task* setting can contribute to the execution of these de-triangulation strategies and so can paradoxical interventions, *interpretations* and *confrontation*. The triangulation of the therapist is a danger in all *systems therapy* but is particularly problematic in *conjoint marital therapy*. Strategies for de-triangulating the therapist fall into two kinds. The first, described by Broderick (1983), is the conscious effort on the part of the therapist to engage in a *symmetrical* relationship with each member of the pair. The second, suggested by Minuchin and Fishman (1981), is the reverse and entails the therapist using unbalancing techniques to re-align the system in such a way that its need to triangulate the therapist is dissolved.

BRODERICK, C. B. (1983), *The Therapeutic Triangle* (Sage Publications, London).
MINUCHIN, S. and FISHMAN, H. C. (1981), *Family Therapy Techniques* (Harvard University Press, Cambridge, Mass.).

Developmental stages

See *Stages of development.*

Deviation amplification

A systems process which results from *positive feedback.* It is defined by Maruyama (1968) as 'all processes of mutual causal relationships that amplify an insignificant or accidental kick, build up deviation and diverge from the initial condition'. Unlike many *systems theorists* who have had a tendency to view positive feedback in terms of its self-destructive tendency, Maruyama views positive feedback and the deviation amplification which results as a necessary factor in systems development and the process which enables systems change to occur. Deviation amplification can be seen operating destructively when the disequilibrium which it produces leads to systems chaos. The stress may precipitate dysfunctional solutions aimed at correcting the situation such as (in a family system) the production of an *identified patient* or *scapegoat*; or the procreation of a child in order to dissipate conflict in a marital *sub-system*. The amplification and repetition of false solutions leads to a regressive 'more of the same' approach to problem solving. The development of deviance and its amplification through the mutual needs and interaction of the deviant and non-deviant members of a group has been studied extensively by sociologists such as Goffman and Becker amongst many others. As a systems process, deviation amplificaton is neither functional nor dysfunctional but may be either. The systems therapist can deliberately amplify deviation in order to create a return, through a reaction, to the status quo, or in order to stabilise the system at a new level of functioning.

GOFFMAN, L. (1971), 'Deviation-amplifying processes in natural groups' (in Haley, J. (ed.), *Changing Families*, Grune & Stratton, New York).
MARUYAMA, M. (1968), 'The second cybernetics: deviation-amplifying mutual causal processes' (in Buckley, W. (ed.), *Modern Systems Research for the Behavioral Scientist*, Aldine, Chicago).

Devil's pact

A technique used by *strategic therapists* and those using *focused problem resolution* whereby a promise of compliance is extracted from the client before the content of a *task* is revealed. The client is put into a *therapeutic double bind*, for whether he accepts or refuses the challenge he has to take a new risk. The technique is indicated when a client has failed to comply with previous treatment approaches or tasks suggested by the therapist, yet is continuing to request help.

WATZLAWICK, P. *et al.* (1974), *Change: Principles of Problem Formation and Problem Resolution* (W. W. Norton, New York).

See also *Symptom prescription.*

Diagnosis

Literal Greek 'dia' meaning 'through', and 'gnosis', 'knowledge'. The analysis and classification of *symptoms* and the relation of symptoms to a dysfunctional situation or psychological disorder or both. Diagnosis is usually preceded by a period of study and evaluation of the patient, his problems, their history, his attempts at dealing with them and his psycho-social environment; and is followed by suggestions for treatment and a prognosis of the likely *outcome* (i.e. the classical model of data accumulation, data interpretation and data classification). However, diagnostic procedures are highly dependent upon the *model* of therapy being used, the theoretical framework that underpins it, the *style* of the therapist and the *agency* and professional discipline from which he is working. For example, many would view diagnosis as the first stage of treatment and would be disinclined to differentiate the two at all clearly. Menninger (1963) for example, comments, 'diagnostic assessment is treatment', and for many *family therapists* 'diagnosis and treatment are concurrent not consecutive activities' (Walrond-Skinner 1976).

A broad division exists between those therapists who recognise some commonalities between patient problems (e.g. people in *crisis* or suffering *bereavement* or from phobias,

anxiety states, depression, etc.) and are therefore prepared to classify them according to a nosological system using *phenotypic* and *genotypic* methods (for example psychodynamically based therapists, medically oriented therapists and behaviour therapists); and those who emphasise the essential uniqueness of every patient problem and who are therefore critical of attempts to diagnose because it appears to involve 'pigeonholing' patients (for example humanistic, client-centred, existential and radical therapists). The difference between the two groups hinges in part on whether diagnosis is viewed mainly as a planning stage for treatment (which would commend itself to the second group) or whether it necessarily involves the ascertaining of causes, the categorisation of problems and the *labelling* of the patient (which would be acceptable to many in the first group but not to the second). For a discussion of the different purposes of diagnosis see Meehl (1973).

The concept of diagnosis derives from medical terminology. Thus for the psychiatrist, Redlich and Freedman (1966) define diagnosis as the 'systematic observation, recording and classifying of pertinent information. In medicine, these procedures are called diagnosis. By means of the diagnostic process, physicians attempt to determine the nature of the disease with which they are confronted and also to distinguish one disease from another.' Behaviour therapists, while accepting the need to classify particular problems, replace the medically derived schemes with that of a functional or *behavioural analysis*. Kanfer and Saslow (1965) discuss behavioural analysis as an alternative to diagnostic classification. Other phenotypic forms are discussed in Katz *et al.* (1968).

Arbuckle (1970) defines the meaning of diagnosis for the counsellor in terms which are clearly derived from the *medical model*: 'the analysis of one's difficulties and the causes that have produced them . . . the determination of nature, origin and maintenance of ineffective, abnormal modes of behaviour'. But he goes on to suggest that part of this determination must involve the reflexive process of examining and developing the client-counsellor relationship. Laing (1968), who represents an existentialist viewpoint, carries this idea further: 'diagnosis is dia: through; gnosis: knowledge of. Diagnosis is appropriate for social situations, if one understands it as seeing through the social scene . . . the way one sees through the situation changes the situation. [Thus,] social diagnosis is a process, not a single moment. It is not an element in an ordered set of before-after events in time [even though] in the medical model such a sequence is the ideal.' Minuchin (1974) discusses diagnosis in relation to family therapy and outlines six major areas that require consideration: family structure; system flexibility; place on the *enmeshed/disengaged* continuum; strengths in the family's ecology; developmental stage; and the function of the *identified patient's* symptoms for the *system* as a whole. Identifying the membership of the family *system* is also an essential preliminary in family diagnosis.

Hogan (1979) asks 'whether diagnostic skills are in fact essential for the effectively functioning therapist' and comments that this 'is currently a hotly contested issue'. Opinions range as to whether it is vital for the responsible treatment of patients, to whether it is dangerous in terms of its labelling potential and its proven accuracies, to whether it is simply harmless but redundant. Menninger (1963) proposes a unifying definition in an attempt to bridge these different viewpoints: 'to diagnose is to differentiate, to distinguish, to designate. It is to recognise, to have knowledge of or to come to an understanding of.'

Diagnostic interviews often adopt some structured design. Projective and other *personality tests* such as *Rorschach, TAT, repertory grids*, etc., may be employed; or in family therapy a *genogram* or *family sculpting*; or in *play therapy* the child's play and drawings. Beck (1962), Hogan (1979) and others have discussed the extraordinarily wide variations in psycho-diagnostic classification that exist and suggest that the validity and reliability of diagnosis is exceptionally poor. On the whole, non-professionals make as good or better diagnostic judgments in terms of nosology than do professionals, even on such gross variables as whether the individual is deemed to be psychotic, neurotic or normal. Rosenhan (1973) reports a fascinating and now famous experiment in which he and seven colleagues complained of one symptom of schizophrenia (the hearing of voices) and although they afterwards showed no abnormality whatsoever, each was detained in a psychiatric hospital for a mean length of stay of nineteen days.

Regardless of the ethical and technical difficulties inherent in diagnosis, most psychotherapists seem to suggest that continuing attempts need to be made to overcome these problems for the sake of training, research and practice. Ways of assessing more subtle and elusive patient variables such as *coping behaviours* and *ego strengths* need to be developed. Strupp (1978) for example, comments that 'diagnosis is a process that calls for the exercise of significant clinical skills. It must be systematic and it must lead to prognostic judgments that can be translated into therapeutic operations as well as outcome evaluations.' In addition, relevant methods of diagnosis need to be developed for the different psychotherapeutic approaches.

AMERICAN PSYCHIATRIC ASSOCIATION (1980), 'Diagnostic and statistical manual of mental disorders' (*DSM III*, 3rd edn, APA, Washington, DC).

ARBUCKLE, D. S. (1970), *Counseling: Philosophy, Therapy and Practice* (2nd edn), Allyn & Bacon, Boston).

BECK, A. T. (1962), 'Reliability of psychiatric diagnoses: 1. A critique of systematic studies' (*Am. J. of Psychiatry*, vol. 119, pp. 210-16).

HOGAN, D. B. (1979), *The Regulation of Psychotherapists* (vol. 1, Ballinger, Cambridge, Mass.).

KANFER, F. J. and SASLOW, G. (1965), 'Behavioural analysis: an alternative to diagnostic classification' (*Archives of General Psychiatry*, vol. 12, pp. 529-38).

KATZ, J. and ASSOCIATES (1968), *No Time for Youth: Growth and Constraint in College Students* (Jossey-Bass, San Francisco).

LAING, R. D. (1968), 'Interventions in social situations' (reprinted in Walrond-Skinner, S. (1981), *Developments in Family Therapy*, Routledge & Kegan Paul, London).

MEEHL, P. E. (1973), *Psychodiagnosis: Selected Papers* (University of Minnesota, St. Paul, Minnesota).

MENNINGER, K. (1963), *The Vital Balance: The Life Process in Mental Health and Illness* (Viking, New York).

MINUCHIN, S. (1974), *Families and Family Therapy* (Tavistock, London).

REDLICH, F. C. and FREEDMAN, D. (1963), *The Theory and Practice of Psychiatry* (Basic Books, New York).

RICHARDSON, H. (1973), 'The historical approach to the theory of diagnosis' (*Brit. J. of Psychiatry*, vol. 122, pp. 245-50).

ROSENHAN, D. I. (1973), 'On being sane in insane places' (*Science*, vol. 179, pp. 250-8).

STRUPP, H. H. (1978), 'Psychotherapy research and practice: an overview' (in Garfield, S. L. and Bergin, A. E., *Handbook of Psychotherapy and Behavior Change*, Wiley, New York).

WALROND-SKINNER, S. (1976), *Family Therapy: The Treatment of Natural Systems* (Routledge & Kegan Paul, London).

Diagrams, therapeutic use of

Diagrams can be used in individual work, family or group work to develop the patient's self-awareness, clarify *goals*, increase self-esteem, clarify role relationships, define areas of difficulty, etc. Examples are the *genogram*, *sociogram*, *lifespace* drawing, *Johari's window*, *lifeline* etc. Some minimum structure is provided for the externalisation of cognitive and effective experience but the patient is still free to use the diagrammatic form to explore his intra- and interpersonal experience. Cox (1978) describes two types of visual display system which can be used both therapeutically with the patient and to help the therapist record information.

COX, M. (1978), *Coding the Therapeutic Process* (Pergamon Press, London).

See also *Chronogram, Psychobiogram*.

Differentiation

Term used by Bowen (1966) and other family therapists to describe a position on a continuum which represents the polar opposite from that of the undifferentiated ego mass. When an individual has become differentiated from other members of his family, he shows little evidence of *ego* fusion and he is able to function at an optimal level in relation to others, relating intimately but without fusion. Bowen (1966) has developed what he calls a *differentiation of self scale* which allows the therapist to measure the extent of family members' differentiation. Differentiation of self is regarded as a major *goal* of the treatment process. The term is also used in a similar sense regarding the relationship between *subsystems* within a family group.

BOWEN, M. (1966), 'The use of family theory in clinical practice' (*Comprehensive Psychiatry*, vol. 7, pp. 345-74).

See also *Individuation, Self-actualisation, Self-realisation*.

Differentiation of self scale

A clinical measure of *differentiation* introduced by Bowen (1966). It is an attempt to conceptualise all human functioning on the same continuum. Complete differentiation of self (equivalent to complete emotional maturity) is assigned a notional value of 100 on a scale from 0 to 100. The lowest level of differentiation (or *undifferentiated ego mass*) is at the bottom of the scale and the highest level of differentiation lies at the top. Detailed profiles for a series of points on the scale are given. The lower the person is on the scale, the more likely he is to become symptomatic and to find difficulty in engaging in functional *communication*.

BOWEN, M. (1966), 'The use of family theory in clinical practice' (*Comprehensive Psychiatry*, vol. 7, pp. 345-74).

Digital

A form of *communication* which uses words and which therefore relies on *symbolism* to express its meaning. Used in contrast to *analogic*, the concept is derived from two models. First, the biological model of the nervous system where the neurons receive information through the synapses. The information is passed or inhibited at the synaptic gap so that the firing or inhibition of the neuron conveys binary digital information to the organism. Second, the cybernetic model of the digital computer, whereby data and instructions are processed in the form of numbers with only an arbitrary correspondence between the information itself and the 'language' through which it is expressed. Digital communication is logical and linear but is 'one removed' from that which it represents. As Bateson and Jackson (1964) point out, 'there is nothing particularly five-like in the number five; there is nothing particularly table-like in the word table.' Digital communication is considered by communication theorists to convey the *content* and information aspects of communication as distinct from the *relational context*, which is conveyed by the analogic mode. Digital communication is of a much higher degree of complexity, versatility and abstraction than the analogic mode. It can express qualifications, negatives and a range of subtleties that are outside the scope of analogic communication. In a sense one can say that it is what distinguishes man from other animals (except, perhaps, dolphins and their genre who may possess this capacity). More importantly, from the point of view of psychotherapy, it is the dual potential of the two modes that enables such a rich and complex pattern of communication to develop and also gives rise to its dilemmas (See *Communication*). Digital communication reflects the *secondary process* of the functional and conscious aspects of the *ego*.

BATESON, G. and JACKSON, D. (1964), 'Some varieties of pathogenic organisation' (in Rioch, D. (ed.), *Disorders of Communication*, vol. 42, Research Publications, Association for Research in Nervous and Mental Disease, pp. 270-83).
WATZLAWICK, P. *et al.*, *Pragmatics of Human Communication* (W. W. Norton, New York).

See also *Causality*.

Dilation
The term used by Kelly to describe the way in which a person broadens his perceptual field in order to re-organise it on a more comprehensive level.

See also *Cognitive complexity, Personal construct theory*.

Direct analysis
A method of analytic psychotherapy suitable for psychotic patients, developed by Rosen (1953). As the psychotic's consciousness is overwhelmed by the products of his *unconscious*, the unconscious is open and available for the *analyst* to work with in a direct way. The analyst aims to make explicit to the patient the 'unconscious' products which are already perceived and experienced in the patient's consciousness. The analyst's main tool is the establishment of a positive *transference* and a relationship with the patient which seeks to counteract the damage inflicted by negative experiences and privations experienced in early childhood. *Interpretations* are therefore direct and because the unconscious is revealed by the patient's words and/or *non-verbal* cues, the analyst does not have to encounter or interpret *resistance*. Rosen also utilises a technique similar to *symptom prescription* which he refers to as 're-enacting the psychosis'. Scheflen (1961) discusses and evaluates this and other aspects of Rosen's work. Although used primarily with highly disturbed patients, Rosen has also applied the principles of direct analysis to those with neurotic disorders. Direct analysis is practised and taught under Rosen's supervision at the Direct Psychoanalytic Institute, at Doylestown, Pennsylvania.

ROSEN, J. N. (1953), *Direct Analysis: Selected Papers* (Grune & Stratton, New York).
ROSEN, J. N. (1962), *Direct Psychoanalytic Psychiatry* (Grune & Stratton, New York).
ROSEN, J. N. (1968), *Selected Papers on Direct Psychoanalysis* (Grune & Stratton, New York).
SCHEFLEN, A. E. (1961), *A Psychotherapy of Schizophrenia: Direct Analysis* (Charles C. Thomas, Springfield, Ill.).

Direction

A basic interviewing skill in which the therapist tells the client what to do. The term is usually reserved for the intra-session situation, with the terms *task, prescription, advice* and *homework assignment* used for directions about events outside the session. Three dimensions of effective direction giving have been identified by Ivey and Gluckstern (1976): appropriate verbal and non-verbal behaviour to support the direction; *concreteness* of expression; and checking out with the client whether or not the direction has been heard and understood. Directions are given by therapists using all psychotherapeutic models although their frequency increases along a continuum from *psychoanalysis* (very few) to the *behavioural* and *strategic therapies* (many). *Existential, psychoanalytic, client-centred* and *humanistic* therapists usually maintain that directives are normally inappropriate and counter-productive and should be used as sparingly as possible.

IVEY, A. and GLUCKSTERN, N. (1976), *Basic Influencing Skills: Leader and Participant Manuals* (North Amherst, Mass., Micro Training).

See also *Interview, Microskill, Non-directive.*

Disavowal

See *Denial.*

Disengaged

Term used by Minuchin (1974) to describe a type of family *system* which is characterised by rigid boundaries. The roles and functions of family members are rigidly defined and alteration between roles and functions even under stress is very limited. For example, it becomes difficult for father to take over mother's nurturing tasks when she is incapacitated and difficult for mother to take on the organisational aspects of the family (if this is how they are normally shared out) when father withdraws temporarily or permanently from the family group. Members of disengaged *sub-systems* may function autonomously, have a skewed sense of independence and find

co-operative sharing difficult. Stress signals from individuals and sub-systems are not quickly picked up or correctly interpreted until the level of stress has become quite high and may have resulted in the production of *symptoms.* Disengagement usually describes a relative form of interaction and need not be dysfunctional unless it is very pronounced. When pronounced, it leads to rootlessness and insecurity in individual family members and an inability to enter into secure commitments within sub-systems.

MINUCHIN, S. (1974), *Families and Family Therapy* (Tavistock, London).

See also *Cohesion, Differentiation, Enmeshed, Homeostasis.*

Displacement

The means by which an *object* of the individual's instinctual desire is replaced by another and *libido* is rechannelled into the new object. Alternatively, it can be used to protect a cherished object by channelling negative feelings away to another. Displacement is a defence against anxiety – a signal from within the *ego*, when threatened with frustration or loss of the desired object or of being overwhelmed by a *drive.* The ego aims to find a substitute which resembles as closely as possible the originally desired object of the drive. During the process of maturation, the ego is able to tolerate less similarity between the two and the resemblance between the original object and its replacement usually gets wider. The mechanism is also seen at work in the production of *symptoms* and the use of *symbols* (see *Symbolism* in *dreams* whereby the *latent content* of a dream is revealed through displacement on to the *manifest content.* Displacement facilitates *condensation.* The process of displacement resembles the way in which an individual or family makes use of a *metaphor* or *myth* to express their anxiety, the decoding of which becomes one of the tasks of the therapeutic process.

Dissociation

A term introduced into nineteenth-century

psychology and psychiatry by Janet and adopted in Freud's early theories of hysteria but dropped and superseded by repression. It is the separating off of mental contents such as thoughts, feelings and phantasies from the individual's conscious awareness. The mental contents which are thus separated off can be either conscious or unconscious, and although they are disowned and separated from the rest of the personality, they are not necessarily *repressed* or *projected* on to someone else. They tend to be made up of aggressive and sexual impulses and fantasies. The separated off contents may start to function independently as in the case of schizophrenia, or they may simply lie in abeyance. The therapeutic task involves helping the patient to re-integrate these disowned parts of the self.

See also *Splitting, Trading of dissociations.*

Distance regulator

An individual who is subjected to the *triangling* process of a dyad and is used by the dyad as a homoestatic *regulator*. The term was introduced by Byng-Hall (1980) in the context of *family therapy*. He suggests that a third party, often a child or an in-law, is used by the marital pair to regulate the degree of intimacy/distance with which they feel comfortable and to ward off the feared catastrophe of total abandonment or total fusion. Because of the stresses involved in this role, the distance regulator is prone to become the *identified patient*. The distance regulator can play a functional as well as a dysfunctional role for the dyad, as in the case of a father's proper intrusiveness into the mother-infant dyad, preventing ongoing *symbiosis*. The therapist's task is to displace the distance regulator, take on the role himself and to convert it from a pathological into a healthy one. Ultimately this involves handing back responsibility for distance regulation to the couple itself.

BYNG-HALL, J. (1980), 'Symptom bearer as marital distance regulator: clinical implications' (*Family Process*, vol. 19, pp. 355-65).
BYNG-HALL, J. and CAMPBELL, D. (1981), 'Resolving conflicts arising out of distance regulation' (*J. of Marital and Family Therapy*, vol. 7, pp. 321-30).

See also *Coalition, Fit (marital), Go-between process.*

Distancing

Term used by Adler to describe a strategy by which the stressed or insecure person tries to cope with problems. Adler describes four modes of distancing: retrogression; cessation; *ambivalence*; and the creation of false obstacles. In each case the individual tries to preserve his self-esteem by placing distance between himself and the perceived threat from the environment. The term is also used more generally to describe the degree to which an individual is incapable of forming intimate relationships.

Divorce therapy

See *Conciliation.*

Double bind

A term introduced by Bateson *et al.* (1956) to describe the *paradox* created by the 'unresolvable sequences of experiences' which confront the schizophrenic in his interpersonal *context* and which renders his own unconventional communicational habits appropriate to that context. He is placed in a 'no win' situation with regard to the injunctions and predictions of the other party so that whatever he does defines him as either mad or bad. Laing (1965) uses the term *mystification* for what is essentially the same process.

Bateson *et al.* (1956) define the necessary ingredients for a double bind situation as being the following:

(a) two or more persons, in some form of interpersonal relationship;

(b) the 'victim' experiences the double binding communication repeatedly so that it becomes his habitual expectation;

(c) a primary negative injunction, commanding a certain action or behaviour under threat of punishment, such as the withdrawal of love or the expression of disapproval;

(d) a secondary injunction which conflicts

with the first at the *metacommunicative* level, e.g. 'do not take any notice of my demands on you'; 'do not see me as making a demand on you, I only want what you want';
(d) escape from the interpersonal field is impossible because the relationship has a survival value for the 'victim'.

Although developed in order to explain the nature of schizophrenic communication, the concept of the double bind has provided a rich field of research and has been applied to a much wider range of interpersonal disorders than the specific area of schizophrenia. It has become a major explanatory principle in the *systemic therapies* and in helping to understand the aetiology of *symptoms* in interpersonal rather than intrapsychic terms; and Bodin (1981) suggests that 'it stands as perhaps the most definitive landmark in the revolutionary shift from an individual to a systems focus in concepts of psychopathogenesis'.

Watzlawick *et al.* (1968) have added important further characteristics of double binding communication. They stress that there are different degrees of psychological disturbance induced by double binding communication: everyone is likely to be subject to *some* double binds during his life, yet not everyone is schizophrenic. Only repeated exposure within a survival relationship produces severe pathology. Where double binding is chronic, it will become a habitual expectation of all human relationships. Moreover, a double bind is a mutual interactive process whereby both parties, not only the apparent 'victim', is caught in the double bind.

BATESON, G. *et al.* (1956), 'Toward a theory of schizophrenia' (*Behavioral Science*, vol. 1, pp. 251-64).
BERGER, M. M. (ed.) (1978), *Beyond the Double Bind: Communication and Family Systems* (Brunner/Mazel, New York).
BODIN, A. M. (1981), 'The interactional view: family therapy approaches of the MRI' (in Gurman, A. S. and Kniskern, D. P., *Handbook of Family Therapy*, Brunner/Mazel, New York).

HALEY, J. (1973), *Uncommon Therapy: The Psychiatric Techniques of Milton H. Erikson* (W. W. Norton, New York).
JACKSON, D. D. (ed.) (1968), *Human Communication*, vols 1 and 2 (Science & Behavior Books, Palo Alto, Calif.).
LAING, R. D. (1965), 'Mystification, confusion and conflict' (in Boszormenyi-Nagy, I. and Framo, J. (eds), *Intensive Family Therapy*, Harper & Row, New York).
SLUZKI, C. E. and RANSOM, D. C. (eds) (1976), *Double Bind: The Foundation of the Communicational Approach to the Family* (Grune & Stratton, New York).
WATZLAWICK, P. *et al.* (1968), *Pragmatics of Human Communication* (W. W. Norton, New York).
WATZLAWICK, P. and WEAKLAND, J. H. (1977), *The International View: Studies at the MRI* (W. W. Norton, New York).

Doubling

Technique used in *psychodrama* whereby an *auxiliary ego* plays the part of the *protagonist's* inner self or double, speaking and commenting as though he was the protagonist. The terms alter ego and double are used interchangeably. Blatner (1973) refers to the use of the double as 'the heart of psychodrama'. Its main functions are to promote as full a range as possible of the protagonist's feelings and emotional experiences; to give him support so that he may be helped to take more risks in the *enactment* and to provide a means of giving more empathic and effective suggestions for the future management of his situation. The therapist makes it clear that the protagonist is free to correct the double if he feels he is inaccurately expressing his feelings or thoughts. The therapist may instruct the protagonist to repeat the double statements and that only if they are thus repeated will they be responded to by other participants in the enactment.

The technique of doubling produces an *intensification* of the protagonist's experience, maximising the feelings, enlarging on the content or verbalising the protagonist's *nonverbal communication* and *defence mechanisms*.

103

The therapist may direct the double to play a specific part of the protagonist's personality or use several doubles for different parts. Any or all of the auxiliary egos in an enactment may also be given doubles. Doubling can be used effectively in *family therapy* and *marital therapy*, the therapist or *co-therapy* pair acting as the couple's doubles. In *multiple family* and *multiple couples therapy* members of the group can effectively double for each other, either spontaneously or as directed by the therapist. Doubling is also a useful device in *empathy* training, where members of a training group work as doubles for a *simulated* or *role played* situation.

BLATNER, H. A. (1973), *Acting-In: Practical Applications of Psychodramatic Methods* (Springer, New York).
STARR, A. (1977), *Psychodrama: Rehearsal for Living* (Nelson Hall, Chicago).

See also *Action techniques*.

Dream

Mental images which are produced by the *unconscious* during sleep. According to psychoanalytic theory, a dream has both a *manifest* and a *latent content*. Dreaming is an unwilled and spontaneous activity, having the function of both communicating and withholding communication about the self. As Rycroft (1979) comments, dreaming is the 'sleeping form' of the imagination. Freud (1900) came to attach such importance to dreams as a means of gaining access to the unconscious that he described them as the 'royal road' to the patient's unconscious processes. He asserted that a dream represents the fulfilment of a wish of a sexual nature which is repressed from consciousness but 'committed' into awareness in a disguise through dream *symbolism*.

The main mechanisms employed by the unconscious to conceal the repressed wish are *condensation* and *displacement*, through which the wish is transformed into the manifest content of the dream. Jung emphasised the creative functions of dreaming and, in contrast to Freud, felt that the main purpose of a dream

is to communicate rather than disguise repressed material. Jung asserted that dreams draw on the *collective unconscious* and that they approximate to *myths* and other collective symbols that elucidate the human condition. Adler believed that dreams are problem-solving efforts and represent the patient's tentative solutions to current problems rather than wish fulfillments.

ALTMAN, L. (1969), *The Dream in Psychoanalysis* (International Universities Press, New York).
FREUD, S. (1900), 'The interpretation of dreams' (*Standard Edition*, vols 4 and 5, Hogarth Press, London).
FREUD, S. (1901), 'On dreams' (*Standard Edition*, vol. 5, Hogarth Press, London).
FREUD, S. (1923), 'Remarks on the theory and practice of dream interpretation' (*Standard Edition*, vol. 19, Hogarth Press, London).
JUNG, C. G. (1934), 'The practical use of dream analysis' (in *The Practice of Psychotherapy*, Collected Works, vol. 16, Routledge & Kegan Paul, London).
RYCROFT, C. (1979), *The Innocence of Dreams* (Hogarth Press, London).

Dream interpretation

Freud's discovery was that *dreams* have a meaning and represent an unacknowledgeable wish. The wish is disguised in a symbol which is unique for the individual at the time and is frequently taken from very recent memories ('the day's residues'). The analysis and interpretation of dream material is mainly, though not entirely, confined to the psychoanalytic therapies and their derivatives. Freud taught that the dream should be analysed into its elements and the patient asked to free associate to each. The first and last elements of the dream are seen as being especially important, as the sequence of elements and the way in which the story in the dream unfolds. The timing and manner of the interpretation of dream material requires great care, so as to avoid raising the patient's *censorship* or breaching his *defence mechanisms*. Boss (1958) describes the way the therapist approaches dreams phenomenologically in *Daseinanalysis*, seeing them as revealing the type of experiences to which the patient is open and receptive or, for the moment, shut off. Some symbols that occur in dreams are held, at least by Freudians, to be universal in their meaning, whilst others are viewed as idiosyncratic to the individual dreamer.

BLUM, H. P. (1976), 'The changing use of dreams in psychoanalytic practice: dreams and free associations' (*Int. J. of Psychoanalysis*, vol. 57, pp. 315-24).

BOSS, M. (1958), *The Analysis of Dreams* (Philosophical Library, New York).

FRENCH, T. and FROMM, E. (1964), *Dream Interpretation* (Basic Books, New York).

JUNG, C. G. (1961), *Memories, Dreams and Reflections* (Collins/Routledge & Kegan Paul, London).

KHAN, M. M. R. (1976), 'The changing use of dreams in psychoanalytic practice: in search of the dreaming experience' (*Int. J. of Psychoanalysis*, vol. 57, pp. 325-30).

Dream work

Term introduced by Freud to describe the operation by which the *latent content* of a *dream* is transformed into the *manifest content* of images and events which the dreamer can recall when he awakes. Dream work is accomplished through the mechanisms of distortion, *condensation*, *displacement* and *secondary elaboration*.

Drive

According to psychoanalytic theory, a mental representation of a bodily need, having its source within the body and an aim (to eliminate tension) and an object through which the drive achieves its aim. Freud (1905) introduced his theory in his *Three Essays on the Theory of Sexuality*. He suggests that the origin of the drives lies 'on the frontier between the mental and physical', in other words, that they are partly bodily and partly psychic in origin.

The term is a translation of the German word 'Treib', variously translated as drive or instinct (see Bettelheim 1983). Freud suggested that the drives or instincts which all have their origins in the *id* are paired and are thus dualistic. He subdivided the life instincts into the sexual instincts and the life preservation instincts; but in his later writings he viewed *libido* as the energy of *all* the life instincts. In 1920, Freud introduced a new theory of instincts (Freud, 1920) in which he contrasted life instincts (both libido and the ego instincts) with a *death instinct*. This later revision was not adopted by clinical *psychoanalysis* or *ego psychology* but has been adopted by the *Kleinian school* of psychoanalysis and has led to different views about the nature of anxiety and of the *defence mechanisms* against anxiety. Some *object relations* theorists dispense with a theory of instincts altogether, notably Fairbairn.

Freud viewed his theory of the instincts as rooted both in biology and in *metapsychology*. In his later writing (1932) he recognised that 'the theory of the instincts is, so to say, our mythology. Instincts are mythical entities, magnificent in their indefiniteness.' Instincts can be transformed or *sublimated* and still find a satisfactory elimination of tension. They may also be forced back into the *unconscious* through *repression* where they may become the source of psychological disturbance through the ensuing build-up of tension. Freud's reduction of all human aspiration and activity to the satisfaction of base instinctual drives was challenged at the time and is still much criticised.

As Ellerberger (1970) points out, much of Freud's early work on instincts was foreshadowed by Adler and Freud acknowledged Adler's importance in the development of his theory of the instincts. Jung disagrees with Freud's emphasis on the sexual nature of the instincts, and Sullivan, Horney and the *interpersonal school* of psychoanalysis emphasises the cultural conflicts rather than the instinctual ones. Humanistic therapists have criticised the lack of orientation to the whole person particularly evident in Freud's views regarding the instincts and the *reductionism* that the theory involves.

BETTELHEIM, B. (1983), *Freud and Man's Soul* (Constable, London).
ELLERBERGER, H. F. (1970), *The Discovery of the Unconscious* (Allen Lane, London).
FREUD, S. (1905), 'Three essays on the theory of sexuality' (*Standard Edition*, vol. 7, Hogarth Press, London).
FREUD, S. (1920), 'Beyond the pleasure principle' (*Standard Edition*, vol. 18, Hogarth Press, London).
FREUD, S. (1932), 'New introductory lectures on psychoanalysis' (*Standard Edition*, vol. 22, Hogarth Press, London).

See also *Approach avoidance conflict.*

Drop out
See *Single session therapy, Termination.*

Dualism
See *Cartesian.*

Dying, psychotherapeutic work with

The initiation of effective psychotherapeutic work with the dying is dependent upon establishing that the person has reached the terminal stage of his life; but the point at which a person is considered to be dying is variously defined, depending on the criteria being used. For example, a person may be deemed to be dying when a physician arrives at such a prognosis or when a person accepts such a prognosis or when carers or relatives relinquish hope. Pattison (1977) describes three phases which result from a person's awareness of the fact that he is dying: acute crisis; a chronic living-dying phase; and a terminal phase. The experience of dying, for the patient and his relatives, is highly dependent upon the patient's position in the life cycle (Backer *et al.* 1982). Pattison (1977) describes the degree to which various ego *defence mechanisms* are used during different stages of the life cycle. Hinton (1967) states that the majority of people have a terminal period of life before death, requiring special care and lasting for a few days or weeks and not usually exceeding three months. Increasing numbers of people now die in hospital rather than at home and these are

likely to experience anxiety generated by the separation from familiar people and surroundings as well as by their other fears stemming from being terminally ill.

Hinton (1967) has shown that, regardless of what they were told, the majority of dying patients realise that their death is imminent. He and others have further shown that the opportunity to talk about their impending death is viewed positively by most patients. Thus the therapist or counsellor must be prepared to talk about the patient's death at the point at which he indicates that he is ready to do so. This preparedness frees the individual to move through a psychological transition from disbelief to realisation to acceptance. The therapist's task includes enabling the patient to ventilate a range of emotions including anger, despair and disappointment; recognising his reality and thus confirming his sense of identity; reassuring him as to the helper's continuing availability and support throughout the length of his illness; helping him to remain involved in making plans for his life and taking responsibility for plans for his family, so far as he is able to do so; assisting him to attend to any 'unfinished business' he may feel is important, either of a practical or an emotional nature; maintaining his hope for the life he has left; facilitating communication between the patient and his relatives, including helping them to say goodbye to each other; and enabling him to explore the spiritual aspects of his situation if he wishes to do so, through the services of a priest, minister, rabbi or other religious representative. Individual work is the chief method employed with the dying, but some writers report the use of group work (Goodyear 1977), family work and multiple family groups (Adams 1978). The particular needs of dying children are discussed by Sahler (1978), Wilkenfeld (1977) and Burton (1974).

ADAMS, M. (1978), 'Helping the parents of children with malignancy' (*J. of Paediatrics*, vol. 93, pp. 734-8).
AINSWORTH-SMITH, I. and SPECK, P. (1982), *Letting Go* (SPCK, London).

BACKER, B. *et al.* (1982), *Death and Dying: Individuals and Institutions* (Wiley, New York).
BURTON, L. (1974), *Care of the Child Facing Death* (Routledge & Kegan Paul, London).
GOODYEAR, C. (1977), 'Group therapy with advanced cancer patients' (in Pritchard *et al.*, *Social Work with the Dying Patient and his Family*, Columbia University Press, New York).
HINTON, J. (1967), *Dying* (Penguin, London).
LAMERTON, R. (1980), *Care of the Dying* (2nd edn. Penguin, Harmondsworth).
PATTISON, E. M. (ed.) (1977), *The Experience of Dying* (Prentice-Hall, New Jersey).
SAHLER, D. (ed.) (1978), *The Child and Death* (Mosby, St Louis).
WILKENFELD, L. (ed.) (1977), *When Children Die* (Kendal/Hunt, Iowa).

Dynamic

Term used with various meanings within the psychoanalytic approach to psychotherapy. According to Ellenberger (1970), the term was coined in the eighteenth century by Gottfried Wilhelm Leibniz and applied to mechanics. It was taken over first by Herbart who applied it to psychology in order to distinguish between static and dynamic states of consciousness. Second, Fechner, during the nineteenth century, applied the term to psychic energy. Third, Charcot and others used the term to distinguish between organic and *functional* illnesses. Fourth, it was used to distinguish between repressive and evolutionary forces. Freud (1910) adopted the term to denote the presence of inherent movement and conflict within the *psyche*. In particular, he used the term to describe the permanent condition of the *unconscious* in which movements to make psychic material *conscious* are continually opposed by contrary forces. The term is also used synonymously with *psychodynamic* to describe any psychological theory or therapeutic approach which concerns itself with unconscious *drives* and processes, and their interaction.

ELLENBERGER, H. F. (1970), *The Discovery of the Unconscious* (Allen Lane, London).

FREUD, S. (1910), 'Five lectures on psychoanalysis' (*Standard Edition*) vol. 11, Hogarth Press, London).

See also *Depth psychology*.

Dysfunctional

An inappropriate, unhealthy or maladaptive *process* or *structure* which produces problems for an individual, relationship or group. The term can also be applied descriptively direct to the individual, relationship or group which is experiencing the problem.

Dystonic

See *Ego alien*.

E

Eclectic psychotherapy

An approach *to* and a trend *within* psychotherapy which encourages the selection of ideas and methods from a range of different theoretical orientations or schools, sometimes with an attempt to create a new systematic approach. For example, Thorne (1967) argues for an integrative psychology built upon a systematic theoretical foundation and leading to eclectic clinical practice. Far from being an unsystematic, atheoretical 'cook book' approach, the approach which he advocates is built upon principles of consistency, comprehensiveness and systematic synthesis. The *therapist variable* is usually viewed as more important than technical purity and the personality and *style* of the therapist is seen as the determinant of how and what he chooses to use as his techniques of treatment.

Whilst eclecticism is discouraged by many because it may lead to lack of rigour and difficulty in evaluating the *process* or *outcome* of treatment, recently there have been clearly discernible trends in the direction of eclecticism. These have been noted by Garfield and Kurtz (1977).

One aspect of this development is the

attempt by some workers to merge ideas from humanistic or insight approaches with behavioural approaches. *Learning-based client-centred therapy, multi-modal therapy* and *cognitive therapy* are all examples of this. Others have been described by Wachtel (1977). Disillusionment with the search for the one effective method of psychotherapy in all cases, as well as a growing recognition that the micro activities of therapists within a therapy session do not differ markedly or consistently from each other in relation to their school of therapy, have contributed to the trend towards eclecticism.

GARFIELD, S. L. (1980), *Psychotherapy: An Eclectic Approach* (Wiley, New York).
GARFIELD, S. L. and KURTZ, R. (1977), 'A study of eclectic views' (*J. of Consulting and Clinical Psychology*, vol. 45, pp. 78-83).
GOLDFRIED, M. R. (1982), *Converging Themes in Psychotherapy* (Springer-Verlag, New York).
PROCHASKA, J. O. (1979), *Systems of Psychotherapy: A Transtheoretical Analysis* (Dawsey Press, Homewood, Ill.).
THORNE, F. C. (1967), *Integrative Psychology* (Clinical Publishing, Brandon, Vt.).
THORNE, F. C. (1973), 'Eclectic psychotherapy' (in Corsini, R. (ed.), *Current Psychotherapies*, Peacock, Itaska, Illinois).
WACHTEL, P. L. (1977), *Psychoanalysis and Behavior Therapy: Toward an Integration* (Basic Books, New York).

Economic model

The economic model was Freud's attempt to generate a scientific psychology, based on the physical principle of the conservation of energy (Freud 1895). He postulated a law of conservation of psychic energy, and conceived of the mind as an apparatus or network through which energy flows from bodily stimulation to muscular discharge. In between, pathological blockages may give rise to the damming up of energy and its abnormal discharge through symptoms. Although the economic model remained to some extent a permanent feature of Freud's thought, it was partly superseded by his development of the *topographical model* and the *structural model*.

FREUD, S. (1895), 'Project for a scientific psychology' (*Standard Edition*, vol. 1, Hogarth Press, London).

See also *Metapsychology*.

Eco-system
See *Supra-system*.

Ego
One of the three *agencies* which compose the structure of the *psyche*. In the earliest psychoanalytic writings (prior to the *structural model* in 1923) the ego was viewed as the 'self' of everyday language.

The ego is the central agency of the personality, whose task it is to mediate the conflicting demands of the *superego*, the *id* and those of external reality. Freud (1923) described the ego as owing service 'to three masters and it is consequently menaced by three dangers: from the external world, from the libido of the id and from the severity of the superego'. The ego employs *censorship* to modify the instinctual *drives* and signals anxiety when the contents of the id threaten to overwhelm it, whilst its own *defence mechanisms* protect it from threat from the external world. Freud saw the task of analysis as the expansion of the scope and functioning of the ego at the expense of the id; although occasionally he seemed to see the antagonism between the two as being less sharp.

The ego has a range of functions, including observation, *reality testing*, rational thought and perception. It functions largely within the conscious domain except for its defence mechanisms which are unconscious processes. According to Freud, the ego develops gradually out of the id through having to adapt to the demands of external reality. It is built up through the *introjection* of part *objects* and *object relations*. Melanie Klein however, conceives of the ego as existing embryonically from birth and of being capable of distinguishing the self from the object. And so, from the beginning it uses primitive defence mechanisms such as *splitting* and *projection*.

Anna Freud (1937) emphasised the ego and its functions as a primary dimension of psychoanalytic study. This was a novel development, for as she points out (1937), whenever 'research was deflected from the id to the ego, it was felt that here was a beginning of apostasy from psychoanalysis as a whole'. Hartmann (1964) enormously expanded the Freudian theory of the ego and clarified many of its functions. The emphasis placed on the ego by Anna Freud, Hartmann and others became the primary emphasis in much psychoanalytic theory and practice and led to the development of *ego psychology* which has tried to broaden many psychoanalytic concepts and find links with other disciplines such as psychophysiology and child development studies.

FREUD, A. (1937), *The Ego and the Mechanisms of Defence* (Hogarth Press, London).
FREUD, S. (1921), 'Group psychology and the analysis of the ego' (*Standard Edition*, vol. 18. Hogarth Press, London).
FREUD, S. (1923), 'The ego and the id' (*Standard Edition*, vol. 19, Hogarth Press, London).
HARTMANN, H. (1964), *Essays on Ego-psychology* (International Universities Press, New York).

Ego alien

A term used in *ego psychology* to describe the unacceptability to the *ego* of the urges, demands or expectations of one of the other psychic *agencies* or of the outside world. The term is used interchangeably with the term ego dystonic. Part of the therapeutic process involves enabling the patient to convert those urges and expectations that hinder the ego's development from being *ego syntonic* to becoming ego alien. Only when they become ego alien is the patient motivated towards change.

Ego ideal

A structure within the *psyche* by which the *ego* measures its performance and achievements. It acts as a model for the ego and is the

performance goal to which the ego aspires. The term is often used interchangeably with that of ideal self, against which the actual self is measured. Much of the impetus for closing the gap between the ego and the ego ideal is derived from the demands of the *superego*. Originally, Freud (1923) saw the superego and the ego ideal as indistinguishable but in his later writings, the superego is viewed as the motivating agency by which the ego conforms more closely to the ego ideal. The ego ideal may be externalised and replaced by actual people – a revered or idealised teacher or leader for example, who then becomes the ego's model.

FREUD, S. (1923), 'The ego and the id' (*Standard Edition*, vol. 19, Hogarth Press, London).

Ego instincts

See *Drive*.

Ego psychology

A psychoanalytic theory which focuses upon the *ego* and its functions as the centre of psychoanalytic study rather than the *id* or the instincts or *drives*. Ego psychology developed out of Freud's (1923) study of the ego and its relationship to the id and was considerably developed and expanded by Anna Freud in her *Ego and the Mechanisms of Defence* (1937). Important early work was also contributed by Federn (1952). But the major proponents of ego psychology in its most developed form are Erikson, Hartmann, Kris and Lowenstein. Between them, these major figures in the psychoanalytic field have developed a concept of the ego which goes considerably further than Freud's theoretical framework and places ego psychology alongside *object relations* theory as one of the major departures from classical psychoanalytic theory. Important concepts include an emphasis on the autonomous functions of the ego, which are not influenced by unconscious drives, such as cognition, perception, attention, memory, planning and foresight, and on the synthetic role of the ego's desexualised, neutralised energy. The attention of ego psychologists is turned towards ego-initiated processes rather than to its enforced responses to the libidinal drives. The ego is seen primarily as enabling the regulation and adaptation of the personality to external reality. The therapeutic consequences of this emphasis on the ego's role has led to a realisation that important intrapsychic work can be accomplished without the prolonged analysis of the unconscious contents of the id. A concentration on *ego strengths* and on the adaptive potential of the ego have led to briefer treatments including the development of *crisis intervention*.

ERIKSON, E. H. (1968), *Identity: Youth and Crisis* (Faber & Faber, London).

FEDERN, P. (1952), *Ego Psychology and the Psychoses* (Basic Books, New York).

FREUD, A. (1937), *The Ego and the Mechanisms of Defence* (Hogarth Press, London).

FREUD, S. (1923), 'The ego and the id' (*Standard Edition*, vol. 19, Hogarth Press, London).

HARTMANN, H. (1958), *Ego Psychology and the Problem of Adaptation* (International Universities Press, New York).

HARTMANN, H. (1964), *Essays on Ego Psychology* (International Universities Press, New York).

HARTMANN, H. *et al.* (1964), 'Papers on psychoanalytic psychology' (*Psychological Issues*, vol. 4).

RAPAPORT, D. (1959), 'A historical survey of psychoanalytic ego psychology' (*Psychological Issues*, vol. 1, pp. 5-17).

Ego state

A term used in *transactional analysis* to describe a coherent system of feelings with its related set of behaviour patterns. Berne (1961) introduced the idea of a tripartite division of the personality into the three ego states of Parent (or Extereo Psyche), Adult (or Neo Psyche) and Child (or Archaeo Psyche). Although each division is influenced respectively by the psychoanalytic constructs of *superego*, *ego* and *id*, they are qualitatively different from them. They are dynamic and observable states and at any particular time the individual will be operating primarily from one or other of these three aspects of his or her personality. When a particular ego state is in executive control of the personality, it is described as 'cathected' (see *Cathexis*).

Berne (1966) defines the Parent ego state as a 'set of feelings, attitudes and behaviours which resemble those of a parental figure'. These include the individual's memories of what the *actual* Parent symbolised and his *parataxic* distortion of what he now *believes* the Parent symbolised for him. When this ego state is dominant, the individual operates in terms of what he perceives to be correct and appropriate behaviours as seen through the Parent. The Child ego state is defined by Berne (1966) as the 'feelings, attitudes and behaviours which are relics of the individual's childhood'. When the Child state dominates, the individual speaks, feels and thinks more or less as a child of approximately eight years old or younger. His behaviour is therefore impulsive and spontaneous and although this can lead to irrational and self-destructive consequences, transactional analysts tend to emphasise the autonomous and creative aspects of this ego state. The Adult ego state which emerges gradually over the years is defined by Berne (1966) as exhibiting 'three kinds of tendencies: personal attractiveness and responsiveness, objective data-processing and ethical responsibility'. Later descriptions emphasise the unemotional, decision-making, computing functions of the Adult state which realistically appraises the behaviour of Parent and Child. The first stage in therapy is to perform a *structural analysis* of the individual's ego states. To determine which ego state is cathected at any given point, a behavioural, social, historical and phenomenological diagnosis is undertaken and an *egogram* is constructed.

BERNE, E. (1961), *Transactional Analysis in Psychotherapy* (Grove Press, New York).

BERNE, E. (1966), *Principles of Group Treatment* (Oxford University Press, New York).

BERNE, E. (1977), *Intuition and Ego States*

(Harper & Row, San Francisco).
THOMSON, G. (1972), 'The identification of ego states' (*Transactional Analysis Journal*, vol. 2, pp. 196-211).

Ego strength
The extent to which the *ego* has libidinal energy freely available for it to use. This is dependent upon the amount of energy left over after its use by the ego in *defence mechanisms*. The less that is used for defences, the more strongly the ego discharges its functions of *reality testing*, cognition, perception and observation and the more is it able to cope with the demands of the other *agencies* and with the challenges of the external world.

Ego syntonic
A term used in *ego psychology* to describe the acceptability to the *ego* of the urges, demands or expectations of one of the other psychic *agencies* or of the outside world. In addition, Berne used the term in relation to *ego states* and asserted that behaviours may be syntonic with one ego state and dystonic with another. Those urges and demands which are acceptable to the ego are termed ego syntonic while those which are not and which therefore cause conflict are termed dystonic or *ego alien*.

Egogram
A biograph used in the early, structural analytic stage of *transactional analysis*. It indicates how much energy is being expended upon five subdivisions of the three *ego states*. These subdivisions consist of the Critical Parent, Nurturing Parent, Adult, Free Child and Adapted Child. These five energies are present to some degree in each person but the variation between them gives each individual a unique personality profile. This profile is illustrated by the egogram. It is hypothesised that an energy constancy exists, so that a high reading on some of these states will be compensated for by a low reading on others. A person's egogram remains fixed unless he consciously decides to change its balance. The egogram reflects the kind of person one is and

the types of problems which may be encountered. Egograms cannot be typed or be described as functional or dysfunctional since they are related to the personality need and aspirations of each individual. However, problems generally arise if a gross imbalance exists, with one ego state extremely high and another extremely low.

DUSAY, J. (1972), 'Egograms and the constancy hypothesis' (*Transactional Analysis Journal*, vol. 2, no. 3, July).
DUSAY, J. (1977), *Egograms* (Harper & Row, New York).

Eidetic psychotherapy
Literal Greek 'eidetikos', 'idos', meaning 'form', or 'image'. A method of psychotherapy which makes systematic use of the natural images of consciousness in the identification and resolution of psychological disturbance. The image or idetic is, according to Sheikh and Jordan (1981), a self-organising nucleus within the *psyche*. Each idetic has a visual core which is either the memory of an actual event in the past or an image from the *unconscious*. To this visual image is attached profound meaning and affect with the power to direct the personality either towards functional development or the production of *symptoms*. Idetics are thought of as being bi-polar, representing negative and positive elements. Psychological disturbance may result from the quasi-separation of the visual core of the image from its meaning and affect; fixation on the negative whole (see *Wholeness*) of the idetic; or *repression* of a significant aspect of the image's meaning.

Building on Allport's (1924) early work, Ahsen (1965, 1968, 1977) developed idetic psychotherapy into a fully worked out approach to therapeutic change. Ahsen suggests that the idetic image has both a genetic and a developmental origin. The former represents the individual's genetically endowed tendency towards wholeness; the latter, all those significant experiences which leave residual core images and which later help or hinder development. The aim of therapy is to restore the lost connections between the image and its affect and meaning; shift the individual's attention to the neglected pole of the image (and especially to the positive end); and to uncover repressed idetics which can contribute to growth and development. Ahsen's approach is underpinned by a *holism* which views the idetic as a unifying potential within the personality and which postulates the need for a continuous dialectic between forces of *equilibrium* and forces of change. Ahsen's ideas have been incorporated into other methods of psychotherapy – for example, Lazarus's *multi-modal* approach, and they have much in common with other holistic and *humanistic* approaches. Therapy is conducted both with individuals and in groups.

AHSEN, A. (1965), *Idetic Psychotherapy: A Short Introduction* (Nai Mat Booat, Lahore, Pakistan).
AHSEN, A. (1968), *Basic Concepts in Eidetic Psychotherapy* (Random House, New York).
AHSEN, A. (1977), *Psycheye: Self Analytic Consciousness* (Random House, New York).
ALLPORT, G. W. (1924), 'Idetic imagery' (*Brit. J. of Psychology* vol. 15, pp. 99-120).
SHEIKH, A. A. and JORDAN, C. S. (1981), 'Eidetic psychotherapy' (in Corsini, R. J. (ed.), *Handbook of Innovative Psychotherapies*, Wiley, New York).

See also *Focusing, Guided fantasy, Imagery.*

Eigenwelt
Literal German meaning 'own world'. The term is used in *existential* approaches to psychotherapy to describe the individual's awareness of the self, so as to understand the subjective meaning of the external world for the self. It embraces all that goes to make up a human being's relationship with his or her self. Binswanger uses the term, along with *Mitwelt* and *Umwelt*, to describe the three modes or world regions of *Dasein*.

Electra complex
A term introduced by Jung (1913) to denote the feminine equivalent of the *Oedipus complex*. In Greek mythology, Electra took vengeance

on her mother Clytemnestra for murdering her husband Agamemnon and thus robbing Electra of her beloved father. Jung suggested that a conflict between love and hate existed for the little girl in relation to her parents which paralleled the conflict for the little boy. Freud (1931), however, rejected the term and asserted that the feminine experience was not analogous to the male one. The term is not much used, either in the psychoanalytic literature or generally in the field of psychotherapy.

FREUD, S. (1931), 'Female sexuality', (*Standard Edition*, vol. 21, Hogarth Press, London).
JUNG, C. G. (1913), 'The theory of psychoanalysis' (in *Freud and Psychoanalysis, Collected Works*, vol. 4, Routledge & Kegan Paul, London).

Element
Term used by Kelly to describe the people, things or events which are interpreted and controlled by a person's system of *constructs*. An element is equivalent to an *object*, the term used to describe the same phenomenon in psychoanalytic theory. Elements which fall within a construct's *range of convenience* are controlled by it, whilst those which fall outside are not. To the extent that a construct is permeable, new elements will be admitted into its sphere of control. A subordinate construct acts as an element in the *context* of one which is superordinate.

KELLY, G. A. (1955), *The Psychology of Personal Constructs* (W. W. Norton, New York).
KELLY, G. A. (1963), *A Theory of Personality* (W. W. Norton, New York).

Emergence
See *Pole.*

Emotional flooding approaches
A group of therapies identified by Olson (1976) and Prochaska (1979) which all rely on their power to stimulate intense emotional experiences in the patient and produce *catharsis*. Whilst they differ in their theoretical

rationale and the techniques used, they share the common assumption that emotional and psychological disorders can best be helped by encouraging the direct release of blocked emotions in the therapeutic session. Emotional flooding therapies include *Reichian therapy*; *bio-energetics*; *primal therapy*; *flooding*; and *implosion*.

OLSON, P. (1976), *Emotional Flooding* (Human Sciences Press, New York).
PROCHASKA, J. O. (1979), *Systems of Psychotherapy* (Dorsey Press, Homewood, Ill.).

Empathy

Literal Greek meaning 'to suffer with' or 'alongside'. Empathy is probably the most important of the *core conditions* described by Rogers as essential factors in all psychotherapeutic relationships. The term is associated particularly with Rogers's *client-centred therapy* where it is usually described as 'accurate empathy'. In 1979, Rogers described empathy as the ability of a person to perceive the situation of another as if it were his own, without ever losing the 'as if' quality of the perception. It involves an active process of trying to enter the perceptual world of another as accurately and sensitively as possible in order to understand the other's thoughts, feelings and behaviour from his point of view. It involves adopting an accepting and non-judgmental attitude to the client and to his experiences, enabling the confirmation and validation of his self, which in turn enables his negative self-concept to change. Rogers and Truax (1967) describe empathy as 'the ability of the therapist accurately and sensitively to understand experiences and feelings and their meaning to the client during the moment to moment encounter of psychotherapy'.

Barrett-Leonard (1981) has described the three stages involved in empathic interaction: the empathic resonance by person A in response to person B; A's attempt to *convey* his responsive understanding to B; and B's reception of A's empathic response. The process can continue over time, with stage one remaining the core feature. Raskin (1974) has showed that therapists from a wide variety of contrasting schools rank empathy among the highest qualities which a therapist can possess. Levels of accurate empathy have been measured and found by Bergin and Strupp (1972) to be correlated with a high degree of client self-exploration and with a high degree of confidence in interpersonal relations on the part of the therapist (Bergin and Solomon 1970).

Aspry (1972) and others have shown that empathy can be taught and that it is most successfully taught within an empathic climate.

Despite the complexity of the research issues involved, there seems to have been a resurgence in confidence in the correlation between high levels of therapist empathy and positive therapeutic outcome. Rogers (1975) has clarified the distinction between empathy and *identification* by noting the essential 'as if' quality of the therapist's efforts to understand the patient's world. Curtis (1981) has shown that an inverse relationship exists between the amount of therapist *self-disclosure* and the perceptions of his empathy on the part of the client. Empathy remains one of the most studied relationship variables that occur in the client-therapist transaction and a large body of research is suggestive of its major contribution to positive outcome in therapy.

ASPRY, D. (1972), *Toward a Technology for Humanizing Education* (Research Press, Champaign, Ill.).
BARRETT-LEONARD, G. T. (1981), 'The empathy cycle: refinement of a nuclear concept' (*Journal of Counseling Psychology*, vol. 28, pp. 91-100).
BERGIN, A. E. and SOLOMON, S. (1970), 'Personality and performance correlates of empathic understanding in psychotherapy' (in Hart, J. T. and Tomlinson, T. M. (eds), *New Directions in Client Centred Therapy*, Houghton Mifflin, Boston).
BERGIN, A. E. and STRUPP, H. H. (1972), *Changing Frontiers in the Science of Psychotherapy* (Aldine-Atherton, Chicago).

CURTIS, J. (1981), 'Effect of therapist self disclosure on patients' impressions of empathy, competence and trust' (*Psychological Reports*, vol. 48, pp. 127-36).

MITCHELL, K. M. *et al.* 'A re-appraisal of the therapeutic effectiveness of accurate empathy, non-possessive warmth and genuineness' (in Gurman, A. and Razin, A., *Effective Psychotherapy*, Pergamon, New York).

KATZ, R. L. (1963), *Empathy* (Collier Macmillan, London).

RASKIN, N. J. (1974), 'Studies of psychotherapeutic orientation: ideology and practise' (*Research Monograph One*, American Academy of Psychotherapists, Florida).

ROGERS, C. R. (1975), 'Empathic: an unappreciated way of being' (*The Counseling Psychologist*, vol. 3, pp. 2-10).

ROGERS, C. R. and TRUAX, C. B. (1967), 'The therapeutic conditions antecedent to change: a theoretical view' (in Rogers, C. R. (ed.), *The Therapeutic Relationship and its Impact: A Study of Psychotherapy with Schizophrenics*, University of Wisconsin Press, Madison).

Empty nest syndrome

Term used to describe the sense of loss accompanying the post-parenthood phase of the life cycle when children have left home. A relatively new phenomenon, it is often associated with severe depression in one or both parents, brought about by the juxtaposition of the parents' mid-life crisis, role loss, especially for the mother, and the absence of children for use in *detouring* conflict within the marital *sub-system*. The use of *family therapy*, *marital therapy* and *rational emotive therapy* can successfully alleviate problems associated with this stage.

ROBERTS, C. L. and LEWIS, R. A. (1981), 'The empty nest syndrome' (in Howells, J. G. (ed.), *Modern Perspectives in the Psychiatry of Middle Age*, Brunner/Mazel, New York).

Enactment

The dramatic interpretation of a problem or conflict by the patient, family or members of a group. Enactment of a present or projected problem is sometimes distinguished from re-enactment of a past difficulty but on the whole the terms are used interchangeably. Enactment is used as a major tool in *psychodrama* and in many *action techniques*. A scene is portrayed which depicts interpersonal tension or intrapsychic conflict, using some type of active and often non-verbal medium. In a group work setting, members of the group can be used to enact an individual's problem situation, becoming his *auxiliary ego* and using *role play* and *simulation* to portray a sequence of events occurring between the individual's significant others. Enactment can also be used to portray how the individual *would like* a situation to be resolved. It can be used in *family therapy* for the same purposes, family members playing themselves or each other. Minuchin and Fishman (1981) describe enactment in family therapy as 'the technique by which the therapist asks the family to dance in his presence'. Asking the individual to 'show' rather than 'talk about' the problem enables the therapist to gain a much clearer picture of the dimensions of the difficulty. The therapist can use enactment in any of the *systemic therapies* to help bring about the treatment goals; mother can be helped to control her children right now, a couple to talk to each other attentively, a teenager to negotiate more privileges from his parents, etc. As such, enacting the problem and its solution is a major tool in the systemic therapies. The use of physical movement and expression also increases the involvement of the patient, promoting his self-awareness and the impact of interpersonal sequences and intrapsychic experience on himself and others is increased. *Family sculpting* and *family choreography* are particular types of enactment.

MINUCHIN, S. and FISHMAN, H. C. (1981), *Family Therapy Techniques* (Harvard University Press, Cambridge, Mass.).

Enantiodromia

The tendency for everything to move towards its opposite. The term is used by Jung to describe the dynamic relationship between pairs of opposites such as *progress* and *regres-*

sion; consciousness and *unconsciousness*; extroversion and introversion (see *Psychological types*). When opposites combine or synthesise, not only is *libido* generated, but the resultant 'third' product will display characteristics different from those of the original components. This is a way of describing what happens in psychological development. The process is not static: the 'third' product will generate its own opposite, and so on. In the process, each 'pole' is regulated by the other and the greater the tension and interconnectedness within the pair, the greater the energy that is generated.

JUNG, C. G. (1953), *Two Essays on Analytical Psychology* (Routledge & Kegan Paul, London).

Encounter

Term used in *humanistic psychology*, *client-centred therapy*, the *human potential movement* and *existential* approaches, to describe a creative, present-centred meeting between persons, involving a deep level of sharing, mutual participation and reciprocity. Moreno (1914) appears to be the first to have used the term in this sense: he describes the encounter between two persons as 'a meeting of two: eye to eye, face to face. And when you are near I will tear your eyes out and place them instead of mine, and you will tear my eyes out and place them instead of yours. Then I will look at you with your eyes and you will look at me with mine.' Moreno describes the term as being derived from the French 'rencontre' and the German 'Begegnung' and describes it as a meeting on the most intensive level of experience: 'It is an intuitive reversal of roles, a realization of the self through the other; it is identity, the rare, unforgotten experience of total reciprocity' (Moreno 1959).

FROMM-REICHMANN, F. and MORENO, J. L. (1959), *Philosophy of the Third Psychiatric Revolution* (New York).
MORENO, J. L. (1914), quoted in Johnson, P. (1959), *The Psychology of Religion* (New York).

Encounter groups

The encounter group provides a highly eclectic range of personal growth experiences. Encounter groups developed as part of the *human potential movement* during the 1960s, being influenced by the growth of *T-group training* and other sensitivity training models. An encounter group provides an intensive group experience which is designed to put group members into closer touch with themselves and with each other. The group leader may use a range of techniques drawn from *psychodrama*, *Gestalt*, etc., to enable members to relate to each other with more openness and honesty and to develop self-awareness and self-responsibility. *Action techniques* and non-verbal encounters are more typical of encounter group work than prolonged verbal reflections. The focus is on the personal growth of individual members rather than on the *group process*.

The encounter movement espouses a set of fairly coherent values, including a belief in *holism*; a belief that emotional health depends on an individual being honest and open in his significant relationships and that an individual has the power to choose what happens to him, both inside and outside the group, and that he, and not the group leader or any other group member, is responsible for what happens to him. Encounter group leaders stress that encounter is a way of life and not simply a therapeutic technique.

Several practitioners have been responsible for developing the basic format of encounter group work, probably the most influential being William Schultz (1975), whose practice and writing has significantly shaped the movement. Schultz advocates a group size of between eight to fifteen members, meeting several times over a period of four or five days in a residential setting. In addition, the work of Carl Rogers (1970) on basic encounter and the 'intensive group experience', the *marathon* models of encounter developed by Bach (1966), Stoller (1972) and Mintz (1971) and the confrontational leaderless groups developed at Synonon, one of the original *therapeutic communities*, have all contributed to the encounter group culture. A great deal of controversy occurred during the 1960s about the possible dangers of encounter groups. The lack of screening for gross mental disturbance, the highly confrontational style of some group leaders in working with resistance and the lack of therapeutic follow-up for members who had in some cases sustained severe emotional trauma, all contributed to the concern. The work of Yalom and his associates and other researchers who have investigated encounter group casualties is reviewed by Hogan (1979). More recently Kaplan (1982) has undertaken a detailed review of the injurious effects of encounter groups and suggests that these stem primarily from a disconnection between the group leader and one of the group members. This disconnection results from the leader *splitting* and disowning his own anxieties and disabilities, *projecting* them into the group member and then attacking and rejecting them in that person.

BACH, G. R. (1966), 'The marathon group: intensive practise of intimate interaction' (*Psychological Reports*, vol. 18, pp. 995-1002).

BURTON, A. (ed.) (1969), *The Theory and Practice of Encounter Groups* (Jossey-Bass, San Francisco).

HOGAN, D. B. (1979), *The Regulation of Psychotherapists* (Ballinger, New York).

KAPLAN, R. E. (1982), 'The dynamics of injury in encounter groups' (*Int. J. of Group Psychotherapy*, vol. 32, pp. 163-87).

LIEBERMAN, M. A. *et al.* (1973), *Encounter Groups: First Facts* (Basic Books, New York).

MINTZ, E. E. (1971), *Marathon Groups: Reality and Symbol* (Appleton-Century-Crofts, New York).

MORENO, J. L. (1969), 'The Viennese origins of the encounter movement' (*Group Psychotherapy*, vol. 22).

ROGERS, C. R. (1970), *Carl Rogers on Encounter Groups* (Penguin, Harmondsworth).

SCHULTZ, W. C. (1975), *Elements of Encounter* (Bantam Books, New York).

STOLLER, F. H. (1972), 'Marathon groups: toward a conceptual model' (in Solomon, L. N. and Berzon, B. (eds), *New Perspectives on Encounter Groups*, Jossey-Bass, San Francisco).

Enmeshed

Term used by Minuchin (1974) to describe a type of family *system* which is characterised by a diffuse *boundary*. The roles and functions of family members are not well defined and the transactional style of the system tends towards fusion. The lack of *sub-system differentiation* discourages autonomy and growth in individuals, and enmeshment which occurs across generational sub-systems (mother-maternal grandmother; father-daughter, etc.) produces the type of pathological triad which Haley (1967) and others have noted as particularly dysfunctional. Enmeshment, however, usually describes a relative form of interaction and is likely to occur in different degrees at different points in the life cycle. For example, mother and young child are likely to be functionally enmeshed temporarily at the 'expense' of father – but later the situation will reverse to leave mother less proximal and father more engaged. Enmeshment is only dysfunctional if it becomes inflexible and prevents change, growth and adaptation over a period of time.

HALEY, J. (1967), 'Toward a theory of pathological systems' (in Watzlawick, P. and Weakland, J. (eds), 1977, *The International View*, W. W. Norton, New York).

MINUCHIN, S. (1974), *Families and Family Therapy* (Tavistock, London).

See also *Cohesion, Differentiation, Disengaged, Symbiosis.*

Entropy

The disorganisation and lack of pattern or structure in a *system*. Used in contrast to *negentropy*, the term indicates the tendency of systems to degenerate into *runaway* and to move towards what Bateson (1972) calls 'mixedness and muddle'. Applied to natural systems such as the family, the term indicates the family's tendency to degenerate into chaos unless it can make use of *negative feedback* and develop rules for conducting its own processes and developing its own structure. In a *closed system*, changes in entropy always lead to runaway and therefore destruction. In an *open system*, entropy can be delayed or offset both by using negative feedback and by processing *positive feedback* in such a way that new energy and information is transformed and redistributed to the environment.

BATESON, G. (1972), *Steps to an Ecology of Mind* (Granada, London).

Envy

A central concept in *Kleinian* theory. *Life instincts* and *death instincts* are seen as being inherent, so that the *object* related to may attract both love and hate. Early in development the infant may experience hate towards his good objects. This initial life problem is resolved at first by the methods employed in the *paranoid-schizoid position*. However the merger of a primary kind of hate into a love relation remains a possibility throughout life and takes the form of hating the good object simply for its goodness. Rosenfeld (1965) describes schizophrenic states as deriving from prolonged early states of envy, the schizophrenic suffering from a particularly intense confusion between love and hate.

KLEIN, M. (1957) 'Envy and gratitude' (in *The Writings of Melanie Klein*, vol. 3).
ROSENFELD, H. A. (1965), *Psychotic States* (Hogarth Press, London).

Epigenesis

The capacity for development and growth which resides in every human being from before birth. The term is particularly associated with E. H. Erikson's work on the *stages of development* of the life cycle. Erikson suggested that the formation of the *ego* and the consequent development of identity continues throughout life and can be clearly seen to occur within eight distinct phases, spanning the individual's existence from birth to death. Different aspects of the personality become highlighted during each phase and sociocultural factors are viewed as being as important as *intrapsychic* ones in shaping the course of development. The concept corrects an imbalance that prevails in some approaches to psychoanalytic theory in which psychic development occurring during infancy is

viewed as determining the course of later development.

ERIKSON, E. H. (1950), *Childhood and Society* (Penguin, Harmondsworth).
ERIKSON, E. H. (1968), *Identity, Youth and Crisis* (W. W. Norton, New York).

Epistemology

Literal Greek 'episteme', meaning knowledge. The branch of philosophy concerned with the nature and scope of knowledge. Epistemology is concerned with theories about the method or grounds of knowledge. It is seen to be necessary when doubts arise as to how much of what we think we know of the world around us is really true, and how much is invention, or indeed the development of doubts about whether we have *any* knowledge of the world as it really is. Epistemology is not concerned with the psychology of claims to knowledge, nor with their history, nor with the interest served by them. It is concerned with grounds for such claims and in particular whether there are grounds sufficient to warrant a claim to knowledge in certain types of context. A belief may be true and yet a claim to knowledge unwarranted, if good and sufficient reasons for believing it to be true are lacking. Hence the concern with the different types of grounds that warrant claims to knowledge.

Epistemology is thus a way of conceptually organising the world and it gives rise to theories, paradigms, *models* and *metaphors* within whatever particular field of enquiry is under discussion. Approaches which differ sharply in their theoretical framework and methods may yet share the same undergirding epistemology. An epistemology may shift and change in what Kuhn (1962) has described as a series of discontinuous leaps. One such leap within psychotherapy was the leap to *holism* upon which the *humanistic* approaches are predicated. The term has been made popular in the psychotherapeutic field by Bateson (1973, 1979) who used it first in relation to anthropology and the field of *communication* studies. From there it has been adopted by the *systemic* theorists (e.g. Keeney 1982, 1983,

117

Dell 1982, and others) to describe the shift made from one way of thinking to another. As well as building upon holistic ideas of synthesis and non-reductionism, systemic epistemology moves from an interest and concentration upon substance (as in Newtonian physics) to an interest and concentration upon pattern and form (as in cybernetics) and further, as Dell (1982) points out, into order through fluctuation and coherence as contrasted with simple *homeostasis*.

In some respects, the term epistemology has almost become coterminous with the idea of the system view, because of the ubiquity of its current usage. Piaget (1971), for example, pointed out in his genetic epistemology that all the modern sciences, both natural and social, deal with organised totalities or 'systems'. However, in the view of Bateson and other systemic and communication theorists, all psychotherapeutic approaches, beyond the systemic approach, continue to subscribe to the old 'Newtonian' epistemology, whilst the systemic epistemology, by contrast, cuts across an ever-wider range of disciplines and includes, as Capra (1982) and others point out, physics and the natural sciences, so that the systemic therapies are linked into a far wider world of thought and conceptual development. Humanistic psychologists would certainly argue however that their own epistemology of holism is as crucially different from *psychoanalysis* and *behaviourism* as the communication theorists' cybernetic-systemic model is from the non-systemic approaches.

AYER, A. J. (1956), *The Problem of Knowledge* (Penguin, Harmondsworth).

BATESON, G. (1973), *Steps to an Ecology of Mind* (Granada, London).

BATESON, G. (1979), *Mind and Nature: A Necessary Unity* (Dutton, New York).

CAPRA, F. (1982), *The Turning Point* (Wildwood House, London).

DELL, P. (1982), 'In search of truth: on the way to clinical epistemology' (*Family Process*, vol. 21, pp. 407-14).

HAMLYN, D. W. (1970), *The Theory of Knowledge* (Macmillan, London).

KEENEY, B. (1982), 'What is an epistemology of family therapy?' (*Family Process*, vol. 21, pp. 153-68).

KEENEY, B. (1983), *Aesthetics of Change* (Guilford Press, New York).

KUHN, T. (1962), *The Structure of Scientific Revolutions* (University of Chicago Press, Chicago).

PIAGET, J. (1971), *Genetic Epistemology* (W. W. Norton, New York).

PRIGOGINE, I. (1980), *From Being to Becoming* (Freeman, San Francisco).

DE SHAZER, S. (1982), 'Some conceptual distinctions are more useful than others' (*Family Process*, vol. 21, pp. 71-83).

SPENCER-BROWN, G. (1979), *Laws of Form* (Allen & Unwin, London).

Equifinality

The fact that in living systems, the same result can arise from different initial conditions. In other words, objectives can be achieved using varying inputs and in different ways, because it is the ongoing *process* occurring in the system that determines its consequences. As Watzlawick *et al.* (1968) point out, 'If the equifinal behavior of open systems is based on their independence of initial conditions, then not only may different initial conditions yield the same final result, but different results may be produced by the same "causes".' The principle of equifinality has led to the emphasis in the *systemic* therapies on the importance of current interaction, *phenotypic* assessment and the *a-historical* approach rather than on an examination of past behaviour and its linear causal relationship to the present.

WATZLAWICK, P. *et al.* (1968), *Pragmatics of Human Communication* (W. W. Norton, New York).

See also *Circular causality*.

Equilibrium

A state of balance. The tendency to reduce tension to as low a level as possible which is brought about in living *systems* by the process of *homeostasis*. The term is usually reserved for the way in which basic organic and mechanical systems (i.e. relatively *closed systems*) create a state of internal balance within their structures but it is also used as a loose equivalent to homeostasis, rather than simply describing the product of it. The concept of balance is to be found in many theories of personality. Freud's concept of energy balance, for example, exemplifies his view that there is a tendency within the *psyche* to reduce tension as far as possible. In Lewin's *field theory*, equilibrium is understood as operating within the individual and within the individual's psychological field. The term implies stillness and stasis, the state of balance being determined by the initial conditions of the system.

See also *Drive, Equifinality, Feedback, Morphogenesis, Morphostasis*.

Erikson, Erik Homburger (1902-1979)

Born in Denmark, Erikson's parents separated before his birth and he went with his mother to live in Karlsruhe, Germany, where she remarried. Erikson first studied art at Karlsruhe, continuing his studies at Munich and then in Florence. His career as an art teacher was broadened out by an invitation to help teach the children of patients being analysed by Sigmund and Anna Freud in Vienna. He entered analysis with Anna Freud and completed his analytic training at the Vienna Psychoanalytic Institute in 1933. Having left Germany during the rise of the Nazi regime, Erikson came into contact with anthropologists at Harvard University where he worked with Gregory Bateson and Margaret Mead as well as with the psychologists Kurt Lewin and Henry Murray. In 1939 he went to California where he continued his analytic work with children and undertook research into children's play. During this period he became deeply interested in the child-rearing practices and cultural patterns of other social and racial groups such as the Yurok Indians, interests which he was to pursue both in other parts of the USA and, during the 1960s, on the Indian subcontinent. His contributions to psychoanalytic theory have been extensive and,

because of the breadth of his interests, he has been able to integrate ideas and insights from the different fields of *psychoanalysis*, anthropology and psychology. The concepts for which he is best remembered include his theory of *epigenesis*; the idea of a continuing exploration of identity throughout the life cycle (see *Stages of development*) and the essential influence of social and cultural factors on the formation of the *ego*. He also developed an interest in applying the insights of psychoanalysis to the lives of great historical figures and he wrote psychological biographies of Luther and Gandhi. Erikson pursued a lifelong interest in underprivileged and impoverished children and the Erikson Institute for Early Childhood Education was established in Chicago to help train teachers for work in inner-city and poor rural areas.

See also *Stages of development, Ego psychology*.

Erogenous zone

Areas of the body which act as seats of sexual excitement, principally the oral, anal and genital areas. Freud (1905) introduced the idea that the oral, anal and genital orifices provided the source of special sensations which created psychic energy (*libido*). He suggested that the activities that occur around these orifices, such as sucking, biting, expulsion and retention, all have a perverse sexual function. The *reductionism* and ubiquity of this explanation has been much criticised, although Kline (1972) suggests that the lack of empirical evidence for the erotic nature of these zones may be due to the methodological problems involved in researching the issue.

FREUD, S. (1905), 'Three essays on the theory of sexuality' (*Standard Edition*, vol. 17, Hogarth Press, London).
KLINE, P. (1972), *Fact and Fantasy in Freudian Theory* (Methuen, London).

Est

An acronym for Erhard Seminar Training and Latin for 'is', Est is a form of psychological training developed by Wernar Erhard in 1971. The Est standard training is approximately sixty hours long and is usually presented on two successive weekends. In addition, there are pre-, mid- and post-training seminars of about three and a half hours long which occur during the evenings before, during and after the training weekends. About 250 participants take part in the training at any one weekend. The training format includes lectures by the trainer; 'processes' or guided experiences which trainees participate in with closed eyes; and sharing, when trainees communicate their experiences to the trainer and/or the class. Four principal topics are addressed during the training: belief, experience, reality and self. The trainer makes use of a charismatic style and *social influence* techniques designed to engage the compliance of trainees. *Confrontation* is used systematically to get trainees to examine the criteria they use to determine what is real in their lives. On the final day, the trainer gives a six-hour discourse which is entitled 'Anatomy of the Mind' and is designed to move the trainees towards 'recontextualisation' and the goal of training which Erhard describes as 'getting it'. 'At the end of this process . . . trainees experience a transformation – a shift in the *nature* of experiencing – from thinking that things (the *contents* of experience) determine and define what one experiences (mind) to experiencing self as the context, or source of the *way* they experience' (Erhard and Gioscia, 1979).

The contextual shift of the trainees' perception of reality achieved in Est training is akin to *reframing* techniques used in *strategic therapy*. Many criticisms have been made of Est training: its severe confrontational style, its ability to humiliate and degrade trainees and the high fees that are charged. Finkelstein *et al.* (1982), however, found that the majority of trainees were satisfied with the training and they suggested that *catharsis* is probably an important ingredient of its efficacy.

ERHARD, W. and GIOSCIA, V. (1979), 'Est: communication in a context of compassion' (in Masserman, J., *Current Psychiatric Therapies*, vol. 18, Grune & Stratton, New York).

FENWICK, S. (1976), *Getting It: The Psychology of Est* (Lippincott, New York).
FINKELSTEIN, P. *et al.* (1982), 'Large group awareness training' (*Annual Review of Psychology*, vol. 5, pp. 15-39).
RHINEHART, L. (1976), *The Book of Est* (Holt, Rinehart & Winston, New York).

Ethics

The values and norms which guide the psychotherapist in the exercise of his or her professional duties to the patient, to society, to the profession and to him or her self. Ethical problems abound in psychotherapy and they have become more complex with the increased diversity of methods. Various codes of practice have been established by professional associations and institutes, which attempt to offer guidelines for the practitioner and some protection for the patient, but in Britain, the *regulation* of psychotherapists and hence their ethical practice remains uncontrolled by law. From a broad perspective, the whole practice of psychotherapy has been criticised as unethical *per se* by writers such as Fourcault, Szasz, Cooper and the radical therapists, because, as they would see it, psychotherapy has an inherent tendency to act as a normalising and therefore repressive agent of society. These writers are particularly critical of the way in which the individual is measured against an artificial, societal norm of mental health in the *diagnosis* of pathology, often with assumptions derived from the *medical model* which may be inappropriate to emotional, psychological and situational difficulties.

Ethical problems can be summarised under five headings and include those that arise from the personality, skill and *competence* of the therapist; the relationship between the therapist and the patient; the method of psychotherapy and the techniques used; the type of patient being treated and the freedom with which he is able to give his informed consent to treatment and the demands made by third parties on the therapeutic process such as the therapist's *agency* or the referrer of the case.

First, the *therapist variable*. The contributions to the therapeutic process made by the therapist include his personality make-up, his own varying emotional needs, his knowledge base, technical skill and therapeutic *experience*, all of which contribute to his competency. By recognising the importance of *training*, there is a recognition that it is unethical to practise psychotherapy with insufficient knowledge, skill or experience. By providing training, the patient is protected to some extent from the therapist's deficits in these areas, although, by the same token, he must necessarily be exposed to the efforts of trainee psycho-therapists if the latter are to increase in competence. Other aspects of the therapist variable are more difficult to evaluate. The personality of the therapist has been found to be a critical factor in some studies of patient *deterioration* but assessing the *psychonoxious* effects of personality is much harder to achieve than assessing technical skill and knowledge.

Second, the therapeutic relationship, involving the meshing together of the needs, strengths and weaknesses of therapist and patient, provides many areas of ethical difficulty. Apart from blatant, conscious dis-honesty or immoral behaviour, the therapist's *counter transference* may lead him or her to exploit the patient on an *unconscious* level. The need to be helpful, avoid patient hostility, be nurturant, controlling, potent, rescue victims, or simply 'be successful' may all lead the therapist to create patient dependency, enter into *collusions* or act out his or her sexual attraction or punitive impulses towards the patient. However, whilst erotic contact between therapist and patient is always inappropriate and unethical (with the possible exception of sexual surrogates in *sex therapy*), non-erotic touching, as Holroyd and Brodsky (1977) point out, is often highly beneficial to the patient and to the relationship and it may not always be easy to draw a clear boundary between these very different ways of relating. Sex therapy creates particular ethical dilemmas in this respect with its use of surrogates in some cases, for people present-ing without partners and the need for the therapist to be relatively free from sexual

conflicts, guilt and competitiveness. Where fee paying is involved, the therapist may uncon-sciously link the size of the fee to his feeling of self-worth leading to financial exploitation. Value conflicts between patient and therapist may get subsumed within the therapist's views of the patient's psychopathology rather than confronted in a straightforward way. Tsoi-hoshmund (1976) has drawn attention to the way in which changing social values (for example, the development of feminism) need to be taken account of in practice. The power imbalance between patient and therapist may lead the therapist to use techniques for helping psychological disturbance, to attack inappro-priately the patient's differing and threatening value system. Many have suggested too (e.g. Kovel 1982) that the therapist's own values must be internally coherent and consistent with the therapy that he or she is practising.

Third, the method of psychotherapy and the techniques used may involve difficult ethical decisions, revolving around a tension between the 'ends' and 'means' of therapy. Directive therapies such as *behaviour therapy, behaviour modification, strategic therapy, provocative therapy, rational emotive therapy*, etc., are more specific and pro-active in their techniques and they are therefore more obviously open to scrutiny for potential abuse. *Non-directive* therapies employ more reactive techniques but the fact that *social influence* operates subtly in all thera-peutic relationships means that *psychoanalysis, client-centred therapy* and the *humanistic* therapies generally are also liable to misuse of their techniques. Premature in-depth *inter-pretations* or pressure to *self-disclose*, for example, may be as intrusive and unacceptable as many more obviously intrusive directive techniques. In the behavioural therapies, the use of coercion, *punishment*, and *aversive therapy* are very obviously open to abuse. Suggestions for the protection of the patient receiving these interventions include his active participation in the planning of treatment and use of *contracts*, his choice of or acceptance of the treatment *goals*, the selection by the therapist of the least punitive, coercive and intrusive treatment intervention compatible

121

with achieving these goals and the provision of alternative interventions if the patient is unwilling to participate. The exercise of covert control in strategic therapy and the use of non-compliance-based techniques such as *symptom prescription, paradox* and the *therapeutic double bind* appears to flout most agreed ethical norms of patient participation and self-determination and can perhaps only be justified on the grounds that they can successfully relieve grossly dysfunctional and hence painful situations that have been unresponsive to other methods.

Properly validated *outcome* research is in itself an ethical imperative, when deciding on the use of particular methods and techniques. As Bergin (1982) points out, 'It is one of the anomalies of the behavioral and psychiatric sciences that methods of intervention can still be invented, used and paid for by the public without a shred of standard empirical evidence to demonstrate efficacy and absence of harmful effects. This kind of proliferation is a professional scandal.' Outcome research has amply demonstrated the existence of deterioration as a result of psychotherapy in some cases and it remains as valid an expectation as always for the clinician to be able to select his method and intervention techniques so as to at least do the sick no harm. This is a particularly important requirement for the newer approaches and those where there is little preliminary screening of patients and/or where the level of *confrontation* and therefore of stress, may be high – in for example, *encounter groups, marathon group therapy* and *Est.*

Fourth, the vulnerability or special circumstances of some patients makes informed consent harder to achieve and they thus require special ethical sensitivity. Children's rights, for example, in *conciliation* work and *family therapy* as well as in *child analysis* and *child psychotherapy*, need particular attention, especially when very young children are involved. They may need protection from the frightening emotions of their parents and opportunities to withdraw or they may need support and help in making their voice heard.

Irreconcilable conflicts may arise between the needs of adolescents and parents in family treatment or between the needs of children and the needs of an elderly grandparent, whereby one or other apparently has to leave the home. The vulnerability of several weak members within the unit may make highly conflicting demands on the therapist. Care needs to be taken with the mentally handicapped and the imprisoned that they are not unwittingly coerced into participating in a *token economy* or other treatment regime because there seems to be no alternative. Roth *et al.* (1977) discuss some of the difficulties of gaining informed consent and suggest that many judgments of patient competency reflect social considerations and societal biases. Gaining informed consent from any patient group for the conduct of *process* and *outcome* research and for the use of clinical material (whether written or audio visual) for teaching or research purposes requires the development of rigorous standards of behaviour and practice.

Fifth, the demands of third parties such as a court, the agency personnel, the referrer or the patient's relatives may lead to breaches of confidentiality. Information exchange is made easier with the growth of computers and data banks and therefore requires even more stringent consideration. Confidentiality is not an absolute, but in most circumstances the patient has a right to expect that the confidences he has entrusted to the therapist will not be disclosed nor used by him for any other purpose without his informed consent. When using clinical material for teaching (especially audio visual material) it needs to be properly disguised. Confidentiality in group work or family therapy needs full discussion and clear agreements at the outset of treatment as to who will be made party to the confidences shared. Recent legislation allowing clients of certain statutory agencies to have access to their files places extra responsibilities upon therapists working in these agencies to ensure that what is on the file is in the client's best interests.

Finally, the therapist has an ethical duty to himself, to prevent *burn out* and to ensure his continuing competence through ongoing education and professional stimulation. He also has the duty to protect his family or close emotional *network* from damaging incursions from his professional life.

BERGIN, A. E. (1982), 'Sixtyfour therapies – but who will evaluate them?' (*Contemporary Psychology*, vol. 27, pp. 685-6).
BOLTON, N. (ed.) (1979), *Philosophical Problems in Psychology* (Methuen, London).
COREY, G. *et al.* (1979), *Professional and Ethical Issues in Counseling and Psychotherapy* (Brooks-Cole Publishing, Monterey, Calif.).
ERIKSON, R. C. (1977), 'Walden III: toward an ethics of changing behavior' (*J. of Religion and Health*, vol. 16, pp. 7-14).
HOLROYD, J. and BRODSKY, A. (1977), 'Psychologists' attitudes and practices regarding erotic and non-erotic physical contact with patients' (*Am. Psychologist*, vol. 32, pp. 834-9).
ILLICH, I. *et al.* (1977), *Disabling Professions* (Marion Boyars, London).
KOVEL, J. (1982), 'Values, interests and psychotherapy' (*Am. J. of Psychoan.*, vol. 42, pp.109-19).
MACKIE, J. M. (1977), *Ethics* (Penguin, Harmondsworth).
ROTH, L. H. *et al.* (1977), 'Tests of competency to consent to treatment' (*Am. J. of Psychiatry*, vol. 134, pp. 279-84).
STOLZ, S. *et al.* (1978), *Ethical Issues in Behavior Modification* (Jossey-Bass, San Francisco).
SZASZ, T. (1965), *The Ethics of Psychoanalysis* (Delta, New York).
TSOI-HOSHMUND, L. (1976), 'Marital therapy and changing values' (*Family Co-ordinator*, vol. 25, pp. 51-6).
WATSON, D. and WALROND-SKINNER, S. (in press), *Ethical Problems in Family Therapy* (Routledge & Kegan Paul, London).
WILE, D. B. (1977), 'Ideological conflicts between clients and psychotherapists' (*Am. J. of Psychotherapy*, vol. 31, pp. 437-49).

See also *Labelling*.

Executive sub-system
See *Sub-system*.

Existential analysis
See *Logotherapy*.

Existential psychotherapy
A trend within and an approach to psychotherapy, influenced by such existential philosophers as Kierkegaard, Heidegger and Sartre, and the phenomenology of Husserl. Existential psychotherapy arose out of a dissatisfaction with what was perceived to be the reductionist and mechanistic aspects of *psychoanalysis*. Instead, the idea of the individual's existence or capacity to 'stand out' or transcend self through self-consciousness and self-reflection is the fundamental idea behind this approach. Existential psychotherapists, who include Binswanger, Boss, May and Laing, concern themselves with how the patient experiences life rather than with *diagnosis* or with understanding the *causality* of his problems. They emphasise the importance of the current and immediate moment of experience, and stress the importance of consciousness, personal identity, the unity of the person and the search for meaning in life. They view pathology as arising from the need to defend against *alienation* from self and others and the anxiety generated by the threat of immediate experience. This leads to rigid and restrictive behaviour, a clinging to the past and a desire to impose a false order on the present and future.

Although strongly anti-technical, some existential psychotherapists make use of *confrontation, focusing, paradoxical intention* and other techniques used in a variety of other therapeutic approaches. More important, however, is their emphasis on a participatory dialogue between patient and therapist, which needs to take place within an authentic and equal relationship. The aim of existential therapy is to enable the individual to take responsibility for his own being in the world (*Dasein*); to become autonomous and to develop the capacity to move beyond the self into full *encounter* and community with other human beings. Binswanger (1967) adopts the term existential analysis to describe his therapeutic approach, while Boss (1971) uses the term *Daseinanalysis*. May (1975) draws particular attention to the individual's capacity for exercising intentionality, making ethical choices, devoting himself to high ideals and engaging in loving relationships, the cost of all these abilities being the possibility of experiencing anxiety and inner crisis. Laing (1967a) draws attention to the part played by the family and other social institutions in creating limitation and stress for the individual, whose only authentic response may be to choose madness.

Although often more confrontational in style, existential psychotherapy has many similarities with the humanistic approaches, particularly in its emphasis on *holism*, the therapeutic efficacy of the relationship between therapist and patient and its focus on present-centredness. It is however best considered as an influence or trend within psychotherapy as a whole rather than as a discrete method. It represents the polar opposite to the technical, *behavioural* and *strategic* models and while it can be criticised for its elusiveness, it provides an antidote to the mechanical aspects of the latter approaches and is an attempt to grapple with the problems of meaninglessness and extinction which have to be faced in our increasingly anomic and threatened nuclear society.

BINSWANGER, L. (1967), *Being-In-The-World* (Harper & Row, New York).
BOSS, M. (1971), *Existential Foundations of Medicine and Psychology* (Aronson, New York).
EDWARDS, D. G. (1982), *Existential Psychotherapy* (Gardner Press, New York).
FRANKL, V. (1973), *Psychotherapy and Existentialism* (Penguin, Harmondsworth).
LAING, R. D. (1967a), *The Divided Self* (Penguin, Harmondsworth).
LAING, R. D. (1967b), *The Politics of Experience* (Penguin, Harmondsworth).
MACQUARRIE, J. (1972), *Existentialism* (Penguin, Harmondsworth).
MAY, R. (1975), *The Courage to Create* (Bantam, New York).
MAY, R. *et al.* (eds) (1958), *Existence* (Simon & Schuster, New York).
RUITENBECK, H. (ed.) (1968), *Psychoanalysis and Existential Philosophy* (Dutton, New York).
WARNOCK, M. (1970), *Existentialism* (Oxford University Press, Oxford).
YALOM, I. D. (1981), *Existential Psychotherapy* (Basic Books, New York).

Experience

The level of a therapist's experience has been studied as a variable in *process* and *outcome* studies. Gurman and Razin (1977) suggest that there are several dimensions which differentiate experienced from inexperienced therapists: the experienced therapist can display flexibility, even when subscribing to a particular therapeutic approach; can evaluate accurately differences in patient functioning; has worked with a few patients from each diagnostic category; is relatively free from self-preoccupation during his time with a patient; is relatively immune from patient attacks or seductions; and has worked in full-time clinical work for three or four years. Auerbach and Johnson (1977) have reviewed the studies which have compared therapist experience and inexperience, under three headings: the behaviour of therapists during the therapy session; their attitudes; and the outcome achieved by each group. With regard to therapist behaviour, they found that experienced therapists are more talkative, commit themselves more and take the initiative more often in the session. Experienced therapists are also shown to develop more satisfying therapeutic relationships, as judged by their ability to establish the *core conditions* satisfactorily, with less defensiveness and distance. Regarding attitude, several studies analysed by Auerbach and Johnson showed that experienced therapists are more active, reveal more of themselves, believe more strongly that affect is important in therapy and formulate more specific *goals*. With regard to outcome, the findings were far less clear. Auerbach and Johnson found that only five out of twelve studies indicate that experienced therapists achieve a superior outcome. Those who have researched into the outcome achieved by non-professional therapists have found that equally good results are obtained and although lack of professional training and inexperience are not equivalent variables, it is likely that non-professionals will have less experience overall since many are doing short-term voluntary jobs prior to *training*. Other studies suggest either no difference or that the experienced therapists only do better with better educated patients. This contrasts with Bergin's (1971) study in which he found that there was a modest relationship between experience and positive outcome regarding correlations between therapist inexperience and *deterioration*. Meltzoff and Kornreich (1970) conclude that on the whole a correlation exists between high levels of experience and positive outcome and Glass (1976) suggests that where there seems to be a negative correlation, this can be explained by the fact that more experienced therapists presumably deal with more difficult and disturbed patients with a poorer prognosis.

Such uncertainties raise subtle questions about therapist careers and '*burn out*' and suggest both that there may be an optimum amount of experience required for positive outcome to occur and that a more refined understanding of the behaviours that bring about positive change is required, including patient-therapist matching and, where appropriate, therapist-therapist matching. In a study of *co-therapy* pairs, for example, working as *family therapists*, Rice *et al.* (1972) found that experienced pairs and inexperienced pairs achieved roughly equivalent outcome, but that both were superior to a mixed experienced-inexperienced team.

AUERBACH, A. H. and JOHNSON, M. (1977), 'Research on the therapist's level of experience' (in Gurman, A. S. and Razin, A. M., *Effective Psychotherapy*, Pergamon Press, New York).

BERGIN, A. (1971), 'The evaluation of therapeutic outcomes' (in Bergin, A. E. and Garfield, S. L. (eds), *Handbook of Psychotherapy and Behavior Change*, Wiley, New York).

GLASS, G. V. (1976), *Primary, Secondary and Meta Analysis of Research* (paper presented as presidential address to the 1976 annual meeting of the American Educational Research Association, San Francisco, Calif.).

GURMAN, A. S. and RAZIN, A. M. (1977), Footnote 1 to Auerbach and Johnson, op. cit.

MELTZOFF, J. and KORNREICH, M. (1970), *Research in Psychotherapy* (Atherton Press, New York).

RICE, D. G. *et al.* (1972), 'Therapist experience and "style" as factors in co-therapy' (*Family Process*, vol. 11, pp. 1-12).

See also *Attraction, Competence, Expertness*.

Experiential family therapy

An approach to *family therapy* which emphasises the importance of the actual experiences that are transacted between therapist and family and between family members themselves, within the therapy session. Its principal advocate is Carl Whitaker and his colleagues, David Keith, Thomas Malone and John Warkentin, who work at Atlanta, Georgia.

Experiential family therapy (or symbolic-experiential family therapy as it is also called) has its roots in *existential* ideas and *humanistic* approaches. It emphasises the family's 'process of becoming' whereby the group can make use of its dysfunction, symptoms and craziness to grow forward. Experiential family therapists try to enhance the therapeutic experience of the session, either through the use of *action techniques* (De'Ath 1981) or through engagement and *encounter* with the therapists who express their emotions of interest, boredom, intimacy and distance to the family as they experience them. *Co-therapy* is encouraged as a means of engaging in a real relationship alongside the family and in order to free one of the therapists to enter fully into the family *system* alongside a disturbed child or psychotic member. At the same time, Whitaker de-emphasises theory and technical approaches to treatment. Instead, he stresses the need for the therapist to win the battle of initiative and control over the structure of therapy by his use of self and by a paradoxical approach which he describes as 'the psychotherapy of the absurd.'

DE'ATH, E. (1981), 'Experiential family therapy' (in Walrond-Skinner, S. (ed.),

Developments in Family Therapy, Routledge & Kegan Paul, London).

KEMPLER, W. (1981), *Experiential Psychotherapy with Families* (Brunner/Mazel, New York).

NAPIER, A. Y. and WHITAKER, C. (1978), *The Family Crucible* (Harper & Row, New York).

NEIL, J. R. and KNISKERN, D. P. (1982), *From Psyche to System: The Evolving Therapy of Carl Whitaker* (Guilford Press, New York).

WHITAKER, C. A. (1975), 'Psychotherapy of the absurd' (*Family Process*, vol. 14, pp. 1-16).

WHITAKER, C. A. and MALONE, T. P. (1953), *The Roots of Psychotherapy* (Blakiston, New York).

WHITAKER, C. A. and KEITH, D. V. (1981), 'Symbolic-experiential family therapy' (in Gurman, A. S. and Kniskern, D. P., *Handbook of Family Therapy*, Brunner/Mazel, New York).

Experimenter effect

The way in which the experimenter may unwittingly influence the results of a psychological experiment. Also known as the Rosenthal effect, after its main discussant. The discovery that, even in the most scientifically conducted experiments with human subjects, an objective experimenter's attitude, approach, speech, etc., can significantly affect outcome, led to the current interest in the *therapist variable* in psychotherapy and recent efforts to discriminate between the effects of the therapist's personality from treatment techniques as agents of change in the therapeutic process.

ROSENTHAL, R. (1966), *Experimenter Effects in Behavioural Research* (Appleton-Century-Crofts, New York).

Expertness

The therapist's perceived *competence* in psychotherapy as judged by the patient. This variable has been studied along with *experience* and *attraction* as a constituent of the patient's perceptions of the therapist's *credibility*. Schmidt and Strong (1970) and Strong and Schmidt (1970) have shown, not surprisingly, that a combination of expert behaviours and credentials produce more change in subjects' ratings

of their achievement motivation than a combination of inexpert behaviours and lack of credentials. Their studies also indicate however that the interviewer's behaviour influenced the subject's opinion of his expertness more than his credentials but that neither was effective alone in altering the subject's opinion. Ratings of the therapist's expertness after watching video tapes of an actual session were however in almost inverse proportion to the amount of experience, though this is not typical of research findings into the relation of expertness and *experience*. (See *Experience*.)

SCHMIDT. L. D. and STRONG, S. R. (1970), 'Expert and inexpert counselors' (*J. of Counseling Psychology*, vol. 17, pp. 115-18).

STRONG, S. R. and SCHMIDT, L. D. (1970), 'Expertness and influence in counseling' *J. of Counseling Psychology*, vol. 17, pp. 81-7).

SPIEGEL, S. B. (1976), 'Expertness, similarity and perceived counselor competence' (*J. of Counseling Psychology*, vol. 23, pp. 436-41).

See also *Social influence*.

Extinction

The process whereby a *conditioned response* is reduced to its preconditioned level. In *classical conditioning* the repeated presentation of the *conditioned stimulus* without the *unconditioned stimulus* leads to extinction. In *operant conditioning*, the frequency of the target response decreases following the withdrawal of the *reinforcer* which was maintaining it. For example, the withdrawal of attention from aggressive or hostile members of a group or ignoring inappropriate behaviour in a child. *Avoidance learning* will also be extinguished if the negative consequences of engaging in undesired behaviour cease to occur. Bandura (1969) reviews the different theories which seek to explain the way in which extinction operates and, in view of the variety of explanations, he concludes that the experimental data with human subjects strongly supports a cognitive explanation rather than one based on *learning theory*. Extinction can be successfully combined with other behavioural techniques such as the positive *reinforcement* of incompatible behaviour. Connis and Rusch (1980) show that undesirable behaviour in retarded males remains extinguished if reinforcers for incompatible behaviour are withdrawn sequentially.

Initially, behaviour that has depended upon reinforcers will increase when they are removed. For example, temper tantrums and other attention seeking behaviour is intensified in an attempt to get the reinforcers to operate once more. But this is a temporary phase prior to the lessening of unreinforced behaviour. Extinction may also be achieved by massive exposure to aversive stimuli, either in reality or imaginarily as, for example, in *flooding, implosion* or *negative practice*. It can also be brought about vicariously in feared situations by having the client repeatedly observe that, for a third party, the feared consequences do not follow the feared event. An early reported case is described by Ayllon and Michael (1959) who used extinction procedures to reduce the number of times a retarded woman entered the nurse's office each day. Thomas (1968) points out that resistance to extinction is often high because by the time the individual enters treatment, intermittent reinforcement has been occurring over a long period of time.

AYLLON, T. and MICHAEL, J. (1959), 'The psychiatric nurse as a behavioural engineer' (*J. of Exper. Anal. Behavior*, vol. 2, p. 323).
BANDURA, A. (1969), *Principles of Behavior Modification* (Holt, Rinehart & Winston, New York).
CONNIS, R. T. and RUSCH, F. R. (1980), 'Programming maintenance through sequential withdrawal of social contingencies' (*Behavior Research of Severe Developmental Disabilities*, vol. 1, pp. 249-60).
THOMAS, E. J. (1968), 'Selected socio behavioral techniques and principles: an approach to interpersonal helping' (*Social Work*, vol. 13, no. 12).

Extroversion
See *Psychological types*.

Eysenck personality inventory (EPI)
The Eysenck personality inventory is designed to measure the two personality factors of

neuroticism and extroversion-introversion and was produced by H. J. and S. B. G. Eysenck. In addition to the very similar *Maudsley Personality Inventory*, a lie scale on the EPI can pick up the subject who makes false responses.

See also *Personality tests, Psychological types*.

Eysenck personality questionnaire (EPQ)
The Eysenck personality questionnaire was designed by H. J. and S. B. G. Eysenck. It adds a measurement of psychoticism to the two major factors measured in the *Eysenck personality inventory*, neuroticism and extroversion-introversion.

See also *Maudsley Personality Inventory, Personality tests, Psychological types*.

F

Facilitative conditions
See *Core conditions*.

Fairbairn, W. Ronald D. (1889-1964)
A major figure in the *British school* of *psychoanalysis*, Fairbairn made original contributions to the development of *object relations* theory. He was born in Edinburgh and, graduating in philosophy from Edinburgh University in 1911, he followed this with three years' postgraduate study in divinity and Greek. After active service during the First World War, Fairbairn returned to Edinburgh and qualified in medicine in 1923. After a year's psychiatric experience at the Royal Edinburgh Hospital, he was appointed a lecturer in the Department of Psychology at the University and started private practice in Edinburgh which he continued for the rest of his life. His psychoanalytic work was developed independently and often in great isolation and although he was made a member of the *British Psychoanalytical Society* he did most of his work alone. From 1940 onwards he began making important and original contributions to the

literature. In 1952, he published a seminal collection of papers under the title *Psychoanalytic Studies of the Personality* in which he attempted a synthesis between psychoanalytic theory and social and interpersonal studies. In his *Revised Psychopathology of the Psychoses and Psychoneuroses* Fairbairn describes mental development in terms of the theory of object relationships. Here he also developed his theory of the *ego*, viewing it as divided into three, the libidinal ego, the anti-libidinal ego, and the central ego. Roughly speaking these structures correspond to the *id*, the *superego* and the ego, respectively.

Fairbairn's theoretical postulate of a schizoid position which underlay the *depressive position* had a great influence on Melanie Klein, who was then prompted to describe the clinical evidence for the *paranoid-schizoid position*.

False self

A term introduced by Winnicott (1960) to describe a defensive structure which develops during early infancy if the environment does not provide a nurturing and facilitative condition for the development of the *true self.* Winnicott suggests that the major factor in providing a facilitative condition for early infancy is the *good enough mother.* The false self is similar in conception to Balint's *basic fault.* It emerges when the infant's belief in his own omnipotent self-gratification is impinged on by the environment and the *ego* responds with an experience of *annihilation.*

WINNICOTT, D. W. (1960), 'Ego distortion in terms of true and false self' (in *The Maturational Processes and the Facilitatory Environment,* Hogarth Press, London).

Family choreography

A conceptual outgrowth of *family sculpting* which is technically better suited to representing the fluid and shifting transactional patterns of a family or other group. In practice, the two terms are often used interchangeably, but strictly, the term choreography introduced by Papp (1976) emphasises a method of active intervention in the family system, which stresses the ongoing and circular nature of a *transaction.* Having developed a static picture of their relationships through creating a family sculpture, family members are asked to go repeatedly through the movements which hold this sculpture in being. The therapist is then able to intervene in a variety of ways to help family members change the movement sequence and begin to create new and more functional transactional patterns and emotional alignments within the group.

PAPP, P. (1976), 'Family choreography' (in Guerin, P., *Family Therapy: Theory and Practice,* Gardner Press, New York).

Family constellation

The pattern of relationships between siblings and parents created by the timing and order of the children's birth. Various theorists have suggested that the family constellation is an important parameter for understanding both the individual members' personality structure and the nature of the family *system* itself. Adler (1928) was the first theorist to investigate the importance of sibling position and he suggested that each child developed certain personality traits depending upon whether he is youngest, oldest, or middle child. Toman (1961) expanded and refined the concept to include a two- and three-generational model and developed profiles for individual family members to describe twelve major types. Particular interactions develop between individual family members based on the parental sibling positions and those of their children. Toman suggests (1962) that, with regard to mate selection, some combinations of sibling positions are more likely to lead to a functional marital relationship than others. *Complementary* sibling positions seem more conducive to a successful marriage than *symmetrical* ones, although this observation was not confirmed by Levinger and Sonnheim's (1965) research. Some individuals seem predisposed by their position within the family constellation to take on the role of *identified patient*, particularly if a certain role (for example, the caretaker of aged parents) is allocated to a particular sibling position within each generation. Hines (1973) has shown that first-born adults perform better under social reinforcement conditions and Johnson (1973) showed that they are more concerned with behaving in a socially desirable way, but on the whole the evidence is inconclusive.

ADLER, A. (1928), *Understanding Human Nature* (Allen & Unwin, London).

HINES, G. H. (1973), 'Birth order and relative effectiveness of social and non-social reinforcers' (*Perceptual and Motor Skills*, vol. 136, pp. 35-8).

JOHNSON, P. B. (1973), 'Birth order and Crowne-Marlowe social desirability scores' (*Psychological Reports*, vol. 32, p. 536).

LEVINGER, G. and SONNHEIM, M. (1965), 'Complementarity in marital adjustment: reconsidering Toman's family constellation hypothesis' (*J. of Individual Psychology*, vol. 21, pp. 137-45).

TOMAN, W. (1961), *Family Constellation* (Springer, New York).

TOMAN, W. (1962), 'Family constellation of the partners in divorced and married couples' (*J. of Individual Psychology*, vol. 18, pp. 48-51).

See also *Genogram*.

Family crisis intervention

Psycho-social procedures offered to a family in *crisis*, which combine the concepts of *crisis theory* with those of *family therapy*. Crisis in a family is manifested by a state of time-limited disequilibrium within the family's system of interactional patterns. The crisis may be precipitated by an internal factor, for example a member of the family develops physical or psychiatric symptoms, engaged in delinquent acts, etc.; or by an external factor such as unemployment, housing problems, racial discrimination, problems at work, school, etc.

The components of a crisis outlined in crisis theory are applicable to families, as are the three main types of crisis to which a family, like an individual, may be subjected. Because of the systemic properties of the family group, however, both the individuals and relation-ships between individual family members will be affected. Moreover, both developmental and role-transitional crises may be multiple and interlocking – for example, a family may experience the toddlerhood of one of its members simultaneously with the late adolescence of the parents and the mid-life crisis of grandparents, etc.

Rappoport (1963) and others have described the normal crises of family life and Hadley *et al.* (1974) have explored family patterns of dealing with crisis including the loss or addition of a family member. As when working with individuals, the primary goal of the help giver is to restore the family to its pre-crisis level of effective functioning. A further goal may include the effort to teach the family new *coping behaviour* and skills and thus increase the level of functioning beyond the family's pre-crisis level. A variety of methods of *family therapy* form the basis of family crisis intervention. Umana *et al.* (1980) describe three methods which are commonly used: the psychoanalytic, behavioural and systems approaches. Langsley *et al.* (1968) describe the way in which family treatment is more rapid and intensive when the family is in crisis, with frequent sessions of prolonged duration offered over a short period of time – usually a one- to two-month period. Families in crisis need to be seen as soon as possible after referral; *home visits* are usually indicated and a *team* approach, using several therapists, is common.

HADLEY, T. R. *et al.* (1974), 'The relationship between family developmental crisis and the appearance of symptoms in a family member' (*Family Process*, vol. 13, pp. 207-14).

LANGSLEY, D. G. *et al.* (1968), *The Treatment of Families in Crisis* (Grune & Stratton, New York).

RAPOPORT, R. (1963), 'Normal crises, family structure and mental health' (*Family Process*, vol. 2, pp. 68-80).

UMANA, R. F. *et al.* (1980), *Crisis in the Family – Three Approaches* (Gardner Press, New York).

See also *Multiple impact therapy*.

Family healer

Family member who takes responsibility for reducing conflict between other members of the family group, either functionally or through *detouring* it away from the stressed dyad. The family healer may try to act as a therapist himself to other family members; or he may call in outside assistance explicitly or covertly, by developing symptoms.

ACKERMAN, N. W. (1968), *Treating the Troubled Family* (Basic Books, New York).

See also *Distance regulator, Identified patient, Scapegoat.*

Family myth

A pattern of mutually agreed but distorted roles adopted by a family as a shared defence against the anxiety provoked by some avoided theme, *phantasy*, past event or forbidden wish. The term was first used in relation to families by Ferreira (1963, 1965) and has since been developed by Byng-Hall (1973, 1979, 1982). Byng-Hall (1973) suggests that the myth represents a compromise between family members whereby each individual's defences can be maintained through the development of the myth, using mechanisms of *unconscious* mutual *collusion*. Byng-Hall (1973) points out that the 'family myth is related to the general area of how one drama, recognised by all, hides and controls another, perhaps diametrically opposed, repudiated family scene'. As is the case with the *manifest content* of a *dream*, the purpose of the family myth is both to conceal and reveal the repudiated drama. It allows it to be denied or projected outside the family altogether and yet enables family members to maintain a symbolic connection with the repudiated material. Fearful themes such as incest, death and disintegration can be contained without threatening the integrity of the group. However, the effort to maintain the myth is often costly in terms of psychic energy and requires the continuous collusion of all family members. Family myths are, according to Ferreira, important means of maintaining *homeostasis*. They may be inherited over several generations and be 're-edited' to fit the new defensive needs of the current situation. A family may enter treatment when they perceive that their family myth has been breached. The therapist's task is to enable the family to engage directly with what they perceive to be a potentially calamitous family drama and to build a new consensus of mutually agreed role relationships based on the actual needs and possibilities of the present instead of on the mythology inherited from the past.

BYNG-HALL, J. (1973), 'Family myths used as defence in conjoint family therapy' (*Brit. J. of Med. Psychology*, vol. 46, pp. 239-50).
BYNG-HALL, J. (1979), 'Re-editing family mythology during family therapy' (*J. of Family Therapy*, vol. 1, pp. 2-14).
BYNG-HALL, J. (1982), 'Family legends: their significance for the family therapist' (in Bentovim, A. *et al.*, *Family Therapy: Complementary Frameworks of Theory and Practice*, Academic Press, London).
FERREIRA, A. (1963), 'Family myths and homeostasis' (*Arch. Gen. Psychiatry*, vol. 9, pp. 457-63).
FERREIRA, A. (1965), 'Family Myths: the covert rules of the relationship' (*Confin. Psychiat.*, vol. 8, pp. 15-20).
STIERLIN, H. (1973), 'Group fantasies and family myths' (*Family Process*, vol. 12, pp. 111-25).

See also *Fit (marital), Folie à deux*

Family relations indicator (FRI)

A *projective test* devised by Howells and Lickorish (1962) for assessing the feelings and attitudes of a child towards his family. A series of thirty-three pictures of various family *subsystems* are presented to the child and each is replicated three times to allow for cross-checking the validity of the child's responses. He or she is asked to say what he or she thinks the people in the picture are saying or doing. The replies are summarised using the following headings to indicate the relationship that appears to exist between parent and child: punitive actions, verbal hostility, deprivations, indifference and positive relationship.

HOWELLS, J. G. and LICKORISH, J. R. (1962), *The Family Relations Indicator* (Oliver & Boyd, Edinburgh).

Family relationship test

An interpersonal relations perception technique developed by Scott for assessing the relationships of a hospitalised patient and his parents and the cultural image that each holds of mental illness. Patient, mother and father are asked to use a set of provided terms to describe the way they see themselves, each other, and how they expect each of the others to see them. A scoring procedure is provided.

SCOTT, R. D. and ASHWORTH, P. L. (1965), 'The "axis value" and the transfer of psychosis' (*Brit. J. of Medical Psychology*, vol. 38, pp. 97-116).

Family romance

Term introduced by Freud (1909) to describe the tendency of the individual to 'invent' a story about his origins and his family. For example, that he was adopted, the son of rich parents, illegitimate, etc. One of the purposes of the invention is to come to terms with his or her fears of sexuality and the exclusivity of the parental relationship to which he is an outsider. Freud thought that such phantasies originated during the Oedipal phase. The concept of *family myth* includes the idea of family romance, although it is concerned with the interconnecting elements of the whole family's phantasies.

FREUD, S. (1909), 'Family romances' (*Standard Edition*, vol. 9, Hogarth Press, London).

Family sculpting

A technique used in *family therapy* whereby the relationships between family members are recreated in space through the formation of a physical tableau. This *tableau vivante* symbolises the emotional position of each member of the family in relation to the others. The therapist asks one member of the family (or each family member in turn) to place the rest of the family in physical positions which most clearly represent his view of the family interaction. The 'sculptor' may be asked to put himself into the sculpture or simply to engage the therapist as an *auxiliary ego* to take his place in it for him. Family members may also be asked to sculpt the way they *would like* the family to be and to adopt the positions of several different members in turn to see how the position 'feels'. Thus, the technique can be used for *diagnosis* or to establish treatment *goals* and the use of different family members as sculptors allows discrepancies in understanding and aspiration to be revealed. As an *action technique*, sculpting enhances the involvement of small children and other less verbal members of the family.

DUHL, F. J. (1973), 'Learning, space and action in family therapy: a primer of sculpture' (in Bloch, D., *Techniques of Family Psychotherapy*, Grune & Stratton, New York).
HEARN, J. and LAWRENCE, M. (1981), 'Family sculpting I – some doubts and some possibilities' (*J. of Family Therapy*, vol. 3, pp. 341-51).
HEARN, J. and LAWRENCE, M. (1985), 'Family sculpting II – some practical examples' (*J. of Family Therapy*, vol. 7, pp. 113-31).
JEFFERSON, R. M. (1972), 'Some notes on the use of family sculpture in therapy' (*Family Process*, vol. 17, pp. 69-76).
PAPP, P. (1973), 'Family sculpting in preventive work with "well families" ' (*Family Process*, vol. 12, pp. 197-212).
SIMON, R. M. (1972), 'Sculpting the family' (*Family Process*, vol. 11, pp. 49-57).

See also *Family choreography*.

Family therapy

A treatment modality directed towards producing change in the family system and rendering its members a-symptomatic. The basic treatment medium is the *conjoint interview* and the *unit of treatment* is the family group and not the *identified patient*. Family therapy emerged at several different places in the USA almost simultaneously during the 1950s. Workers at Palo Alto and New York were probably the first to develop their ideas systematically, and in Britain the credit for the first paper on family therapy must go to John Bowlby at the Tavistock Clinic, London (Bowlby 1949). However, family theorists differ as to the way they define the family for the purposes of treatment, some suggesting (e.g. Laing 1979) that as many family members as possible should be convened and others, that a focal *sub-system* (e.g. Minuchin 1974; Haley 1980), such as the marital pair, creates the optimal platform for conducting systems change. Broderick and Schrader (1981) outline the history of the development of family therapy since its beginnings in the 1950s, its relationship to *psychoanalysis, marital therapy* and group work and the prominent figures that have helped shape its identity as a modality alongside individual and group work methods.

There are now several different schools of family therapy, including *structural family therapy, strategic therapy* (which includes some individual approaches as well), *transgenerational family therapy, behavioural family therapy, experiential family therapy, brief focal family therapy*, and *psychoanalytic family therapy*. Family theory draws upon *systems theory*, psychoanalytic theory, *communication* theory, *learning theory* and *group dynamics* for its main theoretical constructs, each school emphasising a different mixture of influences. Family therapy has developed a range of related subspecialties during the thirty years it has been actively practised, including *multiple family therapy, multiple couples therapy, multiple impact therapy, network intervention* and *conjoint marital therapy*. It has proved to be a fertile area for creating new intervention techniques and for promoting a therapeutic philosophy which seeks to avoid the *labelling* of individuals. It is based on principles of *holism* and the belief that *symptoms* and psychological difficulties of all sorts stem from *interpersonal* relationships rather than (although not to the exclusion of) *intrapsychic* mechanisms.

Gurman and Kniskern (1981) summarise the mushrooming number of *outcome* studies that have been produced and Gale (1979) discusses some of the problems involved in family therapy research. Major professional family therapy journals include *Family Process*, *Journal of Marital and Family Therapy, The American Journal of Family Therapy* and (in Britain) *The Journal of Family Therapy*. Associations of family therapy have been formed in the United States and in Britain to promote practice and teaching.

BOWLBY, J. (1949), 'The study and reduction of group tension in the family' (reprinted in Walrond-Skinner, S. (1981), *Developments in Family Therapy*, Routledge & Kegan Paul, London).

BRODERICK, C. B. and SCHRADER, S. S. (1981), 'The history of professional marriage and family therapy' (in Gurman and Kniskern, see below).

GALE, A. (1979), 'Problems of outcome research in family therapy' (in Walrond-Skinner, S. (ed.), *Family and Marital Psychotherapy*, Routledge & Kegan Paul, London).

GROUP FOR THE ADVANCEMENT OF PSYCHIATRY (1970), *The Field of Family Therapy* (vol. 7, Mental Health Material Centre, New York).

GURMAN, A. S. (ed.) (1981), *Questions and Answers in the Practice of Family Therapy* (Brunner/Mazel, New York).

GURMAN, A. S. and KNISKERN, D. P. (eds) (1981), *Handbook of Family Therapy* (Brunner/Mazel, New York).

HALEY, J. (1980), *Leaving Home* (McGraw-Hill, New York)

HOFFMAN, L. (1981), *Foundations of Family Therapy* (Guilford Press, New York).

KASLOW, E. (1983), *The International Book of Family Therapy* (Brunner/Mazel, New York).

LAING, R. D. (1979), *Address at the Annual Conference of the American Association for Marriage and Family Therapy* (Washington, DC, October 1979).

MINUCHIN, S. (1974), *Families and Family Therapy* (Tavistock, London).

OLSON, D. H. and MILLER, B. C. (1983), *Family Studies Review Yearbook* (Sage, New York).

WALROND-SKINNER, S. (1976), *Family Therapy: The Treatment of Natural Systems* (Routledge & Kegan Paul, London).

WALROND-SKINNER, S. (1984), 'Whither

family therapy: twenty years on' (*J. of Family Therapy*, vol. 6, pp. 1-16).
WOLMAN, B. B. (ed.) (1983), *Handbook of Marital and Family Therapy* (Plenum Press, New York).

Family transference
The term is used in slightly different ways but usually indicates the *network* of transferred images and relationships, derived from family members' individual experiences of past significant relationships. The concept is used in psychoanalytic approaches to *family therapy* to describe the interlocking process that occurs on an *unconscious* level between family members' intrafamilial *transferences*. Intrafamilial transference usually crosses generations, so that a mother may transfer on to her child the relationship she had with *her* mother; or on to her husband the relationship she had with her father or brother. Intrafamilial transference is considered to be more significant in family therapy than the transference that occurs between family members and the therapist. The term was originally coined by Boszormenyi-Nagy and Framo (1962) to account for the tendency of some individual patients to transfer on to the hospital setting and staff their own family network of relationships. The term was then extended to mean the way in which individuals transfer on to their current relational context (i.e. their current family or other social network) significant introjected family images and relationships from the past.

BOSZORMENYI-NAGY, I. and FRAMO, J. L. (1962), 'Family concept of hospital treatment of schizophrenia' (in Masserman, J. (ed.), *Current Psychiatric Therapies*, vol. 2, Grune & Stratton, New York).

See also *Family myth, Fit (marital), Imago.*

Federn, Paul (1871-1950)
Federn was born in Vienna, the son of a well-known physician. He trained first as a paediatrician and later, after meeting Freud in 1902, he entered psychoanalytic training. He joined Freud's inner circle and took an active role in

the Viennese Psychoanalytic Society, describing himself as Freud's Apostle Paul. Later, during the last decade of Freud's life, he was looked upon as Freud's deputy, representing Freud at professional and social occasions and continuing to promote his influence. Immediately before the Second World War, Federn emigrated to the United States, where after a long period of illness, he finally committed suicide. His scientific work reflected a particular interest in the study and treatment of psychosis and in the development of *ego psychology*. His best known books are *Analysis of Psychotics* (1933) and *Ego Psychology and Psychosis* (1952), published posthumously.

Feedback
A general term derived from *communication* theory but used more loosely than, for example, *feedback loop* to describe the therapist's response to the patient's behaviour, expression of feelings, etc. The purpose of feedback is the use of information (output) to modify the patient's behaviour, develop *insight* and close the gap between his or her actual performance and experience and the *goals* of treatment (input).

Feedback provides a means of overcoming communication problems that arise from discrepant detonative and *metacommunicational* levels and from the inaccurate encoding or decoding of messages. To be maximally effective, feedback should be immediate, specific and offered within an accepting and supportive framework. Lieberman *et al.* have shown that feedback overload in group work settings is an important contributor to the *deterioration* effect in psychotherapy.

LIEBERMAN, M. A. *et al.* (1973) *Encounter Groups: First Facts* (Basic Books, New York).

See also *Interview, Knowledge of results, Microskill.*

Feedback loop
A circular process by which an output of a *system* is subsequently processed as an input. A classic example is the thermostat in a heating system which reacts negatively to increasing

output and thus regulates the system's behaviour. Feedback is also the means by which both new information from the environment is introduced into a system and stability is maintained. Feedback can be either *positive* leading to change and variation or *negative* producing stability and *homeostasis*. A balance between both types of feedback is essential for the optimal functioning of a system.

See also *Bio-feedback*.

Female sexuality

Freud's early work mapped out the development of the little boy's sexuality (Freud 1905), but his attempts to translate this to the development of the little girl were contrived and unconvincing. Although he later (Freud 1931) attempted a full review of his ideas on female sexuality, these were really prompted by the work of female analysts such as Lou Andreas Salome, Anna Freud, Karen Horney, Melanie Klein and Hélène Deutsch. There has been much interest in recent years by feminist writers in the psychoanalytic view of femininity (Mitchell 1974, Chodorow 1978, Sayers 1982, Chasseguet-Smirgel 1985).

CHASSEGUET-SMIRGEL, J. (1985), *Creativity and Perversion* (Free Association Books, London).

CHODOROW, N. (1978), *The Reproduction of Mothering* (University of California Press, Berkeley).

FREUD, S. (1905), 'Three essays on the theory of sexuality' (*Standard Edition*, vol. 7, Hogarth Press, London).

FREUD, S. (1931), 'Female sexuality' (*Standard Edition*, vol. 21, Hogarth Press, London).

MITCHELL, J. (1974), *Psychoanalysis and Feminism* (Penguin, Harmondsworth).

SAYERS, J. (1982), *Biological Politics* (Tavistock, London).

See also *Feminist psychology, Feminist therapy, Penis envy.*

Feminist psychology

An approach to psychology which attempts to redress the imbalance imposed by the past lack of recognition and devaluing of feminist concerns. Personality theories and a variety of psychological concepts have been heavily affected by the cultural and societal views regarding masculinity and femininity but not until the rise of the women's movement in the 1960s has there been a systematic attempt to scrutinise psychological theory for its sexist bias against women. Various researchers have shown that there is bias in sample selection, meaning that women are often under-represented or that research results are misinterpreted. For example, in studies of *leadership* in groups, generalisations have been drawn from research on all-male groups and then used as though applicable to human groups in general. Walker (1981), for example, explores the differences in the structure, goals, interpersonal relationships, communication patterns and developmental sequence in female therapy groups as compared with mixed groups. She found that mixed groups tend to be more oriented to interpersonal issues, to be more competitive, and that communication tends to be male-dominated. Female groups encourage the sharing of interpersonal issues, explore the social determinants of personal problems, are more co-operatively oriented and use more intimate and expressive communication.

The idea of women being deficient in some way has been a major premise of Freudian psychoanalytic theory, seen most clearly in Freud's concepts of *penis envy*, the *castration complex* and the deficiency of the female *super-ego*. Although many psychoanalytic writers (e.g. Horney, Adler and others) have tried to redress this view, feminist writers are usually highly critical of psychoanalytic theory and it is indeed hard to see how psychoanalytic theory can be regarded as helping forward a more equitable view of women. Broverman *et al.* (1970) too have shown how the characteristics regarded as desirable and typical of mental health are those associated with males and they conclude that a mentally healthy woman is typically viewed as a mentally unhealthy adult.

The recently explored concept of

androgyny has provided a fruitful way into a discussion of these issues. Two broad views of androgyny are currently found: first, the *integrative* view, whereby the differences between the sexes are regarded as much less important than the similarities. Williams (1979) and others have shown that the androgynous person, with a balance of feminine and masculine characteristics, is both physically and psychologically healthier. The integrative view is therefore directed towards identifying the sources of gender difference and reducing their effects. Second, the *complementary* view of androgyny recognises that there are important gender differences between the feminine and masculine, reflected in the way men and women think, the symbols they use and their different approaches to instrumental behaviour on the one hand and expressive, interpersonal behaviour on the other. Various studies suggest that women exhibit greater facility and interest in the sphere of interpersonal relationships than men; their interests are synthetic rather than analytic and their mode of learning is experiential rather than didactic. Feminist theologians have pointed to the distinctive contribution which women can make to spirituality and moral values and they call for the patriarchal Churches to incorporate and recognise the feminine in their language, liturgy and leadership (Ruether 1975). The complementary view of androgeny stresses the need for a new recognition of the worth of feminine insights and values and a rebalancing of social norms and cultural values in their favour.

Feminist therapy, *radical therapy* and various *self-help* groups are attempts to overcome the perceived negative effects of sexual stereotyping in the field of psychotherapy as a whole.

BERN, S. L. (1974), 'The measurement of psychological androgyny' (*J. of Consulting and Clinical Psychology*, vol. 42, pp. 155-62).
BROVERMAN, I. K. *et al.* (1970), 'Sex role stereotypes and clinical judgements of mental health' (*J. of Consulting and Clinical Psychology*, vol. 34, pp. 1-7).

GLENNON. L. M. (1979), *Women and Dualism* (Longman, London).
HARTNETT, O. *et al.* (eds) (1979), *Sex Role Stereotyping* (Tavistock, London).
MITCHELL, J. (1974), *Psychoanalysis and Feminism* (Penguin, Harmondsworth).
RUETHER, R. R. (1975), *New Women, New Earth: Sexist Ideologies and Human Liberation* (Seabury Press, New York).
WALKER, L. S. (1981), 'Are women's groups different?' (*Psychotherapy: Theory, Research and Practice*, vol. 18, pp. 240-5).
WILLIAMS, J. (1979), 'Psychological androgyny and mental health' (in Hartnett *et al.* op. cit.).

Feminist therapy

An approach to psychotherapy that has developed out of the philosophy and value base which underpins the women's movement. Feminist therapy reacts to the strong sexist bias that many women feel exists in the major personality theories and in their systems of psychotherapy, particularly in the views of Freud and the techniques of classical *psychoanalysis*. Feminists vary as to whether they see feminist therapy as a set of values from which to practise a variety of existing therapies, or as an approach in its own right, or, as Tennov (1976) suggests, as a means of highlighting the damage caused to women by much traditional psychotherapy. As a relatively new approach, it is not surprising that there are elements of all three strands in much feminist writing.

Common elements in the feminist approach to psychotherapy include the debunking of psychological mythology regarding sex differences, particularly concepts such as *penis envy* and the *castration complex*; the development of a new awareness of the value of the female body and its functions; an emphasis on the development of equal responsibility, talents, skills and power in women; a removal of sex role differentiation; an acceptance of the fusion between personal and political goals regarding change and development; and an emphasis on the egalitarian nature of the therapeutic relationship.

Much feminist therapy is conducted in

groups, using *consciousness raising* as the major element. *Action techniques* and *assertiveness training* are used to help women express their frustration and move on to find new self-esteem and develop new confidence and skills. Individual therapy is also used, where *modelling* by an empathic and accepting female therapist is an important element. Family and couples therapy (Hare-Mustin 1978) can also be approached from a feminist perspective and has great potential for undoing harmful sexist experiences within the family of origin and the current marriage. Some feminist therapy, however, can be criticised for losing or avoiding a systemic focus.

BRODSKY, A. and HARE-MUSTIN, R. (eds) (1980), *Research on Psychotherapy with Women* (Guilford Press, New York).

CARTER, E. *et al.* (1982), *Mothers and Daughters (Monograph Series*, vol. 1, no. 1, The Women's Project in Family Therapy, Washington DC).

CHASE, K. (1977), 'Seeing sexism: a look at feminist therapy' (*State and Mind*, March/April, pp. 19-22).

EICHENBAUM, L. and ORBACH, S. (1982), *Outside In ... Inside Out* (Penguin, Harmondsworth).

FRANKS, V. and BURTLE, V. (1974), *Women in Therapy* (Brunner/Mazel, New York).

HARE-MUSTIN, R. (1978), 'A feminist approach to family therapy' (*Family Process*, vol. 17, pp. 181-94).

LLEWELYN, S. and OSBORNE, K. (1983), 'Women as clients and therapists' (in Pilgrim, D. (ed.), *Psychology and Psychotherapy*, Routledge & Kegan Paul, London).

RAWLINGS, E. I. and CARTER, D. K. (1977), *Psychotherapy for Women* (Thomas, Springfield, Ill.).

SAYERS, J. (1982), *Biological Politics: Feminist and Anti-feminist Perspectives* (Tavistock, London).

TENNOV, D. (1976), *Psychotherapy: The Hazardous Cure* (Archer Press, New York).

See also *Female sexuality, Feminist psychology, Radical therapy*.

Ferenczi, Sandor (1873-1933)

Ferenczi was born in Miskolc, Hungary, the fifth of eleven children. He graduated in medicine from the University of Vienna in 1894. In 1908 he met Freud and began his psychoanalytic training. He became one of the inner circle of psychoanalysts practising in Vienna and remained a close friend of Freud's until his death, despite Freud's reservations about Ferenczi's later innovations in technique. In 1913 he founded the Hungarian Psychoanalytic Society and began his own innovative work. His first important book was *Stages in the Development of the Sense of Reality* in which he described the infant's experience of omnipotence. His most important contribution, however, was in innovating new technical approaches to *psychoanalysis*, both forms of which are described under the heading *active technique*.

Field theory

The application of field theory to psychology was undertaken by Kurt Lewin, who produced from it a theory of personality and an approach to psychotherapy. It emphasises the *context* in which human behaviour and development take place. Lewin's work was published during and soon after the Second World War and focused attention on the individual-in-his-psycho-social environment rather than on the individual as an isolated entity. His work thus set the scene for the *conjoint systemic* and interactional therapies which were to develop during the 1950s.

Lewin viewed behaviour as a function of the way in which the individual perceives his psychological field at any one time. Field theory asserts that the individual's behaviour is influenced by the relationship of his goals, the *forces* in the field and the strength of the *vector* and *valence* operating between the individual and the objects with which he interacts. The way in which he perceives his psychological field is determined by his *cognitive structure* or blueprint for evaluating his inner and outer experiences. The cognitive structure can be changed through learning and in this respect Lewin anticipated the work of the *cognitive restructuring approaches.* Normal development consists in the individual becoming progressively familiar with his psychological field or *lifespace* and able to distinguish past, present and future accurately. Both the lifespace and the concept of time become progressively more differentiated as development occurs. Field theory is related to *Gestalt psychology* but puts greater emphasis on social and motivational forces. Lewin extended his ideas to both the marital relationship and to the functioning of groups and he undertook seminal work in relation to *leadership* in groups and prepared the way for the development of the *T-Group*.

DE RIVERA, J. (1976), *Field Theory as Human-science* (Gardner Press, New York).
LEWIN, K. (1935), *A Dynamic Theory of Personality* (McGraw-Hill, New York).
LEWIN, K. (1948), *Resolving Social Conflicts* (Harper & Row, New York).
LEWIN, K. (1951), *Field Theory in Social Science* (Greenwood Press, Westport, Connecticut).
MARROW, A. J. (1969), *The Practical Theorist: The Life and Work of Kurt Lewin* (Basic Books, New York).

Fight/flight

See *Basic assumption behaviour.*

Figure-ground

A concept derived from *Gestalt psychology* and used in *Gestalt therapy*. Perls (1969) suggests that all experience lies on a continuum, between the 'foreground' of an individual's awareness, when a need becomes pressing, and the 'background' experience of awareness when the need is met. The unmet need presses for attention as a figure against the ground of other experience. When satisfied, it moves into the ground of awareness and another need takes its place as figure. The satisfaction of the need completes a 'Gestalten'. The aim of Gestalt therapy is to help the individual become aware of the continuous process of 'Gestalten' formation, dissolution and reformation.

PERLS, F. S. (1969), *Gestalt Therapy Verbatim* (Real People Press, Moab, Utah).

Filial therapy

A group work method introduced by Guerney (1964) in which parents are taught *play therapy* techniques for use with their children. Parents are taught in groups through demonstrations and practice sessions. Parents then conduct play sessions at home with their child, keeping written records which they then use to report back to the group meeting. When parents have participated in about a dozen play therapy sessions at home, the group leader helps them to apply principles of child management to situations outside the play session, adding behavioural techniques of *reinforcement* to the *non-directive* skills used in the play session. Treatment usually lasts about nine months in all. The approach has the multiple effect of acting as a therapeutic medium for the children, a learning laboratory for the parents and as a means of improving relationships between parent and child. The method has also been used with foster parent groups and with step-parents, to assist the bonding process.

GUERNEY, B. G. (1964), 'Filial therapy: description and rationale' (*J. of Consulting Psychology*, vol. 28, pp. 304-10).
GUERNEY, L. (1976), 'Filial therapy program' (in Olsen, D. H. (ed.), *Treating Relationships*, Graphic Publishing, Lake Mills, Iowa).

See also *Paraprofessional.*

FIRO tests

Developed by William Schutz, a *humanistic psychologist*, the fundamental interpersonal relationships orientation tests (FIRO) analyse how people react to and feel about others, i.e. their interpersonal behaviour. They measure three psychological dimensions: inclusion – an individual's need to communicate with and associate with others; affection – an individual's need for love, affection and friendship; and control – an individual's need to exercise authority over others. Several scales are available, including FIRO-B and FIRO-F, geared towards behaviour and feelings respectively; and MATE, the marital attitudes evaluation, measuring the degree of satisfaction at the level of behaviour and feelings of any closely involved couple.

All the tests are relatively short, consisting of six or more scales of nine items each. The tests measure the relative strength of needs within the individual; they are not designed to compare a person with others, and therefore no norms are available. Unsuitable for statistically based research, they are of great value in counselling or therapeutic settings.

SCHUTZ, W. C. (1958), *FIRO: A Three-Dimensional Theory of Interpersonal Behavior* (Rinehart & Winston, New York).
SCHUTZ, W. C. (1967), *The FIRO Scales* (revised 1978) (Consulting Psychologists' Press, Palo Alto, Calif.).

First order change

One of two types of therapeutic change postulated by Watzlawick *et al.* (1974) and referring to change that occurs within a given system or frame of reference but which does not change the system itself. A wide range of therapeutic interventions fall into this category. *Tasks* and *homework assignments* designed to promote competence, increase problem solving skills and develop *coping behaviour* in general fall into the category of first order change interventions. From the point of view of the *theory of types* first order change occurs between the same levels or within the same class of behaviours, while *second order change* occurs when a shift is made to a higher or *meta* level of experience and analysis.

Watzlawick *et al.* (1974) use the analogy of speed change in a car to compare the two types: first order change is brought about by depressing the accelerator pedal; second order change is produced by changing gear. *Strategic therapists* emphasise the importance of distinguishing between the two types of change. First order change interventions operate at a logical level and depend on linear causal thinking. However, if a range of first order change interventions have already been applied and the problem continues to get worse, applying more of the same first order interventions will contribute to the main-

tenance of the problem, not to its solution. When the solution to the problem has become the problem, second order interventions are indicated.

WATZLAWICK, P. *et al.* (1974), *Change: Problem Formation and Problem Resolution* (W. W. Norton, New York).

See also *Causality*.

Fit (marital)

A mutual *collusion* which determines the initial choice of marital partner and which enables the relationship to remain in being. The term was introduced by workers using a psycho-analytic approach to *marital therapy* (Dicks 1967; Pincus *et al.* 1962). Dicks (1967) and others suggest that the initial choice of marital partner is significantly influenced by the parental model, choice occurring on the basis of identification with an idealised parental figure or on the basis of repudiation of a negative one. In terms of this parameter, a person tends to choose a partner who resembles the parent with whom he was most closely bonded as a child or who possesses the opposite characteristics of a parent with whom he or she experienced an unsatisfactory relationship. In the first case, a fit is achieved through replication of an idealised past experience; in the second, through the creation of a wished for but unattained past situation. In either case, the current reality is determined by needs stemming from the past and difficulties are likely to arise when the partner cannot live up to the required role.

The second main parameter of choice arises from the person's perception of the features and deficits in his own personality. Marital partnering may then take place on the basis of *symmetrical* choice, i.e. the individual chooses someone who is perceived to have similar characteristics as the self, or on the basis of *complementary* choice, where the individual chooses someone who seems to have different or opposite characteristics to the self. In extreme cases the individual may split off the idealised and desired parts of the self, projecting them into the other, idealising the partner and denigrating the self; or, conversely, he or she may split off undesirable parts, project them into the partner and attack and repudiate the other as the container of all the 'badness' that exists in the relationship. A marital fit is produced by the collusive role relationships attained by the pair but although it is a powerful tool in maintaining *homeostasis*, it greatly restricts the ability of each partner and the relationship as a whole to develop and adapt to new situations such as the birth of children and other developmental or role transitional *crises*. As Pincus (1962) points out, the unrecognised or unconscious aspects of each partner's personality is often revealed in the other. The therapist's task is to help each to recognise the marital fit and its basis in the past or in the split-off aspects of each person's personality, help the individuals mourn for the past, re-integrate the denied and repudiated aspects of the self and establish a relationship with the other based on the mutual acceptance of each partner's real personality.

BANNISTER, K. and PINCUS, L. (1965), *Shared Fantasy in Marital Problems* (Tavistock Institute of Human Relations, London).

DICKS, H. V. (1967), *Marital Tensions* (Routledge & Kegan Paul, London).

PINCUS, L. (ed.) (1955), *Marriage: Studies in Emotional Conflict and Growth* (Methuen, London).

PINCUS, L. *et al.* (1962), *The Marital Relationship as a Focus for Casework* (Tavistock Institute of Human Relations, London).

See also *Family myth, Folie à deux, Projective identification, Quid pro quo (marital)*.

Fixation

In classical *psychoanalysis*, the idea that the *drive* development can, in part, remain stuck at an earlier stage, type of *object* or type of relationship, which is inappropriate to the chronological age that the person has actually reached. Although fixations are inevitable features of normal development, they may be seen as sources of significant pathology, either as the outcome of excessive stimulation and inappropriate drive gratification or as a result of excessive drive frustration. A child may remain fixated on his mother as a result of rejection and frustration by her or as a result of excessive gratification by her (Oedipal fixation).

Freud used the term in two ways: first to denote the fixation of a memory, an idea or a *symptom*, and second, to describe the fixation of the *libido* to a stage, type of object, etc. Freud links fixation with *repression*, viewing fixation as its first stage; and he also links it with *regression*, viewing fixation as the end point to which regression proceeds. For example, an adult who has regressed to the behaviour of early childhood might be described as having libidinal development fixated at the *oral* or *anal stage* and certain characterological features would be seen as associated with the stage at which fixation had occurred.

FREUD, S. (1905), 'Three essays on the theory of sexuality' (*Standard Edition*, vol. 7, Hogarth Press, London).

FREUD, S. (1915), 'Repression' (*Standard Edition*, vol. 14, Hogarth Press, London).

Fixed role therapy

A form of *brief therapy* developed by Kelly and derived from the principles of *personal construct theory*. Fixed role therapy is one of Kelly's important contributions to therapeutic practice as distinct from theory, yet even here Kelly (1973), in keeping with his emphasis on the client as a scientist, described fixed role therapy as an investigation, where the client is the chief investigator and the therapist the research supervisor. Fixed role therapy consists in the client adopting the role of another person (often this is the role of the person that the client would like to be) and enacting this role for a period of several weeks. Client and therapist meet together regularly during the period, and at the end the client evaluates the total experience with the help of the therapist.

The therapist first helps the client write a self-characterisation and then a sketch of the role that he will enact. The enactment sketch should include aspects of the character that the client finds difficulty in portraying but which he would like to integrate into his reportoire of responses.

The client is then asked to pretend that his own self has gone on holiday for a few weeks and that the new person is here instead. The enactment script is read by the client four times a day. During the course of the enactment, the client tries out at least five important interpersonal encounters. At the end of the period, the enactment script is abandoned, but the client is helped to integrate whatever he has found valuable from the enacted role into his own personality.

Fixed role therapy is not widely used in its original form and has been criticised by Rogers (1956) because of its intellectual approach. Even so, in a modified form it can be useful in initiating or helping to terminate therapy or as a means of moving forward when therapy has reached an impasse. It has obvious parallels with Moreno's *psychodrama* and with other forms of *role play*.

BONARIUS, J. C. (1970), 'Fixed role therapy : a double paradox' (*Brit. J. of Medical Psychology*, vol. 43, pp. 213-19).
KARST, T. O. and TREXLER, L. D. (1970), 'Initial study using fixed role and rational-emotive therapy in treating public speaking anxiety' (*J. of Consulting and Clinical Psychology*, vol. 34, pp. 360-6).
KELLY, G. A. (1973), 'Fixed role therapy' (in Jurjevich, R. M. (ed.), *Direct Psychotherapy: Twentyeight American Originals*, University of Miami Press, Coral Gables, Florida).
ROGERS, C. R. (1956), 'Intellectualized psychotherapy' (*Contemporary Psychology*, vol. 1, pp. 357-8).

Flight into health
A term used to describe the process whereby a patient may claim to be relieved of his *symptoms* or problems prematurely. The term is used in the psychoanalytic literature and denotes the way in which the patient's fear of the treatment, the therapist and/or the prospect of change outweighs his perception of the benefits to be gained.

See also *Reaction formation, Secondary gain.*

Flight into illness
The term was originally used by Freud (1905, 1909) to denote the way in which a person tries to evade or reduce the tension of a psychic conflict by developing *symptoms*. The concept appears to be indistinguishable from the idea of indirect gains derived from illness.

FREUD, S. (1905), 'Fragment of an analysis of a case of hysteria' (*Standard Edition*, vol. 7, Hogarth Press, London).
FREUD, S. (1909), 'Some general remarks on hysterical attacks' (*Standard Edition*, vol. 9, Hogarth Press, London).

See also *Secondary gain.*

Flooding
The exposure of the patient to massive doses of the anxiety-provoking stimuli, usually *in vivo*. Flooding techniques are aimed at bringing about *extinction* of the undesired behaviour, using an approach that is in contrast to the step-by-step procedures of *systematic desensitisation*. In contrast to the low arousal of the desensitisation situation, the patient undergoes repeated high arousal experiences until extinction occurs. As with *implosion* (often used interchangeably with flooding), *shaping, behavioural rehearsal, covert modelling* and *modelling*, flooding applies the principle of high and frequent exposure to the evoking stimuli. Thus, exposure is the means of habituating the patient to the fearful stimuli and extinguishing his fear (Marks 1978a).

Flooding has been successfully used with phobic and obsessional patients and is almost entirely confined to use with these problems. Gelder (1975) compared the effects of flooding and systematic desensitisation and concluded that both techniques were equally effective and superior to the control. They showed that flooding is most effective when carried out with an anxiety-reducing drug and with the patient's knowledge of this, suggesting that the most effective formula is continuous exposure to phobic situations under conditions that prevent the development of anxiety. Rachman *et al.* (1973) evaluated the effectiveness of flooding, modelling and a combination of the two, in comparison with *relaxation training*. All three exposure techniques proved superior to relaxation but were indistinguishable one from the other. Boudewyns and Shipley (1982) suggest that flooding is superior to *negative practice*. But Emmelkamp and Mersch (1982) conclude that although flooding is superior in the short term, *cognitive restructuring approaches* are more effective in the treatment of agoraphobia when tested after a longer period. A crucial unanswered question which Marks (1978b) poses is why should exposure to the anxiety-provoking stimuli sometimes *produce* phobias and at other times *cure* them?

BOUDEWYNS, P. A. and SHIPLEY, R. H. (1982), 'Confusing negative practice with flooding: a cautionary note' (*Behaviour Therapist*, vol. 5, pp. 47-8).

EMMELKAMP, P. M. and MERSCH, P. P. (1982), 'Cognition and exposure in vivo in the treatment of agoraphobia: short term and delayed effects' (*Cognitive Therapy and Research*, vol. 6, pp. 77-90).

GELDER, M. (1975), 'Flooding: results and problems from a new treatment for anxiety' (in Thompson, T. and Dockens, W. (eds), *Applications of Behavior Modification*, Academic Press, New York).

MARKS, I. M. (1972), 'Flooding (implosion) and related treatments' (in Agras, W. S. (ed.), *Behavior Modification: Principles and Clinical Applications*, Little Brown, Boston).

MARKS, I. M. (1978a), 'Exposure treatments' (in Agras, W. S. (ed.), *Behavior Modification: Principles and Clinical Applications*, 2nd edn, Little Brown, Boston).

MARKS, I. M. (1978b), 'Behavioral psychotherapy of adult neurosis' (in Garfield, S. and Bergin, A. E., *Handbook of Psychotherapy and Behavior Change*, Wiley, New York).

RACHMAN, S. *et al.*. (1973), 'The treatment of obsessive-compulsive neurotics by modeling and flooding in vivo' (*Behavior, Research and Therapy*, vol. 11, pp. 463-71).

Focal formulation

The systematic arrangement of information gathered about a family during the assessment stage and entered under seven headings in nine columns on a focal formulation sheet. This method of analysing the gathered information is used in *brief focal family therapy* but is adaptable as a tool for other methods of intervention requiring systematic recording during the assessment phase. The seven headings are as follows: family and professional composition; current complaint; reported past events in previous and current family systems (two columns); surface action, reported and observed (two columns); meanings active in the family; therapist's speculation; and requisite changes.

GLASER, D. *et al.* (1984), 'Focal family therapy: the assessment stage' (*J. of Family Therapy*, vol. 6, pp. 265-73).

Focal hypothesis

A summarised statement used in *brief focal family therapy*, arrived at after the assessment of an individual or family and including the following four elements:

(a) The *symptom* is stated in interactional terms.

(b) The symptom is *reframed* in terms of its function and underlying meaning for the family.

(c) The feared anxiety or disaster which is avoided by the presence of the symptom is stated.

(d) The salient and unresolved past experience(s) and their links to the family's current dysfunction are outlined.

The focal hypothesis is arrived at after information has been systematically gathered and entered on a *focal formulation* sheet. By drawing out the therapist's salient observations of the family, the focal hypothesis is intended to link symptoms, surface action, depth meanings and historical events and thereby to capture the essence of the family's problem. It produces a guiding formulation for understanding the treatment *goals* and the means by which these may be met.

BENTOVIM, A. (1979), 'Towards creating a focal hypothesis for brief focal family therapy' (*J. of Family Therapy*, vol. 1, pp. 125-36).

KINSTON, W. and BENTOVIM, A. (1983), 'Constructing a focal formulation and hypothesis in family therapy' (*Australian J. of Family Therapy*, in press).

Focal psychotherapy

A form of brief psychoanalytic psychotherapy developed by Balint (1972) and Malan (1963, 1976) at the Tavistock Clinic, London. These workers have adapted psychoanalytic techniques and concepts to a brief model of treatment which does not exceed forty sessions. The term 'focus' was used by earlier writers (e.g. Feinsinger 1948; French 1958) to describe the way in which the patient is encouraged to focus on specific material and to work on a 'focal conflict', i.e. one that is nearest to the surface in the patient's current life.

The idea of developing a focus for treatment lies at the heart of this approach and workers using focal psychotherapy emphasise the way in which intensive interpretive work directed towards the focal problem can result in profound restructuring of the personality. In order to attend single-mindedly to the focal problem, the therapist guides the patient during sessions by means of selective *interpretations*, selective attention and selective neglect (Malan 1976). However, so long as the correct focus has been chosen, workers maintain that in-depth restructuring of the *psyche* can nevertheless be achieved. As with other forms of brief psychoanalytic psychotherapy, a careful selection of patients is made and only those who are judged to have sufficient *ego strength*, have problems which can be defined within a current life situation and are sufficiently motivated, are accepted. The main therapeutic tool is interpretation, including interpretation of the *transference*. Malan (1963) has demonstrated a high level of positive *outcome* using this approach.

BALINT, M. *et al.* (1972), *Focal Psychotherapy* (Tavistock, London).
FEINSINGER, T. E. (1948), 'Psychiatric interviewing: some principles and procedures in insight therapy' (*Am. J. of Psychiatry*, vol. 105, p. 87).

FRENCH, T. M. (1958), *The Integration of Behavior* (University of Chicago Press, Chicago).
MALAN, D. H. (1963), *A Study of Brief Psychotherapy* (Plenum Press, New York).
MALAN, D. H. (1976), *The Frontier of Brief Psychotherapy* (Plenum Press, New York).

Focal therapy record sheet (FTRS)

A recording tool used in *brief focal family therapy* allowing the therapist to monitor the therapeutic process, the changes that take place between sessions and the final outcome of treatment. The sheet includes seven headings as follows: therapeutic aims; feedback from family and inter-session events; content of sessions as it relates to the *focal formulation*; information which enlarges the focal formulation; area of focal formulation to be worked on; therapist's aims and strategies; and the criteria for improvement which have been met.

FURNISS, T. *et al.* (1983), 'Clinical process recording in focal family therapy' (*J. of Marital and Family Therapy*, vol. 9, pp. 147-70).

Focus of convenience

The primary application of a *construct* for which the user finds it maximally useful. Kelly suggested that, although a variety of *elements* will fall within a construct's *range of convenience*, some will be better described by it than others and these former constitute the construct's focus of convenience.

KELLY, G. A. (1955), *Psychology of Personal Construct* (W. W. Norton, New York).
KELLY, G. A. (1963), *A Theory of Personality*, (W. W. Norton, New York).

Focused problem resolution

A form of *brief therapy* developed originally at the Brief Therapy Project formed as part of the Mental Research Institute (MRI), Palo Alto, California, in 1967. The basic premises are that all problems are essentially behavioural and that the problem behaviour is maintained by other behaviours within the client's current environment. Treatment is therefore focused on the client's current experience and does not investigate the aetiology of problem behaviours. Both for the therapist and for the client, an understanding of the origin of the problem behaviours is considered to be redundant. Usually a maximum number of ten one-hour sessions is offered, during which the main presenting complaint is the focus of intervention. The client's belief that the problem he presents for treatment *is* a problem rather than a *symptom* of it is accepted by the therapist.

The therapist seeks to achieve the minimum possible change that is required to resolve the *presenting problem* and when this is achieved, therapy is terminated. A *team* approach is preferred, with one member working with the client or family in the room and the others consulting from behind a *one-way screen.*

Focused problem resolution grew out of the interactional and *systemic* ideas of *family therapy*, the hypnotic work of Milton Erikson (Haley 1973) and the *strategic therapy* of Haley and others, including earlier work which took place at the MRI (Bateson *et al.* 1956; Watzlawick *et al.* 1968; Watzlawick *et al.* 1974). Therapists are prepared to see either an individual or a family group, depending on who is motivated to come for therapy. Focused problem resolution differs sharply from many forms of family therapy in its emphasis on symptom removal and its focus on the presenting complaint. However, its emphasis on active intervention and *homework assignments* is shared with Minuchin's *structural family therapy* and various forms of *behaviour therapy*, and its preoccupation with tactics and strategies to bring about change is similar to *strategic therapy*. Its premise that psychological and emotional problems are actually situational difficulties of interaction between people is a belief shared at a fundamental level by all family therapists.

Therapists using this approach assume that the locus of problem-maintaining behaviour lies in the client's *attempted solution* to the problem. Therapeutic intervention therefore focuses on interrupting and changing the attempted solution, within an interactional context. *Goals* are limited to small, clearly definable pieces of behaviour, based on the belief that small achievements prompt the client on to further self-induced changes, thus changing the vicious spiral of chronic problem behaviour into a beneficent spiral of positive change. A six-stage scheme for treatment is routinely used with each case: introduction to the treatment set-up (there is no screening and no waiting list); specific definition of the problem to be treated; assessment of the behaviour which maintains the problem; establishment of treatment goals to define the minimum sufficient change required to eliminate the problem; selection and application of behavioural interventions (including the use of *paradox*, *reframing*, use of *pessimism*, *tasks*, and other directed behaviour change).

Therapists using this approach claim that it differs from other forms of brief therapy in its reliance on radically different premises rather than simply being an attenuated form of long-term treatment. It is considered appropriate for problems of chronic duration as well as of acute onset. Therapists rely chiefly on patients' self-report for evaluating *outcome*. Thus, at the beginning and end of treatment, the therapist relies on the patient's judgment as to what the problem is and whether it has been relieved. Both can be criticised as naive and oversimplistic, given the complexity of most people's intrapersonal and intersystemic difficulties, but notwithstanding these reservations, the outcome reported by Weakland *et al.* (1974) of 72 per cent success or significantly improved compares favourably with other forms of brief and long-term treatment.

BATESON, S. *et al.* (1956), 'Toward a theory of schizophrenia' (*Behavioral Science*, vol. 1, pp. 251-64).

FISCH, R. *et al.* (1982), *The Tactics of Change: Doing Therapy Briefly* (Jossey-Bass, San Francisco).

HALEY, J. (1973), *Uncommon Therapy* (W. W. Norton, New York).

WATZLAWICK, P. *et al.* (1968), *Pragmatics of Human Communication* (W. W. Norton, New York).

WATZLAWICK, P. *et al.* (1974), *Change: Principles of Problem Formation and Problem Resolution* (W. W. Norton, New York).
WEAKLAND, J. H. *et al.* (1974), 'Brief therapy: focussed problem resolution' (*Family Process*, vol. 13, pp. 141-68).

Focusing

A technique introduced by Gendlin (1962) whereby the patient is asked to attend to his or her feelings about a problem in a series of stages, recognise their uniqueness and validity and allow a 'felt sense' to form which enables new perceptions of the problem and possible courses of action to emerge. Gendlin (1978) has developed a series of focusing instructions which the therapist gives to the patient, leaving silent periods in between for the internal work to proceed. These consist of asking the patient to attend to how his or her body feels inside; gain an awareness of the feelings that exist; allow a problem to emerge and gain a sense of it as a whole; pay attention to the one most salient feeling that begins to emerge; allow it to begin to change; put fresh words and pictures to the changed feeling that best capture its essence; and to relax and reflect upon the changes that have occurred.

Focusing tries to address the patient's difficulties very directly; rather than talking about them, the therapist tries to have an immediate impact on them. The experience is centred in the patient's body. The therapist enables the patient's felt sense, experienced in his body, to tackle the problem and to answer the questions which the problem poses. In the process, the patient gains *insight*, experiences emotional release or *catharsis* and becomes freer to decide to try out new behaviours. Focusing is a technique used in *existential* and *humanistic* approaches to psychotherapy.

GENDLIN, E. T. (1962), *Experiencing and the Creation of Meaning* (Free Press, New York).
GENDLIN, E. T. (1978), *Focusing* (Dodd, New York).
KANTOR, S. and ZIMRING, F. M. (1976), 'The effects of focusing on a problem' (*Psychotherapy: Theory, Research and Practice*, vol. 13, pp. 255-8).

Folie à deux

Two people in close association who share the same delusional idea. The concept involves the contagion of one person by the psychopathology of the other, in a linear causal relationship. An extension of the condition to three and four people has been reported as a folie à trois and a folie à quatre respectively, or simply as a folie communique or a folie à famille. The concept predates *systemic* views of psychopathology but Sonne *et al.* (1962) use it to explain the need for a particular *resistance* encountered in *conjoint* work, whereby a vital member of the *system* absents himself from treatment in order to protect the dyad or system from change. Gralnick (1942) reviewed the literature and described the essential process as 'the psychosis of association'. Recently, Wikler (1980) has looked at the phenomenon from a systems perspective and suggests that the shared delusions present in the folie à famille are a more extreme version of the shared *family myths* found in less pathological situations.

GRALNICK, A. (1942), 'Folie à Deux – the psychosis of association' (*Psychiatric Quarterly*, vol. 16, pp. 491-520).
SONNE, J. *et al.* (1962), 'The absent member manoeuvre as a resistance in family therapy of schizophrenia' (*Family Process*, vol. 1, pp. 44-62).
WIKLER, L. (1980), 'Folie à famille: a family therapist's perspective' (*Family Process*, vol. 19, pp. 257-68).

See also *Absent member manoeuvre*.

Folie communique
See *Folie à deux*.

Force
Term used by Lewin in *field theory* to describe the tendency towards movement within the individual's psychological field. Forces influence the individual's possibilities and opportunities for action. According to Lewin (1951), 'the construct force characterises, for a given point of the life space, the direction and strength of the tendency to change.' The force may be either *intrapsychic* or environmental in origin.

LEWIN, K. (1951), *Field Theory in Social Science* (Greenwood Press, Westport, Conn.).

Foulkes, Sigmund Heinrich (1898-1976)
Sigmund Foulkes, pioneer in methods of *group psychotherapy* and *group analysis*, was born in Karlsruhe, Germany in 1898. He was the youngest of five children. After serving in the German army during the First World War, he began his medical studies in 1919, first at Heidelberg and later at Munich and Frankfurt, where he received his MD in 1923. After postgraduate studies at Frankfurt and two years' study of neurology under Kurt Goldstein, Foulkes began his psychoanalytic and psychiatric studies in Vienna in 1928. His training analyst was Hélène Deutsch and during this time he worked with Heinz Hartmann and other prominent psycho-analysts. In 1930, he joined the recently founded Frankfurt Psychoanalytic Institute and was put in charge of the clinic. On the invitation of Ernest *Jones*, he left Germany in 1933 and settled in London, changing his name from Fuchs to Foulkes and becoming a naturalised British subject. In the early 1940s he began to develop psychoanalytic group work and introduced group work methods at the Northfield Military Hospital, Birmingham, transforming the hospital into a *therapeutic community*. He began to hold regular meetings with others interested in group psychotherapy and in 1952 he founded the Group Analytic Society (London), remaining its president until 1970. Some of his most important books include *Introduction to Group Analytic Psychotherapy* (1948), *Group Psychotherapy* (with E. Anthony, 1957), *Therapeutic Group Analysis* (1964) and *Group Analytic Psychotherapy* (1975). In 1967 he founded the journal *Group Analysis* and remained its editor until 1975.

Free association
The patient's spontaneous uncensored self-expression to the therapist or analyst within the treatment situation. Free association became the 'fundamental rule' of psycho-analytic technique and was, to a large extent,

synonymous with the whole psychoanalytic method, superseding the pre-analytic methods of hypnosis and suggestion and developing from Jung's early work on *word association*. By encouraging the patient to say whatever comes into his mind to the *analyst*, the *ego*'s *censorship* is bypassed and access is afforded to the patient's *unconscious*. Free association remains the unique form of com-munication between patient and analyst and a primary tool of *psychoanalysis*, standing in opposition to the structured, task-focused approach of the *behavioural therapies*. Although enquiry into the patient's *dreams* may provide a starting point, the analyst's task is to refrain from providing any prompt which might encourage the patient consciously to select his material. The activity required in free associa-tion runs counter to all previous experience and violates the rules of normal communica-tion. It imposes a new and unfamiliar task on the *analysand*, requiring what Kris (1952) has called a 'regression in the service of the ego'.

BELLACK, L. (1961), 'Free association: con-ceptual and clinical aspects' (*Int. J. of Psycho-analysis*, vol. 42, pp. 9-20).
FREUD, S. (1910), 'Five lectures on psychoanalysis' (*Standard Edition*, vol. 11, Hogarth Press, London).
KRIS, E. (1952), *Psychoanalytic Explorations in Art* (International University Press, New York).
ZILBOORG, G. (1952), 'Some sidelights on free association' (*Int. J. of Psychoanalysis*, vol. 33, pp. 489-95).

See also *Stream of consciousness*.

French school (of psychoanalysis)
The oldest section of the French school of psychoanalysis is the Psychoanalytic Society of Paris, founded in 1926 by Marie Buonaparte, Laforgne, Allendy, Lowenstein and others. Splitting and sub-grouping has been particu-larly prevalent amongst French psychoanalysts, and after the Second World War the French Society of Psychoanalysis was formed, led by Jacques Lacan and Daniel Lagache. Since then, this group has further sub-divided, with

Jacques Lacan forming his own Freudian School of Paris, and this in turn has given birth to a 'Fourth Group' made up of some of Lacan's followers. Thus, the major sub-groups of the French school consist of the Psychoanalytic Society of Paris; the French Society of Psychoanalysis; the Freudian School of Paris; and Le Quatrième Groupe. A major difference exists between the French Society's emphasis on a historic interpretation of the *unconscious* and the Freudian School's emphasis on the linguistic structure of the unconscious. Because of the interest shown in Lacan through recent translations of his work into English, this entry will focus on the Freudian School of Paris.

Lacan's ideas have had wide political, literary and cultural influence in France. His writings are, however, notoriously complex and this, together with the fact that they are not easy to translate, has, until recently, reduced his influence in the English-speaking world. Lacan believes that the theory of linguistics provides an appropriate metatheory for psychoanalysis and that its adoption resolves some of the dilemmas inherent in Freud's original *metapsychology*. 'If psychoanalysis is to become instituted as the science of the unconscious one must set out with the notion that the unconscious is structured like a language' (Lacan 1978).

Lacan describes a three-fold ordering of the psychoanalytic field, the imaginary, the symbolic and the real, and he suggests that it is important that the analyst avoids confusing one with another. Lacan's concept of the imaginary, or first stage of development, is based on the idea that the *ego* is built up initially from its own reflection, or image. This is perceived literally during what Lacan calls the 'mirror phase' in which the baby catches sight of itself in a mirror (see also *Winnicott*). Thus the baby anticipates, in an imaginary way, its own inner unity and the mastery of its environment which is to follow, stemming from future development of its ego. By the symbolic order, or second stage, Lacan suggests that the individual begins to participate in pre-existing symbolic systems of culture, especially that of

language. The structure of the unconscious can be compared with the symbolic structure of language and thus it is possible to apply the rules of linguistics to uncovering and understanding the symbolism of the unconscious which is formed through the mechanisms of metonymy and *metaphor*. Moreover, the therapeutic ingredients of the analytic process reside in the symbolic level of the analyst's language and his method of using it; and the therapeutic task of psychoanalysis is the restoration of full speech to the patient. The third order of development is the real, which should not be confused with external reality. According to Sheridan, Lacan's (1977) translator, the real 'stands for what is neither symbolic nor imaginary and remains foreclosed to analytic experience . . . which may be approached, but never grasped.'

Prior to the imaginary stage, the baby is incompletely formed. He is 'a broken egg' or 'une hommelette' and during this 'premature' phase of life, the baby experiences *alienation*. Maturity is judged by how near or far the individual is being 'a language user', language granting him the possibility, as Wolheim (1979) puts it, 'of articulating reality, outer and inner. It can now have thoughts, form desires and enter into relations with others.' In the imaginary stage, the infant engages in a dyadic relationship (between himself and his image); in the symbolic stage he engages in three-person relationships (between himself, the sign or language and the other). The prevailing *phantasy* of the imaginary stage is the phallus and of the symbolic stage the Name-of-the-Father, or sum of all rule-governed activity, especially speech.

Lacan has introduced many controversial techniques into his practice of psychoanalysis: for example, the ten-minute therapeutic session and the extremely attenuated training period for new analysts. The linguistic emphasis that permeates the whole of Lacan's work has led to a discussion of the use of his ideas within a theory of interpersonal therapy and Poster (1978) discusses Lacan's contribution to a language of the family.

GORNEY, J. E. (1982), 'The clinical application of Lacan in the psychoanalytic situation' (*Psychoanalytic Review*, vol. 69, pp. 241-8).
LACAN, J. (1977), *Ecrits: A Selection* (translated by Sheridan, A., Tavistock, London).
LACAN, J. (1978), *The Four Fundamental Concepts of Psychoanalysis* (translated by Sheridan, A., Hogarth Press, London).
LEMAIRE, A. (1977), *Jacques Lacan* (Routledge & Kegan Paul, London).
MANNONI, M. (1970), *The Child, His 'Illness' and the Other* (Pantheon, London).
POSTER, M. (1978), *Critical Theory of the Family* (Pluto Press, London).
SCHNEIDERMAN, S. (1983), *Jacques Lacan* (Cambridge, Mass., Harvard University Press).
TURKE, S. (1979), *Psychoanalytic Politics: Freud's French Revolution* (Burnett Books, London).
WILDEN, A. (1968), *The Language of the Self* (Johns Hopkins University Press, Baltimore).
WOLHEIM, R. (1979), 'Psycholinguistic guru' (in *The New York Review of Books*, 25 January).

Freud, Anna (1895-1982)
Pioneer in *child analysis* and *child psychotherapy*, Anna Freud was the youngest of Sigmund Freud's six children and the only one to become a psychoanalyst. Born in Vienna, she trained first as a teacher and then as an *analyst*. During the 1920s she lectured on analytic work with children, an area of work in which she broke entirely new ground. In 1930, she published her first major book, *Psychoanalysis for Teachers and Parents* and in 1937, her seminal work on *The Ego and the Mechanisms of Defence*. She and her father escaped to England from the Nazis in 1939 and she remained living and working in Hampstead, London, until her death in 1982. Her diagnostic and analytic work with children is set out in two major books, *Normality and Pathology in Childhood* (1965) and *The Psychoanalytic Treatment of Children* (1946). In 1947 she founded the Hampstead Child Therapy Course and in 1952 the Hampstead Clinic. From this centre, her influence spread to many aspects of education and child care, beyond her primary focus on child analysis, and a

nursery school attached to the clinic enabled the integration between her different interests to continue until she died. She is also noted for her work with her colleague Dorothy Burlingham on children separated by evacuation during the Second World War from their parents. She saw her task as the development and consolidation of her father's theories, often in the face of criticism and opposition from other schools of psychoanalysis.

See also *Continental school of psychoanalysis*.

Freud, Sigmund (1856-1939)
Sigmund Freud, the founder of *psychoanalysis* was born in Freiberg, Moravia, in 1856, of Jewish parents. He was the eldest of seven children from his father's second marriage. When he was three, the family moved first to Leipzig and then to Vienna. In 1873 he began his medical studies and received his MD from the University of Vienna in 1881. He followed this with postgraduate studies in the natural sciences and spent six years doing research under Ernst Brucke who believed in the possibility of reducing psychological processes to physiological laws. After a period of residency at the Viennese General Hospital, Freud went to Paris to study hypnosis under Jean Charcot. In 1886 he married Martha Bernays, began work in a children's hospital and began too, his collaborative work with Joseph Breuer on the psychological treatment of hysteria. The death of his father in 1896 precipitated a period of painful self-reflection, which developed into a lifelong *self-analysis* and a rich source of new insight into psychological processes and the aetiology of psychic disturbance. In 1902, he was appointed professor at the University of Vienna and later that year began meeting with interested colleagues in his home on Wednesday evenings. This Wednesday Society formed the beginnings of the first Psychoanalytic Society. Here Freud and his early followers, Jung, Adler, Stekel and Ferenczi, explored and developed the major themes of psychoanalytic study – infantile sexuality, the exploration of the *unconscious*, and the study of *dreams*, building on work that had already been developed

147

by workers in other fields. The influences that contributed to Freud's major work on personality and his institution of psychoanalysis were very varied and included the work of Pierre Janet, Charles Darwin and Franz Brentano. Freud was a prodigious writer, the Standard Edition of his works being published by the Hogarth Press, London. Many of his discoveries were published in the form of case studies (Anna O, Little Hans, The Wolf Man, Dora). After a brilliantly successful and productive life, Freud experienced great suffering towards the end. In 1923, he discovered that he had cancer of the jaw and before his death he underwent over thirty operations. His daughter Sophie and his grandson died the same year, and with Hitler's rise to power, he had to experience first the burning of his books in 1934 and then exile to England in 1938. He died the following year, leaving his daughter Anna in England, the only one of his six children to become a psychoanalyst.

Fromm, Erich (1900-1980)
Fromm was born in Frankfurt, Germany in 1900, the only child of Jewish parents. He studied sociology, philosophy and psychology at Frankfurt and Munich Universities and received his doctorate in 1922 from the University of Heidelberg. He undertook his psychoanalytic training at the Berlin Psychoanalytic Institute where he met Karen Horney. Although his early psychoanalytic practice was classical and was modelled closely on the work of Freud, his interest in social and cultural factors led him to attempt a new integration of social and psychological ideas. He emigrated to the United States in 1933 and taught psychoanalytic psychology at the New School for Social Research, New York, and developed his professional association with Harry Stack Sullivan, Karen Horney and Frieda Fromm-Reichmann, whom he married but later divorced. Although he is usually thought of as a neo-Freudian and as a member of the *interpersonal school* of psychoanalysis, he thought of himself as remaining closer to Freud's work than Sullivan or Horney. Nevertheless, his prolific writings reflect his strong interest in socio-cultural influences and

the effect of social and political conditions on personality development. Fromm experienced some difficulty in advancing his work in New York because of his lack of a medical degree, and in 1943 he left the American Institute of Psychoanalysis and joined the William Allenson White Foundation. In 1949 he went to live in Mexico where he continued his writing. In 1974 he moved to Switzerland, where he died in 1980. Some of his best known books include *The Art of Loving* (1956), *The Escape from Freedom* (1941), *The Crisis of Psychoanalysis* (1970) and *Anatomy of Human Destructiveness* (1973).

Fromm-Reichmann, Frieda (1889-1957)
Frieda Fromm-Reichmann was born in Karlsruhe, Germany, the oldest of three sisters. She studied medicine at the University of Königsberg, receiving her MD in 1914. During the First World War she worked alongside Kurt Goldstein, caring for brain injured soldiers, and after the war she worked with Schutz, collaborating with him in his *autogenic training* methods. Becoming familiar with Freud's writings, she trained as an *analyst* and, with her husband Erich Fromm, founded the Psychoanalytic Training Institute of South West Germany. In 1935 she emigrated to the USA and began work at Chestnut Lodge, Rockville, Maryland. She was greatly influenced by Harry Stack Sullivan in the development of her particular approach to *psychoanalysis* which she called *intensive psychotherapy*. Her major works are *Principles of Intensive Psychotherapy* (1950) and *Psychoanalysis and Psychotherapy: Selected Papers* (1974). The novel *I Never Promised You a Rose Garden* by Hannah Greene describes her approach to therapy.

Function
See *Process*.

Functional
Used in two ways: first, in contrast to organic, to indicate that an individual's *symptoms* and disturbance relate to psychological and/or social factors, impaired or deficient learning, lack of problem solving skills, etc., but not to

organic impairment or disease; second, in contrast to *dysfunctional*, to indicate an adaptive, healthy, well-functioning individual, relationship or group.

Functional analysis
See *Behavioural analysis*.

Functional family therapy
See *Behavioural family therapy*.

Functional professional
See *Paraprofessional*.

Fundamental postulate
Term used to describe the basic premise upon which Kelly's *personal construct theory* rests. Kelly's (1955) fundamental postulate runs as follows: 'A person's processes are psychologically channelised by the ways in which he anticipates events.' The postulate, which is elaborated in eleven *corollaries*, captures the essence of Kelly's theory, i.e. it is concerned with individuals, construed as forms of motion and the fact that the individual's psychological life is structured in a flexible yet non-random way by the way in which he predicts future reality.

KELLY, G. A. (1955), *The Psychology of Personal Constructs* (W. W. Norton, New York).
KELLY, G. A. (1963), *A Theory of Personality* (W. W. Norton, New York).

Fundamental rule
See *Free association*.

G

Game
Term introduced by Berne (1961) to describe a defensive, ulterior *transaction* occurring between two people and operating on contradictory overt and covert levels. Berne suggests that games are experienced in different degrees of seriousness and different levels of consequence to the players. The game players operate from three distinct roles: those of victim, persecutor and rescuer. These roles are interchangeable and players may switch backwards and forwards between them during the course of a game. Games usually become stereotyped and predictable and result in both players experiencing bad feelings or what Berne calls 'rackets'. Games serve to protect the individual from authentic and intimate relationships and to provide a self-reinforcing pattern of negative relationship experiences. Berne (1961) describes a varied selection of commonly played games. The therapist's task in *transactional analysis* is to enable the patient to engage in more complementary communicational transactions and to develop a more straightforward, authentic method of relating to others. Techniques which the therapist may use to achieve this include *confrontation*, *psychodrama*, *insight*, *Gestalt* techniques and emotional *working through* of childhood experiences – depending on the 'school' of transactional analysis being practised.

BERNE, E. (1961), *Transactional Analysis in Psychotherapy* (Grove Press, New York).

Generalisation
The degree to which learning or experience gained in an artificial setting such as therapy or training sessions can be transferred to the real-life situation in which the client or trainee must actually function. In behavioural terms, generalisation involves the transfer of effects to *responses* or *stimuli* that have not been directly the focus of *reinforcement* or *conditioning*. Generalisation is a fundamental principle of *learning theory* and therefore of *behaviour therapy*, but it is also fundamental to the therapeutic efficacy of the *transference* relationship in *psychoanalysis* and to all forms of psychotherapy other than those where the psycho-social situation itself is the focus of treatment.

Transfer can be either positive or negative – that is, the learning in one situation can either have a helpful or a detrimental effect on another situation. Successful positive transfer of learning is enhanced by a specific focus on the behaviour to be changed or learned; by proximity of the behaviour or learning to the real-life situation; and by opportunities to practise the changed behaviour both in the artificial and the real life situation, through *covert modelling*, *role play* and *behavioural rehearsal*. In the residential setting, Heiner (1975) distinguishes between internal generalisation, between different parts of the treatment programme, and external generalisation, between the treatment programme and the outside world. Kazdin and Bootzin (1972) have suggested a variety of techniques that increase generalisation and suggest that behaviours should be selected that will come under the control of naturally occurring reinforcers when the client returns to his natural environment. Therapists who advocate the use of *coping skills interventions* suggest that there is a greater degree of generalisation to other stress-inducing situations when using these approaches compared with *counter conditioning* techniques.

The greater use of community treatment facilities, *home visits* and the involvement of parents, significant others and collaterals in treatment programmes all illustrate a greater understanding of the determinants of successful generalisation. In addition, the use of treatment interventions directed towards the *pathogenic system* itself means that the concept of generalisation has in these instances been superseded.

KAZDIN, A. E. and BOOTZIN, R. R. (1972), 'The token economy: an evaluative review' (*J. of Applied Behavior Analysis*, vol. 5, pp. 343-72).
HEINER, H. (1975), 'Self control in individual and group behavior modification programmes for emotionally disturbed children' (in Thompson, T. and Dockens, W., *Applications of Behavior Modification*, Academic Press, New York).

Genital stage

The stage of psycho-sexual development usually associated with adolescence but also used to describe a period between the *phallic stage* and *latency* in psychoanalytic theory, when actual sexual relationships with another becomes the major aim of sexual excitement and pleasure. Genital sexuality is considered to be the form of libidinal expression in which love, concern and altruism become normal and dominant features. Freud (1905) suggested that the full expression of the genital stage in adolescence is prefigured in infancy, 'the only difference lies in the fact that in childhood . . . the primacy of the genitals has been effected only very incompletely or not at all.' Moreover, Freud suggested that, as in the phallic stage, the infant's interest in the genitals is focused on the penis, whether the child is a boy or a girl. Klein (1928) agreed that the genital stage made its appearance in infancy with strong sexual feelings associated with the genitals but, as with the phallic stage, she asserted that a girl's interest was also focused on her own genitals. Although Erikson (1950) does not distinguish the genital and phallic stages he underlines the early genital experience, viewing it as marked by experiences of inclusion and intrusion.

ERIKSON, E. H. (1950), *Childhood and Society* (Penguin, Harmondsworth).
FREUD, S. (1905), 'Three essays on the theory of sexuality' (*Standard Edition*, vol. 7, Hogarth Press, London).
KLEIN, M. (1928), 'Early stages of the Oedipus conflict' (in *Contributions to Psychoanalysis*, Hogarth Press, London).

See also *Stages of development*.

Genogram

A graphic device for gathering and recording family history, based on the idea of a family tree. The genogram can be used with individuals, couples, families or in group work settings, whenever the method of psychotherapy values the use of *genotypic* material. The individual is asked to describe his family in response to the therapist's questions, who then draws out the individuals, their relationships, and significant dates and events on a blackboard or piece of paper, using standard symbols. Alternatively, the individual may be asked to construct his own genogram between sessions as a *homework assignment*. When constructed within a *family therapy* session, the genogram allows the therapist to link past and current events, check out the different views family members hold of significant family members and events in the past, elucidate *family myths* and clarify current affective material that can be surveyed and discussed in the less threatening context of the past.

GUERIN, P. J. and PENDERGAST, E. G. (1976), 'Evaluation of family systems and genograms' (in Guerin, P. (ed.), *Family Therapy: Theory and Practice*, Gardner Press, New York).
LIEBERMAN, S. (1980), *Transgenerational Family Therapy* (Croom Helm, London).
WATCHEL, E. F. (1982), 'Family psyche over three generations: the genogram revisited' (*J. of Marital and Family Therapy*, vol. 8, pp. 335-43).

See also *Action techniques, Diagnosis, Family constellation, History taking, Transgenerational family therapy.*

Genotype
The genetic constitution or history of the individual, family or group which may exert a causative influence on his or her development and behaviour. Genotypic *diagnosis* is a form of personality assessment which attempts to discover and classify the underlying causes of behaviour, both in terms of hereditary traits and underlying *psychodynamics*. According to Hogan (1979), 'genotypic classification is inferential in nature . . . and it is the research on genotypic diagnosis that has stirred the most controversy and put the value of diagnosis for therapeutic purposes most in doubt.' Nevertheless, even present-centred therapies, such as most forms of *family therapy, cognitive therapy, behaviour therapy* and others, often undertake some exploration of patient history through techniques such as a *genogram*.

HOGAN, D. (1979), *The Regulation of Psychotherapists*, vol. 1 (Ballinger, Cambridge, Mass.).

See also *History taking, Phenotype.*

Genuineness
The degree to which the therapist is freely and deeply himself and relates to the client in an unfeigned and undefensive manner. One of the *core conditions* described by Rogers as being essential within the psychotherapeutic relationship. It is often used interchangeably with authenticity and *congruence*, although congruence is also viewed as the means by which genuineness and authenticity are achieved and expressed. Rogers and Truax (1967) view genuineness as the precondition for *empathy* and *unconditional positive regard*, neither of which 'can possibly be meaningful in the relationship unless they are real. Consequently unless a therapist is, both in these respects and others, integrated and genuine within the therapeutic encounter, the other conditions could scarcely exist to a satisfactory degree.'

Genuineness is a quality of being on the part of the therapist, leading to an authentic presentation of himself so far as this is possible for him and resulting in *self-disclosure* on the part of the client. The client's need to believe that the therapist genuinely feels empathy and unconditional regard for him has led some writers (e.g. Watkins 1978) to make the further suggestion that the therapist must therefore be completely open and 'disclosed' in all his dealings with the client. This presents a variety of difficulties for the therapist. For example, he may feel obliged to convey honestly to the client the full range of his feelings, including negative ones – which may or may not be therapeutic for the client. Second, he may feel obliged to disclose the techniques he is using which may be contra-indicated in the case of some approaches (e.g. *strategic therapy*). This logical corollary is however, specifically disallowed by Barrett-Leonard (1962), and most other therapists and researchers: whilst 'the highly congruent individual is completely honest, direct and sincere in what he conveys, he does not feel any compulsion to communicate his perceptions or any need to withhold them for emotionally self protective reasons.' The debate about genuineness hinges to some degree on the relative weighting placed on technical vs. *relationship factors* in therapy and also on the distinction made between a core self and peripheral manifestations of it which may vary even while the individual continues to be authentic.

BARRETT-LEONARD, G. T. (1962), 'Dimensions of therapist response as causal factors in therapeutic change' (*Psychological Monographs*, vol. 76, no. 43, whole no. 562).
ROGERS, C. R. and TRUAX, C. B. (1967), 'The therapeutic conditions antecedent to change: a theoretical view' (in Rogers, C. R. (ed.), *The Therapeutic Relationship and its Impact*, University of Wisconsin Press).
WATKINS, J. G. (1978), *The Therapeutic Self* (Human Sciences Press, New York).

Gestalt psychology

Literal German meaning 'form' or 'whole'. The Gestalt approach to psychology was developed in Germany during the 1930s and 1940s by Wertheimer, Kohler (1930) and Koffka (1935) based on the early work of the philosopher and psychologist von Ehrenfels. Their work sprang out of a dissatisfaction with both *psychoanalysis* and *behaviourism* and the inability of these theories to deal with the person as a whole. In contrast, Gestalt psychologists suggest that the individual perceives and responds to configurations as wholes. Their ideas were influential in the development of *humanistic psychology* and found particular clinical expression in *Gestalt therapy*.

KOFFKA, K. (1935), *Principles of Gestalt Psychology* (Harcourt, Brace & World, New York).
KOHLER, W. (1930), *Gestalt Psychology* (Liveright, New York).

Gestalt therapy

A method of therapy developed by Fritz Perls which stresses an *a-historical, existential* approach and which aims to help the individual to be self-supportive and self-responsible. The primary therapeutic tool is the development of awareness of what is going on within the self at any given moment.

According to Yontef (1971) Gestalt therapy helps the patient gain 'awareness of the process of awareness' and 'brings self-realisation through Here-and-Now experiments in directed awareness'. The approach is *holistic* in that it is directed to the whole person in his environment. It draws upon the theoretical insights of *Gestalt psychology* and it has been influenced technically by both *psychodrama* and the *body therapies*.

Gestalt therapy is practised in both the individual and the group work setting, although the group work approach is more usual. Its principles have also been applied in *family therapy* (Kempler 1974) and in *art therapy* (Rhyne 1973). The therapist attends to the patient's behaviour, *non-verbal communication*, breathing pattern and evidence of tensions in the here-and-now experience of the session, pointing them out to the patient and asking him what they mean. Typically, the patient takes the *hot seat* and may be encouraged to act out the roles he perceives significant others to be playing in his life, as well as the different aspects of his own personality which he has *suppressed* or disowned through *projection, introjection* and dissociation. The abandonment or integration of these disowned parts into the personality enables the individual to complete his 'Gestalten', meet his needs and accept himself as he is and thereby diminish his psychic conflict. Perls used the language of Gestalt psychology to suggest the way in which the individual's needs become a figure in relation to the ground of his experience. Perls (1969) points out that 'the most important fact about the figure-background formation is that if a need is genuinely satisfied, the situation is changed'.

A criticism levied against Gestalt therapy by both the *body* and *depth* therapists is that it can be superficial in its approach to profound psychic conflict. It may help patients get in touch with their needs but may not teach them the skills or wisdom to deal with them.

FAGAN, J. and SHEPPARD, I. L. (eds) (1970), *Gestalt Therapy Now* (Science & Behavior Books, Palo Alto, Calif.).

HATCHER, C. and HIMMELSTEIN, P. (eds) (1976), *The Handbook of Gestalt Therapy* (Jason Aronson, New York).

HIMMELSTEIN, P. (1982), 'A comprehensive bibliography of Gestalt therapy' (*Catalog of Selected Documents in Psychology*, vol. 12, MS 2421).

KEMPLER, W. (1974), *Principles of Gestalt Family Therapy* (Kempler Institute, Costa Mesa, Calif.).

PERLS, F. S. (1969), *Gestalt Therapy Verbatim* (Real People Press, Moab, Utah).

PERLS, F. S. (1973), *The Gestalt Approach: An Eye-witness to Therapy* (Science & Behavior Books, Palo Alto, Calif.).

RHYNE, J. (1973), *The Gestalt Art Experience* (Magnolia Street Publications, Chicago).

RIET, V. VAN DER *et al.* (1980), *Gestalt Therapy* (Pergamon Press, New York).

YONTEF, G. M. (1971), *A Review of the Practice of Gestalt Therapy* (Brunner/Mazel, New York).

Ghosts from the past

The presence of an *intrapsychic object* derived from the memory of a dead relative which significantly influences current family relationships. Paul (Paul and Grosser 1965) defines ghosts from the past as dead family members who survive pathologically within several current family systems. The network of internalised objects thus created produces a fixed *equilibrium* within the *system* which prevents change from occurring.

PAUL, N. L. and GROSSER, G. H. (1965), 'Operational mourning and its role in conjoint family therapy' (*Community Mental Health Journal*, vol. 1, pp. 339-45).

See also *Family transference, Family myth, Shadow of the ancestor.*

Gifts

The giving of gifts by the patient to the therapist has been studied mainly in the context of psychoanalysis. Freud (1917) linked the production of faeces with the infant's first experience of his ability to give gifts and gifts given to the *analyst* are usually considered to be a form of *acting out* from the patient's infantile self. Freud (1917), however, clearly expected that gifts would be given by patients: 'those who question this derivation of gifts [as above] should consider their experience of psychoanalytic treatment, study the gifts they receive as doctors from their patients and watch the storms of transference which a gift from them can rouse in their patients.' Stein (1965) suggests that gifts are similar to the *manifest content* of *dreams* and may express through *condensation* several meanings. She discusses gifts as forms of *communication*, as a defence and as a form of magic action. Gifts may also be viewed as manipulations, as restitution for actual or phantasied harm done to the therapist or, at the end of a successful treatment, simply as a mature expression of gratitude. Most therapists advise the acceptance of small gifts, but the action will probably also call for *interpretation* of its significance.

FREUD, S. (1917), 'On transformation of instinct as exemplified in anal eroticism' (*Standard Edition*, vol. 17, Hogarth Press, London).

SILBER, A. (1969), 'A patient's gift: its meaning and function' (*Int. J. of Psychoan.*, vol. 50, pp. 335-41).

STEIN, H. (1965), 'The gift in therapy' (*Am. J. of Psychotherapy*, vol. 19, pp. 480-6).

See also *Transitional object.*

Glover, Edward (1888-1972)

A foremost exponent of *psychoanalysis* in Britain, Edward Glover trained first in biology and the basic sciences and later in medicine. He trained as a psychoanalyst at the Berlin Institute of Psychoanalysis, undergoing his personal analysis with Karl Abraham. He took a leading part in the organisation of the British Psychoanalytic Society in 1924, and for the next twenty years taught at the Society and wrote some of his major works. Glover was influential in encouraging Melanie Klein to settle in London and was an early advocate of her innovative techniques. However, after the 'Controversial Discussions' within the British Society (see *Continental school of psychoanalysis*)

Glover felt unable to support the Kleinian approach and he resigned from the Society in 1944. The following year he published a searching critique of the Kleinian approach and a considerable amount of his later work was devoted to underscoring the scientific nature of psychoanalysis as proposed by Freud and the need to exclude what he perceived to be the 'wild surmises' and unscientific dilutions of psychoanalytic theory and technique introduced in the newer developments. He produced over one hundred scientific works and one of his most important contributions to psychoanalytic study, beyond his rigorous restatement of the classical Freudian position, was his concept of ego-nuclei, in which he suggested that the primitive *ego* is a compromise formation, consisting of autonomous ego-nuclei. His most important works include *Basic Mental Concepts* (1947), *The Technique of Psychoanalysis* (1955), and *The Birth of the Ego* (1968).

Goal (treatment)

The object or end towards which the treatment process is aimed. Treatment goals in some therapeutic approaches are method-specific: for example, in *psychoanalysis* the treatment goal for all patients is to render unconscious material conscious, in *client-centred therapy* it is to increase *self-actualisation*, and in *family therapy* it is to restructure the *system* and to bring about a more fully functioning family group. In most *strategic* and *behavioural therapies* treatment goals are client-specific and organised pragmatically in the light of the *presenting problem*.

Johnson and Matross (1977) suggest that 'the goals for therapy are a combination of the individual goals of the persons involved'; and Johnson and Johnson (1975) comment that 'goals are important as they provide guides for action, the basis for evaluating the success of therapy and the motivating force for both the client and the therapist to promote client growth and change'. The client's goals are based upon his perceived needs, some of which he may be only partly aware of. The therapist's goals are derived from his particular approach to psychotherapy and the normative mode of mental health which helps him arrive at a *diagnosis* and a treatment plan.

Treatment goals may be explicit or covert. If they are explicit, as in the case of the *cognitive*, behavioural and *brief therapies*, they are arrived at by a process of negotiation between therapist and client. If they are covert, as in the strategic therapies, the explicitly agreed upon goal may serve as a screen for the achievement of the covert goal. Where the model of therapy postulates a presenting (explicit) and an underlying (covert) problem it will also tend to postulate an immediate (explicit) and a long-term (covert) goal. Immediate, interim and long-term goals may, however, be used in most psychotherapeutic approaches in order to break down the client's difficulties into more easily perceived and manageable portions. Parloff (1976) distinguishes between intermediate (or mediating) goals and ultimate goals: 'mediating goals are those which reflect the clinician's assumptions regarding the necessary steps and stages through which a patient must progress if the treatment is to be effective ... [these goals] permit the attainment of the ultimate goals [which] go beyond such ... mediating variables' as the clinician's inferences regarding the resolution of the patient's conflicts.

The relationship between goal and *task* may overlap considerably, with the same event being viewed both as a long-term end towards which the client is working (goal) and as an intermediate means by which it is achieved (task). Whether an event is viewed as a goal or as a means of achieving a goal depends on how the event is construed. For example, enabling an adolescent to leave home may be the treatment goal or it may be the means by which the goal of conflict resolution between the marital pair is explicitly revealed and worked on. Moreover, the client may present his treatment goal in the shape of the problem which he is experiencing. Separating out problem from goal is an early task of therapy, since the problem may merely be the only soluton to his life situation which the client can envisage when he enters therapy. Thus the formulation and expansion of the client's goals form an important part of the early stage of treatment in, for example, *problem solving interventions, humanistic* approaches, behavioural, cognitive and brief therapies and in many forms of group and family therapy.

Goals should be specific, measurable and attainable if the treatment process is to be realistically linked to an evaluation of *outcome.* Goals may address different levels of the individual, group or family's functioning, and therefore they may be multiple and require some ordering in terms of their priority. They may be modified and reassessed as treatment proceeds. Choosing inappropriate goals, including goals that are not in the client's best interest or are too vague and unreachable, is likely to produce *deterioration* in the client.

JOHNSON, D. W. and JOHNSON, R. T. (1975), *Learning Together and Alone* (Prentice-Hall, Englewood Cliffs, New Jersey).
JOHNSON, D. W. and MATROSS, R. (1977), 'Interpersonal influence in psychotherapy' (in Gurman, A. S. and Razin, A. M., *Effective Psychotherapy*, Pergamon Press, New York).
MCGLASHAN, T. H. and MILLER, G. H. (1982), 'The goals of psychoanalysis and psychoanalytic psychotherapy' (*Archives of General Psychiatry*, vol. 39, pp. 377-88).
PARLOFF, M. B. (1976), 'The narcissism of small differences and some big ones' (*Int. J. of Group Psychotherapy*, vol. 26, pp. 311-19).

Goal attainment scaling (GAS)

A research tool developed by Kiresuk and Sherman (1968) for the evaluation of treatment *outcome.* GAS requires that individual *goals* are established prior to the outset of treatment. For each goal specified, a graded scale is devised with a series of likely outcomes, ranging from most to least favourable. The goals and the scale are made specific enough for them to be examined after treatment has been completed by an impartial judge. GAS enables multiple goals to be established, each specifically addressed to the individual patient's requirements and allowing an exact measure of degree of attainment to be

assessed. The procedure has also been used in *marital* and *family therapy* outcome research (Woodward *et al.* 1978).

KIRESUK, T. and SHERMAN, R. (1968), 'Goal attainment scaling' (*Community Mental Health*, vol. 4, pp. 443-53).
WOODWARD, C. A. *et al.* (1978), 'The role of goal attainment scaling in evaluating family therapy outcome' (*Am. J. of Orthopsychiatry*, vol. 48, pp. 464-76).

Go-between process

Term introduced by Zuk (1966) to describe the transactions that occur between the family therapist and family members within the three role functions of go-between, side taker and celebrant. He defines the go-between as the member of the therapy group who sets the rules for communicating. Just as the go-between process is more than the functioning of the go-between role, so the go-between role itself is more than that of mediator, since the person taking this role may be intrusive and confronting as he moves between family members. The side taker is the member of the therapy group who sides with or against others in family conflict; and the celebrant is the one who certifies and celebrates important family events. Any of these three roles may be carried either by the family therapist or by a member of the family but it is important, according to Zuk, that the therapist remains in charge of the go-between process as a whole, including deciding who shall play each role. Zuk describes four variations of the go-between process, all of which can be used to influence and shift the network of relationships in the family.

ZUK, G. H. (1966), 'The go-between process in family therapy' (*Family Process*, vol. 5, pp. 162-78).

See also *Coalition, Strategic therapy.*

Goldstein, Kurt (1878-1965)

Kurt Goldstein was born in Kattowitz in Germany in 1878. He studied medicine at the University of Breslau, receiving his MD in

1903. In 1914 he went to Frankfurt and established an institute for the rehabilitation of psychiatric and neurological casualties during the First World War, where he worked for a period with Frieda Fromm-Reichmann. During this time he produced a range of publications on visual perception, brain diseases and aphasia, and also papers on psychotherapy and on motivational problems. In 1927, Goldstein helped to found the International Society for Psychotherapy. In 1930 he became professor of neurology at the University of Berlin but left at the beginning of Hitler's rise to power. In 1935 he emigrated to the United States and took posts successively at Columbia University and Tufts Medical School. His importance lies in his influence on a variety of schools and individuals, including *Gestalt psychology*, *existential psychotherapy* and through Fromm-Reichmann on *psychoanalysis*. But in particular, his emphasis on the dynamic internal relationship of individuals as wholes gave impetus to the development of a holistic approach to understanding the patient, found particularly in *humanistic psychology*.

Good enough mother

A term introduced by Winnicott to describe the part played by the mother or mother substitute in creating a basic facilitating environment for an infant's healthy psychological development. Winnicott (1960) suggests that the mother's ability to be 'good enough' depends upon her ability to meet the absolute dependence and omnipotence of the infant by adapting herself more or less completely to his or her needs. By discovering that external reality is predictable and reliable, through the mother's anticipation of those needs, the infant is gradually able to forego his phantasies of omnipotence and begin to relate to the external world in terms of the constraints of the *reality principle*. This leads to the development of the infant's *true self*. If the mother is not able to produce a 'good enough' facilitating environment, and thus to keep at bay the 'unthinkable anxiety' of disintegration and total oblivion which the infant fears may overwhelm him, he develops instead a *false*

self. This development of a false self which originates in the failed relation between mother and infant has a parallel in Balint's concept of *basic fault*.

HARRIS, M. (1975), 'Some notes on maternal containment in "good enough"' mothering' (*J. of Child Psychotherapy*, vol. 4, pp. 35-51).
WINNICOTT, D. W. (1960), 'Ego distortion in terms of true self' (in *The Maturational Processes and the Facilitating Environment*, Hogarth Press, London).

Greek chorus

A therapeutic *team* used in *family therapy* to observe a therapist at work from behind a *one way screen*. It is used to comment on the interaction of the family *system* and on the process of therapy. The team acts as a *participant-observer* to the session, following the pattern of the audience at tragic dramas in ancient Greece. It can be used by the therapist to support one or more family members; to take sides with different *sub-systems*; polarising and thereby clarifying the important issues for the family; to create surprise or confusion by sending ambiguous messages into a family that is particularly resistant to the therapist; or to form a therapeutic *triangle*, the therapist taking one view and the observers the opposite view of what course the family should follow. The procedure to be followed has to be worked out in advance between members of the group and the therapist. A common practice is for the therapist to explain to the family that he or she will retire to discuss the session with the group towards the end. The therapist may then return to the family with a written message which is read out to them, using one of the positions described above. This particular use of a therapeutic team is usually given primary importance in the various forms of *strategic therapy*. Breunlin and Cade (1981) describe the five aspects of a successful message as follows: its function, target, timing, content and delivery.

BREUNLIN, D. C. and CADE, B. W. (1981), 'Intervening in family systems with observer messages' (*J. of Marital and Family Therapy*,

vol. 7, pp. 453-60).
CADE, B. W. (1980), 'Resolving therapeutic deadlocks using a contrived team conflict' (*Int. J. of Family Therapy*, vol. 2, pp. 253-62).
PALAZZOLI, M. S. *et al.* (1978), *Paradox and Counter Paradox* (Jason Aronson, New York).
PAPP, P. (1980), 'The Greek chorus and other techniques of paradoxical therapy' (*Family Process*, vol. 19, pp. 45-57).
STORM, C. L. and RITCHIE, A. (1982), 'Innovative adaptations of the team approach: from a Greek chorus to a duet' (*Family Therapy*, vol. 9 pp. 209-13).

See also *Hypothesis, Live supervision, Paradox, Prescription.*

Grief
A normal, time-limited reaction of intense sorrow following the loss of an emotionally significant person through death or separation, the loss of part of the self, the loss of material objects or the loss of a previous stage in the life cycle. For Freud (1917), the grieving process allows ties with the lost *object* to be broken through the withdrawal of *libido*. He describes grief as 'work' and identified a period of between one to two years as the normal period for the accomplishing of this work. For Bowlby (1980), grieving is an attempt to re-establish ties rather than of withdrawing them. Most bereaved people recover from intense grief reactions after about six months. According to Marris (1974), the process of normal grief is a working out of conflicting impulses. Grief, as the cost of attachment, is a theme both in folklore and in the literature on *attachment theory* (Bowlby 1980).

Grief can be sub-divided into three types: anticipatory grief, acute grief and morbid or pathological grief. Anticipatory grief is grief that is expressed in advance of what is perceived to be an inevitable loss. Kubler-Ross (1970) describes five stages of anticipatory grief in the dying: denial and isolation, anger, bargaining, depression and acceptance. Anticipatory grief ends when the actual loss takes place and in the case of the bereaved, it merges into acute grief. The evidence as to whether or not anticipatory grief is helpful to the bereaved in terms of their long-term

adjustment is contradictory. (The arguments are summarised in Backer *et al.* 1982.) Lindermann (1944) identified a pattern of reactions discernible during acute grief. Acute grief falls into three main sub-phases: shock (focused on the past and characterised by alarm and denial); realisation (focused on the present and characterised by intermittent denial, searching behaviour, preoccupation with the lost object accompanied by idealisation and identification with the lost person, regression, crying and various somatic symptoms, depression and helplessness, guilt, anger and shame); and integration (focused on the future and characterised by acceptance, a return to physical, social and psychological well-being, or by a refusal to accept the loss and a continuation of depression, somatic symptoms and vulnerability to other losses). Parkes (1965) defines three categories of pathological grief: inhibited grief (where expected reactions are either absent or distorted); chronic grief (where reactions are prolonged); and delayed grief (where reactions are postponed and experienced more severely at a later date). Factors predisposing a person to experience a pathological grief reaction include separation and loss of a significant person in early childhood, although, as Rutter (1972) has pointed out, the evidence for this is inconclusive. Other factors described are the absence of an effective support network, the perception of the death as sudden and untimely, the experience of a previous mental illness and the existence of a strongly ambivalent relationship with the deceased (Smith 1982). The loss of a child is often perceived to be so abnormal as to increase the likelihood of denial and distortion (Anthony and Koupernick 1973). It is also likely that parents will experience severe guilt and shame because of their position as caretakers in relation to the child. With the loss of a spouse, Pincus (1976), has suggested that couples whose marriage was based on *identification* fare worse when one dies than those whose relationship was based on *projection*.

ANTHONY, E. J. and KOUPERNICK, A. (eds) (1973), *The Child in his Family: The Impact of*

Disease and Death (Wiley, New York).

BACKER, B. *et al.* (1982), *Death and Dying* (Wiley, New York).

BOWLBY, J. (1980), *Attachment and Loss: Vol. 3 – Loss* (Hogarth Press, London).

FREUD, S. (1917), 'Mourning and Melancholia' (*Standard Edition*, vol. 14, Hogarth Press, London).

KUBLER-ROSS, E. (1970), *On Death and Dying* (Tavistock, London).

LINDERMANN, E. (1944), 'Symptomatology and management of acute grief' (*Am. J. of Psychiatry*, vol. 101, p. 141).

MARRIS, P. (1974), *Loss and Change* (Routledge & Kegan Paul, London).

PARKES, C. M. (1965), 'Bereavement and mental illness, part two' (*Brit. J. of Med. Psychology*, vol. 38, p. 13).

PARKES, C. M. (1972), *Bereavement: Studies of Grief in Adult Life* (Tavistock, London).

PINCUS, L. (1976), *Death and the Family* (Faber & Faber, London).

RUTTER, M. (1972), *Maternal Deprivation Re-assessed* (Penguin, Harmondsworth).

SCHOENBERG, B. *et al.* (1974), *Anticipatory Grief* (Columbia University Press, New York).

SMITH, C. R. (1982), *Social Work with the Dying and Bereaved* (BASW/Macmillan, London).

Group analysis

A method of *group psychotherapy* based on psychoanalytic principles. Freud (1921) laid the foundation for the development, discussing the way in which changes in the psychology of the individual transform the psychology of the group and how changes in the group help to create the structure of the individual's *psyche*. He stressed the opposition between neurosis and group formation and clearly foresaw the therapeutic possibilities of groups in the healing of neurosis. According to Anthony (1983), Freud was the first great group-analytic psychologist, even though he never followed through his preliminary theorising into any fully developed model of what was to become group analysis.

Group analysis was developed in its present form in Britain by S. H. Foulkes and his associates out of his work during the Second World War at the Northfield Hospital, Birmingham and later at the Maudsley Hospital, London. Other important contributors to the development of group analysis have been Anthony, Bion, Slavson, Ezriel, Sutherland and Pines. Anthony (1972) describes three main approaches. First, the individual-oriented approach, which is essentially the analysis of the individual and the *transference* in the presence of the group, together with the analysis of his or her interactions with others. Slavson in particular developed this approach in the United States. Second, the integrative approach, which focuses on both the individual patient and the group and the relationship between the two. This is the primary method used in group analysis. Third, the group-as-a-whole approach, where the group itself is the chief focus of therapy and where there is primary emphasis on group interaction, group roles and group themes. Bion and Ezriel utilised this method but it has been somewhat criticised by Bar-Levav (1980) and others.

Group analysis makes different demands on the therapist and requires him to deal with the here-and-now relationships between group members as well as their symbolic and representative meaning for the individual's intrapersonal world. Thus, three different worlds overlap: the patient's intrapsychic reality, the intragroup world of relationships between group members and the external interpersonal world from which group members come. The task of the therapist or 'conductor' is to help members of the group gain understanding and *insight* into each of these aspects and into the relationship between them. In the classical group analytic situation, eight patients (four men and four women) meet once or twice a week with the conductor for one and a half hours. *Co-therapy* is not used except for training purposes. The meetings take place at the same time and place each week and group members are discouraged from meeting socially between sessions. The group sits in a circle and members communicate with each other using free floating discussion and working on current conflict situations both within the group and in the individual's outside life. The conductor-therapist facilitates the group process, offers *interpretations*, helps the decoding of *symptoms*, and assists the process of *working through* and the gaining of insight. As well as the classical psychoanalytic framework, group analysis makes use of *object relations* theory, *systems theory*, the theory of small group behaviour and the understanding of *group dynamics* developed in the *Tavistock group training* model. Group analysis has been influential in the development of other methods of group psychotherapy as well as providing one of the models for *psychoanalytic family therapy*.

ABSE, D. W. (1974), *Clinical Notes on Group Analytic Psychotherapy* (John Wright, Bristol).
ANTHONY, E. J. (1972), 'The history of group psychotherapy' (in Kaplan, H. J. and Sadock, B. J. (eds), *The Evolution of Group Therapy*, Jason Aronson, New York).
ANTHONY, E. J. (1983), 'The group-analytic circle and its ambient network' (in Pines, M. (ed.), *The Evolution of Group Analysis*, Routledge & Kegan Paul, London).
BAR-LEVAV, R. (1980), 'The group-as-a-whole approach: a critical evaluation' (in Wolberg, L. R. and Arunson, M. L., *Group and Family Therapy*, 1980, Brunner/Mazel, New York).
BION, W. R. (1961), *Experiences in Groups* (Tavistock, London).
FOULKES, S. J. (1964), *Therapeutic Group Analysis* (Allen & Unwin, London).
FOULKES, S. J. (1975), *Group Analytic Psychotherapy* (Gordon & Breach, London).
FOULKES, S. J. and ANTHONY, E. J. (1973), *Group Psychotherapy: The Psychoanalytic Approach* (revised edn, Penguin, Harmondsworth).
FREUD, S. (1921), 'Group psychology and the analysis of the ego' (*Standard Edition*, vol. 18, Hogarth Press, London).
PINES, M. (ed.) (1983), *The Evolution of Group Analysis* (Routledge & Kegan Paul, London).
PINES, M. (ed.) (1984), *Bion and Group Psychotherapy* (Routledge & Kegan Paul, London).
RICE, C. A. (1981), 'Three perspectives on psychoanalytic group therapy' (*Am. J. of Psychiatry*, vol. 138, pp. 62-4).

Group composition

The pattern of characteristics belonging to group members which go to make up the culture of the group as a whole. The composition of a group has a powerful effect upon the execution of its task and its ability to maintain itself in being. Thus, *group structure, group process*, group performance and therapeutic *outcome* are all related to the manner in which the group is composed.

Broadly speaking, two different views are taken regarding the method of composing a group: the first maximises heterogeneity and the second maximises homogeneity. In practice a mixture of these two elements is usually necessary, since each caters for different elements of group life. Homogeneity between group members increases *affiliation* between members and improves the *cohesion* of the group, improving its chances of remaining in being. On the other hand, heterogeneity increases the group's resources and thereby increases its problem solving capability. Hoffmann and Maier (1961) show that groups with varied personalities, mixed sexes and conflicting attitudes towards dominant solutions to problems are more successful in solving problems. The danger is that the level of discomfort and stress engendered by this heterogeneity may lead to the break-up of the group. For this reason, Yalom (1975) asserts that cohesiveness is a more important variable and should be the 'primary guideline in the composition of therapy groups'.

Following Whitaker and Leibermann (1964) and Foulkes and Anthony (1957), Yalom suggests that the group therapist needs to organise maximum heterogeneity within the patients' conflict areas and coping skills and maximum homogeneity in their degree of vulnerability and *ego strength*. The therapist should try to reduce the tendency of a group to use an obvious isolate as a *scapegoat* by avoiding putting a much older person into a mid-twenties group, a man into a women's group, or including other, more subtle isolating characteristics which a patient may have. Some therapists make use of *FIRO tests* and other diagnostic tools to predict the behaviour of individual patients in a prospective therapy group and this may help to create optimal group composition. Others have experimented with diagnostic groups prior to the initiation of the therapy group. *Multiple couples* groups and *multiple family* groups are usually composed of couples and families from a similar developmental stage in the life cycle (see *Stages of development*).

FOULKES, S. H. and ANTHONY, E. J. (1957), *Group Psychotherapy: The Psychoanalytic Approach* (Penguin, Harmondsworth).
HOFFMANN, L. R. and MAIER, N. R. F. (1961), 'Quality and acceptance of problem solutions by members of homogeneous and heterogeneous groups' (*J. of Abnormal and Social Psychology*, vol. 62, pp. 401-7).
WHITAKER, D. and LIEBERMANN, M. (1964), *Psychotherapy Through the Group Process* (Atherton Press, New York).
YALOM, I. D. (1975), *The Theory and Practice of Group Psychotherapy* (2nd edn, Basic Books, New York).

Group dynamics
The scientific study of groups, their formation, organisation, task performance, decision making processes and problem solving capacities. The study of group dynamics developed as a branch of social psychology and the term is used interchangeably with small group research. Kurt Lewin played a major part in the early study of group dynamics during the 1930s, using an artificial laboratory setting to study and extrapolate the principles of group life. Aspects of group life which together make up the dynamics of the group include its *leadership style of*, degree of *cohesion*, shared values and norms, *structure* and *process*. As studies have progressed, they have paid increasing attention to more detailed aspects of group life, for example, patterns of dominance, competition and co-operation and the means by which members are attracted to each other and form *affiliations*, *alliances* and *coali-*

tions. Differences between male, female and mixed groups have also recently been studied and show that a variety of generalisations drawn from early research fail to take into account this important variable.

ARGYLE, M. (1969). *Social Interaction* (Methuen, London).
BONNER, H. (1959), *Group Dynamics: Principles and Applications* (Ronald Press, New York).
CARTWRIGHT, D. and ZANDER, A. (eds) (1968), *Group Dynamics: Research and Theory* (3rd edn, Tavistock, London).
HARE, A. P. (1976), *Handbook of Small Group Research* (2nd edn, Collier Macmillan, London).
SHORE, M. (1981), *Group Dynamics: The Psychology of Small Group Behavior* (McGraw-Hill, New York).

See also *Group analysis, Group composition, Group psychotherapy, T-group training, Tavistock group training*.

Group process
The dynamic interaction between group members and their tasks, functions and roles as manifested in their reciprocal relationships and in their verbal and *non-verbal communication*. The interaction between the individual and the group as a whole is an important aspect of group process and there is an oscillating tension within groups between the needs of the individual and the needs of the group. The behaviour and performance of individuals in a group has been shown to be different from when individuals are working alone.

Douglas (1983) points out that the development of the group through certain well-defined phases should not be equated with all that is meant by group process, although group development is an important *part* of group process. Group development has been studied by various researchers. Tuckman (1965) suggests that there are four main stages of development: forming, where group members test out the situation they are in, discover the group's task and rely heavily on the group leaders; storming, where members form *coalitions* against leaders, struggle for power and show *resistance* to the task; norming, where these conflicts are sufficiently resolved for members to work on the task and develop some *cohesion* and accepted culture; and performing, where energy is released for problem solving and task work. A final stage, *mourning*, should also be included, to mark members' disengagement from the task and from the group when the group's life comes to an end. These stages often overlap and do not always follow on from one another in an orderly sequence.

Bales (1950) and Thibaut and Kelly (1959) studied group functions and suggested that groups are continuously concerned with two sets of functions: task functions, directed towards problem solving and the achievement of the group's goals, and maintenance functions, directed towards servicing the group and building cohesion. Different leaders normally take on these two functions.

Hare (1976) suggests that the enormous variety of interactions in groups can be reduced to four basic factors: dominance vs. submissiveness; positive vs. negative social emotional behaviour; task-oriented (instrumental) vs. group maintenance (expressive) behaviour; and conformity to the group norms vs. non-conformity, shown by withdrawal and resistance. Bion (1961) has identified other aspects of group process in his description of *work group* and *basic assumption* behaviour, two aspects of group process which usually alternate throughout a group's life. The group therapist, as a *participant-observer* of group process, must attend continually to its development and help to foster the optimal climate for group members' development.

BALES, R. F. (1950), *Interaction Process Analysis* (Addison-Wesley, Cambridge, Mass.).
BION, W. R. (1961), *Experiences in Groups* (Tavistock, London).
CATHCART, R. S. and SAMOVA, L. A. (1970), *Small Group Communication: A Reader* (W. C. Brown, Dubuque, Iowa).
DOUGLAS, T. (1983), *Groups* (Tavistock, London).

HARE, A. P. (1976), *Handbook of Small Group Research* (2nd edn, Collier Macmillan, London).
LACOURSIÈRE, R. (1980), *The Life Cycle of Groups* (Human Sciences Press, New York).
PRICE, A. K. (1969), 'Individual, group and inter-group processes' (*Human Relations*, vol. 22, pp. 565-84).
THIBAUT, J. W. and KELLY, H. H. (1959), *The Social Psychology of Groups* (Wiley, New York).
TUCKMAN, B. W. (1965), 'Developmental sequence in small groups' (*Psychological Bulletin*, vol. 63, pp. 384-99).

Group psychotherapy

A form of psychotherapy directed towards *stranger groups* of patients who come together at regular intervals for the purposes of treatment and change. Group psychotherapy is a generic term used to describe a variety of approaches, differing widely in their theoretical bases and treatment techniques.

J. H. Pratt, an American physician, was probably the first person to make systematic use of a therapeutic group, using a mixture of didactic teaching and social interaction between group members. Adler's work with teachers and parents in the early European child guidance clinics and schools demonstrated an early use of group methods (Dreikurs 1959).

Three broad sub-divisions began to develop: the action-based methods originating with Moreno; the psychoanalytic approaches derived from Freud; and the humanistic, client-centred methods of Rogers. Moreno's work was developed first in Vienna in the 1930s and later in the United States, where his approach became known as *psychodrama*. Moreno's work was influential upon other action-based group methods such as *encounter groups, sensitivity training, transactional analysis* and *Gestalt therapy* groups.

Psychoanalytic approaches were developed in the United States by early pioneers such as Burrow (1927), Schilder and Slavson; and in Britain by Foulkes, Anthony and others. The psychoanalytic approaches are now primarily represented by the Freudian method of *group analysis* but Jungians too have developed some group psychotherapy (Whitmont 1964), although Jung, as Illing (1957) points out, was basically opposed to it. Besides his influence on the encounter group movement, Carl Rogers encouraged the use of client-centred group therapy, both as an adjunct to individual work and as a method in its own right. The therapist uses the *core conditions* to assist group members to develop more *congruency* in their interpersonal relationships. More recently, different forms of behavioural group therapy have developed. Rose (1977) describes the way in which the whole range of behavioural techniques are used and the group is directed by the therapist according to a pre-set programme. The presence of the group enhances the effect of some behavioural techniques such as positive *reinforcement* and *modelling*.

Many other derivations of these basic models are used, particularly in the effort to offer *supportive psychotherapy* to large numbers of people who are linked by some common anxiety or problem. Therapeutic groups for the bereaved, for foster parents, for alcoholics and for children in residential care are among the many applications of group therapy methods. Particular uses of group therapy are to be found in *multiple family* groups and *multiple couples* groups, both using a mixed model of group therapy and family/marital therapy. Yalom (1975) has provided a wide-ranging overview of the field and he has made a major contribution in attempting to isolate the curative factors in group psychotherapy.

BLOCH, S. (1981), 'Group psychotherapy' (*Brit. J. of Psychiatry*, vol. 138, pp. 117-69).
BLOCH, S. *et al.* (1981), 'Therapeutic factors in group psychotherapy' (*Arch. Gen. Psychiatry*, vol. 38, pp. 519-26).
BURROW, T. (1927), 'The group method of analysis' (*Psychoanalytic Review*, vol. 14, pp. 268-80).
COCHE, E. and DIACE, R. R. (1981), 'Integrating research findings into the practice of group psychotherapy' (*Psychotherapy: Theory, Research, and Practice*, vol. 18, pp. 410-16).
DOUGLAS, T. (1976), *Group Work Practice* (Tavistock, London).

DOUGLAS, T. (1978), *Basic Group Work* (Tavistock, London).
DREIKURS, R. (1959), 'Early experiments with group psychotherapy' (*Am. J. of Psychotherapy*, vol. 13, pp. 882-91).
ILLING, H. A. (1957), 'C. G. Jung on the present trends in group psychotherapy' (*Human Relations*, vol. 10, pp. 77-83).
KELLERMAN, H. (1979), *Group Psychotherapy and Personality* (Grune & Stratton, New York).
MARÉ, P. B. DE (1972), *Perspectives in Group Psychotherapy* (Allen & Unwin, London).
MORENO, J. L. (1957), *The First Book on Group Psychotherapy* (Beacon House, New York).
ROSE, S. D. (1977), *Group Therapy: A Behavioral Approach* (Prentice-Hall, Engelwood Cliffs, New Jersey).
SHAPIRO, J. L. (1978), *Methods of Group Psychotherapy and Encounter* (Peacock Publishers, Itasca, Ill.).
WHITAKER, D. S. (1985), *Using Groups to Help People* (Routledge & Kegan Paul, London).
WHITMONT, E. C. (1964), 'Group therapy and analytical psychology' (*J. of Analytical Psychology*, vol. 9, no. 1).
YALOM, I. D. (1975), *Theory and Practice of Group Psychotherapy* (Second Edition, Basic Books, New York).

Group structure

The relatively stable patterns of relationships which arise out of the *group process* or ongoing interaction between the members of the group. The structure of a group largely depends upon the assignment of different roles between group members and on the resulting pattern of role relationships that emerges. Roles become differentiated in terms of authority and responsibility. Authority roles are determined by the degree of freedom which an individual has for initiating actions and influencing decisions. Responsibility is defined in terms of a group member's perception of and commitment to the group task. Several group members may carry authority and responsibility roles, some designated formally and others carried informally. The *leadership* style exercised by the formal leaders helps to influence the development of the group's structure and the successful execution of the group's task is dependent on the way in which the development of *alliances, coalitions* and *affiliations* between group members and between members and leaders occurs.

Group structure can be further understood by examining the difference between formal and informal roles. Besides the formal roles, a developed group structure, as Hare (1976) points out, will produce a variety of informal roles. These may include the supporter, the clown, the nurturer, the silent member, the *scapegoat*, etc. Both formal and informal roles are required by the group in order to take care of its instrumental task functions and its expressive maintenance functions, and to promote both task performance and *group cohesion* respectively. Even when a formal structure is provided with a hierarchy and a set of designated positions, the group will establish its own informal structure.

AGAZARIAN, Y. and PETERS, R. (1981), *The Visible and Invisible Group* (Routledge & Kegan Paul, London).

DOUGLAS, T. (1983), *Groups* (Tavistock, London).

HARE, A. P. (1976), *Handbook of Small Group Research* (2nd edn, Collier Macmillan, London).

HOMANS, G. C. (1950), *The Small Group* (Random House, New York).

MILLS, R. (1967), *The Sociology of Small Groups* (Prentice-Hall, Englewood Cliffs, New Jersey).

OLMSTEAD, M. S. (1959), *The Small Group* (Random House, New York).

SHORE, M. E. (1974), *An Overview of Small Group Behavior* (General Learning Press, Morristown, New Jersey).

SPROTT, W. J. H. (1958), *Human Groups* (Penguin, Harmondsworth).

Group therapy interaction chronogram (GTIC)

A tool devised by Cox (1973) for recording the content and process of *group psychotherapy* sessions. A chronogram sheet consists of ten circles (one for each member of the group) printed in the shape of a clock face, each circle being divided in half, with one half subdivided again. The right hand quadrant is used to record material from the beginning of the session; the lower half of the circle, material from the main body of the session; and the left hand quadrant, material from the ending phase. Content is recorded by abbreviated comments in the appropriate section of each circle and process is recorded in an interaction lattice by arrows between group members in a similar way to a *sociogram* with + and − used to denote positive and negative feelings. The chronogram is filled in with the salient events that occur during the session for each group member, creating a sequence of individual motifs as well as a record over time of the development of the group's life as a whole. If two therapists are working together with a group, each fills in a chronogram sheet and a comparison between the two allows differences in the perceptions of the *co-therapy* pair to be checked. The GTIC is suitable for recording any method of group psychotherapy. Blank GTIC forms can be obtained from Bocardo and Church Army Press Ltd, Temple Road, Cowley, Oxford.

COX, M. (1973), 'The group therapy interaction chronogram' (*Brit. J. of Social Work*, vol. 3, pp. 243-56).

See also *Diagrams*.

Guided fantasy

The encouragement of fantasy experiences by the client within a structured situation, to achieve a range of therapeutic *goals*. Guided fantasy can be used with both individuals and in group work. The therapist provides the client with an image to initiate the fantasy and then encourages him to follow his explorations of this image wherever they may lead. The client is encouraged to use *free association* and to allow *unconscious* material to come to the surface in developing the themes of the fantasy. The therapist prompts, encourages and brings the fantasy experience to a close. Afterwards he may analyse the material with the client in terms of its meaning and *symbolism* in a similar way to a *dream*, or he may leave the client to continue working on and integrating the material in a less conscious way after the session has ended. Guided fantasy can be used as an *action technique* in groups, one person beginning to fantasise out loud and other group members adding to it to build up a composite image. Guided fantasy can be highly task-focused. For example, the therapist can structure the experience for the individual or group, who share a problem, so that they explore a particular set of fearful images in order to try and overcome a particular fear or anxiety. Guided fantasy is used in *Gestalt therapy, systematic desensitisation, sex therapy* and *cover modelling*. Papp (1980) describes the way in which fantasy can be used as an ingredient of *family choreography*, in *multiple couples therapy*. Guided fantasy is also being used in the treatment of cancer patients to help them overcome or ameliorate some of the effects of the disease and its treatment (Lyles 1982).

KELLY, G. F. (1972), 'Guided fantasy as a counseling technique with youth' (*J. of Counseling Psychology*, vol. 19, pp. 355-61).

LEUNER, H. (1969), 'Guided effective imagery' (*Am. J. of Psychotherapy*, vol. 23, pp. 4-22).

LYLES, J. (1982), 'Efficacy of relaxation training and guided imagery in reducing the awareness of cancer chemotherapy' (*J. of Consulting and Clinical Psychology*, vol. 50, pp. 509-24).

PAPP, P. (1980), 'The use of fantasy in a couples' group' (in Andolfi, M. (ed.), *Dimensions of Family Therapy*, Guilford Press, New York).

H

Hartmann, Heinz (1894-1970)

Heinz Hartmann, an outstanding contributor to psychoanalytic theory, was born in Vienna of a family professionally distinguished in medicine and the arts. He received his MD from the University of Vienna in 1920.

Between 1920 and 1934 he was a member of the staff of the Psychiatric and Neurological Institute of Vienna University. After his own psychoanalytic training he quickly took a leading role in the development of *psychoanalysis*, becoming a *training analyst* of the Vienna and Paris Psychoanalytic Institutes. He left Austria in 1938 to escape the Nazis. Arriving in the USA in 1941, he joined the New York Psychoanalytic Institute, becoming its medical director between 1948 and 1951. From 1952 to 1954 he was president of the New York Psychoanalytic Society and he was subsequently president and honorary president of the International Psychoanalytic Association. His contributions to the development and clarification of psychoanalytic theory were massive, centring in particular around the development of *ego psychology*. Alongside Anna Freud and Ernst Kris, he founded and remained an editor of *Psychoanalytic Study of the Child*. His most important publications were *Ego Psychology and the Problem of Adaptation* (1939) in which he extended Freud's theory of pathology to a general theory of normal development, and *Essays on Ego Psychology* (1964).

Helplessness

Term used in both the behavioural and the psychoanalytic literature. Freud (1926) used the idea of helplessness to contrast the baby's dependence with his experience of his mother's omnipotence. The baby's motor helplessness leads to frustration and tension and in turn this leads to psychic helplessness because of the inability of the psyche to deal with the tension which is generated. Seligman (1975) describes a condition which he calls learned helplessness, in which the individual fails to see that his responses can affect the outcome of his particular predicament. Helpless is first learned through experiencing an inescapable situation which produces, through the mediating cognition of independence, a failure to connect the aversive *stimulus* with an escape *response*. Learned helplessness can be prevented by early experiences of mastery over outcomes and can often be treated through *coping skills interventions*.

ABRAHAM, L. Y. *et al.* (1978), 'Learned help-lessness in humans: critique and reformula-tion' (*J. of Abnormal Psychology*, vol. 87, pp. 49-74).

FREUD, S. (1926), 'Inhibitions, symptoms and anxiety' (*Standard Edition*, vol. 20, Hogarth Press, London).

SELIGMAN, M. E. P. (1975), *Helplessness: On Depression, Death and Development* (Freeman, San Francisco).

See also *Coping behaviour*.

Hierarchy

The term is generally used to describe an organisation of persons, *sub-systems*, behaviours or *constructs* arranged in a descending order, with all those below the first being subordinate. The term is used in *behaviour therapy* to describe the construction of a set of problem behaviours or anxieties prior to the use of *systematic desensitisation*; in *systems theory* to describe the relationship of sub-systems within a system; in family theory to describe the relationship of individuals or sub-systems to each other; in *personal construct theory* to describe the relationship between subordinate and superordinate *constructs*; and in group dynamics to describe the patterns of dom-inance and submissiveness in groups. The term is derived from biology where it is used to describe the stratified and organised order of nature.

Two problems arise in the application of the concept to social systems and to therapeutic aims; the equation of hierarchy with organisa-tion and the covert or overt stipulation that one particular type of hierarchy is being indicated. Rather, the concepts of organisation and predictable though flexible structure are to be preferred. As Capra (1982) points out, 'the important aspect of the stratified order in nature is not the transfer of control but rather the organisation of complexity.' Maruyama (1967, 1979) discusses hierarchical thinking as a culture-bound phenomenon. The con-cept of hierarchy can be and has been mis-interpreted in the psychotherapeutic field to justify the promotion by the therapist of culturally specific patterns of family and marital organisation. Skynner (1976), for example, goes so far as to say that 'the optimal pattern for family functioning is one which the *father* in general accepts the ultimate respons-ibility and the authority which goes with this' (italics mine). Such a conclusion naturally provokes the sort of feminist critique offered by Gray (1979). By contrast, most research would suggest that the optimal pattern for the functioning of groups and families requires the existence of clear boundaries; well-defined roles; a balance between *cohesion* and *differentiation*; congruent *communication* processes; and the ability to adapt its organisa-tion to meet new challenges (Olson *et al.* 1979). The use of the term is in fact open to such misinterpretation that some theorists suggest its abandonment. Capra (1982), for example, suggests that 'to avoid confusion we may reserve the term "hierarchy" for those fairly rigid systems of domination and control in which orders are transmitted from top down. . . . By contrast, most living systems exhibit multileveled patterns of organization characterised by many intricate and non-linear pathways along which signals of information and transaction propagate between all levels, ascending as well as descending.'

CAPRA, F. (1982), *The Turning Point: Science, Society and the Rising Culture* (Wildwood House, London).

GRAY, D. E. (1979), *Why the Nigger Green?* (Round Table Press, Wellesley, Mass.).

MARUYAMA, M. (1967), 'The Navaho phil-osophy: an aesthetic ethic of mutuality' (*Mental Hygiene*, April).

MARUYAMA, M. (1979), 'Mindscapes: the limits to thought' (*World Future Society Bulletin*, Sept.-Oct.).

OLSON, D. H. *et al.* (1979), 'Circumplex model of marital and family systems' (*Family Process*, vol. 18, pp. 3-28).

SKYNNER, A. C. R. (1976), *One Flesh, Separate Persons* (Constable, London).

History taking

The elucidation of the relevant factors in the patient's past which enables the therapist to develop an accurate *diagnosis* of his disturbance and aids his treatment plan. The activity stems from a medical approach to psychological treatment which traditionally stresses the need to investigate three main areas: first, heredity, including constitutional and physical factors; second, the environmentally related experience of the individual and his relationships; and third, the socio-economic facts of his life. Psychotherapists vary widely as to their views about history taking. There is a broad division between psychoanalytic approaches which stress a genotypic view of history taking and the behavioural approaches which stress a phenotypic view. In the former, history is required not only to make an accurate diagnosis but also to implement treatment procedures, such as *abreaction* and *catharsis*. More fundamentally still, *psychodynamic* or *depth psychologies* are based on the premise that their curative factor is *insight* into the roots of psychic conflict and the *working through* of that understanding in the present. An understanding of the past and of the patient's history is the prerequisite for change in the present. This leaves a range of psychotherapies which adopt an *a-historical* approach to treatment altogether, the therapist preferring to know very little about the patient or family before he or she meets them and then focusing on a 'here-and-now' approach to current conflict. History is only attended to as it unfolds naturally during the course of treatment and its understanding is not seen to be essential for change to occur.

Typically, psychoanalytically based therapies make use, first, of initial diagnostic interviews, when a history of the patient's current problems is taken and his resources, *ego strengths*, habits, relationships and medical history are examined. Second, the therapist notes his conscious emotional attitudes, aspirations and motivations. Third, any unconscious associative data provided by the patient's memories, *dreams*, daydreams, *non-verbal communication* and the analyst's exper-

ience of the patient's *transference* to him and his own *counter transference* to the patient. Behavioural therapies emphasise a detailed investigation of the *presenting problem* and its history as well as the history of the immediate circumstances which surround the problem. But the purpose of history taking in the behavioural therapies is in order to initiate detailed treatment planning, set *homework assignments*, prescribe *tasks*, etc., rather than to classify the patient's problem and/or his personality type.

Methods of history taking range from dependence upon a formal protocol such as that given by Menninger (1962) and the use of questionnaires, to the use of *action techniques*, *genograms* and sequential *family sculpting*, covering major crisis points in the patient's life. Supplementary data may be acquired from the patient's relatives and other collaterals. In those group treatments which work from a psychoanalytic base, it is customary to take the patient's history in individual sessions before introducing him to the group. In psychoanalytically oriented *family* and *marital therapy*, on the other hand, a family history is elucidated during the early sessions, from the family group as a whole, often using a *genogram*.

MENNINGER, K. (1962), *A Manual for Psychiatric Case Study* (Grune & Stratton, New York).

NOVEY, S. (1968), *The Second Look: The Reconstruction of Personal History in Psychiatry and Psychoanalysis* (Johns Hopkins Press, Baltimore, Maryland).

See also *Genotype, Phenotype*.

Holding

See *Containment*.

Holism

Literal Greek 'holos', meaning 'whole'. Holism is a unitary approach to understanding the world. It takes the view that all *systems*, physical, biological and social, are composed of interconnecting *sub-systems* which create a whole that is more than the sum of these parts.

The whole itself can only be explained as a totality. The term can be applied either to the individual, whose cognitive, affective and physical processes are viewed as interconnected; or to the person in relation to his environment, where the individual is seen as an integral part of his psycho-social *context* with which he is in continual interaction.

Holism can therefore be contrasted with *reductionism* which attempts to study the whole by analysis into its constituent parts. Advocates of holism suggest that the study and aggregation of parts loses essential information about the relationship *between* the parts or what Bateson describes as 'the pattern that connects'. A broad division exists in the field of psychotherapy between those approaches which emphasise a holistic non-linear approach to the person and/or his situation (the *systemic therapies*, *client-centred therapy*, *Gestalt therapy*, *eidetic psychotherapy*, *humanistic psychology*, *existential* and *phenomenological* approaches) and those which emphasise the linear analysis of the constituent parts of the person and his problem (*behaviour therapy*, some forms of *strategic* and *brief therapy*, and *crisis intervention*). *Psychoanalysis* reveals elements of both approaches, depending upon the particular school, but in its original, classical form it was and is primarily 'analytic'.

BATESON, G. (1979), *Mind and Nature* (Dutton, New York).
BAYNES, C. F. and WILHELM, R. (translators) (1967), *The I Ching* (Princeton University Press, Princeton, New Jersey).
CAPRA, F. (1975), *The Tao of Physics* (Shambala, Berkeley, Calif.).
THOMAS, L. (1974), *The Lives of a Cell: Notes of a Biology Watcher* (Bantam Books, New York).

See also *Hologram, Nonsummativity, System, Systems theory*.

Holistic education

A method of helping the whole person to develop and integrate the physical, aesthetic, intellectual, spiritual, social and emotional sides of himself. It emerged from the *encounter group* movement and has been influenced by body techniques, *psychodrama* and *group dynamics* ideas. The emphasis is on an educational process whereby the educator creates the conditions and atmosphere for the learner to respond. When the learner chooses to respond, growth occurs. The theory rests on three principles: that the educator will help the learner to focus on all aspects of the learner's personality; that the focus will be on the truth (i.e. maximising the learner's self-awareness); that the responsibility for what happens to him in the therapy rests with the client and both learner and educator are only responsible for themselves, not for each other.

Like any other method, holistic education contains various implicit or explicit assumptions about the individual person and his relationship to society. These include the development of self-determination, freedom, and agreement between individuals as the only necessary basis for action; openness, self-awareness, self-responsibility and a strong emphasis on rewards for 'healthy' living, based on the belief that people have limitless possibilities if only they make the right choices. The approach is optimistic and emphasises learning rather than therapy. It suffers from the same limitations and incurs the same criticisms as other approaches that broadly fall within the *human potential movement*.

SCHUTZ, W. (1973), *Elements of Encounter* (Joy Press, Calif.).
SCHUTZ, W. (1979), *Profound Simplicity* (Bantam, New York).

Hologram

Pattern produced by a technique of lens photography called holography, based on the interference property of light waves. When illuminated, the hologram produces an image of the object photographed in three dimensions. It therefore represents the whole recorded information on any image. If the hologram is broken into fragments, each fragment contains an image of the whole object, similar to Bohm's notion of implicate order where all of reality is portrayed in each of its parts. The hologram has therefore been used as an analogue for the way in which short sequences of client behaviour can be seen as representational of the kernel of the client's or client family's behaviour pattern. This has encouraged therapists (for example, *structural family therapists*) to concentrate their efforts on intervening therapeutically in these small, defined interactional sequences, as a means of altering the whole. Like all analogues, it can also be misleading if taken too far, since part and whole are not identical, and even with a hologram there is some loss of information (the 3-D effect, for example) when it is fragmented. Nevertheless, the accuracy and value of the information retained in the small representative behaviour sequence is of great value to the therapist and may become the main focus of his work.

BOHM, D. (1980), *Wholeness and the Implicate Order* (Routledge & Kegan Paul, London).
COLLIER, R. J. (1968), 'Holography and integral photography' (*Physics Today*, July).
OUTWATER, C. and HAMERSVELD, E. VAN (1974), *Practical Holography* (Pentagel Press, Beverly Hills, Calif.).

See also *Holon, Metaphor.*

Holon

Literal Greek 'holos', meaning 'whole'. (Used with the suffix 'on' to mean particle or part.) A term coined by Koestler (1978) to describe the property of *sub-systems* which make them both parts and wholes. He suggests that each holon has two opposite tendencies; an integrative tendency to function as part of the larger whole and a self-assertive tendency to preserve its autonomy. These two tendencies are opposite but complementary, manifesting both the independent properties of wholes and the dependent properties of parts. The term has been adopted by some family therapists. For example, Minuchin (Minuchin and Fishman 1981) suggests that the term 'is particularly valuable for family therapy, because the unit of intervention is always a holon. Every holon – the individual, the nuclear family, the extended family and the community – is both a whole and a part, not more one than the other, not one rejecting or conflicting with the other.'

He also suggests the essential *isomorphy* of whole and part; 'each whole contains the part and each part also contains the "program" that the whole imposes.' This has important implications for therapy which find expression in the emphasis placed by *structural family therapy* on intervening in small sequences of behaviour which are seen as being representative of the behaviour patterns of the larger whole.

KOESTLER, A. (1978), *Janus* (Hutchinson, London).
MINUCHIN, S. and FISHMAN, H. C. (1981), *Family Therapy Techniques* (Harvard University Press, Cambridge, Mass.).

Home visit

Diagnosis or treatment carried out in the patient's home. Traditionally this is an unusual procedure in the case of psychoanalytic approaches and it is employed more frequently in the newer forms of psychotherapy. The rationale for home visits includes the opportunity given to gain a fuller appreciation of the patient's circumstances, both material and interpersonal; the fact that *generalisation* is more likely to occur when problems that happen mainly in the home, such as behavioural problems in children, are treated as close as possible to their place of origin; in a *crisis* situation; in the case of particular problems such as agoraphobia, when leaving the home or visiting a strange place produces too much anxiety; when the therapist needs to help the patient or family feel more relaxed or, in *family therapy*, when the only possibility of getting crucial family members to attend the session is by going to their home. (This may be a *resistance* which needs testing, or may be due to cultural or religious factors.)

Many therapists are prepared to use a mixture of office space sessions and home visits; others routinely prefer one or the other. Contra-indications for home visits which are usually given include the belief that motivation is tested and increased by expecting the patient or family to come to the therapist's office;

office-based treatment allows the use of special procedures such as *audio visual equipment*, the use of *bio-feedback* apparatus, etc., more difficult to use in the home; the therapist is able to control the treatment more effectively and in some cases, such as group work, *multiple family therapy*, etc., the method may automatically contra-indicate the use of an individual's home on the grounds of practicability. Some approaches, e.g. *transgenerational family therapy*, encourage the patient to make a series of home visits to various relatives.

BLOCH, D. and PROSKI, P. (1973), 'The clinical home visit' (in Bloch, D., *Techniques of Family Psychotherapy*, Grune & Stratton, New York).

See also *Ambience*.

Homeostasis
Literal Greek meaning 'same state'. An *open systems* process which results from *negative feedback*. The term was coined by the biologist William Cannon (1939) to describe the tendency of living organisms to maintain a state of internal balance. Used originally to describe the way in which the body maintained its constant internal temperature, the term was applied to cybernetics and to *systems theory* and through systems theory to the functioning of psycho-social *systems*. The homeostasis or stability of a system is maintained by its ability to process information through a *feedback loop*. Negative feedback triggers the system's *regulator* which, by altering the system's internal condition, maintains homeostasis.

Almost from the beginning, controversy has surrounded the concept of homeostasis. Bertalanffy (1972), for example, in his later writings, suggests that systems theory must move 'beyond the homeostasis principle', particularly in its application to socio-cultural systems. Whilst Jackson (1957) and early writers on systems theory and its application to families made a straight application of the concept from cybernetic models, many systems theorists have found that homeostasis does not provide a sufficiently comprehensive explanation for processes which operate in psycho-social systems. It cannot, for example, explain phenomena such as growth, change and creativity – in short the processes of *schismogenesis* and *differentiation* which are the essential life-enhancing processes of all living systems. Speer (1970), Dell (1982) and others have suggested modifications of the theory to account for the system's growth processes, Speer introducing the concept of *morphogenesis* and Dell the concept of coherence. These concepts avoid some of the early errors whereby the *identified patient* was viewed as a homeostatic *regulator* and all *symptoms* were viewed as efforts to restore the homeostatic balance in the system. Two problems arose from this identification: first, homeostasis was seen as a dysfunctional process; and second, opposition was placed between the interaction of one part of a system with another (the identified patient and 'the rest'), creating a linear explanation of what is essentially a circular series of events. Rather, it is the whole system that coheres to produce a balance between homeostatis and *deviation amplification*, both of which are required to enable the system to maintain its stability and its creative development. Too high a degree of homeostasis operating within a system certainly leads to dysfunction, examples being the *enmeshed* family system or one which can be described as having an *undifferentiated ego mass*. Highly disturbed families are often marked by a high degree of homeostasis and an enormous ability to retain the status quo, despite great efforts on the part of the therapist to initiate change.

BERTALANFFY, L. VON (1972), 'General system theory: a critical review' (in Beishon, J. and Peters, G., *Systems Behaviour*, Open University Press/Harper & Row, London).
CANNON, W. B. (1939), *The Wisdom of the Body* (W. W. Norton, New York).
DELL, P. (1982), 'Beyond homeostasis: toward a concept of coherence' (*Family Process*, vol. 21, pp. 21-39).
JACKSON, D. (1957), 'The question of family homeostasis' (*Psychiatric Quarterly Supplement*, vol. 31, pp. 79-90).
SPEER, D. C. (1970), 'Family systems:

morphostasis and morphogenesis or "Is homeostasis enough?" ' (*Family Process*, vol. 9, pp. 259-78).

Homework assignment

A prescribed *task* which the patient is asked to carry out *between* therapy sessions. The task is specifically related to alleviating the patient's problem and changing the behaviour, affect or cognitions associated with it. As with tasks carried out *within* the therapy session, a homework assignment is a technique used in the directive methods of psychotherapy: *behaviour therapy*; *cognitive behaviour therapy*; *personal construct therapy*; *strategic therapy*; and some forms of *group psychotherapy* and *family therapy*. Shelton and Ackerman (1974) suggest that homework assignments greatly reduce the rate of relapse after *termination* of treatment by increasing the *generalisation* of treatment to other areas of the patient's life.

The patient's active collaboration in understanding the purpose of the homework and formulating its specific content greatly improves its efficacy and the likelihood that it will be attempted. Where the homework involves the practice of some social skill in which the patient is deficient, the task is usually first practised symbolically in the session. For example, a non-assertive patient may practise a homework assignment requesting an interview for a job, by *role playing* the elements of the task with the therapist. Homework assignments are usually graded in terms of their difficulty, the *attempted* assignment being as valuable as the *successfully completed* assignment in terms of generating data and material for discussion in the session. Any attempt at carrying out the homework should be regarded as a success in its own right even if uncompleted, but subsequent assignments should be more carefully monitored in terms of their appropriateness of level, interest etc., for the patient. To promote completion, *self-reinforcement* or *self-punishment* techniques can be used.

Examples of homework assignments include *self-monitoring*; *daily record of dysfunctional thoughts*; the practice of a fixed role

in *fixed role therapy*; *sensate focus exercises*; *bibliotherapy*; and the use of tape recordings in *relaxation training* and *assertiveness training*. Shelton and Ackerman (1974) suggest that when the homework has been agreed, it should be written down in duplicate for the therapist and patient to each keep a copy. They also suggest that homework for the therapist be included, such as listening to a tape of the session, bringing in a book for the patient, etc. This increases the collaborative nature of the exercise. Homework should be reviewed at the beginning of each session (providing opportunities for *positive reinforcement*) and new homework assigned at the end.

MAULTSBY, M. C. (1971), 'Systematic written homework in psychotherapy' (*Psychotherapy: Theory, Research and Practice*, vol. 8, pp. 195-8).
SHELTON, J. L. and ACKERMAN, J. M. (1974), *Homework in Counseling and Psychotherapy* (Charles C. Thomas, Springfield, Ill.).

Horney, Karen (1885-1953)

Karen Horney was born in Hamburg. She studied medicine at the University of Berlin. After training as a psychoanalyst, when she was analysed by Karl Abraham and Hans Sachs, she taught at the Berlin Psychoanalytic Institute between 1920 and 1932 and then emigrated to the USA. She taught at both the Chicago and New York Psychoanalytic Institutes but began to be increasingly critical of Freudian theory, particularly of the biological assumptions and the way in which *female sexuality* was viewed. Her views were expressed in a book, *New Waves in Psychoanalysis*, in 1939. Opposition to her ideas grew and she was prevented from acting as a *training analyst*. In 1941 she founded the American Association for the Advancement of Psychoanalysis and the American Institute for Psychoanalysis which she directed until her death. Horney stressed social and cultural factors in the development of personality and in this she was influenced particularly by Erich Fromm and Harry Stack Sullivan. Along with them, she is usually considered as a member of the *interpersonal school* of psychoanalysis.

Other important books written by Horney include *Self Analysis* (1942), *Our Inner Conflicts* (1945) and *Neurosis and Human Growth* (1950).

Hot seat

Term introduced by Perls (1969) to describe the focus of work in a *Gestalt therapy* group session. Each participant in a Gestalt workshop usually gets the opportunity to get into the 'hot seat' and to become the focus of the therapist's attention. When conducted in a group, Gestalt therapy is primarily dyadic, between the therapist and the occupant of the hot seat, with the rest of the group acting as observers. The group member leaves his place in the group and sits on an empty chair opposite the therapist. While in the hot seat, the patient enacts different aspects of himself, moving from one chair to another and conducting a dialogue between different aspects of the self.

PERLS, F. S. (1969), *Gestalt Therapy Verbatim* (Real People Press, Moab, Utah).

See also *Protagonist*.

Hull, Clark Leonard (1884-1952)

Clark Leonard Hull was born near Akron, New York, in 1884. He gained his PhD in psychology from the University of Wisconsin in 1918. After teaching at the University of Wisconsin, he took up an appointment at Harvard University in 1927. Two years later he moved to Yale and began to develop his major work on the analysis and description of behaviour. Like Watson, Hull viewed psychology as a natural science, subject to the same laws and methods of enquiry. He undertook research into theories of *conditioning* and *reinforcement* and developed mathematical formulae to support behavioural *learning theory*. He had an important influence on the development of *behaviourism* and in 1936 he was made President of the American Psychological Association. In 1943 he published his major work, *Principles of Behavior*, which he modified in 1951 and then extended under the title of *A Behavioral System*.

Human potential movement

A generic term for a group of approaches linked by the common belief that, as Mann (1979) expresses it, 'the normal individual represents a point of departure rather than an objective.' In contrast to most other approaches to psychotherapy, where the primary emphasis is the eradication of pathology, the human potential movement encompasses all those methods which help to fulfil the individual's potential by expanding his awareness and creativity and raising his level of functioning on either the cognitive, affective, behavioural or spiritual spheres. The person who avails himself of these methods is viewed as a participant, not a patient, and the person who acts as a leader or therapist may or may not have formal qualifications in a system of traditional psychotherapy. The human potential movement shades into and is often used synonymously with *humanistic psychology* (see Rowan 1976). The term human potential movement, however, is somewhat broader and encompasses the 'fringe' methods in addition.

Early figures that contributed importantly to the human potential movement were Maslow with his description of the *peak experience* and J. L. Moreno. The movement provides an umbrella for those psychotherapies which emphasise personal growth rather than the detection and treatment of dysfunction. These include *psychosynthesis, holistic education, transpersonal psychology* and *encounter groups*. Therapists working from within a human potential orientation are likely to use a variety of techniques drawn from *psychodrama, transactional analysis, Gestalt, primal therapy*, the *body therapies* and *meditation*. Psychedelic drugs, yoga, acupuncture, creative art and movement, and hypnosis may also be used to release energy, develop self-expression and expand awareness. The model is educative and developmental rather than curative and it has been developed for what Schutz (1971) calls 'normal neurotics', not for those who require intensive psychotherapy. The growth centre has become the usual focus for human potential activities. The first of these was Esalen which opened in Big Sur, California, in the

1960s. Growth centres attract a variety of leaders who offer a range of workshops and other activities to participants. Each participant is expected to take responsibility for his own choice of activity and the extent of his involvement in it. Several growth centres have developed in Britain, operating on similar lines to those in the USA. Criticisms that can be levied against these methods are the superficiality and lack of rigour that may result in little more than a temporary 'high' for participants, the stress on individualism and personal fulfilment and the relative abdication of concern for the individual's membership of and duty to a social group, and a tendency towards novelty for its own sake. The human potential movement remains, however, a rich resource for anyone who experiences a depletion of energy and creativity, including professional therapists. Reason and Rowan (1981) have explored the implications of human potential methods for doing research and they suggest that those who are being studied need to be recruited as co-researchers into the project.

MANN, J. H. (1972), *Learning to Be* (Free Press, New York).
MANN, J. H. (1979), 'Human potential' (in Corsini, R. J., *Current Psychotherapies*, Peacock, Itaska, Ill.).
MILLER, S. (1971), *Hot Springs* (Viking Press, New York).
OTTO, H and MANN, J. H. (eds) (1976), *Ways of Growth* (Penguin, Harmondsworth).
REASON, P. and ROWAN, J. (eds) (1981), *Human Enquiry: A Resource Book of New Paradigm Research* (Wiley, Chichester).
ROWAN, J. (1976), *Ordinary Ecstasy: Humanistic Psychology in Action* (Routledge & Kegan Paul, London).
SCHUTZ, W. C. (1971), *Here Comes Everybody* (Harper & Row, New York).

Humanistic psychology (psychotherapy)
The group of approaches which stress the need to engage the whole person in the psychotherapeutic endeavour. One of the major orientations to psychotherapy, the humanistic approach emphasises the future, in contrast to the past or present emphases of the psychoanalytic and behavioural orientations respectively. The group includes the work of Rogers, Maslow, Allport and Goldstein. They have some views in common with *existential* writers such as Tillich, Binswanger and Laing, and proponents of new forms of group and individual therapy such as Perls and Berne. Abraham Maslow in particular is considered to be one of the major figures behind the development of this approach. The term 'becoming' is frequently found in their literature, originating in Tillich's phrase (Tillich 1960) and reflected in the title of one of Rogers's (1967) seminal works, *On Becoming a Person*.

The humanistic approaches emphasise *relationship factors* in therapy and are anti-technical. Experience and meaning are considered to be the important aspects of the patient's life, rather than his overt behaviour, and these should therefore be of primary concern to the therapist. Jourard (1973), for instance, comments, 'there is a sense in which I regard efforts to foster change in another by environmental control or by shaping techniques or by any means that are not part of an authentic dialogue as in some ways pernicious and mystifying and probably not good for the well-being and growth of the persons to whom these efforts are addressed.' Humanistic psychologists view the therapeutic relationships as a participative endeavour between two human beings both of whom are seeking growth from the relationship. Goals include *self-actualisation*, personal growth, self-understanding and re-education, all of which are far removed from the emphasis of those orientations which stress symptom removal, problem solving or environmental manipulation. Helping the client to clarify his values and beliefs is also an important task of therapy. The American Association of Humanistic Psychology was founded in 1962 and many regard humanistic psychology as the *third force* alongside the behavioural and psychoanalytic approaches to psychotherapy.

BUGENTAL, J. F. T. (ed.) (1967), *The Challenges of Humanistic Psychology* (McGraw-Hill, New York).

ELLIS, A. (1973), *Humanistic Psychotherapy* (Julian Press, New York).

GOBAL, F. (1970), *The Third Force* (Grossman, New York).

JOURARD, S. M. (1973), 'Changing personal worlds' (*Cornell J. of Social Relations*, vol. 8, pp. 1-11).

MASLOW, A. H. (1970), *Motivation and Personality* (2nd edn, Harper & Row, New York).

MAY, R. (1967), *Psychology and the Human Dilemma* (Von Nostrand, Princeton, New Jersey).

ROGERS, C. (1967), *On Becoming a Person* (Constable, London).

TILLICH, P. (1952), *The Courage to Be* (Fontana/Collins, London).

TILLICH, P. (1960), 'Existentialism, psychotherapy and the nature of man' (*Pastoral Psychology*, vol. 11, pp. 10-18).

Humour

The use of humour in psychotherapy has received rather scant attention. Freud (1905) regarded jokes and *parapraxes* as revelations of the *unconscious*. He distinguished between 'the comic', 'wit' and humour, viewing them all as a means by which psychic energy could be discharged and the *ego* protected from the impact of threatening thoughts or events. Drever (1979), in his early dictionary of psychology, infers that the expression of humour, through laughter at least, reflects adversely on the level of maturity in an adult. Moreover, the *core conditions* of therapy, which most methods of psychotherapy stress, reflect qualities of seriousness and maturity which might make humour, by comparison, seem an inappropriate therapist response. Again, the particular circumstances of therapeutic interaction, which normally relate to the patient's problems and pain, may suggest the inappropriateness of humour. (Here a distinction must be made between humour used as an attacking response or as a movement *against* another person, and humour used as a sharing response or as a movement *towards* another person (Chapman and Foot 1976, 1977).)

However, recently various researchers have drawn attention to the functions of humour in social interaction generally which have obvious relevance to psychotherapy: it lowers anxiety, increases intimacy, reduces interpersonal distance, focuses attention on the material being discussed, helps build an alliance and promotes *catharsis*. Kris's (1952) concept of regression in the service of the ego is also relevant to understanding the functional place of humour. It is likely that the appropriate use of humour by the therapist increases his *attraction* and therefore his *social influence* over the patient. It may also increase his creativity (as suggested by the work of Koestler (1976)). Killinger (1977) has discussed the role of humour in individual therapy; Whitaker (1975) in *family therapy*, and Cade (1982) in relation to the functioning of a therapeutic *team*. Humour is often an important component part of other technical interventions such as *reframing*, the use of *parables* and *paradox* (Fry 1963). It is probably used most consciously as a technique by the therapist in *strategic* or *provocative therapy* but most other therapists would value its softening and relaxing effects and try to employ it particularly in the early stages of therapy.

CADE, B.W. (1982), 'Humour and creativity' (*J. of Family Therapy*, vol. 4, pp. 35-42).

CHAPMAN, A. J. and FOOT, H. C. (1976), *Humour and Laughter: Theory, Research and Applications* (Wiley, Chichester).

CHAPMAN, A. J. and FOOT, H. C. (1977), *It's a Funny Thing, Humour* (Pergamon, Oxford).

DREVER, J. (1979), *Dictionary of Psychology* (2nd edn, Penguin, Harmondsworth).

FREUD, S. (1905), 'Jokes and their relation to the unconscious' (*Standard Edition*, vol. 8, Hogarth Press, London).

FRY, W. F. (1963), *Sweet Madness: A Study of Humor* (Pacific Books, Palo Alto, Calif.).

KILLINGER, B. (1977), 'The place of humour in adult psychotherapy' (in Chapman and Foot, op. cit.).

KRIS, E. (1952), *Psychoanalytic Explorations*

in Art (International Universities Press, New York).

KOESTLER, A. (1976), *The Act of Creation* (Hutchinson, London).

MCGHEE, P. E. (1979), *Humor: Its Origin and Development* (W. H. Freeman, San Francisco).

WHITAKER, C. A. (1975), 'Psychotherapy of the absurd' (*Family Process*, vol. 14, pp. 1-16).

See also *Acting out, Joining, Regression, Therapist variable.*

Hypothesis

Literal Greek 'hupotheses', meaning 'foundation'. An initial assumption which serves as a tentative explanation of events, without regard to its truth, and an organising principle from which to examine data. The hypothesis can be retained or abandoned according to whether it is confirmed by the examination of the data. The term is used formally by two schools of psychotherapy, although the process of *diagnosis* must require most therapists to develop tentative hypotheses from which to develop an initial approach to treatment.

The concept holds a central place in Kelly's *personal construct theory*. Each *construct* represents a pair of rival hypotheses, either of which may be applied to a new *element* which the individual seeks to construe. For example, black and white are the rival hypotheses which are set up by the black versus white construct and one or other of the hypotheses is confirmed by an examination of the element in question. The formation of hypotheses lies at the heart of Kelly's view of individual behaviour; and he sees the therapist's task as opening out a range of hypotheses for the client and assisting him with a 'methodology' for testing them.

The concept is also used by the *Milan school* of *family therapy* in relation to the therapist's intervention in the family *system*. Palazzoli *et al.* (1980) suggest that 'the hypothesis establishes

a starting point for the [therapist's] investigation'. The functional value of the hypothesis is seen to rest not upon its accuracy but on the fact that it prompts therapist activity in the session and thus produces more data about the family's relational pattern. It also provides the therapist with a guide or map with which he is more likely to circumvent the family's effort to distract him. The hypothesis, whether right or wrong, introduces a powerful input of the unexpected and the improbable into the family system, thus creating difference. It is of course vital in systems work that the hypothesis is fully systemic and it must therefore make an assumption about the total relational system and include all components of the family.

KELLY, G. A. (1963), *A Theory of Personality* (W. W. Norton, New York).

PALAZZOLI, M. P. *et al.* (1980), 'Hypothesising – circularity – neutrality: three guidelines for the conductor of the session' (*Family Process*, vol. 19, pp. 3-12).

See also *Circular questioning, Focal hypothesis, Paradox, Prescription.*

I

Iatrogenic

Literal Greek 'iatros', meaning 'physician'. Pertaining to an illness or psychological disturbance caused or induced by the therapist's *diagnosis* or treatment interventions.

See also *Deterioration, Pathogenesis.*

Id

One of the three *agencies* which between them

compose the structure of the *psyche*, according to psychoanalytic theory. The id represents the major portion of the *unconscious*, although it is not co-terminus with it, since both the *ego* and the *superego* have unconscious aspects. Freud suggested that the three agencies cannot be sharply divided and that both the ego and superego merge into the id. Freud (1923) viewed the id as 'a chaos . . . filled with energy reaching it from the instincts. It has no organisation, produces no collective will but only a striving to bring about the satisfaction of instinctual needs subject to the observance of the pleasure principle.' In its lack of organisation and its complete unconsciousness it stands in contrast to both the ego and the superego.

Freud proposed an evolution of the id, the individual's first total state of being. The ego and the superego both develop out of the id, each agency retaining its own functions as the others develop but also being subject to modifications by them. The task of *psychoanalysis*, according to Freud, is to increase the functioning of the ego at the expense of the id and in a famous dictum he suggested that 'where id was, there shall ego be'. However, this way of viewing the agencies as being profoundly antagonistic with each other produces problems, since the id is also the creative ferment of energy by which the ego and superego are sustained, a position emphasised more fully in Freud's later exposition of the *structural model* which becomes his 'new typography' of the mind.

The notion of positive creative aspects of the id was more clearly developed by Jung (1963) and he emphasised the need to use the ego to integrate rather than to overcome the id. Haman (1969) suggests that the id is best understood as a way of acting that conforms to the infantile mode – irrational, unrestrained and heedless of consequences or contradictions. Such spontaneous action can either be aggressively egocentric or creatively part of lateral thinking and hence independent and novel in its results.

FREUD, S. (1923), 'The ego and the id' (*Standard Edition*, vol. 19, Hogarth Press, London).

HAMAN, A. (1969), 'What do we mean by id?' (*J. of Am. Psychoanalytic Ass.*, vol. 17, pp. 353-80).

JUNG, C. G. (1963), *Memories, Dreams and Reflections* (edited by Jaffe, A., Collins and Routledge & Kegan Paul, London).

SCHUR, M. (1963), *The Id and the Regulatory Principles of Mental Functioning* (International Universities Press, New York).

Idealisation

A *defence mechanism* whereby a particular *object* of a sexual *drive* is overvalued in order to protect it from the *ambivalence* of the subject's feelings or from the fear of persecution by that object. The protection of the object is achieved through *splitting* it from the negative feelings it engenders and defining it as a wholly 'good' object. The *denial* of fear (for example, of women) may lead to the idealisation of the feared object which then becomes something to be worshipped from a distance rather than related to. An *identification* may be made with the idealised object which helps to form the person's *ego ideal*.

Idée fixe

A fixed idea which dominates the mind and becomes an obsession.

Identification

A form of internalisation by which the individual can model aspects of his or her self upon others. According to Freud's later views, it is an important means by which the personality is formed and the *ego* and *superego* developed. The mechanism is of central importance in *psychoanalysis* and in understanding the way in which many psychotherapeutic processes operate. *Empathy* and *mimesis*, for example, are dependent upon the therapist's ability to identify to a large extent (though not completely) with the patient. Imitation and *modelling* depend for their success on the extent of the identification achieved with the model. Freud came to view identification as of central

IDENTIFICATION

importance: 'identification is not simple imitation but a simulation on the basis of a similar aetiological pretension; it expresses a resemblance and is derived from a common element which remains in the unconscious' (Freud 1900). Jung suggested that identification is distinguished from imitation by the fact that identification is an unconscious imitation. Whilst identification is an inevitable and important developmental process in childhood, the growth towards progressive *differentiation* is a hallmark of growing maturity. Erikson (1968) discusses the place of identification in the formation of identity and concludes that 'identity formation arises from the selective repudiation and mutual assimilation of childhood identifications and their absorption in a new configuration'.

In addition, identification is used in the psychoanalytic literature to describe several overlapping processes. First, in the formation of *symptoms*, Freud (1950) suggested that a symptom is the means by which an individual denies a feeling or wish. For example, a man's impotence may shield him from his repudiated identification with an aggressively penetrating male figure. Second, the narcissistic identification with qualities in others, perceived as being similar to qualities in the self. Pincus (1960), Dicks (1967) and others have described the way in which overidentification between marital partners may be used as a defence against handling difference. Third, identification arising from loss, where the individual unconsciously or consciously tries to become like the lost love object in order to lessen the sense of separation and its accompanying anxiety. Fourth, the identification with authority figures, first of all with parental figures during the phase when the *Oedipus complex* is being resolved, and later with other significant authority figures. Identification in this sense is based on a mixture of love and fear and leads to the formation of conscience and the superego, made up of internalised aspects of the parental figures with which the individual then identifies. Klein (1955) developed the concept further, distinguishing identification through *introjection* from identification

through *projection* which she called *projective identification*.

The term can be distinguished from *incorporation* and introjection, both of which are methods by which identification is achieved. Schafer (1976) has criticised the unnecessary complexity of the concept and its use of the spatial metaphor. He suggests that identification simply means that 'in order to develop as a specific person, one must have models; one cannot and does not have to create one's idea of being fully human by one's self'. The connection between the concepts of identification, identity formation and the development of the self, however, remains a central topic in contemporary psychoanalysis.

Bandura (1969) and other behavioural therapists emphasise the continuous nature of the identification process throughout life and the need to study the effect of a variety of models, not simply the parental model. The concept of identification is one of the major links between the psychoanalytic and social learning theories of development (Mussen and Eisenberg-Berg 1977).

BANDURA, A. (1969), *Principles of Behavior Modification* (Holt, Rinehart & Winston, New York).
DICKS, H. V. (1967), *Marital Tensions* (Routledge & Kegan Paul, London).
ERIKSON, E. H. (1968), *Identity, Youth and Crisis* (Faber & Faber, London).
FREUD, S. (1900), 'The interpretation of dreams' (*Standard Edition*, vol. 4, Hogarth Press, London).
FREUD, S. (1950), 'The origins of psychoanalysis' (*Standard Edition*, vol. 1, Hogarth Press, London).
JUNG, C. G. (1921), 'Psychological types' (*Collected Works*, vol. 6, Routledge & Kegan Paul, London).
KLEIN, M. (1955), 'On identification' (*New Directions in Psychoanalysis*, Maresfield Reprints, Karnac, London).
MEISSNER, W. W. (1970, 1971, 1972), 'Notes on identification' (*Psychoanalytic Quarterly*, vols 39, 40, 41, pp. 563-89, 277-302, 224-60).
MUSSEN, P. and EISENBERG-BERG, N.

(1977), *Roots of Caring, Sharing and Helping* (W. H. Freeman, San Francisco).
PINCUS, L. (ed.) (1960), *Marriage: Studies in Emotional Conflict and Growth* (Methuen, London).
SCHAFER, R. (1976), *A New Language for Psychoanalysis* (Yale University Press, New Haven, Conn.).

Identified patient

Term used in *family therapy* to describe a member of the family who is presenting an overt problem for treatment, in the form of a behaviour problem, illness, psychosomatic disturbance or psychiatric disorder. The term is used to indicate that the family therapist assumes that the family *system*, not the individual, is disordered in some way and should therefore be the *unit of treatment*. The terms of index patient and designated patient are used interchangeably, whilst the terms *scapegoat*, *distance regulator*, *family healer* and *regulator* refer to roles taken by family members which often propel the individual towards carrying the role of the identified patient. Family theorists vary as to the way in which they explain the relationship of the identified patient to the family system, the manner in which this member should be approached by the therapist and the relationship between symptomatic improvement of the identified patient and systems change in the family when assessing *outcome* in family therapy. Family members who are at some transitional point in the life cycle (e.g. toddlers, adolescents, adults at their mid-life crisis) are predisposed to carry this role and the *symptom* which they present is seen by some theorists as having a symbolic relationship with the family dysfunction which it represents. Other predisposing factors include a physical abnormality of some kind, and a particular position within the *family constellation*.

Imagery

The inner representation of objects and events created at will by the conscious mind. The use of imagery has been somewhat neglected in psychotherapy, although Freud was initially enthusiastic about its use. Later he abandoned it in favour of *free association* and its use generally falls between the two schools of the behavioural and psychoanalytic approaches. Behavioural methods divert attention away from the patient's inner image to his external behaviour, whilst *psychoanalysis* concentrates on his unconscious *phantasies*. However, several recent approaches make use of the patient's capacity to produce imagery including *psycho-imagination therapy*, *eidetic psychotherapy*, *guided fantasy* and, to a lesser extent, *psychosynthesis* and *multi-modal therapy*. Imagery is also used in *cognitive therapy*, *systematic desensitisation*, *implosion*, and the *covert* approaches to modelling and sensitisation.

CRAMPTON, M. (1974), *An Historical Survey of Mental Imagery Techniques in Psychotherapy* (Quebec Centre for Psychosynthesis, Montreal).
DESOILLE, R. (1966), *The Directed Daydream* (Psychosynthesis Research Foundation, New York).
SHORR, J. B. (1974), *Psychotherapy Through Imagery* (Intercontinental Medical Book Corporation, New York).
SHORR, J. B. *et al.* (1980), *Imagery: Its Many Dimensions and Applications* (Plenum Press, New York).
SINGER, J. L. (1974), *Imagery and Daydream Methods in Psychotherapy and Behavior Modification* (Academic Press, New York).

Imaginary

See *French school of psychoanalysis*.

Imago

Term introduced by Jung in 1911-12 and adopted in psychoanalysis. When 'imago' is used instead of 'image', this is to underline the fact that images are generated subjectively, particularly those of other people. That is, the object is perceived according to the internal state and dynamics of the subject. There is the additional specific point that many images (e.g. of parents) do not arise out of actual personal experiences of parents of a particular character, but are based on unconscious *phantasies* or derived from the activities of the *archetypes*. For example, an infant will tend to image his or her mother as a life-giving fertility Goddess or, alternatively, as a death-dealing witch. Clearly, the mother will fit neither of these imagos in her personal reality.

An imago which has operated in a person over time will develop to the point where it functions like an expectation, or rather a filter through which experiences of certain categories of people are perceived. Hence, an imago leads to feelings and behaviour towards others as well as to how they are imaged.

JUNG, C. G. (1921), 'Psychological types' (*Collected Works*, vol. 6, Routledge & Kegan Paul, London).

See also *Complex*.

Implicitness
See *Pole*.

Implosion
A variation of *flooding* techniques introduced by Stampfl, whereby the anxiety-eliciting stimuli to which the patient is exposed are thoughts and *imagery*. Stampfl and Levis (1967, 1968) describe the technique and the theory upon which it rests. Using the principles of *classical conditioning* they suggest that anxiety is the *conditioned response* to images and thoughts about fearful objects and events. The images and thoughts are the *conditioned stimuli* whilst the actual object or event is the *unconditioned stimulus*. Therefore, if the conditioned stimulus is presented repeatedly in the absence of the unconditioned stimulus, *extinction* will occur. The patient's instinct is to avoid the conditioned stimulus and therefore extinction does not occur. The aim of therapy is therefore to prevent the patient's avoidance of the conditioned stimuli.

Stampfl considered many of the evoking stimuli to be psychodynamic in origin and implosion therapy draws on some principles of psychoanalytic theory as well as *learning theory*, providing an unusual bridge between the two. As in *systematic desensitisation*, a *hierarchy* is

employed of anxiety-provoking thoughts, but it is used to heighten and not reduce the anxiety. The goal is to escalate the anxiety until the patient is finally unable to experience it at all. Barrett (1969) has compared the effects of systematic desensitisation and implosion and found that although both methods were equally effective initially, some patients who had received implosion had relapsed after six months follow up. Wolpe (1973) advocates a cautious attitude towards implosion because, although effective, it can produce side effects and can exacerbate some neuroses. The terms 'flooding' and 'implosion' are often used interchangeably.

BARRETT, C. L. (1969), 'Systematic desensitisation vs. implosion therapy' (*J. of Abnormal Psychology*, vol. 74, pp. 587-93).
HOGAN, R. A. (1968), 'The implosive technique' (*Behavior Research and Therapy*, vol. 6, pp. 423-31).
STAMPFL, T. G. and LEVIS, D. J. (1967), 'Essentials of implosive therapy: a learning therapy based psychodynamic behavioral therapy' (*J. of Abnormal Psychology*, vol. 72, p. 496).
STAMPFL, T. G. and LEVIS, D. J. (1968), 'Implosive therapy, a behavioral therapy' (*Behavior Research and Therapy*, vol. 6, p. 31).
WOLPE, J. (1973), *The Practice of Behavior Therapy* (2nd edn, Pergamon, New York).

See also *Abreaction, Catharsis*.

Incest taboo
Prohibition against sexual relationships between near kindred which operates universally and finds expression in the laws of most societies. Freud (1913) asserted that the incest taboo was introjected by each individual at the resolution of the *Oedipus complex*. In many cultures, initiation ceremonies at puberty act to reinforce the idea that the mother and sister are forbidden to the young male as sexual objects. Jung (1911) criticised Freud's emphasis on the literal importance of the incest taboo and his inability, as Jung felt, to grasp the symbolic significance of incest.

FREUD, S. (1913), 'Totem and taboo' (*Standard Edition*, vol. 13, Hogarth Press, London).

JUNG, C. G. (1911), 'Symbols of transformation' (*Collected Works*, vol. 7, Routledge & Kegan Paul, London).

Incestuous fixation
See *Modes of relatedness*.

Incorporation
The bodily mode whereby *introjection* and *identification* is achieved. The *object* is introduced into the body in *phantasy* becoming part of an *internal world* of objects. The individual can then act in relation to the internal object – possess it, destroy it, and/or identify with it. Freud introduced the term when discussing the development of the *oral stage* of development and he linked the concept with that of introjection (Freud 1925). The ambivalent dependence of the infant on the mother creates a need to possess her lovingly or destroy her out of fear. Klein (1955) and Riviere (1955) develop the ideas described by Freud (1917) and Abraham (1924) and connect the impulse to incorporate an object to the fear of its loss and ultimately to the loss of life itself. Thus the infant tries to compensate for his lost incorporation within the mother's womb by incorporating the mother into himself, through his mouth. Other orifices can serve to incorporate a loved object, the most obvious being the incorporation of the penis into the vagina. Incorporation is often the means by which identification occurs. Isaacs (1952) discusses the way in which the individual comes to realise that what he has 'taken inside' was an image rather than an actual bodily object. Some primitive types of physical incorporation can still be found, however, in some societies where the object with which the individual wishes to identify is eaten and is thus physically incorporated into the body. An example of the practice continues in the Christian sacramental practice of eating the Body and Blood of Christ (in the form of bread and wine) in order to identify with the Person of Christ.

ABRAHAM, K. (1924), 'A short history of the development of the libido', in *Collected Papers* (Hogarth Press, London).

FREUD, S. (1917), 'Mourning and melancholia' (*Standard Edition*, vol. 14, Hogarth Press, London).

FREUD, S. (1925), 'Negation' (*Standard Edition*, vol. 19, Hogarth Press, London).

ISAACS, S. (1952), 'The nature and function of phantasy' (in *Developments in Psychoanalysis*, edited by Riviere, J., Hogarth Press, London).

KLEIN, M. (1955), 'On identification' (in *New Directions in Psychoanalysis*, Maresfield Reprints, Karnac, London).

RIVIÈRE, J. (1955), 'The unconscious phantasy of an inner world reflected in examples from literature' (in *New Directions in Psychoanalysis*, Maresfield Reprints, Karnac, London).

Index patient
See *Identified patient*.

Individual psychology
An approach to personality and psychotherapy introduced by Alfred Adler. Adler described 'the science of individual psychology [as developing] out of the effort to understand that mysterious creative power of life which expresses itself in the desire to develop, to strive, to achieve and even to compensate for defeats in one direction by striving for success in another'. Like Jung, Adler was an early disciple of Freud, but became dissatisfied with Freud's emphasis on sexuality in the development of normal and abnormal personality structure. He was the first to break with Freud and form his own school of psychotherapy. In contrast to Freud, Adler suggested that the young child's experience of powerlessness and *helplessness* was at least as important, and probably more so, than early infantile sexuality. From the beginning, he sees human life as being goal-oriented towards the future and thus each individual is challenged to overcome his powerlessness and the obstacles in the way of him achieving the fulfilment of his particular goals.

Adler called this consistent goal of orientation on the part of each individual, his 'style of life'. The style of life is made up of the individual's pattern of relationships with others and his problem solving activities as well as the goals he has set himself. Adler suggested that what he called '*social interest*' is an innate tendency and that all personality growth leads to increased social interest. For Adler, therefore, interpersonal relationships are of primary importance in enabling or disabling the growth of personality. Neurotic responses arise from low social interest and are expressed by a variety of *distancing* mechanisms.

Adler's belief in powerlessness as a universal experience led him to postulate three frequent pathological responses to this situation: the *inferiority complex*, the *superiority complex* and *masculine protest*. For Adler, the *family constellation* provided an important means of understanding the effect on the individual of the family of origin and he drew attention to the significance of sibling relationships as well as relationships between the child and his parents.

The object of individual psychology is to help the patient adopt a more socially useful lifestyle; increase his social interest and thus improve his interpersonal relationships; and enable him to abandon his need for either a superiority or inferiority complex. As Ansbacher and Ansbacher (1956) comment, Adler's emphasis is on social relationships rather than biological factors, the self rather than the id and the supergo, the striving for self-actualisation rather than the sex instinct and the present situation rather than early experiences'. In individual psychology the therapist creates a climate of encouragement and optimism, uses *interpretations* and suggestions which are particularly directed towards making unrealistic goals conscious and bringing into awareness the patient's feelings of inferiority and compensatory superiority. Although Adler's school of individual psychology has attracted fewer followers than those of Freud or Jung, he has had considerable influence on adherents of other schools and modalities. His emphasis on social relations and interpersonal behaviour

has influenced *family therapy* somewhat (see, for example, Liebermann 1980) and his emphasis on ego development rather than on the development of the unconscious drives of the individual helped pave the way for the later work on *ego psychology*. His interest in self-direction and education gave impetus to educational schemes for parents and children and the development of child guidance clinics, the first of which he founded in Vienna. The Vienna child guidance clinic pioneered several new therapeutic approaches including the first recorded experiments with *co-therapy* and some early uses of group work. As Ellenberger (1970) points out, Adler's ideas have permeated the whole field of psychoanalysis and beyond in subtle and far-reaching ways.

ADLER, A. (1924), *The Practice and Theory of Individual Psychology* (Littlefield, Adams, Totowa, New Jersey).
ADLER, A. (1928), *Understanding Human Nature* (Allen & Unwin, London).
ADLER, A. (1933), *Social Interest: A Challenge to Mankind* (Capricorn Books, New York).
ANSBACHER, H. L. and ANSBACHER, R. R. (eds) (1956), *The Individual Psychology of Alfred Adler* (Harper & Row, New York).
ANSBACHER, H. L. (1974), 'Adler and Virchow: new light on the name "individual psychology" ' (*J. of Individual Psychology*, vol. 30, pp. 43-52).
ELLENBERGER, H. F. (1970), *The Discovery of the Unconscious* (Allen Lane, London).
LEIBIN, V. M. (1981), 'Adler's concept of man' (*J. of Individual Psychology*, vol. 37, pp. 3-4).
LIEBERMANN, S. (1980), *Transgenerational Family Therapy* (Croom Helm, London).

Individuation

A term used by Jung to describe the process of psychological development over a lifetime in which a person learns who he or she was 'intended to be', quite distinct from all others. Individuation involves the achievement of selfhood, *self-realisation* and emotional maturity and is brought about by a gradual fulfilment of the person's individual capacities and functions. The process also involves facing and integrating the dark or shadow aspect of the self; a *progression* away from the stereotyped image of the *persona* and a growth towards *differentiation* from the contents of the *collective unconscious*. Far from the self preoccupation of individualism, Jung (1917) suggested that since a person's 'very existence presupposes a collective relationship, it follows that the process of individuation must lead to more intense and broader collective relationships and not to isolation'. Individuation also suggests the individual's goal-oriented striving towards the future and it thus has a teleological facet, differentiating Jung's concept of psychological goals from those of Freud.

JUNG, C. G. (1917), 'The psychology of the unconscious' (in *Two Essays on Analytical Psychology, Collected Works*, vol. 7, Routledge & Kegan Paul, London).

Induction

The process whereby the therapist is persuaded by an individual patient, family, couple or group to collude with the *dysfunctional* situation which he is trying to change. The process is usually *unconscious* and results in a loss of therapeutic leverage. It should be distinguished from the *joining* and *accommodation* processes in which the therapist consciously engages the patient or family on their own terms with a view to developing compliance, overcoming *resistance* and creating the conditions for change to occur. Strategies for avoiding or reducing induction include the use of supervision or consultation; *co-therapy* or the use of a *team* in family and marital work; and the use of *audio visual equipment*.

See also *Collusion, De-triangulation*.

Inferiority complex

Term introduced by Adler to describe a style of life developed around feelings of weakness and insignificance. The powerlessness which Adler believed to be the general experience of all human infants may be accentuated by the experience of actual organ inferiority or the experience of being female. The goal of therapy is to enable the individual to overcome his feelings of inferiority and develop new self-esteem without needing to overcompensate by striving for power or superiority over others. Erikson (1950) viewed inferiority as the penalty for not achieving the expansion of ego identity at the fourth stage of the life cycle (see *Stages of development*), through learning how to make things and create.

ANSBACHER, H. L. and ANSBACHER, R. R. (eds) (1956), *The Individual Psychology of Alfred Alder* (Harper & Row, New York).
ERIKSON, E. H. (1950), *Childhood and Society* (Penguin, Harmondsworth).

See also *Helplessness, Individual psychology, Superiority complex*.

Insight

A term used in several different ways in psychotherapy. Zilboorg, Marmour and others have commented on the uncertainty of its origins and meaning. Its main usages can be summarised as follows. (1) In accord with common usage of everyday speech, insight can be defined as the penetration of a situation, leading to a special kind of understanding. Natural insight of this kind is equivalent to intuition and seems to be a capacity that some possess and some do not (for example, artists, poets, mystics or 'natural therapists'). The term carries implications of depth and suddenness and, as in lateral thinking, it has an unexpected quality. Hence gaining insight involves seeing beneath the surface of a person or situation, perhaps for the first time. (2) Cognitive or intellectual insight, by which a new pattern is perceived between cause and effect, creating new opportunities for effective problem solving (for example, in scientific enquiry). (3) Emotional insight, by which new awareness is gained about feelings, motives and relationships. When used in relation to the self, it is thus equivalent to self-awareness. (4) In *psychoanalysis*, an awareness of the relationship between past experience and current behaviour, especially in relation to *unconscious* conflict now made *conscious* by *interpretations* and the *working through* process.

Anna Freud (1981) reviews two contrasting opinions in the psychoanalytic literature: one that maintains that the task of analysis is to restore to the patient the insight which he had before the onset of the neurosis, and another that views psychoanalysis as helping the patient to develop an altogether deeper level of insight impossible without therapy.

Although these four usages overlap considerably, it is possible to distinguish three broad usages in psychotherapy: cognitive/intellectual insight (or awareness, as Bandura (1969) terms it) recognised by behaviour therapists; psychoanalytic insight, recognised by all schools of psychoanalysis and *depth psychology*; and emotional insight, recognised in most forms of non-behavioural psychotherapy, in the humanistic therapies and many forms of group, *family* and *marital therapy* which do not fall into the first two categories. *Strategic therapy* and its derivatives, however, tend to discount insight of any kind as being redundant to the therapeutic process.

Considering the central position given to insight in many psychotherapies, very little systematic research has been devoted to the subject. All schools emphasise a great many features of the therapeutic process as instrumental in bringing about change over and above the acquisition of insight, and even within psychoanalysis insight was not originally emphasised as a major curative factor. Subsequently, however, the concept came to acquire a central position. As Menninger (1958) points out, insight is the 'simultaneous identification of the characteristic behaviour pattern' in three distinct situations: in the patient's childhood, in his contemporary behaviour and in his response to the analytic situation. It is this triple connection that is characteristic of the psychoanalytic use of the term, but it also subsumes the idea of cognitive and emotional insight – for both are necessary if full insight is to be achieved. There remains considerable discussion within psychoanalysis regarding the exact nature of insight. As Marmour (1962) has pointed out, 'to a Freudian it means one thing, to a Jungian another, to a Rankian, a Horneyite, an Adlerian or a Sullivanian, still another.' He goes on to comment on the power of the analytic relationship to elicit the responses and insights which are approved by the analyst. Moreover, the relative weighting of insight compared with other factors such as a *corrective emotional experience* in the relationship with the analyst is a matter of debate, with those of the *Freudian* and *Kleinian schools* laying greatest emphasis on insight as the primary factor.

Bandura (1969) suggests that the acquisition of insight is more a process of conversion to the therapist's belief system than a process of patient self-discovery. Thus, according to this idea, the therapist has the option of choosing a description and cause of the problem that is likely to promote change and then converting the client to his *hypothesis* (see *Attribution theory*). Bandura suggests that the process of gaining insight is quite independent of gaining help for the problems for which the patient approached the therapist in the first place. Hence, high levels of insight may be acquired without any associated behavioural changes. As Bandura points out, behaviour therapists, whilst discounting the concept of insight used in the psychoanalytic sense, nevertheless invoke a concept of awareness. Awareness is defined by Bandura as 'correct verbalisation of response-reinforcement contingencies'. Behaviour therapists are engaged in a similar debate regarding whether awareness of the stimulus-response connection precedes, succeeds or is redundant to the process of behaviour change. The inter-relationship between insight and behaviour change remains a complex and unresolved matter.

BANDURA, A. (1969), *Principles of Behavior Modification* (Holt, Rinehart & Winston, New York).

BLACKER, K. H. (1981), 'Insight: clinical conceptualisation' (*J. of the Am. Psychoan. Assoc.*, vol. 29, pp. 659-71).

FREUD, A. (1981), 'Insight: its presence and absence as a factor in normal development' (*Psychoanalytic Study of the Child*, vol. 36, pp. 241-9).

MARMOUR, J. (1962), 'Psychoanalytic therapy as an educational process' (in Masserman, J. J. (ed.), *Science and Education*, vol. 5, Grune & Stratton, New York).
MATROSS, R. P. (1975), 'Insight and attribution in counselling and psychotherapy' (*Office for Student Affairs Research Bulletin*, University of Minnesota).
MENNINGER, K. (1958), *Theory of Psychoanalytic Technique* (Imago, London).
VALENSTEIN, A. F. (1981), 'Insight as an embedded concept in the early historical phase of psychoanalysis' (*Psychoanalytic Study of the Child*, vol. 36, pp. 307-15).
WICKLUND, D. (1972), *A Theory of Objective Self-awareness* (Academic Press, New York).
ZILBOORG, G. (1952), 'The emotional problem and the therapeutic role of insight' (*Psychoanalytic Quarterly*, vol. 21, pp. 1-24).

Insight approaches
See *Depth psychology*.

Instinct
See *Drive*.

Integration
The process whereby the separated parts of the personality or *psyche* are brought into a unified whole and the individual achieves a relatively harmonious relationship with himself and with the external world. Erikson (1950) views integrity or integration as the final goal of mature human development, achievable in the last phase of life – and the total lack of integration as leading to despair. According to the *Freudian* and *Kleinian schools* of *psychoanalysis* the human psyche begins as a disorganised chaos and moves towards the integration with the development of the *ego*. Integration is hindered by the operation of *defence mechanisms* which defend the ego from anxiety by *splitting* and *repression* of parts of the self. The aim of psychoanalysis is to enable a greater degree of integration within the personality to take place. The term is particularly associated with the *humanistic* approaches of Maslow, Allport and Rogers who emphasise that psychotherapy should be directed to the whole person and towards helping him to become unified, integrated or *self-actualised*.

ERIKSON, E. H. (1950), *Childhood and Society* (Penguin, Harmondsworth).

See also *Differentiation, Individuation*.

Integrity groups
A form of self-help practised in groups along the principles established by Hobart Mowrer. Mowrer first introduced a form of individual therapy which focused upon encouraging the client to disclose the aspects of his life about which he felt guilty. Mowrer prompted client *self-disclosure* by *modelling* the self-disclosure of his own deficiencies. Later he moved from the individual to work with groups and currently these groups operate as self-help groups. Mowrer's work originated from a dissatisfaction with the way personal guilt is handled in orthodox psychotherapy. Mowrer believes guilt needs to be recognised, 'confessed' to another and when the reason for the guilt involves another person, retribution made to that person for any wrong that has been committed. Mowrer uses the language of theology but the techniques of psychotherapy. For example, the therapist or group leader may encourage the individual to undertake *homework assignments* and to make journeys to distant relatives to resolve long-standing difficulties with them, in a way that is similar to that used in *transgenerational family therapy*. Mowrer stresses the three principles of honesty (through self-disclosure), responsibility (through making amends) and mutual involvement (through concern for others). Currently, integrity groups have become part of the self-help movement, with professionals used as catalysts and teachers of the method rather than as therapists. Training groups for students in the mental health disciplines are also run in some American academic departments. Introspection, self-disclosure and *feedback* from other group members and commitment to them regarding their intention of behaving differently are the chief tools of behaviour change.

MOWRER, O. H. (1964), *The New Group Therapy* (Van Nostrand Reinhold, Princeton, New Jersey).

MOWRER, O. H. (1966), 'Integrity therapy: a self-help approach' (*Psychotherapy: Theory, Research and Practice*, vol. 3, pp. 114-19).

MOWRER, O. H. and VATTANO, A. J. (1976), 'Integrity groups: a context for growth in honesty, responsibility and involvement' (*J. of Applied Behavioral Science*, vol. 12, pp. 419-31).

Integrity therapy

See *Integrity groups*.

Intellectualisation

A *defence mechanism* whereby the *ego* seeks to protect itself from emotional conflict by dealing with the conflict cognitively rather than emotionally. The term is used primarily to describe a particular way in which the patient uses psychoanalytic treatment. Anna Freud (1937) described this as the ego's attempt 'to lay hold on the instinctual processes by connecting them with ideas which can be dealt with in consciousness'. Intellectualisation is a normal process in enabling an individual to 'make sense' of himself and the world around him. Although it can be a severe block in the treatment situation, preventing real, affective '*working through*' from taking place, it can be used constructively in treatment. In situations of high emotional arousal and severe conflict, the therapist may need to help the individual or family to bypass the affective content temporarily by encouraging the use of intellectualisation. The mechanism is obviously related to the mechanism of *rationalisation*.

FREUD, A. (1937), *The Ego and the Mechanisms of Defence* (Hogarth Press, London).

Intensification

A technique of *structural family therapy* described by Minuchin for increasing the emotional impact of a therapeutic intervention and therefore increasing its effectiveness. The technique is used with *resistant* family structures where it is difficult for the therapist to make any impact. Intensification techniques include repetition of content, where the therapist repeats a point many times over during the session, either describing it in exactly the same way or using different approaches and *metaphors* to arrive at the same issue; repetition of theme, where the therapist uses the principle of *isomorphy* to work on a theme of *enmeshment*, conflict resolution, etc. through the transactions that occur in different *sub-systems* during the session; prolonging the time during which a transaction takes place until some resolution, or new learning is achieved; and changing physical (and therefore emotional) positions between family members and between the family and the therapist by moving members closer or further apart, getting on the floor to speak to a child, etc. *Action techniques* such as *family sculpting* are also important means of intensifying relationship problems and portraying their potential solution and intensification is also achieved by using an *auxiliary ego* or by *doubling*.

MINUCHIN, S. and FISHMAN, H. C. (1981), *Family Therapy Techniques* (Harvard University Press, Cambridge, Mass.).

See also *Enactment*.

Intensive psychotherapy

A derivative of *psychoanalysis*, intensive psychotherapy aims at basic structural changes in the personality via the formation and resolution of the *transference*. *Interpretation* is used as a primary technique but the transference does not develop as systematically or intensely as in psychoanalysis. Other main differences between intensive psychotherapy and psychoanalysis is the more focused approached, more limited goals (major structural change in the personality is not attempted), less *regression*, greater activity on the part of the therapist, and greater focus on the here and now experiences of the patient's life. Therapeutic sessions take place two or three times a week. Curative factors include supportive and educative as well as interpretative interventions and the overall intention is to foster the growth and development of the ego. The term was introduced by Fromm-Reichmann (1950) to describe her approach to psychoanalysis. Her theoretical stance derives from the *interpersonal school* of psychoanalysis. Although she emphasises more direct methods of approaching the patient's material, through *questioning* for example, rather than *free association* alone, she clearly considered psychoanalysis in its various forms to be the only valid type of intensive psychotherapy.

CHESSICK, R. (1974), *The Technique and Practice of Intensive Psychotherapy* (Jason Aronson, New York).

CHESSICK, R. (1977), *Intensive Psychotherapy of the Borderline Patient* (Jason Aronson, New York).

FROMM-REICHMANN, F. (1950), *Principles of Intensive Psychotherapy* (University of Chicago Press, Chicago).

Interaction process analysis

A method of observing and recording the internal processes of different types of small group, introduced by Bales (1950). Bales established a set of twelve categories of types of interactions in which group members engage when they participate in groups, including therapy groups. He divided these twelve categories into positive and negative interactions that occur in six areas: defining the situation; developing a value system for evaluating alternative solutions; making decisions; dealing with tension; members influencing or controlling each other; and maintenance of the group. The first three of these six areas are concerned with the group's task and actions occurring in these areas are described by Bales as instrumental. The second three are concerned with maintaining the socio-emotional life of the group and are described by Bales as expressive. Bales (1955) suggests that normally about two-thirds of the actions of group members are directed towards task performance and the group's goals and about one-third are directed towards the socio-emotional needs of the group. Hare (1962) suggests that where a group shows a higher level of task-focused interactions than the two-thirds level, this may indicate that

group members have other opportunities to give each other socio-emotional support; or that the group has developed a high level of positive functioning over a period of time and therefore it requires less socio-emotional maintenance; or that members are colluding with each other in establishing a shared defence against dealing with tension, conflict and difference.

BALES, R. F. (1950), *Interaction Process Analysis: A Method for the Study of Small Groups* (Addison-Wesley, Cambridge, Mass.).

BALES, R. F. (1955), 'How people interact in conferences' (*Scientific American*, vol. 92, pp. 31-5).

HARE, A. P. (1962), *Handbook of Small Group Research* (Free Press, New York).

See also *Group process, Sociogram.*

Internal world

A term used loosely to describe the internalised *objects*, events and relationships which help to form the individual's *mental apparatus*. The internal world is partly *conscious* and partly *unconscious*, and it is contrasted with the external world of objective reality. Melanie Klein (1940) describes the relationship of the two as follows: 'When external situations which [the child] lives through become internalised – and I hold that they do from the earliest days onwards – they follow the same pattern: they become "doubles" of real situations.' The internal world is created as a result of the operation of unconscious *phantasy* and is conceived of as a psychic 'space' into which objects are drawn from the external world through *introjection* and *incorporation* and expelled from the internal world through *projection* and *projective identification*. Although a metaphor, the concept is afforded a very 'realistic' quality in psychoanalytic literature, particularly amongst analysts of the *Kleinian school*. Rivière (1955) interprets the rejection of the concept of an inner world as a resistance to the anxiety it engenders. However, it should be borne in mind that the literalism that is apparent in Kleinian writers' conceptualisation relates to the pre-verbal and concrete experiencing of internal processes which the baby is believed to have. Stripped of its literalism, the idea of an internal world is acceptable to most schools of psychotherapy other than the most radical behaviourist.

KLEIN, M. (1940), 'Mourning and its relation to manic-depressive states' (in *Contributions to Psychoanalysis*, Hogarth Press, London, 1948).
RIVIÈRE, J. (1955), 'The unconscious fantasy of an inner world reflected in examples from literature' (in Klein, M. *et al.* (eds), *New Directions in Psychoanalysis*, Maresfield Reprints, Karnac, London).
SCHAFER, R. (1976), *A New Language for Psychoanalysis* (Yale University Press, Newhaven, Conn.).

Internalisation

The process whereby the individual transfers a relationship with an external *object* into his *internal world*. The term is also used to describe the transfer of the object itself into the internal world in *phantasy* but in this usage it becomes synonymous with *introjection*. It is also used as a generic term to describe all the psychic processes such as introjection, *incorporation* and *identification* which involve the making internal of what has been expressed as external through permanent mental representation in the internal world. Hartmann (1939) views the process of individual and societal development as one of 'progressive internalisation': 'Evolution leads to an increased independence of the organism from its environment, so that reactions which originally occurred in relation to the external world are increasingly displaced into the interior of the organism.'

Melanie Klein laid great stress on the processes of internalisation as a means of building up the child's internal world. She suggests that there is a continuous interaction between the internalised person or relationship and its external counterpart and this constant interaction in the infant's mind provides an incentive for *reality testing* and the development of the *ego*. Schafer (1976) has severely criticised the concept: 'Internalisation

is a spatial metaphor that is so greatly incomplete and unworkable that we would do best to avoid it in psychoanalytic conceptualisations.' He suggests that internalisation refers to a phantasy, not to a process, a point with which Meissner (1979, 1981), however, sharply disagrees. Meissner suggests that the spatial metaphor inherent in the concept of internalisation and in other concepts such as introjection is the best that can be achieved to convey the necessary meaning at present.

HARTMANN, H. (1939), *Ego Psychology and the Problems of Adaptation* (International Universities Press, New York, 1958).
MEISSNER, W. W. (1979), 'Critique of concepts and therapy in the action language approach to psychoanalysis' (*Int. J. of Psychoanalysis*, vol. 60, pp. 291-310).
MEISSNER, W. W. (1981), *Internalisation in Psychoanalysis* (International Universities Press, New York).
SCHAFER, R. (1976), *A New Language for Psychoanalysis* (Yale University Press, Newhaven, Conn.).

Interpersonal

That which occurs between persons as contrasted with *intrapersonal* or *intrapsychic* which occurs between parts of the person. Hence, the processes and events which are social or contextually related. Interpersonal therapies are concerned with focusing on relationship problems and social issues, either *in vivo* as in the *conjoint* and group therapies or through work with the individual, as with the *interpersonal school* of *psychoanalysis* and other interpersonal individual approaches.

Interpersonal perception method

A method of analysing and recording dyadic relationships introduced by Laing and his collaborators (Laing, Phillipson and Lee 1966). The method is based upon Laing's understanding of and metaperspective on relationships as involving the self's view of the other, the other's view of the self and the self's awareness of the awareness and view of the other about the self. The self's identity, according to Laing, becomes 'refracted through the media of the different inflections of "the other" ' and thus the self undergoes change in and through its perception of the awareness and evaluation of others. The interpersonal perception method is based on this idea and is made up of a questionnaire, comprising sixty 'issues' – for example, 'is sorry for'. The sixty issues embrace such factors as interdependence and autonomy, concern, disparagement, areas of contention, confusion and denial of autonomy. Each issue is expressed four times as follows: She is sorry for me; I am sorry for her; she is sorry for herself; I am sorry for myself. The subject or patient is instructed to record how true each of these four statements are and also to record how his or her partner would answer them. The questionnaire yields one thousand four hundred and forty answers when completed by two people. The methodology has a similarity to the double dyad technique in *repertory grid* methods but it has proved even more complex to use fruitfully in clinical practice. White (1982) suggests ways in which the instrument can be used as both a diagnostic and an evaluative technique in counselling.

LAING, R. D., PHILLIPSON, H. and LEE, A. L. (1966), *Interpersonal Perception* (Tavistock, London).
WHITE, J. (1982), 'The application of Laing's interpersonal perception method to the counselling context' (*Family Therapy*, vol. 9, pp. 167-73).

Interpersonal school (of psychoanalysis)

Term used to describe a group of American psychoanalysts who replaced the biological emphasis of Freud with a concern for interpersonal relationships and the individual's social and cultural environment. The group, which is also termed 'neo-Freudian', included Harry Stack Sullivan, Karen Horney and Erich Fromm, and after Horney and Fromm had arrived in the USA, from Germany, the three worked in close association for some years. Brown (1961) describes the interpersonal approach as a 'left-wing' development within

psychoanalysis. This description stems from the modifiability of human nature which the interpersonal school stresses, rather than the deterministic conclusions they believe are inherent in a biological approach.

The interpersonal school was influenced by Adler, and each of the members of this group reflect themes and interests from Adler's work, particularly his concept of *social interest*. They were also influenced by the work of the American anthropologists Margaret Mead and Ruth Benedict, whose work on primitive tribes of the Pacific showed the widely different cultural patterns that pertained in other cultures. Sullivan (1940) stressed the indivisibility of the individual from his environment and suggested that 'the environment flows through the living cell, becoming its very life in the process'. He proposed that there was no qualitative difference between normals and the psychologically disturbed and that problems and disturbances were matters of degree, because 'everyone is much more simply human than otherwise'. From his focus on interpersonal relationships, Sullivan was led to an interest in *communication* and he identified three *referential processes*, an understanding of which enables communication to be productive. He outlined a theory of human development in which he placed these communication modes alongside the developmental stages and the individual's basic social needs, emphasising that the individual's development can only occur communally.

Horney also proposed that psychological disturbance arose from disturbed interpersonal relationships. She saw the goal of human striving as *self-realisation*. For Horney, this could only be achieved through effective interpersonal relationships. She (1945) suggests that individuals characteristically move either towards, against or away from others, and that extreme reliance on one of these trends creates vulnerability, anxiety and dependence. The individual needs to be able to use all three appropriately in his interpersonal relations. Horney focuses on some of the destructive aspects of contemporary Western culture for the healthy development of the individual: its competitiveness; its emphasis on personal choice and freedom, when in reality both are often very limited; and the overvaluing, and thus the overstressing, of love and intimate relations as the solution to all life's problems. One of Horney's major contributions was a discussion of *female sexuality* and psychology and she has done much to challenge Freud's views of women expressed in his concepts of *penis envy* and the *castration complex*. Like Adler, Horney (1967) offered alternative explanations of the data from which Freud drew his conclusions that women are fundamentally inferior to men, and she paved the way for a much more complete and complementary understanding of the relationship between the sexes.

Like Horney and Sullivan, Fromm criticised the biological basis of Freud's theories and he emphasised instead the part played by social relations in the formation of the individual. He suggested that there are basic organic *drives* which are common to all individuals but that the differences *between* individuals can only be accounted for by interaction with society and the social process. Fromm was influenced by Marx, but rejected his exclusive emphasis on sociological factors, just as he had rejected Freud's exclusive focus on biology. He (1973) identified five basic human needs as 'a frame of orientation and devotion; rootedness; unity; effectiveness and stimulation'. Achieving these constitutes freedom; failure to achieve them in some degree may persuade the individual to escape into authoritarianism or destructiveness. He described five *modes of assimilation* and three *modes of relatedness*, one of which predominates, though not exclusively, in each individual. The interpersonal school's stress on the reciprocal relationship of the individual and his social environment did much to redress the balance in this respect in Freudian theory and it paved the way for the development of social theories and those concerned with the *conjoint* treatment of families and *networks*. Institutes where psychoanalysis is practised according to the interpersonal school include the William Allenson White

Institute and the Karen Horney Institute, both in New York. Anchin and Kiesler (1982) provide an overview of the current status of the interpersonal approach and show how rich is the potential for an interpersonal perspective within a focus that retains the individual as the patient. They show too how a variety of cross-fertilising influences have now been brought to bear on interpersonal psychotherapy including ideas from *brief therapy* and from *strategic therapy*.

ANCHIN, J. C. and KIESLER, D. J. (eds) (1982), *Handbook of Psychotherapy* (Pergamon Press, New York).
BROWN, J. A. C. (1961), *Freud and the Post-Freudians* (Penguin, Harmondsworth).
FROMM, E. (1973), *The Anatomy of Destructiveness* (Fawcett, Greenwich, Conn.).
HORNEY, K. (1945), *Our Inner Conflicts* (W. W. Norton, New York).
HORNEY, K. (1967), *Feminine Psychology* (W. W. Norton, New York).
SULLIVAN, H. S. (1940), *Conceptions of Modern Psychiatry* (W. W. Norton, New York).
SULLIVAN, H. S. (1955), *The Interpersonal Theory of Psychiatry* (W. W. Norton, New York).

Interpretation

A communication from therapist to patient designed to elucidate the *unconscious* meaning and repressed wishes which lie beneath his *dreams, free association*, use of *symbolism, resistance, symptoms* and/or feelings towards the therapist expressed through the *transference*. Within *psychoanalysis*, the purpose of an interpretation is to make the unconscious conscious or to raise the *primary* to the *secondary process*. Although interpretation is the chief tool of the *analyst* and his primary form of activity in the treatment, interpretation is also used in many other forms of psychotherapy and within other modalities such as *family therapy* and *group psychotherapy*. Rules governing the level, type and timing of interpretations relate to different approaches to psychoanalysis and to different forms of psychotherapy. The activity involves, first, an understanding of the material by the therapist, and second, the communication of that understanding to the patient in a manner which will be acceptable to him, that is, *ego syntonic*. Care must be taken that the interpretation does not break the patient's *defence mechanisms* prematurely or brutally. The interpretation of *dreams* was offered by Freud (1900) as a paradigm for all interpretations, although Jung (1954) criticised what he felt to be Freud's stereotyped interpretations of dream symbols. Strachey (1934) formulated an influential model of the way a 'mutative' interpretation results in change in the intrapsychic structure.

Most psychoanalytic theorists emphasise the importance of transference interpretations over all others, though Leites (1977) has challenged this view. In her discussion of transference interpretations, Segal (1973) suggests that a full transference interpretation 'should include the current external relationship in the patient's life, the patient's relationship to the analyst and the relation between these and the relationships with the parents in the past', though she admits that this is seldom possible to do fully.

In psychoanalysis, interpretation is generally regarded as the tool which holds greatest potential for being either curative or harmful to the patient. The function of an interpretation is to promote *insight* and bring about *integration* within the *psyche* and an interpretation that brings about these changes in the patient is termed a mutative interpretation.

CHESHIRE, N. M. (1975), *The Nature of Psychodynamic Interpretation* (Wiley, London).
FRENCH, T. (1970), *Psychoanalytic Interpretations* (Quadrangle Books, Chicago).
FREUD, S. (1900), 'The interpretation of dreams' (*Standard Edition*, vols 4 & 5, Hogarth Press, London).
JUNG, C. G. (1954), 'The practical use of dream analysis' (*Collected Works*, vol. 16, Routledge & Kegan Paul, London).
LEITES, N. (1977), 'Transference interpretations only?' (*Int. J. of Psychoanalysis*, vol. 58, pp. 275-87).
SEGAL, H. (1973), *Introduction to the Work of Melanie Klein* (Hogarth Press, London).
SPRINGMAN, R. R. (1970), 'The application of interpretations in a large group' (*Int. J. of Group Psychotherapy*, vol. 20, pp. 333-41).
STRACHEY, J. (1934), 'The nature of the therapeutic action of psychoanalysis' (*International Journal of Psychoanalysis*, vol. 15, pp. 127-59).

Interview

A face-to-face encounter between the therapist (interviewer) and the patient, couple, family or group (interviewee(s)). The interview is the therapist's primary tool and one of the chief means by which the direct therapeutic process is conducted. In those methods which do not make use of *homework assignments* or *tasks*, it is the sole means. Kahn and Connell (1957) define an interview as a 'specialized pattern of verbal interaction – initiated for a specific purpose, focussed on some specific content area, with consequent elimination of extraneous material'.

The purpose and *ambience* of an interview are of great importance in determining its form. The purpose is in part determined by whether it is a *diagnostic* interview, a treatment interview, or a follow-up interview for the evaluation of *outcome*. In the first and the third, data collection will play a particularly important part, but there is a further distinction to be made in this respect within a treatment interview, between what Palazzoli *et al.* (1975) describe as the 'search for information' and the 'conclusion' (or intervention). Here, information gathering and intervention are clearly distinguished in this treatment model, yet both form an ongoing part of the treatment.

The process of an interview is determined by the method and approach being used, the *unit of treatment* to which therapy is directed and the *goals* of treatment. Regardless of the approach being used, however, certain interviewing skills such as *clarification, questioning, confrontation*, support and the giving of *feedback* are almost always required, although they will be demonstrated in different ways and in varying degrees according to the therapeutic approach being used.

The therapeutic interview takes place in a specific *context* within a contractual relationship between two or more people, the therapist and client or client group, who usually relate to each other exclusively through these specialised role relationships. It involves a special kind of *communication* designed to achieve the treatment goals. Davis (1971) has discussed interviews in terms of a mutual influence model, in which each of the participants tries to gain the advantage in the interaction. Considerable initial advantages lie on the side of the therapist and many traditional therapist behaviours are, Davis suggests, strategies designed to maintain this advantage. Clearly therapists whose model views *social influence* as an important aspect of the therapist's armamentarium will overtly try to maximise this influence over the patient. But all therapists, as Haley (1963) and others have pointed out, employ covert strategies to maintain their advantage within the interaction of the interview. 'The therapist maintains an appearance of inscrutability and while indicating that he knows what the patient must do to get better, insists that he must discover this for himself. Techniques involving mystification and ambiguity are common' (Haley 1963).

An interview has three phases, the opening and closing phases and the main body of the interview in the middle. Each of these phases has its own particular requirements of the therapist. The degree of structure which the therapist imposes within the interview is highly dependent on his *style* including his style of leadership and his therapeutic method. First and last interviews require special attention. The way in which the first interview is handled is likely to determine whether or not the client continues in treatment. Interviewing techniques during the early phase of treatment will normally focus on building up the *therapeutic alliance* and overcoming the client's *resistance*. Procedures for the first interview have been discussed in relation to different methods. Haley (1976), for example, has suggested that in *family therapy*, a first interview involves a social stage, a problem-eliciting stage, an interaction stage, and a goal setting stage. Stierlin *et al.* (1980) have also provided a detailed description of the first interview in family therapy.

Special techniques for interviewing children, adolescents, conducting interviews in groups, with families, with older people, with the dying and with the severely deprived, have been developed, making use of games, *action techniques*, drawings, *play*, *diagrams* and *structured exercises*. Most of the literature on interviewing skills and the process and structure of interviews relates to specific methods of therapy and to the different professional disciplines involved. Much of it, however, concerns generic principles which, with modification, are applicable to most therapeutic situations.

BESSELL, R. (1972), *Interviewing and Counselling* (Batsford, London).

DAVIS, J. D. (1971), *The Interview as Arena* (Stanford University Press, Stanford, Calif.).

DEUTSCH, F. and MURPHY, W. F. (1960), *The Clinical Interview* (International Universities Press, New York).

FENLASON, A. *et al.* (1962), *Essentials in Interviewing* (Harper & Row, New York).

HALEY, J. (1963), *Strategies of Psychotherapy* (Grune & Stratton, New York).

HALEY, J. (1976), *Problem Solving Therapy* (Harper & Row, New York).

KAHN, R. and CONNELL, C. (1957), *The Dynamics of Interviewing* (Wiley, New York).

LABOV, W. and FANSHEL, D. (1977), *Therapeutic Discourse: Psychotherapy as Conversation* (Academic Press, New York).

MATARAZZO, J. and WIENS, A. N. (1972), *The Interview* (Aldine Atherton Press, New York).

PALAZZOLI, M. S. *et al.* (1975), *Paradox and Counterparadox* (Jason Aronson, New York).

RICHARDSON, S. *et al.* (eds) (1965), *Interviewing* (Basic Books, New York).

STIERLIN, H. *et al.* (1980), *The First Interview with the Family* (Brunner/Mazel, New York).

See also *Contract, Microskill, Structured interview*.

Interviewing skill

See *Interview, Microskill.*

Intrapersonal

That which occurs within persons as contrasted with *interpersonal.* Hence, cognitive and affective events, such as the operation of the defences, the emotional experiences of fear, love, hate etc., the workings of conscience and the creative processes of thought and imagination. Intrapersonal therapies are all those therapies which are directed to the patient's *internal world* whether they take place in the individual or the group work setting.

See also *Intrapsychic.*

Intrapsychic

That which occurs within the *psyche* – hence the operation of the *ego, id* and *superego* and the relationships between them; and the interaction between the *conscious,* the *unconscious* and the *preconscious.* The different forms of *psychoanalysis* and *group analysis* are primarily concerned with understanding and modifying the patient's intrapsychic world.

Introjection

A form of *internalisation* by which *objects,* feelings and situations are transposed from the outside world into the person's *internal world.* Introjection thus holds the opposite meaning to *projection* but has similarities with the terms *incorporation,* internalisation and *identification.* The term introjection was originated by Ferenczi (1909) to describe the way in which pleasurable aspects of the outside world are introduced into the *ego* to become the objects of *phantasy.* The introject becomes the possession of the ego rather than the object of the ego's identification, although, as Melanie Klein points out (Klein 1955), 'identification as a sequel to introjection is part of normal development.'

In his studies of melancholia, Freud (1917) concluded that the process originated in the earliest development of the individual and that, along with identification, introjection was a major contributory process in the formation

of the ego and *superego.* Unlike Freud and Klein, Jung viewed the child as having a discrete personality from the beginning and that introjection is used as a defence against the fear of separateness rather than as a building block of normal development. Freud and others (for example, Erikson) use the term also to refer to the transposition of feelings as well as of objects into the internal world. Thus, feelings of blame may be introjected, leading to a masochistic response, or feelings of aggression, leading to sadism. Klein, however, reserves the term for the passing in of objects or part objects into the ego or superego. Heimann (1952) discusses the importance of the concept in Melanie Klein's work.

The purpose of introjection is to keep the self in contact with important objects when physically separated from them. This also protects the ego from anxiety, either by bringing into it good objects, to strengthen it against the outside world, or lost objects which can thus be retrieved and retained for ever (for example, during the *mourning* process). Conversely, the introjection of 'bad' objects allows the ego to possess them and thereby control them. Family therapists have made use of the concept to show how several family members may introject a lost family member. Paul and Grosser (1965) show how *'ghosts from the past'* may survive within the living family group, to form a pathological network which operates to maintain a fixed family *equilibrium.*

FERENCZI, S. (1909), 'Introjection and transference' (in *First Contributions to Psychoanalysis,* Hogarth Press, London, 1952).

FREUD, S. (1917), 'Mourning and melancholia' (*Standard Edition,* vol. 14, Hogarth Press, London).

HEIMANN, P. (1952), 'Certain functions of introjection and projection in early infancy' (in Klein, M., *Developments in Psychoanalysis,* Hogarth Press, London).

KLEIN, M. (1955), 'On identification' (in *New Directions in Psychoanalysis,* Tavistock Publications, London).

PAUL, N. L. and GROSSER, G. H. (1965),

INTROVERSION

'Operational mourning and its role in conjoint family therapy' (*Community Mental Health Journal*, vol. 1, pp. 339-45).
SCHAFER, R. (1976), *A New Language for Psychoanalysis* (Yale University Press, Newhaven, Conn.).

Introversion
See *Psychological types.*

Isomorphy
Literal Greek meaning 'same form'. A term adopted from chemistry, to describe something which corresponds with or has the same form as something else. The discovery of isomorphism between subjects that have hitherto been considered to be discrete allows the application of theory and technique from one area to another. Hence the understanding of the individual as a *system*, for example, allows the application of *systems theory* to the functioning of intrapsychic processes and a greater degree of convergence between individual, group and systems therapies. The discovery that systems themselves are basically isomorphic allows the similarities between couples, families, *stranger groups*, organisations, *networks*, etc., to be exploited in treatment. Similarly, the basic isomorphy between therapist and patient is the crucial factor enabling *empathy* to be experienced, *joining* operations to take place and the *core conditions* of therapy to be established. Isomorphy refers to a principle and does not describe an absolute. Obviously, the similarity between therapist and patient is not absolute and it is their *relative* isomorphy that enables the therapist to see the way forward towards change.

See also *Hologram, Intensification, Metaphor.*

J

Jackson, Donald, De Avila (1920-1968)
Don Jackson, a family and marital therapist,

and a major contributor to the development of communications theory, began his professional career in individual psychodynamic therapy. After training in medicine, Jackson undertook his psychoanalytic training at the Washington-Baltimore and San Francisco Psychoanalytic Institutes. In 1951 he entered private practice in Palo Alto and took up a consultative and training appointment to the Veteran Administration Hospital where he worked primarily with schizophrenics. Here he had the opportunity of studying the cyclical nature of schizophrenia, the relationship of the patient and his relatives and the interlocking pathology that is revealed between them. His paper on 'The question of family homeostasis', given as a lecture in 1954, marked his break with individual models of psychopathology. Soon afterwards he made contact with Gregory Bateson and in 1954 he joined Bateson and his colleagues Haley, Fry and Weakland in their work on the communicational nature of schizophrenia. As a psychoanalyst and psychiatrist, Jackson was able to provide the project team with direct access to schizophrenic patients and their families. The major paper which emanated from this group, 'Toward a theory of schizophrenia' (1956), introduced the concept of the *double bind* and laid the foundations for the development of the *systemic therapies*. Jackson's future work included investigations of psychosomatic disorders and their relationship to family pathology, further efforts to refine the concept of family *homeostasis* and efforts to classify different types of relationships, and in all these areas he was a vigorous writer. He died suddenly in 1968 at the age of 48.

Jamming
An intervention designed to reduce the information value of *communication* in situations of interpersonal conflict. The therapist may use this technique when one party is involved in accusing or checking up on the behaviour of another in such a way that the undesired behaviour is exacerbated rather than reduced. For example, an adult daughter may be instructed, in front of her mother, to give the

same report of her day's events to her mother, regardless of what she has actually been doing. Mother then realises that however hard she enquires, she cannot rely on the accuracy of the information she receives and so will stop eliciting it. She cannot demand that her daughter does otherwise than as the therapist instructs, since she is likely to have taken her daughter to the therapist for help in the first place. Mother thus changes her behaviour in relation to her daughter and thus changes the relationship between them. The purpose of this technique is to interrupt a destructive sequence of interaction and enable new interpersonal behaviours to develop.

A	B
Known to self and others	Unknown to self but known to others
C	D
Known to self but unknown to others	Unknown to self and unknown to others

FISCH, R. *et al.* (1982), *Tactics of Change: Doing Therapy Briefly* (Jossey-Bass, San Francisco).

Janet, Pierre (1859-1947)
Pierre Janet was born in Paris in 1859. He gained his Docteur des Lettres from the University of Paris in 1889 and his MD in 1893. Between 1890 and 1894 he worked in the psychological laboratories at the Salpetrière Hospital under Charcot where he studied hypnosis. In 1920 he moved to the Collège de France and began to develop a system of psychopathology and to relate ideas derived from both clinical and academic psychology to the study of hysteria. In 1907 he published *The Major Symptoms of Hysteria*. The development of his ideas regarding hysteria led him to conceive of the mind as divided into *conscious* and *unconscious* parts, the contents of the unconscious being converted into symbolic forms. Janet's ideas bore a close resemblance to Freud's and the two men engaged in controversy as to which could rightly claim to have originated some of the concepts. Amongst his major writings are *Principles of Psychotherapy* (1924) and *Psychological Healing* (1925).

Johari's window
A four-celled model of the personality, drawn in relation to the way it is affected by *feedback* and *self-disclosure*. Cell A, which is known both to self and to others, is the public area of the self; Cell B, which is unknown to self but known to others, is where self-awareness is lacking but motives, feelings and behaviour are obvious to others; Cell C, which is known to self but unknown to others, is the private or secret self; and Cell D, which is unknown to self and unknown to others is the *unconscious* self. Johari's window is used as a cognitive aid in some therapeutic groups to help the group member decrease the amount of material in Cell B through feedback from other group members and the therapist; and in Cell C through self-disclosure. Material in Cell D is either left untouched or is approached obliquely through related areas which begin to allow *repression* to lift. The name of the window is derived from its originators, Joe Luft and Harry Ingram.

LUFT, J. (1966), *Group Processes: An Introduction to Group Dynamics* (National Press, Palo Alto, Calif.).

Joining
Term used by Minuchin and other family therapists to describe techniques for developing a *therapeutic alliance*. Although the term is mainly used within the context of family therapy, the concept is equally relevant for the formation of a therapeutic alliance with individuals and groups. Joining techniques include support, use of self, *humour*, validation of individuals' concerns and points of view, *reflection* of what the family is describing and

offering to the therapist, *tracking*, *mimesis* and *maintenance*.

Difficulties in joining occur when therapist and family or client espouse very different value systems or ideologies; where the therapist can find few or no characteristics that attract him to the client or where the family or couple are so embattled that there seems to be no space left for the therapist to enter the arena. Although joining techniques are required most plentifully at the beginning, they go on being needed throughout the course of treatment. Minuchin and Fishman (1981) speak of joining as an 'operation which functions in counterpoint to every therapeutic intervention'. The movement towards the family made by the therapist in joining techniques is a strategy for encouraging the family's movement towards the therapist in accepting the restructuring interventions he will make later.

MINUCHIN, S. and FISHMAN, H. C. (1981), *Family Therapy Techniques* (Harvard University Press, Cambridge, Mass.).

See also *Accommodation*.

Joke
See *Humour, Parapraxis*.

Jones, Ernest Alfred (1879-1958)
Ernest Alfred Jones, a prominent leader in the psychoanalytic movement, was born at Garaton, Glamorganshire, Wales in 1879. He studied medicine at the University of London and gained his MD in 1903. In 1908 he met Freud and became a member of Freud's inner circle. He was recognised as the leader amongst English-speaking analysts and, through his writings and his presidency of the International Psychoanalytic Association between 1920 and 1924, he was accepted as a leading figure amongst analysts worldwide. In 1920 he founded the *International Journal of Psychoanalysis* and remained its editor until 1939. Having taken a leading role in introducing psychoanalysis to England, he recognised the importance of Melanie Klein's work and decided to invite her to come and work in London, which she did in 1926. He expended considerable effort in defending psychoanalysis from attack and in preventing the movement from breaking up when the new approaches to theory and practice began to develop. Nevertheless, he set an uncompromising standard and maintained that all psychotherapy that was not psychoanalysis is merely rapport therapy or suggestion. His writings were collected together in *Papers on Psychoanalysis* but his best-known work remains his three-volume biography of Freud, published between 1953 and 1957, which he dedicated to Anna Freud, 'true daughter of an immortal sire'.

Jung, Carl Gustav (1875-1961)
Originator of *analytical psychology*, Jung was one of the pioneering psychoanalysts and an early disciple of Freud. Born in Kessivil, Thurgau, to a Protestant pastor and his wife, Jung spent his early childhood near Basle. He studied medicine at the University of Basle but from his youth, his interests were very broad and he read widely, studying philosophy, language and theology. In 1900 he moved to Zurich where he worked with Bleuler. In 1903 he married Emma, who herself later contributed to the literature of analytical psychology, and they producd a son and four daughters. Jung undertook early experiments on *word association* and in 1907 he met Freud and became a member of the Vienna Psychoanalytic Circle, along with Adler, Abraham, Ferenczi and others. Freud and Jung engaged in a regular correspondence between 1906 and 1913 and in 1911 he became the first president of the International Psychoanalytic Society. Freud regarded him as the 'crown prince' of the movement and his heir apparent. By 1914, however, Jung's views had diverged so widely from those of Freud that he broke his association with him, to the considerable pain of both men. The recent publication (Jung 1983) of a series of lectures given by Jung to his student fraternity has stimulated discussion about neo-Freudian influences upon him. These lectures, written in 1895-6 when Jung was 20 or 21 years old and had never heard of

Freud, anticipate many of his more mature concerns. In recent years, in many centres, something of a rapprochement has occurred between the followers of Jung and Freud.

Like Adler, Jung introduced a new name for his own type of *psychoanalysis*. Much of Jung's prolific writings (published in English as the *Collected Works* in twenty volumes) are devoted to trying to understand the individual as a whole person, in his spiritual and collective aspects as well as in terms of his biological and individual needs. Jung travelled widely in later life, visiting Africa and studying primitive cultures. He spent most of his later life at Kusnacht and at Bollingen on Lake Zurich where he practised and wrote.

JUNG, C. G. (1983), 'Supplementary volume A', *Collected Works* (Routledge & Kegan Paul, London).

K

Kelly, George Alexander (1905-1967)
George Kelly, the founder of *personal construct theory*, was born near Perth, Kansas, in 1905, the only child of a Presbyterian minister and his wife. He studied physics and mathematics at Park College, Kansas, and later some economics and sociology before concentrating on psychology at the University of Iowa, where he gained his PhD in 1931. The same year he took up an appointment at Fort Hays State College in the relatively isolated area of Western Kansas, remaining there for twelve years. Here he came face to face with people who were struggling with the economic depression and for whom formal education was a waste of time and the prospect of a job or career was remote. He became involved in a helping capacity with those who were coping with severe economic deprivation and developed his psychological and psycho-therapeutic premises from his work with this population. He pursued an optimistic approach to the possibility of change,

encouraging his clients to adopt the position of a scientist, testing *hypotheses*, experimenting, and revising his or her findings in the light of that experience. Kelly's unorthodox approach brought him into opposition with the psychiatric establishment but despite this he developed his work in both clinics and schools in the area. Influenced originally by Freud, he later turned to the writings of Korybski, Moreno and others, which led him to develop what he described as 'a radical approach to psychotherapy'. His theory is set out in a two-volume work entitled *The Psychology of Personal Constructs* which finally brought him recognition as a major theorist.

See also *Fixed role therapy, Repertory grid*.

Kin network therapy
See *Network intervention*.

Kinesics
See *Non-verbal communication*.

Klein, Melanie (1882-1960)
Melanie Klein, the pioneer of several developments in *psychoanalysis*, was born in Budapest in 1882. She was the youngest child of a Viennese Jewish doctor and his wife and from an early age she had hoped to study medicine. However, she married when she was twenty-one and it was not until after her children were born that she became interested in psycho-analysis. She was analysed first by Ferenczi and later by Karl Abraham whose particular interest in the early stages of infantile develop-ment encouraged her to turn her attention to working with children. In 1921 she became a child therapist at the Berlin Psychoanalytic Institute and in the same year she published her first paper entitled 'The development of a child' (in *Contributions to Psychoanalysis*). In 1926 she came to London at the invitation of Ernest Jones and the rest of her life was spent in England, writing, practising and teaching. Although she was a devoted follower of Freud, she developed several concepts which were at variance with his theories. During the early 1940s the rift had become so great between

'Kleinians' and 'Classical Freudians' that the two groups formed as separate parts of the *British Psychoanalytical Society* and developed their own forms of training. Klein's followers are often known as the English school of psychoanalysis. Her major contributions to practice were in the field of child analysis, *child psychotherapy* and *play therapy*. Her main contributions to theory were the early origins of the *Oedipus complex* and the precursors of the *superego*; the nature of early ('psychotic') anxiety; the primitive *defence mechanisms*; and the concepts of the *depressive position* and the *paranoid-schizoid position*. Her main writings include *Contributions to Psychoanalysis* (1948), *New Directions in Psychoanalysis* (ed.) (1955), *The Psychoanalysis of Children* (1960), and *Our Adult World and Other Essays* (1963).

MELTZER, D. (1978), *The Kleinian Development* (Clunie Press, Strathtay, Perthshire).

Kleinian school (of psychoanalysis)

Term used to distinguish the work of Melanie *Klein* and her followers from the *British school* of *psychoanalysis*. Melanie Klein was invited to settle in London in 1926 by Ernest *Jones*. A specifically English trend was developing at that time encouraged by Jones and Edward *Glover*, to which Klein contributed increasingly radical developments.

Many of Klein's formulations challenge Freud's theory, although Segal is at pains to point out that they should be regarded as a development of Freud's later work rather than as opposing it. Klein's major contributions to psychoanalytic theory can be summarised as follows: the discovery of the *paranoid-schizoid* and the *depressive positions*; the understanding of the *Oedipus complex* and the *superego* as occurring in the early months of life rather than at three or four years; the understanding of the importance of *phantasy* and symbolisation in the formation of the *internal world*, and the delineation of *projective identification*. In addition to her theoretical formulations, Klein played a major part in pioneering the techniques of *child analysis* and it was out of her observations and work with very young

children that her theoretical developments originated. Amongst Klein's more controversial concepts is her literal use and application of the *death instinct*.

The Kleinian and *continental* schools, the latter led by Anna Freud, grew widely apart during the early 1940s, and during 1943-4 what came to be known as the Controversial Discussions took place. The Kleinian School's papers produced during these discussions were published under the title of *Developments in Psychoanalysis*. The discussions between the two groups did not bring an integration of views but rather a sharper polarisation. This ultimately led to changes in the structure of the British Psychoanalytical Society whereby both the followers of Klein and those of Anna Freud do some of their training separately and some of it together, alongside a third group of 'eclectic' analysts drawn from both groups and from other influences. Many would currently view the Kleinian school as the dominant influence in British psychoanalytic circles today.

MACKAY, N. (1981), 'Melanie Klein's metapsychology: phenomenological and mechanistic perspectives' (*Int. J. of Psychoan.*, vol. 62, pp. 187-9).
MELTZER, D. (1978), *The Kleinian Development* (Clunie Press, Strathtay, Perthshire).
MELTZER, D. (1981), 'The Kleinian expansion of Freud's metapsychology' (*Int. J. of Psychoan.*, vol. 62, pp. 177-85).
SEGAL, H. (1973), *Introduction to the Work of Melanie Klein* (Hogarth Press, London).
SEGAL, H. (1979), *Klein* (Collins, London).

Knowledge of results

A form of *feedback* provided during *training* or therapy which enables the trainee or patient to modify his behaviour as a result of being told about his progress. Knowledge of results may be provided concurrently, as the *task* is being performed; for example, the therapist's comments on a couple's efforts to discuss a contentious issue productively, or a supervisor's feedback to a trainee given during the course of an interview through the *bug in ear* device. Both examples also employ ideas from *shaping* and positive *reinforcement* techniques if they involved giving praise and encouragement alongside the feedback. Knowledge of results may also be terminal, that is provided *after* a task has been completed. The former is more useful when the learning task is conceived of as primarily technical, and the latter when more complex learning is involved. Delay in giving knowledge of results is disruptive to concurrent feedback but learning is relatively unaffected by delay when terminal feedback is given. Thus the concurrent feedback which may be given in training when a *one-way screen* or bug in ear is used, needs to be delivered promptly and focus specifically upon the *microskill* being used.

ANNETT, J. (1969), *Feedback and Human Behaviour* (Penguin, Harmondsworth).
HOLDING, D. H. (1965), *Principles of Training* (Pergamon, Oxford).

See also *Audio visual equipment.*

Kris, Ernst (1900-1957)
Kris, one of the chief exponents of *ego psychology*, was born in Vienna in 1900. He studied art history at the University of Vienna and received his PhD in 1922. During the 1930s he came to Britain and worked with the BBC during the Second World War, studying German radio propaganda. He left Britain and settled in the USA in 1944 and began to apply psychoanalytic concepts to the study of art. His psychoanalytic studies led him to extend Freud's concept of the *ego* and, along with other workers in the field, notably Anna Freud and Heinz Hartmann, he suggested that the ego possessed a range of autonomous functions such as cognition, perception and *reality testing* which were independent of the *id*. In 1952 he published his *Psychoanalytic Explorations in Art* where he introduced the concept of *regression* in the service of the ego and a variety of ideas which sought to understand the nature of creative work. In association with Hartmann and Lowenstein he published a series of papers on ego psychology and with Hartmann

and Anna Freud he founded the publication the *Psychoanalytic Study of the Child.*

L

Labelling
The process by which the individual names, categorises and interprets behaviour and *objects*. In this broad sense, labelling is a universal process by which a person makes sense of his world, through using language to interpret and 'hold' the meaning of experiences. The label acquires a *symbolism* by which the labeller can understand and relate to that which has been labelled.

The term is also used more narrowly to describe the process whereby a labeller confers a deviant status upon an individual, predisposed in some way to carry that status. The conferred label implies the acquisition of a role in relation *to* others and a set of responses and expectations *from* others, particularly from members of the labelled person's psychosocial system. The conferred status has to be accepted and the behaviour and expectations which accompany the role have to be learned. Subsequently the role and behaviours will be internalised unless interrupted and changed by formal or informal therapeutic intervention. The psychotherapeutic literature on labelling draws heavily upon the extensive researches undertaken by sociologists such as Goffman, Becker, Lemert, Scheff and others.

Labelling complicates *diagnosis* since if the process of labelling a person as mentally ill, sick, deviant, etc., is thus dependent upon an interaction between several variables, this complex of variables itself has to be considered in assessing or diagnosing psychological disturbance in the individual. Moreover the *type* of label conferred may depend as much on the perceptions and *stereotypes* of the labeller, the availability of treatment facilities and the professional interest of relevant therapists as on any objective assessment of the patient's *presenting problem* or *symptom*. A variety of studies have noted the wide variations in the incidence of schizophrenia, for example, even though there is little to suggest an intrinsic explanation in terms of patient population. The reason appears instead to lie in the therapists' variations in labelling habits. Moreover some problems or 'conditions' are culturally specific and will be labelled as sick, mad or bad in some contexts but not in others.

Labelling performs a function for the labelled person, who may derive *primary* or *secondary gains* from the label and from the new role which results, for the labeller, who may gain in status by comparison, and for the social group or society which contains them both. The social group may, for example, feel freed and 'unburdened' by the labelling of some of its members as sick or deviant, as for example in the *scapegoating* process. The relationship between labeller and labelled person is regulated and/or altered by the other party, each deriving his status and role from the other. Thus the therapist possesses his status and identity as a therapist, *because* the help seeker has been labelled as a patient; family members are able to become carers and protectors *because* the patient has accepted the *sick role*; or a marital partner can function well *because* a marital *fit* has been established by the acceptance of dependency by the other partner. Scheff (1966) has drawn attention to certain stages involved in the labelling process and to the *rituals* which accompany them.

Simply removing an individual's label may serve to change his behaviour or emotional experience in some instances. (See *Fixed role therapy*, *Reframing*.) Usually, however, new patterns of behaviour need to be learned and the new role and status in the community needs to be built up before the individual can relinquish his label. Moreover the attitudes and expectations of others such as family members may need to change and the burden of deviance, sickness or 'abnormality' shared out amongst the group.

Positive aspects of the labelling process have been noted by researchers into the *therapist variable* and into *social influence* within the psychotherapeutic process and they have

shown that therapists who acquire the label of expert do better with some patients. *Radical therapists* have been particularly fierce in their opposition to the effects of labelling and, as they would see it, the artificial acquisition of deviancy. A range of viewpoints on labelling and associated phenomena are discussed by Wing (1978).

BECKER, H. (1963), *Outsider: Studies in the Sociology of Deviance* (Free Press, New York).
GOFFMAN, E. (1963), *Stigma: Notes on the Management of Spoiled Identity* (Penguin, Harmondsworth).
HORWITZ, A. V. (1982), *The Social Control of Mental Illness* (Academic Press, New York).
LEMERT, E. (1967), *Human Deviance, Social Problems and Social Control* (Prentice-Hall, Englewood Cliffs, New Jersey).
MITCHELL, A. (1973), 'What's on your label?' (*Mind and Health Magazine*, pp. 32-5).
SCHEFF, R. (1966), *Being Mentally Ill* (Aldine Press, Chicago).
SZASZ, T. (1973), *Ideology and Insanity* (Calder & Boyars, London).
WING, J. K. (1978), *Reasoning About Madness* (Oxford University Press, Oxford).

See also *Attribution theory, Deviation amplification, Identified patient.*

Lacan, Jacques (1901-1981)
Jacques Lacan, a brilliant and unconventional leader of the *French school* of *psychoanalysis*, is intimately connected with the turbulent history of psychoanalysis in France during the twentieth century. He undertook his psychoanalytic training in Paris during the 1930s and was influenced by Hegel and by developments in literature and philosophy which were showing themselves in avant-garde circles in France during that period. He was an early supporter of the philosopher Martin Heidegger. Lacan's work is marked by, first, his claim to an extreme fidelity to Freud and by close exegesis of his writings, and second, by the idea of the *unconscious* being structured like a language and hence being susceptible to psycholinguistic tools for its analysis. In 1953, Lacan and others broke from the Psycho-

analytic Society of Paris and formed the French Society of Psychoanalysis and he made this the occasion for elaborating the main ideas behind his theories in his *Discour de Rome*. The Society of Psychoanalysis later sub-divided twice more, with Lacan on each occasion claiming to represent the true psychoanalytic orthodoxy even though his own developments in both theory and technique took him further and further away from most other schools of analysis. He became something of a cult figure in France, holding regular afternoon meetings in Paris, open to the general public. His major writings, which have recently been translated into English, include *Ecrits* (1966) and *The Four Fundamental Concepts of Psychoanalysis* (1978).

Lacuna
A gap experienced as a temporary lapse in memory, affect or action, or a more permanent missing aspect of the personality. For example, a delinquent may be described as having lacunae in his *superego* or a patient may complain of experiencing something 'missing' in his inner self, an experience which Balint describes as *basic fault*.

Laddering
A procedure devised by Hinkle (1965) for use in *personal construct therapy*. It enables the therapist to find out the position of any of the client's *constructs* within the *hierarchy* of his construct system. For each construct elicited, the client is asked to say by which *pole* he would prefer to be described. He is then asked the reason for his choice and this in turn generates a further (superordinate) construct. The construct 'ladder' can be developed in this way until the client's overarching construct is reached at the top of the pyramid. Hinkle showed that the more resistant to change a construct is, the more likely it is to be superordinate in the construct hierarchy.

HINKLE, D. N. (1965), 'The change of personal constructs from the viewpoint of a theory of implications' (unpublished thesis, quoted in Bannister, D. and Fransella, F., *Inquiring Man*, Penguin, Harmondsworth).

Laqueur, Peter (1909-1979)
Pioneer in *multiple family therapy*, Peter Laqueur was born in Königsberg, Germany, and grew up in different parts of Germany until his family moved to Holland when he was ten. He was one of five children and the son of a professor of endocrinology. He studied medicine at the University of Amsterdam, following his father into endocrinology. He married in 1937, moving to Argentina to work in 1939. During the Second World War he worked as a double agent for the Allies and after the war he emigrated to the United States. He settled in New York, taking a post at Mount Sinai Hospital. It was at this point that he became interested in psychiatry and he started by doing a residency at Creedmoor State Hospital, New York. He soon started seeing large groups of patients with their families together, gradually reducing the size of the group to ten families. In 1968, after moving to Vermont, he began to write about and video tape his work and to develop a regular format whereby three to five families were seen together in a group at any one time. Much of his time was spent in teaching and giving workshops. He did not produce any books but made a considerable number of contributions to journals and to collections of papers.

Large group
The large group can be defined as any group which is composed of more than twelve and usually more than about twenty members, who are linked together by shared beliefs, rituals, behaviours, norms and a common purpose. The individual's identity is strongly influenced by the social role he carries within the large group or groups to which he belongs. Following Le Bon's (1895) classic study of the psychology of crowds, Freud (1921) discussed two examples of the large group, the army and the Church. He viewed group psychology primarily in terms of the large group and as being concerned with the individual 'as a member of a race, of a nation, of a caste, of a profession, of an institution or as a component part of a crowd of people who have been

organised into a group at some particular time for some definite purpose'. The large group is however usually distinguished from communities and other large social structures by the fact that its members are able to meet face to face within a primary group structure.

The large group began to be studied as an entity in its own right in the 1940s. Two types were distinguished. First, the naturally formed large group such as a Church congregation, a social club, a football team, etc. Galanter (1981) points out that there are inherent therapeutic properties within the natural large group: 'there is an innate relationship within the individual between neurotic distress and alienation from a large group, on the one hand, and between psychological well-being and affiliation on the other.' Second, with the development of the *therapeutic community*, with its regular large group meetings, the artificially formed large group was viewed as a unit for psychotherapeutic and/or sociotherapeutic intervention. The growth in *self-help* groups such as Alcoholics Anonymous has also focused attention on the therapeutic potential of the artificially formed large group.

Two main views are taken regarding the aims and tasks of therapy in the large group: those of such as Edelson (1970) who describe the process as sociotherapy and believe that the group should focus on reality tasks and the actual interpersonal problems that exist between members; and those of such as Kreeger (1975) who describe the process as psychotherapy and who believe that psychoanalytic methods can be employed and *interpretations* of the *group process* can usefully be made. Kreeger (1975) identifies several typical aspects of large group process: the tendency of the large group to split into sub-groups; the abundance of psychotic mechanisms; the powerful forces that surface within the large group; and its capacity to become dependent upon its leader(s). De Mare (1975) draws clear distinctions between the small and the large therapeutic group. He suggests that the latter manifests more clearly the characteristic features of group dynamics, whilst in the small group there is often a tendency to revert to

intra-personal material and the analysis of individual members. He sees the besetting problem of the large group as 'mindlessness' or 'group think'.

The physical conditions for conducting large group psychotherapy usually include the provision of a double circle of seating, suitable for twenty to a hundred people. The group may be either open or closed and meets together regularly for one and a half to two hours with either a single leader or conductor, or a team. If a *team* of conductors is employed, its members need to meet together regularly after therapy sessions to share their impressions and insights, as in the case of any other model of *co-therapy*.

The large group stands midway between the individuals' experiences of small groups through the family group and other intimate networks and the social experiences of belonging to a nation, political party, religious organisation, school, factory, etc. Psychotherapy conducted in a large group setting is often combined with small group psychotherapy and/or individual treatment, though some (for example Kreeger 1975) would maintain that the individual can gain maximum benefit from large group psychotherapy alone. Its potential usefulness in relieving broader social, political and international tensions remains largely unexplored, although it has become a tool that has been effectively used in industry and business organisations. The large group and its interrelationship with a variety of small group situations is a primary focus for training and study in *T-group training* and *Tavistock group training*.

See also *Network intervention, System, Systems theory*.

DE MARE, P. (1972), 'Large group psychotherapy – a suggested technique' (*Group Analysis*, August).
DE MARE, P. (1975), 'The politics of large groups' (in Kreeger, L., *The Large Group: Dynamics and Therapy*, Constable, London).
EDELSON, M. (1970), *Sociotherapy and Psychotherapy* (University of Chicago Press, Chicago).

FREUD, S. (1921), 'Group psychology and the analysis of the ego' (*Standard Edition*, vol. 18, Hogarth Press, London).
GALANTER, M. (1981), 'Cohesiveness in the large group: a sociobiological perspective' (in Kellerman, H. (1981), *Group Cohesion*, Grune & Stratton, New York).
KREEGER, L. (ed.) (1975), *The Large Group: Dynamics and Therapy* (Constable, London).
LE BON, G. (1895), *The Crowd: A Study of the Popular Mind* (Hogarth Press, London, English translation 1920).
SPRINGMANN, R. (1970), 'A large group' (*Int. J. Group Psychotherapy*, vol. 20.

Latency

The period between infancy and adolescence. For Freud and his followers, this period, which lasts from the provisional resolution of the *Oedipus complex* at about the age of five or six to the onset of adolescence, is marked by the absence of any specific sexual development. Freud saw it as a period of waiting, during which memories and wishes remaining from the early infantile period are repressed. Psychoanalytic theorists who have focused less exclusively on sexual development, such as Erikson (1950), point out the important social and cognitive developments that are occurring for the child during this period. Not only is the child leaving the family group to embark on full-time schooling but he or she is having to learn to create and use his environment in a satisfying way and develop social skills by learning to interact with others in peer relationships. Erikson suggests that the stage is marked by satisfying industry and task identification which serve as an apprenticeship for the full creativity of adulthood. If this stage is not negotiated successfully, the child may experience a sense of inferiority and futility. Piaget's work on the development of cognition has underlined the important cognitive developments taking place during latency.

ERIKSON, E. H. (1950), *Childhood and Society* (Penguin, Harmondsworth).

See also *Stages of development*.

Latent content

The unconscious content and meaning of a *dream* which is expressed through the *manifest content* of stories and images. The latent content is revealed through decoding the symbols and analysing the elements of the dream in the context of the dreamer's past history and current experiences. The latent content thus revealed gives access to the patient's *unconscious* processes.

FREUD, S. (1900), 'The interpretation of dreams' (*Standard Edition*, vols 4 and 5, Hogarth Press, London).

Lateralisation

Specialisation of brain function in such a way that the left and right hemispheres are each responsible for different areas of activity. Sperry's (1968) split brain research and other neuro-physiological research into brain function has suggested important ways in which each hemisphere may be responsible for the performance of different psychic functions. Whereas the left side of the brain controls language, logical thought sequences and analytic and mathematical modes, the right side controls perceptual and construction tasks, creative and artistic expression, *non-verbal communication* and the synthesizing of fragmentary information into wholes.

Russell (1979) has shown how there is a remarkable consistency across cultures as to the way in which the two sets of functions are perceived. Because of the crossover connections of the nerve pathways, the left side of the brain controls the right side of the body and all right-sided activities and it is these 'left brain' activities which have traditionally been seen as superior, dominant and of much greater value than those controlled by the right brain and expressed on the left side. Even linguistically, we think of 'right' as associated with being correct, superior and good, whereas 'left' (following the Latin 'sinister') is thought of as inferior, clumsy and even evil. The left-handed (right brain) activities are also associated with femininity and as Capra (1982) points out, 'the deep-rooted preference

201

for the right side – that controlled by the left brain – in so many cultures makes one wonder whether it may not be related to the patriarchal value system' of Western society. Deikman (1971) suggests that the left and right hemispheres are characterised respectively by 'active doing', compared with 'receptive perceiving' and which Ornstein (1972), Capra (1982) and others suggest is demonstrated in the Western emphasis on science, technology and the exploitation of the world's resources, compared with Eastern acceptance and diffusion which tends towards the synthesis of opposites through *paradox*.

Stevens (1982) points out the parallels between these researches and Freud's distinction between the *primary process* of the *unconscious* (right brained and intuitive) and the *secondary process* of *conscious* functioning (left brained and rational). Rossi (1977) and Stevens (1982) discuss the way in which Jung's thinking foreshadowed much of this work and how his division of the *psychological functions* was essentially a division between left brain and right brain capacities. Stevens (1982) suggests that 'there is reason to suppose that the Jungian attitude and functional types may be subject to cerebral lateralization – the left hemisphere subserving the extroverted attitude and thinking function, the right contributing to the introverted attitude and intuitive and sensation functions, while the feeling function is mediated by both hemispheres acting in conjunction via the corpus callosum'. The linking by *communication* theorists of the *analogic* mode with right brain functioning and the *digital* mode with the left brain has opened the way to a fuller exploitation of the potential of *metaphor, paradox* and *parable* in the service of therapeutic change. *Strategic therapists* in particular have made use of the relatively unexplored potential of the right brain and by bypassing the logical, analytic scrutiny of the left side, by paradoxical techniques, have been able to devise ways of overcoming patient *resistance*.

CAPRA, F. (1982), *The Turning Point* (Wildwood House, London)

DEIKMAN, A. (1971), 'Biomodial consciousness' (*Archives of General Psychiatry*, vol. 125, pp. 481-9).

EDWARDS, B. (1982), *Drawing on the Right Side of the Brain* (Collins, London).

LURIA, A. R. (1973), *The Working Brain* (Basic Books, New York).

ORNSTEIN, R. E. (1972), *The Psychology of Consciousness* (W. H. Freeman, San Francisco).

ROSSI, E. (1977), 'The cerebral hemispheres in analytical psychology' (*J. of Analytical Psychology*, vol. 22, pp. 32-51).

RUSSELL, P. (1979), *The Brain Book* (Routledge & Kegan Paul, London).

SPERRY, R. W. (1968), 'Hemisphere disconnection and unity in conscious awareness' (*Am. Psychologist*, vol. 23, pp. 723-33).

STEVENS, A. (1982), *Archetype: A Natural History of the Self* (Routledge & Kegan Paul, London).

Leadership

Leadership in groups is of two kinds: formal, where the leader is appointed by the organisation, and informal or emergent, where the leader arises out of the group's interaction. The qualities, attributes and characteristics of leaders have been studied in order to try to isolate the critical variables of effective leadership. The topic is of great importance to psychotherapists acting as leaders in various types of group work and in group training, and also to those who act as consultants to *teams*, organisations and institutions in order to help them when they are experiencing problems of leadership. An early study of leadership undertaken by Lewin *et al.* (1939) examined three styles: authoritarian, democratic and laissez-faire. They found that the democratic leader was most effective in enabling the group to engage with its task and maintain its socio-emotional well being. Authoritarian leaders provoked more hostility, attention seeking and critical behaviour in the group, whilst democratic leaders evoked more co-operation, praise and constructive suggestions. More recent studies have suggested a number of factors which help a leader to assist the group in accomplishing both its task and main-tenance functions. Fiedler (1967) suggests that leaders who direct themselves to accom-plishing the group task require a high level of power and influence, whilst leaders who are more concerned with socio-emotional maintenance functions require only a moderate amount of influence. House (1971) has shown that structuring behaviour by the leader is most effective when the task is unclear, and maintaining, supportive behav-iour, when the task is unpleasant or boring. He also suggests that an effective leader needs to emphasise the relationship between group members' individual needs and the overall task of the group or organisation. Vroom and Yetton (1974) have shown that individual decisions made by the leader are more time-effective than group decisions, group members are more committed to decisions in which they have participated and the more complex the task, the more information and consultation is required to reach a satisfactory decision. Various studies have shown that a leader's influence is related to the quality and quantity of his interventions in a group, and Hollander (1978) suggests that his status is in-creased in proportion to his commitment and contribution to the group's values and goals.

FIEDLER, F. E. (1967), *A Theory of Leadership Effectiveness* (McGraw-Hill, New York).
HOLLANDER, E. P. (1978), *Leadership Dynamics: A Practical Guide to Effective Relationships* (Free Press, New York).
HOUSE, R. J. (1971), 'A path-goal theory of leader effectiveness' (*Administrative Science Quarterly*, vol. 16, pp. 321-38).
LEWIN, K. *et al.* (1939) 'Patterns of aggressive behavior in experimentally created social climates' (*J. of Soc. Psychology*, vol. 10, pp. 271-301).
RICE, A. K. (1965), *Learning for Leadership* (Tavistock, London).
VROOM, V. H. and YETTON, P. W. (1974), *Leadership and Decision-making* (Wiley, New York).

See also *Cohesion, Group dynamics, Group process*.

Leadership style
See *Leadership*.

Learned helplessness
See *Helplessness*.

Learning-based client-centred therapy
An integration between *behaviour therapy* and *client-centred therapy*. This was first attempted by Truax and Carkhuff (1967) in their seminal book on the practice and training of psycho-therapists. In this book they offer 'a tentative step toward a constructive encounter between the emerging behavior therapy and traditional conversation therapy'. Martin (1972) believes that a sufficiently complex learning view of emotional disorders is needed to provide a basis for explaining the efficacy of client-centred therapy. He further believes that an integration between the two models restrains the behaviour therapies from becoming mechanistic or oversimplistic. Naar (1970) discusses the peaceful co-existence of client-centred therapy and behaviour therapy but also points to some of the philosophical dilemmas inherent within this integration. For example, client-centred therapy presupposes that the client is capable of directing the course of therapy, whilst the behavioural therapies emphasise the importance of the therapist controlling and directing the therapeutic pro-cess. Naar approaches this dilemma by offer-ing the client a range of specific behavioural techniques for him to choose to work on with the therapist. The client will repeatedly attempt to approach the elements of his con-flict and in this sense has a self-actualising tendency, but the therapist is a necessary agent in the client's efforts to problem solve and thus become self-actualised.

The relationship which the therapist creates with the client and which Rogers believes to be efficacious because it provides the necessary and sufficient conditions for the client's capacities to develop is perceived instead as a *counter conditioning* agent whereby the client is enabled to cope with the anxiety of examining the elements of his conflict. The *process* by which the therapist is responsive to the client's initiative is the same in client-centred therapy but the *explanation* of what is happening differs and the extent to which the therapist offers the client behavioural tools for dealing with his conflicts is much greater. Proponents of this approach argue that both the client-centred therapist's *core conditions* and behavioural techniques are required in effective therapy.

MARTIN, D. G. (1972), *Learning Based Client Centred Therapy* (Brooks Cole, Calif.).
NAAR, R. (1970), 'Client centred and behavior therapies: their peaceful co-existence' (*J. of Abnormal Psychology*, vol. 7, pp. 155-60).
TRUAX, C. B. and CARKHUFF, R. R. (1967), *Toward Effective Counseling and Psychotherapy* (Aldine, Chicago).

Learning theory

A set of principles which seek to explain the way in which behaviour is modified in response to changes in the individual's environment. It is the theoretical framework which underpins *behaviour therapy* and *behaviour modification* and their derivatives, and it is therefore one of the major frameworks within the therapeutic field. All the later behavioural therapies are derived from the learning principles developed by Pavlov, Thorndike, Watson, Tolman, Hull, Skinner and Wolpe and their work contributed to the theory of *conditioning*, motivation and habit formation and paved the way for the use of these principles in therapy. Wolpe (1952) defines learning as follows: 'Learning may be said to have occurred if a response has been evoked in temporal contingency with a given sensory stimulus and it is subsequently found that the stimulus can evoke the response although it could not have done so before. If the stimulus could have evoked the response before but subsequently evokes it more strongly, then, too, learning may be said to have occurred.' Problems are learned and can therefore be unlearned: defective learning can be corrected and deficient learning can be supplemented.

Learning theory is operationalised in several different forms, the chief being *classical conditioning*, *operant conditioning* and *modelling*.

Each method relies on intervening in and manipulating the S-R model of the *behavioural sequence* in a different way. Learning theory's clearly articulated premises and scientific basis renders its methods particularly accessible to investigation and measurement and behaviour therapists have produced one of the largest bodies of research studies into the *process* and *outcome* of psychotherapy. Dollard and Miller (1950) set out to translate psychoanalytic concepts into learning theory terms and to form some bridges between the two conceptual frameworks.

DOLLARD, J. and MILLER, N. (1950), *Personality and Psychotherapy* (McGraw-Hill, New York).
EYSENCK, H. J. (1959), 'Learning theory and behaviour therapy' (*J. of Mental Science*, vol. 105, p. 61).
KANFER, F. H. and PHILLIPS, J. S. (1970), *Learning Foundations of Behavior Therapy* (Wiley, New York).
MOWRER, O. H. (1960), *Learning, Theory and Behavior* (Wiley, New York).
SKINNER, B. F. (1953), *Science and Human Behavior* (Macmillan, New York).
WOLPE, J. (1952), 'Experimental neurosis as learned behavior' (*Brit. J. of Psychology*, vol. 4, p. 243).

Left brain
See *Lateralisation*.

Lewin, Kurt (1890-1947)
Lewin was born in Prussia, the second of four children. He studied first at the University of Freiburg and then gained a PhD in psychology at the University of Berlin in 1914, studying under Carl Stumpt. Founder of field theory, Lewin was influenced in his early work by the school of *Gestalt psychology*. He emigrated to the United States in the early 1930s, teaching first at Cornell University and then in 1944 becoming director of the Research Centre for Group Dynamics, Massachusetts Institute of Technology. Here he continued work on his concepts of *field theory* and *group dynamics*, producing a huge amount of scientific work.

Much of it appeared in somewhat obscure journals and the impact of his work was further hindered by the fact that his writing was split almost evenly between English and German, making a complete overview of his work in either language difficult. Lewin had a considerable influence on the whole development of social psychology and on the development of *T-group training* and *encounter groups*. His ideas are most clearly stated in *A Dynamic Theory of Personality* (1935), *Principles of Topological Psychology* (1936) and *Contributions to Psychological Theory* (1938). He died at Newtonville, Massachusetts, in 1947.

Libido

The psychic energy, usually sexual in character, which drives the individual towards the gratification of desires and the achievement of life goals. In his early writings, Freud (1905) contrasts the sexual and the self-preservative instincts, using the term libido for the first. Later on, libido is used to describe both. In 1923, Freud suggested that the *ego* should be regarded as 'a great reservoir of libido from which libido is sent out *to* objects and which is always ready to absorb libido flowing back *from* objects'. The term is a hypothetical construct used to describe the energy of the *psyche*, existing in various forms and related to the *erogenous zones*.

FREUD, S. (1905), 'Three essays on sexuality' (*Standard Edition*, vol. 7, Hogarth Press, London).
FREUD, S. (1923), 'Two encyclopaedia articles' (*Standard Edition*, vol. 18, Hogarth Press, London).

See also *Cathexis, Drive, Life instinct, Metapsychology*.

Life instinct

A major category of instincts. It is sometimes referred to as Eros (Greek for love) and contrasted by Freud (1920) with the *death instinct* and including the sexual and self-preservative instincts. Originally, Freud had drawn a contrast between the sexual instincts (*libido*) and the self-preservative instincts, but latterly the contrast was drawn between life and death instincts. The purpose of the life instincts is to bring about greater unity and wholeness within the *psyche* in contrast to the fragmenting tendency of the death instinct.

FREUD, S. (1920), 'Beyond the pleasure principle' (*Standard Edition*, vol. 18, Hogarth Press, London).

Lifeline

An exercise for reviewing the significant events of an individual's past life. The lifeline can either be drawn freely across a large sheet of paper, indicating the troughs and peaks when life was perceived as going well or badly, or it can be encased in the form of a 'snake' or a river provided in printed form by the therapist. The client may record the dates and affects surrounding the event and several lines can be drawn, using different colours to depict different aspects of the person's life. This enables the therapist to gain an idea of the way in which these different aspects interweave. Lifelines can be used with individuals, families or groups.

See also *Diagrams, therapeutic use of.*

Lifespace

A term used by Lewin in field theory to describe the psychological space or psychosocial *context* in which the individual is embedded at any particular time. To understand the individual's behaviour, his position in the lifespace has to be ascertained. This includes his physical surroundings, his membership of a family and other social groupings, his physical, mental and emotional capabilities, the obstacles and opportunities that surround him and the goals which he is trying to achieve. His lifespace can be changed through learning and re-education. These occur either by the individual *moving* within his lifespace (out of some unpleasant group, into some new activity, etc.), i.e. leaving the field, or *changing his perception* of his goals or the means of achieving them.

Linear causality
See *Causality*.

Live supervision
The term is used in three different ways. (a) First, it describes a *co-therapy* relationship where one therapist is the supervisor and one is in training (Kempster and Sevitsky 1967). Both interact with the patient or family 'as if' they were a co-therapy team but the supervisor takes the lead and remains responsible for the treatment. (b) A method of supervision which enables concurrent *feedback* and *knowledge of results* to be given to the trainee from a supervisor or *team* who observe the interview from behind a *one-way screen*. The supervisor may use a bug in ear device or telephone (see *Audio visual equipment*) to instruct, affirm or redirect the trainee; or he may enter the therapy session and take over the therapeutic work for part of the session. A clear *hierarchy* is established, whereby the supervisor is in control of the therapist, who is in control of the family. This method of supervision is used primarily in *conjoint marital* and *family therapy* and is described by a variety of writers as cited below. Russell (1976) suggests that live supervision is too intrusive and distracting to the learning process to be effective, but most writers feel that its learning potential outweighs any disadvantages it may have. (c) Smith and Kingston (1980) and Kingston and Smith (1983) describe a particular form of live supervision without a one-way screen whereby the supervisor sits in the room with the trainee but outside the circle of interaction. He or she offers comments to the therapist on the content and process of the interview as it occurs, in exactly the same way as if a screen was in use. The major difference is that the patient or family hears exactly what the supervisor says. The supervisor, however, does not engage in any direct interaction with the family. Again, the advantages of concurrent feedback and knowledge of results are present and also the disadvantage of intrusion. Various kinds of live supervision used in family therapy are discussed in Whiffen and Byng-Hall (1982), including a particular type developed

by Pegg and Mannachio (1982) at the Centre for Therapeutic Communication, London, whereby supervisor, trainees, family and therapist all work in the same room together.

All these methods can be used as regular working arrangements between peers as well as training devices, and in this case the roles of 'supervised' and 'supervisor' will alternate from case to case. Finally, Constantine *et al.* (1984) draw attention to the *meta* process of live supervision of the supervision process and the advantages to be gained from developing a clear hierarchy of roles, functions and responsibilities in a highly complex learning/teaching format.

BIRCHLER, G. (1975), 'Live supervision and instant feedback in marriage and family therapy' (*J. of Marriage and Family Counseling*, vol. 1, pp. 331-42).

CONSTANTINE, J. A. *et al.* (1984), 'Live supervision-of-supervision in family therapy' (*J. of Marital and Family Therapy*, vol. 10, pp. 95-7).

GERSHENSON, J. and COHEN, M. (1978), 'Through the looking glass: experiences of two family therapy trainees with live supervision' (*Family Process*, vol. 17, pp. 225-30).

HARE-MUSTIN, R. (1976), 'Live supervision in psychotherapy' (*Voices*, vol. 17, pp. 21-4).

KEMPSTER, S. and SEVITSKY, E. (1967), 'Training family therapists through live supervision' (in Ackerman, N. W. *et al.* (ed.), *Expanding Theory and Practice in Family Therapy* Family Service Association of America, New York).

KINGSTON, P. and SMITH, D. (1983), 'Preparation for live consultation and live supervision when working without a one-way screen' (*J. of Family Therapy*, vol. 5, pp. 219-33).

MONTALVO, B. (1973), 'Aspects of live supervision' (*Family Process*, vol. 12, pp. 343-59).

PEGG, P. F. and MANNACHIO, A. J. (1982), 'In on the act' (in Whiffen, R. and Byng-Hall, J., see below).

RUSSELL, A. (1976), 'Contemporary concerns in family therapy' (*J. of Marriage and Family Counseling*, vol. 2, pp. 243-50).

SMITH, D. and KINGSTON, P. (1980), 'Live supervision without a one-way screen' (*J. of Family Therapy*, vol. 23, pp. 379-87).
WHIFFEN, R. and BYNG-HALL, J. (1982), *Family Therapy Supervision* (Academic Press, London).

Logical types
See *Theory of types.*

Logotherapy
Literal Greek 'logos', meaning 'word', 'meaning'. A method of psychotherapy introduced by Victor Frankl, based upon the premise that life is unconditionally meaningful and that the major task of psychotherapy is to help the patient to discover this meaning for his or her life. Logotherapy (or existential analysis, as Frankl originally called it) asserts the existence of three fundamental concepts: freedom of the will, the will to meaning, and the meaning of life. Although the individual's freedom of will is always circumscribed by circumstances and the physical and psychological conditions of his life, Frankl (1969) suggests, first, that he can, nevertheless, always be free 'to take a stand on whatever conditions might confront him'. Thus, Frankl counters the tendency towards *reductionism* and determinism that he sees in other systems of psychotherapy by the individual's potential for rising above even the most adverse conditions. Second, Frankl (1969) suggests that an individual's basic need and tendency is 'to find and fulfil meaning and purpose' and the discovery of meaning in itself produces a sense of fulfilment. Meaning is conceived of by Frankl as an objective phenomenon which the individual is required to find and to which he must respond. Third, the individual has to find his own *unique* meaning of life – the logotherapist cannot find it for him. The search involves facing the fact that whilst some circumstances can be changed, others cannot and finding and responding to the meaning of life will then require an acceptance of the suffering that may be involved.
Frankl (1967) stresses a holistic approach to the person as a physical-psychological-spiritual totality and he sees transcendence as the 'essence of existence'. To gain fulfilment the individual has to go beyond the search for *self-actualisation* and become other-directed. This may include seeing oneself as accountable for one's life before God or some other eternal perspective. Frankl uses the terms 'existential frustration' to describe the individual's sense of meaninglessness, and 'existential vacuum' to describe the sense of emptiness which results. He understands the current conditions of life in the Western world as making people particularly prone to the experience of an existential vacuum. Individuals can be helped to move out of this vacuum by finding meaning through love, work, suffering and death.
Frankl sees logotherapy as offering a kind of intervention which is mid-way between psychotherapy and spiritual counselling and as supplementing rather than supplanting either. Logotherapy examines the individual and his *symptoms* in terms of responsibility. It does not deal directly with the symptom but rather with the individual's attitude to it. Special techniques introduced by Frankl are the *paradoxical intention* and *dereflection.*

FRANKL, V. E. (1955), *The Doctor and the Soul: From Psychotherapy to Logotherapy* (Knopf, New York).
FRANKL, V. E. (1967), *Psychotherapy and Existentialism* (Simon & Schuster, New York).
FRANKL, V. E. (1969), *The Will to Meaning: Foundations and Applications of Logotherapy* (New American Library, New York).
FRANKL, V. E. (1978), *The Unheard Cry for Meaning* (Simon & Schuster, New York).

See also *Psychosynthesis, Teleology, Transpersonal psychotherapy.*

M

Maintenance
A *joining* technique described by Minuchin (1974) in relation to *family therapy* by which a

dysfunctional part of the structure of the family group is temporarily supported by the therapist. The therapist accommodates himself to the family both at the beginning of his contact with them, to build up a *therapeutic alliance*, and also at points during the therapy when the anxiety level of family members has risen. This may involve the therapist accepting the family's rule that one person speaks for everyone, or that a symbiotic relationship exists between mother and daughter, or that father's drinking habits are a non-negotiable subject, etc. The therapist adopts the strategy of maintaining, by his apparent acceptance or support, the dysfunctional set in order to gain the family's confidence and lower their *resistance* to change at a later point.

MINUCHIN, S. (1974), 'Structural family therapy' (in Caplan, G. (ed.), *Am. Handbook of Psychiatry*, vol. 3, Basic Books, New York).

See also *Accommodation*.

Malpractice

Improper or negligent treatment of a patient by the therapist. This may take an active form, for example, verbal or physical abuse, sexual or financial exploitation, or a passive form, for example, subjecting the patient to the therapist's inexperience or incompetence, or using inappropriate treatment interventions and thus increasing the risk of negative effects from the treatment.

See also *Deterioration, Outcome, Pathogenesis, Psychonoxious, Regulation*.

Mandala

A Sanskrit word meaning 'magic circle', a mandala is traditionally used as a symbol of unity and wholeness. Primarily, Jung (1951) regarded the appearance of mandala symbols in his patients' *dreams* and drawings as indicative of movement towards *individuation* when the Self is depicted as 'a composite whole in mandalas that are drawn spontaneously by our patients'. But he was also aware of the possible defensive usages to which mandalas may be put, binding together a personality which is in fact shattered. The mandala originates in

Hindu philosophy and is used in the East and West as a focus for *meditation*.

JUNG, C. G. (1951), 'Aion' (*Collected Works*, vol. 9, Routledge & Kegan Paul, London).

Manifest content

The dream images and descriptive narrative which forms that part of a *dream* which can be recalled on waking. The manifest content is alternatively viewed as either a way of disguising the *latent content* (Freud) or as a means of revealing it (Jung). According to Freud, it is produced by the *dream work*. There has been a tendency amongst some writers to dismiss the manifest content as of little value, but Freud (1940) in his later writings corrected this imbalance and stressed the way in which dreams can arise from the *ego* as well as the *id* and how the manifest content itself can be extremely expressive of the ego's conflict.

FREUD, S. (1900), 'The interpretation of dreams' (*Standard Edition*, vols 4 and 5, Hogarth Press, London).
FREUD, S. (1940), 'An outline of psychoanalysis' (*Standard Edition*, vol. 23, Hogarth Press, London).

Manipulation

The management of a person or situation with adroitness and skill, including the use of unethical means, if they appear necessary for achieving the desired ends. Within psychotherapy, the term is often used synonymously with *social influence*. But Johnson and Matross (1977) argue that the two should be distinguished. 'Manipulation is a certain type of influence . . . [it involves] influencing others in ways they do not fully understand and with consequences which are undesirable for them but highly desirable for oneself.' This distinction begs various questions. By this definition, are the covert, non-compliance-based techniques utilised in *strategic therapy* manipulative or not? The patient obviously 'does not fully understand them'; if he did they would probably lose their efficacy. Yet strategic therapists are no more likely to want to produce undesirable consequences for their patients than any other kind of therapist. On the other hand, all therapists may engage in more manipulation than they would care to admit to, under pressure to produce results. For example, in what is a notoriously difficult field to evaluate, the therapist may be prepared to manipulate the interaction between his interventions, the length of treatment and the timing of follow-up so as to maximise the positive showing of his work, or he may be unprepared to open his work to scrutiny by impartial observers, or he may engage in subterfuge regarding the patient's progress in order to prevent premature *termination* and his (the therapist's) consequent loss of self-esteem. Any or all of these procedures are manipulative although they may not cause any harm to be done to the patient. Manipulation normally involves the use of duplicity and violates the basic ethical principle of respect for persons by infringing their autonomy, even when the underlying purpose is the recipient's greater good.

JOHNSON, D. W. and MATROSS, R. (1977), 'Interpersonal influence in psychotherapy' (in Gurman, A. S. and Razin, A. M., *Effective Psychotherapy*, Pergamon, New York).
LINDLEY, R. (in press), 'Family therapy and respect for people' (in Watson, D. and Walrond-Skinner, S. (eds.) *Ethical Problems in Family Therapy*, Routledge & Kegan Paul, London).

See also *Ethics*.

Marathon group therapy
Falling under the general heading of the *human potential movement*, marathon group therapy is an intensive type of *encounter group* experience, introduced by Bach (1966), which takes place over an extended period of time, usually between twenty-four and forty hours. Bach makes use of *confrontation*, group pressure and *feedback* to help group members to relate to each other less manipulatively, more authentically and without relying on the normal social rules of interaction. Having experienced what Bach describes as authentic communication in the marathon group, participants are encouraged to use the same kind of

spontaneous 'levelling' in their significant relationships outside the group. Twelve to eighteen participants take part, usually with a *co-therapy* pair, and the proceedings may be video taped and played back to group members at a two-month follow-up session. The aim of a marathon group is to allow members to *encounter* each other more genuinely and to experiment with new ways of relating. Bindrim (1971) reports experiences of a nude marathon and concludes that this particular form of marathon enables participants to explore the differences between sensuality and sexuality and to enjoy sensual pleasure without that being confused with sexual involvement.

BACH, G. R. (1966), 'The marathon group: intensive practice of intimate interaction' (*Psychological Reports*, vol. 18, pp. 995-1002).
BACH, G. R. and GOLDBERG, H. (1974), *Creative Aggression* (Avon, New York).
BINDRIM, P. (1971), 'A report on a nude marathon' (in Siroka, R. *et al.*, *Sensitivity Training and Group Encounter*, Grosset & Dunlap, New York).
MINTZ, E. E. (1971), *Marathon Groups: Reality and Symbol* (Appleton-Century-Crofts, New York).

See also *Multiple impact therapy*.

Marital schism and skew
See *Schism, Skew*.

Marital therapy
See *Behavioural, Collaborative, Combined, Concurrent* and *Conjoint marital therapy, Multiple couples therapy*.

Masculine protest
Term introduced by Adler to describe the compensatory process by which women overcome their feelings of inferiority by striving to gain the power of men. Adler also used the term to describe a general striving for power in both men and women, but in his later writings it is reserved for the first usage. Adler viewed woman's feelings of inferiority as stemming from early socialisation and the limitations placed by society on her role, and not from an

innate biological inferiority. He recommended education of both sexes in equality and co-operative living.

See also *Individual psychology*.

Maslow, Abraham Harold (1908-1970)
Abraham Maslow was one of the most influential leaders of *humanistic psychology* as a *third force* within the psychotherapeutic field. He was born in New York in 1908, the eldest of seven children of Jewish parents. His childhood left him nervous and shy and it was not until his later years at school that he began to gain in confidence. He studied psychology at the University of Wisconsin and was exposed to the work of Ruth Benedict, Margaret Mead and Bronislaw Malinowski and the behaviourist John Watson. He studied under Harry Harlow and he also read Freud during this period. He received his PhD in 1934 and from 1937 to 1951 he taught at Brooklyn College, working mainly with underprivileged youth. He gained some training and experience as a therapist and spent time with leading therapists such as Alfred Adler, Karen Horney and Erich Fromm in New York. The Second World War had a profound effect on Maslow and in response to its horror and suffering he began to develop his own theory of human motivation, emphasising the normality of human growth and studying the *hierarchies* of human *needs* in terms of problem solving, perception and cognition. This led him to his major work on *self-actualisation, peak experiences* and the development of a humanistic approach to psychotherapy. In 1951 he took the chair of psychology at Brandeis University where he taught until just before he died. He took a major part in the founding of the Esalen Institute at Big Sur, California, the first centre for the *human potential movement*. Some of his most important books include *Motivation and Personality* (1954), *Toward a Psychology of Being* (1962) and *The Farther Reaches of Human Nature* (1971).

Maudsley Personality Inventory (MPI)
Developed by H. J. Eysenck, the MPI is one of the most frequently used research instruments into personality assessment in Britain. A forty-eight item self-rating questionnaire, it is designed to measure the two personality factors of neuroticism-normality and extraversion-introversion. It has large-scale supportive experimental and statistical studies and has been widely standardised.

See also *Personality tests, Psychological types*.

Mediation (divorce)
See *Conciliation*.

Medical model
An explanation of the aetiology, function and treatment of psychological disorders based on the view that they are physiological phenomena. Proponents of the medical model take the view that psychological problems are ultimately reducible to some form of disease which is either transmitted by heredity and/or is environmentally produced, and that they can be treated as a special case of illness. Mental 'illness' can therefore be classified into separate entities, each with an appropriate aetiology, treatment and prognosis, discernible through *history taking* and *diagnosis*. The help seeker is a patient and is expected to adopt the *sick role* with its rights and privileges, in exchange for being *labelled* as ill. The helper is medically trained or at least accountable to a medically trained person. The medical model remains the basic model for much psychotherapeutic practice but has come increasingly under attack from many different quarters. Szasz (1961) and other *radical therapists* have pointed to its controlling function over the 'ownership' of psychotherapy amongst professionals and its creation of dependency and stigmatisation for the help seeker. New insights from sociology, anthropology, psychology and *systems theory* have pointed to the multi-faceted nature of *causality* in psychological disorders. Moreover, the paucity of *outcome* results from medically based approaches, combined with some excellent results from people who have no training at all, have encouraged other professionals to lay

claim to their right to direct the course of psychotherapy, according to an array of different *models* and approaches. A wealth of research has shown that *empathy* and other *core conditions* are more validly linked with positive outcome than is medical training or a medical orientation to problem solving. The medical model is *reductionist* and incompatible with a holistic approach to psychological disorder. Torrey (1974) comments that 'the medical model is equivalent to the model of the sun revolving around the earth'. Pendleton (1983) offers an integration of physical, psychological and social components which provides an alternative orientation without abandoning some of the useful rigour of a medical approach. The appropriateness of the medical model for psychoanalysis has recently been discussed in the *Journal of the American Academy of Psychoanalysis* (vol. 10, 1982). Whilst Rogawiski (1982) concludes that it *is* still appropriate, others feel that its use will retard rather than advance psychoanalysis.

MACKLIN, R. (1973), 'The medical model in psychoanalysis and psychotherapy' (*Comprehensive Psychiatry*, vol. 14, pp. 49-69).

PENDLETON, D. A. *et al.* (1983), *The Consultation: An Approach to Learning and Teaching* (Oxford University Press, Oxford).

PILGRIM, D. (1983), 'Politics, psychology and psychiatry' (in *Psychology and Psychotherapy*, Routledge & Kegan Paul, London).

ROGAWISKI, A. S. (1982), 'Is the medical model appropriate for psychoanalysis?' (*J. of Am. Academy of Psychoan.*, vol. 10, pp. 113-22).

SSASZ, T. S. (1961), *The Myth of Mental Illness* (Dell Publishing, New York).

TAYLOR, F. K. (1976), 'The medical model of the disease concept' (*Brit. J. of Psychiatry*, vol. 128, pp. 588-94).

TORREY, E. F. (1974), *The Death of Psychiatry* (Chiltern, Radnor, Pa.).

Meditation

The induction of a self-conscious state of inner calm, produced within an altered state of consciousness. Deep meditation also brings about changes in the frequency and pattern of the brain waves with an increase in alpha and theta waves. There may be synchronisation of waves between the two hemispheres of the brain in some forms of meditation. Other physiological responses include a decreased respiratory rate and increased body warmth. Several different approaches have become popular in the West, including transcendental meditation (TM), Zen and Zazen meditation. Meditation is used as an adjunct to psychotherapy with a range of patient problems and as a means of self-training for the therapist. It has its roots in Eastern religions and philosophies, notably Buddhism and Zen. Its purpose as a method of psychotherapy or as an adjunct to other methods is to increase relaxation, help in the management of stress, develop self-esteem, increase concentration, develop awareness of present-centredness and increase *insight*. Meditation involves the patient in the paradoxical process of becoming sharply aware of his mental processes as they are occurring and then rising above them into a state of unawareness.

Meditation training takes place either individually or in a group. It may include some *relaxation training* and breathing exercises, or the use of a mantra and/or a *mandala*, but basically it consists in sitting quietly for a fixed period of time, usually with closed eyes, and emptying the mind of thoughts, phantasies, hopes and desires. The mantra and mandala work on the principle of the *reciprocal inhibition* of competing thoughts and anxious feelings. Research into the effectiveness of meditation is conflicting, but several reports (Shapiro 1980; Shapiro and Walsh 1980) have suggested its efficacy for a range of psychological disorders. Carrington and Ephron (1976) have pointed to its use as an adjunct to other forms of psychotherapy. Research provides a fairly consistent picture of the effectiveness of meditation in lowering the anxiety levels of patients so that highly charged emotional material can be brought to the surface. Carrington (1977) has shown how meditation can be used to help lift *repression*, and Rachman (1981) has described a method of clinical meditation that can aid the psychotherapist's own personal and professional growth and his ability to explore difficult clinical issues in his practice.

CARRINGTON, P. (1977), *Freedom in Meditation* (Anchor Press, New York).
CARRINGTON, P. and EPHRON, H. S. (1976), 'Meditation as an adjunct to psychotherapy' (in Arieti, S. and Chrzanowski, G. (eds), *The World Biennial of Psychotherapy and Psychiatry*, Wiley, New York).
CROOK, J. H. (1980), *The Evolution of Human Consciousness* (Oxford University Press, Oxford).
NARANJO, C. and ORNSTEIN, R. E. (1971), *On the Psychology of Meditation* (Viking Press, New York).
RACHMAN, A. W. (1981), 'Clinical meditation in groups' (*Psychotherapy: Theory, Research and Practice*, vol. 18, pp. 252-8).
SHAFII, M. (1973), 'Silence in the service of the ego: a psychoanalytic study of meditation' (*Int. J. of Psychoan.*, vol. 54, pp. 431-43).
SHAPIRO, D. (1980), *Meditation: Self-regulation Strategy and Altered States of Consciousness* (Aldine Press, New York).
SHAPIRO, D. and WALSH, R. (eds) (1980), *The Science of Meditation: Theory, Research and Practice* (Aldine Press, New York).
WALLACE, R. K. (1970), 'Physiological effects of transcendental meditation' (*Science*, vol. 167, pp. 1751-4).
WEST, M. (1979), 'Meditation' (*Brit. J. of Psychiatry*, vol. 135, pp. 457-67).

See also *Autogenic training, Existential psychotherapy, Self-help, Transpersonal psychotherapy*.

Mental apparatus

The three *agencies* of the *psyche* or the three levels of consciousness at which they operate. Although Freud used the expression as a *metaphor* or fiction, the models which he constructed were physical ones, based on the comparison with a mechanical apparatus. This has led to the same criticisms which have been levelled against other aspects of Freudian *metapsychology*. However, the model usefully describes the dynamic processes that operate within the psyche and the systemic relationship between them.

See also *Topographical model*.

Meta

Literally a Greek preposition meaning 'with', 'after' or 'about'. Used in English as a prefix, meaning a change of position or conditions, or belonging to a higher or second order kind. The prefix is used to express differences in the hierarchy of the therapeutic relationship (the therapist takes a meta position); differences in the kind of communication (metarule, *metacommunication*); differences in the level of theorising (metatheory, *metapsychology*); and differences within the *theory of types*.

See also *Communication, First order* and *Second order change*.

Metacommunication

A *communication* about a communication. A metacommunication is a comment both on the literal content of the message and on the relationship of the communicators and can be expressed either verbally or non-verbally or both at the same time. Metacommunication is more often, though not always, conveyed in the *analogic* rather than the *digital* mode. Satir (1967) contrasts the metacommunicative level with the detonative level which is the level of literal content and suggests that human beings 'cannot not metacommunicate'. Problems arise when there is a lack of congruency between the metacommunicative and detonative levels (for example, a mother telling her child she loves him but holding him stiffly and coldly), or when the metacommunication which is sent is misinterpreted by the receiver. Confusions and contradictions between the two levels may lead to a variety of impasses. These are comprehensively discussed by Watzlawick *et al.* (1968), Watzlawick *et al.* (1974) and Watzlawick (1978).

SATIR, V. (1967), *Conjoint Family Therapy* (Science and Behavior Books, Palo Alto, Calif.).
WATZLAWICK, P. *et al.* (1968), *Pragmatics of*

Human Communication (W. W. Norton, New York).
WATZLAWICK, P. *et al.* (1974), *Change: Principles of Problem Formation and Problem Resolution* (W. W. Norton, New York).
WATZLAWICK, P. (1978), *The Language of Change* (Basic Books, New York).

See also *Communication, Double bind.*

Metaphor
An indirect method of *communication* by which two discrete elements are juxtaposed, the comparison between the two serving to create new meaning. One of the two elements may be familiar and is used analogously to throw light upon the meaning of the second; or the new meaning is brought about by the interaction between two elements normally considered to be quite unconnected. Black (1962) describes metaphor as a 'distinctive mode of achieving *insight*'. In psychotherapy, such insight relates both to the therapist's need to decode and understand the patient's metaphors and his conscious use of metaphor to enable the patient to gain insight and/or to create change. Modern linguistic studies have shown how *all* language is a metaphorical expression of inner experience and external reality and a means of linking the two together. Therefore therapist and patient will always be engaged in a process of uncovering the meaning of each other's metaphors arising out of the normal requirements of using language.

Both metaphor and symbol involve comparison but the comparison functions differently in each. With symbolisation, the symbol *represents* something else; with a metaphor it is said to *be* something else. The therapist can choose to interpret the patient's metaphors or work within them. The decoding of the patient's metaphors, expressed in word or action, lies at the heart of psychoanalytic *interpretation*. For example, the therapist may interpret a woman's discussion of the chaotic state of her kitchen as a reference to her *ambivalence* about wanting to be a nurturing person. Working *within* the metaphor rather than interpreting it has been used in particular in *strategic therapy*. Cade (1982), for example, describes how a couple who were finding the open discussion of their sexual problems very difficult, shifted the conversation to the decoration of their house. The wife explained: 'I do the stripping, he gets on with the job, then I have to clear the mess up after him.' The therapist, by entering into a discussion of their house decorating conflict – a metaphor for the sexual problem – can lead them to begin to resolve their sexual difficulties without them being aware that this is what is being discussed. Milton Erikson (Erikson and Rossi 1979) suggests the importance of using metaphor with highly resistant patients. The metaphor is organically related to the subject that the patient is resisting and yet is apparently removed from it. Since it is difficult for the patient to resist a suggestion that he or she is not conscious of receiving, he is likely to accept it within the metaphor but apply it within the central issue which he would otherwise be unable to discuss. Minuchin (1974) and other *structural family therapists* make use of small activities, *tasks* and *homework assignments* as metaphors for problem solving within the area of dysfunctional realtionships. De Shazer (1980) also discusses the use of metaphorical tasks in *family therapy.*

ANDOLFI, M. *et al.* (1983), *Behind the Family Mask* (Brunner/Mazel, New York).
BLACK, M. (1962), *Models and Metaphors* (Cornell University Press, Ithaca, New York).
CADE, B. (1982), 'Some uses of metaphor' (*Australian J. of Family Therapy*, vol. 3, pp. 135-40).
DE SHAZER, S. (1980), 'Brief family therapy: a metaphorical task' (*J. of Marital and Family Therapy*, vol. 6, pp. 471-6).
ERIKSON, M. H. and ROSSI, E. L. (1979), *Hypnotherapy: An Explanatory Casebook* (Irvington Publishers, New York).
GORDON, D. (1978), *Therapeutic Metaphors* (Meta Publications, Calif.).
MINUCHIN, S. (1974), *Families and Family Therapy* (Tavistock, London).

See also *Analogic, Digital, Isomorphy, Model, Parable, Paradox, Psycholinguistics.*

Metapsychology

A theory of psychology and, more specifically, the more theoretical concepts of *psychoanalysis*. Freud (1917) introduced the term to describe his own contributions to psychology and he originally intended to publish a book entitled *Preliminaries to Metapsychology*. He suggested the use of the term to describe the theories which explain the clinical hypotheses and constructs of psychoanalysis. Used in this sense, the term metapsychology is equivalent to metatheory or *epistemology* but applied to the particular body of knowledge which psychoanalysis comprises. Freud also used the term to denote the theoretical structure of his theories as compared with the classical theories current in his own day. Elements of psychoanalytic theory that can particularly be described thus are Freud's three models of mental functioning, the *economic model*, the *topographical model* and the *structural model*; his developmental point of view; the theory of the *unconscious*; his notion of *life* and *death instincts* and of *libido*.

Metapsychology is currently under attack. Outside psychoanalysis, critics point out the unscientific nature of the metapsychological basis of psychoanalysis. The hypothetical, interpretative nature of the data, as Klein (1976) points out, makes it peculiarly difficult to develop a firm empirical base for testing the theories of psychoanalysis. Inside the psychoanalytic movement, several theorists have proposed the abolition or revision of metapsychology but argue for the retention of the clinical theory. They suggest that the two are separable, although it is doubtful whether Freud (1937) would have agreed. 'Without metapsychological speculation and theorising – I had almost said "fantasising" – we shall not get another step forward,' he wrote in 1937. Klein (1976), however, suggests that the two *are* separable and should be separated, whilst Gill (1976) and Pribram and Gill (1976) go further and suggest that the metapsychological basis of psychoanalysis is a positive handicap. Schafer (1976) suggests other difficulties: 'Freud, Hartmann and others deliberately used the

language of forces, energies, functions, structures, apparatus and principles to establish and develop psychoanalysis along the lines of a physicalistic psychobiology. It is inconsistent with this type of scientific language to speak of intentions, meanings, reasons or subjective experience', yet these are at the heart of psychoanalysis.

Several writers, however, have defended the metapsychology of psychoanalysis. Modell (1981) argues strongly for 'a modification but not the elimination of metapsychology' and Brenner (1980) points out that Freud's metapsychology performs the necessary function of any theoretical framework, supporting practical methods and distinguishing psychoanalysis from other theories of psychology that are oriented merely to the conscious.

Interestingly, Bettelheim (1983) has shown that the excessively mechanistic language, which is the focus of so many of these criticisms is the result of the particular translations into English from Freud's original German which Bettelheim claims is much more humanistic.

BETTELHEIM, B. (1983), *Freud and Man's Soul* (Constable, London).

BRENNER, C. (1980), 'Metapsychology and psychoanalytic theory' (*The Psychoanalytic Quarterly*, vol. 49, pp. 189-214).

FREUD, S. (1917), 'A metapsychological supplement to the theory of dreams', (*Standard Edition*, vol. 14, Hogarth Press, London).

FREUD, S. (1937), 'Analysis terminable and interminable' (*Standard Edition*, vol. 23, Hogarth Press, London).

GILL, M. (1976), 'Metapsychology is not psychology' (in Gill, M. and Holzman, P. (eds), *Psychology vs. Metapsychology*, Psychological Issues, Monograph 36, International Universities Press, New York).

KLEIN, G. (1976), *Psychoanalytic Theory* (International Universities Press, New York).

MODELL, A. (1981), 'Does metapsychology still exist?' (*Int. J. of Psychoan.*, vol. 62, pp. 391-401).

PRIBRAM, G. and GILL, M. (1976), *Freud's*

'Project' Reassessed (Basic Books, New York). SCHAFER, R. (1976), *A New Language for Psychoanalysis* (Yale University Press, Newhaven, Conn.).

Meyer, Adolf (1866-1950)

Adolf Meyer, a Swiss psychiatrist, was born near Zurich in 1866. He gained his MD from the University of Zurich in 1892 and then underwent further training in Germany, France and England. In 1894 he emigrated to the United States and took positions in various psychiatric hospitals and teaching institutions. From 1909 to 1942 he was professor of psychiatry and director of the Henry Phipps Psychiatric Clinic at Johns Hopkins University. It was here that he made major contributions both to psychiatric practice and to the training of psychiatrists in a holistic approach to psychological disorder. During his leadership, the Henry Phipps Clinic was the foremost psychiatric training centre in the English-speaking world. Meyer introduced a model of *psychobiology* which integrated the biological, psychological and sociological influences upon the patient as being causative in producing his *symptoms* and psychological disorder. He promoted the view that the patient's behaviour could only be understood if there was some effort to understand his personality structure in its context. His interest in preventative work was influential upon later developments in community mental health. In contrast to many psychiatrists of the period, Meyer adopted an optimistic approach to even the most grossly disturbed patients, and he encouraged the use of a range of occupational, recreational and after-care programmes, all novel approaches at that time.

Microskill

Interviewing skills used by therapists of all orientations and within all therapeutic modalities. These include the use of *direction, feedback, advice, questioning, reflection, clarification* and *attending*. Although the frequency and manner with which they are used depends on the method of psychotherapy and the *style* of the therapist, they are, in some measure, the generic interviewing skills of all psychotherapists. Ivey and Authier (1978) distinguish between *attending* skills (in which they include reflection, minimal encouraging responses, (*tracking*), support, paraphrasing, clarification and questioning) and *influencing* skills (in which they include the giving of directions, expressions of content (advice), expression of feeling (*self-disclosure*) and *interpretation*). Microskills can be distinguished from therapist qualities and therapist attitudes. They are the behavioural expression of the *core conditions* of therapy and the means by which techniques specific to different methods of intervention are operationalised.

IVEY, A. E. and AUTHIER, J. (1978), *Micro Counseling* (2nd edn, Charles C. Thomas, Springfield, Ill.).
IVEY, A. and GLUCKSTERN, N. (1974), *Basic Attending Skills: Leader and Participant Manuals* (North Amherst, Mass., Microtraining).
IVEY, A. and GLUCKSTERN, N. (1976), *Basic Influencing Skills: Leader and Participant Manuals* (North Amherst, Mass., Microtraining).
PATTERSON, C. H. (1974), *Relationship Counseling and Psychotherapy* (Harper & Row, New York).

See also *Interview*.

Milan school (of family therapy)

See *Strategic therapy*.

Milieu therapy

See *Social therapy*.

Mimesis

A *joining* technique described by Minuchin (1974) in relation to *family therapy* by which the family's style, affect, culture and mood are incorporated by the therapist into his own interactions with them. Mimesis is one way in which the therapist *accommodates* to the family as it reveals itself to him through the medium of *non-verbal* or *analogic communication*. The therapist engages spontaneously in a form of adaptation, by modulating his use of language, *humour*, posture, gesture and mood, to fit in with the family. This includes the building up of a differential relationship with different age groups and the appropriate use of language with children, babies, old people, etc. The process is equally relevant and necessary in work with individuals and groups.

MINUCHIN, S. (1974), 'Structural family therapy' (in Caplan, G. (ed.), *Am. Handbook of Psychiatry*, vol. 3, Basic Books, New York).

See also *Accommodation, Empathy, Maintenance, Tracking.*

Minimum sufficient network

A concept introduced by Skynner (1971) to indicate the importance of engaging in treatment a sufficiently autonomous psychological structure. The term is usually employed in relation to *systemic therapies* but Skynner originally applied it to work with individuals as well. He suggests that the 'network' of psychological functions needed for autonomous operation (i.e. *ego strength, superego* control and *id* mastery) must be sufficient to enable the patient to benefit from individual psychotherapy. In relation to *family therapy*, the term means that the operative family *system* must be engaged, although in accordance with the principle of parsimony it should include only the minimum number of individuals in the nuclear or extended family that are required to make therapeutic change possible.

SKYNNER, A. C. R. (1971), 'The minimum sufficient network' (*Social Work Today*, vol. 9, pp. 3-7).

See also *Absent member manoeuvre.*

Minnesota Multiphasic Personality Inventory (MMPI)

The MMPI is a self-rating questionnaire developed by two American clinicians, Hathaway and McKinley, a psychologist and a psychiatrist respectively. The subject is asked to respond 'true', 'false' or 'can't say' to a collection of 550 questions, such as: 'I believe I am being plotted against'; 'I wish I could be as happy as others seem to be'; 'I have very few quarrels with members of my family.' Scoring of the test is objective and the results yield scores on

ten scales: hypochondriasis, depression, hysteria, psychopathic deviate, masculinity-feminity, paranoia, psychosthenia, schizophrenia, hypomania and social introversion.

A group of control keys identifies or allows for unusual response styles: thus the K (lie) scale is based on the number of improbable responses to certain items and often picks up subjects who are faking their responses or whose answers are in other ways untrustworthy. Widely used in clinical research, there is no simple translation from test scales to descriptive information and the clinician has to rely on his clinical experience and knowledge of other response profiles.

HATHAWAY, S. R. and McKINLEY, J. C. (1943), *Manual For the Minnesota Multiphasic Personality Inventory* (Psychological Corporation, New York).

Mirror phase

See *French school of psychoanalysis.*

Mirror phenomena

A term used in *group psychotherapy* and *group analysis*. The group situation becomes a 'hall of mirrors' whereby the individual group member is confronted with various aspects of his social, psychological or body image. By scrutinising these reflections he can, according to Foulkes and Anthony (1957), 'discover his real identity and link it up with past identities'. In the infant's early development, mirror reactions help him to differentiate the self from the not-self, and this concept has been used particularly fruitfully by Lacan who describes a mirror phase of early psycho-social development. (See *French school of psychoanalysis.*) In group psychotherapy, the group member uses the reflections of the self he perceives in others to build up his personal and social identity, through *identification* with and *projection* on to other members of the group. Foulkes called mirror phenomena part of a set of group-specific factors.

FOULKES, S. H. and ANTHONY, E. J. (1957), *Group Psychotherapy* (Penguin, Harmondsworth).

See also *Condenser phenomena, Resonance, Chain phenomena.*

Mirror-image disagreement
Term used by Stanton and Schwartz (1964) to describe the tendency towards polarisation that occurs in triads. When two individuals are in conflict over a third, the opposing views are retained at an amplified level regardless of whether one of the pair changes his position. When one changes his position the other does so that the third party remains caught between the conflicting dyad. It thus has the effect of a *homeostatic* mechanism. Although the process was noted by Stanton and Schwartz in the context of organisations, it has relevance for work with other groups and families and was adopted by researchers into pathological triads.

STANTON, A. and SCHWARTZ, M. (1964), *The Mental Hospital* (Basic Books, New York).

See also *Communication, Detouring, Identified patient, Scapegoat, Triangle, Triangulation.*

Mitwelt
Literal German meaning 'with the world'. The term is used in *existential* approaches to psychotherapy to describe the individual's network of relationships in which inter-personal encounters are experienced between the self and others. Binswanger uses the term, along with *Eigenwelt* and *Umwelt* to describe the three modes or world regions of *Dasein*.

Modality
Type of therapeutic intervention classified according to its *unit of treatment*. Hence, *group psychotherapy*, individual psychotherapy, *family therapy, marital therapy* and *network intervention* are all treatment modalities. The term can be distinguished from the terms approach (e.g. psychoanalytic, behavioural, humanistic, etc.); method (e.g. *client-centred, group analytic, Gestalt*); technique (e.g. *prescription, modelling, interpretation*, etc.); and *microskill (e.g. clarification, confrontation, questioning*, etc.), although in practice these terms are often used inter-changeably. The unit of analysis increases in generality from a modality at the top, through an approach, method, technique and micro-skill. Thus techniques are built up from microskills, methods from techniques, approaches from methods and modalities from approaches.

Model (for psychotherapy)
An analogue or pattern on which to base the practice of a type of psychotherapy. The term is often used synonymously with theory in psychotherapy, although strictly speaking a model is an explanatory representation of a theory rather than the theory itself. Two types of models are commonly used in psycho-therapy. First, the paradigmatic, used as a basic *metaphor* for a whole theoretical approach. Traditionally the *medical model* has claimed a large following but this has come under increasing attack, despite the almost inevitable retention of such 'medically' oriented terms as therapy, treatment, diag-nosis, patient and therapist. A major alternative is the educational model which proposes that psychological problems are created by maladaptive or deficient learning. Some forms of *behaviour therapy, cognitive therapy* and the *problem solving interventions* make use of this model as well as *parenting skills training, social skills training*, various *group therapies* and *learning-based client-centred therapy*. Other models found to be appropriate by different practitioners are the growth model, which stresses *self-actualisation* and expanded awareness as overall goals (*human-istic psychology, existential psychotherapy, psycho-synthesis*); the morality model in which the help seeker is expected to take responsibility for his or her behaviour and its consequences (*Morita therapy, Nakian therapy, integrity groups*) and the systems/environmental model whereby the individual's problem is viewed as a function of a problem community or *system* and he or she either needs rescuing from it or the system itself needs to change (*systemic therapies, radical therapy, feminist therapy*). The adoption of a particular model by the psychotherapist is probably highly dependent upon his person-ality and his own training resources.

217

The second type of model used is that which highlights features of a psychological process in the individual or group by analogy to some physical entity. Used in this way, the term is more or less equivalent to that of metaphor. Examples are the central heating system and many other engineering models used to illustrate the systemic properties of families or groups; and the hydraulic model which lies at the heart of Freudian theory.

BLACK, M. (1962), *Models and Metaphors* (Cornell University Press, New York).

COLLINS, L. (ed.) (1975), *The Use of Models in the Social Sciences* (Westview, Boulder, Colorado).

SIEGLER, M. and OSMOND, M. (1974), *Models of Madness, Models of Medicine* (Macmillan, New York).

Modelling

A term used to describe the principle underlying a variety of vicarious learning procedures such as imitation, observational learning, mirroring, *mimesis* and *identification*. The relation between these concepts is viewed differently by different theorists but Bandura (1969) suggests that essentially the same learning process is involved in all of them. According to Bandura (1969) modelling involves the acquisition of new modes of behaviour and the modification of existing behaviour patterns through the observation of other people's behaviour and its consequences for them. The information that observers gain from models is converted to covert perceptual-cognitive images and covert mediating rehearsal responses that can later be used as symbolic clues for new overt behaviour. By observing a model engaged in a fear of activity, the patient experiences the vicarious *extinction* of his fears and learns new *coping behaviour*. Differences in the characteristics of the patient and the model do not seem to affect the modelling process although similarity in degree of fearfulness, for example, is useful.

Modelling involves a complex set of procedures including extinction, *coping skills interventions* and positive *reinforcement*. Bandura

suggests that when attempting to extinguish fears, it is helpful to use a graduated *hierarchy*, so that the model begins with the least feared activity. Meichebaum (1971) suggests that coping models are more effective than mastery models in reducing fear and others suggest that guided participation alongside the modelling is helpful in increasing the effectiveness of the modelling procedure. Etringer *et al.* (1982) compared the effects of modelling with an equally credible *placebo* and found that modelling was clearly superior.

BANDURA, A. (1969), *Principles of Behavior Modification* (Holt, Rinehart & Winston, San Francisco).

ETRINGER, B. D. *et al.* (1982), 'Behavioural, affective and cognitive effects of participant modelling and an equally credible placebo' (*Behavior Therapy*, vol. 13, pp. 476-85).

MEICHEBAUM, D. (1971), 'Examination of model characteristics in reducing avoidance behavior' (*J. of Personality and Social Psychology*, vol. 17, pp. 298-307).

See also *Behavioural rehearsal*, *Systematic desensitisation*.

Modes of assimilation

Term used by Fromm (1947) to describe five basic character orientations. These are: receptive – the belief that happiness and the source of good exists outside the self and the individual can only passively please others and conform; exploitative – good things exist outside the self and they therefore must be taken from others by force and manipulation; hoarding – good things are in short supply and they must therefore be held on to; marketing – everything is a commodity and the individual is a salesman of his qualites and a buyer of the affections and contributions of others; productive – the individual relates to the world productively and generatively through the participation of his intelligence, emotion and sensory responses with others, with himself and with the environment. The goal of life and the task of therapy is to develop the productive orientation and the full realisation of the individual's potential.

FROMM, E. (1947), *Man for Himself* (Fawcett, New York).

See also *Interpersonal school (of psychoanalysis), Modes of relatedness.*

Modes of relatedness

Term used by Fromm (1964) to describe three characteristic ways of relating to the world. These are: necrophilous – the concentration on death, the past, the destruction of life and an admiration of tradition and law and order; biophilous – the love of life and the experience of the basic polarity in life as being between male and female, instead of between those with the power to kill and those without; incestuous fixation – dependence on others to provide security, protection and admiration, leading to a desire to regress to the womb or cling to one all-providing relationship. Only the biophilic mode allows the individual to engage in loving, mature relationships through which he or she can engage productively with others without losing the separateness and integrity of the self.

FROMM, E. (1964), *The Heart of Man* (Harper & Row, New York).

See also *Interpersonal school (of psychoanalysis), Modes of assimilation, Pseudotherapeutic.*

Moreno, Jacob Levi (1889-1974)

Moreno was born in Bucharest in 1889. Five years later his family moved to Vienna and in 1910 he began his studies in philosophy at the University of Vienna. He went on to study medicine, receiving his MD in 1917. His interests were very wide and included theology, literature and poetry. While in Vienna, he published a literary magazine called *Daimon* and wrote books on philosophy and poetry including *The Words of the Father* which considers man's relationship to God. In 1925 he moved to the USA and began his prodigious contributions to *group psychotherapy, psychodrama*, sociometry and the *encounter group* movement. In 1932, he coined the term group psychotherapy and his influence was powerful in its early develop-

ment. His original interest in dramatic re-enactments of problem situations had been awakened while at the university of Vienna and during the period 1914-1921 his informal encounters playing with children in the city parks led him to see the potential of psychodrama. In 1936, he founded the Moreno Sanitorium for the practice and teaching of psychodrama, and in 1942 he established institutes in New York City and at Beacon, New York, for the training of group therapists and psychodrama practitioners. In 1937 he founded the journal *Sociometry* and ten years later he began to publish *Sociatry* which together eventually became the present journal entitled *Group Psychotherapy, Psychodrama and Sociometry*. After his marriage to Zerka Toeman in 1949, they travelled together widely, giving lectures and demonstrations and leading workshops. Moreno was a prolific writer, his best-known works being his three-volume treatise on psychodrama. In psychodrama, perhaps his most important field of study, he succeeded in integrating a therapeutic approach which combines attention to the patient's body, mind and spirit and enables the cognitive, affective and behavioural aspects of the personality to be developed.

Morita therapy

A method of therapy developed by Shoma Morita, a Japanese psychiatrist, during the early years of the twentieth century. It combines elements of Western and Eastern approaches to the treatment of psychological disorders. Although its main influence remains within Japan, it has, since the 1960s, attracted some attention in the United States (Reynolds 1976). The method focuses attention on the patient's abilities and the opportunities that exist for him *now* to live a fulfilling life, regardless of his *symptoms*. The Morita therapist ignores symptoms and concentrates, via a systematic four-phase programme, on helping the patient to live his life productively, whether or not his symptoms remain. The classic form of this programme is as follows. Phase one consists of a four- to seven-day period of absolute bed rest, complete isolation and almost total sensory deprivation, and patient leaving his bed only to eat and to visit the toilet. No activities or amusement of any kind are permitted. This enables the patient to experience an awareness of self and his needs and motivates him to receive help. In phase two, the patient leaves his bed for daily therapy, group meetings and sessions with an individual therapist. He is encouraged to define his life goals and the means by which these may be achieved. Bathing and some light work are allowed. Phase three allows vigorous manual work and increased interaction with staff members, and phase four involves intensive therapy sessions, group interaction and re-involvement with the community.

The format has been considerably modified for use in the United States and is done on an out-patient basis. A daily diary-keeping task is usually imposed, to provide material for the therapy sessions and to enable the therapist to focus the client on acceptance of his feelings and symptoms as they are and yet acting productively and responsibly regardless of these difficulties. Morita therapists are directive in their approach and repeatedly refocus the client on living actively in the present. Some behavioural techniques such as positive *reinforcement* are commonly used and the de-emphasis on *symptoms* and pathology may act as an *extinction* procedure. Morita therapy involves a commonsense approach to character training, summarised by Reynolds (1981) as the recognition of purpose, the acceptance of feelings and the control of behaviour. Its emphasis on adjustment rather than change might be criticised by some schools of therapy.

HARPER, R. A. (1975), *The New Psychotherapies* (Prentice-Hall, Englewood Cliffs, New Jersey).
O'HARA, K. and REYNOLDS, D. K. (1968), 'Changing methods in Morita psychotherapy' (*Int. J. of Soc. Psychiatry*, vol. 14, pp. 305-10).
REYNOLDS, D. K. (1976), *Morita Psychotherapy* (University of California Press, Berkeley).

REYNOLDS, D. K. (1981), 'Morita psychotherapy' (in Corsini, R. J. (ed.), *Handbook of Innovative Psychotherapies*, Wiley, New York).

See also *Character training approaches.*

Morphogenesis

Term introduced by Maruyama (1968) to describe the way in which a living *system* possesses the capacity for change and development. The process is brought about by *positive feedback* which leads to deviation amplification and is comparable to the term *schismogenesis* used by Bateson. It is used in contrast to *morphostasis* and *homeostasis*. In relation to families, Wertheim (1973) describes a form that she calls induced morphogenesis, a term which indicates the extent to which a family is likely to respond to the interventions of a therapist. Morphogenesis, as Speer (1970) points out, is the essential adaptive growth-promoting property of a natural system which accounts for its ability to meet developmental *crises* and create new forms.

MARUYAMA, M. (1968), 'The second cybernetics: deviation-amplifying mutual causal processes' (in Buckley, W. (ed.), *Modern Systems Research for the Behavioral Scientist*, Aldine, Chicago).
SPEER, D. C. (1970), 'Family systems: morphostasis and morphogenesis or "Is homeostasis enough?"' (*Family Process*, vol. 9, pp. 259-78).
WERTHEIM, E. (1973), 'Family unit therapy and the science and typology of family systems' (*Family Process*, vol. 12, pp. 361-76).

Morphostasis

Term introduced by Maruyama (1968) to describe the way in which a living *system* maintains its internal constancy and stability. The term is used as a contrast to *morphogenesis* and is equivalent to *homeostasis*. As Speer (1970) points out, however, the juxtaposition of the two terms morphostasis and morphogenesis emphasises their essential interconnectedness and this helps avoid the error of emphasising one at the expense of the other. In particular it avoids the error of suggesting that one or the other tendency is undesirable. Wertheim (1973) distinguishes between consensual morphostasis and forced morphostasis. Consensual morphostasis refers to the genuine stability of the family system, consensually validated by its members, whilst forced morphostasis refers to a condition of apparent stability brought about by a power imbalance between members. The former allows morphogenic processes to take place whilst the latter does not.

MARUYAMA, M. (1968), 'The second cybernetics: deviation-amplifying mutual causal processes' (in Buckley, W. (ed.), *Modern Systems Research for the Behavioral Scientist*, Aldine, Chicago).
SPEER, D. C. (1970), 'Family systems: morphostasis and morphogenesis or "Is homeostasis enough?" ' (*Family Process*, vol. 9, pp. 259-78).
WERTHEIM, E. (1973), 'Family unit therapy and the science and typology of family systems' (*Family Process*, vol. 12, pp. 361-76).

Mourning

The period of time which follows a bereavement and which allows the expression of *grief* through a variety of culturally defined, ritual acts. Averill (1975) distinguishes grief and mourning, viewing grief reactions as involving physiological and psychological processes, whilst mourning has its basis in the customs and mores of the culture. Grief and mourning may or may not occur simultaneously, but most clinical writers feel that a period of ritualised mourning helps prevent a pathological grief reaction. Rosenblatt *et al.* (1976) studied the mourning behaviours and customs of seventy-eight cultures and concluded that people in all societies experience the death of a close significant other as a loss and, typically, mourn for that loss. A variety of death ceremonies occur during the mourning period, according to the cultural mores of the bereaved. These often involve a final ceremony which indicates the end of the mourning period, the breaking of ties and the transition to a new life without the deceased. They found that the mourning of spouses for each other is the loss which is most frequently ritualised in most societies. Women are usually allowed or expected to express their grief through mourning more than men. Mourning rituals are frequently linked with religious observance and practice and Gorer (1965) concludes that the decline in formal religious belief, especially in Western societies, has removed some of the guidelines for the practice of mourning. Liebermann (1978) has described the way in which a procedure called 'forced' mourning can be used to enable an individual to complete the grief process satisfactorily. Paul and Grosser (1965) and Liebermann (1978) describe two similar techniques which they describe as operational mourning and forced mourning respectively, whereby a patient or family group is helped to convert a morbid or arrested grief reaction into a normal process of mourning.

AVERILL, J. R. (1975), 'Grief: its nature and significance' (in Carr, A. C. *et al.* (eds), *Grief: Selected Readings*, Health Sciences Publishing, New York).
GORER, G. (1965), *Death, Grief and Mourning in Contemporary Britain* (Cresset, London).
LIEBERMANN, S. (1978), 'Nineteen cases of morbid grief' (*Brit. J. of Psychiatry*, vol. 132, pp. 159-73).
PAUL, N. and GROSSER, G. (1965), 'Operational mourning and its role in conjoint family therapy' (*Community Mental Health Journal*, vol. 1, p. 339).
ROSENBLATT, P., WALSH, R. and JACKSON, D. (1976), *Grief and Mourning in Cultural Perspective* (HRAF Press, New Haven, Conn.).

Multi-modal therapy

An approach to psychotherapy developed by Lazarus (1973, 1976, 1981) which focuses on seven interacting aspects of treatment: behaviour, affect, sensation, imagery, cognition, interpersonal relationships and drugs (a term which Lazarus uses to cover a range of biological factors and treatments). These seven form the acronym Basic Id which is used as a shorthand name for multi-modal treatment. Lazarus emphasises the need for a technical eclecticism in order to focus on the physical, cognitive and affective aspects of the personality. Only by so doing will durable change be brought about. The method is theoretically based on an educative model and social *learning theory* forms the major theoretical influence. Lazarus also makes use of a *systemic* understanding of the ways in which the seven modalities interact, so that interventions made in one area will have consequences for the others. Lazarus divides the therapeutic task into four parts: systematic assessment of the client's specific problems under the seven headings; the development of a treatment plan, organised in relation to each of the Basic Id categories; the implementation of the treatment plan using a range of techniques. These include, where appropriate, a combination of behavioural techniques, *relaxation training, meditation, assertiveness training, cognitive restructuring approaches, family* and *marital therapy, imagery* techniques, *bibliotherapy* and a variety of *homework assignments* and '*in vivo*' exercises. The fourth stage is called refinement, whereby successful techniques are further developed and unsuccessful ones abandoned. Multi-modal therapy has much in common with behavioural and cognitive therapies but, because of its technical eclecticism, it has links with many others too. It provides a rich resource of organised therapeutic possibilities for a range of client problems.

LAZARUS, A. A. (1973), 'Multi-modal behavior therapy: treating the "basic id" ' (*J. of Nervous and Mental Disease*, vol. 156, pp. 404-11).

LAZARUS, A. A. (1976), *Multi-Modal Behavior Therapy* (Springer, New York).

LAZARUS, A. (1981), *The Practice of Multi-Modal Therapy* (McGraw-Hill, New York).

See also *Eclectic psychotherapy, Rational emotive therapy*.

Multiple appeal

A term introduced by Hartmann (1951) to describe the multi-faceted effect of a psycho-analytic *interpretation*, whereby it impinges on several levels of the psychic system simultaneously.

HARTMANN, H. (1951), 'Technical implications of ego psychology' (in *Essays on Ego Psychology*, International Universities Press, New York).

Multiple couples therapy

The treatment of a group of married couples simultaneously. The approach combines the techniques of *conjoint marital therapy* with those of *group psychotherapy*. Groups are comprised usually of three or four couples and a therapist or *co-therapy* pair. Therapists vary as to their criteria for selecting couples for a group. Some prefer to choose couples of a similar stage in their family life cycle, others advocate a heterogeneous group. Other selection criteria are sometimes used, such as similarity between *presenting problem*. Assessment sessions may be organised, during which the therapist meets the couple together and each partner separately, prior to their joining the group. Framo (1981) includes sessions with each couple's family of origin at some stage in the treatment.

Rules regarding confidentiality, extraneous meetings between participants, absences, etc., are agreed, and the length, duration and venue for sessions are established during the early stage of treatment. There are two formats which can be used for running the group: the time can be allocated equally between the four couples, or members can participate freely throughout the session as in any other group work setting. Alternatively, a mixture of the two formats may be employed during the course of the group's life. Powerful therapeutic aspects of multiple couples therapy are its help in normalising experiences felt by a couple to be abnormal and guilt-provoking, its ability to increase *empathy* and enable couples to see their partner in a different light, and its effect in broadening attitudes and improving problem solving skills through *modelling* and *feedback* from group members.

ALGER, I. (1976), 'Multiple couple therapy'

(in Guerin, P., *Family Therapy: Theory and Practice*, Guilford Press, New York).

FRAMO, J. (1973), 'Marriage therapy in a couples group' (in Bloch, D. (ed.), *Techniques of Family Psychotherapy*, Grune & Stratton, New York).

FRAMO, J. (1981), 'Marital therapy with sessions with family of origin' (in Gurman, A. S. and Kniskern, D. P., *Handbook of Family Therapy*, Brunner/Mazel, New York).

LOW, P. and LOW, M. (1975), 'Treatment of married couples in a group run by a husband and wife' (*Int. J. of Group Psychotherapy*, vol. 25, pp. 54-66).

Multiple family therapy

The treatment of a group of families simultaneously. Two therapists separately pioneered this approach. Lacquer (1976) developed this work out of a desire to maximise the benefits of *conjoint family therapy*, whilst Bowen's (1976) work grew out of his particular approach of *transgenerational family therapy*. Like *multiple couples therapy*, it combines elements of conjoint and *stranger group* work. There are several differences between Bowen and Lacquer's approach to multiple family therapy. Bowen feels that three to four families is the optimal number. He works with each family individually for half an hour in front of an 'audience' formed by the other three families. Lacquer tends to work with a slightly larger group. He uses *structured exercises* initially to speed up the process of group *cohesion* and thereafter the group interacts freely with families being worked with by the therapist and other family members acting as his 'co-therapists'. A variety of *action techniques* such as *family sculpting* are used. Bowen's multiple family therapy is focused around the therapist's efforts to *coach* family members (mainly the marital pair) to develop greater *differentiation* from their families of origin. Both Bowen and Lacquer believe multiple family therapy to be the treatment of choice for most psychological disturbances, in preference to working with individuals or with one couple or family alone.

BOWEN, M. (1976), 'Principles and tech-

niques of multiple family therapy' (in Guerin, P., *Family Therapy: Theory and Practice*, Gardner Press, New York).

LACQUER, H. P. (1976), 'Multiple family therapy' (in Guerin, P., *Family Therapy: Theory and Practice*, Gardner Press, New York).

STRELNICK, A. H. (1977), 'Multiple family group therapy: a review of the literature' (*Family Process*, vol. 16, pp. 307-35).

Multiple impact therapy

An approach developed by MacGregor *et al.* (1964) in which an interdisciplinary *team* of professional therapists meet intensively with a family group in *crisis* over a short, sustained period of time. Sessions are held with different *sub-systems*, individuals and various combinations of family members. The therapeutic team also works in different combinations and meets together regularly throughout the period. The experience usually lasts for a weekend or other two-day period, during which an understanding of the family's problems is gained and a variety of interventions may be made to shake the defensive system and open out new options for change to occur. Recommendations, *tasks* and *direction* may be given, but no further therapy occurs until the family is followed up several months later. The approach is not used very frequently, though it clearly has potential as a form of *crisis intervention* directed towards the family group as a whole.

MACGREGOR, R. (1962), 'Multiple impact psychotherapy with families' (*Family Process*, vol. 1, pp. 15-29).

MACGREGOR, R. *et al.* (1964), *Multiple Impact Theory with Families* (McGraw-Hill, New York).

See also *family crisis intervention*.

Multiple psychotherapy

See *Co-therapy*.

Music therapy

Alvin (1966) defines music therapy as 'the controlled use of music in the treatment, rehabilitation, education and training of adults and children suffering from psychical, mental and emotional disorder'. The use of music as a diagnostic and treatment tool in psychotherapy is mainly confined to work within psychiatric hospitals and *therapeutic communities*. Its use developed during the 1950s, first in the United States and later in Britain and other parts of Europe. Music is used both in the passive sense of engaging patients as listeners, and actively, enabling them to participate in music making. In both these ways, music can be used to calm and relax anxious or overactive patients, stimulate the depressed and isolated, provide a means of *non-verbal communication* for the inarticulate or withdrawn and evoke and allow the expression of strong feelings. In the group setting, participation in music making can be a tool for developing relationships and enabling isolated individuals to co-operate together to achieve a group goal. For children and other patients who are physically unco-ordinated and/or handicapped in some way, music making can help them learn better co-ordination. Some success in acquiring a new skill may also serve to increase self-esteem. Listening to music acts as a stimulus and a means of freeing the imagination and can be particularly helpful with mentally handicapped patients. Used for these purposes, music therapy is an adjunct to hospital or institutional treatment and, as with *art therapy* and *dance therapy*, can be used alongside other methods of psychotherapy. During the last twenty years, the training and recognition of music therapists has been formalised.

ALVIN, J. (1965), *Music For the Handicapped Child* (Oxford University Press, Oxford).
ALVIN, J. (1966), *Music Therapy* (J. Baker, London).
CHARLESWORTH, E. A. (1982), 'Music, psychology and psychotherapy' (*Arts in Psychotherapy*, vol. 9, pp. 191-2).
GASTON, E. T. (1968), *Music in Therapy* (Macmillan, New York).
MICHEL, D. E. (1976), *Music Therapy* (Charles C. Thomas, Springfield, Ill.).

Mutual story telling technique

A technique introduced by Gardner (1969, 1971, 1975) for use in *child psychotherapy*. The therapist elicits a story from the child, gains some sense of its psychodynamic meaning and then tells the child another story, using the same setting and characters but introducing a healthier resolution. By using material and language that has been elicited from the child, the therapist is more likely to 'be heard' by him. Gardner suggests too that the therapist's *interpretations* conveyed via the story bypass the *conscious* and are received directly by the *unconscious*.

Gardner introduces the idea to the child by asking him if he'd like to take part in a make-believe television story telling programme. The child is then welcomed and introduced to the 'audience' and invited to tell a make-believe story. The therapist may ask a few questions at the end, to help him gain an accurate understanding of its psychodynamic content, and he then proceeds to tell the child a story designed to help interpret and resolve some of his conflicts. Gardner advocates the use of this technique for children between the ages of four and twelve, experiencing a range of psychological disorders.

GARDNER, R. A. (1969), 'Mutual story telling as a technique in child psychotherapy and psychoanalysis' (in Masserman, J. (ed.), *Current Psychiatric Therapies*, vol. 14, Grune & Stratton, New York).
GARDNER, R. A. (1971), *Therapeutic Communication with Children* (Jason Aronson, New York).
GARDNER, R. A. (1975), *Psychotherapeutic Approaches to the Resistant Child* (Jason Aronson, New York).

Mystification

Term used by Laing (1965) to describe the way in which 'one person (p) seeks to induce in the other some change necessary for (p's) security'. The interpersonal process is seen especially clearly in families where there is a schizophrenic member. The function of mystification is to maintain the status quo needed by the rest of the family which the schizophrenic member is endangering. Mystification produces a confusion in the individual's sense of self which, like the analogous phenomenon the *double bind*, makes him progressively more and more insecure in his own self-identity. Mystification also 'makes it difficult for the one person to know "who" the other is, and what is the situation they are "in". He does not know where he "is" any more' (Laing 1969). Laing views mystification as a process which occurs preeminently in *dysfunctional* families, but also in other social *systems* including the political system.

LAING, R. D. (1965), 'Mystification, confusion and conflict' (in Boszormenyi-Nagy, I. and Framo, J. (eds), *Intensive Family Therapy*, Harper & Row, New York).
LAING, R. D. (1969), *The Divided Self* (Penguin, Harmondsworth).

See also *Nexus, Praxis*.

Myth

A fictional or semi-fictional story which conveys an important hidden truth, concerning the inner meaning of the universe and of human life. The power of a myth lies in its ability to make sense of otherwise overwhelming aspects of human existence. From early on, the term carried the pejorative sense of 'false' as opposed to 'true', but the positive meaning of myth as conveying serious but not literal truth is accepted in modern studies of myth. It is in this sense that it is used in psychotherapy. Myths are viewed as being important orienting truths for individuals, families and societies. Myths are close to symbols in that they represent reality but do so by means of a story. The reality represented by a myth is some basic aspect of human experience such as birth, sexuality, procreation, destructiveness, mortality and the struggle between good and evil. The raw materials for both personal and social myths may lie in Jung's concept of the *archetype* and the primordial images of the *collective unconscious* and myths provide a means of gaining access to these archetypal

motifs. Mythical stories provide the basis for a variety of psychoanalytic constructs such as the *Oedipus complex*, the *Electra complex, narcissism*, etc., each of which embodies some major existential problem facing human beings. Whilst Jung paid great respect to their broad mythic dimension, some overliteral *interpretation* of basic mythology can devalue their broad and universal meaning. *Family myths* have been studied as a means of transmitting shared meaning from one generation of the family to another.

Myths operate chiefly at an *unconscious* level and act as *homeostatic* mechanisms, producing *cohesion* and stability within an individual, group or society. May (1973) points out that the patient's mythology is an endeavour to make sense of the objective world and to bridge the gap between the distorted self and external reality. 'The aim of therapy ought to be not to rationalize or dry up the mythologizing process, but to make it less compulsive, to free the patient to use it constructively and to help him to experience the myths he moulds as bridges between him and his fellow men as well as ways of interpreting his human experience.' Understanding, interpreting and synthesising the individual or family's mythology forms a part of many psychotherapeutic approaches. Ehrenwald (1966) points out that all of us live and benefit through 'doctrinal compliance . . . with the myths' and customs of period and culture and that mental health is essentially 'a syndrome of adaptation of a given individual in a given culture [i.e. mythology] at a given time'.

CASSIRER, E. (1946), *Language and Myth* (Harpers, New York).
EHRENWALD, J. (1966), *Psychotherapy: Myth and Method* (Grune & Stratton, New York).
MAY, R. (1973), 'The function of myth in sickness and health' (in Wittenberg, E. G. (ed.), *Interpersonal Explorations in Psychoanalysis*, Basic Books, New York).

See also *Metaphor, Parable, Symbolism*.

N

Naikan therapy

A character building approach to therapy which has some similarities to *Morita therapy* and more particularly to the approaches used in *integrity groups*. Naikan therapy was developed in Japan by Isshin Yashimoto, a Japanese priest and businessman. Its practice is almost entirely confined to Japan but the work of Reynolds has recently introduced it to the United States. Naikan therapy first involves meditative reflection on three themes: what has been received from others, what has been returned to them and the troubles that have been caused to them by the client. This three-fold reflection is followed by the 'confession' of deficiencies and misdeeds, first to the therapist, then to a peer group and then to the client's significant others. Finally, the client is encouraged, where possible, to make reparation to those he has wronged and to show his gratitude to those from whom he has received help and nurturance. Like Morita therapy. Naikan is disinterested in *symptoms* and expects that they will disappear as a result of the character building process of therapy. Clients spend one week undertaking this three-fold reflection alone from 5 a.m. to 9 p.m. each day, punctuated by a period when these reflections are shared with the therapist. The therapist's task is to assign the topics for reflection (mother is usually the first topic and then other significant figures in the client's past and current life), listen empathically to the client's reflections at regular intervals and offer some words of encouragement. Basically, the therapist structures the week's experience for the client but does not intervene directly other than by giving the topics for reflection. Two group meetings take place during the week in which the therapist gives a lecture and answers questions. On the last day, clients meet together and those who wish to may talk about the week's experience before the whole group.

Naikan therapy encourages the client to gain control of his response to his environment through bringing into awareness the positive aspects of even apparently damaging experiences. (The concept has similarities with *reframing*.) He is enabled to take responsibility for his own deficiencies by facing them and then trying to repair them. His self-esteem is increased by reflecting on what he receives from others despite the trouble he has caused them. Naikan therapy may be criticised by *depth psychologists* and directive approaches for being superficial and naive but the moratorium it offers to mildly disturbed clients allows them the opportunity to gain a new perspective on their current behaviour and an encouraging new awareness of positive influences in their life.

REYNOLDS, D. K. (1977), 'Naikan therapy: an experiential view' (*Int. J. of Soc. Psychiatry*, vol. 23, pp. 252-64).
REYNOLDS, D. K. (1981), 'Naikan psychotherapy' (in Corsini, R. J., *Handbook of Innovative Psychotherapies*, Wiley, New York).
REYNOLDS, , D. K. (1983), *Naikan Therapy: Meditation for Self-Development* (University of Chicago Press, Chicago).

See also *Character training approaches*.

Narcissism

The process whereby the individual directs love and admiration primarily to himself. The term is derived from a Greek myth in which a youth, Narcissus, falls in love with a young girl, Echo, and thus with himself, for she is only able to mirror and echo what she perceives in Narcissus. Freud (1914) used the term to describe both a primary and a secondary self-love, the first being the infant's early love of himself prior to his ability to form *object relations* and the second being the turning back on to the self of *libido* which has been directed towards an *object* but which has subsequently been withdrawn. In its psychoanalytic usage, the term is a controversial one and there is a recent extensive literature on the subject. (See for example, Sandler *et al.* 1976; Grunberger 1979.) Whilst in one sense narcissism is a defensive activity which disrupts the development of healthy interpersonal relationships, narcisssism properly understood, as Dare and Holder (1981) point out, 'represents a positive contribution to the overall level of self-esteem'. It would now be generally agreed that a distinction should be made between narcissistic object choice where libido has become *fixated* on the self and objects similar to the self, and appropriate self-interest and self-regard. In the latter case, a high level of self-esteem enables the individual to create satisfying and reciprocal interpersonal relationships.

DARE, C. and HOLDER, A. (1981), 'Developmental aspects of the interaction between narcissism, self-esteem and object relations' (*Int. J. of Psychoan.*, vol. 62, pp. 323-37).
FREUD, S. (1914), 'On narcissism: an introduction' (*Standard Edition*, vol. 14, Hogarth Press, London).
GRUNBERGER, B. (1979), *Narcissism* (International Unversities Press, New York).
HAMILTON, V. (1982), *Narcissus and Oedipus* (Routledge & Kegan Paul, London).
PULVER, S. (1970), 'Narcissism: the term and the concept' (*J. of American Psychoan. Assoc.*, vol. 18, pp. 319-41).
SANDLER, J. *et al.* (1976), 'Frames of reference in psychoanalytic psychology – X: narcissism and object love in the second phase of psychoanalysis' (*Brit. J. of Med. Psychology*, vol. 49, pp. 267-74).

Necrophilous
See *Modes of relatedness.*

Needs, hierarchy of
A central concept in the theories of Abraham Maslow. He describes five levels of human need: physiological, safety, love, esteem and *self-actualising.* The lower physiological and safety needs must be relatively satisfied first, then moving up the *hierarchy* until it becomes possible to realise self-actualisation needs. He described the first two levels as lower needs and the second three as higher needs and he further suggested that self-actualisation, the fifth level, is not an end point in the individual's development but generates new desires called 'metaneeds'. These include the

desire for *peak experiences*, metavalues (such as beauty, unity, truth and justice), creativity and transcendent spiritual experiences. This idea of a progression through a hierarchy of needs has been criticised by Maddi (1968) as not conforming to the life experience of many creative individuals who lacked the fulfilment of basic physiological or safety needs and yet managed to produce exceptional creative achievements.

MADDI, S. R. (1968), *Personality Theories – A Comparative Analysis* (Dorsey Press, Homewood, Ill.).
MASLOW, A. H. (1976), *The Farther Reaches of Human Nature* (Penguin, Harmondsworth).

Negative effects
See *Deterioration.*

Negative feedback
A *systems* process in which the rules of transformation in the *feedback loop* tend to dampen any variation in initial input. Negative feedback leads to *homeostasis* and the restoration of the system's state of internal balance. The stability that is induced may be desirable or undesirable. For example, when a family system is facing a new phase in its life cycle and consequent developmental changes in its members, negative feedback can push the system towards a resistive 'no change' reaction in an attempt to preserve an earlier stability. On the other hand a state of internal stability is an essential condition of optimal systems functioning, enabling points of growth and change to occur beneficially and undestructively. The term is used in *communication* theory and the *systemic therapies.*

See also *Positive feedback.*

Negative fit
The degree to which the therapist responds in ways that fit the patient's fears and negative expectations of the way significant people have responded to him in the past. Singer and Luborsky (1977) suggest that negative fit describes a phenomenon 'that partly involves a reaction between the patient's *transference*

and the therapist's *countertransference'*. Various types of therapist-patient fit have been described. Singer and Luborsky suggest that two major fits can be distinguished. The first involves the patient's fear of rejection combined with the therapist's lack of acceptance or interest; the second, the patient's expectation of dependency combined with the therapist's need to be directive and domineering.

SINGER, B. A. and LUBORSKY, L. (1977), 'Countertransference: the status of clinical versus quantitative research' (in Gurman, A. S. and Razin, A. M., *Effective Psychotherapy*, Pergamon Press, New York).

Negative practice
A reactive inhibition procedure introduced by Dunlap (1932) whereby the patient engages in repeated practice of the undesired behaviour until exhaustion is reached. Dunlap used the technique with patients suffering from tics and from stuttering. The deliberate evocation of the habit has the effect of controlling its involuntary appearance. The technique, which has been used more recently by Yates (1958) and others for the treatment of tics, is reminiscent of some of the paradoxical techniques of *strategic therapy*. Boudewyns and Shipley (1982) emphasise the distinction between negative practice and *flooding* and suggest that negative practice is less effective.

BOUDEWYNS, P. A. and SHIPLEY, R. H. (1982), 'Confusing negative practice with flooding: a cautionary note' (*Behavior Therapist*, vol. 5, pp. 47-8).
DUNLAP, K. (1932), *Habits: Their Making and Unmaking* (Liveright, New York).
YATES, A. J. (1958), 'The application of learning theory to the treatment of tics' (*J. of Abnormal Social Psychology*, vol. 56, p. 175).

Negative therapeutic reaction
The inability of the patient to tolerate progress in treatment. Negative therapeutic reaction is distinguished in the psychoanalytic literature from *regression* accompanying a *transference neurosis* and from a form of negative *transference*. However, as it appears to result directly from the treatment interventions, it has logically to be regarded as an aspect of the deterioration effect (see *Deterioration*). Jaffe (1981) suggests that it results from the patient perceiving his/her progress and approval by the therapist as a threat to his/her autonomy. The fear of fusion with the therapist propels him to express his negativism by deterioration. Levy (1982) suggests that when negative therapeutic reaction is based on borrowed guilt (as described by Freud 1923) its resolution is more amenable to analysis. Negative therapeutic reaction led Freud to postulate a new instinct theory that included a drive towards repeating the original traumatic suffering (the *death instinct*). The negative therapeutic reaction has also been attributed to *envy*.

FREUD, S. (1923), 'The ego and the id' (*Standard Edition*, vol. 19, Hogarth Press, London).
JAFFE, A. M. (1981), 'The negative therapeutic reaction' (*Psychotherapy: Theory, Research and Practice*, vol. 18, pp. 313-19).
LEVY, J. (1982), 'A particular kind of negative therapeutic reaction based on Freud's "borrowed guilt" ' (*Int. J. of Psychoan.*, vol. 63, pp. 361-8).

Negentropy
Term coined by Schroedinger (1945) to describe the degree of pattern or structure that exists within a *system*. Used in contrast to *entropy*, the term indicates the extent of the system's capacity for organising and assimilating new information. Applied to natural systems such as the family, the term indicates the family's capacity to operate in a non-chaotic way, although too high a degree of negentropy leads to a rigid and maladaptive *homeostasis* in the system. The *open system* allows entropy to be transformed into negative entropy through its ability to transform its resources and redistribute them to the environment.

SCHROEDINGER, E. (1945), *What is Life?* (Cambridge University Press, Cambridge).

Neo-Freudian

See *Interpersonal school (of psychoanalysis)*.

Network

The group of significant others, family members, neighbours and friends who play an ongoing social role in relation to the patient or family group in treatment. A network differs from a group in that it exists beyond the constraints of space and time. It can stay intact even when long intervals elapse between meetings of its members and even though the whole network is never convened. It may include dead persons, animals and *transitional objects* from the past. Speck and Attneave (1973) view a network as the layer surrounding the family unit that mediates between the family and the larger society. It is analogous to the tribe that exists in other cultures. A major part or the whole of a network may be convened at family reunions, weddings, funerals or when one or more members become ill or identified as having a problem. Therapeutic approaches which make particular use of the concept are *network intervention*, the *systemic therapies*, *social therapy* and *crisis intervention*.

SPECK, R. and ATTNEAVE, C. (1973), *Family Networks* (Pantheon Books, New York).

See also *Ritual*.

Network intervention

A type of *systems therapy* directed to the patient or family group's *network*, introduced into the United States by Speck, Attneave and Rueveni. These writers describe network intervention as a method of last resort, suggested after individual treatment or *family therapy* has been tried and failed. The intervention *team* consists of three or four members and the network is made up of between about forty to a hundred persons. The family who have requested help are invited to call together all those people who they feel are involved in their problem or who could act as a useful resource in solving it. Support systems for every family member are encouraged – some of which may overlap and others be quite

independent of each other. The network is likely to include professionals involved with the family, for example the GP, the DHSS official, the local authority housing officer, as well as relatives, friends and neighbours. Prior to the network meetings, the team meets with the family to discover the problem and once or twice as a team to plan strategy. Meetings with the network usually occur on about one to six occasions and last the whole evening. Speck and Attneave (1973) describe a six-stage process in developing the network interevention. First, retribalisation, where the network is helped to feel some common bond. The leader of the team explains the purpose of the meeting and suggests that everyone link hands, hum, sway, etc., to experience their common purpose. Second, polarisation, where sub-groups are set up, which potentially conflict and are in competition with each other, each group meeting to discuss its own perspective on the problem and mobilising its own energy. The team moves around the room or hall encouraging the sub-groups and watching for the emergence of informal leaders. Third, mobilisation of the resources which have surfaced in the sub-groups, encouraging the informal leaders to lead support groups for the family members. Fourth, resistance, when the process gets bogged down, members of the network become destructive and a sense of depression overwhelms the exercise. Fifth, breakthrough – the team helps the network move out of their stalemate using *structured exercises*, support, encouragement and retribalisation techniques. Sixth, resolution, when some feeling of accomplishment is achieved and some tangible help for the family is agreed or given. Network therapy can be used with a variety of intractable family problems and is particularly useful with *symbiotic* problems. It can also be used to help resolve problems within organisations. Beels (1981) discusses the importance of the social revolution in relation to schizophrenic patients and describes the way in which some clinical programmes incorporate social network concepts. Foulkes (1981) presents an overview of the complex nature of social network intervention, its positive and negative effects and the different network constellations that can be covered for different clinical problems.

BEELS, C. C. (1981), 'Social network as the treatment of schizophrenia' (*Int. J. of Family Therapy*, vol. 3, pp. 310-15).

FOULKES, E. F. (1981), 'Social network therapies: an overview' (*Int. J. of Family Therapy*, vol. 3, pp. 316-20).

SPECK, R. *et al.* (1972), *The New Families* (Basic Books, New York).

SPECK, R. and ATTNEAVE, C. (1973), *Family Networks* (Pantheon Books, New York).

SPECK, R. and RUEVENI, U. (1969), 'Network therapy: a developing concept' (*Family Process*, vol. 8, pp. 182-91).

SPECK, R. V. and SPECK, J. L. (1979), 'On networks: network therapy, network interventions and networking' (*Int. J. of Family Therapy*, vol. 1, pp. 333-7).

RUEVENI, U. (1979), *Networking Families in Crisis* (Human Sciences Press, New York).

See also *Multiple impact therapy, Social therapy*.

Neuro-linguistic programming

Neuro-linguistic programming (NLP) is a model developed by Bandler and Grinder (1975, 1976, 1979, 1981, 1982) to describe how the brain works in terms of its language function, how language use interacts with other brain functions and how our knowledge about the functions of both can be used systematically to enable human beings to achieve more satisfying choices in their patterns of behaviour. Bandler and Grinder's early work led them to develop a transformational grammar of behaviour which they then went on to apply to an analysis of several therapists' work – including Fritz Perls, Virginia Satir and Milton Erickson, whose major focus lies in using and altering the *communication* patterns between clients and their significant others.

NLP is a development of the work done on communication theory by Bateson, Jackson, Erickson and Haley and uses techniques of *reframing, mimesis* (or the matching of gestures, body posture and voice tone of the client by the therapist) and the careful scrutiny of *non-*

verbal communication. Techniques specific to NLP include bridging, anchoring and the use of eye movements as an almost exact language.

Bridging involves the therapist in translating the experiences of family members who are expressing themselves through different representational systems. Bandler and Grinder argue that each person has a preferred mode of representing experience to himself and to others, based upon the different sensory modalities of taste-smell, sight, hearing and body movement. Thus, people who use words derived from a visual mode may find it difficult to communicate with someone who uses auditorily derived words. The bridging process involves the therapist in either translating both parties' modes into neutral, nonsensory words or helping each to understand the experience in terms of the other's representational system.

Anchoring involves the therapist in developing in the client a new set of *conditioned stimuli*, for getting a required response. Dilts *et al.* (1979) describe anchoring as a means of accessing and reaccessing the client's representations. The therapist may use any representation system for doing this and by touch, voice tone or other means will seek to establish in the client an anchor for evoking the desired but essentially unrelated experience. For example, the client is asked to experience the desired feeling and when he says that he is doing so, the therapist applies pressure to his left shoulder. After several repetitions, the pressure to the shoulder should, of its own accord, trigger the desired feeling in the client. In practice, it is hard to see how the technique of anchoring differs significantly from the behavioural technique of *conditioning*.

NLP therapists make very precise analyses of the client's eye movements as a means of gaining access to his internal state. Bandler and Grinder (1975) suggest that 'the eye scanning movement up and left is a common way people use to stimulate that hemisphere as a method for accessing visual memory. Eye movements up and right conversely stimulate the left cerebral hemisphere and constructed images – that is visual representations of things a person has never seen before.' By asking questions which focus on different representational systems, the therapist can learn to calibrate the client's eye movements in fine and precise detail. This helps the therapist to discover leads into his internal state by observing his range of eye movements.

Research into the efficacy of NLP is only embryonic but its proponents claim that it enables movement to be achieved in clinical situations which have apparently reached an impasse. It is a limited model for understanding human behaviour rather than a full-scale theory and it clearly owes many of its ideas to *behaviour therapy*'s attention to specific observable data; to the assumption of *unconscious* processes central to *psychoanalysis* and the adoption of many of the tenets of communication theory.

BANDLER, R. and GRINDER, J. (1975), 'Patterns of the hypnotic techniques of Milton H. Erickson MD' (Meta Publications, Cupertino, Calif.).
BANDLER, R. and GRINDER, J. (1976), *Structure of Magic* vols 1 and 2 (Science and Behavior Books, Palo Alto, Calif.).
BANDLER, R. and GRINDER, J. (1979), *Frogs into Princes* (Real People Press, Moab, Utah).
BANDLER, R. and GRINDER, J. (1981), *Transformations: Neuro-linguistic Programming and the Structure of Hypnosis* (Meta Publications, Cupertino, Calif.).
BANDLER, R. and GRINDER, J. (1982), *Reframing* (Real People Press, Moab, Utah).
DILTS, R. (1983), *Applications of Neuro-Linguistic Programming* (Meta Publications, Cupertino, Calif.).
DILTS, R. *et al.* (1979), *Neuro-Linguistic Programming* (Meta Publications, Cupertino, Calif.).
GRINDER, J. *et al.* (1973), *Guide to Transformational Grammar* (Holt, Rinehart & Winston, New York).

See also *Psycholinguistics*.

Neurotic paradox
The self-perpetuating and self-defeating behaviour that occurs in repeated *dysfunctional* behaviour even when the patient is conscious of its destructive consequences to himself and/or others. Examples include drug addiction, alcoholism, phobias and repeated delinquency. Explanations for the self-defeating repetition include the *secondary gains* that such problem behaviour may produce and the reduction in fear of other events which may be contingent upon the avoidance element of the problem behaviour. The *extinction* of these fears cannot occur since the avoidance of the feared stimulus brought about by the problem behaviour makes it impossible for the individual to discover that the reason for his fear may no longer exist.

EYSENCK, H. J. (1976), 'The learning theory model of neurosis: a new approach' (*Behaviour, Research and Therapy*, vol. 14, pp. 251-67).
MOWRER, O. H. (1948), 'Learning theory and the neurotic paradox' (*Am. J. of Orthopsychiatry*, vol. 18, pp. 571-610).

See also *Avoidance learning*.

Neutrality
The belief held by most psychoanalysts that the therapist must adopt a neutral stance in relation to the patient, his *phantasies*, *projections* and the *transference*. The idea of neutrality developed as an important distinguishing feature within *psychoanalysis* as against methods of suggestion in which the therapist deliberately sought to influence the patient. By being neutral he can act as a blank screen on to which the patient can project his past conflictual relationships which in turn enables the patient to re-live them, *work through* them and resolve them. The therapist expresses his neutrality by refusing to respond to the patient's emotional influence, by not reacting with anger or sadness to material which would normally elicit these emotions, by being completely impartial regarding religious, political or social values and by refusing to share with the patient any of his own personal circumstances. Freud stressed that uncontrolled *counter transference* reactions interfere

with the therapist's neutrality and he advised the therapist to show the patient 'nothing but what is shown to him' (Freud 1912). The expression has become a frequently used definition of the proper attitude of the analyst within the therapeutic situation but the term itself is not to be found in Freud's writings.

In a more general sense, neutrality is used synonymously with impartiality – a mode of being which is thought to be appropriate for therapists to adopt in most forms of therapy. The therapist refuses to take sides or to judge the patient or his behaviour, although the difficulties involved in achieving this consistently are considerable and most would agree that it is necessarily a relative rather than an absolute concept. The *Milan school* of *family therapy* emphasises neutrality as a major therapeutic position, enabling them to remain outside the family *system* and thus to retain their therapeutic leverage. For them, neutrality is a direct consequence of their technique of *circular questioning* and they suggest that neutrality involves the therapist operating from a meta-level vis-à-vis the family, without which the therapist is unable to be effective. Conversely, some forms of therapy advocate the *abandonment* of therapeutic neutrality altogether in favour of techniques designed to challenge, confront or raise the patient's anxiety level. (See, for example, *intensification, unbalancing, provocative therapy, short-term anxiety-provoking therapy*.)

FREUD, S. (1912), 'Recommendations for physicians on the psychoanalytic method of treatment' (*Standard Edition*, vol. 12, Hogarth Press, London).
PALAZZOLI, M. S. *et al.* (1980), 'Hypothesizing – circularity – neutrality' (*Family Process*, vol. 19, pp. 3-12).

See also *Self-disclosure, Social influence.*

Nexus

Literal Latin 'nectere', meaning 'to bind'. Term used by Laing to describe the means by which the individuals which compose a family or group are bonded together. He defines nexus as 'a group whose unification is achieved

through the reciprocal interiorisation by each of each other'. The bonding is entirely mutual rather than serial and the nexus only exists in so far as it is present in each individual member of the group. Laing builds the concept upon Sartre's idea of a bonded group. The nexus is threatened by any member who leaves or threatens to leave the group.

LAING, R. D. (1962), 'Series and nexus in the family' (in *New Left Review*, vol. 15).

See also *Cohesion, Family transference.*

Nominalisation

A distorted form of *communication* whereby a process word or verb appears as an event word or noun, indicating a static instead of a changeable situation. Bandler and Grinder (1975) use the term to help identify the way in which the client uses linguistic distortion as a means of creating or crystallising problem behaviour. They suggest that reversing nominalisation (i.e. helping the client first to identify what they are doing and then using verbs instead of nouns) enables him to see that what he had considered to be a past event beyond his control is actually an ongoing process which can be changed.

BANDLER, R. and GRINDER, J. (1975), *The Structure of Magic* (vol. 1, Science and Behavior Books, Palo Alto, Calif.).

See also *Reframing.*

Non-directive

An attempt by the therapist to engage in an equal, participative relationship with the client rather than organise the therapeutic experience for him. The term non-directive therapy was used first by Rogers to describe his work but latterly he abandoned it in favour of the term *client-centred therapy*. The accurate definition of the term is fraught with difficulty because of its use in varying contexts and sometimes for different polemical purposes. Although it is often used by adherents of *humanistic psychology* as a way of differentiating their work from directive therapies and especially from the *behaviour therapies*, it begs the question as to whether it is in fact ever possible to be non-directive. Social psychological research has shown that the process of *social influence* is ubiquitous within human encounters. Moreover, most therapists consider it important to structure the context of therapy in terms of time boundaries, venue, length of treatment, etc., and in this sense they are not being non-directive. Regarding the process and content of the therapy, Frank (1973) and others have shown that all therapy is a process of active persuasion and influence on the part of the therapist and that even in the most client-oriented, 'non-directive' methods, the therapist is engaged in a self-conscious and deliberate effort to help the client to change. Some therapists (e.g. Whitaker 1975) distinguish between a directive intention in relation to the structure of the therapy and a non-directive intention in relation to its process and content. The term can therefore still be useful in distinguishing between the aims and intentions of the therapist and whilst some can be described as intending a directive approach to structure, content and process, others would attempt to reduce as much as possible the therapist's direction of these variables. Non-directiveness, as Pope (1977) points out, is probably best regarded as a stylistic dimension of the therapist rather than an attribute of a particular 'school' of therapy. Viewed from this perspective, Friedman and Dies (1974) show that directive and non-directive therapist *styles* affected different types of client differently, with highly defensive clients responding adversely to a more directive therapist.

FRANK, J. D. (1973), *Persuasion and Healing* (2nd edn, Johns Hopkins Press, Baltimore).
FRIEDMAN, M. L. and DIES, R. R. (1974), 'Reactions of internal and external test anxious students to counseling and behaviour therapies' (*J. of Consulting and Clinical Psychology*, vol. 42, p. 921).
POPE, B. (1977), 'Research on therapeutic style' (in Gurman, A. S. and Razin, A. M., *Effective Psychotherapy*, Pergamon Press, New York).)

STRUPP, H. (1977), 'A reformulation of the dynamics of the therapist's contribution' (in Gurman, A. S. and Razin, A. M., *Effective Psychotherapy*, Pergamon Press, New York).
WHITAKER, C. (1975), 'The growing edge' (in Haley, J. and Hoffman, L., *Techniques of Family Therapy*, Basic Books, New York).

Non-possessive warmth
See *Unconditional positive regard.*

Non-specific factors
Factors involved in the therapeutic relationship which are not specific to any one approach and which cannot be described in terms of consciously applied method. They are sometimes regarded as no more than those elements which belong to any satisfying human relationship, such as respect, hope, mutual stimulation, understanding and regard. Others would want to include the therapist's conviction about the effectiveness of his treatment and the patient's perception (justified or not) of the therapist's *expertness, experience, attraction* and *credibility.*

Researchers and therapists vary as to the extent to which non-specific factors are recognised as part of the psychotherapeutic process or as being contributory factors to a positive therapeutic *outcome.* For example, *client-centred* and *humanistic* therapists would describe non-specific factors as the *core conditions* of therapy and would regard them as the essential and sufficient ingredients of therapy. Therapies using other approaches would regard them as being necessary to the process but not sufficient in themselves to bring about change. Frank (1961) studied non-specific factors by investigating the similarities between various forms of psychotherapy, healing in primitive societies, and religious experience. Later, Frank (1971) isolated six non-specific factors which are common to most forms of psychotherapy. These are: an intense, emotionally charged, confiding relationship with a helping person; an acceptable explanation of the patient's problem; new information about the ways in which it may be helped; an expectation of help on the part of the patient;

an experience of progress or success during the course of therapy; and the emotional arousal of the patient. Strupp (1977) points out that although we have not gone very far in teasing apart the nature or effect of non-specific factors, their recognition as such is clearly an advance on calling them simply 'spontaneous remission'.

FRANK, J. D. (1961), *Persuasion and Healing: A Comparative Study of Psychotherapy* (Johns Hopkins Press, Baltimore, revised edn, 1973).
FRANK, J. D. (1971), 'Therapeutic factors in psychotherapy' (*Am. J. of Psychotherapy*, vol. 25, pp. 350-61).
FRANK, J. D. (1978), *Psychotherapy and the Human Predicament* (Schocken Books, New York).
STRUPP, H. H. (1977), 'A reformulation of the dynamics of the therapist's contribution' (in Gurman, A. S. and Razin, A. M., *Effective Psychotherapy*, Pergamon Press, New York).

See also *Relationship factors, Social influence, Therapist variable.*

Nonsummativity
A term confined to *systems theory* meaning that a system's whole is more than the aggregate of its summated parts. Nonsummativity or *holism* is the fundamental premise upon which systems theory is built emphasising the need to study and intervene in *systems* as wholes.

Non-verbal communication (NVC)
Aspects of social behaviour other than language that provide information concerning attitudes, emotions and cognition. Several other terms are used in the literature to convey the same meaning – for example, visible behaviour, bodily communication, body movement and non-verbal behaviour. NVC can be divided into several categories: non-verbal phonation, which includes voice tone, pitch, stress and pace, laughter, grunts, 'uh-hums' and marks of annoyance, etc.; body movement or kinesics, such as facial expression, eye contact and gaze, proxemics, gestures and body contact; and the use of external presentations of self such as dress and the use

of *ritual* and objects to convey information.
Argyle (1969, 1975, 1978) is one of the foremost researchers in Britain in this area. He suggests that NVC has three broad functions: to comment on and elaborate verbal communication so that its meaning is better understood; to manage synchronisation, so that the conversation can be passed back and forth between different contributors with the minimum of difficulty; and to provide *feedback* through an almost continuous commentary of non-verbal signals. Much NVC occurs outside conscious awareness and as such it is less censored and is therefore a rich source for gaining understanding into a person's emotions and attitudes. Even when a person is trying to hide his opinions or emotions, these are often betrayed through some aspect of NVC. NVC is culturally specific and to some extent also dependent on the type of individual personality, sex difference and differences in social class.

A vast amount of research has been conducted into NVC by social psychologists, many of their findings being of considerable practical use to the therapist. For example, attentiveness on the part of the listener is conveyed through well defined non-verbal signals such as frequent eye contact, sitting within a certain proximity, with an alert, slightly forward-bending posture and using frequent head nods and 'uh-hums', 'ah-has', etc. Argyle *et al.* (1972) showed that NVC overrules verbal communication when the two conflict. Eye contact facilitates *self-disclosure* but if prolonged unduly or with too much intensity it may be experienced as overwhelming. Proximity and eye contact need to be related – the nearer the therapist sits to the patient the more he or she must allow for breaks in eye contact. Proximity is an indicator of intimacy/formality and can be manipulated according to which of these the therapist wishes to emphasise. Since *attraction* has been found to be an important variable in the therapeutic relationship, increasing the patient's desire to continue in therapy, physical appearance is important as a means of increasing interpersonal attraction. Ekman and Friesen (1974) and others have shown that the face offers a particularly transparent display of emotional states and learning to decode these forms a part of therapist training and a part of some forms of psychotherapy, for example, *social skills training*. Congruity within NVC and between NVC and verbal communication enhances the effectiveness of the communication process.

Gladstein (1974) reviewed the literature on NVC related to counselling/psychotherapy and commented that three-quarters of it had appeared since the mid-1960s. The upsurge in interest in NVC is presumably related to the development of forms of therapy which make much greater use of action and body movement than did classical *psychoanalysis* or *behaviour modification*. Breunlin (1979) points out that NVC needs to be considered on three levels. First, the organismic level, where it is *expressive* of the individual's emotion, *intrapsychic* processes and psychopathology. Mahl (1967) has conducted studies of NVC in patients undergoing psychoanalysis and has noted the way in which it provides indicators of intrapsychic states. Ellsworth and Carlsmith (1968) showed that subjects respond favourably to eye contact when the verbal content of discussion is favourable but not when it is unfavourable. The second level suggested by Breunlin is the interpersonal level, where NVC is *communicative*. Here the work of the communication theorists has shown the relationship between *analogic* NVC and *digital* verbal communication, the former qualifying the latter and acting as a *metacommunication* upon it. The third level is the social group or family group level where NVC is seen as a function of the group itself. Scheflen (1963) showed how NVC plays a vital role in regulating group activity and functions to preserve the group in being and to ensure that it achieves its aims. Scheflen (1964) also found that postural shifts were particularly important in providing information about relationships in the group. People with similar views often adopt similar postures and individuals take up physical positions in a group according to whether they feel close to others or oppose them, sitting next

to them or opposite them respectively. Moreover, Hall (1966) showed that the distance that separates the interactants in a group (i.e. the proxemics) is partly related to the nature of the interaction as well as the nature of the relationships. Breunlin (1979) provides a very useful guide to the way in which NVC can be interpreted and managed in *family therapy*.

ARGYLE, M. (1969), *Social Interaction* (Methuen, London).

ARGYLE, M. (1975), *Bodily Communication* (Methuen, London).

ARGYLE, M. (1978), *The Psychology of Interpersonal Behaviour*, 3rd edn (Penguin, Harmondsworth).

ARGYLE, M., ALKEMA, F. and GILMOUR, R. (1972), 'The communication of friendly and hostile attitudes by verbal and non-verbal signals' (*European Journal of Social Psychology*, vol. 1, pp. 385-402).

BIRDWHISTELL, R. (1970), *Kinesics and Context: Essays on Body Motion Communication* (University of Pennsylvania Press, Philadelphia).

BREUNLIN, D. (1979), 'Non-verbal communication in family therapy' (in Walrond-Skinner, S. (ed.), *Family and Marital Psychotherapy*, Routledge & Kegan Paul, London).

EKMAN, P. and FRIESEN, W. V. (1974), 'Nonverbal behaviour and psychopathology' (in Friedman, R. J. and Katz, M. M. (eds), *The Psychology of Depression*, Winston, Washington, DC).

ELLSWORTH, P. C. and CARLSMITH, J. M. (1968), 'Effects of eye contact and verbal content on affective responses to a dyadic interaction' (*J. of Personality and Social Psychology*, vol. 10, pp. 15-20).

GLADSTEIN, G. A. (1974), 'Non-verbal communication and counseling/psychotherapy: a review' (*Counseling Psychologist*, vol. 4, pp. 34-57).

HALL, E. (1966), *The Silent Language* (Fawcett, Greenwich, Conn.).

MAHL, G. F. (1967), 'Some clinical observations on non-verbal behavior in interviews' (*J. of Nervous and Mental Diseases*, vol. 144, pp. 492-505).

SCHEFLEN, A. E. (1963), 'Communication and regulation in psychotherapy' (*Psychiatry*, vol. 26, pp. 126-36).

SCHEFLEN, A. E. (1964), 'The significance of posture in communication systems' (*Psychiatry*, vol. 27, pp. 316-31).

SCHEFLEN, A. E. (1976), *Human Territories: How We Behave in Space-Time* (Prentice-Hall, Englewood Cliffs, New Jersey).

O

Object

A real or phantasied person or aspect of a person which is felt to satisfy or frustrate an individual's need. The term does not imply reification, but is used in contrast to 'subject'. Freud (1915) used the term in two main ways: first to describe the recipient of the goal-directed focus of an instinctual drive, usually a part object, such as a part of the body; and second, as a focus of attraction to the *ego*, usually a whole object or person. For Melanie Klein (1952), the concept was of central importance to her theoretical framework and she suggested that the infant learned first to relate to part objects (the mother's breast, the penis) during the *paranoid-schizoid position* of early infancy. Later, as he begins to move into the *depressive position*, he begins to relate to whole objects. Both part and whole objects are subject to the *splitting* process by which they are conceived of as either 'good' and reassuring or 'bad' and persecutory and they become the prototypes, according to Klein (1952), of all gratifying and persecutory experiences in the external world. In the earliest stage of development, the infant's rudimentary concept of external objects is mediated by his own perceptions and *phantasies*. Their designation as 'good' or 'bad' arises both from their own ability to satisfy or frustrate and from the baby's *projections* of goodness and badness into them.

In psychoanalytic theory, the individual's *internal world* is stored with objects. Examples of internal objects are the *superego* and the *ego ideal* and the relationship of these objects to each other creates a complex and powerful internal experience. Mechanisms such as *introjection* and *projection* provide the means whereby external and internal objects are experienced. From the baby's own concrete viewpoint, projection and introjection literally involve the passing of objects in and out of his internal world. For him this process may be frightening and overwhelming both because of the introjection of the object when it is experienced as extremely powerful and the projection of the object which may then be experienced as lost. Later, with the development of the ego's capacities and functions, the individual gains the capacity to relate more fully to external objects and to hold on to them symbolically even when they are absent.

FREUD, S. (1915), 'Instincts and their vicissitudes' (*Standard Edition*, vol. 14, Hogarth Press, London).

KLEIN, M. (1952), 'Some theoretical conclusions regarding the emotional life of the infant' (in Rivière, J. (ed.), *Developments in Psychoanalysis*, Hogarth Press, London).

Object relations

A development of Freud's ideas to describe the interaction between *object* and subject. Object relations theory was developed principally, though not entirely, after Freud and in reaction to what was perceived to be the inherent limitations of the instinctual, intrapersonal emphasis of Freudian concepts. Freud viewed the satisfaction or inhibition of instinctual *drives* as the primary determinant of early development and his emphasis and interest was therefore upon the subject experiencing those drives. In contrast, object relations theory shifts the emphasis to the object and libidinal drives are viewed as the effort to find an appropriate object rather than simply to satisfy an impulse. Moreover, the term object relation suggests an interactional relationship between subject and object. Although the difference between Freud and later theorists is more a matter of emphasis, important distinctions in practice do follow from the two approaches.

Object relations theory was developed from the work of two different principal theorists. First from Klein's view of the *ego* and its relationship with internal, part or whole objects. The part or whole objects are not passive but hold the power to affect the ego in some way, for example to persecute or to reassure. Moreover, they possess attributes such as 'goodness' and 'badness'. Second, from Fairbairn's object relations theory, which built upon Klein's work and emphasised the essentially object-seeking goals of all early ego development. Fairbairn's concern is with objects with whom the individual must learn to relate, not simply as vehicles for the gratification of the individual. He stated that people are 'object-seeking' and not 'pleasure-seeking'. Maturity in interpersonal relationships becomes the goal of the whole maturation process. Although Fairbairn's own work remained primarily concerned with the individual's internal world, the *British school* of *psychoanalysis* which formed around Fairbairn broadened the emphasis and paved the way for those family and marital therapists who take object relations theory as a major theoretical construct in their clinical work (for example, Dicks 1967; Boszormenyi-Nagy 1967; Shapiro 1979).

BOSZORMENYI-NAGY, I. (1967), 'Relational modes and meaning' (in Zuk, G. and Boszormenyi-nagy, I. (eds), *Family Therapy and Disturbed Families*, Science & Behavior Books, New York).

DICKS, H. V. (1967), *Marital Tensions* (Routledge & Kegan Paul, London).

FAIRBAIRN, W. R. D. (1952), *Psychoanalytic Studies of the Personality* (Tavistock, London).

FAIRBAIRN, W. R. D. (1963), 'Synopsis of the object relations theory of the personality' (*Int. J. of Psychoan.*, vol. 44, pp. 224-5).

GUNTRIP, H. (1968), *Schizoid Phenomena, Object Relations and the Self* (Hogarth Press, London).

KERNBERG, O. (1976), *Object Relations Theory and Clinical Psychoanalysis* (Jason Aronson, New York).

SCHARFF, D. E. (1982), *The Sexual Relationship: An Object Relations View of Sex and the Family* (Routledge & Kegan Paul, London).

SHAPIRO, R. (1979), 'Family dynamics and object relations theory' (in Feinstein, S. and Giovacchini, P. (eds), *Adolescent Psychiatry*, vol. 7, University of Chicago Press, Chicago).

SUTHERLAND, J. D. (1963), 'Object relations theory and the conceptual model of psychoanalysis' (*Brit. J. of Med. Psychology*, vol. 36, pp. 109-24).

Oedipus complex

A triangular conflict experienced during the *phallic stage* in children between three and five years whereby, according to Freudian psychoanalytic theory, the loving desire for the parent of the opposite sex as a love object reaches a climax. Consequently, feelings of intense rivalry with the same-sex parent who is the actual love partner occur. The conflict re-appears during adolescence and is finally resolved when the young person is able to choose somebody outside the nuclear family as his love object in a mature *genital* love relationship. The passing of the intensity of Oedipal feelings for the parents marks, in Freudian theory, the moment of full ego development with the concomitant ability to engage in *object relations*. Freud used the *myth* of Oedipus Rex to describe the fundamental elements of the concept. In the original story, Oedipus, in search of his origins, falls in love with his mother and murders his father. Sophocles used the myth in a tragic drama to describe not only the individual's tragedy but that of the whole human race. Freud's use of the myth reflects both aspects. Originally, Freud asserted that the Oedipal triangle affected both girls and boys in the same way but later he altered this view and rejected also Jung's coinage of the term *Electra complex* to describe what Jung believed to be a symmetrical event for girls. By contrast, Freud (1924) asserted that for boys, the Oedipal conflict is resolved due to the perceived *threat* of castration by father, a threat which encourages him to give up his incestuous desires for mother. For girls, however, the development of the Oedipus complex has itself involved a switch of love object from mother, her original attachment, to father. For her, the Oedipus complex culminates in the *recognition* of her lack of a penis, which produces the gradual awareness in her of her compensatory abilities, for which mother is the model. The resolution of the Oedipus complex leads to the formation of the *superego* by the *internalisation* of the prohibitions and taboos which become evident to the child during this phase. The *repression* of Oedipal wishes at this point provides a source of irrational guilt in later life.

Melanie Klein (1945) asserted that the Oedipus complex appeared much earlier in the development of the infant, starting during the first year of life, during the *depressive position*. Jung (1956) criticised Freud for what he felt to be the too literal use of the symbolism of the Oedipal myth and more particularly Freud's view that an unresolved Oedipus complex is the origin of all future neurotic disturbance. Jung felt that this over-emphasised the part played by the remote past in the aetiology of psychological problems. Recently, Loewald (1979) has emphasised that the Oedipus complex is never destroyed or overwhelmed as Freud had indicated, but that it persists in varying degrees throughout adult life.

Freud's universal application of the myth to society as a whole (Freud 1913) has also been criticised as being irrelevant to cultures which are not based upon dual parentage in a nuclear family. It can be argued, however, that even in different cultural situations, the Oedipal triangle of desire and rivalry is worked out, using the different elements of whatever social system that pertains. Freud has also been criticised for implying that all revolutionary conflict in society is merely an *acting out* of the Oedipal conflict writ large, an interpretation which would of course dismiss the actual facts of economic and political grievance as causative in social upheaval. Although Gabriel (1983) cogently defends Freud from this attack, the way in which Freud's tendency to reduce social phenomena to psychological

ones, particularly in relation to the Oedipal myth, appears to produce a conservative effect.

Although chiefly concerned with intra-psychic events, one of the major contributions that Freud's elaboration of the Oedipus complex has made to psychotherapy is the central place which it gives to the real relationships within the triangle of mother, father and child. Intrasystemic concepts such as *triangling* and *detouring* are directly derived from the original Oedipal triangle; and the highlighting of this central family relationship laid the foundation for the development of psychotherapeutic approaches to the whole family, at a later date.

FREUD, S. (1913), 'Totem and taboo' (*Standard Edition*, vol. 13, Hogarth Press, London).

FREUD, S. (1924), 'The dissolution of the Oedipus complex' (*Standard Edition*, vol. 19, Hogarth Press, London).

GABRIEL, Y. (1983), *Freud and Society* (Routledge & Kegan Paul, London).

HAMILTON, V. (1982), *Narcissus and Oedipus* (Routledge & Kegan Paul, London).

JUNG, C. G. (1956), 'Symbols of transformation' (*Collected Works*, vol. 5, Routledge & Kegan Paul, London).

KLEIN, M. (1945), 'The Oedipus complex in the light of early anxieties' (in *Contributions to Psychoanalysis*, Hogarth Press, London).

LOEWALD, H. W. (1979), 'The waning of the Oedipus complex' (*J. of Am. Psychoan. Assoc.*, vol. 27, pp. 751-75).

One-way screen

Specially prepared glass inserted into a wall dividing an interviewing room from an observation room. The screen allows the observers to view the interview without being seen by therapist or patients. One-way viewing screens have been used in small group and family research for years, and also to observe children at play during *play therapy* sessions. The one-way screen is a relatively new introduction into psychotherapy, but is now used frequently both in treatment and in the training of therapists, particularly in group work and in the *systemic therapies*.

CADE, B. W. and CORNWELL, M. (1983), 'The evolution of the one-way screen' (*Aust. J. of Family Therapy*, vol. 4, pp. 73-80).
CORNWELL, M. and PEARSON, R. (1981), 'Cotherapy teams and one-way screen in family therapy practice and training' (*Family Process*, vol. 20, pp. 199-209).
MACKIE, R. and WOOD, J. (1968), 'Observations on two sides of a one-way screen' (*Int. J. of Group Psychotherapy*, vol. 18, pp. 177-85).
VENKATRAMAIAH, S. R. (1974), 'Low-cost one-way vision screens for unobserved observation in child guidance clinics' (*Child Psychiatry Quarterly*, vol. 7, pp. 14-15).
WOLMAN, R. N. (1970), 'Through the one-way mirror: an analysis of the dynamics in the observation of psychotherapy' (*Psychotherapy: Theory, Research and Practice*, vol. 7, pp. 108-10).

See also *Greek chorus, Live supervision, Team.*

Open system

A *system* which is characterised by permeable boundaries and is open to inputs from the environment. All biological and social systems have to be open to some extent in order to survive, but the *degree* to which they are open describes the extent to which they are capable of increasing their variety through the process of *morphogenesis.* An open family or group allows its members to move out and new members to enter with ease. It can make use of resources within the environment and thus reduce the burden on its members and its vulnerability to stress.

See also *Closed system, Feedback loop, Homeostasis.*

Open-ended questioning

The posing of questions which cannot be answered by a closure response, such as the simple 'yes' or 'no' elicited by a leading question. Instead, an open-ended question demands elaboration and self-revelation from the respondent. Open-ended questions are useful in the early stages of treatment since they allow the client to focus on the material which is of greatest importance to him,

uncontaminated by the therapist's bias, and they afford the therapist maximum data, although of a somewhat unstructured kind, from which to develop a *diagnosis.* Questioning can move from open-ended to specific and focused, as the diagnosis is clarified and treatment develops. Although any form of question is a directive technique, when compared with no questions at all (as in *free association*), open-ended questioning is more typical of the *non-directive* approaches such as *client-centred therapy. Behavioural* and *strategic* approaches are more likely to use specific focused questioning from the start. Ivey and Authier (1978) point out that open questions more often begin with 'what' and 'how' whereas closed questions more often begin with 'is', 'are', 'do' or 'did'. Closed questions can be useful in slowing the pace of an *interview* where the client is moving too rapidly into painful or complex material.

IVEY, A. E. and AUTHIER, J. (1978), *Micro Counseling* (Charles C. Thomas, Springfield, Ill.).
PAYNE, S. (1951), *The Art of Asking Questions* (Princeton University Press, Princeton, New Jersey).

See also *Circular questioning, Microskill.*

Operant

A *response* emitted by an individual or other organism which can be described in terms of its effect upon the environment. Emphasis is on consequence and not cause and it stands in contrast to the *classical conditioning* focus on the connection between *stimulus* and response.

Operant conditioning

The process whereby behaviour is seen as being a function of its consequences and thus the subject's *response* is viewed as being instrumental in producing those consequences. As the response is effective in producing a result, it is called an *operant.* In contrast to *classical conditioning*, operant conditioning focuses on changing the response pattern of the subject. The name of B. F. Skinner is linked with the development of operant conditioning. Observing a rat's efforts to get food, Skinner showed that it could be trained to make a positive response on its own behalf, first by trial and error, contingent upon hunger, and then in response to the *reinforcement* received by its success in obtaining food. There are two main differences between operant and classical conditioning. With classical conditioning, the reward is not dependent upon the subject's performance, whilst with operant conditioning the subject exercises some active control over the consequences of his action. Second, the responses which can be effected by classical conditioning are mainly involuntary responses and somatic responses, whereas operant conditioning applies mainly to the voluntary responses of the subject.

Operant conditioning principles have given rise to a varied group of techniques used in *behaviour therapy*, including the *contingency management* approaches of positive and negative reinforcement, *punishment* and *response cost*, as well as the environmental application of these principles contained in the running of a *token economy*. Operant conditioning does not focus on *causality* or on the individual's perception, motivation, beliefs or purpose. Skinner suggests that any data other than observable behaviour are mere 'explanatory fictions' and he rejects all inferential data such as *cognitive structure*, *unconscious* processes, *ego states* and any other non-behavioural concept. Recently, Skinner (1981) has described operant conditioning as 'a kind of selection by consequences, a causal mode found only in living things or in machines made by living things'.

Of all behavioural approaches, operant conditioning has been most severely criticised from several different viewpoints because of its *reductionism*, materialism, manipulation and simplistic approach to the complexity of human existence. Rogers (1963) makes a swingeing attack on some of the inconsistencies which lie within Skinner's approach: 'From what I understand Dr Skinner to say, it is his understanding that though he might have thought he *chose* to come to this meeting, might

have thought he had a purpose in giving this speech, such thoughts are really illusory. He actually made certain marks on paper and emitted certain sounds here simply because his genetic make-up and his past environment had operantly conditioned his behavior in such a way that he as a person doesn't enter into this.' In replying to Rogers, Skinner said that he accepted Rogers's characterisation of his presence at the joint meeting which they were attending at the time. Kazdin (1978) provides an overview of the current status of operant techniques.

KAZDIN, A. E. (1978), 'The application of operant techniques' (in Garfield, S. and Bergin, A. (eds), *Handbook of Psychotherapy and Behavior Change*, Wiley, New York).

ROGERS, C. R. (1963), 'Learning to be free' (in Farber, S. M. and Wilson, R. (eds), *Control of the Mind*, vol. 2, McGraw-Hill, New York).

SKINNER, B. F. (1953), *Science and Human Behavior* (Macmillan, London).

SKINNER, B. F. (1969), *Contingencies of Reinforcement* (Appleton-Century-Crofts, New York).

SKINNER, B. F. (1981), 'Selection by consequences' (*Science*, vol. 213, pp. 501-4).

Oral stage

The first psycho-sexual stage of human development, occurring during the first one to two years of life, and first described by Freud (1905). The mouth acts as the *erogenous zone* from which sexual pleasure is achieved and a relationship with the outside world is established. The acts of incorporating and eliminating food (by the mouth) and the sensual pleasure of mouthing, sucking, kissing, eating, etc., provide the baby with its chief means of *communication* with the outside world, and these modes provide the physical analogues for the psychological processes of *incorporation* and *projection*.

Abraham (1924) sub-divided the oral stage into two: oral-dependent, characterised by the early sucking relationship, and oral-aggressive, characterised by the biting and nibbling activities which become possible when babies' teeth develop, which Abraham thought was at about six months. Melanie Klein adopted this sub-division, relating the oral-dependent phase to the baby's desire to incorporate the breast as 'good' *object* and the oral-aggressive phase to the baby's desire to attack the breast, when perceiving it as 'bad' object. In Erikson's (1950) analysis of the eight developmental stages of man, he suggests that successful transition through the oral stage is characterised by basic trust which allows for the development of mutual recognition between mother and baby (see *Stages of development*). Unless basic trust is established, dependency and mistrust are likely to develop in adulthood. The societal and cultural concomitant of the oral stage, according to Erikson, is religious faith. Farrel (1981) and others have criticised the erotic nature of the oral stage postulated by Freud and also the cultural and social extrapolations made by Erikson.

ABRAHAM, K. (1924), 'A short study of the development of the libido, viewed in the light of mental disorders' (*Selected Papers*, Hogarth Press, London).
ERIKSON, E. H. (1950), *Childhood and Society*, (Penguin, Harmondsworth).
FARRELL, B. A. (1981), *The Standing of Psychoanalysis* (Oxford University Press, Oxford).
FREUD, S. (1905), 'Three essays on the theory of sexuality' (*Standard Edition*, vol. 7, Hogarth Press, London).

See also *Stages of development*.

Orgone energy
A cosmic energy defined by Wilhelm Reich as the orgasmic energy which charges all living substances with life. Reich believed that this energy was experienced most fully and directly in the orgasmic reflex and that the task of psychotherapy is to release this energy in the patient. The term orgone is intended to reflect both its organic and orgasmic sources.

See also *Character analysis, Character armour, Reichian therapy*.

Orgone therapy
See *Reichian therapy*.

Orgonomy
See *Reichian therapy*.

Outcome
Research conducted into the results of psychotherapy. The study of outcome focuses on the conditions and determinants of therapeutic benefits. Several issues form the background to the study of outcome in psychotherapy.

(1) After a period when the study of outcome was virtually abandoned as too complex, in favour of the study of *process*, outcome is again receiving considerable attention. This can only be an appropriate development since all discussion of process, technique, method and other variables must ultimately be related to an evaluation of their outcome for the patient.

(2) Early studies were based on an effort to show that one approach was superior to others, and until fairly recently debates about outcome have been fought on ideological rather than empirical lines.

(3) Many outcome studies have been concerned with the study of gross variables such as: does psychotherapy, of whatever kind, 'work', as compared with no psychotherapy at all? A complicating factor here is that it is likely that *all* forms of therapeutic intervention produce *some* benefit in *some* circumstances and although there is an enormous literature investigating the results of a particular method of work compared with no psychotherapy at all, it is hard to draw any meaningful conclusions from such studies.

(4) The effort to show that one type of psychotherapy is superior to all others in all situations has also frequently been undertaken. These studies have been reviewed by Luborsky *et al.* (1975) who found that only insignificant differences were established between the outcome achieved by different approaches. Sloane *et al.* (1975) compared the results of

psychoanalytic and behaviour therapies and came to a similar conclusion and other review studies have shown that in relation to various comparisons, this is a recurrent finding. Instead, researchers are turning their attention to much more specific analyses of which type of intervention with which type of patient and problem under what circumstances and with what therapist can effective change be produced? Moreover it is generally agreed throughout the field that for change to appropriately be claimed to have occurred, it must be capable of demonstration, be relatively permanent and be attributable to the activity which has occurred between therapist and patient. These criteria of change presuppose agreement between therapists of different orientations on the purpose and objectives of psychotherapy, which is itself very hard to establish, although it is generally recognised now that changes of affect, cognition and behaviour should all be evaluated.

(5) The evaluation of outcome is further complicated by phenomena that may or may not be extraneous to the psychotherapeutic process such as *spontaneous remission* and *placebo* effect. Eysenck (1952, 1966) initiated one of the longest-lasting debates in psychotherapy when he claimed that psychotherapy achieves no better results than would occur anyway by spontaneous remission. Progress has been made however in understanding these phenomena and also in detailing the methodological and psychometric requirements for designing outcome studies (e.g. Fiske *et al.* 1970).

Smith and Glass (1977) have undertaken a meta-analysis of outcome studies. Goldstein and Stein (1976) believe that we have now reached the stage of undertaking outcome-related process studies, whereby an interactionist view of the outcome question is the only valid approach to adopt. Suggestions for the future direction which outcome research should take have been discussed for individual psycho-

therapy by Bergin and Lambert (1978). *Client-centred therapy* and *behaviour therapy* have both produced large numbers of studies showing a positive outcome and Bergin and Suinn (1975) comment that the weight of the evidence now 'supports the notion of significant improvement . . . in psychotherapy, with improvement rates averaging about 67%'. The outcome of treatment in other modalities has received considerably less attention. Bednar and Kaul (1978) reviewed the outcome research on group therapies and comment that the bulk of the literature is so inadequate methodologically that no valid inferences can be drawn from it. They describe a selection of the best studies, covering a range of different group work methods, and discuss their findings. Gurman and Kniskern (1978) were able to locate over 200 relevant studies conducting research into *marital* and/or *family therapy*. Because of the comparatively recent development of family and marital research, Gurman and Kniskern consider studies of gross rates of improvement useful. Examining seventy-seven studies of non-behavioural family and marital therapy, they found that there was a 71 per cent and 61 per cent improvement respectively. They found that family and marital therapy produced significantly better results than individual treatment for marital problems, anorexia, many childhood behaviour problems, juvenile delinquency and sexual dysfunction. The outcome of *brief therapy* has been reviewed by Butcher and Koss (1978). They suggest that brief behavioural therapies produce the most rapid change within the short-term models and that, overall, short-term methods achieve as good results as long-term approaches.

BEDNAR, R. L. and KAUL, T. J. (1978), 'Experiential group research: current perspectives' (in Bergin, A. E. and Garfield, S. L., *Handbook of Psychotherapy and Behavior Change*, Wiley, New York).

BERGIN, A. E. and LAMBERT, M. J. (1978), 'The evaluation of therapeutic outcomes' (in Bergin, A. E. and Garfield, S. L., *Handbook of Psychotherapy and Behavior Change*, Wiley, New York).

BERGIN, A. E. and SUINN, R. M. (1975), 'Individual psychotherapy and behavior therapy' (*Annual Review of Psychology*, vol. 26, pp. 509-55).

BUTCHER, J. N. and KOSS, M. P. (1978), 'Research of brief and crisis-oriented therapies' (in Bergin, A. E. and Garfield, S. L., *Handbook of Psychotherapy and Behavior Change*, Wiley, New York).

EYSENCK, H. J. (1952), 'The effects of psychotherapy: an evaluation' (*Journal of Consulting Psychology*, vol. 16, pp. 319-24).

EYSENCK, H. J. (1966), *The Effects of Psychotherapy* (International Science Press, New York).

FISKE, D. *et al.* (1970), 'Planning of research on effectiveness of psychotherapy' (*Archives of General Psychiatry*, vol. 22, pp. 22-32).

GOLDSTEIN, A. P. and STEIN, N. (1976), *Prescriptive Psychotherapies* (Pergamon Press, New York).

GURMAN, A. S. and KNISKERN, D. P. (1978), 'Research on marital and family therapy: progress, perspective and prospect' (in Bergin, A. E. and Garfield, S. L., *Handbook of Psychotherapy and Behavior Change*, Wiley, New York).

GURMAN, A. S. and KNISKERN, D. P. (1981), 'Family therapy outcome research: knowns and unknowns' (in *Handbook of Family Therapy*, Brunner/Mazel, New York).

LAMBERT, M. J. *et al.* (1983), *The Assessment of Psychotherapy Outcome* (Wiley, New York).

LUBORSKY, L. *et al.* (1971), 'Factors influencing the outcome of psychotherapy – a review of quantitative research' (*Psychological Bulletin*, vol. 75, pp. 145-85).

LUBORSKY, L. *et al.* (1975), 'Comparative studies of psychotherapies: "Is it true that everyone has won and all must have prizes?" ' (*Archives of General Psychiatry*, vol. 32, pp. 995-1008).

MELTZOFF, J. and KORNREICH, M. (1970), *Research in Psychotherapy* (Atherton Press, New York).

MILLER, T. I. (1980), *The Benefits of Psychotherapy* (Johns Hopkins Press, Baltimore).

MINTZ, J. (1977), 'The role of the therapist in assessing psychotherapy outcome' (in Gurman, A. S. and Razin, A. M. (eds), *Effective Psychotherapy*, Pergamon Press,. New York).

SLOANE, R. B. *et al.* (1975), *Psychotherapy versus Behaviour Therapy* (Harvard University Press, Cambridge, Mass.).

SMITH, M. L. and GLASS, G. V. (1977), 'Meta-analysis of psychotherapy outcome studies' (*American Psychologist*, vol. 132, pp. 752-60).

STRUPP, H. H. and HADLEY, S. W. (1979), 'Specific versus non-specific factors in psychotherapy – a controlled study of outcome' (*Archives of General Psychiatry*, vol. 36, pp. 1125-36).

TREACHER, A. (1983), 'On the utility or otherwise of psychotherapy research' (in Pilgrim, D., *Psychology and Psychotherapy*, Routledge & Kegan Paul, London).

P

Pairing

See *Basic assumption behaviour.*

Parable

A fictional story with a moral point composed by the therapist to expound, by analogy, the meaning of some real events or circumstances in the patient's life. As Cade (1982) points out, 'in such stories, significant features of the story line and facets of the relationships between the participants or components should stand in a direct analogic correspondence to events and relationships of importance to the client and his circumstances.' The story used may be taken from work with another patient and represent a piece of successful problem solving that another person has actually achieved in an analogous situation, or the story may be a fiction composed by the therapist in such a way that *advice* is given to the patient in an indirect way. Adams and Chadbourne (1982) describe the use of imaginative stories in the treatment of obese patients. Alternatively, the story may be taken from literature – a biblical parable, for example. The degree to which the story overtly relates to the patient's situation varies according to how resistant or anxious he or she is; the higher the degree of anxiety, the greater the likelihood that a covert connection should be chosen by the therapist. In either case, however, the essential ingredient is the symbolic connection between the story told and the patient's problem.

ADAMS, C. H. and CHADBOURNE, J. (1982), 'Therapeutic metaphor: an approach to weight control' (*Personnel and Guidance J.*, vol. 60, pp. 510-12).
CADE, B. W. (1982), 'Some uses of metaphor' (*Australian J. of Family Therapy*, vol. 3, pp. 135-40).
FELLNER, C. (1976), 'The use of teaching stories in conjoint family therapy' (*Family Process*, vol. 15, pp. 427-33).
TESELLE, S. (1975), *Speaking in Parables: A Study in Metaphor and Theology* (SCM Press, London).

See also *Mutual story telling technique, Metaphor, Myth, Symbolism.*

Paradox
Bateson, Watzlawick and other workers at the Mental Research Institute, Palo Alto, California, have been instrumental in developing the use of paradox in psychotherapy. Paradox is defined by Watzlawick *et al.* (1968) as 'a logical contradiction following consistent deductions from correct premises'. They go on to distinguish three types of paradox:

(a) Logico-mathematical paradoxes: according to the *theory of types*, whatever forms a collection cannot at the same time be a member of that collection (e.g. the term 'flowers' cannot itself be described as a flower in the way that a dandelion is a flower).

(b) Paradoxical definitions: definitions that are inherently paradoxical because of their language, such as Epimedes the Cretan's famous statement, 'all Cretans are liars'. In order to avoid such a paradoxical definition, language must be viewed as having both a detonative (or informational) level and a *metacommunicative* level, allowing comments on the informational level to be made from a *meta* position.

(c) Pragmatic paradoxes: the giving of an injunction or a prediction by someone who is in a position of power superior to the other, where the injunction can only be obeyed through disobeying it and where it is impossible for the inferior to step outside the superior's frame of reference. A classical example of a paradoxical injunction is the instruction to 'be spontaneous': to comply with the injunction, the recipient will have to do so within a frame of non-compliance, since one cannot, by definition, be spontaneous to order.

Pragmatic paradoxes that operate within interpersonal relationships were shown by Bateson *et al.* (1956) to create a *double bind* for the inferior member of the relationship. They can however, also be used effectively in treatment and a considerable amount of work has been done in developing paradox as a therapeutic technique, especially by *strategic therapists*.

Therapeutic double binds, symptom prescription, the *Devil's pact* and *reframing* are examples, together with a range of other paradoxical interventions, described by Watzlawick (1978) as 'blocking the left hemisphere', i.e. the rational and logical area of the brain. Other types of paradoxical intervention used therapeutically include confusion techniques which take the problem out of the frame of reference prescribed by the patient by confusing him, a technique used particularly creatively by Erikson (see Haley 1973); the creation of an illusion of alternatives, where the patient is forced to choose between two courses of action, as though no other choice is possible (for example, between 'having another appointment here tomorrow or at home next week'); rehearsing a relapse, i.e. predicting a relapse into symptomatic behaviour after change has been achieved, as a means of *preventing* it; and displacing a symptom temporarily on to something less handicapping (see *Symptom substitution*).

Rohrbaugh *et al.* (1977) have divided paradoxical interventions into three types: prescribing strategies, restraining strategies, and positioning, in which the therapist takes up a position which is designed to counter the patient's view, by the therapist's acceptance of it (for example, *pessimism*). Weeks and L'Abate (1979) offer a classification of techniques of paradox as follows: individual vs. systemic; prescriptive vs. descriptive; direct insight vs. indirect insight; direct vs. cryptic; time-bound vs. time-random; reframing vs. relabelling; and specific vs. general. Haley (1976) outlines eight stages in undertaking a paradoxical intervention: patient-therapist relationship is defined as attempting to bring about change; a clearly defined problem has been elucidated; clearly defined goals established; the therapist offers a plan and a rationale; the therapist gently disqualifies other authorities on the problem, for example, a spouse or a parent; the therapist observes the response of the patient and continues to encourage the usual behaviour (i.e. he reinforces 'no change'); the therapist avoids taking credit for any change that occurs. Omer (1981) reviews three theories of paradoxical treatment: Frankl's *paradoxical intention*; the behavioural technique of *counter conditioning*; and Haley's concept of the therapeutic double bind.

Paradox can be as powerful therapeutically in bringing about change as it is pathologically in causing *dysfunction*. If the patient's motivation for change is high, however, the use of paradoxical interventions is usually unnecessary and should be avoided. Their potency resides in enabling the therapist to unblock extremely complex, interpersonal situations that have hitherto proved to be resistant to all therapeutic efforts.

BATESON, G. *et al.* (1956), 'Toward a theory of schizophrenia' (*Behavioral Science*, vol. 1, pp. 251-64).

HALEY, J. (1963), *Strategies of Psychotherapy* (Grune & Stratton, New York).

HALEY, J. (1973), *Uncommon Therapy* (W. W. Norton, New York).

HALEY, J. (1976), *Problem Solving Therapy* (Jossey-Bass, San Francisco).

L'ABATE, L. and WEEKS, G. R. (1978), 'A bibliography of paradoxical methods in the psychotherapy of family systems' (*Family Process*, vol. 17, pp. 95-8).

OMER, H. (1981), 'Paradoxical treatments: a unified concept' (*Psychotherapy: Theory, Research and Practice*, vol. 18, pp. 320-4).

ROHRBAUGH, M. *et al.* (1977), 'Paradoxical strategies in psychotherapy' (unpublished manuscript, quoted in Stanton, below).

STANTON, M. D. (1981), 'Strategic approaches to family therapy' (in Gurman, A. S. and Kniskern, D. P., *Handbook of Family Therapy*, Brunner/Mazel, New York).

WATZLAWICK, P. (1978), *The Languages of Change* (W. W. Norton, New York).

WATZLAWICK, P., BEAVEN, J. H. and JACKSON, D. D. (1968), *Pragmatics of Human Communication* (W. W. Norton, New York).

WATZLAWICK, P. *et al.* (1974), *Change: Principles of Problem Formation and Problem Resolution* (W. W. Norton, New York).

WEEKS, G. R. and L'ABATE, L. (1979), 'A compilation of paradoxical methods' (*Am. J. of Family Therapy*, vol. 7, pp. 61-76).

WEEKS, G. R. and L'ABATE, L. (1982), *Paradoxical Psychotherapy* (Brunner/Mazel, New York).

WITTGENSTEIN, L. (1956), *Remarks on the Foundations of Mathematics* (Blackwell, Oxford).

Paradoxical injunction

See *Paradox*.

Paradoxical intention

A technique introduced by Frankl (1969) whereby 'the patient is encouraged to do, or wish to happen, the very things he fears'. The technique is based on an understanding of the effects of anticipatory anxiety and the power of the *self-fulfilling prophecy*. As with *negative practice*, *implosion* and *flooding*, the aim of paradoxical intention is to reverse the patient's instinctive avoidance of the feared event or object and break the vicious circle by which the anticipatory anxiety itself produces *symptoms*. As in the case of *symptom prescription*, the patient is frequently instructed to do deliberately what he believes to be occurring involuntarily.

FRANKL, V. E. (1969), *The Will to Meaning* (New American Library, New York).

See also *Paradox*.

Paranoid-schizoid position

A term introduced by Melanie Klein to describe a normal developmental process occurring during the first three or four months of life. It is, to quote Hannah Segal (1973), 'the earliest phase of development. It is characterised by the relation to part *objects*, by *splitting* in the *ego* and the object and paranoid anxieties.' Initially the ego perceives only part objects – the mother's breasts, hands, etc. The infantile ego is very precarious and easily overwhelmed by feelings of persecution and fears of *annihilation*. In an attempt to get rid of these feelings and preserve a sense of well-being, they are split off, disowned and *projected* outside. But then the sense of persecution is felt to come from outside, i.e. from the object such as the breast, into which the baby's angry feelings have been projected. Thus, objects in the outside world are experienced as being themselves bad and persecutory. To the hungry baby, the absent feeding breast/ mother is experienced as a bad present object, rather than as a good absent one. The experiences are sharply split between idealised, good on the one hand, and persecutory, bad on the other. In this position, the two aspects cannot be held in mind together. Things tend to be experienced as all good or all bad, not as a mixture of both, as if to try and keep the feelings of *idealisation* uncontaminated, while retaining control over both good and bad feelings.

The transition from paranoid-schizoid position to *depressive position*, normally proceeding later during the first year of life, depends very much on the baby's experience of external objects, especially the mother and

her capacity to help modify the baby's feelings of excessive persecution and anxiety arising from within it. As Segal (1973) points out, 'the fantasy of the ideal object merges with and is confirmed by gratifying and feeding experiences from the real, external mother, while the fantasy of persecution similarly merges with real experiences of deprivation and pain which are attributed by the infant to the persecutory object'.

Klein (1946) thought schizophrenic disorders were rooted in the paranoid-schizoid position. In those patients an excess of aggression (perhaps constitutional) results in excessive splitting of objects and of the self, with a mounting anxiety associated with the fear of fragmentation or annihilation.

KLEIN, M. (1946), *The Writings of Melanie Klein*, vol. 3 (Hogarth Press, London).
KLEIN, M. (1952), 'Notes on some schizoid mechanisms' (in Rivière, J. (ed.), *Developments in Psychoanalysis*, Hogarth Press, London).
KLEIN, M. (1952), 'Some theoretical conclusions regarding the emotional life of the infant' (in Rivière, J. (ed.), *Developments in Psychoanalysis*, Hogarth Press, London).
SEGAL, H. (1973), *Introduction to the Work of Melanie Klein* (Hogarth Press, London).

See also *Good enough mother, Kleinian school, Position (paranoid-schizoid and depressive)*.

Parapraxis

A slip of the tongue or of the pen, momentary amnesia regarding names and other errors which, according to Freud (1901), demonstrate the intrusion of *unconscious* mental processes into the *conscious* world of the normal individual. Freud suggested that *censorship* operates in some of these situations to repress material which is unacceptable to the *ego* and thus brings about the 'mistake'.

FREUD, S. (1901), 'The psychopathology of everyday life' (*Standard Edition*, vol. 6, Hogarth Press, London).

Paraprofessional

A person who is untrained in the mental health

disciplines and without formal training in counselling or psychotherapy and yet who gives therapeutic help to others. Other terms such as functional professional, non-professional, volunteer or lay professional are also used. Three sub-groups can be distinguished: first, all those who provide informal help to others in their day-to-day life – e.g. friends, work colleagues, housewives, shopkeepers; second, those whose work involves a psychotherapeutic element over and above their main professional involvement with others – e.g. lawyers, teachers, priests, GPs; third, helpers who are organised to help others in a voluntary capacity, under the guidance of a professional therapist – e.g. Samaritans, good neighbour services, ancillary workers attached to professional departments, etc.

During the 1960s and 1970s, with the enormous increase in the use of paraprofessionals, there was a surge of interest in the comparative effectiveness of professionals and non-professionals. Durlak (1971) reviewed the thirteen studies published and concluded that in no case was the work of the paraprofessional found to be inferior, and in six of the studies the paraprofessionals achieved superior therapeutic results to the professional psychotherapists. This corroborated the work of Gurin *et al.* (1960) who, in a nationwide American survey, found that paraprofessionals were more frequently consulted by those needing help and gave more satisfaction to the help seeker than the professional therapist. Such findings have been replicated across a wide range of client settings and they call into question the validity of the *spontaneous remission* factor in therapy and also the need for prolonged training and academic qualifications for therapists. However, as Gurman and Razin (1977) point out, there are often differences in patient populations, treatment *goals* and *outcome* criteria between the practices of paraprofessionals and accredited professional therapists which must be borne in mind when outcome results are being compared. As a comparison, the use of volunteers ancillary to social work, the only major mental health discipline to make routine use of paraprofes-

sionals, has been studied in Britain by the Aves Committee (1969) and by Holme and Maizels (1978). Few, however, were engaged in psychotherapeutic activities.

ANTHONY, W. A. and CARKHUFF, R. R. (1977), 'The functional professional therapeutic agent' (in Gurman, A. S. and Razin, A. M., *Effective Psychotherapy*, Pergamon Press, New York).
AVES COMMITTEE (1969), *The Voluntary Worker in the Social Services* (Allen & Unwin, London).
CARKHUFF, R. R. (1968), 'The differential functioning of lay professional helpers' (*J. of Counseling Psychology*, vol. 15, pp. 117-26).
DURLAK, J. A. (1971), 'The use of non-professionals as therapeutic agents' (abstracted in *Dissertation Abstracts International*, vol. 32B. pp. 2999-3000).
GURIN, G. *et al.* (1960), *Americans View Their Mental Health* (Basic Books, New York).
GURMAN, A. S. and RAZIN, A. M. (1977), 'Editors' footnote 8 to Chapter 6, The functional professional therapeutic agent' (in Gurman, A. S. and Razin, A. M., *Effective Psychotherapy*, Pergamon Press, New York).
HOLME, A. and MAIZELS, J. (1978), *Social Workers and Volunteers* (British Association of Social Workers/Allen & Unwin, London).

See also *Regulation (of psychotherapists), Self-help.*

Parapsychology

The study of all those psychological phenomena which are beyond the normal and which cannot therefore be explained in terms of natural scientific laws and principles. Included are the experiences of clairvoyance, telepathy, psychokinesis, extrasensory perception, déjà vu, dowsing and thought control. Having for years been considered outside the realm of proper psychological interest, parapsychology has recently gained in respectability and is the subject of a considerable amount of scientific interest.

BELOFF, J. (ed.) (1974), *New Directions in Parapsychology* (Paul Elek, London).

WHITE, R. (ed.) (1976), *Surveys in Parapsychology* (Scarecrow Press, Metuchen, New Jersey).

WOLMAN, B. B. (ed.) (1977), *Handbook of Parapsychology* (Van Nostrand Reinhold, New York).

See also *Synchronicity, Transpersonal psychology.*

Parataxic

See *Referential processes.*

Parental child

Term used in *structural family therapy* to describe a child who takes on a role in the *executive sub-system*. In the single-parent family, the formation of an executive sub-system through an *alliance* between the single parent and parental child may be *functional* for the whole family. In a two-parent family, a diffuse *boundary* around the parental sub-system may encourage an alliance between one parent and a parental child to the exclusion of the other parent and to the detriment of the family structure.

MINUCHIN, S. (1974), *Families and Family Therapy* (Tavistock, London).

Parenting skills training

Preventative programmes designed to develop and enhance parental competence in caring for and bringing up their children. Training for parenthood has only recently developed as a separate provision and at present programmes are more commonly found in the United States than in Britain. American approaches emphasise group training through the medium of 'schools for parents' for which a variety of handbooks and manuals have been prepared. Rutter *et al.* (1983) have summarised the skills required for effective functioning within the parental role. These include skills in communication, coping with stress and shaping behaviour; the development of consistent and reliable attitudes and behaviour; the acquisition of knowledge to practise the behaviour and attitudes; and 'permitting circumstances' such as adequate housing and other facilities that are conducive

to the execution of those skills, attitudes and knowledge.

Lewis *et al.* (1976), in an American study, concluded that although there was no one 'right' way of parenting, several variables seemed important: leadership provided by a clear parental coalition; power that is not exercised in an authoritarian manner, but with negotiation with children occurring; and communication that is clear, with individual differences accepted and high levels of personal autonomy and responsibility emphasised. De'Ath (1983) summarises three approaches to the teaching of parenting skills. First, a functional approach, whereby *problem solving interventions* are adopted for a particular family with an emphasis on *behaviour modification* and *social skills* development offered by professional workers to help parents learn how to modify their children's behaviour. This approach is usually offered within a *family therapy* context. Second, a therapeutic approach, whereby a counsellor or befriender seeks to build a nurturing relationship with the parent in order to help him or her introject this model and use it in relation to their children. The aim is to support and develop the parent's own sense of competency within his or her home (Van der Eyken 1982). Third, an educational approach, whereby preparation for parenthood is offered through schools to older children and within the community by such agencies as the Pre-School Playgroup Movement and the Open University, both in Britain.

ABIN, R. R. (1976), *Parenting Skills – Workbook and Training Manual* (Human Sciences Press, New York).

DE'ATH, E. (1983), 'Teaching parenting skills' (*J. of Family Therapy*, vol. 5, pp. 321-35).

GORDON, T. (1970), *Parent Effectiveness Training (PET)* (Peter H. Wyden, New York).

LEWIS, J. et al. (1976), *No Single Thread* (Brunner/Mazel, New York).

RUTTER, M et al. (1983), 'Parenting in two generations' (in Madge, N. (ed.), *Families at Risk*, Heinemann Educational, London).

VAN DER EYKEN, W. (1982), *Home Start – A*

Four Year Evaluation (Home Start Consultancy, Leicester).
WOLFSON, J. (1982), 'Tools for teaching parenting skills' (in Pugh, G., *Can Parenting Skills Be Taught?*, National Children's Bureau, London).

Part object
See *Object*.

Participant-observer
The simultaneous or oscillating experience of observing a phenomenon, participating in its being and observing that participation. The term is contrasted with non-participant observation, in which the therapist or researcher views events from the outside. Traditionally, non-participant observation has been regarded as more objective and as yielding more valid data from which to arrive at a *diagnosis* or to conduct treatment. The concept of participant observation has been stressed, however, in *humanistic psychology* and in the *existential psychotherapies*. The reflexive nature of the therapist's role is a key feature, yielding a special, and no less valid form of data. It leads to the development of therapeutic qualities such as *genuineness* and *congruence*. The ability to experience and convey *empathy*, for example, ultimately rests on the ability to be both a participant and an observer. Participant observation is most clearly demonstrated in some of the existential therapies and in, for example, *experiential family therapy*. Therapist *self-disclosure* and *transparency* are other manifestations of a participant observer position.

The concept is in opposition to the dualistic *Cartesian* split between opposites. For this reason, it does not figure in classical *psychoanalysis* although current statements about psychoanalytic technique suggest a developing use of *empathy*, a closing of the gap between participant-patient and observer-analyst with a greater emphasis on the involvement of the analyst as a real person. Likewise, behavioural therapies usually view the therapist as a non-participant observer but more recent interest in the therapist/patient relationship indicates a change in emphasis. The concept of partici-pant observation rests on the ability to separate and to integrate the experience of being subject and object, described by Winnicott (1962) in terms of early infancy as the baby's ability to relate to 'subjective objects'. The ability to become a particpant observer can be learned and when observation is of the self, it is a key element in the development of *insight*. Experiences gained in therapeutic *training* and in *T-group training*, *psychodrama* and other group work methods can increase the ability to act as a participant observer.

WINNICOTT, D. W. (1962), 'Ego integration in child development' (in *The Maturational Process and the Facilitating Environment*, Hogarth Press, London).

Pathogenesis
Literally from 'pathogen', an agent causing disease. A term used by Vandenbos and Karon (1971) to describe the way in which a therapist can act as a harmful agent to the patient. They suggest that this occurs when the therapist makes use (either consciously or unconsciously) of the patient's dependency to satisfy his own personal needs for power, sexual contact, etc., at the expense of the patient. Vandenbos and Karon assessed therapist pathogenesis by means of the *Thematic Apperception Test* and found that patients of benign therapists were functioning at higher levels after six months' treatment compared with patients of pathogenic therapists. Pathogenic therapists were thus found to be less clinically effective than benign ones.

VANDENBOS, G. E. and KARON, B. P. (1971), 'Pathogenesis – a new therapist personality dimension related to therapeutic effectiveness' (*J. of Personality Assessment*, vol. 35, pp. 252-60).
KARON, B. P. and VANDENBOS, G. R. (1972), 'The consequences of psychotherapy for schizophrenic patients' (*Psychotherapy: Theory, Practice and Research*, vol. 9, pp. 111-19).

See also *Deterioration*, *Iatrogenic*, *Malpractice*, *Psychonoxious*.

Patient position

A term used by *strategic therapists* and those using *focused problem resolution* to describe the world seen through the help seeker's eyes, including his reality, his value system and his *goals*, however absurd or distasteful they may appear to be to the therapist. The therapist starts from the patient's view or position on his problem and the way in which he feels it should be handled. Therapists from other schools usually do the same, though they may not use the same term. The purpose is to maximise the patient's compliance with the therapy by couching explanations, *interpretations* or suggestions for action in a language and belief system acceptable to the patient. *Resistance* is thus circumvented instead of being confronted head-on.

FISCH, R. *et al.* (1982), *Tactics of Change: Doing Therapy Briefly* (Jossey-Bass, San Francisco).

Pavlov, Ivan Petrovich (1849-1936)

Pavlov was born in Ryazan, Russia, in 1849. He entered the University of St Petersburg in 1870 and graduated in natural sciences in 1875. He then began his medical studies at the Military Academy, gaining his MD in 1883. After spending a few years studying under Carl Ludwig in Leipzig, Pavlov returned to Russia and took up his post as professor of pharmacology at the Military Medical Academy in 1890, later becoming professor of physiology. Pavlov's professional life was devoted to understanding the process of *conditioning* which, he believed, underlies the way in which animals and human beings learn. His seminal work in this field provided the foundation for later work on *learning theory*. His early observations of the way in which dogs begin to salivate when stimuli associated with feeding are provided had first prompted his interest in learning and conditioning. By 1901 he had named the reflexive *response* to a *stimulus* the *conditioned* reflex, and he spent the rest of his life refining and developing these ideas. In 1904 he received the Nobel Prize for his work on the physiology of digestion.

Peak experiences

A term employed by Abraham Maslow to describe the high points in an individual's experience of life. They occur through aesthetic appreciation, a sense of unity with others and experiences of love. Maslow felt that peak experiences help to shape a person's identity.

MASLOW, A. H. (1976), *The Farther Reaches of Human Nature* (Penguin, Harmondsworth).

Penis envy

Term introduced by Freud to describe the female response to her lack of male genitals. Freud inherited the generally held beliefs of his time in asserting that 'anatomy is destiny' and that a woman's lack of a penis rendered her inferior physiologically, psychologically and socially. Because of the way in which the *Oedipus complex* is resolved, her psychological inferiority derives from the less mature *super-ego* which results. Socially, she is inferior because of her minor contribution to cultural and community life. Penis envy leaves women more disposed towards jealousy and shame than men. Its resolution occurs when the little girl's wish for a penis becomes both a wish for a baby and subsequently a wish to receive a penis into herself during sexual intercourse.

From the beginning, Freud was highly criticised for these assertions by Jung (who suggested different but complementary psychologies of men and women); by Adler (who suggested the superior psychology of women); by Suttie (who pointed out the comparable jealousy experienced by fathers at the possession of the infant by the mother); by Horney and other female psychoanalysts, who suggested that women's envy of men arose from their disadvantaged relationship and not from penis envy. Freud has been particularly criticised outside psychoanalytic circles for the determinism of the concept of penis envy, and especially by *radical* and *feminist therapists*. Horney suggests that an equally plausible concept is men's envy of women's biological creativity, leading them both to overcompensate in other areas of life and to depreciate women out of envy and fear.

FREUD, S. (1931), 'Female sexuality'
(*Standard Edition*, vol. 21, Hogarth Press,
London).
HORNEY, K. (1939), *New Ways in
Psychoanalysis* (W. W. Norton, New York).
HORNEY, K. (1967), *Feminine Psychology*
(W. W. Norton, New York).
SAYERS, J. (1982), *Biological Politics: Feminist
and Anti-feminist Perspectives* (Tavistock,
London).
SUTTIE, I. (1935), *The Origins of Love and Hate*
(Penguin, Harmondsworth).

See also *Female sexuality*.

Perls, Fritz (1893-1970)

Fritz Perls was born in Berlin where he
studied medicine at the University of Berlin.
He continued his studies at the Berlin and
Vienna Institutes of Psychoanalysis and was
analysed by Wilhelm Reich. After receiving his
MD, Perls went to Frankfurt in 1926 to assist
Kurt Goldstein at his Institute for Brain
Damaged Soldiers. Here, as well as being
exposed to Goldstein's ideas, Perls met his
future wife Laura, who received her DSc from
Frankfurt University in 1932. She became
extremely influential in the future development of *Gestalt therapy*. Other important
influences on Perls during this period were the
Gestalt psychologists Koffka and Kohler. In
1934, during the rise of Nazism in Germany,
Perls left for South Africa, where he established his own analytic practice and founded
the South African Institute of Psychoanalysis.
During the next ten years, however, he began
developing a variety of revisions to classical
psychoanalytic theory. By 1947, when his first
book was published, it was clear that a new
system of psychotherapy was emerging from
Perls's thought. With the rise of apartheid in
South Africa, Perls left in 1946 for the United
States and, together with his wife Laura, he
founded the New York Institute for Gestalt
Therapy. The term Gestalt therapy was first
used as the title of a book published by Perls
and co-authored by Ralph Hefferline and Paul

Goodman in 1951. During the 1950s, the New
York Institute was the centre of Perls's work.
From here he practised, taught and wrote, and
a wide variety of seminars and teaching workshops were mounted. Gestalt therapy training
was developed and intensive workshops
offered in other parts of the United States. In
1955 a second institute was founded at
Cleveland. In 1960 Perls moved to the west
coast and much of his later work was conducted from the Esalen Institute, California,
until his death in 1970.

Persona

The Latin word for 'mask', used by Jung
(1968), to describe 'a complicated system of
relations between individual consciousness
and society, fittingly enough a kind of mask,
designed on the one hand to make a definite
impression upon others, and, on the other, to
conceal the true nature of the individual'. A
persona is necessary for consistent interaction
with other people, but too great an identification with the persona may obliterate the real
person within. The persona can help keep the
shadow in check by means of the consciously
held values with which it may be associated.

JUNG, C. G. (1953) 'Two essays on analytical
psychology' (*Collected Works*, vol. 7, Routledge
& Kegan Paul, London).

Personal construct theory/therapy

A psychological theory developed by Kelly
(1955, 1963) which describes a theory of
personality and a method of psychotherapy. In
developing his theory, Kelly (1963) sought to
avoid some of the dilemmas he found in other
psychological theories. His hope for personal
construct theory was that it could be 'a
dynamic psychology without the trappings of
animism, a perceptual psychology without
passivity, a behaviourism in which the behaving person is credited with having some sense,
a learning theory in which learning is considered so universal that it appears in the
postulate . . . and a view of personality which
permits psychotherapy to appear both lawful
and plausible'.

The theory is worked out with great care and in a step-by-step logical progression. It is built upon a *fundamental postulate* and eleven supporting *corollaries* which set out the basic framework of the theory. The underlying assumption is described as *constructive altern-ativism*, which seeks to assert an optimistic view of a person's ability to control rather than be controlled by circumstances. This emphasis, derived from Kelly's early exper-iences of working with unemployed and underprivileged groups in rural Kansas during the American depression of the 1930s, prompted him to formulate a theory which would enable the individual to maximise his choices even in the most unpromising situations.

Kelly suggested that the individual developed bipolar *constructs* by which he made sense of the events and people he encoun-tered. The events and people became the *elements* which are construed or interpreted by the constructs. Constructs have a variety of properties or formal aspects and these can be more or less helpful to the individual in his task of predicting and therefore controlling events. The task of the psychotherapist is to increase the individual's *cognitive complexity* by increas-ing the permeability of his construct system without endangering its structure. A particular contribution made to psychotherapeutic technique is Kelly's *fixed role therapy*, and his *repertory grid* technique gave a new assessment tool to clinicians and researchers.

Kelly's theories have been less influential than many of his contemporaries', although he has a considerable following among psycho-logists both in Britain and America. Although a theory of individual personality functioning and therapy, personal construct theory has also been applied to work with families and groups.

BANNISTER, D. and FRANSELLA, F. (1971), *Inquiring Man* (Penguin, Harmondsworth).
BANNISTER, D. (ed.) (1970), *Perspectives in Personal Construct Theory* (Academic Press, London).
BANNISTER, D. (ed.) (1977), *New Perspectives in Personal Construct Theory* (Academic Press,

252

London).
BANNISTER, D. and MAIER, J. M. M. (1968), *Evaluation of Personal Constructs* (Academic Press, London).
KELLY, G. A. (1955), *The Psychology of Personal Constructs* (W. W. Norton, New York).
KELLY, G. A. (1963), *A Theory of Personality* (W. W. Norton, New York).
MANCUSO, J. C. and ADAMS-WEBBER, J. R. (eds) (1982), *The Construing Person* (Praeger, New York).
PROCTER, H. (1981), 'Family construct psychology: an approach to understanding and treating families' (in Walrond-Skinner, S. (ed.), *Developments in Family Therapy*, Routledge & Kegan Paul, London).

Personal Orientation Inventory (POI)

A self-report instrument for measuring *self-actualisation* developed by Shostrom (1963) in collaboration with Abraham Maslow. The POI consists of 150 paired choice items such as 'I am afraid to be myself – I am not afraid to be myself'. The client chooses the one from each pair which best describes him or her. The POI provides the therapist with measures of the client's inner-directedness and the degrees to which he or she lives in the present. The POI is used primarily by *humanistic psychologists* and *client-centred therapists* to evaluate *outcome*.

SHOSTROM, E. L. (1963), *Personal Orientation Inventory* (San Diego).
SHOSTROM, E. L. (1963), *Manual for the Personal Orientation Inventory* (Edits, San Diego).

Personal unconscious
See *Unconscious*.

Personality assessment
See *Diagnosis* and *Personality tests*.

Personality tests
The wide range of personality tests available to clinicians reflects the differing current theories of personality structure, dynamics and development. In addition to radically different views of the person, therapists have

other disagreements which are reflected in their approach to personality testing. Probably the major disagreement is crystallised in the 'clinical' versus 'statistical' argument. The related argument separates proponents of 'subjective' tests from proponents of 'objective' tests. In essence, proponents of objective tests often view personality as an ultimately measurable entity with a different number of traits or dimensions which make it possible to make predictions about a person fairly accurately and scientifically. Such tests are often standardised on a large representative sample of the population with the use of, at times, complex statistical methods. They are often criticised as being less valid and reliable than is claimed, and criticised too for tapping rather superficial aspects of the personality and therefore yielding information which is clinically barren.

Proponents of subjective tests are usually more interested in the dynamic forces in a person's life, particularly in the early years, which have helped to mould him. This 'depth' approach is considered by its proponents to provide a more vital and more clinically rich view of the person with his hopes, fears and unconscious conflicts. Critics of such tests comment on their lack of validity and reliability and the part played by the interference of the subjective judgment of the clinician (see *Experimenter effect*).

The majority of personality tests fall into two major categories: projective tests and rating tests. As a generalisation, projective tests are often deemed to be 'subjective' and rating tests 'objective', though such a distinction into subjectivity and objectivity is a relative matter since, in essence, even so-called objective tests, despite being scored objectively, still rely on the subjective judgment of the test compiler to determine which items to include and how such items should be worded. Projective tests, including the *Rorschach* and the *Thematic Apperception Test*, are based on the notion that a person, in response to a stimulus which is often ill-defined, will 'project' or 'read himself into' the given framework, thereby revealing his values, fears, conflicts,

mode of functioning, view of the world and his relationships within it. Typically, the subject may be required to respond to a picture or word or to complete an incomplete sentence, and his responses will be interpreted at length and in depth by a skilled clinician.

Rating tests can be either self-rating or ratings done by others, the former being more popular. Typically, the subject has to reply to a questionnaire or series of items with a 'true' or 'false' response. An analysis of a person's responses is usually fairly short, sometimes mechanised, to give a profile of a person on certain psychological 'traits' or 'dimensions'. Such tests include the *Minnesota Multiphasic Personality Inventory*, the *Sixteen Personality Factor Questionnaire* and the *Maudsley Personality Inventory*.

In recent years, tests have been developed which tap the subject's own personal concepts and his construction of the world rather than the concepts and constructs of the test compiler or interpreter. Such a test is Kelly's *Repertory Grid* test. Tests of group, family and marital functioning have also been developed for use in the therapeutic evaluation of group and systems work.

Whatever psychological tests are used, it is important to validate them against other information, for instance, developmental history, observed behaviour, situational performance or other psychological tests in order to have as full and valid a picture as possible.

PERVIN, L. A. (1980), *Personality: Theory, Assessment and Research* (Wiley, London).
RABIN, A. I. (ed.) (1981), *Assessment with Projective Techniques* (Springer, New York).

Pessimism
A position taken by the therapist in relation to the patient which conveys a more gloomy attitude to his problems or progress than the patient himself holds. Used as a paradoxical technique by *strategic therapists*, it relies upon mobilising the patient's non-compliance. Its purpose is to encourage the patient to move towards a contrasting optimistic view and to motivate him towards change.

PETS (THERAPEUTIC USE OF)

See also *Ego alien, Enantiodromia, Paradox, Self-fulfilling prophecy.*

Pets (therapeutic use of)

The use of animals in the *diagnosis* and treatment of psychological dysfunction. Corson and Corson (1979) used the term pet-facilitated psychotherapy to emphasise that the use of animals is an additional tool to be used in conjunction with other forms of psychotherapy. They describe the use of animals as 'an effective instrument for developing meaningful non-verbal and verbal communication and re-socialization and as an adjunct and stepping stone to other forms of therapy and to reasonably independent functioning'. Corson and Corson have experimented with dogs in helping the aged and institutionalised to develop greater social abilities as a preliminary to helping them to relate more fully to human beings. Mugford and M'Comisky (1975) have also used dogs and caged birds with the elderly, the housebound and institutionalised individuals. Byng-Hall (1982) describes several ways in which the inclusion of pets in *family therapy* sessions can provide valuable sources of information about the family and symbolic means by which family members can represent both their problems and their potential solutions. Sherick (1981), in a discussion of the analysis of a nine-year-old girl, suggests that the child's intense involvement with a variety of pets served as both a *resistance* and as a means of *communication*. Brickel (1982) offers some theoretical explanation for the effectiveness of pet facilitation therapy on the grounds of the competing response theory of *extinction*, via attention shifts. Pets are viewed as emotionally distracting stimuli that allow exposure to anxiety-generating stimuli, enabling extinction to occur. Mackler (1982) argues that dysfunctional families often present with unmanageable pets – the pet's well-being is however allowed to overide all other concerns. He suggests that conflict resolution and maximum family functioning may be achieved through the treatment of the pet alongside, or even instead of the treatment of the family (!).

BRICKEL, C. M. (1982), 'Pet facilitated psychotherapy: a theoretical exploration via attention shifts' (*Psychological Reports*, vol. 50, pp. 71-4).

BYNG-HALL, J. (1982), 'Grandparents, other relatives, friends and pets' (in Bentovim, A. *et al., Family Therapy: Complementary Frameworks of Theory and Practice*, Academic Press, London).

CORSON, S. A. and CORSON, E. O. (1979), 'Pets as mediators of therapy' (in Masserman, J. H. (ed.), *Current Psychiatric Therapies*, Grune & Stratton, New York).

MACKLER, J. L. (1982), 'Teaching an old dog new tricks' (*Family Therapy*, vol. 9, pp. 305-10).

MUGFORD, R. A. and M'COMISKY, J. G. (1975), 'Some recent work on the psycho-therapeutic value of cage birds with old people' (in Anderson, R. S. (ed.), *Pet Animals and Society*, Williams & Wilkins, Baltimore).

SHERICK, I. (1981), 'The significance of pets for children' (*Psychoan. Study of the Child*, vol. 36, pp. 193-215).

Phallic stage

The third developmental stage of human development in the life cycle occurring between about four and five years. The term phallus rather than penis is used to indicate its symbolic meaning and to denote the predominantly masturbatory rather than object-directed nature of the sexual urge. Freud (1923) described the stage originally to indicate the time when an 'interest in the genitals and in their activity acquires a dominating significance'. According to Freud, interest in the penis for both the boy and the girl becomes the centre of sexual attention. Just as in the *anal stage*, Freud noted a polarity between activity and passivity, so in the phallic stage he suggested that the two phantasies of the possession of a penis and its castration were opposed in the mind of the child. Many theorists, particularly female ones such as Klein and Horney, disagree with this polarity and suggest that the little girl's interest is focused on her vagina in a similar way to the boy's interest in his penis. For Freud and some later analysts, the pride in the possession and display of the penis (phallic narcissism) is a crucial model and precursor for a variety of forms of exhibitionism. The absence of a penis to display is thought by this group of analysts to pose crucial problems for female development, which is usually coped with by the little girl developing pleasure in the display of her whole body which is manifested in dancing, horse riding and the love of display through clothes, jewellery, make-up, etc. The culture-bound nature of these views is clear, but see Mitchell (1974) for a sympathetic feminist critique.

The importance of the phallic stage lies in its correspondence with the *Oedipus complex*, the resolution of which prepared the way for the *genital stage* which is experienced fully in adolescence. In his analysis of the eight developmental stages, Erikson (1950) suggests that the phallic stage is characterised by the development of initiative and role experimentation. If this stage is not accomplished satisfactorily, the child experiences guilt and role *fixation* or inhibition. He views the establishment of conscience as the societal concomitant of the phallic stage and in this he follows Freud who suggested that the development of individual conscience was a result of Oedipal resolution.

ERIKSON, E. H. (1950), *Childhood and Society* (Penguin, Harmondsworth).
FREUD, S. (1923), 'The infantile genital organisation' (*Standard Edition*, vol. 19, Hogarth Press, London).
MITCHELL, J. (1974), *Psychoanalysis and Feminism* (Penguin, Harmondsworth).

See also *Stages of development.*

Phantasy

An imagined scene or event, described by Freud as emanating from either the *conscious, preconscious* or *unconscious* parts of the *psyche*. According to Freud, phantasies arise out of unfulfilled wishes and they are efforts on the part of the individual to bring about their fulfillment. The mental picture evoked may be purely a product of the imagination or it may be rooted in a distorted memory from the past.

Unconscious phantasies are discernible in the *manifest content* of *dreams*, whilst phantasies that arise within consciousness take the form of reveries or daydreams. Melanie Klein reserved the term solely for phantasies arising from the unconscious (though from the unconscious *ego* as well as the *id*) and the *Kleinian school* of *psychoanalysis* distinguishes between the word spelt with a 'ph' meaning unconscious phantasy and the word spelt 'fantasy' meaning conscious daydreams, fictions or artistic and poetic licence. American writers and others, however, tend not to make this distinction.

Klein greatly extended Freud's discussion of the subject. She viewed phantasy as a universal phenomenon but its nature and the way in which it is related to external reality determines whether it becomes creative or pathological for each individual. Phantasy is the means by which the *internal world* is constructed and it is the basic process through which the mechanisms of *projection, introjection, incorporation* and *projective identification* operate. It also provides the material through which the *transference* relationship with the analyst is established. Isaacs (1952), Rivière (1955) and Segal (1963), writing from a Kleinian perspective, have contributed seminal papers on the subject by describing the analysis of the phantasy life of very young children and the way in which phantasy can be seen operating in the inner worlds of literary figures. Isaacs draws out the fundamental role of phantasy in all unconscious processes and in particular the relationship of phantasy to the individual's instincts or *drives*. 'Phantasy is . . . the mental corollary, the psychic representative, of instinct. There is no impulse, no instinctual urge or response which is not experienced as unconscious phantasy.' And she goes on to suggest that 'all impulses, all feelings, all modes of defence are experienced in phantasies which give them mental life and show their direction and purpose'. As Segal (1979) points out, 'phantasy is not considered by Klein and Isaacs as a pure id phenomenon, but as an elaboration by the ego of impulses, defences and object relationships.'

In *stranger groups* or natural systems such as families and marital pairs, phantasies may be shared between the individuals in the group. Bannister and Pincus (1965) have described the process in marital pairs, and Bion (1961) in the stranger group situation.

BANNISTER, K. and PINCUS, L. (1965), *Shared Phantasy in Marital Problems* (Institute of Marital Studies, London).
BION, W. R. (1961), *Experiences in Groups* (Tavistock, London).
FREUD, S. (1900), 'The interpretation of dreams' (*Standard Edition*, vols 4 and 5, Hogarth Press, London).
ISAACS, S. (1952)·, 'The nature and function of phantasy' (in Klein, M. *et al.*, *Developments in Psychoanalysis*, Hogarth Press, London).
KLEIN, M. (1958), 'On the development of mental functioning' (*Int. J. of Psychoanalysis*, vol. 39, p. 136).
RIVIÈRE, J. (1955), 'The unconscious phantasy of an inner world reflected in examples from literature' (in Klein, M. *et al.* (ed.), *New Directions in Psychoanalysis* (Maresfield Reprints, Karnac, London).
SEGAL, H. (1963), 'Contributions to the symposium on phantasy' (*Int. J. of Psychoan.*, vol. 44).
SEGAL, H. (1979), *Klein* (Collins, London).

Phenomenology

The word may be used in a wide sense to refer to any descriptive study of a given subject, free from an attempt to provide theoretical explanations. It is also the name of a philosophical movement which began in Germany in the early twentieth century and whose leading member was Edmund Husserl.

Adequate description of the would-be science of phenomenology is still being developed. It is said to be descriptive of 'phenomena' as they appear to us in 'immediate experience'. But this raises the problem of what are phenomena? They are said by phenomenologists to be not empirically observable matters of fact, but 'essences', 'intuited' as a result of reflections upon arbitrarily chosen examples, considered with 'existence

bracketed' and are the subjects of statements about 'intentional' acts. All these features are elusive and their conception is therefore problematic. Further, phenomenology is said not to involve presuppositions. As Schmitt (1967) puts it, 'phenomenology does not need any true but unexamined premises; the truth of all its premises can be tested by examining the phenomena.' Provided a clear account of the nature of phenomena can be developed this can be achieved by the method mentioned above – that of 'bracketing existence' – that is, by suspending belief in the existence of objects, because of the presuppositions carried by the conceptual framework within which those objects are identified.

These philosophical ideas gave rise to phenomenological psychology which attempts the re-evaluation of perceived internal, external and interpersonal events. Thinkers such as Karl Jaspers, Aron Gurwitsch, Erwin Strauss, Eugene Minkowski and Ernest Schachtel all emphasise the living of experience in the here-and-now world of the present moment or 'lived time' as Minkowski describes it. Present-centred and holistic psychotherapeutic approaches have drawn on these ideas and *existential psychotherapy*, *Gestalt therapy* and *client-centred therapy* make considerable use of them.

GURWITSCH, A. (1931), *Human Encounters in the Social World* (Duquesne University Press, Pittsburgh).
GURWITSCH, A. (1957), *The Field of Consciousness* (Duquesne University Press, Pittsburgh).
HUSSERL, E. (1927), 'Phenomenology' (in *Encylopaedia Britannica*, trans. Solomon, C. V., 14th edn, vol. 17, pp. 699-702).
MINKOWSKI, E. (1933), *Lived Time* (Northwestern University, Evanston, Ill.).
SCHMITT, R. (1967), 'Phenomenology' (in Edwards, P., *Encyclopaedia of Philosophy*, vol. 6, Macmillan, London).
STRAUSS, E. (1966), *Phenomenological Psychology* (Basic Books, New York).

Phenotype

The observable characteristics and surface behaviours and interactions of an individual, family or group, which may be causally related both to *genotype* and to the environment. Phenotypic and genotypic classifications are both used in *diagnosis*. Phenotypic classifications stress what groups or individuals *do* ('here and now' material), whilst genotypic classifications stress what a group or individual *is* ('there and then' material).

See also *A-historical.*

Philosophical psychotherapy

A cognitive approach to psychotherapy introduced by Sahakian (1974, 1976) based on the belief that the curative effects of psychotherapy lie in helping to alter the patient's attitude to his problems, frustrations and life situation. The role of the therapist is to help the patient achieve a philosophical acceptance of whatever it is that he or she wishes to change or eliminate. Moreover, the therapist helps the patient to 'eliminate the tension created by the determination to gain mastery over the symptoms and the symptoms themselves . . . dissipate'. Philosophical psychotherapy has a considerable amount in common with ideas behind *reframing* and also some similarities with *rational emotive therapy* in its emphasis on changing the patient's belief system, and with other *cognitive restructuring approaches.*

SAHAKIAN, W. S. (1974), 'Philosophical psychotherapy' (*Psychologia*, vol. 17, pp. 179-85).
SAHAKIAN, W. S. (1976), *Psychotherapy and Counseling: Techniques in Intervention* (2nd edn, Rand McNally, Chicago).

Placebo

Literal Latin 'placere', meaning 'to please'. Shapiro and Morris (1978) have traced the history of the term and comment that its earliest definition in connection with therapy appeared in 1795 in Motherby's *New Medical Dictionary*. Here it was defined as 'a common-place method or medicine'. This original definition was erroneously transformed into 'a common-place method *of* medicine' and this subtle change brought about a concentration on medical procedures to the exclusion of other methods. As the use of drugs became more important in the practice of medicine, the term placebo became equated with and limited to the use of an inert substance which nevertheless brings about change in the patient. With the growth in non-pharmacological treatments and the developments of psychotherapy, the use of the term has reverted to its broad original meaning. Currently the term is used in research to describe any substance or procedure that does not affect the condition being evaluated in any specific way. In psychotherapy it can be defined as any therapy or component of therapy which produces non-specific effects unaccounted for by the active component of the therapy. It may take the form of an unfocused interview or asking the patient to report on his *symptoms* regularly. Although no active work is undertaken, these procedures may nevertheless effect change in the patient. The change is presumed to be brought about by *non-specific factors* such as hope, suggestion, expectancy, and/or some 'explanation' of the problem which reassures the patient. These beneficial effects are known as placebo effects. Placebos can, however, also have negative effects or no effect at all. Strupp (1973) points out that the placebo effect can either be deplored as an unwelcome hindrance in evaluating the effects of psychotherapy or be acknowledged as an impressive set of phenomena which, although not well understood, deserve acknowledgment in their own right. Fish (1973) has suggested ways of deriving maximum therapeutic effect from the placebo. McCardel and Murray (1974) showed that in group work, for a group given an attention placebo therapy was as effective as in groups where active interventions occurred. Shapiro and Morris (1978) have pointed out that increasing our understanding as to how the placebo operates will also serve to increase our understanding of the way in which the specific components of psychotherapy may be effective.

PLAY THERAPY

FISH, J. M. (1973), *Placebo Therapy* (Jossey-Bass, San Francisco).

FRANK, J. D. (1973), *Persuasion and Healing: A Comparative Study of Psychotherapy* (Johns Hopkins Press, Baltimore).

MCCARDEL, J. and MURRAY, E. J. (1974), 'Non-specific factors in weekend encounter groups' (*J. of Consulting and Clinical Psychology*, vol. 42, pp. 337-45).

SHAPIRO, A. K. and MORRIS, L. A. (1978), 'The placebo effect in medical and psychological therapies' (in Bergin, A. E. and Garfield, S. L. (eds), *Handbook of Psychotherapy and Behavior Change*, Wiley, New York).

STRUPP, H. H. (1973), 'On the basic ingredients of psychotherapy' (*J. of Consulting and Clinical Psychology*, vol. 41, pp. 1-8).

Play therapy

A technique introduced into *child analysis* and *child psychotherapy* by Hug-Hellmuth (1921). Play therapy is used in child psychotherapy for both *diagnosis* and treatment. It enables the child to use a natural medium to express his *phantasies* and emotions, communicate with the therapist, engage in *reality testing* and, with the help of the therapist, develop new understanding and resolution of psychic conflict.

Play therapy originated in the psychoanalytic treatment of children. Although it remains an important technique in psychoanalytic treatment, it is now used in a variety of other treatment approaches for children and their families. It was recognised early on as of importance to *psychoanalysis*, Karl Abraham commenting in 1924 that 'the future of psychoanalysis lies in play analysis' (quoted in Klein 1955). Both Anna Freud (1947) and Melanie Klein (1932) made use of play therapy within child analysis. Their use of it was somewhat different, however, and has led to two main approaches being taken to play therapy, as reflected in the *Kleinian* and *continental schools* of psychoanalysis respectively. Klein substituted free play for *free association* on the grounds that play, not words, is the natural medium through which the young child expresses himself. Anna Freud, whilst agreeing that play is indispensable in creating 'a real dependency on me' (Freud 1947) and thus forming a relationship with the therapist, felt that Klein's view of play, as equivalent to free association in the adult, was unjustifiable. Anna Freud's followers thus use play therapy to establish a positive relationship with the therapist, whilst in the Kleinian approach, play is the primary medium for diagnosis, *interpretation* and therapeutic change. Other play techniques were developed by Lowenfeld at the Institute of Child Psychology.

Winnicott (1968, 1971) has pointed out that play, which enables a therapeutic experience to take place, occurs when both patient and therapist are prepared to enter into the play as fully as possible; 'psychotherapy is done in the area of overlap between the playing of the patient and the playing of the therapist.' As well as creating an atmosphere of trust and confidence by entering into the play with the child and helping to form a positive relationship with him, the therapist's task includes providing suitable play material, setting limits regarding safety and physical aggression and helping the child to gain maximum benefit from the experience by expanding his understanding of his problems and helping him to find a way out of them. Separation anxiety, fears, destructive impulses, obsessive-compulsive behaviour and social isolation can all usefully be worked on through play therapy

Suitable play material usually includes dolls, puppets or other figures that can be used to express relationship difficulties; paper, clay, finger paints, crayons, etc., for drawing and modelling; and water and sand for free expression. Ideally, a playroom is made available, often fitted with a *one-way screen* so that the therapist can observe one or more children at play and/or can help parents to understand the meaning of their child's play. The therapist may also demonstrate to an observing parent how they might play more productively with their child. Each child's toys are, ideally, kept for him in a separate locked container. The use of play therapy in *family therapy* has been discussed by Keith and Whitaker (1981).

AXLINE, V. M. (1947), *Play Therapy: The Inner Dynamics of Childhood* (Houghton Mifflin, Boston).

AXLINE, V. M. (1964), *Dibs: In Search of Self* (Gollancz, London).

BRUNER, J. et al. (1976), *Play – Its Role in Development and Evolution* (Basic Books, New York).

ERIKSON, E. H. (1972), *Play and Development* (W. W. Norton, New York).

FREUD, A. (1947), *The Psychoanalytic Treatment of Children* (Hogarth Press, London).

HAMBRIDGE, G. (1955), 'Structured play therapy' (*Am. J. of Orthopsychiatry*, vol. 25, pp. 601-15).

HUG-HELLMUTH, H. VON (1921), 'On the technique of child analysis' (*Int. J. of Psychoan.*, vol. 2, pp. 287-305).

JERNBERG, A. M. (1979), *Theraplay* (Jossey-Bass, San Francisco).

KEITH, D. V. and WHITAKER, D. A. (1981), 'Play therapy: a paradigm for work with families' (*J. of Marital and Family Therapy*, vol. 7, pp. 243-54).

KLEIN, M. (1932), *The Psychoanalysis of Children* (Hogarth Press, London).

KLEIN, M. (1955), 'The psychoanalytic play technique' (in *New Directions in Psychoanalysis*, Hogarth Press, London).

PIERS, M. (ed.) (1971), *Play and Development* (W. W. Norton, New York).

RICKARBY, G. and EGAN, P. (1981), 'Family therapy in the playroom' (*Int. J. of Family Psychiatry*, vol. 2, pp. 221-35).

SCHAEFER, C. E. and O'CONNOR, K. J. (1983), *Handbook of Play Therapy* (Wiley, New York).

WINNICOTT, D. W. (1968), 'Playing: its theoretical status in the clinical situation' (*Int. J. of Psychoan.*, vol. 49, pp. 591-9).

WINNICOTT, D. W. (1971), *Playing and Reality* (Penguin, Harmondsworth).

See also *Acting out, Mutual story telling technique, Squiggle game.*

Pleasure principle

A theory of motivation postulated by Freud, whereby the individual's behaviour is guided by his desire to seek pleasure and avoid unpleasure. Freud (1920) contrasted the pleasure principle which serves the needs of the id with the *reality principle* which serves the needs of the *ego*. It is not clear how Freud defines pleasure. Sometimes it seems to be equated with a total absence of tension, which begs the question as to how then to understand the existence of pleasurable tension; sometimes it is viewed as the maintenance of constancy regarding the level of tension; and sometimes it seems to be viewed as the satisfaction of need. The debate regarding the psychoanalytic meaning of pleasure continues. The search for pleasure and the avoidance of unpleasure may be an *unconscious* as well as a *conscious* process. Modification of the pleasure principle is gradually achieved by the operation of the reality principle after the ego has developed in maturity and this enables the individual to come to terms with the demands of external reality and their limitation upon his pleasure seeking activities. The pleasure principle serves a regulatory function analogous to the concept of *homeostasis*.

FREUD, S. (1911), 'Formulations on the two principles of mental functioning' (*Standard Edition*, vol. 12, Hogarth Press, London).

FREUD, S. (1917), 'Mourning and melancholia' (*Standard Edition*, vol. 14, Hogarth Press, London).

FREUD, S. (1920), 'Beyond the pleasure principle' (*Standard Edition*, vol. 18, Hogarth Press, London).

RYCROFT, C. (1962), 'Beyond the reality principle' (in *Imagination and Reality*, Hogarth Press, London).

Poetry therapy

The use of poetry to stimulate the patient to express his emotions and to promote identification with parallel emotions expressed by the poet. Poetry therapy is usually conducted in groups, often in an in-patient setting and as an adjunct to some form of individual treatment. The therapist can either bring written material from poets to the group for discussion or stimulate patients to write their own. If the former, the therapist tries to choose material that will allow the patient to identify vicariously with the emotions expressed and thus gain *insight* into his own *internal world*. Writing poetry allows patients to express *preconscious* or *unconscious* material which can be analysed in a similar way to *dreams*. The use of *Zen telegrams* as a warm-up technique for a poetry therapy group is described by Clancy and Lauer (1978), and Schloss and Grundy (1978) show how poetry therapy can be combined with *action techniques*. As in *bibliotherapy*, the reading or writing of a poem may be given as a *homework assignment*.

CLANCY, M. and LAUER, R. (1978), 'Zen telegrams: a warm-up technique for poetry therapy groups' (in Lerner, A. (ed.), *Poetry in the Therapeutic Experience*, Pergamon Press, New York).

LERNER, A. (ed.), (1978), *Poetry in the Therapeutic Experience* (Pergamon Press, New York).

LIPPIN, R. A. (1982), 'Poetry and poetry therapy: a conversation with Arthur Lerner' (*Arts in Psychotherapy*, vol. 9, pp. 167-74).

SCHLOSS, G. A. (1976), *Psychopoetry: A New Approach to Self Awareness Through Poetry Therapy* (Grosset & Dunlap, New York).

SCHLOSS, G. A. and GRUNDY, D. E. (1978), 'Action techniques in psycho poetry' (in Lerner, A. (ed.), *Poetry in the Therapeutic Experience*, Pergamon Press, New York).

Pole

The end point of a *construct*. Kelly, in his elaboration of *personal construct theory*, asserted that each construct has two poles, one at either end of its dichotomy. The *elements* at each pole are like each other in relation to the construct and are unlike the elements at the other pole. The relationship between the two poles is one of contrast. Kelly used the terms 'likeness end' to refer to the pole where one set of elements is grouped and 'contrast end' to refer to the opposite pole. He also used the terms emergence and submergence (or implicitness), respectively, to refer to the pole that embraces most of the immediately perceived *context* and

the pole which embraces least. Thus, in the context 'sparrows and hawks are feathered whilst cats are not' (or 'are furry'), 'feathered' is the emergent pole of the construct 'feathered-furry' while furry is implicit and may not be articulated as such. The term is also used in a similar way in *eidetic psychotherapy* to describe the contrasting positive and negative aspects of the eidetic.

KELLY, G. A. (1955), *The Psychology of Personal Constructs* (W. W. Norton, New York).

KELLY, G. A. (1963), *A Theory of Personality* (W. W. Norton, New York).

Position (paranoid-schizoid and depressive)

The terms *paranoid-schizoid position* and *depressive position* were introduced by Melanie Klein. They can most helpfully be thought of in relation to each other because of the dynamic and continuing interaction between the different states of mind to which they refer. Each describes a normal developmental stage of infancy, the paranoid-schizoid position occurring first, and the beginnings of the depressive position occurring later during the first year of life. The term 'position' is used rather than stage to denote the fact that the more primitive aspects of mental functioning associated with the paranoid-schizoid position are rarely, if ever, completely absent in any individual although the extent to which they continue to operate during adult life varies greatly from one person to another.

See also *Stages of development*.

Positive connotation

A special type of *reframing* defined by Palazzoli *et al.* (1975) in which the relationship between the *symptoms* and the behaviour of the other members of the patient's family *system* is made explicit in a benign way. The placing of a positive connotation by the therapist on all attitudes and behaviours of the patient and the rest of the family has the effect of putting all family members on the same level and therefore changing their systemic interactions. Palazzoli *et al.* suggest that 'the primary function of the positive connotation of all the observable behaviours of the group is that of permitting the therapist's access to the systemic model'. The positive connotation is one of the most powerful ingredients of the *interview* and it is instrumental in enabling the patient and family's acceptance of the *prescription*. This is because what is being positively connoted is the homeostatic tendency of the system and not the *homeostasis*-producing behaviour of its members; and the therapist is thus defining himself as in *alliance* with the homeostatic tendencies of the system. Since it is assumed that change is highly threatening to the system, the family is thus enabled to perceive the therapist as less of a threat. As Palazzoli *et al.* emphasise, it is essential that the non-verbal aspects of the therapist's positive message to the family should be congruent, with no hint of sarcasm or other contradictory features present.

The positive connotation of the family's apparently *dysfunctional* behaviour has two further therapeutic functions: it defines the relationship between family members and between family and therapist in such a way that the definition is unlikely to be disqualified; and because it is given within the context of therapy, it faces the family with a contradiction. The family is implicitly placed in a *paradox* since, despite the therapist's assurance that their behaviour is appropriate, they are still left with a symptomatic member. The paradox imposes a pressure, between the approval of the therapist, the discomfort engendered by the symptom, and the link that has been made between the symptom and the behaviours of others, and all become the triggers for change to begin.

PALAZZOLI, M. S. *et al.* (1975), *Paradox and Counter Paradox* (Jason Aronson, New York).

Positive feedback

A systems process in which the rules of transformation in the *feedback loop* lead to *deviation amplification*. Positive feedback leads to change and variation within the *system*. The change that is induced may be desirable or undesirable. For example, positive feedback that continues unchecked leads the system to *runaway* and ultimately to its own destruction. The *symmetrical* fights of a marital couple can be of this order and lead to such a result. On the other hand, positive feedback is a means whereby novelty and variation is introduced to the system, such as new ideas, new members and new values, all of which are essential for the development and optimal functioning of the system.

Practice

See *Behavioural rehearsal*.

Praxis

Literal Greek meaning 'doing'. Term used by Laing (Laing and Cooper 1964), following Sartre (1960) and Marx to distinguish what a person does (praxis) from the impersonal series of events and happenings occurring in a group or family to which no one is the author and which Laing calls *process*. Praxis, therefore, has human authorship, assumes intentionality and implies responsibility. Unintelligible, alienated behaviour can therefore be rendered intelligible by converting 'process' back into 'praxis'. Laing's aim in using Sartre's distinction between praxis and process is to assert that a family or group is not an organism in its own right and that the processes of a group can always be traced to an aggregate of individual praxes. Thus, the group or family whole can never be grasped as a whole even though, through its process, it appears both to be and to act as a whole. Laing's view of praxis should be contrasted with *systemic therapists'* views as expressed for example in terms such as *holon* and *holism*. The idea of praxis is a somewhat problematic one within the systemic therapies and even within Laing's own theoretical framework, it seems to cause difficulties when considered alongside his concept of *nexus*. In so far as the term implies an effort to distinguish the tendencies of groups and families to produce fusion rather than *differentiation* among members, the term is a useful one.

LAING, R. D. and COOPER, D. (1964), *Reason and Violence: A Decade of Sartre's Philosophy, 1950-1960* (Tavistock, London).
SARTRE, J. P. (1960), *Critique de la raison dialectique* (Gallimard, Paris).

See also *Mystification, Symbiosis*.

Preconscious

The region of the mind described by Freud as lying between the *conscious* and the *unconscious*, the so-called 'ante-chamber' to consciousness. The term is only used by psychoanalytic writers. Its contents are made up of memories which, although not present within consciousness, are accessible to it because the *censorship* which operates between the unconscious and preconscious is absent, except in the sense that Freud described when he talked of a mild secondary censorship. Material in the preconscious can therefore be described as *suppressed* or temporarily forgotten and not *repressed*. Preconscious material can usually be brought into consciousness at will. Its mode of operation is nearer to the conscious than to the unconscious and its activity is governed by *secondary process*. Nevertheless, descriptively, the preconscious is often equated with the unconscious, since both can be described as being, for the present moment in time, 'not conscious'. The preconscious plays an important part in psychoanalytic treatment, because the process of *working through*, during which an *interpretation* is emotionally assimilated, is actually a process whereby unconscious material is assimilated into the preconscious. As Freud frequently pointed out, the mere verbal interpretation of unconscious material directed to the patient's conscious is quite insufficient to bring about change.

FREUD, S. (1915), 'The unconscious' (*Standard Edition*, vol. 14, Hogarth Press, London).

See also *Topographical model*.

Premack principle

The use of a high probability behaviour to *reinforce* a low probability behaviour. Premack (1965) suggests that by observing an individual's behaviour or questioning him about it, the therapist can determine which behaviours will be reinforcing to those which he wishes to encourage. Thus, for a person who likes ice cream, eating ice cream will be a high probability behaviour and *therefore* will act as a reinforcer for those behaviours which he is trying to develop. The Premack principle offers an explanation of the way in which reinforcement operates and provides a means for selecting appropriate *reinforcers*.

PREMACK, D. (1965), 'Reinforcement theory' (in Lavine, D. (ed.), *Nebraska Symposium on Motivation*, University of Nebraska Press, Lincoln).

Prescription

A statement offered by the therapist to an individual or family about their situation and problems, together with an implied or explicit suggestion regarding the course of action they should take. The term is taken from medical terminology and, as with a pharmacological prescription, it is offered to the individual or family after a consultation and after the therapist has arrived at a *diagnosis* regarding the nature of the problem. Prescriptions may take the form of *tasks* which are suggested from within the context of the various forms of *behaviour therapy*. However, the term is usually reserved for describing the comments and suggestions made by *strategic therapists*, particularly those who subscribe to the Milan model of strategic therapy. Although the prescription is based on the systemic *hypothesis* which the therapists have arrived at, the prescription is seldom an identical rendering of the hypothesis. As Hoffman (1981) points out, 'the hypothesis respects the circularity of family events as far as possible. When translated to a prescription, a linear *epistemology* is unavoidably adopted.' However, the linear statement is usually a reversal of the family's own linear explanation of its situation. It is therefore a new *punctuation* of events which moves the family towards a more complete or a more circular understanding of its systemic processes.

HOFFMAN, L. (1981), *Foundations of Family Therapy* (Basic Books, New York).

See also *Direction*.

Presenting problem
The complaint which brings the client to the therapist for help. Depending upon the type of therapy being used, the problem presented by the client may or may not be construed by the therapist as the target towards which his interventions should be directed. There are several positions which therapists of different persuasions may adopt: the presenting problem is regarded as the client's 'admission ticket' to therapy and the choice of problem is seen as being arbitrary – as soon as the client allows, the presenting problem is disregarded in favour of seeking for one or more under-lying problems with which to work; or the presenting problem is regarded as *symbolic* of the client's underlying difficulties – within the psychoanalytic therapies the presenting problem is seen as a conscious manifestation of *unconscious* or *preconscious* conflict; or the presenting problem is regarded as synony-mous with the problem itself and therefore forms the material with which the therapist works – *behaviour therapies, strategic therapies* and many who use different forms of *brief therapy* or *crisis intervention* would adopt this view.

Regardless of the specific problem pre-sented, therapists from different theoretical orientations are likely to hold different assumptions about the general nature of presenting problems. For example, behav-ioural and strategic therapists conceive of all problems as *behavioural*; humanistic therapists view them as *existential* and as therefore involving basic identity difficulties; psycho-analytic therapists conceive of problems as involving *intrapsychic conflict*; family therapists are likely to assume that the individual's presenting problem is symptomatic of a *dys-functional family system*; and group therapists, that the individual's presenting problem is an *interpersonal* one. The therapist's professional discipline is also likely to affect his basic assumption about presenting problems. The way in which the therapist handles the presenting problem is thus highly dependent upon these basic assumptions and upon his theoretical orientation.

See also *Symptom, Labelling, Problem solving interventions*.

Primal scene
Infantile experience of, or *phantasy* about, parental sexual intercourse. Freud (1918) suggested that whether or not the child actually witnessed parental intercourse or merely imagined it, anxiety and guilt was aroused which could become the source of neurotic disturbance in later life.

FREUD, S. (1918), 'The wolf man: from the history of an infantile neurosis' (*Standard Edition*, vol. 17, Hogarth Press, London).
IKAMEN, P. and RECHARDT, E. (1981), 'Primal scene fantasies and cathexis of self as reflected in the psychoanalytic situation' (*Scandinavian Psychoan. Review*, vol. 4, pp. 75-93).

Primal therapy
A method of psychotherapy developed by Janov (1970, 1971) which aims to unblock repressed, painful feelings about the many unmet early needs of childhood and through *catharsis* to enable them to be re-integrated into a more functional lifestyle. The theory behind primal therapy derives ultimately from Otto Rank's work on *birth trauma*. On witnessing a patient improving after screaming out his pain-ful, raging feelings regarding his parents, Janov experimented with ways of helping patients to regress and to relive the painful effects of early childhood. *Trauma* is experienced both before and during birth as well as in the early months of post-uterine life so that the *regression* must take in these very early experiences. The pain is kept out of awareness by three 'gates', the somatosensory, affective and cognitive pain gates, which protect the individual from re-experiencing the pain in later life but at the cost of neurotic *symptoms* and psychological disorders. Janov believes that the task of

therapy is to free the patient from this pool of pain, draining it away through the active catharsis of the painful feelings.

Therapy consists of an initial week's period of isolation, during which the patient is deprived of all sensory stimuli. This helps him to let early experiences begin to emerge into consciousness. During the therapy sessions, the therapist encourages the client to talk about these memories in the present tense as though they were happening now, entering into the early experience of rejection, deprivation and frustration as fully as possible. Therapy is directive and confrontative and the therapist tries to disarm the patient and to break through his defences. Janov acknowledges the stress that this involves for the patient, and for the first three weeks the therapist is available for consultation on a twenty-four-hour basis. Therapy sessions take place as frequently as necessary during this period after which the patient joins a group for daily two-hour meetings to experience continued catharsis. The release of emotions and the accompanying pain takes place through kicking, screaming, crying and shouting. The final phase of treatment, which may last for up to a year, is undertaken partly at home and partly through regular group meetings.

The patient is encouraged to confront his memories whenever they come into consciousness on the principle that each time some catharsis occurs, a little more of the pool of pain is drained away. The aim of therapy is for the patient to bring into conscious awareness the repressed pain of the past so that neurotic symptoms disappear. The patient becomes able to let go of unrealistic hopes regarding the past and to enter into his present relationships and endeavours more fully. In particular, the patient disengages from his longings for what his parents might have given him. Janov (1971) has claimed very high success rates for primal therapy, although data reported in Holden's (1975) survey suggests that some patients experience continuing and even increased problems after treatment. Like other *emotional flooding approaches*, primal therapy is psychologically violent and stressful

for the patient but its adherents believe it to be effective in producing durable relief for long-standing problems. Prochaska (1979) summarises the many criticisms that can be made of primal therapy. The centre for its teaching and practice is the Primal Institute, Los Angeles, which is directed by Janov. The Institute publishes the *Journal of Primal Therapy*.

HOLDEN, E. M. (1975), 'The primal questionnaire: patients' reports on changes during primal therapy' (in Janov, A. and Holden, E. M. (1975), see below).
JANOV, A. (1970), *The Primal Scream* (Putman, New York).
JANOV, A. (1971), *The Anatomy of Mental Illness* (Putnam, New York).
JANOV, A. and HOLDEN, E. M. (eds) (1975), *Primal Man: The New Consciousness* (Crowell, New York).
PROCHASKA, J. O. (1979), *Systems of Psychotherapy* (Dorsey Press, Homewood, Ill.).

Primary gain

A direct benefit derived from a *symptom* or psychological disorder such as a reason for not going to work, to school, taking an examination, etc.

See also *Flight into illness, Secondary gain.*

Primary process

The mode of functioning which characterises the *unconscious* part of the *psyche* and therefore the *id*. It is congruent with the operation of the *pleasure principle*. Freud introduced the concept alongside his elaboration of the unconscious. Primary processes can be seen operating most clearly in *dreams*, when they make use of the mechanisms of *displacement* and *condensation*. They stand in contrast to the orderly functioning of *secondary process*. Rycroft (1962) criticises the view that primary process is inherently maladaptive.

FREUD, S. (1900), 'The interpretation of dreams' (*Standard Edition*, vols 4 and 5, Hogarth Press, London).
RYCROFT, C. (1962), 'Beyond the reality principle' (in *Imagination and Reality*, Hogarth Press, London).

Primitive defence mechanisms
See *Defence mechanisms*.

Privation therapy
See *Active technique*.

Problem solving interventions
Techniques used to develop a goal-directed, graduated approach to improve an individual's or family's abilities. D'Zurilla and Goldfried (1971) point out that *symptoms* such as anxiety and depression may be due to the patient's inadequate attempts at resolving certain situational problems in his life. Thus the symptoms may abate when new problem solving skills have been learned. Problem solving interventions are allied to both *cognitive behaviour therapy* and *coping skills interventions*, but they can trace their ancestry back to John Dewey (1933) and his descriptive work on the thought processes of a human being when confronted with a problem. Dewey asserted that effective problem solving involves the active pursuit of a well-defined and orderly sequence of steps and suggested a five-phase sequence: recognising the problem, defining the problem, collecting data regarding possible solutions and exploring their merit, selecting the best solution, and taking steps to carry it out. Others have elaborated and refined this sequence (for example, by building in an evaluation step at the end) but it has remained the basis for the problem solving approach. Mahoney (1977) has developed an 'apprenticeship format' whereby the patient adopts a 'scientific approach' to personal problem solving. Using a seven-step format, Mahoney enables the patient, in addition to learning the problem solving model, to develop general attitudes towards *self-monitoring, functional analysis* and the evaluation of the consequences of actions, all of which provide a new orientation towards problem situations. Blechman (1974) and Haley (1976) have adapted the approach to work with families.

BLECHMAN, E. A. (1974), 'The family contract game: a tool to teach interpersonal problem solving' (*Family Co-ordinator*, vol. 23, pp. 269-81).
DEWEY, J. (1933), *How We Think* (D. C. Heath, New York).
D'ZURILLA, T. J. and GOLDFRIED, M. R. (1971), 'Problem solving and behaviour modification' (*J. of Abnormal Psychology*, vol. 78, pp. 107-26).
HALEY, J. (1976), *Problem Solving Therapy* (Jossey-Bass, San Francisco).
MAHONEY, M. J. (1977), 'Personal science: a cognitive learning theory' (in Ellis, A. and Grieger, R. (eds), *Handbook of Rational Psychotherapy*, Springer, New York).
SPIVACK, G., PLATT, J. J. and SHURE, M. D. (1976), *The Problem Solving Approach to Adjustment* (Jossey-Bass, San Francisco).

Process
An organised series of events that occur within a course of individual action, interaction or *transaction* within or between individuals. Both *intrapsychic* and *interpersonal* process takes place within a functional *context* from which it can be clearly distinguished in the same way that figure and ground (see *Figure-ground*) can be said to be distinguished in *Gestalt psychology*. The term implies motion and change as distinct from the static concept of *structure* or the terminal concept of *outcome*. Thus, a social group can be characterised by its process, i.e. its *communication* sequences, rules, and the behavioural and symbolic interactional events occurring between members. Likewise, an individual can be described in terms of *intrapersonal* process, i.e. the way in which his *mental apparatus* functions, his use of *defence mechanisms*, and his use of *primary* and *secondary process*. In therapeutic work, the *diagnosis* of process takes the form of *phenotypic* assessment.

Laing (Laing and Cooper 1964) uses the term in contrast to that of *praxis* to indicate an impersonal description of the events that are taking place. In the evaluation of therapeutic work, research into outcome is contrasted with research into process. The latter is concerned with the assessment of variables such as the therapist's instrumental and expressive activity, the degree to which he is able to mobilise the *core conditions* of therapy, the intervention techniques that he consciously employs, the relationship between patient and therapist including *transference* and *counter transference* phenomena and the communication sequences that occur within the therapy session. Process research is also concerned with investigating a range of patient variables and the interaction between these and the therapist. Orlinsky and Howard (1978) distinguish four major facets of process that occur within social relationships and apply these to the therapeutic process: co-oriented activity (the therapeutic, interactional aspect of the relationship); concurrent experience (the phenomenological dimension of social events); dramatic interpretation (the symbolic formulation of meaning and value); and regular association (the normative, prescriptive patterns of relatedness that bind the participants of the relationship together). They further distinguish between the micro and macro cosmic view of process, a distinction that is time-related: the short-term microcosmic series of events which make up 'what is going on' in an *encounter* and the long-term cumulative changes that emerge from a series of encounters. Pinsof (1981) has undertaken a similar exercise in relation to *family therapy*. Linking research into process variables with outcome research is of primary importance if those factors which are foremost in promoting positive therapeutic change are to be effectively isolated.

LAING, R. D. and COOPER, D. (1964), *Reason and Violence: A Decade of Sartre's Philosophy 1950-1960* (Tavistock, London).
ORLINSKY, D. E. and HOWARD, K. I. (1978), 'The relation of process to outcome in psychotherapy' (in Garfield, S. L. and Bergin, A. E. (eds), *Handbook of Psychotherapy and Behavior Change*, 2nd edn, Wiley, New York).
PINSOF, W. (1981), 'Family therapy process research' (in Gurman, A. S. and Kniskern, D. P. (eds), *Handbook of Family Therapy*, Brunner/Mazel, New York).

See also *Group process*.

Progression

Term used by Jung to describe the movement of *libido* which has an opposite direction from that of *regression*. The forward movement of progression satisfies the demands of the *ego*, and is concerned with active adaptation to the demands of reality in the external world. Jung emphasised the rhythmic need of the individual's psychic energy to flow between the two poles of progression and regression, each having a regulatory function for the other.

JUNG, C. G. (1953), *Two Essays on Analytical Psychology* (Routledge & Kegan Paul, London).

See also *Enantiodromia*.

Projection

The process whereby the individual places outside himself and into another feelings or attributes which belong within, and comes to view the mental image thus produced as objective reality. It is described as a *defence mechanism* and as such it may have a role in *symptom* formation. It has the effect of making the individual particularly aware of those things in others which he refuses to recognise in himself. Freud first discussed projection in paranoia in 1896. Later (1911) he suggested that projection is used to eliminate destructive wishes from the self and that the external world is first defined as a location for bad feelings. He describes the way in which projection often involves, in addition, a transformation or reversal of affect: 'What should have been felt internally as love is perceived externally as hate.' As with the opposite *ego* defences, *introjection* and *incorporation*, Freud located the origins of projection at the *oral stage* of development. He maintained that, as with the process of *identification*, the ability to project presupposed the awareness of difference between the ego and the outside world, but projection is also part of the process of developing that *differentiation*. Abraham (1924) linked projection with the anal-phase – Klein considered that the mechanism of projection is the means by which the infant begins to differentiate the self from the not-self, and that it is first being used as a defence against destructive anxiety during the *paranoid-schizoid position*. Freud maintained that it was feelings and affect which were expelled through projection and thus disowned, whilst for Klein and her followers, the thing projected was the 'bad' *object* itself, or in some cases the 'good' object in order to keep it safe. Jung suggested that projection is closely akin to *transference* and is a mechanism in the formation of the therapeutic transference. He asserted that the main objects of projection were the parental *imagos* and the therapeutic process involved the gradual withdrawal of these projections from the outside world, leading towards an *integration* of the personality.

ABRAHAM, K. (1924), 'A short study of the development of the libido viewed in the light of mental disorders' (in *Selected Papers*, Hogarth Press, London).

FREUD, S. (1896), 'Further remarks on the neuro-psychoses of defence' (*Standard Edition*, vol. 3, Hogarth Press, London).

FREUD, S. (1922), 'Psychoanalytic notes on an autobiographical account of a case of paranoia' (*Standard Edition*, vol. 12, Hogarth Press, London).

See also *Defence mechanisms*.

Projective identification

A term introduced by Melanie Klein (1946) to describe the *splitting* of the *ego* during early infancy, the *projection* of parts of the self (in contrast to projection of objects), into others, primarily the mother and her breast, and the subsequent *identification* with the split off 'bad' parts of the self, now located in the other. The key idea is that what is projected is simultaneously identified with as part of the self and is not (as in the case of projection) seen as part of the other. The term is, however, a controversial one and may often be used loosely, which leads to considerable confusion. For this reason some writers (e.g. Meissner 1980) have suggested its abandonment altogether.

Klein introduced the term in a paper on schizoid mechanisms and she discussed it again when considering the mechanism of identification (Klein 1955). She describes it as originating in the *paranoid schizoid position* (Klein 1946) and she sees it as part of normal development, although if engaged in persistently, it may lead to an impoverishment of the ego (if the projected objects are 'good'), or depersonalisation, a fear of imprisonment (claustrophobia), or to the creation of a hostile, retaliatory and persecuting external world (if the projected objects are 'bad'). Klein appears to derive the concept from an interactional view of the relationship between *introjection* and projection. Either projection may precede introjection or vice versa. When the latter occurs, the mechanism is sometimes called introjective identification. For example, the individual may project 'bad' parts of the self into the other, identify with them and then introject them back into the self; or he may introject 'good' or 'bad' objects into the self and then project them into the other (to preserve them safe or to escape from their power). The parts which are projected and introjected may not of course be the same: Segal (1973) gives an example of a child projecting the baby part of herself into the analyst and introjecting the analyst as 'mother' into herself to enable her to care for the 'baby' self now located in the analyst.

The problem in using the term arises from a failure to retain a firm connection between the concepts of projection and identification, resulting in fusion with one or other of these two concepts. Projective identification is a *defence mechanism* employed by the ego to protect it against the anxieties of being persecuted by and separated from others. As such it can lead, if excessive, to pathological manifestations and a divorce from reality, but it is also part of normal development, retaining useful functions in adult life. Segal (1973), for example, suggests that projective identification is an early form of *empathy* helping the individual to learn how to step into the shoes of another. She also suggests that it forms the basis of the earliest form of symbol formation. Bion (1959) elaborated the way in which the mechanism works in the therapeutic situation, both with individuals and groups, and Ogden (1979) suggests four ways in which the individual can make use of the mechanism: as a defence whereby unwanted or internally endangered parts of the self can be disowned yet kept alive in another; a mode of communication whereby one exerts pressure on another person to experience feelings similar to one's own; a way of experimenting with object relatedness, the projector perceiving the other as different from self but sufficiently undifferentiated to share feelings, etc.; and as a pathway to change, by which the projector can identify with and therefore learn from the way in which the recipient of his projections handles them. A further possibility, however, is manifested in the *scapegoating* process whereby the individual attacks in the other what cannot be tolerated in the self.

Workers from other psychoanalytic perspectives have examined the concept. For example, Malin and Grotstein (1966) suggest the differentiation of three important elements: the projection, the creation of an 'alloy' of external object plus projected self, and re-internationalisation. *Family* and *marital therapists* working from within a psychoanalytic framework have found the term rich in potential. For example, Box (1978) discusses the importance of projective identification in understanding the way in which feelings and roles can become locked in one family member, rendering him the *scapegoat*, while other family members can relate with these disowned parts of the self through identifying with them in the other. Zinner and Shapiro (1972) have discussed the process in families where the adolescent is presenting with symptoms.

Bion, W. (1959), 'Attacks on linking' (*Int. J. of Psychoan.*, vol. 40, pp. 308-15).
Box, S. (1978), 'An analytic approach to work with families' (*J. of Adolescence*, vol. 1, pp. 119-33).
Klein, M. (1946), 'Notes on some schizoid mechanisms' (in *Developments in Psychoanalysis*, Hogarth Press, London).
Klein, M. (1955), 'On identification' (in *New*

Directions in Psychoanalysis, Maresfield Reprints, Karnac, London).
Malin, A. and Grotstein, J. (1966), 'Projective identification in the therapeutic process' (*Int. J. of Psychoan.*, vol. 47, pp. 26-31).
Meissner, W. W. (1980), 'A note on projective identification' (*J. of the A. Psychoan. Assoc.*, vol. 28, pp. 43-67).
Ogden, T. H. (1979), 'On projective identification' (*Int. J. of Psychoan.*, vol. 60, pp. 357-72).
Segal, H. (1973), *Introduction to the Work of Melanie Klein* (Hogarth Press, London).
Zinner, J. and Shapiro, R. (1972), 'Projective identification as a mode of perception and behaviour in families of adolescents' (*Int. J. of Psychoan.*, vol. 53, pp. 523-30).

See also *Defence mechanisms*.

Projective tests
See *Personality tests*.

Protagonist
Term used in *psychodrama* to describe the person who is the subject of the psychodramatic *enactment*. This person may be either a patient or a trainee. With the help of the therapist or group leader, the *auxiliary ego* and the audience the protagonist re-enacts important conflicts, memories, suppressed emotions or future worries to the point where these can be *worked through* to some form of resolution.

See also *Hot seat*.

Prototaxic
See *Referential processes*.

Provocative therapy
A method of psychotherapy introduced by Farrelly and Brandsma (1974) out of dissatisfaction with *client-centred therapy*. It is a directive method which has links with both *rational emotive therapy* and paradoxical interventions. It aims to elicit from the client behaviours and affect which are more appropriate, functional and self-enhancing than those he is currently manifesting, using

techniques of *confrontation, feedback, paradox, humour* and *action techniques*. The therapist tends to play the role of devil's advocate to goad the client into altering his self-concept, behaviour or both. Provocative therapists abandon most of the cautions which most schools of therapy consider essential and provide an abrasive, stimulating experience mainly through the *manipulation* of the client-therapist relationship. Other techniques employed by provocative therapists include negative *modelling*, where the therapist mirrors the client's behaviour back to him in exaggerated form, and the use of the *therapeutic double bind*. Provocative therapy has been used with groups, couples and families as well as with individuals. It is open to many obvious criticisms and can be rather easily abused, but according to its developers it has produced successful results with long-term hospitalised psychotic patients and other hard-to-help client groups.

FARRELLY, F. and BRANDSMA, J. (1974), *Provocative Therapy* (Meta Publications, Cupertino, Calif.).

Proxemics
See *Non-verbal communication.*

Pseudohostility
Term introduced by Wynne (1961) to describe a shared family defence used to prevent the recognition of feelings of tenderness, affection or sexual attraction which family members are unable to handle. Wynne contrasts pseudohostility, which is produced by defensive splits between family members, with the complementary phenomenon of *pseudomutuality*. The pseudohostile split that occurs between two or more family members is produced by a complementary alignment between other family members as well as enabling that alignment to continue. Wynne views this process as a homeostatic mechanism operating particularly clearly in schizophrenogenic families. Zuk (1971) and others use the term slightly differently to indicate the masking of a more pervasive, deeply entrenched hostility existing either between the pseudohostile sub-group or experienced in relation to a third party. 'Pseudohostility may be directed by one family member against another, toward whom the first does not really feel the greatest animosity, but whom he finds a convenient scapegoat' (Zuk 1971).

WYNNE, L. (1961), 'The study of intra-familial alignments and splits in exploratory family therapy' (in Ackerman, N. W. *et al.* (eds), *Exploring the Base for Family Therapy*, Family Service Association of America, New York).
ZUK, G. H. (1971), 'Family therapy' (in Haley, J., *Changing Families*, Grune & Stratton, New York).

See also *Circular causality, Homeostasis, Scapegoat.*

Pseudomutuality
Term introduced by Wynne (1961) to describe a shared family defence used to prevent the *differentiation* or separation from the family of individual family members or *sub-systems*, which is a process perceived as a threat to the integrity of the family system. Wynne contrasts pseudomutuality, which is produced by seemingly close alignments between family members, with the complementary phenomenon of *pseudohostility*. The pseudomutual alignments are produced by a complementary split between other family members, as well as enabling that split to take place. Like pseudomutuality, Wynne views this process as a homeostatic mechanism, operating particularly clearly in schizophrenogenic families.

WYNNE, L. (1961), 'The study of intra-familial alignments and splits in exploratory family therapy' (in Ackerman, N. W. *et al.* (eds), *Exploring the Base for Family Therapy*, Family Service Association of America, New York).

See also *Circular causality, Coalition, Homeostasis, Rubber fence.*

Pseudotherapeutic
A defensive manoeuvre on the part of an

individual, couple, family or group to relieve pain or distress through a false solution. Examples are the *pseudomutual* behaviour of family members who fear the existence of conflict; the *folie à deux*; *basic assumption behaviour* in groups; the operation of a *family myth*; or the self-destructive activities of an individual who engages, for example, in substance abuse. Some pseudotherapeutic activities may be less destructive than others, for example the individual who seeks to repair, in choosing a marital partner, the *lacunae* he experiences in his own personality, or the couple who try to make up for the emptiness of their own relationship by having a baby. The therapist has to decide whether to challenge pseudotherapeutic solutions early on in treatment or whether to offer a *positive connotation* and accept the efforts being made to bring about change, even though those efforts themselves may be *dysfunctional*.

See also *Defence mechanisms, Fit (marital)*.

Psyche

Literal Greek meaning 'breath' or 'spirit'. The *mental apparatus* made up of the three *agencies* – the *id*, the *ego* and the *superego*, and the three levels of consciousness, the *conscious*, the *pre-conscious* and the *unconscious*. Used in this sense, the term is a psychoanalytic concept, but it is also used more broadly to describe the mind or the self.

Psychoanalysis

A general psychology and psychotherapeutic method originated by Sigmund Freud. Alongside *behaviourism* and *humanistic psychology*, psychoanalysis stands as one of the three major orientations to psychotherapy. Freud (1923) gave the following definition of psychoanalysis: 'Psychoanalysis is the name (1) of a procedure for the investigation of mental processes which are almost inaccessible in any other way, (2) of a method (based upon that investigation) for the treatment of neurotic disorders, and (3) of a collection of psychological information obtained along those lines which is gradually being accumulated into a

new scientific discipline.' Its main purpose is to make *unconscious* material *conscious*, using the method of *free association* on the part of the patient, and *interpretation* by the *analyst*, particularly of the patient's *dreams*, his *resistances* and of the *transference* which develops between patient and *analyst*. It would be hard to overestimate the enormous contribution made by psychoanalysis, not only to the obviously relevant fields of psychotherapy and psychology but also to culture, literature, art and philosophy (Gabriel 1983). Most varieties of psychotherapy draw upon the richness of psychoanalytic concepts to a greater or lesser extent and many adopt its methods as well. It claims to be the only body of theory that derives from work with patients, in contrast to other therapies which employ imported theory from other scientific disciplines.

Sandler *et al.* (1972b) list five 'basic assumptions' that underpin psychoanalysis: the generality and applicability of its concepts to both normal and abnormal behaviour; its belief in the existence of a *mental apparatus* which has a three-fold structure and which functions in close relationship to the physiological systems of the body; the concept of psychological adaptation whereby the mental apparatus attempts to produce a 'steady state' in which conflict is reduced as far as possible; its psychic determinism, whereby mental phenomena are believed to have causes analogous to physical ones; and its understanding of mental life as comprising both a conscious and an unconscious world in which unconscious material is only brought into consciousness using particular vehicles such as dreams and *parapraxes* and via the technique of free association in the psychoanalytic treatment situation.

Several broad schools of psychoanalysis can be distinguished: Freudian (followers of Sigmund and Anna Freud); Jungian (followers of Carl Jung, who describe their work as *analytical psychology*; Adlerian (followers of Alfred Adler, who describe their type of psychoanalysis as *individual psychology*; the *interpersonal school* of Harry Stack Sullivan and Karen Horney; the *Kleinian* or English *school* of Melanie Klein and her followers; the *object relations* or *British school* of Fairbairn, Guntrip, Balint and Winnicott; the school of Wilhelm Reich and others; and the *French school*. In addition, we can distinguish *psychoanalytic family therapy*; *group analysis*; several *brief therapies* derived from psychoanalysis, and a variety of approaches to *marital therapy* based on psychoanalytic principles. Each of the main schools of psychoanalysis has developed its own methods of *training* and accreditation, differing in content and method to some extent but all requiring a *training analysis*. Most of the major schools are focused upon a training institute in the country of practice and many major national and international journals are published in the field, the most important being the *International Journal of Psychoanalysis*, the *Journal of Analytical Psychology*, the *Psychoanalytic Quarterly Review*, the *International Review of Psychoanalysis*, and the *Journal of the American Psychoanalytic Association*.

The literature is now voluminous and a variety of developments, modifications and adaptations in theory and technique have continued to be made since Freud and Jung made their own massive written contributions to the field. For example, the part played by the 'real' relationship between patient and analyst and the relationship between the patient's real world and his disorder is now given more attention; a greater emphasis is placed on the *ego* as compared with the *id* with the subsequent development of *ego psychology*; the criticisms of the metapsychological content of psychoanalysis and the debate about the value of 'action language' as a possible substitute (Schafer 1976); the development of what has come to be called *'self psychology'* by Kohut (1971, 1977) and his followers and the technical approaches to narcissistic disorders being refined by this group; the contrasting work of Kernberg (1980), and his elaboration of object relations theory and the effort to strike a better balance between the understanding of Oedipal and pre-Oedipal phases of development.

A range of major criticisms have been levied

against psychoanalysis and important disagreements within the field continue (Schafer 1976; Calef and Weinshel 1979; Frank 1979; Farrell 1981). Several of the new developments in the field outlined above are aimed at addressing some of the long-standing criticisms. The main criticisms of psychoanalysis are as follows:

(1) *Psychoanalytic discoveries are peculiar to the psychoanalytic setting in the consulting room.* Freud claimed that his theories were universally applicable but they were developed from a very narrow sample of Viennese society in the early part of this century and may not therefore apply to all other cultures in all other ages.

(2) *Psychoanalysis overemphasises sexuality* in the aetiology of dysfunction to the exclusion of most other determinants. Both Jung and Adler criticised Freud for this over emphasis and their own models are much less constrained by it. Farrell (1981) summarises the current discussion.

(3) *Psychoanalysis is untestable and therefore unscientific.* Many efforts have been made to study psychoanalytic concepts and procedures objectively but in view of the lack of empirical evidence they remain inconclusive (Kline 1972; Eysenck and Wilson 1973; Fisher and Greenberg 1977). Eysenck, for example, a major critic, argues that 'what is true is not new and what is new is not true' in psychoanalysis, though Kline and other researchers find this blanket rejection invalid. A discussion of whether or not psychoanalysis fulfills the criteria for a science can be found in Will (1980) and Fielding and Llewelyn (1982).

(4) *Psychoanalysis is deterministic.* Because it is derived from a biological, fixed view of human nature and gives such emphasis to the way past experiences causally influence the present, it is pessimistic about change.

(5) *Psychoanalysis is repressive politically.* Marxist critiques of Freudian theory point to the absence of any idea of historical evolution, without which Freudian con-

cepts appear to reinforce and uphold the social status quo.

(6) *Psychoanalysis is anti-feminist.* Psychoanalytic concepts such as the *castration complex* and *penis envy* view women in terms of a deficiency model.

(7) *Psychoanalysis ignores social and interpersonal dynamics* by regarding intrapsychic processes as the determinants of pathology or health. Other therapists would regard the family and society as having a much bigger part to play in enabling or disabling the individual.

(8) *Psychoanalysis is elitist*, because of its cost in time and money. Few troubled individuals can afford either the time or the money to engage in a full psychoanalytic treatment which may mean seeing the analyst for up to five sessions per week for forty-eight weeks of the year.

(9) *It is uncertain whether or not psychoanalysis is effective.* The research evidence for psychoanalysis is even more inconclusive than for other methods of psychotherapy.

Many of these criticisms can be applied equally to other methods and it is only fair to say that the whole field of psychoanalysis has become progressively broader, more open to other influences and more self critical in recent years.

BRENNER, C. (1973), *An Elementary Textbook of Psychoanalysis* (International Universities Press, New York).

BROWN, J. A. C. (1961), *Freud and the Post-Freudians* (Penguin, Harmondsworth).

CALEF, V. and WEINSHEL, E. M. (1979), 'The new psychoanalysis and psychoanalytic revisionism' (*Psychoan. Quarterly*, vol. 48, pp. 470-91).

EYSENCK, H. and WILSON, G. (eds) (1973), *The Experimental Study of Freudian Theories* (Methuen, London).

FARRELL, B. A. (1981), *The Standing of Psychoanalysis* (Oxford University Press, Oxford).

FIELDING, R. G. and LLEWELYN, S. P. (1982), 'Psychoanalysis as a human science' (*Brit. J. of Med. Psychology*, vol. 55, pp. 13-17).

FISHER, S. and GREENBERG, R. P. (1977), *The Scientific Credibility of Freud's Theories and Therapy* (Harvester Press, New York).

FRANK, A. (1979), 'Two theories or one? Or none?' (*J. of Am. Psychoan. Assoc.*, vol. 27, pp. 169-207).

FREUD, S. (1923), 'Two encyclopaedia articles' (*Standard Edition*, vol. 18, Hogarth Press, London).

GABRIEL, Y. (1983), *Freud and Society* (Routledge & Kegan Paul, London).

KERNBERG, O. (1980), *Internal World and External Reality* (Jason Aronson, New York).

KLEIN, G. S. (1976), *Psychoanalytic Theory: An Exploration of Essentials* (International Universities Press, New York).

KLINE, P. (1972), *Fact and Fantasy in Freudian Theory* (Methuen, London).

KOHUT, H. (1971), *The Analysis of the Self* (International Universities Press, New York).

KOHUT, H. (1977), *The Restoration of the Self* (International Universities Press, New York).

MCGUIRE, W. (ed.) (1974), *The Freud/Jung Letters* (Hogarth Press and Routledge & Kegan Paul, London).

RYCROFT, C. (ed.) (1968), *Psychoanalysis Observed* (Penguin, Harmondsworth).

SANDLER, J. *et al.* (1972a), 'Frames of reference in psychoanalytic psychology – II The historical context' (*Brit. J. of Med. Psychology*, vol. 45, pp. 133-42).

SANDLER, J. *et al.* (1972b), 'Frames of reference in psychoanalytic psychology – III A note on the basic assumptions' (*Brit. J. of Med. Psychology*, vol. 45, pp. 143-7).

SCHAFER, R. (1976), *A New Language for Psychoanalysis* (Yale University Press, New Haven, Conn.).

WILL, D. (1980), 'Psychoanalysis as a human science' (*Brit. J. of Med. Pschology*, vol. 53, pp. 201-11).

Psychoanalytic family therapy

Despite Freud's (1912) own opposition to the idea of treating family relationships (he confessed himself to be 'utterly at a loss' in relation to them), *psychoanalysis* has nevertheless had an important influence on *family therapy* generally and on psychoanalytic family therapy in particular. Psychoanalytic family therapy is an approach to family therapy which emphasises *unconscious* processes and the interlocking pathology of members of the family group. Family therapists who advocate this approach transpose many theoretical ideas from psychoanalysis to the treatment of the family, viewing it as a 'single psychic entity' (Zinner and Shapiro 1972). Thus, *transference*, *counter transference* and the relationship which the therapist establishes with the group are viewed as of great importance, and concepts such as *secondary gains* derived from the symptomatic behaviour of the *identified patient* and *defence mechanisms* such as *projective identification* are incorporated into the theoretical framework. Skynner (1976) makes use of concepts derived from *group analysis* in addition.

Treatment techniques involve helping the family to gain *insight* into its dysfunctional processes and their relationship with the past through the therapist's use of *interpretation*, the *genogram* and elaborations of the *family myth* and avoided theme. Techniques such as *family sculpting* may also be used to increase the family's understanding of its relationship patterns. Treatment tends to be reasonably long-term.

ACKERMAN, N. W. (1958), *Psychodynamics of Family Life* (Basic Books, New York).
ACKERMAN, N. W. (1959) 'The psycho-analytic approach to the family' (in Masserman, J. (ed.), *Individual and Family Dynamics*, Grune & Stratton, New York).
ACKERMAN, N. W. (1968), *Treating the Troubled Family* (Basic Books, New York).
BELL, J. E. (1962), *Family Group Therapy* (Bookstall Publications, Bristol).
BOX, S. *et al.* (1982), *Psychotherapy with Families* (Routledge & Kegan Paul, London).
DARE, C. (1981), 'Psychoanalysis and family therapy' (in Walrond-Skinner, S., (ed.), *Developments in Family Therapy*, Routledge & Kegan Paul, London).
FREUD, S. (1912), 'Recommendations for physicians on the psychoanalytic method of treatment' (*Standard Edition*, vol. 12, Hogarth Press, London).

PINCUS, L. and DARE, C. (1978), *Secrets in the Family* (Faber & Faber, London).
RICHTER, H. E. (1974), *The Family as Patient* (Souvenir Press, London).
SKYNNER, A. C. R. (1976), *One Flesh: Separate Persons* (Constable, London).
ZINNER, J. and SHAPIRO, R. (1972), 'Projective identification as a mode of perception in families of adolescents' (*Int. J. of Psychoan.*, vol. 53, pp. 523-30).

Psychoanalytic group therapy

See *group analysis*.

Psychobiogram

A life chart devised by Meyer (1919) for recording chronological data about the patient in various areas of his life. Meyer's purpose was to show 'how simply, controllably and suggestively the facts can be brought into a record'. The chart consists of a series of parallel columns for the patient's age, type of disturbance, duration of disturbance, family and social data, job changes, etc. The dates of all significant events are recorded. The chart enables the therapist and patient to observe connections between various aspects and events in the patient's life at particular stages in his life cycle. The psychobiogram has been adapted for use by therapists from many different orientations to help show the complex lateral and vertical connections between life events. A similar tool has been devised by Duhl (1981), called the Boston Family Chronological Chart, for use with family groups.

DUHL, F. J. (1981), 'The use of the chronological chart in general systems family therapy' (*J. of Marital and Family Therapy*, vol. 7, pp. 361-74).
MEYER, A. (1919), 'The life chart and the obligation of specifying positive data in psychopathological diagnosis' (from *Contributions to Medical and Biological Research*, Paul B. Hoeber, New York).

See also *Chronogram, Diagrams, Psychobiology*.

Psychobiology

An approach to psychotherapy introduced in the United States by the Swiss psychiatrist Adolf Meyer at the turn of the century. Although largely forgotten now, Meyer's approach was novel and influential during the first half of the twentieth century up until the Second World War. It encouraged a comprehensive and eclectic approach to psychological disorder based on observation of the objective facts of the patient's life, including his psychosocial *context*. Meyer introduced a special kind of chart which he called the *psychobiogram* which enabled connections between significant events in the patient's life to be made. Meyer encouraged a focus on the patient's immediate problem and an effort to understand its meaning in terms of the patient's interpersonal and social circumstances and in terms of his developmental history. He was critical of blanket diagnoses and the *labelling* of patients. Instead, he encouraged an optimistic approach to change and a many-levelled approach to treatment including the progressively 'deep' understanding of the patient's *psyche* in individual interviews, supportive help between interviews according to the patient's needs, 'habit training', to show the patient how to modify his behaviour and lifestyle to make it more personally productive, environmental manipulation to create a more favourable living situation where possible, and supportive after-care. Ideas from Meyer's work have been carried on in the various forms of *social therapy*, *vector therapy* and *network intervention*.

MEYER, A. (1957), *Psychobiology: A Science of Man* (Charles C. Thomas, Springfield, Ill.).

Psychocalisthenics

A holistic group approach that stresses therapy as an educative process. It was initiated by Oscar Ichazo who developed the approach during the 1960s at Arica in Chile. In 1971 he began to found centres in the United States for the study of what has come to be called Arica training. Ichazo emphasises the need for a spiritual awakening within Western culture if its destructive tendencies and spiritual impoverishment are to be reversed. This he believes is best achieved by the assimilation of Eastern values which have as their goal the individual's experience of a loving unity with the created order. The group becomes the chief tool for enabling individuals to lose the fears which have produced their defensiveness and inauthentic behaviour. Exercises to re-integrate the body and spirit with the mind enable group members to reverse the over-emphasis on intellectual skills which have led to the impoverishment of their whole self.

ICHAZO, O. (1976), *Arica Psychocalisthenics* (Simon & Schuster, New York).

See also *Body therapies, Holistic education, Transpersonal psychology*.

Psychodiagnosis

See *Diagnosis* and *Personality tests*.

Psychodrama

A method of *group psychotherapy* introduced by Moreno into the United States in 1925. According to Moreno (1946), psychodrama is the 'science which explores truth by dramatic methods. The psychodramatic method uses mainly five instruments – the stage, the subject or patient, the director, the staff of therapeutic aids or *auxiliary egos*, and the audience.' Each of these participants has a unique role to play. The stage enables the patient to express himself freely in relation to both past and present: the therapist is the director and acts as a bridge and an interpreter between the patient and the other participants; the auxiliary egos portray the imagined or real persons in the patient's life drama; and the audience acts as a sounding board, contributing ideas but also entering into the drama and gaining vicarious help for its members' analogous problems.

Psychodrama is a *holistic, existential* approach and has much in common with *Gestalt therapy* and, in terms of its philosophy, with *client-centred therapy*. It emphasises the need for the past to be re-enacted in the here-and-now of the present. Cognitive, affective and behavioural functioning are all stressed, and behaviour change is seen as taking place after *catharsis* has occurred and *insight* been achieved. These can be promoted by engaging the patient's body and mind together in dramatic *enactments* and re-enactments of his problems within the context of a therapeutic group. Emphasis is on the *process* rather than on the content of interactions and on the spontaneity and creativity of the patient.

A therapeutic session consists of warm-up exercises for the therapist and the group; the choice of *protagonist* and auxiliary egos; the *coaching* of the auxiliary egos; the enactment of the protagonist's problem; the introduction of special techniques such as *doubling* and the highlighting of particular aspects of the protagoniost's personality and situation; *working through* the problem or conflict situation using repeated *role play, role reversal* and *modelling* by other group members showing how they would handle the problem; and closure, when group members offer *feedback* and support and all engage in a debriefing session. A psychodrama group usually consists of between six and fourteen people, meeting for about one and a half to three hours on a weekly or twice-weekly basis. Groups may be closed and meet for a fixed number of sessions, or be open-ended. Either one or several group members may act as protagonists during a session.

Psychodramatic techniques have given birth to a wide variety of other methods and approaches, influencing in particular the development of Gestalt therapy and *transactional analysis*. A range of *action techniques* owe their origin to psychodrama and many of these are used in *family* and *marital therapy* (e.g. *family sculpting, family choreography*) and in *behavour therapy* (e.g. *behavioural rehearsal*), as well as in other methods of group psychotherapy. Psychodramatic techniques can be particularly effective when used to work on group or institutional problems and therapies and members' response to them.

BLATNER, H. A. (1973), *Acting In: Practical Applications of Psychodramatic Methods* (Springer, New York).

GREENBERG, I. A. (ed.) (1974), *Psychodrama:* *Theory and Therapy* (Behavioral Publications, New York).

GREER, V. J. and SACKS, J. M. (1973), *Bibliography of Psychodrama* (Greer, New York).

HASKELL, M. R. (1975), *Socio-analysis: Self Direction via Sociometry and Psychodrama* (Role Training Associates, Los Angeles).

LEVERTON, E. (1977), *Psychodrama for the Timid Clinician* (Springer, New York).

MORENO, J. L. (1946, 1959, 1969), *Psychodrama: Vols 1, 2 and 3* (Beacon House, New York).

STARR, A. (1977), *Psychodrama: Rehearsal for Living* (Nelson-Hall, Chicago).

YABLONSKY, I. (1976). *Psychodrama* (Basic Books, New York).

Psychodynamic

Relating to a theory of interacting mental forces, operating within the *psyche*. Thoughts, feelings and behaviour are viewed as the manifestation of inner *drives* and their interaction with each other within the psyche. Thus, all psychological theories which use the concept of inner drives and forces can be described as psychodynamic.

See also *Depth psychology, Psychoanalysis*.

Psycho-imagination therapy

A method of psychotherapy introduced by Shorr (1972, 1974, 1977) which uses the patient's conscious *imagery* as a systematic tool in the treatment process. It is based on an integration of *phenomenology* and the interpersonal approaches of Harry Stack Sullivan. Shorr views imagery as at the heart of the individual's consciousness and as an important means of gaining access to his *internal world*. Shorr uses a number of categories of imagery, some of which are: spontaneous imagery, directed imagery, self-image imagery, dual imagery, body imagery, sexual imagery, parental imagery and depth imagery. Psycho-imagination therapy uses two main techniques. First, the elicitation of imagery, by asking the patient to close his or her eyes. The image may be elicited or provided by the therapist from one of the above categories. Second, a therapeutic dialogue, in which the therapist works with the material that the imagery produces. Third, the use of various methods of *questioning*: finish-the-sentence questions, introduced at an appropriate point in the session can provide further material of importance; self and other questions, where the patient is asked to define him or her self as he perceives others define him; and most-or-least questions, to sharpen the patient's awareness of his self-image, attitudes and values. (A similar technique is employed by those who use *circular questioning*.) Psycho-imagination therapy is useful in focusing a patient who is inclined to use *intellectualisation and denial* on the core problem, and the imagery produced by the patient acts as a prognostic indicator regarding the progress being made. Imagery becomes richer and more hopeful as the patient works through conflicts and gets to grips with repressed material. Psycho-imagination therapy can be conducted in groups as well as in the one-to-one situation.

SHORR, J. E. (1972), *Psycho-imagination Therapy* (Intercontinental Medical Book Corporation, New York).

SHORR, J. E. (1974), *Psychotherapy Through Imagery* (Intercontinental Medical Book Corporation, New York).

SHORR, J. E. (1977), *Go See the Movie in Your Head* (Popular Library, New York).

Psycholinguistics

The application of the principles and theories of linguistics to psychology, psychotherapy and *psychoanalysis*. Although the study of language acquisition and learning has a long history, the study of psycholinguistics proper is a more recent development. Yet the two remain closely associated. Two main approaches have been taken. First, there is the behaviourist approach of Watson and Skinner. Watson suggests that language is learned by certain sounds being associated with certain referents, resulting in the building up of a pattern of linear relationships between

words. Skinner views language acquisition and use as a special case of learning and it is thus dependent upon the same principles of *reinforcement* to be found in *operant conditioning*. Second, there is the work of Noam Chomsky (1978), who challenged the behaviourist view of a stimulus-response model, and suggests instead the existence of a 'language acquisition device' which is part of the original endowment of the child and does not develop as part of his cognitive development. From this point of view, language does not develop as a linear collection of units acting as stimuli to the next in line but is generated as formal wholes. Other approaches have stressed the inter-actional *context* of language acquisition and use, and the way in which the type of language that is used and acquired strongly determines the individual's view of self and his/her environment. Bernstein (1977), for example, suggests that a restricted and an elaborated language code is used by the working class and middle classes respectively, determining their views of each other and reducing their ability to communicate with each other. Similarly, *feminist psychologists* (e.g. Lakoff 1973) have shown how much current language use favours the continuing patriarchal model of society.

The field is now an extremely broad and complex one but it has had the effect of increasing the psychotherapist's awareness of the role and function of language for the individual and for the psychotherapeutic process. Within *psychoanalysis* there are several ways in which language is being studied as an important aspect of the individual's experience and as a significant variable in the psychotherapeutic process. Jacques Lacan has been a prominent figure in the use of linguistic tools and concepts within the *French school* of psychoanalysis. He refers to his therapeutic work as 'textual analysis' and, following the linguist Saussure, Lacan suggests that the *unconscious* is structured like a language, made up of signifiers which have been repressed and which are inaccessible except through language. The task of psychoanalysis is to understand the relationship between the signifier and that which it signifies. Shapiro (1979) shows how psychoanalysts already make use of many linguistic concepts in their work and that linguistic analysis could profitably be used more formally by them. Schafer (1976) has suggested that psychoanalysts should rethink the language that they use both in their theoretical formulations and in clinical practice and should substitute an 'action language' for some of the metapsychological constructs used at present.

Outside psychoanalysis, communication theorists have explored language in terms of its *digital* and *analogic* properties and the role of *metacommunication* and *non-verbal communication*. *Labelling* theorists have examined the prescriptive effect of conferring positive and negative labels on patients. Various therapeutic techniques exploit the power of language to confer and alter meaning beneficially or adversely. For example, *paradox, metaphor, reframing*, and the *therapeutic double bind*.

BERNSTEIN, B. (1977), *Class, Codes and Control: Theoretical Studies Towards a Sociology of Language* (Routledge & Kegan Paul, London).

CHOMSKY, N. (1965), *Aspects of the Theory of Syntax* (MIT Press, Cambridge, Mass.).

CHOMSKY, N. (1978), 'Language and unconscious knowledge' (in Smith, J. S. (ed.), *Psychoanalysis and Language*, vol. 3).

GREENE, J. (1972), *Psycholinguistics* (Penguin, Harmondsworth).

JULIA, P. (1983), *Exploratory Models in Linguistics* (Princeton University Press, Princeton, New Jersey).

LAKOFF, R. (1973), 'Language and woman's place (*Language and Society*, vol. 2, pp. 45-79).

SCHAFER, R. (1976), *A New Language for Psychoanalysis* (Yale University Press, New Haven, Conn.).

SHAPIRO, T. (ed.) (1979), *Clinical Psycholinguistics* (Plenum Press, New York).

SMITH, J. S. (ed.) (1978), *Psychoanalysis and Language* (Yale University Press, New Haven, Conn.).

SNOW, C. E. and FERGUSON, C. A. (1977), *Talking to Children – Language and Acquisition*

(Cambridge University Press, Cambridge).

STEINBERG, D. (1982), *Psycholinguistics: Language, Mind and World* (Longman, London).

Psychological functions

Term used by Jung to describe four primary modes of psychic functioning: feeling, thinking, sensation and intuition. Jung suggested that whilst all four are employed by each person, each individual uses one 'superior function' through which he tends to perceive and relate to the external world. Jung (1921) comments that 'sensation establishes what is essentially given, thinking enables us to recognise its meaning, feeling tells us its value and finally, intuition points to the possibilities of the whence and whither that lie within the immediate facts'. Jung felt that the psychological functions could be observed as forming themselves into recognisable *psychological types*. He suggested that each individual's 'superior function' will characterise him typologically, and that this in turn will be oriented towards either extraversion or introversion. Thus, a thinking type of person may be either extraverted or introverted and this will characterise the way in which he expresses his superior function. Rossi (1977) has suggested that these four psychological functions may be associated with the *lateralisation* of the left and right hemispheres of the brain, with thinking forming part of the left brain's activity, intuition and sensation belonging to the right brain and feeling being mediated by both hemispheres acting in conjunction.

JUNG, C. G. (1921), 'Psychological types' (*Collected Works*, vol. 6, Routledge & Kegan Paul, London).

JUNG, C. G. (1933), *Modern Man in Search of a Soul* (Routledge & Kegan Paul, London).

ROSSI, E. (1977), 'The cerebral hemispheres in analytical psychology' (*J. of Analytical Psychology*, vol. 22, pp. 32-51).

Psychological types

The term is commonly associated with Jung's classification of people into extraverts and introverts. However, the effort to categorise and understand people in terms of 'types' can be traced back to antiquity and forward to the major contemporary contributions of Eysenck (1953, 1970, 1973). Historically, the categorisation into types goes back at least to Galen, the physician of the second century AD who, following Hippocrates, suggested that there were four basic temperaments based on the humours – melancholic, choleric, sanguine and phlegmatic. Kretschmer (1925) and later Sheldon (1940) made detailed studies of the relationship between psychological types and physique.

The categorisation made by Jung into extraversion and introversion had been suggested before by the Dutch psychologist Heimans and the Austrian psychiatrist Goss, amongst others, and Kretschmer and Rorschach published descriptions of systems centred on the distinction between these two types almost simultaneously with Jung. Jung, however, developed the concept further and suggested that all human beings could be placed somewhere on the continuum between introversion and extraversion. In his description of these two types, Jung comments, 'to the [extravert], the world of relationships is the important thing; for him it represents normality, the goal of desire. The [introvert] is primarily concerned with the inner pattern of his life, with his own self-consistency.' In the case of the extravert, *libido* naturally flows to the outside world and to the external objects; with the introvert, libido naturally flows towards objects in the *internal world* and reflection is preferred to activity. Jung suggests that a high degree of introversion or extraversion arouses a compensatory process in the *unconscious* from the attitude which is subdued – leading to an extraversion of the introvert and vice versa.

In his book *Psychological Types*, Jung traces the influence of these two attitudes on the development of philosophy, religion, art and psychology and he acknowledges their history. He stresses the normality and variability of each of the two broad types and the fact that each individual possesses characteristics of each type, so that only the relative *predominance* of the one or the other determines the type.

Later, Jung broadened this typology to include, additionally, four basic *psychological functions*. The reconciliation and integration of the potentially opposite trends of introversion and extraversion is the goal which is reached when *individuation* is achieved.

Eysenck has researched extensively into the field of extraversion and introversion and he has developed the *Eysenck personality inventory* for classifying individuals as extraverts and introverts. Morris (1979) has investigated the interpersonal behaviour of each type, and interest amongst psychologists in the experimental study and measurement of this dimension of personality has grown.

Jung's classification was to a great extent an intuitive one, derived from his clinical observations of patients. Eysenck's, by contrast, was derived experimentally from large numbers of people and has been refined as a research tool. The two typologies overlap a good deal but they are not identical and Eysenck (1970) has been somewhat at pains to distinguish the current experimental studies from Jung's work. More recently, however, several Jungian personality type tests have been developed and there is an extensive literature describing them (e.g. Wheelwright 1964, Myers 1962).

EYSENCK, H. J. (1953), *The Structure of Human Personality* (Methuen, London).

EYSENCK, H. J. (ed.) (1970), *Readings in Extraversion-Introversion* (Staples Press, London).

EYSENCK, H. J. (1973), *Eysenck on Extraversion* (Staples, Crosby & Lockwood, London).

JUNG, C. G. (1921), 'Psychological types' (*Collected Works*, vol. 6, Routledge & Kegan Paul, London).

JUNG, C. G. (1954), 'Fundamental questions of psychotherapy' (*Collected Works*, vol. 16, Routledge & Kegan Paul, London).

KRETSCHMER, E. (1925), *Physique and Character* (Harcourt, New York).

MORRIS, L. W. (1979), *Extraversion and Introversion: An Interactional Perspective* (Wiley, London).

MYERS, I. (1962), *The Myers-Briggs Type*

Indicator (Consulting Psychologists Press, Palo Alto, Calif.).

SHELDON, W. H. (1940), *The Varieties of Human Physique: An Introduction to Constitutional Psychology* (Harper, New York).

WHEELWRIGHT, J. *et al.* (1964), *Jungian Typology: the Gray Wheelwright Test Manual* (Society of Jungian Analysts, San Francisco).

Psychonoxious
Literally, psychologically harmful. The harmful qualities or characteristics of the therapist.

See also *Deterioration, Iatrogenic, Pathogenesis.*

Psychoprophylaxis
All those activities and approaches which act as preventative mental health measures, analogous to prophylactic measures taken in the field of physical health.

See also *Crisis intervention, Holistic education, Parenting skills training, Self-help, Social therapy.*

Psychosynthesis
A method of psychotherapy developed by the Italian psychiatrist Roberto Assagioli, as a contrast to what he perceived to be the limitations of *psychoanalysis*. Assagioli was an early disciple of Freud's and Freud debated the value of psychosynthesis in public on several occasions. In 1919 he commented that 'psychosynthesis is achieved during analytic treatment without our intervention, automatically and inevitably'. But later he had become more dismissive: 'I cannot imagine . . . that any new task for us is to be found in this psychosynthesis. . . . I should say it is nothing but a meaningless phrase.'

Whilst retaining the classical psychoanalytic understanding of the *unconscious*, Assagioli believed that Freud's picture of the psychic world was an unbalanced one because of its absence of a spiritual dimension. He proposed a counterbalancing *superconscious* in which the individual could find his transpersonal Self, the repository of the most positive and constructive aspects of his personality. Contact with this Self enables the patient to gain the

courage to explore the less acceptable parts of himself. Whilst Assagioli emphasised the importance of bringing the unconscious into conscious awareness, he believed that this is insufficient of itself to bring about change. In contrast to psychoanalysis, Assagioli suggested that right understanding does not necessarily lead to right action. In addition, the patient's will has to be trained so that he can apply the *insight* he has gained in therapy to the day-to-day decisions of his ordinary life. The direction of the will involves its motivation, decision making, affirmation, planning and execution of the proposed plan. The therapeutic process enables the patient to take responsibility for his feelings and behaviour through the direction of his will.

Assagioli has linked psychosynthesis with *existential psychotherapy.* The individual's search for meaning is viewed as being of central importance, 'particularly the meaning which each individual *gives* to life or is *looking for* in life' (Assagioli 1976). Like existential psychotherapists too, Assagioli recognises the importance of personal and spiritual values, the individual's moral responsibility for the choices he makes and the place of suffering within the individual's life. There are affinities too with other approaches. With *humanistic psychology* it shares an emphasis on the recognition and acceptance of positive, creative and joyous experiences and the therapeutic goal of *self-actualisation*, and with *logotherapy*, the search for meaning.

Psychosynthesis encourages a technical eclecticism. Therapists use cathartic techniques to release powerful negative emotions and a variety of *action techniques*. A combination of therapeutic entry points along the mind-body-affective axis are selected according to the needs of the individual patient. Guided *imagery, meditation,* and *Gestalt,* for example, may be used to reveal unconscious material. Whatever the primary technique used, the therapist helps the patient integrate the work on all three levels of functioning. The overall goal of psychosynthesis is the integration of all the polarities that exist within the patient through a unifying approach to the theoretical and technical aspects of therapy.

ASSAGIOLI, R. A. (1976). *Psychosynthesis: A Manual of Principles and Techniques* (Penguin, Harmondsworth).

ASSAGIOLI, R. A. (1973), *The Act of Will* (Viking, New York).

FREUD, S. (1919), 'Lines of advance in psychoanalytic therapy' (*Standard Edition*, vol. 17, Hogarth Press, London).

VARGIU, J. (1983), *The Realisation of the Self: A Psychosynthesis Book* (J. P. Tarcher, Los Angeles).

Psychotherapy

The task of defining psychotherapy is extraordinarily complex. Definitions abound, ranging from the extremely narrow (e.g. only *psychoanalysis* can properly be regarded as psychotherapy) to the extremely inclusive (any type of benign personal influence which is brought to bear on an individual or a group for the purpose of relieving problems or enhancing life experiences can be regarded as psychotherapy). Whilst the former definition would exclude everyone except trained psychoanalysts (and possibly only the Freudian variety of those), the latter would include the *psychotherapeutic* activities of *paraprofessionals* and the work of priests, teachers, doctors and nurses, etc , as well as many taxi drivers, shopkeepers and next-door neighbours. Thus, in practice, it is usual for the term to be narrowed down, first, to include only the activities of trained professionals whose practice does *not* include other major components (such as nursing and teaching). But in addition, several other exclusions are sometimes made which are more problematic: the term psychotherapy may for example be restricted to the use of verbal interventions, so that art, music, dance, etc., are thereby excluded. Thus, the deceptively simple definition offered by Brown and Pedder (1979) of psychotherapy as 'essentially a conversation which involves listening to and talking with those in trouble with the aim of helping them understand and resolve their predicament', although broad, limits psychotherapy to an insight-oriented, verbal experience. Second, the recipients of psychotherapy may be restricted to those who are diagnosed as having a *recognisable psychological problem*, and the term would then not include 'growth' or self-actualising activities for 'normal' people. Third, the term is often reserved for work done on feelings, cognitions and other mental processes and is thereby contrasted with *behaviour therapy* which is then viewed as a different type of activity altogether.

Several other problems have to be addressed. Should psychotherapy be viewed primarily as an art or as a science or as somewhere in between? If the former, emphasis will be placed on personal charisma, on the *therapist variable* and on *relationship factors*; if the latter, on techniques and skills. Should the *model* for psychotherapy be medical, educational, moral or growth? Are the roots of the problems to which psychotherapy is directed biological, social, existential or are they problems of maladaptive learning? Should the *unit of treatment* be restricted to individuals or should it properly include couples, groups, families and other networks? Is there one or are there many theories of change? The problem of defining psychotherapy was recognised by the Professions Joint Working Party (1978) who felt that because of the impossibility of defining the term, only the indicative and not the functional *regulation* of psychotherapists could be recommended.

The scope of this dictionary implies that the present writer views psychotherapy as including both behavioural and non-behavioural approaches; both verbal and active therapies; as including orientations that are derived from medical, educational, moral and growth models; as accepting multivariate theories of aetiology and theories of change; and as an activity which is directed towards a range of treatment units. Thus, Winnicott's (1971a) delightful definition of psychotherapy as having to do with 'two people playing together' would have to be challenged because of its restriction to the one-to-one situation. Whilst accepting these broad parameters it nevertheless seems important to distinguish psycho-therapy as a primary focus from all those activities such as general medicine, social work, nursing, teaching, etc., which contain major *psychotherapeutic* elements, reserving the term psychotherapy for the former. Moreover, the term is more logically confined to practitioners who have some training in the method they are practising and should not therefore include the work of paraprofessionals. Frank (1973) offers a generally accepted definition, suggesting that psychotherapy is that type of *social influence* exerted by a trained and socially sanctioned healer on a person or persons who suffers and who is seeking relief, through a defined series of contacts.

BERGIN, A. E. and GARFIELD, S. (eds) (1978), *Handbook of Psychotherapy and Behavior Change* (Wiley, New York).
BLOCH, S. (1979), *Introduction to the Psychotherapies* (Oxford University Press, Oxford).
BLOCH, S. (1982), *What is Psychotherapy?* (Oxford University Press, Oxford).
BROWN, D. and PEDDER, J. (1979), *Introduction to Psychotherapy* (Tavistock, London).
CORSINI, R. J. (ed.) (1978), *Handbook of Innovative Psychotherapies* (Wiley, New York).
CORSINI, R. J. (ed.) (1979), *Current Psychotherapies* (Peacock, Itasca, Ill.).
FRANK, J. D. (1973), *Persuasion and Healing: A Comparative Study of Psychotherapy* (Johns Hopkins Press, Baltimore).
GURMAN, A. S. and RAZIN, A. M. (1977), *Effective Psychotherapy* (Pergamon Press, New York).
HARPER, R. A. (1975), *The New Psychotherapies* (Prentice-Hall, Englewood Cliffs, New Jersey).
PROCHASKA, J. O. (1979), *Systems of Psychotherapy: A Transtheoretical Analysis* (Dorsey Press, Homewood, Ill.).
PROFESSIONS JOINT WORKING PARTY (1978), *Statutory Registration of Psychotherapists*.
STORR, A. (1979), *The Art of Psychotherapy* (Secker & Warburg, London).
STRUPP, H. H. (1978), 'Psychotherapy research and practice: an overview' (in Bergin and Garfield, op. cit.).
WINNICOTT, D. W. (1971a), *Playing and Reality* (Penguin, Harmondsworth).
WINNICOTT, D. W. (1971b), *Therapeutic Consultations in Child Psychiatry* (Hogarth Press, London).
WOLBERG, L. (1978), *The Technique of Psychotherapy* (3rd edn, Grune & Stratton, New York).

Punctuation

A linear organisation of systemic behavioural events. The term is used to describe the way in which the same transactional sequence can be described from different viewpoints. For example, in a dyadic *transaction* in which the wife withdraws each time the husband complains, the wife punctuates this sequence causally by saying that she withdraws *because* the husband complains. By contrast, the husband, punctuating the same sequence causally, says that he complains *because* she withdraws. The problem lies in their inability to *metacommunicate* and in their belief that such a sequence has a beginning and an end which, if discovered, will lead to the solution of their disagreement. Watzlawick *et al.* (1968) show that 'the nature of a relationship is contingent upon the punctuation of the communicational sequences between the communicants'. Effective therapeutic interventions include metacommunicating about the process of punctuation and making a paradoxical intervention to alter the nature of the punctuation.

WATZLAWICK, P. *et al.* (1968), *The Pragmatics of Human Communication* (W. W. Norton, New York).

Punishment

A *stimulus* which decreases the frequency of the *response* which it follows. It is similar to *response cost* in that it effects a *decrease* in the succeeding response, but differs from response cost in that it consists of the addition of a new stimulus. Although a punishing stimulus may be unpleasant or painful, punishment is defined independently of whether the consequence appears to be aversive. Thus, *self-monitoring* is technically a punishment if it serves to decrease the frequency of the problem behaviour being monitored. Punishment is on the whole an ineffective way of producing behaviour change unless used in combination with positive *reinforcement.*

AZRIN, N. H. and HOLZ, W. C. (1968), 'Punishment' (in Honig, W. K. (ed.), *Operant Behavior*, Appleton-Century-Crofts, New York).

CHURCH, R. (1963), 'The varied effects of punishment' (*Psychological Review*, vol. 70, p. 369).

Q

Q Sort

A measurement of self-concept developed from the work of William Stevenson at the University of Chicago. The client is given a pack of cards each bearing a self-descriptive statement such as 'I am a submissive person', 'I am a hard worker', etc. The client is asked to sort the cards into a number of piles, usually nine or eleven, along a continuum from most to least characteristic of the client, as he perceives himself. Variations on this procedure include asking the client to sort the cards in accordance with his *ideal* self-concept; from the viewpoint of a particular age in his life; how his wife/mother, etc., might have sorted them, etc. Correlations between these variations may be calculated to discover the client's degree of self-esteem and the discrepancy between his self-concept and his perception of the views of others. The test, which may be administered at intervals during treatment or before and after treatment, is used as an *outcome* measure, particularly amongst *client-centred* and *humanistic psychologists*. Increases in correlations between actual and ideal self and between self and others'

perceptions are regarded as evidence of positive outcome. A considerable number of sets of items are available for the therapist's use with different types and ages of clients although the reliability of items is uncertain and so too is the degree to which the client's responses are subject to social desirability effects.

Questioning

See *Circular questioning, Open ended question*.

Quid pro quo (marital)

Literal Latin meaning 'something for something'. Term introduced by Jackson (1965) to describe the initial bargain entered into by husband and wife. Jackson defines the quid pro quo as 'a metaphorical statement of the marital relationship bargain; that is, how the couple has agreed to define themselves within this relationship'. Jackson suggests that the early phase of marriage is taken up with establishing the rules of the relationship. This involves bargaining and negotiation, the process being partly *conscious* and partly *unconscious*. Out of these negotiations emerges the quid pro quo or contract upon which the relationship is built. In *dysfunctional* relationships, the quid pro quo is built upon a trade-off between the couple, which allows one partner's 'health' to be bought at the expense of the other's *symptoms*. It involves more than an exchange of behaviours but a tacit agreement regarding the definition of the self and the other.

The term is also used to describe a technique of *behavioural marital therapy* (Lederer and Jackson 1968; Stern and Marx 1973). A *contract* is drawn up between husband and wife with the help of the therapist, whereby if one spouse engages in the desired behaviour then the other spouse will also engage in the behaviour that has been requested. (For example, *if* the husband cooks the meal on alternate days then the wife will go out with him once a week – based on the assumption that these are requests that each has made of the other.) Thus, the changes in the behaviours of the spouses are made contingent upon one another. Jacobson and Martin (1976) argue that quid pro quo contracts are more efficient than other kinds because they use as *reinforcers* changed behaviours in the other which the spouses are likely to respond to enthusiastically. However, they may run up against each spouse's *resistance* to starting the process in motion.

JACKSON, D. D. (1965), 'Family rules: the marital quid pro quo' (*Archives of General Psychiatry*, vol. 12, pp. 589-94).

JACOBSON, N. S. and MARTIN, B. (1976) 'Behavioral marriage therapy: current status' (*Psychological Bulletin*, vol. 83, pp. 540-56).

LEDERER, W. J. and JACKSON, D. D. (1968), *The Mirages of Marriage* (W. W. Norton, New York).

STERN, R. S. and MARX, I. M. (1973), 'Contract therapy in obsessive compulsive neurosis with marital discord' (*Brit. J. of Psychiatry*, vol. 123, pp. 681-4).

TSOI-HOSHMAND, L. (1971), 'The limits of quid pro quo in couple therapy' (*Family Co-ordinator*, vol. 24, pp. 51-4).

See also *Collusion, Contingency management, Fit (marital), Metaphor, Reciprocity.*

R

Radical therapy

A group of approaches which hold in common the belief that traditional methods of psychotherapy are themselves the problem that must be changed. Mental illness and psychological disturbance are viewed as last resort solutions to the moral conflicts inherent within intolerable social, political and economic circumstances. Since psychotherapy is seen as trying to adjust the individual to his psycho-social *context* and social/political environment, the problem becomes two-fold. First, how to survive psychotherapy and refuse to be 'adjusted', and second, how to change the oppressive environmental structures which are viewed as causative in producing psychological problems.

Current radical approaches generally rely upon a Marxist analysis of society and they have, as their overall aim, the reorganisation of social and political institutions, to remove racial, sexist and class divisions. Several approaches can be distinguished. First, the anti-psychiatry movement which comprises theoreticians such as Szasz with his views on the 'myth' of mental illness, Goffman (1961) with his attack on the *medical model* and the oppressive effect of institutions, and Laing (1967), Cooper (1967) and their followers whose efforts have been directed at producing alternative communities for understanding mental illness, as well as exposing the repressive effect of the family and other psycho-social networks on the individual. Second, and developing out of the first, the more fully radical position of Steiner *et al.* (1975) who view all psychiatric problems as problems of *alienation* which they define as the experience of being both oppressed and deceived about being oppressed. Liberation involves awareness to act against deception and contact with other human beings to act against alienation. The task of the 'therapist' is to act as a leader of this liberation without in turn becoming a source of oppression. Third, and arising out of the first two, are the whole range of peer group and *self-help* approaches, that span the political/psychotherapeutic interface. These include *feminist therapy, consciousness raising* groups, and peer counselling such as *re-evaluation counselling*. A middle position is taken by the community psychiatry approaches which espouse a far less radical philosophy than some of the above groups but which draw more conservative models and practitioners into the service of structural change. Under the broad heading of community approaches are included the *systemic therapies* concerned with changing an albeit rather narrow psycho-social system, *crisis intervention* which emphasises individual strengths and community resources, and *social therapy*. Sedgwick (1982) provides an up-to-date overview and critique of the radical therapy movement.

AGEL, J. (1971), *The Radical Therapist* (Ballantyne Books, New York).

BROWN, P. (1973), *Radical Psychology* (Tavistock, London).

CLARE, A. (1976), *Psychiatry in Dissent* (Tavistock, London).

COOPER, D. (1967), *Psychiatry and Anti-psychiatry* (Penguin, Harmondsworth).

COOPER, D. (1970), *The Death of the Family* (Penguin, Harmondsworth).

GOFFMAN, E. (1961), *Asylums* (Penguin, Harmondsworth).

HALLECK, S. L. (1971), *The Politics of Therapy* (Harper & Row, New York).

HEATHER, N. (1976), *Radical Perspectives in Psychology* (Methuen, London).

LAING, R. D. (1967), *The Politics of Experience* (Penguin, Harmondsworth).

RT COLLECTIVE (1974), *The Radical Therapist* (Penguin, Harmondsworth).

SEDGWICK, P. (1982), *Psychopolitics* (Pluto Press, London).

STEINER, G. *et al.* (1975), *Readings in Radical Psychiatry* (Grove Press, New York).

Rage reduction therapy

See *Z-process attachment therapy.*

Range of convenience

The extent to which a *construct* is relevant and applicable to the understanding of people and events. According to Kelly's range *corollary*, a construct is convenient for the anticipation of a finite range of events only. For example, the construct tall-short has a range of convenience which includes trees, people and houses, but does not include weather, light or fear. Even though some people will use constructs more comprehensively than others, few if any personal constructs are likely to be applicable to everything.

KELLY, G. A. (1955), *Psychology of Personal Constructs* (W. W. Norton, New York).

KELLY, G. A. (1963), *A Theory of Personality* (W. W. Norton, New York).

Rank, Otto (1884-1939)

Otto Rank was born in Vienna and gained his PhD in philology at the University of Vienna in 1912. He was a member of Freud's inner circle and one of the six members of the circle that guided the development of the psycho-analytic movement. He showed a particular interest in applying Freudian concepts to the interpretation of art, mythology and literature. His most original work, *The Trauma of Birth*, was published in 1923 (1929 in English) and this marked the beginning of a distressing period of conflict with Freud. He finally broke away, leaving Vienna in 1924, to develop his own ideas more freely and to formulate his method of *will therapy*. He settled in the United States, where he founded the Pennsylvania School of Social Work which propagated his theoretical and technical approaches to treatment. Rank's training in philosophy, history and languages, rather than medicine, enabled him to spread the influence of psychoanalytic concepts and to broaden their basis beyond the biological emphasis of Freud. He had a great influence on the development of *humanistic psychology* and on experiential and *existential therapy*. He was a prolific writer but his work tends to be difficult to read and somewhat polemical. His last book, *Will Therapy*, gives the clearest outline of his approach to psychotherapy.

Rankian analysis

See *Will therapy.*

Rapport

A relationship of mutual confidence and understanding that develops between patient and therapist. The term is used in a particular sense by Jung (1954), who links it with the development of the *transference*. He views transference as the patient's attempt to develop a psychological rapport with the therapist. 'The feebler the rapport, i.e. the less the doctor and patient understand one another, the more intensely will the transference be fostered and the more sexual will be its form.' Ultimately, Jung suggests that when the patient's *projections* on to the therapist are recognised for what they are, the transference is at an end and rapport is established through the medium of the real relationship between therapist and patient. Therapists from almost all other approaches emphasise the need to establish rapport by appropriately *joining* the patient and creating the *core conditions* of the therapeutic process. For them, rapport is the means by which both a *working alliance* is formed and the core conditions are facilitated.

JUNG, C. G. (1954), 'The therapeutic value of abreaction' (*Collected Works*, vol. 16, Routledge & Kegan Paul, London).

Rational emotive therapy

A theory of personality and a method of psychotherapy based on the assumptions that an individual's irrational or faulty beliefs are the cause of his *dysfunctional* behaviour and of his destructive self-concept. Rational emotive therapy has elements in common with *cognitive behaviour therapy* and, like it, emphasises the role of cognition in the formation of problem behaviour and affective disorders. The method was introduced by Albert Ellis who proposed an ABC for understanding the relationship between the activating events (A), the destructive consequence that follows it (C) and the irrational belief system (B) about (A) which in fact precipitates (C). Rational emotive therapy emphasises the philosophic disputing (D) of the client's self-defeating beliefs, but although *cognitive restructuring* is the primary approach to treatment, it also utilises affective and behavioural modes of personality change, and the integrating of the three is the method's distinctive feature.

Ellis suggests that people's irrational beliefs fall into three main groups, stemming from the beliefs that: (A) 'I must be competent in everything and approved of by everyone'; (B) 'Others must treat me properly and when they don't they are worthless'; and (C) 'I must have everything I need easily and immediately'. Cognitively, rational emotive therapy teaches the client to change these self-statements into wanting, wishing and preferring instead of needing and demanding. Affectively, it employs *imagery, confrontation* and *structured exercises* to enable the client to experience

himself differently. Behaviourally, it uses a range of techniques such as *operant conditioning, modelling, systematic desensitisation, coping skills interventions* and *homework assignments*. Rational emotive therapy aims both to eliminate *symptoms*, to restructure the personality and to provide the individual with new coping skills (see *coping skills interventions*). It can be used in a group work setting as well as in individual psychotherapy. Recently some work has been done on the evaluation of *outcome*. Smith (1983) examined the changes that occurred in irrational beliefs as a result of rational emotive therapy. As predicted, reliable correlations between changes in beliefs and changes in emotional distress were obtained, but the same held true of the *control group*. Eschenroeder (1982) criticises the theory of rational emotional therapy for its lack of formal structure, its conformity bias and its neglect of the influence of environmental factors on human functioning but Ellis (1982) defends his theory against Eschenroeder's attack.

DE GIUSEPPE, R. *et al.* (1977), 'Outcome studies of rational emotive therapy' (*Counseling Psychologist*, vol. 7, pp. 43-50).
ELLIS, A. (1979), *Reason and Emotion in Psychotherapy* (Citadel Press, Secaucus, New Jersey).
ELLIS, A. (1982), 'A reappraisal of rational emotive therapy's theoretical foundations and therapeutic methods: a reply to Eschenroeder (*Cognitive Therapy and Research*, vol. 6, pp. 393-8).
ELLIS, A. and GRIEGER, R. (1977), *Handbook of Rational-Emotive Therapy* (Springer, New York).
ELLIS, A. and WHITELEY, J. M. (1979), *Theoretical and Empirical Foundations of Rational Emotive Therapy* (Brooks-Cole, Monterey, Calif.).
ESCHENROEDER, C. (1982), 'How rational is rational emotive therapy? A critical appraisal' (*Cognitive Therapy and Research*, vol. 6, pp. 381-91).
MURPHY, R. and ELLIS, A. (1978), *A Bibliography of Materials on Rational Emotive Therapy*

RATIONALISATION

and Cognitive Behavior Therapy (Institute for Rational Living, New York).

SMITH, T. (1983), 'Change in irrational beliefs and the outcome of rational emotive psychotherapy' (*J. of Consulting and Clinical Psychology*, vol. 51, pp. 156-7).

Rationalisation

A *defence mechanism* whereby the individual seeks to 'explain' to himself and others behaviour, motives, attitudes, thoughts or feelings which are otherwise unacceptable. The process is not always considered to be a defence mechanism, but broadly speaking it has the effect of defending the *ego*. For example, racial prejudice may be rationalised by an appeal to the greater good, which can be achieved by all races if 'separate development' is promoted. Rationalisation commonly involves *intellectualisation*.

Reaction formation

A *defence mechanism* against the feared outcome of a repressed wish, whereby the individual behaves as though the opposite were true. For example, the obsessionally clean person may be defending himself against the fear of and wish for the 'dirtiness' of sexuality; the phobic person against a desire for the thing which seems to be feared; or the 'martyred', overzealous husband or wife against his or her resentment at the demands of the partner. The expression of the emotion or the action is determined not by the needs of the other or of what is required by circumstances, but by the *ego*'s need to defend itself from the repressed anxiety.

Reality principle

A regulatory principle of mental functioning which emerges gradually in order to modify the activity of its contrasting principle, the *pleasure principle*. Both form part of the *metapsychology* of *psychoanalysis*. According to Freud, the reality principle develops alongside and in order to assist the development of the *ego* and the elaboration of its functions. The reality principle enables the ego to come to terms with what is real, even though it may be disagreeable, rather than what is merely desired. Its aim is therefore to help the ego postpone the release of tension or the satisfaction of need until a suitable object is available, rather than using a substitute. The development of the reality principle does not supersede the pleasure principle but it enables the ego to suspend temporarily its needs in the interest of external reality until pleasure can again be achieved.

FREUD, S. (1920), 'Beyond the pleasure principle' (*Standard Edition*, vol. 18, Hogarth Press, London).

Reality testing

The process whereby the individual distinguishes between internal *phantasies* and external reality and the means by which he learns to evaluate the external world accurately. According to psychoanalytic theory, reality testing is one of the principal functions of the *ego*, enabling it to form an objective evaluation of the external world and to respond to it appropriately. The process involves the individual in trying out his *hypotheses* through specific actions in the external world, to see whether they can be substantiated or not. For example, the paranoid individual has to test out his paranoid fantasies in the external world in order to discover that his experience of persecution is more appropriately located within than without. Or, an individual has to test out the validity of his hypothesis that all short people are bad-tempered by engaging in a range of interactions with them.

Reality therapy

A method of psychotherapy introduced by William Glasser out of dissatisfaction with *psychoanalysis*. It emphasises the need to help patients face reality and fulfil their basic human needs. Its practice is centred on the Institute of Reality Therapy, Los Angeles, California. It has links with both *cognitive therapy* and *learning theory*, which provides one of the theoretical bases for therapy.

Glasser suggests that all human beings have

two basic psychological needs: the need to love and be loved, and the need to feel that they are worthwhile to themselves and to others. Helping patients fulfil these two needs is the basis of reality therapy. The essential ingredient for fulfilling them is a positive emotional involvement with at least one other person. Thus, at the point when a patient presents for help, he is inevitably lacking a person to care deeply about him and for whom he can care – leading to a sense of isolation and *alienation*. For him to gain help from therapy he must therefore gain or regain involvement, first with the therapist and then with other people. The basic methodology behind Glasser's approach emphasises the creation of a warm involved relationship with the patient; understanding the ways in which the patient's needs are not being fulfilled and rejecting his behaviour which is unrealistic; and teaching him responsibility for himself and for others, by helping him develop ways to meet his needs. Reality therapists enter into a *contract* with the patient and make use of specific, concrete behavioural *tasks*. *Confrontation* of the patient's 'irresponsible' behaviour is an important aspect of treatment.

Therapy emphasises the here and now current situation, is relatively short-term and makes use of both behavioural (tasks, contracts, positive *reinforcement*) and *humanistic* ideas (an involved relationship with the therapist). It is modelled on an educative rather than a medical approach to treatment. It has been criticised for being somewhat moralistic in its emphasis on right and wrong behaviour and simplistic in its disregard for past material and *unconscious* processes. Glasser however has indicated its usefulness in work with seriously disturbed adolescents, with schoolchildren and with psychotics. Its principles can be applied in group work as well as in individual psychotherapy.

BASSIN, A. (ed.) (1976), *The Reality Therapy Reader* (Harper & Row, New York).
GLASSER, W. (1965), *Reality Therapy: A New Approach to Psychiatry* (Harper & Row, New York).

See also *Crisis intervention, Self-help*.

Rebirthing

A regressive therapeutic method introduced by Orr (Orr and Ray 1977) which enables the client to re-experience his own birth and free himself from the negative experiences and belief systems which he developed from this moment onwards. Like Rank, the proponents of this approach consider that the *birth trauma* is the prototype and origin of all later anxiety. The individual's later predisposition towards coping or failing to cope with stressful situations arises from whether or not he was born after prolonged labour, roughly handled at birth and removed from his mother or, conversely, whether he experienced greater continuity and compatibility between his interuterine and extra-uterine existence as suggested by Leboyer (1975) and other advocates of natural childbirth.

Therapy consists in helping the client to re-experience his birth in order to let go of his grievances, originating in the negative experiences surrounding the birth. Originally the rebirthing experience was conducted in a warm pool of water to simulate inter-uterine existence. Currently, rebirthing takes place in a warm, comfortable but dry environment and makes use of two techniques: connected breathing and repeated affirmations which encourage the letting go of what is negative and the acceptance and reiteration of a positive response to the present. *Abreaction* and *catharsis* as used in *primal therapy* are therefore not encouraged. As clients inhale they are encouraged to think of their connection with a positive transcendent Being; as they exhale, they re-establish the fact that they belong to an accepting, created universe. Affirmations consist of single sentences which relate to and reverse the client's specific anxiety or negativity. Rebirthing has connections with both the *character training approaches* and with *transpersonal psychology*.

LEBOYER, F. (1975), *Birth Without Violence* (Knopf, New York).
ORR, L. and RAY, S. (1977), *Rebirthing in the New Age* (Celestial Arts, Millbrae, Calif.).

RECIPROCAL INHIBITION

Reciprocal inhibition

A principle of *counter conditioning* defined by Wolpe (1958) whereby, if a response-inhibiting anxiety can be made to occur in the presence of anxiety-evoking stimuli, it will weaken the bond between these stimuli and the anxiety. Assertive responses, *relaxation training* and mild electric shock are used to inhibit anxiety and it is the principle behind the techniques of *systematic desensitisation* and of *aversion therapy*. The clinical use of reciprocal inhibition was derived from Sherrington's work on spinal reflexes. Gellhorn (1967) discussed its ubiquitous nature outside the clinical situation. Wolpe (1981) discusses the way in which reciprocal inhibition is the common factor in many behavioural treatments and that the alternatives that have been proposed as agents of change are theoretically unacceptable.

GELLHORN, E. (1967), *Principles of Autonomic-somatic Integrations* (Minnesota Press, Mankato, Minnesota).
WOLPE, J. (1958), *Psychotherapy by Reciprocal Inhibition* (Stanford University Press, Stanford, Calif.).
WOLPE, J. (1981), 'Reciprocal inhibition and therapeutic change' (*J. of Behavior Therapy and Experimental Psychiatry*, vol. 12, pp. 185-8).

Reciprocity

The mutual reinforcement of interpersonal behaviour. Both rewards and punishments can be reciprocated although *dysfunctional* relationships are usually characterised by the reciprocation of aversive stimuli in an attempt to control the behaviour of the other. *Behavioural marital* and *family therapists* attempt to interrupt this negative cycle by increasing the couple's exchange of positive behaviours. The principle of reciprocity is fundamental to the behavioural treatment of relationships and usually involves a *quid pro quo* agreement between two people whereby they agree to exchange behaviours desired by the other. The agreement to exchange behaviours is usually formalised into a *contract*. Although this form of 'give to get' negotiation remains an important ingredient of behavioural treatments, it has been criticised on ethical and practical grounds (Leadbeater and Farber 1983). Gurman (1978) points out that whilst behavioural marital therapists stress the desirability of replacing the coercion of one partner by the other by reciprocity, both coercion and reciprocity can be viewed as forms of control at the *meta* level. Although negative control (coercion) is replaced by positive control (reciprocity), both are nevertheless forms of control which may contravene other needful aspects of the marital relationship such as mutual affirmation and acceptance of the other as he or she is.

AZRIN, N. *et al.* (1973), 'Reciprocity counseling: a rapid learning based procedure for marital counseling' (*Behavior, Research and Therapy*, vol. 11, pp. 365-82).
GURMAN, A. S. (1978), 'Contemporary marital therapies' (in Paolino, T. J. and McGrady, B. S., *Marriage and Marital Therapy*, Brunner/Mazel, New York).
LEADBEATER, B. and FARBER, B. (1983), 'The limits of reciprocity in behavior marriage therapy' (*Family Process*, vol. 22, pp. 229-37).
MEAD, D. E. (1981), 'Reciprocity counseling: practice and research', *J. of Marital and Family Therapy*, vol. 7, pp. 189-200).

See also *Contingency management*.

Redefinition

A therapeutic activity by which the therapist seeks both to *accommodate* to the views held by the patient and to alter, by covert and overt means, the patient's or family's view of the problem, in order to adjust it to his own theoretical understandings of their difficulties. Therapists from all modalities and orientations engage in redefinition to some extent. Only through the patient and therapist reaching some common understanding of the problem can the *joining* process take place and the therapist apply the knowledge he derives from a relatively stable theory and set of techniques. Redefinition involves the negotiation of meaning which, if successful, may be a highly therapeutic activity in its own right, since it may involve the patient seeing his problems and their solution in a new and more constructive light. Referring to redefinition in *family therapy*, Andolfi (1979) comments, 'redefinition of the problem for which therapy has been requested is the corner stone on which the entire therapeutic process rests. It is the most creative aspect of therapy, and the one that makes it possible for the family to become the protagonist of its own change in the therapeutic situation.' Except in the brief problem-oriented therapies, most therapists try to redefine the problem to increase its complexity and the range of its possible solutions. Some examples are the inclusion of the *unconscious* determinants of current behaviour (psychoanalytic therapies); the patient's current interpersonal relationships (group therapies); or the transactional relationships that exist in a family or marital system (*systemic therapies*). Each therapeutic method will try to move the patient towards its own belief system in terms of the origin of the problems, the *goals* of treatment and the ways in which these may be reached.

ANDOLFI, M. (1979), *Family Therapy: An Interactional Approach* (Plenum Press, New York).

See also *Attribution theory*, *Labelling*, *Reframing*.

Reductionism

The tendency to reduce wholes to their component parts or lowest common denominator, for the purposes of examination or treatment. Reductionism is seen in the analysis of behaviour into *stimulus* and *response* components; the division of the individual into mental, physical and spiritual aspects or the isolation of individuals from their psycho-social *context*. Radical *behaviourism* and *psychoanalysis* tend to be reductionist in their pure forms, whilst *Gestalt therapy*, *humanistic psychology*, *existential psychotherapy* and the *systemic therapies* stress the need to study and treat the individual as a whole and, if possible, within his psycho-social context. However, reductionism and *holism* are best seen as complementary rather than

opposing forms of description, although the holistic approach has been much needed to redress the balance of the extreme reductionism of some approaches in the past.

Re-evaluation counselling

A form of reciprocal therapeutic help, also known as co-counselling, developed by Harvey Jackins in the United States during the 1950s in which self-directed work between peers meeting together in pairs helps each individual to deal with his or her tensions and emotional pain. Each person in the pair takes turns in being counsellor and client for a fixed period of time, usually for one hour. The counsellor helps the client to discharge pent-up, suppressed painful emotion from the recent or remote past. The client is helped to experience a three-stage cycle of *catharsis*, *insight* or re-evaluation of past traumatic events, and celebration. This may be followed by a fourth stage of goal setting and redirection. The responsibility for the session rests with the person who is taking turns at being the client and he or she is largely self-directed. The task of the person acting as the counsellor is in *attending* fully to what the client is expressing, giving sustained support throughout the hour and offering security for the client's *self-disclosure*. The counsellor does not offer any *interpretations* or *advice* although, if the client gets completely stuck, the counsellor may ask an *open-ended question* or offer a suggestion. Training for co-counselling is conducted by a co-counselling leader and takes place in five-day workshops, in two weekend workshops or in a course of evening sessions. Advanced courses and follow-up days are also held. Client and counsellor are taught to encourage self-affirming statements, talk descriptively rather than analytically, use repetition to uncover emotion and verbalise random thoughts and associations. *Role play* and techniques from *Gestalt therapy* and body work are also used. In Britain, Heron (1973, 1977) has been a leading exponent of co-counselling and one of the chief leaders of training workshops. In 1974 he became one of the founders of Co-counselling International

289

which runs international workshops and provides a forum for discussing theory and practice and encourages the building up of local peer communities as centres of affirmation and support for their members. Help offered in co-counselling avoids some of the dependency problems and the *labelling* processes that are often contingent upon receiving formal psychotherapeutic help, but the method is unsuitable for people who are so disturbed or distressed that they are unable to act as counsellors themselves within a reciprocal relationship.

EVISON, R. and HOROBIN, R. (1979), *How to Change Yourself and Your World* (Co-counselling Phoenix, Sheffield).
HERON, J. (1973), *Re-evaluation Counselling: A Theoretical Review* (Human Potential Research, Guildford, Surrey).
HERON, J. (1977), *Catharsis in Human Development* (University of Surrey, Guildford).
JACKINS, H. (1965), *The Human Side of Human Beings: The Theory of Re-evaluation Counselling* (Rational Island Press, Seattle).
JACKINS, H. (1978), *The Upward Trend* (Rational Island Press, Seattle).
SOUTHGATE, J. and RANDALL, R. (1978), *The Barefoot Psychoanalyst* (AKHPC, London).

See also *Non-directive, Paraprofessional, Radical therapy, Self-help.*

Referential processes
Modes of experience identified by Sullivan (1953) as being fundamental to the individual's understanding of himself and the world and to his ability to communicate with others. Sullivan suggests that there are three referential processes. First, the prototaxic mode includes internal experiences of pain, warmth and sentience which may only be partly *conscious*. This is the earliest mode experienced by the newly born infant. The infant gradually begins to differentiate sequences in the flow of his needs and their gratification and discovers a pattern of signs and symbols which links his need (e.g. for food) with its gratification (e.g. by feeding). Prototaxic communication is pre-verbal and

although it characterises early infancy, it remains a mode of *communication* throughout life. Second, there is the parataxic mode, whereby the individual reads the signs of impending behaviour in the other before that behaviour occurs. A child learns to link the parent's frown with impending angry behaviour and adjust to it accordingly. When this adjustment is made inappropriately and repeatedly in later life to figures who recall the original authority figure, Sullivan describes this process as parataxic distortion and sees it as being equivalent to the *transference* process in psychotherapy. Thus, although parataxic communication uses words, it relates to the other person primarily through distorted images. Third, the syntaxic mode describes consensually validated logical communication between two or more individuals. The child gradually learns to develop consensually validated symbols of communication which are congruent in terms of the detonative and *metacommunicative* levels and the extent to which this becomes possible is the extent to which the individual is enabled to communicate fully with others.

SULLIVAN, H. S. (1953), *The Interpersonal Theory of Psychiatry* (W. W. Norton, New York).

See also *Congruence, Double bind, Interpersonal School (of psychoanalysis), Non-verbal communication, Transaction.*

Reflection
Playing back to the client the feeling state latent within his *communication*. Reflection is an important interviewing skill by which the therapist conveys *empathy*. Patterson (1974) comments that 'reflection responses go somewhat beyond simple acceptance responses . . . reflections of feelings go beyond or behind content. They are responses to the more obvious or clear feelings that the client has about content.' Reflection is used particularly by *client-centred, humanistic* and other *non-directive* therapists. Rogers (1975) has commented on the way in which reflection can be an empty caricature if it is simply understood

as 'repeating the last words the client has said'. To be a therapeutic intervention, reflection needs to convey the therapist's empathic understanding of the client's affect. Reflection which picks up the client's *current* emotional experience accurately is considered to be of particular value.

IVEY, A. and GLUCKSTERN, N. (1976), *Basic Influencing Skills: Leader and Participant Manuals* (Microtraining, North Amherst, Mass.).

PATTERSON, C. H. (1974), *Relationship Counseling and Psychotherapy* (Harper & Row, New York).

ROGERS, C. (1975), *Empathic: An Unappreciated Way of Being* (mimeograph, Center for the Studies of the Person, La Jolla, Calif.).

See also *Clarification, Interpretation, Interview, Microskill.*

Reframing

Changing the conceptual and/or emotional context of a problem so that its meaning is reconstrued in a more facilitative way. The reframing of the patient's reality by the therapist is used as a technique primarily in *strategic therapy* and *structural family therapy* but in a broader sense, the act of entering any type of therapy may serve to reframe the problem into something more manageable for the patient. In other words, although the concrete facts are unchanged, the patient's *perception* of those facts is altered. Korzybski's (1933) notion that the 'map is not territory' has contributed to the idea that it is often possible and psychotherapeutically productive to separate out the concrete facts from the individual's perception of those facts, and the *theory of types* has provided a framework for shifting from *first order* to *second order change* interventions, inherent in the concept of reframing. The concept challenges the notion that there is some objectively measurable 'reality' to which the individual patient must be adjusted or, alternatively, an external reality which must be changed, if the patient is to function productively. Reframing may be used early on in therapy to enable the patient to make some

initial steps towards the treatment *goals*. It may for example be helpful for the therapist to reframe a mother's intrusiveness into her teenage daughter's life as 'concern' or conversely, the teenager's *acting out* as 'showing adventurous initiative, like dad', in order to reduce *scapegoating* and cut through the vicious circle of mutual recrimination and first order change prescriptions, which are preventing any change from occurring. As Watzlawick *et al.* (1974) point out, 'successful reframing must lift the problem out of the "symptom" frame into another frame that does not carry the implication of unchangeability.' The therapist takes the problem and the *resistance* to change as presented by the patient and turns both into tools in the service of producing change.

BANDLER, R. and GRINDER, J. (1982), *Reframing* (Real People Press, Moab, Utah).

KORZYBSKI, A. (1933), *Science and Sanity* (4th edn, International Non-Aristotelian Publishing, Lakeville, Conn.).

MINUCHIN, S. and FISCHMAN, H. S. (1981), *Family Therapy Techniques* (Harvard University Press, Cambridge, Mass.).

WATZLAWICK, P. *et al.* (1974), *Change: Principles of Problem Formation and Problem Resolution* (W. W. Norton, New York).

WITTGENSTEIN, L. (1956), *Remarks on the Foundations of Mathematics* (Blackwell, Oxford).

See also *Attribution theory, Humour, Positive connotation, Redefinition.*

Regression

Reversion to an earlier developmental stage, *ego* functioning, type of *object* or type of relationship from which satisfaction is derived. The process occurs when a person faces an anxiety-provoking situation or a developmental challenge that he feels unable to handle. Regression may be temporary and situation-specific or it may be more long-standing and general. Severe pathological regression can be seen in the schizophrenic's return to childhood or babyhood. Regression is induced in all hospitalisation and in most psychotherapeutic treatments. This is especially true in psychoanalytic treatments where therapeutic regression is a necessary means of enabling the patient and *analyst* to get in touch with the past. It may be encouraged in active forms of group treatment and in methods such as *primal therapy* and *rebirthing* whereby the patient is encouraged to regress and relive the traumatising events of his early infancy and pre-natal life. Kris (1952) calls this and other types of functional regression, such as play and laughter, 'regression in the service of the ego', to distinguish them from the pathological process.

KRIS, E. (1952), *Psychoanalytic Explorations in Art* (International Universities Press, New York).
SCHEIDLINGER, S. (1968), 'The concept of regression in group psychotherapy' (*Int. J. of Group Psychotherapy*, vol. 18, pp. 3-20).

Regulation (of psychotherapists)

Research into the *outcome* of psychotherapy has produced ample evidence for the occurrence of a significant *deterioration* effect for varying proportions of the patient population. Hogan (1979, vol. 4) has given a detailed description of a range of *malpractice* suits in the USA which corroborate the deleterious effects that are experienced by some patients. These factors have emphasised the need to regulate the practice of psychotherapy. However, the *manner* of its regulation is the subject of much disagreement both in the United States and in Britain. Whilst in the USA psychotherapy is the subject of control by state licensing laws, no statutory control exists in Britain. However, as Hogan (1979) argues in an extremely full treatment of the subject, many problems still exist in the United States and there are a variety of negative side effects to statutory control.

In 1971 the Foster Report, produced in Britain as a result of the public's concern over the practice of scientology, recommended that psychotherapy should be regulated by statute. The recommendation was supported by the British Medical Association and the Royal College of Psychiatrists and a working party was set up to see whether there was similar support amongst psychotherapists themselves. In 1978, the working party reported on its conclusions which were that there *should* be a statutory scheme of regulation. It further recommended that 'indicative' rather than 'functional' regulation should be established, protecting the use of the *name* of psychotherapists, psychoanalysts, etc., rather than the *functions* of those persons. Although the latter would obviously exert greater control, the working party pointed to the problems of definition which made it impossible to find a formula which would be both sufficiently exclusive and inclusive for every variety of psychotherapy.

To date no progress has been made in having the working party's recommendations presented to parliament in a bill and the regulation of psychotherapeutic practice in Britain remains up to the professional associations where this is applicable. The position is clearly unsatisfactory. Even for those methods of psychotherapy where the professional association organises training and sets standards, there is very little possibility that a patient will gain redress in a case of suspected malpractice. In those cases where the method is governed by no professional association at all or by one which does not organise training or set standards, the position is even bleaker. Fortunately it is undoubtedly the case that most psychotherapists are self-regulating and that standards of practice and personal codes of *ethics* are generally high. Even so, as the Professions Joint Working Party's (1978) report recognised, a greater degree of accountability could and should be demanded of therapists by their actual and potential patients. Bloch (1982) suggests that the establishment of 'an elected, impartial and judicious committee, composed of representatives of the various caring professions, which is legally granted the power to impose sanctions on a therapist found guilty of malpractice', might be workable and thus hold out some hope of a solution to the problem.

BLOCH, S. (1982), *What is Psychotherapy?* (Oxford University Press, Oxford).

HOGAN, D. B. (1979), *The Regulation of Psychotherapists* (4 vols, Ballinger, Cambridge, Mass.).

HOGAN, D. B. (1982), 'When little is known, what are we to do? The implications of social science research for regulatory policy' (*Professional Practice of Psychology*, vol. 3, pp. 19-25).

PROFESSIONS JOINT WORKING PARTY (1978), *Statutory Registration of Psychotherapists*.

THEAMAN, M. (1982), 'A critical appraisal of Daniel Hogan's position on licenture' (*Professional Practice of Psychology*, vol. 3, pp. 1-18).

Regulator

Term derived from *systems theory* to describe the homeostatic mechanism which, through the action of *negative feedback* maintains the stability or steady state of a *system*. Its application to the treatment of natural psycho-social systems has led sometimes to a linear conception of what is an essentially circular causal process between the regulator and that which is regulated. The *identified patient* and the *symptom* are usually described as systems regulators in *family therapy* but other individuals can unwittingly perform the same function, for example the referral agent or the therapist himself.

See also *Circular causality, Homeostasis*.

Rehearsal

See *Behavioural rehearsal*.

Reich, Wilhelm (1897-1957)

Reich was born into a farming family in Galicia, the German-Ukrainian part of the Austrian Empire. After serving in the Austrian army during the First World War, he studied medicine at the University of Vienna. He came under the influence of Freud and joined the Vienna Psychoanalytic Society in 1920. He soon established his expertise as a practitioner and teacher of *psychoanalysis* and was invited by Freud to join the inner circle of the Society. However, his practice and theoretical descrip-

tions became progressively more unorthodox and his personal life became the subject of increasing rumour. He was suspected of having affairs with patients, a fact which he later confirmed. In 1934 he was expelled from the International Psychoanalytic Society. Thereafter he concentrated on his own approaches to therapy and developed what became known as orgone or vegetotherapy (see *Reichian therapy*). His approach emphasised the role of full orgiastic release and the breaking down of the patient's *character armour*. His political views were greatly influenced by Marx and he remained committed to bringing about a non-oppressive communist society. His book *The Mass Psychology of Fascism*, however, made him enemies amongst Marxists as well as fascists. He fled from Germany in 1933 and spent the last twenty years of his life in the United States where much of his work became progressively more bizarre. He was prosecuted for contravening an injunction preventing him selling his 'orgone accumulator', a box which he believed helped to capture the orgone energy, and in 1957 he was sent to Lewisburg Penitentiary where he died eight months later. His total ostracisation from society by the end of his life initially overshadowed the creativity and many achievements of his earlier work, which are seen in his major writings, *The Function of the Orgasm* (1942) and *Character Analysis* (1945).

Reichian therapy

A method of psychotherapy developed by Wilhelm Reich and called variously orgonomy, orgone therapy, vegetotherapy and *character analysis*. Reich, who was a close associate of Freud in his twenties, saw his theoretical framework as a logical extension of psychoanalytic principles. In particular, he retained and augmented Freud's theory of psychosexual development. The concept of psychic energy of *libido* is given a physical objective existence in the idea of *orgone energy*; and Freud's concept of *fixation* is seen by Reich as being physically represented in the *character armour* of the body's frozen musculature.

Reich suggests that neurosis and psychological disorders of various kinds develop because of the individual's incomplete release of orgone energy. Complete release comes through orgiastic potency which occurs when the individual reaches a sexual climax within a genital union and which produces physical convulsions strong enough to engulf the whole body. The task of the therapist is to unblock the orgone energy through character analysis and by working directly on the muscular armour through breathing, massage and body work. An important ongoing task is to maintain the patient's co-operation and help him or her to gain awareness of his energy blocks and constrictions. This involves interpreting his *resistance* to treatment and working with the *transference*.

As the character armour is loosened through direct work on the seven muscular groups the patient's defensive social facade begins to dissolve and repressed emotions, particularly hate and rage, are released. This work begins with the chest muscles and moves through each group of muscles sequentially, releasing the muscle blocks and the repressed emotions. In the final phase of treatment, when the pelvic muscles are being released, *symptoms* may reappear as the patient's character armour dissolves and he experiences his *helplessness*. At the same time he tries to cope with his newly experienced high energy level. Gradually the patient is able to integrate the loss of his defensive muscular armour and he begins to mobilise his new energy productively.

Reichian therapy has been criticised for its overconcentration on the release of muscular rather than psychological constrictions, its somewhat literal equation of psychic with physical energy and its belief that the acquisition of orgiastic potency is the sum total of the therapeutic endeavour. Moreover, Reich himself made use of several highly controversial practices. Current Reichian practice however would not tolerate the most criticised of these, that is genital sexual relations between patient and therapist, and it is customary for patients now to wear minimal clothing rather than being treated in the nude. Prochaska (1979) quotes Schennum's (1976) work which, in a historical survey of Reichian research, failed to produce any controlled *outcome* studies on its effectiveness. Even so, Reichian therapy has had an important influence on a range of *body therapies* and it has endeavoured to integrate aspects of psychoanalytic therapy with the physical expression and treatment of psychological disorders. The centre for the practice of Reichian therapy is the American College of Orgonomy, New York, which publishes the *Journal of Orgonomy* twice yearly.

BAKER, E. F. (1978), 'Orgone therapy' (*J. of Orgonomy*, vol. 12, pp. 41-54 and pp. 201-15).
PROCHASKA, J. O. (1979), *Systems of Psychotherapy* (Dorsey Press, Homewood, Ill.).
RAKNES, O. (1970), *Wilhelm Reich and Orgonomy* (St Martin's Press, New York).
REICH, W. (1945), *Character Analysis* (Orgone Institute, New York).
REICH, W. (1951), *Selected Writings* (Farrar, Strauss & Giroux, New York).
SCHENNUM, R. (1976), 'Wilhelm Reich's therapy' (unpublished MS. quoted in Prochaska, op. cit.).

Reinforcement

The process of increasing the probability and/or the frequency of a *response* by using an appropriate *reinforcer*. The response which is increased is that which precedes the reinforcer on a succeeding occasion. Reinforcement is divided into two types. Positive reinforcement involves increasing the individual's response through appropriate rewards. The reward may be divided up into parts, so that each step towards the goal can be cumulatively reinforced, as in *shaping* behaviour. Negative reinforcement is the omission or termination of a disliked stimulus. Thus, the avoidance of failing an examination acts as a negative reinforcer to the student's propensity to study. An important variable associated with both positive and negative reinforcement is its time scheduling. Reinforcement may be continuous or intermittent, the former being delivered after each response and the latter being irregular reinforcement delivered either at fixed time intervals or after a certain number of responses. Higher response rates result from short fixed time intervals and behaviour which is acquired through intermittent reinforcement is more resistant to *extinction*.

Reinforcement procedures have been successfully used to modify the behaviour of schizophrenics, delinquents, those with behaviour problems in childhood and clients with sexual disorders. Kazdin (1978) discusses the variables which contribute to the effects of reinforcement programmes. These include the instructions given by therapists, social reinforcement in the form of praise, attention and approval, and modelling produced by the vicarious reinforcement observed in others. He also reviews the comparative studies undertaken, comparing reinforcement with other treatments such as *group psychotherapy*, insight-oriented approaches and chemotherapy and concludes that reinforcement programmes are superior or (in the case of chemotherapy) are either superior or equally as good but produce no adverse side effects. Cautela (1970a, 1970b) has described covert methods of both positive and negative reinforcement.

CAUTELA, J. (1970a), 'Covert reinforcement' (*Behaviour Therapy*, vol. 1, pp. 33-50).
CAUTELA, J. (1970b), 'Covert negative reinforcement' (*J. of Behavior Therapy and Experimental Psychiatry*, vol. 1, p. 273).
KAZDIN, A. E. (1978), 'The application of operant techniques in treatment, rehabilitation and education' (in Garfield, S. and Bergin, A. E. (*Handbook of Psychotherapy and Behavior Change*, Wiley, New York).

Reinforcer

Any *stimulus* which increases the probability and/or the frequency of the *response* it follows. This may be a reward in the case of positive *reinforcement* or the absence of some negative consequence in the case of negative reinforcement. Thus, reinforcers may be either positive or negative. In the example of the Skinner Box, food acts as a positive reinforcer, directly increasing the probability that the animal or bird will depress the lever. The strength of a reinforcer can be measured by the rate of response and the total number of responses before *extinction* occurs. Whether or not a particular stimulus will act as a reinforcer is highly dependent upon a number of variables: for example, the likes and dislikes of the individual and his current need (food for example, will not act as a strong reinforcer unless the person is hungry or unless the food is regarded by him as a particular need or treat). The selection of appropriate reinforcers is therefore an important part of any *contingency management* programme. Premack (1965) has suggested that any high probability behaviour can be used as a reinforcer for low probability behaviour. Thus the selection of suitable reinforcers can be facilitated by observing a client's preferences and using these to reinforce desired behaviour.

PREMACK, D. (1965), 'Reinforcement theory' (in Levine, D. (ed.), *Nebraska Symposium on Motivation*, University of Nebraska Press, Lincoln).

See also *Premack principle*.

Re-labelling
See *Positive connotation, Reframing*.

Relationship factors
A generic term used to describe *therapist variables* such as his personal qualities, characteristics and *style* through which he builds up a relationship with the client and exerts an influence upon him. Relationship factors are distinguishable from the techniques that he uses or the theory upon which they are based. A vast body of research has sought to identify whether and how relationship factors or technical interventions are more important in bringing about a positive therapeutic *outcome*. (See, for example, Gurman and Razin (1977), Bergin (1978).) The formation of a therapeutic relationship with a client is considered to be a fundamental prerequisite of most psychotherapeutic approaches and even those hitherto regarded as the most technically 'pure' now regard a positive therapeutic

relationship as a contributive factor to the treatment. Although relationship factors are generally considered to be important their purpose and management are viewed differently, depending on the approach or school adopted. Many psychoanalytic therapists, for example, consider the 'real' relationship between client and analyst as an interference in the formation of the essential 'artificial' relationship created via *transference* and *counter transference* phenomena. The use of the transference relationship can be regarded as a psychoanalytic 'technique' and, by comparison, the real relationship between client and therapist is contained and reduced as far as possible. On the other hand, Ruitenbeck (1973) discusses ways in which the use of first names, the acceptance of *gifts* and the use of physical touch between *analyst* and patient can all be used appropriately to develop a relationship with the patient which will promote effective treatment. In the behavioural therapies, the technical interventions used are viewed as the agents of change and relationship factors as being either a necessary or an irrelevant adjunct to the treatment programme. Humanistic therapists, however, regard the relationship factors as providing both the necessary and the *sufficient* conditions for change to occur, and they may regard the use of technical interventions as a positive hindrance to the formation of an appropriate therapeutic relationship. After reviewing a very broad list of treatment variables, Bergin (1978) concluded that relationship factors were extremely important: 'It appears that these personal factors are crucial ingredients even in the more technical therapies. This is not to say that techniques are irrelevant but that their power for change pales when compared with that of personal influence. Technique is crucial to the extent that it provides a believable rationale and a congenial modus operandi for the change agent and the client.'

BERGIN, A. E. (1978), 'The evaluation of therapeutic outcomes' (in Bergin, A. E. and Garfield, S. L. (eds) (1978), *Handbook of Psychotherapy and Behavior Change*, Wiley, New York).

GURMAN, A. S. and RAZIN, A. M. (eds) (1977), *Effective Psychotherapy* (Pergamon, New York).
RUITENBECK, H. M. (ed.) (1973), *The Analytic Situation* (Aldine, Chicago).
STRUPP, H. H. (1977), 'A reformulation of the dynamics of the therapist's contribution' (in Gurman, A. and Razin, A., op. cit.).

See also *Client-centred therapy, Core conditions, Social influence*.

Relaxation training

Relaxation training, which was pioneered in clinical practice by Edmund Jacobson (1938), has been developed by a number of workers as an adjunct to various forms of psychotherapy and as a self-contained method for reducing the patient's response to stress. *Meditation*, for example, has made use of simple forms of relaxation training for thousands of years. *Autogenic training* uses relaxation as an important part of its approach. Although Wolpe's *systematic desensitisation* does not necessarily now include relaxation training as a preliminary, Wolpe originally emphasised its use and developed his own approach to it based on Jacobson's work. Relaxation training is also an important component of *anxiety management training, stress inoculation, and various self-help* approaches to the reduction of anxiety and stress, and is used in *sex therapy*, in *eidetic psychotherapy* and in many other approaches.

Relaxation training focuses on the lowering of the patient's level of arousal to stressful events and the development of a less stressful lifestyle. *Bio-feedback* techniques may be used to measure the patient's level of arousal and to provide information on the pattern and frequency of arousal states. Breathing exercises, muscle tensing followed by muscle relaxation, and *imagery* help the patient learn how to relax in the therapy sessions. He or she is then given *homework assignments* requiring the use of the regular pre-recorded audio taped relaxation instructions. The audio tape may be made by the therapist for each patient and thus individually shaped to his needs. The patient plays the tape twice a day and may also be taught to use quick relaxation technique at more regular intervals when he feels his level of arousal increasing. Instructions on diet, exercise and other aspects of the patient's lifestyle are often included. Treatment is usually short-term and is used particularly for various psychosomatic disorders. Lyles *et al.* (1982) have shown that relaxation training may be an effective procedure for helping cancer patients cope with the adverse effects of their chemotherapy and various clinics in Britain and the USA make use of relaxation training for this patient group.

BENSON, H. (1975), *The Relaxation Response* (William Morrow, New York).
JACOBSON, E. (1938), *Progressive Relaxation* (University of Chicago Press, Chicago).
LYLES, J. N. *et al.* (1982), 'Efficacy of relaxation training and guided imagery in reducing the aversiveness of cancer chemotherapy' (*J. of Consulting and Clinical Psychology*, vol. 50, pp. 509-24).
TURIN, A. C. and LYNCH, S. N. (1981), 'Comprehensive relaxation training' (in Corsini, R. J. (ed.), *Handbook of Innovative Psychotherapies*, Wiley, New York).

Repertory grid
A form of sorting test developed by Kelly which enables the relations between an individual's *constructs* and *elements* to be assessed. The raw data is yielded in the form of a matrix whereby elements are ranked or rated against bi-polar descriptive constructs. After analysis by hand or by computer, a finely textured 'map' of the individual's *intrapsychic* space is revealed. Fransella and Bannister (1977) discuss the different types of repertory grid that are commonly used – rated, ranked and implication grids. Elements for the grids are either supplied by the researcher or elicited from the subject and constructs are arrived at by using triads or dyads of elements to elicit the appropriate construct or by *laddering*. Slater (1976, 1977) has discussed and developed detailed research methodology for use with grids and has produced a variety of

computer programmes for their analysis. Repertory grid technique has been adapted for use with groups (Watson 1970) and with couples or families (Ryle and Lipshitz 1975, 1976).

FRANSELLA, F. and BANNISTER, D. (1977), *A Manual of Repertory Grid Technique* (Academic Press, London).
RYLE, A. and LIPSHITZ, S. (1975), 'Recording change in marital therapy with the reconstruction grid' (*Brit. J. of Medical Psychology*, vol. 48, pp. 39-48).
RYLE, A. and LIPSHITZ, S. (1976), 'Repertory grid elucidation of a difficult conjoint therapy' (*Brit. J. of Medical Psychology*, vol. 49, pp. 281-5).
SLATER, P. (1976), *Explorations of Intrapersonal Space* (Wiley, London).
SLATER, P. (1977), *Dimensions of Intrapersonal Space* (Wiley, London).
WATSON, J. P. (1970), 'A repertory grid method of studying groups' (*Brit. J. of Psychiatry*, vol. 117, pp. 309-18).

Repetition compulsion
The tendency unconsciously to repeat painful experiences. It is sometimes viewed as a destructive urge, such as the repeated choice of a violent marital partner, and Freud used the idea in support of his concept of *death instinct*. It can also be viewed as an effort on the part of the *ego* to recreate a situation in order to resolve it. Freud's 'new editions of old conflicts', transferred on to the relationship with the *analyst*, is an example of the positive aspect of repetition compulsion and so too is the way in which, during the *mourning* process, an individual may enter into painful and repetitious *rituals*.

FREUD, S. (1926), 'Inhibitions, symptoms and anxiety' (*Standard Edition*, vol. 20, Hogarth Press, London).

Repression
A process whereby memories, feelings and images are relegated to the *unconscious* and kept out of reach of consciousness. Like all *defence mechanisms*, it is itself an unconscious

process. It is held to be a universal mental process by psychoanalytic theorists and Freud (1914) asserted that 'the theory of repression is the cornerstone on which the whole structure of psychoanalysis rests'. Between 1900 and 1918 Freud described all defence mechanisms as repression, but before and after those years he distinguished them. In the *structural model*, repression and the other defences are always *ego* functions, though they may be 'at the behest' of the *superego* which forbids the idea of memory of certain wished-for relationships or *objects*, or it may be in response to the demands of reality. The effect of repression can be seen in memory loss, such as the total amnesia experienced by most people regarding the events of early infancy. The 'return of the repressed', according to psychoanalytic theory, occurs through *dreams, symptoms* and *parapraxes*, and the translation of these into consciousness is effected by the psychoanalytic process. Some of the dilemmas inherent in this undertaking are discussed by Myerson (1977).

FREUD, S. (1914), 'On the history of the psychoanalytic movement' (*Standard Edition*, vol. 14, Hogarth Press, London).
FREUD, S. (1915), 'Repression' (*Standard Edition*, vol. 14, Hogarth Press, London).
MYERSON, P. G. (1977), 'Therapeutic dilemmas relevant to the lifting of repression' (*Int. J. of Psychoan.*, vol. 58, pp. 453-62).

Resistance
The patient's efforts to obstruct the aims and process of treatment. Resistance is a fundamental concept in *psychoanalysis*, leading Freud to develop his 'fundamental rule' of *free association*, the need for *neutrality* on the part of the therapist and the recognition that access to the *unconscious* could only be gained by indirect methods. Freud regarded resistance as primarily the *ego*'s efforts to prevent unconscious material from breaking through into consciousness, and in his later writings he regarded resistance as a *defence mechanism* employed by the ego, albeit of a particular and unique kind. Freud (1926) distinguishes five

types of resistance: *repression, transference* resistance, resistance manifested by the *secondary gains* of the *symptoms*, the resistance of the *id* and the resistance of the *superego*. Each of these has to be overcome if the patient is to forgo his *symptoms*, integrate unconscious material into consciousness, relax his defence mechanisms and operate in accordance with the *reality principle*. The strength of the resistance is taken as an indicator of the significance of the repressed material. The repeated overcoming of resistance is the reason why treatment, according to psychoanalytic viewpoint, is usually such a prolonged process. Thus it is viewed not as an obstacle to treatment but the way in which the patient reveals, by repeating in the *transference* and in the therapeutic process as a whole, the nature of his or her difficulties. It is by attention to and analysis of the resistances that the patient gradually gains freedom from them. Classical psychoanalysts are careful to foster the positive transference as a technical device to use as a force for overcoming resistances.

Therapists from all orientations recognise the existence of resistance but differ in their explanations of its origin and the approach that they recommend the therapist to take. Bandura (1969), for example, discussing resistance from a social learning point of view, comments, 'If an individual refuses to acknowledge certain thoughts or impulses suggested to him by his therapist, the question remains whether the resistance reveals repressed contents or justifiable incredulity in the face of erroneous interpretations.' Some *behaviour therapists* explain both repression and resistance in terms of *avoidance learning*: if certain thoughts are repeatedly associated with painful experiences they become aversive. Miller (1951) shows how anxiety attached to a spoken word spreads to the thought behind that word through the process of *generalisation*, creating resistance to all attached events, thoughts and memories. *Strategic therapists* and *social influence* theorists view resistance as a major challenge to the therapist and are concerned to design strategies to overcome the patient's resistance to the therapist, to the process of treatment and to the loss of his symptoms. Therapists of the former group rely mainly on indirect methods, such as *symptom prescription* and *paradoxical* interventions, whilst social influence theorists advocate direct methods of producing compliance in the patient. Neither group views the problem of resistance as concerning the repression of (and therefore lack of access to) unconscious material so much as the obstacles it places in the way of the performance of *tasks* and the adoption of new patterns of behaviour. It is seen as self-defeating behaviour on the part of the patient which the therapist must help him overcome to allow the real business of therapy to proceed.

BANDURA, A. (1969), *Principles of Behavior Modification* (Holt, Rinehart & Winston).
FREUD, S. (1926), 'Inhibitions, symptoms and anxiety' (*Standard Edition*, vol. 20, Hogarth Press, London).
MILLER, N. E. (1951), 'Learnable drives and rewards' (in Stevens, S. S. (ed.), *Handbook of Experimental Psychology*, Wiley, New York).
RABKIN, R. (1977), *Strategic Psychotherapy* (Basic Books, New York).
ROSENTHAL, L. (1980), 'Resistance in group psychotherapy' (in Volberg, L. and Arunsen, M., *Group and Family Therapy*, Brunner/Mazel, New York).
WACHTEL, P. L. (ed.) (1982), *Resistance: Psychodynamic and Behavioral Approaches* (Plenum Press, New York).

Resonance
Term introduced by Foulkes and Anthony (1957) to describe a phenomenon specific to *group psychotherapy*. Group members who are fixated at different stages of psychosexual development come into contact with others who are functioning at different levels from themselves. Each member of the group shows a tendency to resonate to any group event according to the level at which he or she is fixated. According to Foulkes, this deep *unconscious* frame of reference is laid down within the first five years of life and pre-

determines the individual's associative responses within the group situation.

FOULKES, S. H. and ANTHONY, E. J. (1957), *Group Psychotherapy* (Penguin, Harmondsworth).

See also *Chain phenomena, Condenser phenomena, Mirror phenomena.*

Response
A behavioural event which follows from a *stimulus* in a *behavioural sequence*. Each member of a sequence is a stimulus in relation to the responses that follow it and a response in relation to the stimulus preceding it. The S-R relationship is a fundamental concept of *learning theory* and *behaviour therapy* and is a major principle behind both *operant* and *classical conditioning*.

See also *Conditioned response, Unconditioned response.*

Response cost
The process of decreasing the probability and/or the frequency of a *response* by the omission or termination of a *stimulus*. As with *punishment*, the response which is decreased is that which the omitted stimulus follows. The term implies that the individual is paying a price for continuing his problem behaviour. The cost may be in the form of the removal of some privilege or reward or the payment of a fine. Kazdin (1971) demonstrated how the withdrawal of tokens from a hospitalised prepsychotic woman dramatically reduced the number of bizarre statements that she made during the course of the day. Even after the withdrawal of tokens had ceased, her use of bizarre statements remained very low. *Time out* is a special type of response cost, when the client is temporarily removed from an environment which is attractive and which is providing positive *reinforcement*. For example, a child may be removed to his bedroom after a temper tantrum. The time out procedure may, in addition to the response cost aspect, involve other active components however. Burchard and Barerra (1972) showed that longer periods

of time out were more successful in reducing the aggression of institutionalised male delinquents, but Repp and Deitz (1974) indicate that as brief a period as thirty seconds time out can reduce aggressive and self-injurious behaviour in young retarded children. Response cost has similarities with *extinction* procedures. However, the latter involves the non-presentation of the rewards which are maintaining the problem behaviour, whilst response cost consists of the forfeiture of rewards which are independent of the problem maintenance.

BURCHARD, J. and BARERRA, F. (1972), 'An analysis of time out and response cost in a programmed environment' (*J. of Applied Behavior Analysis*, vol. 5, pp. 271-82). Kazdin, A. E. (1971), 'The effect of response cost in suppressing behavior in a pre-psychotic retardate' (*J. of Behavior Therapy and Experimental Psychiatry*, vol. 2, pp. 137-41). REPP, A. C. and DEITZ, S. M. (1974), 'Reducing aggressive and self-injurious behaviour of institutionalised retarded children through reinforcement of other behaviors' (*J. of Applied Behavior Analysis*, vol. 7, pp. 313-25). VEINER, H. (1962), 'Some effects of response cost upon human operant behavior' (*J. of the Experimental Analysis of Behavior*, vol. 5, pp. 201-8).

Reverse psychology

An umbrella term sometimes used to describe all therapeutic techniques which are based on encouraging rather than attacking the *symptom*. Rabkin (1977) groups these techniques into three categories: behavioural (*negative practice* and *flooding*), psychodynamic (*paradoxical intention, implosion*), and cognitive (*therapeutic double bind, symptom prescription* and *paradox*).

RABKIN, R. (1977), *Strategic Psychotherapy* (Basic Books, New York).

Right brain

See *Lateralisation*.

Ripple effect

The process whereby therapeutic efforts that are focused on the resolution of one *symptom* or problem area are generalised to others. Spiegel and Linn (1969) report spontaneous improvement in other areas of the patient's life after the removal of the symptom. The ripple effect is the converse of *symptom substitution* and tends to be reported by therapists who subscribe to a behavioural or strategic approach to therapy, although it is a well-known occurrence resulting from all forms of therapy. The ripple effect does not preclude *symptom transfer* to a third party. The usual explanation is that the increased confidence and self-esteem engendered by the successful removal of a troublesome symptom enhances the individual's all-round *coping behaviour*. In working with *systems*, interventions directed towards one member or *sub-system* have a ripple effect on others through the changed perceptions that occur in the third party and through *modelling* of change for others in the group.

SPIEGEL, H. and LINN, L. (1969), 'The "ripple effect" following adjunct hypnosis in analytic psychotherapy' (*Am. J. of Psychiatry*, vol. 126, pp. 53-8).

Ritual

From the Latin 'ritus', meaning 'rite'. A formal pattern of behaviour, culturally prescribed for use in certain specific circumstances. The term includes the social, religious and cultural practices which symbolically convey meaning about an event and those who are participating in it. Role transitional *crises* and changes from one stage in the life cycle to another are frequently marked by ritual, allowing the individual to terminate one phase and pass to another, and enabling others to participate in what Van Gennep (1909) called the 'rites of passage' attendant upon this transition.

Rites of passage are rituals which accompany birth, the attainment of adulthood, marriage and death. Erikson (1977) has drawn attention to the way in which *ego* identity is developed through ritualisation of kinds that are appropriate to different stages of the life cycle. Play, and later *role play*, remain important means of ritualising identity. In psychoanalytic theory, ritual is seen as an attempt to reduce anxiety through undertaking stereotyped, magical actions. This is most obviously to be seen in the pathological rituals of obsessional neurosis. In *communication* theory, ritual is viewed as the intermediary process between *analogic* and *digital* communication. Watzlawick *et al.* (1967) suggests that ritual simulates 'the message material but in a repetitive and stylized manner, that hangs between analogue and symbol'. Van der Hart and Ebbers (1981) discuss how, in *strategic therapy*, rites of separation can be used to help patients take leave of the past. Although the rituals have a common structure, their form and content vary according to the needs of the individual patient. La Gaipa (1982) discusses the use of ritual in helping people disengage from relationships and Kaslow (1981), in describing some rituals that are useful in divorce work, points out how the lack of formal social ritual complicates the process of separation and psychic divorce.

Providing rituals for warm human *encounter* and the acceptance of the other person where these have been absent forms part of many approaches to therapy and in particular these form part of the provision of a *corrective emotional experience*. Palazzoli *et al.* (1978) have developed the use of ritual as a powerful therapeutic technique with dysfunctional family systems. They define a therapeutic ritual as 'an action or series of actions usually accompanied by verbal formulae or expressions which are to be carried out by all members of the family.' Details of the ritual, including its time, place, frequency, etc., are prescribed in detail. Palazzoli *et al.* point out that because it makes use of action and *symbolism*, ritual is closer to the analogic mode of communication than the digital. They conclude that the *prescription* of a ritual for the family to undertake as a *homework assignment* 'is meant not only to avoid the verbal comment on the norms that at that moment perpetuate the family play, but to

introduce into the system a ritualized prescription of a play whose new norms silently take the place of old ones.' Palazzoli *et al.* (1974) describe the use of a funeral ritual in the treatment of a two-year-old anorexic child, with dramatically beneficial results. Exchanging new rituals for old, dysfunctional ones forms a major therapeutic ingredient of *social skills training, problem solving interventions* and *coping skills interventions*, and new rituals for engaging in more productive interpersonal relationships are consciously taught in *sex therapy, marital therapy* and *family therapy*. A variety of rituals surround the structuring of the therapeutic process itself and are engaged in by both therapist and patient, consciously and unconsciously. *Gifts* may form part of the ritual of *termination*, lying on a couch part of the ritual of psychoanalytic treatment, sitting on chairs of equal heights in a circular arrangements part of the ritual of *group psychotherapy*, etc. Because the use of ritual forms such an important part of normal psychological development, it can often usefully be employed by the therapist within the therapeutic situation.

ERIKSON, E. H. (1977), *Toys and Reasons* (W. W. Norton, New York).

KASLOW, F. (1981), 'Divorce and divorce therapy' (in Gurman, A. S. and Kniskern, D. P., *Handbook of Family Therapy*, Brunner/Mazel, New York).

KOBAK, R. R. and WATERS, D. B. (1984), 'Family therapy as a rite of passage' (*Family Process*, vol. 23, pp. 89-100).

LA GAIPA, J. (1982), 'Rules and rituals in disengaging from relationships' (in Duck, S., *Dissolving Personal Relationships*, Academic Press, New York).

PALAZZOLI, M. S. *et al.* (1974), 'The treatment of children through brief therapy of their parents' (*Family Process*, vol. 13, pp 429-42).

PALAZZOLI, M. S. *et al.* (1978), *Paradox and Counter Paradox* (Jason Aronson, New York).

VAN DER HART, J. and EBBERS, J. (1981), 'Rites of separation in strategic psychotherapy' (*Psychotherapy: Theory, Research and Practice*, vol. 18, pp. 188-94).

VAN GENNEP, A. (1909), *Rites of Passage* (Nourry, Paris).
WATZLAWICK, P. *et al.* (1967), *Pragmatics of Human Communication* (W. W. Norton, New York).

Rogerian counselling

See *Client-centred therapy.*

Role play

The structured interaction which results from the adoption of a role other than their usual one, by the patient, group members and/or therapist. The purpose of role play is to give practice in the execution of a skill or the acquisition of an attitude (e.g. *empathy*) for use in real-life situations. Role play is used in *psychodrama, behaviour therapy, assertiveness training, reality therapy, transactional analysis* and a variety of group therapies. It is also used in psychotherapy *training* programmes to enable trainees to increase their levels of empathy, by adopting a variety of patient positions and enacting their problem behaviours. In therapy, role play enables a patient to express anxiety-provoking material more easily, allows him to move from self-criticism to sympathy with his own difficulties and deficits, and provides an opportunity for him to try out new behaviours in a safe environment. Sprakfin *et al.* (1981) suggest that the beneficial effects of role playing are enhanced if participation is voluntary; if the role player is committed to acquiring the behaviour or attitude of the role; if he is encouraged to improvise; and if he is given *feedback* and positive *reinforcement* for an appropriate performance.

CORSINI, R. J. (1966), *Role Playing in Psychotherapy* (Aldine, Chicago).
SPRAFKIN, R. P. *et al.* (1981), 'Structured learning' (in Corsini, R. J., *Handbook of Innovative Psychotherapies*, Wiley, New York).

See also *Fixed role therapy.*

Role reversal

The adoption by the patient of a role which is opposite to that which he usually plays. For example, in *assertiveness training* the patient may be asked to play the part of the feared employer, shopkeeper, headmaster, etc., to enable him to gain skills by the vicarious experience of the opposite role, to reduce its immobilising effect upon him and to gain a more realistic understanding of how the feared person may actually be behaving and feeling. In *marital* and *family therapy* the therapist may suggest that the marital couple or other dyad exchange roles so that husband and wife, parent and child, can experience the problem from the opposite point of view. The experience both increases mutual understanding and often points to new solutions in bringing about conflict resolution. The therapist may also use himself in a role exchange with the patient.

See also *Family sculpting, Psychodrama, Role play, Simulation.*

Rolfing

See *Structural integration.*

Rorschach, Hermann (1884-1922)

Hermann Rorschach was born in Zurich in 1884. He studied medicine at the University of Zurich and after qualifying took a post in a Russian psychiatric hospital in 1913. Returning to Switzerland the following year, he worked in a variety of Swiss psychiatric hospitals, during which time he trained and began to practise as a psychoanalyst. The need to begin research into psychoanalytic treatments and to measure *unconscious* phenomena prompted Rorschach to seek an unstructured *stimulus* that could be used to help patients reveal unconscious or traumatic material. Rorschach's place in the history of psychotherapy is due to the development of his inkblot test. In 1921 he published his *Psychodiagnostics: A Diagnostic Test Based on Perception*, which describes the ten inkblots used, with detailed scoring manuals. The *Rorschach test*, as it became known, was the first in a series of *projective tests* that were developed by others, and is still widely used. Rorschach died prematurely at the age of 38, with his work far from complete.

Rorschach test

This projective *personality test*, developed by the Swiss psychiatrist Hermann Rorschach in 1921, became a very prominent psychometric instrument because clinicians were interested in the descriptions of personality which it yielded. Latterly, a change of emphasis has occurred, from attempted psychiatric classi-fication to a description of the individual's intrapsychic structures. Used extensively in clinical testing, its validity and reliability have been seriously questioned by some psycho-logists. The subject's task is to say what he sees in a series of ten black and white or coloured inkblots whose shape is sufficiently irregular as to permit a wide range of response possibil-ities. The answers he gives are used as indicators of his *phantasies*, personality struc-ture, and overall psychiatric diagnosis. The scoring is systematic and fairly complex. The interpretation of the data is impressionistic and demands considerable experience of a group of inter-related *hypotheses* concerning the nature of the stimulus and of psycho-dynamic theory.

EXNER, J. E. and WEINER, I. B. (1982), *The Rorschach: A Comprehensive System* (3 vols, Wiley, New York).
RORSCHACH, H. (1942), *Psychodiagnostics: A Diagnostic Test Based on Perception* (Huber, Bern).

Rubber fence

Term introduced by Wynne to describe a defensive manoeuvre employed by a family to preserve its frail sense of mutuality and com-plementarity, used particularly to describe schizophrenic families. Wynne suggests that the rubber fence acts as a *boundary* to screen out difference and to prevent members from *differentiating* themselves and from threatening the *nexus* of the family group. 'Family boun-daries thus obscured are continuous but unstable, stretching, like a rubber fence, to include that which can be interpreted as non-complementary' (Wynne, 1958). Searles (1965) points out that the symbiotic relation-ships that are thus created by family members'

turning in towards each other increase the risk of both incest and violence. The rubber fence acts as an effective barrier against the inclusion of a therapist who is perceived as a threat to the family's *cohesion* and *homeostasis*.

SEARLES, H. F. (1965), 'The contributions of family treatment to the psychotherapy of schizophrenia' (in Boszormenyi-Nagy, I. and Framo, J. L. (eds), *Intensive Family Therapy*, Harper & Row, New York).
WYNNE, L. C. *et al.* (1958), 'Pseudomutuality in the family relations of schizophrenics' (*Psychiatry*, vol. 21, pp. 205-20).
WYNNE, L. C. (1961), 'Study of intra-familial alignments and splits in exploratory family therapy' (in Ackerman, N. W. *et al.*, *Exploring the Base for Family Therapy*, Family Service Association of America, New York).

See also *Symbiosis*.

Runaway

The propensity of a *system* to respond to positive *feedback* by an infinite process leading to the disintegration of the system. Some systems writers have tended to view all positive feedback as a destructive process which inevit-ably leads to runaway. More recently, theorists applying systems thinking to families and other natural systems have shown that this is not so and that whilst a destructive runaway *may* result, creative change or *morphogenesis* is an equally possible outcome.

See also *Deviation amplification, Schismogenesis*.

Sachs, Hans (1881-1947)

Hans Sachs was born in Vienna in 1881. He studied law at the University of Vienna, gain-ing his degree in 1904. After reading Freud's writings, he joined Freud's group in 1909 and became one of the 'inner circle' of psycho-analysts, responsible for directing the fortunes of the psychoanalytic movement. Unlike other prominent members of the inner circle such as

Jung and Adler, Sachs remained a devoted follower of Freud. In 1918 he moved to Zurich and opened a private psychoanalytic practice and in 1920 he became director of the Berlin Psychoanalytic Institute and a training analyst for some of the foremost psychoanalysts of that time. After emigrating to the United States, he became a training *analyst* in Boston and a faculty member of the Harvard Medical School. From 1912 to 1938 he edited the psychoanalytic journal *Imago*, and after its suppression by the Nazis he re-established it in the United States. His many writings covered a wide range of psychoanalytic topics including the interpretation of dreams and the application of psychoanalysis to literature and art. He died in Boston in 1947.

Scapegoat

A member of a family or other group who bears the displaced blame or suffering of the rest of the group. The term is taken from the Book of Leviticus in the Old Testament, Chapter 16, where the Jewish custom and ritual for the Day of Atonement are described. Two goats are taken: one is sacrificed to the Lord and the other receives on to its head the sins and rebellions of the whole people of Israel to placate Azazel, a demonic being. It is then driven out into the wilderness to 'escape', thus freeing the community of its burden of sin. Speck (1965) describes the way in which animals and family pets can literally be sacrificed in this way as a means of relieving the family of its tensions. More generally, the phenomenon is seen as a part of family or *group process*, whereby the tension and stress of the group is relieved by the isolation or ostracisation of one of its members (Scheidlinger 1982). The scapegoated member usually possesses one or more characteristics which predispose him or her to attack. These may include a mental or physical handicap or weakness; some other identifying 'difference' such as racial difference, adoption, etc.; or a vulnerable position in the *family constellation*. Ackerman (1964) suggests that specific kinds of scapegoating are characteristic of specific kinds of family pat-

terns and that scapegoating both *acts as* a group defence and *mobilises* different types of group defence to neutralise the most destructive consequences of the scapegoating. The scapegoating process can also be seen at work within societies, where minority groups are blamed for the ills of the community, thus relieving others of taking responsibility for bringing about change. Scheidlinger (1982) suggests that scapegoating occurs in two different but unrelated forms: a short-lived one, characterised by the mechanism of *projection*, and a more complex, persistent one which makes use of the mechanism of *projective identification*.

ACKERMAN, N. W. (1964), 'Prejudicial scapegoating and neutralising forces in the family group' (*Int. J. of Social Psychiatry*, vol. 2, p. 90).
SCHEIDLINGER, S. (1982), 'On scapegoating in group psychotherapy' (*Int. J. of Group Psychotherapy*, vol. 32, pp. 131-42).
SPECK, R. V. (1965), 'The transfer of illness phenomenon in schizophrenic families' (in Friedman, A. S. *et al.*, *Psychotherapy for the Whole Family*, Springer, New York).

See also *Identified patient, Symptom transfer.*

Schism

The division of a group into two opposing subgroups. The term is usually applied to family groups and marital pairs, following Lidz *et al.*, (1957), where the marital *alliance* is weak or non-existent and the couple are often in open warfare. At the same time, strong alliances exist across the generations. These may form between the parent and child of the same or of the opposite sex. The cross-generational alliances serve to increase marital schism and create a schismatic family *system*. Schism is characteristic of *dysfunctional symmetrical* relationships and indicates a chronic failure to achieve any degree of complementarity between the marital pair.

LIDZ, T. *et al.* (1957), 'The intra-familial environment of schizophrenic patients' (*Am. J. of Psychiatry*, vol. 114, pp. 241-8).
SCHAFFER, L. *et al.* (1962), 'On the nature and resources of the psychiatric experience with

the family of the schizophrenic' (*Psychiatry*, vol. 25, pp. 32-45).
WYNNE, L. *et al.* (1958), 'Pseudomutuality in the family relations of schizophrenics' (*Psychiatry*, vol. 21, pp. 205-20).

See also *Skew*.

Schismogenesis

Term introduced by Bateson (1935, 1936) to describe the 'process of *differentiation* in the norms of individual behaviour resulting from cumulative interaction between individuals' (1936). In his studies of different cultural and group relationships, Bateson suggested that one of three results occur following culture contact: complete fusion of the two groups; the elimination of one or both groups or the persistence of both groups in dynamic *equilibrium* within one larger community. The third option requires rules for the construction of the relationship and, depending on how these rules develop, different results will occur. Applying these ideas to interpersonal relationships, Bateson suggests that 'culture contact' between two or more individuals results in a mutually reactive, self-reinforcing process which *either* stops short of producing alteration in the relationship or *system*, *or* proceeds beyond the limits of the previous *homeostasis* and thus creates a novel synthesis and a new equilibrium. When this occurs, the relationship or systems functioning is characterised by schismogenesis. Schismogenesis is therefore a term which describes the continual alteration or progressive change which occurs in relationships and enables coherence to be achieved not through stasis but through continuous movement. Schismogenesis may lead to a *dysfunctional runaway* or it may lead to new creativity. Bateson suggests that this progressive change is one of two kinds: complementary schismogenesis and symmetrical schismogenesis. The concept has been found useful by *systemic therapists* in helping them to understand how change occurs in systems, both naturally and through the introduction of a therapist.

BATESON, G. (1935), 'Culture contact and schismogenesis' (*Man*, vol. 35, pp. 178-83, reprinted in *Steps to an Ecology of Mind*, Granada, London).
BATESON, G. (1936), *Naven* (Cambridge University Press, Cambridge, reprinted 1965 by Oxford University Press, Oxford, with added epilogue).

See also *Complementary*, *Deviation*, *Differentiation*, *Morphogenesis*, *Positive feedback*, *Schism*, *Skew*, *Symmetrical*.

Schizophrenogenic mother

A term introduced by Fromm-Reichmann (1948) to describe the effects that some mothers appear to have in predisposing their children to schizophrenia. The concept is part of a group of related ideas which developed during the late 1940s and 1950s suggesting that the immediate psycho-social *context* surrounding the schizophrenic may play a causative role in producing schizophrenia. The concept is a forerunner of the notion of *double bind* which appeared about ten years later. The idea of the schizophrenic mother, although useful in widening the therapist's field of study beyond the *identified patient*, can be criticised because of its linear causal conception of the relationship between the noxious influence of the mother and its passive reception by the patient.

FROMM-REICHMANN, F. (1948), 'Notes on the development of treatment of schizo-phrenics by psychoanalytic psychotherapy' (*Psychiatry*, vol. 11, pp. 263-73).

See also *Folie à deux* and *Fit (marital)*.

Script

Term introduced by Berne (1961) to describe a blueprint or life plan formulated by the Child *ego state* as a protective compromise between its own needs and the demands of the Parent. The term is used in *transactional analysis* in which the analysis of the individual's life scripts plays an important part. The life script is made up of compensations for the internalised prohibitions of the Parent ego state. Berne (1961) defines scripts and their relationship to *games* as follows: 'Games appear to be segments of larger, more complex sets of transactions called scripts . . . a script is a complex set of transactions, by nature recurrent, but not necessarily recurring since a complete performance may require a whole life time. . . . The object of script analysis is to "close the show and put a better one on the road".'

Berne viewed the life script as the result of the *defence mechanism* of *repetition compulsion*. Transactional analysts since Berne have developed the concept of script and script analysis. Goulding (1972) suggests that components of script development include a parental injunction; the child's decision to obey in order to survive; his effort to meet his own needs; his creation of a life position which enables the injunction to be obeyed *and* his needs to be met; the beginning of a game or racket; and the development of the game to cover a variety of situations. Barnes (1977) describes seven aspects of script analysis all of which deserve the therapist's attention: the counter script which is the part of the individual's life which is adapted to survival; the script proper; the antiscript, devised by the rebellious Child; the episcript or other people's expectations; the current life plan, including all the individual's decisions and strategies of which he is aware; the non-script activities; and the centre or self which is script free and which has the power to re-create its universe each day without relying on a well-worn script. Steiner (1974) has developed important work on the theory of scripts including script checklists, script development and effective ways of therapeutic script analysis.

BARNES, G. (ed.) (1977), *Transactional Analysis after Eric Berne* (Harper & Row, New York).

BERNE, E. (1961), *Transactional Analysis in Psychotherapy* (Grove Press, New York).

GOULDING, R. (1972), 'New directions in transactional analysis' (in Sager, C. J. and Caplan, H. S. (eds), *Progress in Group and Family Therapy*, Brunner/Mazel, New York).

STEINER, C. (1974), *Scripts People Live* (Grove Press, New York).

Second order change

One of two types of therapeutic change postulated by Watzlawick *et al.* (1974) and referring to change directed towards changing change. From the point of view of the *theory of types*, second order change interventions are directed towards the frame of reference of *meta* level, not to the behavioural events themselves. Second order change is applied to the *attempted solution* to a problem, since from this perspective the 'solution' is conceived of as the problem. Characteristic of second order change is its discontinuity with previous approaches and its 'uncommon sense' interventions, which include the use of *paradox*, *symptom prescription*, *therapeutic double binds* and *reframing*. These techniques are directed towards the here and now situation and do not rely on a historical exploration of the *causality* of either the problem or its attempted solution. Second order change avoids the problem posed by the illusion of alternatives inherent in *first order change* interventions, i.e. the idea that there is only a choice between choosing to continue or choosing to stop the undesirable behaviour. Second order change involves instead the recalibration of a *system* through the operation of a *step function*, moving the system on to a different level of functioning. Therapists from many different approaches have pointed to the paradoxical nature of therapeutic change. Beisser (1970), for example, from within the context of *Gestalt therapy*, suggests that 'change can occur when the patient abandons, at least for the moment, what he would like to become and attempt to be what he is'.

BEISSER, A. R. (1970), 'The paradoxical theory of change' (in Fagan, J. and Shepherd, I. L. (eds), *Gestalt Therapy Now*, Science and Behavior Books, Palo Alto, Calif.).

WATZLAWICK, P. *et al.* (1974), *Change: Problem Formation and Problem Resolution* (W. W. Norton, New York).

See also *Calibration, Strategic therapy*.

Secondary elaboration

The tendency to increase the coherence of a *dream*, on awakening, by elaborating its remembered content.

Secondary gain

Secondary advantages which accrue from the patient's *symptom* or illness such as financial compensation, new status conferred by the *sick role* or the satisfactions gained from the *transference*. In practice it is often difficult to distinguish secondary gains from the *primary gains* of the illness.

Secondary process

The mode of functioning characterising the *conscious* and *preconscious* parts of the *psyche*. It is congruent with the operation of the *reality principle* and is the usual means by which the *ego* operates, although *primary process* may influence the ego too. Secondary processes are characterised by reason, judgment, attention and order in contrast to the free-flowing, chaotic activity of primary process.

FREUD, S. (1900), 'The interpretation of dreams' (*Standard Edition*, vol. 5, Hogarth Press, London).

Seduction theory

Freud's very early attempt to understand the origins of neurosis. When hypnotising hysterical patients in the 1880s he found they repeatedly reported early memories of having been sexually abused by adults. At the time he thought that this was an actual traumatic event causing the adult eventually to 'suffer from memories'. Later he realised that the evidence for repressed memories in the *unconscious* was so widespread in adults that what his patients were remembering were probably traumatic *phantasies*, and not actual events.

Self-actualisation

The innate capacity of human beings to grow and develop towards emotional and psychological maturity. The term is used by most *humanistic* therapists to describe the central motivating tendency in life. Goldstein (1934,

1940) recognised self-actualisation as the only ultimate organismic motivating factor, impelling the individual to develop and perfect his or her capacities to the fullest possible extent. Goldstein believed that self-actualisation only occurred through successfully mastered conflict with the environment and that it always entails anxiety. Rogers (1951) also believed that the organism has one basic tendency, that of self-actualisation, and he made use of Goldstein's concept to describe the primary goal of normal development and of therapy. Maslow uses Goldstein's term in the more limited sense of 'desire for self fulfilment'. He views self-actualisation as realising the fullness of one's potential and he places it at the highest level of his hierarchy of human *needs*. For Maslow, self-actualised people are capable of having *peak experiences* more often and more intensely than others, whereby the individual experiences a unity with art, nature and other human beings and the environment to an intense degree.

Because this tendency is thought to exist universally in all human beings, therapists who subscribe to this view of personality (notably the followers of Rogers, Maslow and Goldstein) place great reliance on the self-restorative capacities of the client and they minimise the need for a directive position on the part of the therapist.

The stress induced by having self-actualisation as a life goal within the culture is discussed by Symonds (1980), and the resulting emphasis on achieving self-actualisation for adolescents is discussed by Rakoff (1978). Self-actualisation has been shown to increase using a very wide range of therapeutic interventions.

Many interactionally based therapists would criticise the absolute value placed on self-actualisation as the primary goal of human development and of therapy, on the grounds that it places too high a value on the rights of the individual to develop himself regardless of the cost to others. Goldstein (1940) recognised this problem but felt that love represents 'a higher form of self-actualisation, and a challenge to develop both oneself and the other'. The concept has been attacked for being unclear and unsubstantiated (Butler and Rice 1963; Dollard and Miller 1950). They refute the idea of an innate tendency towards 'growth' and replace it with the idea of 'learning'. Other approaches use terms such as wholeness, maturity and *individuation*.

BUTLER, J. M. and RICE, L. N. (1963), 'Adience, self-actualisation and drive theory' (in Wepman, J. M. and Heine, R. W. (eds), *Concepts of Personality*, Aldine Atherton, Chicago).

COFER, C. N. and APPLEY, M. H. (1964), *Motivation: Theory and Research* (Wiley, New York).

DOLLARD, J. and MILLER, N. E. (1950), *Personality and Psychotherapy* (McGraw-Hill, New York).

GOLDSTEIN, K. (1934), *The Organism* (Beacon Press, Boston).

GOLDSTEIN, K. (1940), *Human Nature in the Light of Psychopathology* (Schocken Books, New York).

MASLOW, A. H. (1970), *Motivation and Personality* (2nd edn, Harper & Row, New York).

RAKOFF, V. (1978), 'The illusion of detachment' (*Adolescent Psychiatry*, vol. 6, pp. 119-29).

ROGERS, C. (1951), *Client-Centred Therapy* (Constable, London).

SYMONDS, A. (1900), 'The stress of self-realisation' (*Am. J. of Psychoan.*, vol. 40, pp. 293-300).

WILKINSON, K. P. (1979), 'Social wellbeing and community' (*J. of the Community Development Society*, vol. 10, pp. 5-16).

Self-actualising therapy

See *Actualising therapy*.

Self-analysis

Systematic investigation of one's own psychic processes using psychoanalytic techniques such as *free association*, the recording and analysis of one's own *dreams* and the investigation of minor *symptoms* such as lapses of memory, headaches, slips of the tongue, etc.

Originally Freud recommended the technique and engaged in self-analysis himself. Later, however, he concluded that such a procedure was a poor substitute for being analysed by someone else. Abraham (1919) believed self-analysis to be a particular form of resistance to *psychoanalysis* but Horney (1942) suggested that it was both feasible and useful, though limited in its results as compared with an analysis by someone else. Currently it is regarded as a highly desirable procedure in its own right, but not as a substitute for one's own therapeutic or *training analysis*. Ticho (1967), Calder (1980) and others have discussed its usefulness as a means of extending the benefits of the training analysis throughout the analyst's subsequent professional life.

ABRAHAM, K. (1919), 'A particular form of neurotic resistance against the psychoanalytic method' (in *Selected Papers*, Hogarth Press, London).

CALDER, K. T. (1980), 'An analyst's self-analysis' (*J. of the American Psychoan. Assoc.*, vol. 28, pp. 5-20).

FLUMMING, J. (1971), 'Freud's concept of self-analysis' (in Marcus, I. (ed.), *Currents in Psychoanalysis*, International Universities Press, New York).

GRINBERG, J. DE EKBOIR and LICHTMANN, A. (1982), 'Genuine self-analysis is impossible' (*Int. Review of Psychoan.*, vol. 9, pp. 75-83).

HORNEY, K. (1942), *Self Analysis* (W. W. Norton, New York).

TICHO, G. (1967), 'On self-analysis' (*Int. J. of Psychoan.*, vol. 48, pp. 308-18).

Self-disclosure

The revelation by the client of his feelings, attitudes and behaviour regarding his current situation and his past experiences. Self-disclosure is an essential client behaviour in most types of psychotherapy and low levels of self-disclosure usually seriously inhibit the therapeutic process. The ability to self-disclose is related to the amount of perceived trust in the person to whom the disclosure is being made (Schlenker *et al.* 1973). Personal trustworthiness reinforces self-disclosing behaviour and further disclosures are also stimulated by the positive and non-judgmental way in which the disclosures are received by the therapist. Johnson and Noonan (1972) have shown that rejection decreases the frequency and depth of self-disclosure. There is some evidence to show that the reciprocation of self-disclosure on the part of the therapist increases trust and therefore increases the frequency and depth of disclosure by the client. A high value is usually placed on early self-disclosure in *self-help* groups and many forms of *group psychotherapy*.

COZBY, P. C. (1973), 'Self-disclosure: a literature review' (*Psychological Bulletin*, vol. 79, pp. 73-91).

JOHNSON, D. W. and NOONAN, M. P. (1972), 'The effects of acceptance and reciprocation of self-disclosures on the development of trust' (*J. of Counseling Psychology*, vol. 19, pp. 411-16).

JOURARD, S. M. and FRIEDMAN, R. (1970), 'Experimenter-subject "distance" and self-disclosure' (*J. of Personality and Social Psychology*, vol. 15, pp. 278-82).

MOWRER, O. H. (1964), 'Freudianism, behavior therapy and "self-disclosure"' (*Behavior Research and Therapy*, vol. 1, pp. 321-37).

SCHLENKER, B. R. et al. (1973), 'The effects of personality and situational variables on behavioural trust' (*J. of Personality and Social Psychology*, vol. 25, pp. 419-27).

See also *Self-disclosure (therapist)*, *Silence*.

Self-disclosure (therapist)

The sharing of some of the therapist's thoughts, feelings and personal data with the client. The subject is a controversial one. The practice is contra-indicated in most psycho-analytic therapies where the disclosure of the therapist's private world would interfere with the development of the *transference*. Human-istic therapists, however, use personal open-ness as a means of reducing the gap between therapist and client. Mowrer is one of the primary advocates of therapist self-disclosure and he has made it an essential core of his

integrity therapy. Jourard (1971) suggests that self-disclosure on the part of the therapist increases the client's ability to self-disclose. Although there is some experimental evidence to support this statement (Bierman 1969), most of the research relates to self-disclosure between peers and therefore may not be relevant to the psychotherapeutic relationship. Dies (1973) has suggested that the value of self-disclosure is enhanced in the later stages of therapy. Weiner (1978) has highlighted the many pitfalls associated with therapist self-disclosure and although it may helpfully build *rapport*, it may also interfere with the therapist's ability to retain his *credibility* and authority. Kaslow et al. (1979), on the other hand, examined self-disclosure in the context of *family therapy* and concluded that the ther-apist's selective use of his own perceptions, values and experiences contributes positively to psychotherapeutic *outcome*.

BIERMAN, R. (1969), 'Dimensions for inter-personal facilitation in psychotherapy and child development' (*Psychological Bulletin*, vol. 72, pp. 338-72).

DIES, R. R. (1973), 'Group therapist self-disclosure: an evaluation by clients' (*J. of Counseling Psychology*, vol. 20, pp. 344-8).

JOURARD, J. (1971), *The Transparent Self* (Van Nostrand Reinhold, Toronto).

KASLOW, F. et al. (1979), 'Family therapist authenticity as a key factor in outcome' (*Int. J. of Family Therapy*, vol. 1, pp. 184-99).

WEINER, W. F. (1978), *Therapist Disclosure* (Butterworth, Boston).

Self-efficacy

A term introduced by Bandura (1977) to explain changes that occur after treatment. Bandura examined several different treatment approaches and concluded that the key to therapeutic change is the client's expectations of his own efficacy. Expectations of personal efficacy stem from four main sources of information: performance and mastery exper-iences; vicarious coping experiences gained from watching others succeed; verbal encouragement; and a low level of emotional arousal. Bandura *et al.* (1977) confirm that different treatment approaches alter expectations of personal efficacy. They suggest that treatments based on performance success produce stronger expectations of personal efficacy than those relying on vicarious experiences, encouragement or the reduction of emotional arousal, a *hypothesis* confirmed in Biran and Wilson's (1981) study of phobics. Moreover, behavioural changes correspond closely to levels of self-efficacy, regardless of treatment approach. An individual's perception of self-efficacy has an important bearing on his ability to engage in *functional* behaviours and activities so that lack of perceived self-efficacy increases a person's susceptibility to psychological disorders.

BANDURA, A. (1977), 'Self-efficacy: towards a unifying theory of behavioral change' (*Psychological Review*, vol. 84, pp. 191-215).

BANDURA, A. *et al.* (1977), 'Cognitive processes mediating behavioral change' (*J. of Personality and Social Psychology*, vol. 35, pp. 125-39).

BIRAN, M. and WILSON, G. (1981), 'Treatment of phobic disorders using cognitive and exposure methods: a self-efficacy analysis' (*J. of Consulting and Clinical Psychology*, vol. 49, pp. 886-99).

Self-fulfilling prophecy

A concept described by Merton (1949) in which a theory's predictions are seen as being responsible for bringing about the 'truth' of the theory. In psychological disturbance, the feared event is brought about by predicting that it will happen. For example, a parent who fears that a child will 'turn against' him may bring this about by repeatedly predicting it. A spouse who fears that he or she is unloved by the other creates that situation by continuously voicing his or her fears of being unloved. The selection of an *identified patient* or *scapegoat* in a family or group may be in accordance with a self-fulfilling prophecy, the elected member being perceived to hold characteristics similar to another deviant member in the family's past. The expectation is conveyed that he or she will

live up to the selected role and those expectations play a part in bringing that about.

Expectancy, however, also plays a part in creating a favourable climate for therapy; the patient's expectation that the therapist will be helpful and skilful enables him to gain help from the therapeutic situation. (See *Non-specific factors* and *Credibility*.) *Strategic therapists* have shown how self-fulfilling prophecies can be used paradoxically by predicting that something will occur which the patient then makes it his business to see does not. Predicting a relapse back into symptomatology, presenting the patient with a *Devil's Pact* and using *pessimism* to promote a counterbalancing optimism in the patient are all examples of the paradoxical use of the self-fulfilling prophecy.

MERTON, R. K. (1949), *Social Theory and Social Structure* (Free Press, Glencoe).

See also *Counter phobic, Family myth, Paradox.*

Self-help

Self-directed therapeutic change gained either alone or through association in pairs or groups with peers who suffer from the same or a similar problem – for example, Alcoholics Anonymous, Weight Watchers, Depressives Anonymous, Gingerbread and the Open Door (Robinson and Robinson (1979) provide a very full list of such groups in Britain). Other groups such as *consciousness raising* groups, feminist groups and liberation groups may combine therapeutic and political/pressure group functions. The limited amount of research that has been conducted in this area points to the positive results obtained. Hurvitz (1970) goes so far as to suggest that professionals should model their behaviour and interventions on self-help groups but Emrick *et al.* (1977), who summarise the research, argue for the distinctions between the two types of therapeutic intervention to be sharply maintained so that clients can make a clear choice.

Other means of gaining self-help are through books, tape recordings or kits which focus on techniques for alleviating a particular symptom or disorder and which do not require the help of either a professional therapist or attendance at a peer group. *Relaxation training* and *assertiveness training*, for example, have been successfully offered using taped instructions. Self-help activities have expanded enormously over the last decade. Reasons for this have been given as the scarcity of professional resources; the growth in community mental health; the high value placed on participation in one's own growth and healing; and the reduction of stigmatisation so that the public admission that one is an alcoholic or drug addict, etc., is now more possible. The development of ideas from *radical therapy* is also undoubtedly an important factor. Glasser (1976) suggests ways of encouraging 'positive addictions' to healthy and growth-promoting feelings and behaviour.

EMRICK, C. D. *et al.* (1977), 'Non-professional peers as therapeutic agents' (in Gurman, A. S. and Razin, A. M., *Effective Psychotherapy*, Pergamon Press, New York).

ERNST, S. and GOODISON, L. (1981), *In Our Own Hands: A Book of Self-Help Therapy* (Women's Press, London).

GLASSER, W. (1976), *Positive Addiction* (Harper & Row, New York).

HURVITZ, N. (1970), 'Peer self-help groups and their implications for psychotherapy' (*Psychotherapy: Theory, Research and Practice*, vol. 7, pp. 41-9).

JOURNAL OF APPLIED BEHAVIORAL SCIENCE, Special Issue (1976), 'Self-help groups', vol. 12.

NEUMANN, M. and BERKOWITZ, B. (1973), *How to be Your Own Best Friend* (Random House, New York).

ROBINSON, D. and ROBINSON, Y. (1979), *From Self-help to Health* (Concord Books, London).

Self-instructional training

A *cognitive restructuring approach* developed by Meichenbaum (1977) directed towards the modification of maladaptive beliefs and cognitions and the development of new skills. Most of Meichenbaum's work has been developed in relation to children's problems, especially impulsivity, but he and colleagues have also related it to schizophrenics, students stressed by performance anxiety and people wanting to improve their creativity. Self-instructional training involves making explicit and then altering the individual's automatic internal dialogue and his negative self-statements; *modelling* the task to be performed with accompanying verbalised self-talk by the modeller; *behavioural rehearsal* by the client accompanied by positive verbalised self-talk; and finally, task performance by the client, accompanied by constructive internal dialogue.

An important part of all self-instructional training is helping the client to generate a range of constructive self-statements which will overcome his negative cognitions. These may be developed through prompting and encouraging the client to produce them and through suggestions and modelling by the therapist. Constructive self-statements receive positive *reinforcement* by the therapist and immediate opportunities for linking to task performance. As Meichenbaum points out, the self-instructional approach is markedly different from the lay concept of 'positive thinking' and relies on the selection of highly individualised positive self-statements, appropriate to the particular client and his specific problem.

MEICHENBAUM, D. (1977), *Cognitive-behavior Modification* (Plenum Press, New York).

See also *Anxiety management training, Cognitive behavioural therapy, Coping skills interventions, Stress inoculation.*

Self-monitoring

The patient's self-observation and recording of his *symptoms* and related behaviour in order to establish a *base line* prior to the introduction of treatment. Originally used as a control procedure for experiments concerned with other issues, self-monitoring is currently recognised as having the dual effect of both providing data for treatment planning and also acting as a treatment agent in its own right. It has disadvantages in both areas. As a means of providing the therapist with objective data, it is subject to bias and dishonesty, although unintentional bias can be reduced by making the client's task quite specific and unambiguous and by providing him with daily recording sheets. In addition to its assessment role, self-monitoring has been shown to be a therapeutic agent and, in some cases, the very act of accurately observing and paying close attention to one's own problem behaviour is sufficient to reduce or even to eliminate it.

Rutner and Bugler (1969) report a case of the virtual elimination of hallucinations in a hospitalised patient after two weeks by this means. Various explanations have been offered for this treatment effect: increased awareness may interrupt the automatic nature of the response sequence; it may encourage *self-reinforcement* or *self-punishment* according to progress made, with the concomitant effects of these procedures, and the prospect of gaining the therapist's approval, may act as a spur to problem reduction. Despite the widely reported beneficial effects of self-monitoring, they are however often variable and short-lived as Mahoney and Arnkoff (1978) point out. They go on to suggest that a variety of issues remain to be clarified, particularly, what are the parameters of its variability and how to tackle the problem of ensuring that self-monitoring is accurately carried out. The technique is mainly used within the *behavioural therapies*.

KANFER, F. H. (1970), 'Self-monitoring: methodological limitations and clinical applications' (*J. of Consulting and Clinical Psychology*, vol. 35, pp. 148-52).
MAHONEY, M. J. and ARNKOFF, D. B. (1978), 'Cognitive and self-control therapies' (in Garfield, S. L. and Bergin, A. E., *Handbook of Psychotherapy and Behavior Change*, Wiley, New York).
RUTNER, I. and BUGLER, C. (1969), 'An experimental procedure for the modification of psychotic behaviour' (*J. of Consulting and Clinical Psychology*, vol. 33, pp. 651-3).
THORENSEN, C. E. and MAHONEY, M. J.

(1974), *Behavioral Self-Control* (Holt, Rinehart & Winston, New York).

Self-psychology

A development of *ego psychology* which adopts some of the concepts of the *Kleinian school* of *psychoanalysis* and *object relations* theory, and attempts to integrate them into the theoretical framework of ego psychology as developed in the United States. It is associated with Jacobson, Kohut, Mahler and Kernberg.

JACOBSON, E. (1954), 'The self and the object world' (in *The Psychoanalytic Study of the Child*, vol. 5, International Universities Press, New York).
KERNBERG, O. (1980), *Internal World and External Reality* (Jason Aronson, New York).
KOHUT, H. (1971), *The Analysis of the Self* (International Universities Press, New York).
MAHLER, M. S., PINE, F. and BERGMAN, A. (1975), *The Psychological Birth of the Human Infant* (Basic Books, New York).

Self-punishment

Punishment administered to the self, contingent upon the occurrence of some undesired response. In contrast to *self-reinforcement*, a very meagre success rate has been reported, presumably because of the difficulty of organising a punishment that is aversive enough to be effective but not so aversive that the client refuses to use it. It should always be used in combination with positive *reinforcement*, self-administered or otherwise.

THORENSEN, C. E. and MAHONEY, M. J. (1974), *Behavioral Self-Control* (Holt, Rinehart & Winston, New York).

Self-realisation

Term often used synonymously with *self-actualisation*. Used specifically by Horney, a member of the *interpersonal school of psychoanalysis*, to describe the goal of all human striving. Horney (1950) contrasted neurosis with self-realisation and suggested that 'the liberation and cultivation of the forces which lead to self-realisation' is the task of psychotherapy and the goal of each human being.

HORNEY, K. (1950), *Neurosis and Human Growth* (W. W. Norton, New York).

Self-reinforcement

Rewards offered to the self, contingent upon the achievement of some desired goal or performance of some desired response. Kanfer (1971) suggests a three-phase model, *self-monitoring*, self-evaluation and self-reinforcement, if performance is deemed to have achieved the predetermined goal. The findings from a large number of studies suggest that self-reinforcement is as effective as external reinforcement, although it is not clear which part of the process is the most powerful in producing behaviour change. Failure may result if the initial goal is set too high.

KANFER, F. H. (1971), 'The maintenance of behavior by self-generated stimuli and reinforcement' (in Jacobs, A. and Sachs, L. B. (eds), *The Psychology of Private Events*, Academic Press, New York).

Sensate focus exercises

Non-genital sensual massage used as a *homework assignment* in the treatment of sexual dysfunction. The technique was introduced by Masters and Johnson (1970). The goal is to create a comfortable, anxiety-free atmosphere for physical contact to take place between the couple and to increase their repertoire of physical interactions. A specific feature emphasises the use of physical touch that is both pleasing to give and pleasing to receive. Afterwards, the couple are encouraged to give each other *feedback* about the ways in which the activity was pleasurable and the ways in which it could have been improved. The technique has similarities with *reciprocal inhibition* and the use of *relaxation training* in *systematic desensitisation*, where the relaxation inhibits anxiety.

MASTERS, W. H. and JOHNSON, V. E. (1970), *Human Sexual Inadequacy* (Little, Brown, Boston, New York).

Sensitivity training

See *Encounter, Encounter groups, Human potential movement, Marathon group therapy, T-group training.*

Separation anxiety

See *Attachment theory.*

Sex therapy

A variety of approaches which take the sexual relationship of the couple or sexual dysfunction of the individual as the focus of treatment. A vast literature now exists on the treatment of sexual dysfunction, using behavioural, strategic, psychoanalytic and group approaches. Sex therapy of varying lengths is a frequent component of *marital therapy*. Early pioneers in research into sexuality paved the way for modern treatments. Freud's work on the importance of sexual energy and his rediscovery of infantile sexuality, Havelock Ellis's researches into the psychology of sex, Wilhelm Reich's work on the origins of sexual oppression, and Alfred Kinsey's compilation of thousands of individual sexual histories, all helped to provide a body of knowledge from which a systematic approach to treatment could be developed. In the 1950s, Masters and Johnson (1966, 1970) began their enormously influential research into sexual dysfunction and its treatment and their therapeutic programme remains the basis for most other treatment approaches that are currently used, even though various modifications have been introduced by other workers.

Basic principles underpinning the Masters and Johnson approach are that, first, treatment must be *conjoint*, and directed to the relationship between the couple, even when, as is usually the case, only one of the partners is presenting a problem. Second, treatment is carried out by a male and female *co-therapy* pair. Third, the relationship between the therapists and the couple is considered to be a primary therapeutic factor. Modifications have been made to these principles by other workers: individuals presenting without partners are treated, sometimes using surrogates, and the work of Matthews *et al.* (1976)

has suggested that no significant advantage is gained by using co-therapists compared with a single therapist. So far as couples are concerned, the marital relationship is recognised by most sex therapists as a primary factor in the aetiology and prognosis of sexual problems. Unless the couple have a reasonably intact relationship, are both motivated for treatment and believe that the problem is to some extent a shared one, sex therapy is unlikely to be helpful.

Masters and Johnson, and the approaches derived from them, offer a systematic course of treatment, some ingredients of which are used regardless of the problem that is presented, others being tailored to the specific problem. The couple is asked to spend two weeks in a hotel near to the clinic and leave behind all occupational and domestic duties (although Crowe (1979) questions whether this residential imperative is absolutely necessary). The couple attends the clinic every day over the two-week period. First, a full sexual history is taken by each therapist working separately with the patient of the same sex. Second, the procedure is repeated but with the patient of the opposite sex. Third, each partner receives a full physical examination (undertaken by a doctor attached to the clinic if the therapists are not medically trained). This ensures that possible physical causes of the problem are eliminated. Fourth, a round table discussion between all four participants takes place and this is continued daily during treatment, during which the couple are encouraged to discuss their problems freely with the therapists and to report progress. The therapists use these sessions to help the couple work on problems revealed in their sexual history and in their marital relationships generally, as well as giving *homework assignments* and offering *interpretations* of the material, if a psychoanalytic approach is being adopted (Kaplan 1974; Scharff 1982). From the fourth day onwards, the Masters and Johnson approach requires the couple to make use of a series of techniques in their hotel room in private. First, a total ban on intercourse is imposed (which has the effect of

reducing 'performance anxiety' and relaxing both partners); second, the couple are asked to practise *sensate focus* exercises; and third, they graduate to genital sensate focus but still keeping a ban on intercourse.

Subsequent interventions are directed towards specific dysfunctions. Crowe (1979) gives a comprehensive list of the common types of sexual dysfunction and their causative factors. The most frequently used techniques for these are as follows: for male impotence and female anorgasmia, a continuation of genital sensate focus exercises, with special instructions to each partner on how to stimulate their own and each other's genital areas and to experiment with different positions when intercourse is permitted; for premature ejaculation, the 'squeeze technique' is recommended, whereby the woman squeezes the glans penis firmly after stimulating it to the point of ejaculation; for inability to ejaculate, the couple concentrates on manual 'super stimulation' of the penis outside the vagina until ejaculation occurs; for vaginismus, *relaxation training* and the use of dilators are recommended; and for low sexual arousal due to tension, lack of information or longstanding inhibitions regarding sexual activity, the therapists provide *counselling, bibliotherapy,* anxiety reduction through *systematic densensitisation* and the use of technical aids such as a vibrator. The needs of particular patient groups, such as homosexual couples, the young, the elderly, the disabled and those who are single and lack confidence in finding a sexual partner, are discussed in specialist books and papers (see Leiblum and Pervin 1980; Ayrault 1982; and Craft and Craft 1982). High success rates are reported by many clinics, especially in the treatment of premature ejaculation, vaginismus and anorgasmia (Lobitz and LoPiccolo 1972).

AYRAULT, E. W. (1982), *Sex, Love and the Physically Handicapped* (SPCK, London).
CRAFT, M. and CRAFT, A. (1982), *Sex and the Mentally Handicapped* (revised edn, Routledge & Kegan Paul, London).
CROWE, M. (1979), 'The treatment of sexual

SHADOW OF THE ANCESTOR

dysfunction' (in Walrond-Skinner, S. (ed.), *Family and Marital Psychotherapy*, Routledge & Kegan Paul, London).

CROWN, S. (1976), *Psychosexual Problems* (Academic Press, London).

FINK, P. J. and GOLDMAN, A. (1981), 'Integrated approaches to sex therapy' (in Masserman, J., *Current Psychiatric Therapies*, Grune & Stratton, New York).

FRANK, O. S. (1982), 'The therapy of sexual dysfunction' (*Brit. J. of Psychiatry*, vol. 140, pp. 78-84).

GILLAN, P. and GILLAN, R. (1976), *Sex Therapy Today* (Open Books, London).

KAPLAN, H. S. (1974), *The New Sex Therapy* (Penguin, Harmondsworth).

KAPLAN, H. S. (1979), *Disorders of Sexual Desire* (Brunner/Mazel, New York).

KROHNE, E. C. (1982), *The Sex Therapy Handbook* (MTP, Lancaster).

LEIBLUM, S. R. and PERVIN, L. A. (1980), *Principles and Practice of Sex Therapy* (Tavistock, London).

LOBITZ, W. C. and LOPICCOLO, J. (1972), 'New methods in the behavioral treatment of sexual dysfunction' (*J. of Behavior Therapy and Experimental Psychiatry*, vol. 3, pp. 265-71).

LOPICCOLO, J. and LOPICCOLO, L. (1978), *Handbook of Sex Therapy* (Plenum Press, New York).

MASTERS, W. H. and JOHNSON, V. E. (1966), *Human Sexual Response* (Little, Brown, Boston).

MASTERS, W. H. and JOHNSON, V. E. (1970), *Human Sexual Inadequacy* (Little, Brown, Boston).

MATTHEWS, A. *et al.* (1976), 'The behavioural treatment of sexual inadequacy: a comparative study' (*Behavioural Research and Therapy*, vol. 14, pp. 427-36).

SCHARFF, D. E. (1982), *The Sexual Relationship: An Object Relations View* (Routledge & Kegan Paul, London).

VAN DER EYKEN, W. (1982), 'Paradoxical strategies in a blocked sex therapy' (*Am. J. of Psychotherapy*, vol. 36, pp. 103-8).

Shadow

Term used by Jung to describe the dark or primitive side of the self which is generally unacceptable to the person concerned and is hence experienced as inferior or uncontrollable. The core of the idea in *analytical psychology* takes two main forms: to indicate the overharsh judgment by an individual of instinctive, impulsive material – infantile elements of *unconscious* life; and to indicate that humanity has an evil, destructive, dark side. This latter usage rests on the manifestation in the *collective unconscious* of such universal images as the devil and the witch and it has therefore an *archetypal* basis. The shadow is kept in check by the *ego* and the *persona* but most of all by consciousness itself. One of the central tasks of psychotherapy, in Jung's view, is to help the individual to accept and come to terms with, or integrate, his shadow. Without this, *individuation* is impossible. The shadow sometimes manifests itself in *dreams*, appearing as a 'shady' character of the same sex as the dreamer but displaying characteristics which the dreamer repudiates or considers to be inferior. The shadow is frequently *projected* on to other individuals, groups or whole societies who are then seen to possess the characteristics that are being repudiated. Jung was fond of saying that everything of substance has a shadow, thus emphasising its naturalness and inevitability.

JUNG, C. G. (1946), 'The fight with the shadow' (*Collected Works*, vol. 10, Routledge & Kegan Paul, London).

JUNG, C. G. (1971), 'Aion' (*Collected Works*, vol. 9, part 2 (Penguin, Harmondsworth).

FRANZ, M. L. VON (1974), *Shadow and Evil in Fairy Tales* (Spring Publications, Zurich).

Shadow of the ancestor

Term introduced by Scott (Scott and Ashworth 1969) to describe the way in which a psychotic illness or shadow of insanity in a close relative affects the parents' attitudes to one of their children. The child is forced into an identification with the 'image' of the ill relative and this identification receives confirmation from any 'disturbance' which is subsequently shown by the child.

315

SCOTT, R. D. and ASHWORTH, P. L. (1969), 'The shadow of the ancestor' (*Brit. J. of Medical Psychology*, vol. 42, pp. 13-32).

See also *Displacement, Family myth, Family transference, Identified patient, Labelling, Scapegoat.*

Shaping

Teaching a new piece of learning or behaviour by reinforcing *responses* which exhibit *successive approximations* to the final response required. Shaping is a major technique employed with mentally handicapped individuals where the total behaviour that is desired, for example, self-feeding, is broken down into small units, each of which, when successfully acquired, can be reinforced.

See also *Operant conditioning, Token economy.*

Short-term anxiety-provoking psychotherapy

A method of *brief therapy* based on psychoanalytic principles and designed for patients unable to make satisfactory relationships and whose disturbance originates in unresolved *Oedipal* problems. Problems relating to general separation difficulty and grief reactions are also suitable for this form of treatment. The selection criteria for patients are strict and rather circumscribed: a clear-cut chief complaint; a history of altruistic relationships with at least one other person during early childhood; an ability to interact flexibly with the evaluator during the initial interview; an above average psychological sophistication and intelligence and high motivation for change. Patients are mainly young adults. The treatment *contract* does not specify the number of sessions in advance as in *time-limited psychotherapy* but patients are told that therapy will take 'a few months'. The average length of treatment is three to four months or from twelve to sixteen interviews. According to Sifneos (1979), the originator of the method, this open-ended contract gives a greater flexibility for the patient to undertake the work.

The therapeutic work consists of the delineation of a psychodynamic focus which underlies the patient's psychological difficulties and which is agreed as the focus for treatment by patient and therapist; the establishment of a *therapeutic alliance*; the active use of anxiety-provoking *confrontation* and *clarification* which penetrates the patient's *resistance*; early *interpretations* of positive *transference* leading to *abreaction* and the use of 'parent-transference links' to interpret connections between the patient's relations with his parents and his transferred attitudes to the therapist. The therapist plays the part of an 'unemotionally involved teacher'.

An important part of the work involves the development of a *corrective emotional relationship*. This enables the patient to resolve the neurotic disturbance which has arisen from unsatisfactory early relationships with his parents. Workers who use this method claim that they are able to help patients to understand the dynamic conflicts underlying their difficulties; provide moderate symptomatic relief; produce general improvement in the patient's relationships with his significant others; increase his self-esteem; develop new problem solving capacities and more appropriate attitudes. Like other brief therapies, this method can be criticised for being a method in search of patients, and as the selection criteria are particularly stringent, the criticism seems particularly appropriate in this case. The method is firmly based on the assumption that *insight* into the roots of the disturbance leads to the relief of pain and behaviour change, in contrast to the anxiety-provoking techniques using chiefly behavioural ideas, such as *flooding* and *implosion*.

DAVANLOO, H. (1978), *Principles and Techniques of Short-Term Dynamic Psychotherapy* (Spectrum Press, New York).
SIFNEOS, P. E. (1968), 'Learning to solve emotional problems: a controlled study of short-term anxiety-provoking psychotherapy' (in Porter, R. (ed)., *CIBA Foundation Symposium on the Role of Learning in Psychotherapy*, J. and A. Churchill, London).
SIFNEOS, P. E. (1972), *Short-Term Psychotherapy and Emotional Crisis* (Harvard

University Press, Cambridge, Mass.).
SIFNEOS, P. E. (1979), *Short-Term Dynamic Psychotherapy: Evaluation and Technique* (Plenum Press, New York).

Sick role
A designation given by one individual or group to another individual whereby, according to Parsons (1951), a deviant status is conferred on the person so labelled, along with the rights and obligations recognised as belonging to the role. The sick role may perform a function not only for the individual so labelled in the form of *primary* and *secondary gains*, but also, he or she may be used as a sacrifice for the sake of the rest of the family or group. Usually, however, the acquisition and acceptance of this label performs a function both for the individual and for his psycho-social system. Within the family, the sick role carried by one member is likely to produce a concerned and united family group as compared with a delinquency label which more often leads to tension and conflict. The sick role performs a protective function for other members and *sub-systems* by increasing *cohesion* and drawing attention away from more threatening areas of dysfunction such as marital conflict or the death or loss of a member. It is a condition of the sick role that the individual accepts that he cannot recover by a *conscious* act of will even though he must desire to get well. Thus his status as a 'sick person' is conditional on his becoming a *patient*.

MECKANIC, D. (1962), 'Some factors in identifying and deconfirming mental illness' (*Mental Hygiene*, vol. 46, pp. 66-74).
PARSONS, T. (1951), 'Illness and the role of the physician: a sociological perspective' (*Am. J. of Orthopsychiatry*, vol. 21, pp. 452-60).

Side taking
See *Unbalancing*.

Silence
Silence is discussed in the psychotherapeutic literature as a strategy of *resistance* by the patient; as a necessary and fruitful part of the

psychotherapeutic process; and as an intervention on the part of the therapist. Originally, in the psychoanalytic therapies, silence was perceived as a resistance (Bengler 1938). Handling the 'silent patient' produced much discussion in terms of the meaning of the silence and the therapeutic technique to be used. Subsequently, as Ferreira (1973) points out, *psychoanalysis* has come to regard silence simply 'as a sort of Wagnerian leitmotif in the drama of psychotherapy'. Silence enables the patient to *free associate*, make connections between his current and past experience and, later in treatment, engage in the *working through* process. Nacht (1964) describes silence as an integrating factor. *Questioning, clarification, reflection, interpretation* or any active intervention on the part of the therapist can interrupt the spontaneous flow of the patient's internal experience, which can perhaps only be expressed in silence.

In all the *non-directive* approaches, the positive value of silence is likely to be stressed. Silence enables therapist and patient to attend to each other and to develop a relationship of depth and intensity. Silence enables words to be heard and *non-verbal communication* to be read. For Khan (1963), the primary function of silence is to communicate – in the case he discusses, intense and prolonged silence is seen as a mode of *acting out*, serving the functions of 'recollecting, integrating and working through' the pathogenic quality of an early relationship. The interactive nature of silence is also well recognised. Ferreira (1973) comments on silence as 'a production which the patient and the therapist share in authorship'. 'It is something that happens *between* people rather than *within* one of them, an occurrence within a relationship.'

These considerations are even more sharply highlighted in *family therapy* and group work approaches. Zuk (1965) and Breunlin and Southgate (1978) identify a strategy which occurs in family therapy and which they describe as 'dysfunctional silencing'. One family member repeatedly silences another in order to prevent change occurring in the *system*. Breunlin and Southgate suggest strategies for interrupting the silencing pattern in the family. In *group psychotherapy* and other group work approaches, the problem, meaning and potential of the 'silent member' has received considerable attention. For some approaches, for example, *meditation* and *relaxation training*, silence is a sine qua non of the method. Whilst the first task for the therapist is to learn to *tolerate* the patient's silence, he or she also needs to know how to help the patient move beyond silence and to resume the use of words. This will be when the therapist judges that the patient is blocking or being defensive because of fear or anger. The therapist then may use a *tracking* device, rephrase and repeat the patient's last statement as a 'prompt', or he may enquire into the nature and reason for the silence.

BENGLER, B. (1938), 'On the resistance situation: the patient is silent' (*Psychoan. Review*, vol. 25, p. 170).
BREUNLIN, D. C. and SOUTHGATE, P. (1978), 'An interactional approach to dysfunctional silencing in family therapy' (*Family Process*, vol. 17, pp. 207-16).
FERREIRA, A. J. (1973), 'On silence' (*Am. J. of Psychotherapy*, vol. 18, pp. 109-15).
KHAN, M. R. (1963), 'Silence as communication' (*Bulletin of the Menninger Clinic*, vol. 27, pp. 300-10).
NACHT, S. (1964), 'Silence as an integrative factor' (*Int. J. of Psychoan.*, vol. 45, pp. 299-303).
ZELIGS, M. A. (1961), 'The psychology of silence' (*J. of Am. Psychoan. Assoc.*, vol. 9, pp. 7-43).
ZUK, G. H. (1965), 'On the pathology of silencing strategies' (*Family Process*, vol. 4, pp. 32-49).

See also *Self-disclosure*.

Simulation
Literal Latin 'simulas', meaning 'like'. A technique used in *training* and therapy whereby an individual enters into the character or situation of someone else, using his/her imagination and internal associations to help bring the character alive. It thus differs from *role play*, which strictly speaking is the enactment of a role, devised by the trainer or therapist and which is therefore essentially external to the role player. When simulating, the trainee engages emotionally with the character, allowing it to evolve out of *preconscious* as well as *conscious* material. Thus, in the process of simulating a young child, an elderly person, or a schizophrenic, the trainee 'finds' these aspects of his own self from within. In practice, the terms simulation and role play are often used interchangeably.

Single session therapy
The complete conduct of therapy within the framework of a single meeting. Two broad categories can be distinguished: single session therapy that is unplanned from the therapist's point of view, and occurs as a result of premature termination by the client after one session; and planned single session therapy which is structured as such by the joint agreement of therapist and client at the outset. The literature reporting the former is far more extensive than the latter and it is only rather recently that planned single session therapy has been explored as a method in its own right. Unplanned single session therapy is frequently discussed in terms of therapeutic 'drop out' (e.g. Silverman and Beech 1979). A variety of studies show that whilst therapists are generally pessimistic about the effects of such once-off contacts, two-thirds of the clients who break off after one session found the contact helpful and they reported that they got what they were seeking for.

There is no reported difference between single sessions that are intentionally therapeutic and those carried out for diagnostic or research purposes only. Both groups show positive outcomes for two-thirds of the clients. Malan *et al.* (1976), for example, followed up forty-five adult neurotic patients who had been seen for a one session evaluation but had received no psychotherapy. They found that a quarter of the patients improved symptomatically and a further quarter 'dynamically' in addition. It has to be admitted, however, that although the authors refute the explanation of *spontaneous remission*, it is hard to see how their

50 per cent is much improvement on Bergin's suggested base line of 43 per cent for spontaneous remission. Others (e.g. Cummings 1977), however, have shown better results and some seem to suggest dramatically that even unplanned or 'non-therapeutic' single session therapy can be remarkably effective.

Bloom (1981) and Spoerl (1975) have reported the use of planned single session therapy. Bloom suggests the following principles: the identification of a salient issue (the concept of salient issue is obviously similar to that of focal conflict in *focal psychotherapy* and a *focal hypothesis* in *brief focal family therapy*); viewing the client's difficulties as an impasse in his normal development; active engagement with the client; sensitive and step-by-step presentation of *interpretations*; timely and empathic responsiveness to the client's expressions of affect; using the session to start a process of problem solving or growth for the client which can continue after the session ends; using a two-hour period to develop through a progression of stages; exercising parsimony over the number of issues to be explored; allowing for the possibility of recurring intermittent consultations along the lines of contact with solicitors and general practitioners.

BLOOM, B. L. (1981), 'Focused single session therapy: initial development and evaluation' (in Budman, S., *Forms of Brief Therapy*, Guilford Press, New York).
CUMMINGS, N. A. (1977), 'Prolonged (ideal) versus short-term (realistic) psychotherapy' (*Professional Psychology*, vol. 8, pp. 491-501).
MALAN, D. H. (1976), *The Frontier of Brief Psychotherapy* (Plenum Press, New York).
ROCKWELL, W. *et al.* (1982), 'Single-session psychotherapy' (*Am. J. of Psychotherapy*, vol. 36, pp. 32-40).
SILVERMAN, W. H. and BEECH, R. P. (1979), 'Are dropouts dropouts?' (*J. of Community Psychology*, vol. 7, pp. 236-42).
SPOERL, O. H. (1975), 'Single session psychotherapy' (*Diseases of the Nervous System*, vol. 36, pp. 283-5).

Sixteen Personality Factor Questionnaire
This is one of a series of self-rating personality questionnaires devised by Raymond B. Cattell. The sixteen personality factors or traits identified and measured include: general intelligence; dominance; *ego strength*; *superego* strength; emotional stability; radicalism; will control; sociability; group adherence; and guilt proneness. The respondent indicates his preferences or dislikes for various life activities. These are then objectively scored, and with a shortened form available, the questionnaire lends itself to research purposes.

CATTELL, RAYMOND B. (1965), *The Scientific Analysis of Personality* (Penguin, Harmondsworth).

See also *Personality tests.*

Skew
An imbalance of power within a marital relationship which renders one of the pair an outsider to a *coalition* formed by the other parent and the children. Covert conflict between the marital pair produces a situation whereby the relationship becomes increasingly a-symmetrical. Skew is characteristic of *dysfunctional complementary* relationships and indicates chronic rigidity in the face of the changing emotional and developmental needs of the group. Although the power imbalance appears to be brought about by one of the parties, both collude in the operation of the skew.

LIDZ, T. (1968), 'Family organisation and personality structure' (in Bell, N. and Vogel, E. (eds), *A Modern Introduction to the Family*, Free Press, New York).
SCHAFFER, L. (1962), 'On the nature and resources of the psychiatric experience with the family of the schizophrenic' (*Psychiatry*, vol. 25, pp. 32-45).
WYNNE, L. *et al.* (1958), 'Pseudomutuality in the family relations of schizophrenics' (*Psychiatry*, vol. 21, pp. 205-20).

See also *Collusion, Folie à deux, Schism.*

Social influence

In psychotherapy, the way in which the therapist consciously exerts an effect upon the patient. A considerable body of social psychological research has revealed the importance of social influence both in the way that *group process* affects individual behaviour and the way in which one individual can determine the attitudes and behaviour of another. The growing recognition of the significance of social influence in psychotherapy can be seen in Frank's (1971) work on the influence of *non-specific factors* in therapy; the importance of the *placebo* effect and suggestion; the nature of interpersonal *attraction*; the perceived *credibility* of the therapist; and the expectancy of the patient. Both an awareness of these factors and a systematic attempt to maximise their power in therapy have developed during the last few years.

Therapists who consciously seek to maximise the use of social influence in relation to the client argue that although this involves *manipulation*, that is an ingredient of all interpersonal relationships. The therapist's task is to use or manipulate the therapeutic situation for the patient's good. This involves, first, increasing the patient's expectancy that therapy will be beneficial, second, creating a position of authority in relation to the patient, and third, using this position to create positive change for him. The conscious manipulation of social influence is primarily directed towards overcoming the patient's *resistance* to change and changing his *cognitive structure* rather than changing his behaviour directly. Therapists who make particularly strong use of social influence factors are those who practise *strategic therapy*. Techniques for maximising the therapist's influence and for altering the patient's cognitive set include *reframing*; the *Devil's pact*; selective *self-disclosure* by the therapist, enhancing the patient's perceptions of the therapist's credibility, *expertness*, *experience* and *attraction*; and *rituals* which induce the patient to change either by providing 'evidence' that he *is* changing (in the form of favourable *feedback*) or 'evidence' that he cannot change (in the form

of the therapist's *pessimism*). In the latter case, the patient is induced to change by a non-compliance strategy.

The therapist sees his task as helping to propel the patient, wittingly or unwittingly, towards the treatment *goals* and to those who find this use of power distasteful, therapists using these techniques point out that *all* therapies, including those who appear to be the most *non-directive*, exercise subtle areas of power and influence over the patient (see Haley 1963). Reservations that have been advanced in relation to the conscious manipulation of social influence are discussed under *ethics*.

CORRIGAN, J. D. *et al.* (1980), 'Counseling as a social influence process: a review' (*J. of Counseling Psychology*, vol. 27, pp. 395-441).

FRANK, J. D. (1971), 'Therapeutic factors in psychotherapy' (*Am. J. of Psychotherapy*, vol. 25, pp. 350-61).

GILLIS, J. S. (1974), 'Therapist as manipulator' (*Psychology Today*, December, pp. 90-5).

GILLIS, J. S. (1979), *Social Influence in Psychotherapy* (Counseling and Monograph Series, no. 1, Pilgrimage Press, Berkeley, Calif.).

GOLDSTEIN, A. P. and STEIN, N. (1976), *Prescriptive Psychotherapies* (Pergamon Press, New York).

HALEY, J. (1963), *Strategies of Psychotherapy* (Grune & Stratton, New York).

HEPPNER, P. P. and DIXON, D. N. (1981), 'A review of the interpersonal influence process in psychotherapy' (*Personal Guidance J.*, vol. 59, pp. 542-50).

HEPPNER, P. P. and HEESACHER, M. (1982), 'The interpersonal influence process in real-life counselling' (*J. of Counseling Psychology*, vol. 29, pp. 215-23).

JOHNSON, D. W. and MATROSS, R. (1977), 'Interpersonal influence in psychotherapy' (in Gurman, A. S. and Razin, A. M. (eds), *Effective Psychotherapy*, Pergamon, New York).

KRAININ, J. M. (1972), 'Psychotherapy by counter-manipulation' (*Am. J. of Psychiatry*, vol. 129, pp. 749-50).

STRONG, S. R. (1968), 'Counseling: an interpersonal influence process' (*J. of Counseling Psychology*, vol. 15, pp. 215-24).

Social interest

Term introduced by Adler to describe the innate interpersonal concerns which, if developed, characterise the well-functioning personality. Adler (1964) considered social interest to be 'the barometer of the child's normality'. Encouraging and increasing social interest is a primary goal of therapy since social interest enables the individual to feel secure in his identity and at one with his social grouping and it enables him to develop a style of life free from both an *inferiority* or a *superiority complex*.

ADLER, A. (1964), *Social Interest: A Challenge to Mankind* (Capricorn Books, New York).

Social skills training

An approach to the treatment of psychological or behavioural disorder based on the belief that the disturbance is caused or made worse by a lack of social competence. The term actually covers quite a broad spectrum of approaches since the concept of social skills has been differently defined by different writers. Van Hasselt *et al.* (1979) suggest that social skills are situation-specific; they are acquired capacities for displaying appropriate responses and they enable people to behave in such a way that their own benefit is maximised without harming others. Trower *et al.* (1978) suggest that the failure of social competence may be primary, leading to rejection and social isolation and to the resulting production of disturbance; or secondary, in that the psychological disturbance itself has led to stigmatisation, rejection and a deterioration in social performance, thus adding to the original source of stress. In either case, systematic training in social skills competency is likely to lead to the patient's recovery or improvement.

Social skills training has been developed in Britain chiefly by Argyle and his associates and it is based on the skills theory developed by Argyle (1969, 1975) from extensive experimental research. The content of skills training is divided up between observation skills (getting information and reading social signals); performance skills (listening, speaking, meshing, appropriate *non-verbal communication*, greetings and partings, initiating conversations, rewarding and assertive skills); and cognitive skills (planning and problem solving). The methods used to teach these skills include guidance, *modelling*, practice and *feedback*.

The trainer first describes the behaviour to be taught and the skills to be learned. Second, he models the behaviour himself or uses a video tape model. Third, the trainee practises the behaviour, using a partner who role plays the other person. During the practice, the trainer and other trainees may watch from behind a *one-way screen* and the trainer may use a bug in ear device to guide the trainee's performance (see *Audio visual equipment*). Fourth, the trainer and other trainees give feedback, replaying an audio or video tape of the trainee's performance. Trainees make a commitment to attend sessions regularly and *homework assignments* are given after each session to enhance practice.

Other models for social skills training have been developed in Britain by Priestley *et al.* (1978). In the United States, Goldstein (1973) uses a structured learning approach. Here, patients are seen in groups of eight to twelve using *co-therapy* pairs. Liberman *et al.* (1975) have developed a similar programme and Johnson (1972) has made use of sensitivity training methods. Eisler and Frederiksen (1980) have used social skills training with marital problems, with children, in work situations and with aggressive patients.

Particular types of social skills training include *assertiveness training, problem solving interventions* and *coping skills interventions*. Outcome studies conducted by Argyle *et al.* (1974) and by Trower *et al.* (1978) comparing social skills training with *psychotherapy* and with *systematic desensitisation* respectively show that social skills training effectively improved the patient's behaviour skills. In the first study, the gains made by patients receiving social skills training persisted longer than those made by the psychotherapy patients, and in the second, social skills training was superior on the more specific items to be changed. There seems to be some evidence that skills training can improve behaviour skills and that at least in terms of out-patients, *generalisation* occurs from training laboratory to the patient's real-life situation in a lasting way.

ARGYLE, M. (1969), *Social Interaction* (Methuen, London).
ARGYLE, M. (1975), *Bodily Communication* (Methuen, London).
ARGYLE, M. (ed.) (1981), *Social Skills and Health* (Methuen, London).
ARGYLE, M. *et al.* (1974), 'Social skills training and psychotherapy: a comparative study' (*Psychological Medicine*, vol. 4, pp. 435-43).
EISLER, R. and FREDERIKSEN, L. (1980), *Perfecting Social Skills* (Plenum Press, New York).
GOLDSTEIN, A. P. (1973), *Structured Learning Therapy* (Academic Press, New York).
GREEN, D. and YEO, P. (1982), 'Attitude change and social skills training: potential techniques' (*Behavioural Psychology*, vol. 10, pp. 79-96).
JOHNSON, D. W. (1972), *Reaching Out* (Prentice-Hall, Englewood Cliffs, New Jersey).
LIBERMAN, R. P. *et al.* (1975), *Personal Effectiveness* (Research Press, Champaign, Ill.).
PRIESTLEY, P. *et al.* (1978), *Social Skills and Personal Problem Solving* (Tavistock, London).
TROWER, P. *et al.* (1978), *Social Skills and Mental Health* (Methuen, London).
TROWER, P. *et al.* (1978), 'The treatment of social failure' (*Behavior Modification*, vol. 2, pp. 41-60).
VAN HASSELT, V. *et al.* (1979), 'Social skills assessment and training for children: an evaluative review' (*Behavioral Research and Therapy*, vol. 17, pp. 417-37).

Social therapy

An umbrella term which embraces two broad groups of approaches: first, the *therapeutic community*, which provides social therapy within a hospital or other institution, and second, community psychiatry where services are offered outside the hospital setting. In both cases the focus of intervention is the patient's relationship with his physical and inter-personal environment.

The term was first used in 1947 by Elliott Jacques in relation to the task of trying to organise social institutions therapeutically. Edelson (1970) explains that social therapy is 'concerned with the situation, with the social system and social conditions . . . with the relations, especially the strains between entities (persons or groups) as these play different parts in achieving the shared goals of the social system and with direct attempts to intervene in and alter this social system'. Ruesh (1970) claims that social therapy is designed 'to alter existing conditions, and approaches this by influencing both the social system and the individual'. He suggests that social therapy includes community psychiatry, *group psychotherapy, family therapy* and the work of therapeutic communities. The therapist engaged in social therapy is therefore likely to be involved in political activity, welfare rights problems and the *manipulation* of the social and physical environment on behalf of his patient. Social therapy conducted inside an institution or therapeutic community focuses upon group relations, staff-patient relation-ships, the way in which decision making is conducted and where power resides. The environment is deliberately structured so as to maximise its therapeutic potential; the value of each individual is stressed and conflict is worked at at a daily community meeting. Pioneering figures in the sphere of the thera-peutic community are Main (1946) who coined the term and founded the Cassel Hospital as a therapeutic community, where the structuring of community life is used as an adjunct to the patient's individual treatment, and second, Maxwell Jones, who developed the prototype for other therapeutic com-munities at the Henderson Hospital and where the community itself is the major influence on the patients, and the main form of treatment. Clark (1977) distinguishes between the therapeutic community proper, as developed by Main and Jones, and a therapeutic milieu which a large number of different kinds of institutions try to provide (see Canter and Canter (1979) for a discussion of these). Laing and his associates have also contributed important ideas to this area through their experimental work at Kingsley Hall and the Arbors Association. Much social therapy is conducted across the boundary of the institution and the community, ranging from the day care and after-care of patients to the particular kind of *crisis intervention* described by Scott and Starr (1981). The Richmond Fellowship Hostels as well as some halfway houses and after-care hostels implement many ideas from the therapeutic community ideology.

In Britain, social therapy in the community is conducted chiefly by social workers, community workers, community nurses, some general practitioners and some community psychiatrists. Caplan (1964), in his seminal work, provided an important theoretical base for the approach and emphasised its *psychoprophylactic* potential. Other contributory influences have been the work of the *interpersonal school* of *psychoanalysis*, the *systemic therapies* (particularly *network intervention*) and group relations training pioneered at the Tavistock Clinic, London. The practice of social therapy presupposes that the practitioner is willing to forgo much of his professional status and rely instead upon the different skills of mobilising a therapeutic *network* of resources for the patient.

ARTHUR, R. J. (1971), *An Introduction to Social Psychiatry* (Penguin, Harmondsworth).

CANTER, D. and CANTER, S. (1979), *Designing for Therapeutic Environments* (Wiley, Chichester).

CLARK, D. H. (1977), 'The therapeutic community' (*Brit. J. of Psychiatry*, vol. 131, pp. 553-64).

EDELSON, M. (1970), *Sociotherapy and Psychotherapy* (University of Chicago Press, Chicago).

JACQUES, E. (1947), 'Some principles of organisation of a social therapeutic institution' (*J. of Social Issues*, vol. 3, pp. 4-10).

JONES, M. (1953), *The Therapeutic Community* (Penguin, Harmondsworth).

JONES, M. (1968), *Beyond the Therapeutic Community* (Penguin, Harmondsworth).

KAPLAN, G. (1964), *Principles of Preventive Psychiatry* (Basic Books, New York).

MAIN, T. F. (1946), 'The hospital as a therapeutic community' (*Bulletin of the Menninger Clinic*, vol. 10, pp. 66-70).

MOUNTNEY, G. (1974), 'Social therapy' (in Varma, V. (ed.), *Psychotherapy Today*, Constable, London).

RAPOPORT, R. N. (1960), *Community as Doctor: New Perspectives on a Therapeutic Community* (Tavistock, London).

RUESH, J. (1970), 'Social psychiatry: an overview' (in *Social Psychiatry*, Routledge & Kegan Paul, London).

SCOTT, D. (1973), 'The treatment barrier' (*Brit. J. of Medical Psychology*, vol. 46, pp. 45-55 and 57-67).

SCOTT, R. D. and STARR, I. (1981), 'A 24-hour family-oriented psychiatric and crisis service' (*J. of Family Therapy*, vol. 3, pp. 177-86).

See also *Supportive psychotherapy, Vector therapy.*

Sociogram

A technique devised by Moreno (1960) for measuring and evaluating *group dynamics*. In particular it enables the therapist to plot, in diagrammatic form, the attitudes of social acceptance and rejection within the group. Members who are isolated can be identified as well as those who are centres of negative or positive interaction.

MORENO, J. L. (ed.) (1960), *The Sociometry Reader* (Free Press of Glencoe, Glencoe, Ill.).

See also *Diagrams (therapeutic use of), Genogram.*

Split

See *Pseudohostility, Pseudomutuality.*

Splitting

Psychoanalytic term used to describe a division into two within the *psyche*. The term is used in three main ways. First descriptively, to indicate the division between the *conscious*, the *preconscious* and the *unconscious* levels and between the three *agencies* of the *psyche* ('horizontal splitting'). Second, the splitting of the *ego*. This entails a simultaneous experience within the ego of two contradictory responses to reality, acceptance and *denial*, without the ego needing to produce a compromise between the two or to repress the one or the other. Freud (1938) developed this concept ('vertical splitting'). Third, the splitting of the *object*. This entails the division of objects into 'good' and 'bad' as a primitive *defence mechanism* against the anxiety of holding the contradictory whole together. This usage was introduced by Melanie Klein who described it as arising from the *paranoid-schizoid position*. It lays the foundations for understanding the process by which individuals may sharply compartmentalise people and relationships in the external world into good and bad and polarise their response accordingly.

FREUD, S. (1938), 'Splitting of the ego in the process of defence' (*Standard Edition*, vol. 23, Hogarth Press, London).
GROTSTEIN, J. S. (1981), *Splitting and Projective Identification* (Jason Aronson, New York).
KLEIN, M. (1948), *Contributions to Psychoanalysis* (Hogarth Press, London).

See also *Defence mechanisms*.

Spontaneous remission

The extent to which a client population improves without benefit of professional therapeutic intervention. Eysenck, Rachman and others have argued that psychotherapy achieves no better results than if the client was left alone. Thus they argue that the burden of proof must rest with psychotherapists to achieve better results than those attributable to spontaneous remission. The spontaneous remission factor therefore provides a base line for assessing the effectiveness of the treatment variable.

The subject is a controversial one and the debate between psychotherapists of various schools with Eysenck, Rachman *et al.* has raged for three decades. Eysenck (1952), using *averaged* figures for the results of psychotherapy, proposed that the gross spontaneous remission rate for neurotic disorders over a two-year period was 65 per cent; but Bergin and Lambert (1978) (amongst many others) reviewed the reports used by Eysenck and Rachman and proposed instead that a median spontaneous remission rate of 43 per cent for untreated cases and a 50 per cent rate for minimally treated cases was more accurate. These figures too obscure the wide variation that is likely to exist and are probably therefore also too high. Part of the variation may be accounted for by including patients with different types of disorders, degrees of disturbance and past history; and part is due to the fact that some therapists produce significant positive effects while others produce negative effects, thus cancelling each other out. The *nature* of the phenomenon of spontaneous remission also needs further investigation. It is likely that many who receive no formal treatment nevertheless receive considerable help from friends, priests, colleagues, etc., and this informal therapeutic help may account for their improvement. The term 'spontaneous' thus may simply denote the fact that the source of therapeutic help is unknown and the fact therefore that therapy-like experiences are likely to account for much so-called spontaneous remission, and this in turn casts the effectiveness level of therapeutic procedures in a much more positive light.

The concept of spontaneous remission raises two interesting possibilities. First, *outcome* studies which purport to show that psychotherapy is effective may actually be examples of self-limiting disturbances. Second, they may be the result of the positive effect of non-professional psychotherapeutic help which has taken place outside the therapy sessions. Recently, Eysenck (1980) has attempted a unified theory of treatment which, he suggests, explains the apparent successes of spontaneous remission and he considers it in relation to several approaches to psycho-therapy including *behaviour therapy*. Most researchers would agree that the results of psychotherapy are much more favourable than the original pessimistic reports suggested. Even if spontaneous remission is a frequent occurrence after a two-year time lapse, various studies have shown (for example, Sloane *et al.* 1975) that psychotherapy significantly accelerates the desired changes.

BERGIN, A. E. and LAMBERT, M. J. (1978), 'The evaluation of therapeutic outcomes' (in Bergin, A. E. and Garfield, S. L. (eds). *Handbook of Psychotherapy and Behavior Change*, Wiley, New York).
EYSENCK, H. J. (1952), 'The effects of psychotherapy: an evaluation' (*J. of Consulting Psychology*, vol. 16, pp. 319-24).
EYSENCK, H. J. (1980), 'A unified theory of psychotherapy, behaviour therapy and spon-taneous remission' (*Zeitschift für Psychologie*, vol. 188, pp. 43-56).
LAMBERT, M. J. (1976), 'Spontaneous remis-sion in adult neurotic disorder: a revision and summary' (*Psychological Bulletin*, vol. 83, pp. 107-19).
RACHMAN, S. (1971), *The Effects of Psycho-therapy* (Pergamon, Oxford).
SLOANE, R. B. *et al.* (1975), *Psychotherapy versus Behavior Therapy* (Harvard University Press, Cambridge, Mass.).

Squiggle game
A drawing game devised by Winnicott (1971) for use in therapeutic consultations with children. The game consists of turns being taken by the child and the therapist to make a mark of some kind, with eyes closed, on a blank sheet of paper. The other person turns the mark into a picture. Winnicott describes the game simply as 'one way of getting into contact with the child'. The technique allows the child to use *non-verbal communication* to express his anxieties and concerns and enables a *therapeutic alliance* to be established through the mutual participation of child and *analyst* in a non-threatening activity. It also enables the parents to participate more fully by seeing the child's drawings and discussing their meaning with the analyst. The game is only a starting point and the usual skills needed in *child psychotherapy* are required for under-standing, interpreting and helping to change the child's *internal world*.

WINNICOTT, D. W. (1971), *Therapeutic Con-sultations in Child Psychiatry* (Hogarth Press, London).

See also *Play therapy, Zen telegram*.

Stages of development
Psychoanalytic theory has generated several formulations of the development of the human being. Freud's classical description states that the infant passes through the *oral* stage in the first year, the *anal* stage in the second year of life, and the *phallic* and *genital* stages from about three years until school age. This is followed by repression of the *libido* during the latency phase until puberty and the development of the mature genital stage. Erikson, a systematic *ego psychologist*, marks out eight stages which are characterised by the specific problems encountered in 'reality relationships'. In sequence these eight stages can be described as follows: basic trust vs. basic mistrust (first year of life); autonomy vs. shame and doubt (second year); initative vs. guilt (third to fifth years); industry vs. inferiority (between seven and eleven years); identity vs. identity con-fusion (from puberty to about twenty years); intimacy vs. isolation (young adulthood); generativity vs. stagnation (childbearing period and ageing); and integrity vs. despair.

Erikson viewed each stage as a crisis for the development of the individual for it is a turning point and a crucial period both of increased vulnerability and of heightened potential. Using an epigenetic approach, Erikson expanded Freud's analysis of the psycho-sexual stages to embrace the whole of the individual's life experience. He also integrated the individual's *intrapsychic* development within a social and relational context.

Mahler *et al.* (1975) focus on the very early phases of development and are concerned with the development of identity. They designate a period from the fourth or fifth month until about the thirtieth or thirty-sixth month as the time of the process of 'separation-individuation' which constitutes the psychological birth of the infant. They describe four sub-phases. *Klein* tended to dismiss rigid chronological phases of development and saw the problems of working through the *depressive position* as a lifelong struggle. However, under the influence of *Fairbairn* she did recognise the existence of the *paranoid-schizoid position* as preceding in time the depressive position.

ERIKSON, E. (1959), *Identity and the Life Cycle* (International Universities Press, New York).
ERIKSON, E. (1968), *Identity, Youth and Crisis* (Faber & Faber, London).
MAHLER, M. S., PINE, F. and BERGMAN, A. (1975), *The Psychological Birth of the Human Infant* (Basic Books, New York).

See also *Epigenesis, Erogenous zone, Instinct.*

Stekel, Wilhelm (1868-1940)

Born in Bukovina (now Rumania) into a German-speaking Jewish family, Stekel became one of the founder members of the Vienna Psychoanalytic Circle and an early student and colleague of Freud. He was an unorthodox and creative therapist who used a unique combination of technique and his own personality in working with patients. He broke with Freud in 1912 and thereafter developed what he called *active analysis*, a brief and more direct form of *psychoanalysis*. For most of his life he was a close friend of Adler and his prodigious literary output (which included fiction, songs and plays as well as psychoanalytic work) was influenced by and influential upon Adler's work. He was immensely successful in his career, travelling widely, lecturing and writing. He was forced to flee Britain after the outbreak of the Second World War and committed suicide shortly afterwards.

Step function

Term introduced by Ashby (1954) to describe one way in which a natural *system* moves from one state to another, involving a discontinuous change. The operation of a step function enables a system to be recalibrated. Thus, the range of speed and the level of road which a car can negotiate changes when a shift from one gear to another takes place. The term is used by *systems therapists* to understand the way in which a family or other *system* changes its pattern of functioning in response to *positive feedback*. The production of *symptoms* in one member of a family is a step function to a new state of being, a family-with-a-symptomatic-member; or the involvement of a therapist or other outside helper is a step function to the new state of being a family-in-therapy. Likewise, promotion for the family's breadwinner may act as a step function, taking the family into a new level of ease, security or tension. After a step function has occurred, the system is recalibrated and a new set of rules is developed to maintain its *homeostasis* at a new level.

ASHBY, W. R. (1954), *Design for a Brain* (Wiley, New York).

See also *Calibration, Deviation amplification, Schismogenesis.*

Stereotype

A term (derived from printing) used to describe a rigid and inflexible impression held of a behaviour, an individual or a group, built up from past interpretations of behaviour and characteristics, and influencing future judgments and perceptions. A stereotype involves an oversimplification and is used to some extent by everyone to reduce the complexity of the external world and enable the individual to relate to it emotionally and cognitively. Stereotypes are relatively impervious to change and do not easily admit the influence of objective data which challenge the assumptions on which they rest. The greater the degree of threat perceived from the external world, the greater the need the individual will feel to employ stereotypes to help him deal with it. Some stereotyped reactions become part of the individual's repertoire of *defence mechanisms*; others, such as phobias and paranoia, become part of a more extreme pathological reaction to the world and require treatment.

See also *Labelling*.

Stimulus

A cue which provokes a *response* and is simultaneous or antecedent to it in a *behavioural sequence*. Each member of a sequence is a stimulus in relation to the responses that follow it and a response in relation to the stimulus preceding it. The S-R relationship is a fundamental concept of *learning theory* and *behaviour therapy* and is a major principle behind both *operant* and *classical conditioning* techniques.

See also *Conditioned stimulus, Unconditioned stimulus.*

Stranger group

Term used to describe a group of two or more unrelated, interacting persons that come together to participate in *group analysis, group psychotherapy, encounter groups* and other forms of therapeutic group work. A stranger group can be distinguished from a natural group such as a family, work group, social group, friendship group, etc., because it only comes together for the purposes of treatment. In contrast, although a natural group may come into treatment as a group, it has a life of its own outside the treatment situation. In practice a stranger group develops a complex *group process* and set of *group dynamics* derived from its composition, structure and its common *goals*, norms and role relationships. Both research and clinical practice distinguish between work done with small groups (about twelve members or less) and large groups (over ten or twelve members).

See also *Group composition, Group structure, T-Group training.*

Strategic therapy

A group of approaches to the treatment of both families and individuals which have developed out of *communication* theory and *systems* theory. Strategic therapists fall into several sub-groups: the Mental Research Institute,

Palo Alto, with Gregory Bateson and Don Jackson (both deceased), John Weakland, Paul Watzlawick, Richard Fisch, Arthur Bodin and Carlos Sluzki; the Washington Family Institute, with Jay Haley and Cloe Madanes; the Milan Associates, with Mara Selvini-Palazzoli and colleagues; the Ackerman Family Institute's Brief Therapy Project, New York; the work of Richard Rabkin; and the work of Gerald Zuk. Milton Erikson and Gregory Bateson have both been seminal influences on the work of all sub-groupings of strategic therapists. Although these groups differ in their approach, all stress the importance of a theory of therapeutic change and clearly articulated techniques for bringing that change about; the need for the therapist to gain a position of power and influence over the client and over the therapy; the acceptance of the *presenting problem* as defined by the family or client; the use of *reframing*; overtly *symptom*-focused and covertly *systems*-focused *goals*; an eclecticism with regard to the *unit of treatment*; the use of a *team* or *live supervision*; and the use of defiance-based techniques such as paradox and *symptom prescription*. Specialised concepts and techniques developed by one or more sub-groups include the use of the *double bind* and its therapeutic possibilities; *ritual*; the *positive connotation*; *focused problem resolution*; and the *Greek chorus. Outcome* results have been impressive and these approaches have been used with a wide range of disorders in individuals, couples and families, although the approach raises difficult questions about *ethics* and its long-term effects (Walrond-Skinner 1984). A *Journal of Strategic and Systematic Therapies* is published in the United States.

BATESON, G. (1972), *Steps to an Ecology of Mind* (Granada, New York).

BATESON, G. (1979), *Mind and Nature: A Necessary Unity* (Dutton, New York).

CADE, B. (1980), 'Strategic therapy' (*J. of Family Therapy*, vol. 2, pp. 89-99).

HALEY, J. (1963), *Strategies of Psychotherapy* (Grune & Stratton, New York).

HALEY, J. (ed.) (1967), *Advanced Techniques of*

Hypnosis and Therapy: Selected Papers of Milton H. Erikson (Grune & Stratton, New York).

HALEY, J. (1973), *Uncommon Therapy* (W. W. Norton, New York).

HALEY, J. (1980), *Leaving Home* (McGraw-Hill, New York).

MADANES, C. (1981), *Strategic Family Therapy* (Jossey-Bass, San Francisco).

PALAZZOLI, M. S. (1975), *Self-starvation: From Individual to Family Therapy in the Treatment of Anorexia Nervosa* (Jason Aronson, New York).

PALAZZOLI, M. S. (1978), *Paradox and Counter-paradox* (Jason Aronson, New York).

RABKIN, R. (1977), *Strategic Psychotherapy* (Basic Books, New York).

ROSEN, S. (1982), *My Voice Will Go With You: The Teaching Tales of Milton H. Erikson* (W. W. Norton, New York).

WALROND-SKINNER, S. (1984), 'Whither family therapy? Twenty years on' (*J. of Family Therapy*, vol. 6, pp. 1-14).

WATZLAWICK, P., BEAVIN, J. H. and JACKSON, D. D. (1967), *Pragmatics of Human Communication* (W. W. Norton, New York).

WATZLAWICK, P., WEAKLAND, J. and FISCH, R. (1974), *Change: Principles of Problem Formation and Problem Resolution* (W. W. Norton, New York).

ZEIG, J. K. (ed.) (1982), *Eriksonian Approaches to Hypnosis and Hypnotherapy* (Brunner/Mazel, New York).

Stream of consciousness

Term coined by William James to contrast the nature of consciousness with the view of the structuralists led by Wundt, who viewed consciousness as consisting of a multiplicity of discrete elements. James saw consciousness as a continuous and constantly changing flow of experience which could be distinguished from the objects of consciousness.

JAMES, W. (1890), *Principles of Psychology* (Dover Press, New York, 1950).

See also *Free association*.

Stress inoculation

An approach to *coping skills intervention*

developed by Meichenbaum (1976) based on the biological model of immunisation. The concept rests on the premise that mastery of stressful situations can be developed and *coping skills* can be increased if the client learns to deal successfully with small doses of threatening material, while defending himself against excessive exposure. Gradually he becomes able to tolerate a stress-inducing situation of greater and greater intensity. Meichenbaum suggests that stress inoculation training involves three phases: the educational phase, in which the client is given a plausible conceptual framework for understanding his stressful reactions; the rehearsal phase, in which he uses *relaxation training* to reduce anxiety and develop positive self-statements regarding the situation; and the application training phase, in which the client is encouraged to try out his new coping skills in a stressful situation *other* than that for which he has sought help. During this phase, the stressful situation is provided by the therapist and takes the form of the administration of unpredictable electric shocks, stress-inducing films, etc. Evaluative studies that have been carried out to date suggest that stress inoculation training is the most effective treatment in reducing avoidance behaviour and in fostering *generalisation* to other situations.

MEICHENBAUM, D. (1976), 'A stress instructional approach to stress management: a proposal for stress inoculation training' (in Sarason, I. and Spielberger, C. D. (eds), *Stress and Anxiety in Modern Life*, Wiley, New York).

See also *Anxiety management training, Self-instructional training*.

Stroke

A term introduced by Berne to describe a unit of recognition. Berne suggests that all social behaviour is motivated by the need for recognition which is only satisfied by the physical, verbal or non-verbal stroking provided by another person. Strokes may be either positive or negative and although positive strokes are much to be preferred, negative strokes (for example, criticism or punishment) are better than no strokes at all. Strokes can also be either unconditional (strokes for being) or conditional (strokes for doing).

The need of the very young for physical strokes was demonstrated by Spitz (1945) and others and transactional analysts postulate the continuing need for physical and emotional stroking throughout childhood and adult life. Since strokes are necessary for survival, an individual will do whatever is necessary to receive the strokes he or she needs. This may include interacting with others through the means of *games*. Transactional analysts suggest that the degree to which an individual receives the strokes he needs leads to four different life positions: 'I'm OK – you're OK' (the individual has a good opinion of himself and others); 'I'm OK – you're not OK' (he has a good opinion of self that is critical of others); 'I'm not OK – you're OK' (he has a low opinion of himself and sees others as more able or more valued than himself); 'I'm not OK – you're not OK' (the individual has a low opinion of himself and of others).

BERNE, E. (1961), *Transactional Analysis in Psychotherapy* (Grove Press, New York).
HARRIS, T. A. (1969), *I'm OK – You're OK* (Harper & Row, New York).
SPITZ, R. (1945), 'Hospitalism: genesis of psychiatric conditions in early childhood' (*Psychoanalytic Study of the Child*, vol. 1, p. 53).

See also *Transactional analysis*.

Structural analysis

The process of identifying and analysing the individual's *ego states*. The term is used in *transactional analysis* to mark an early stage in therapy. Unlike the tripartheid system of psychoanalytic theory, the concept of the ego state is seen by Berne and other transactional analysts as a phenomenological system, based upon here and now observable data. The individual indicates the ego state from which he is operating by his behaviour, language, gestures and other *non-verbal communication*. The use of an ego state is not related to the actual age of the individual, although Parent and Child states naturally predominate during childhood.

Three problems are frequently encountered in the operation of the ego states. First, confusion, where the individual cannot discern which ego state is operating and he slips from one to another at random. The therapist helps the patient clarify and become sensitive to the hallmarks of each different state. Second, contamination, where one ego state intrudes into another, leading to the contamination of the reality perceptions of the Adult. Here, the therapist's task is to confront the patient with the distortion of his beliefs or the irrationality of his behaviour. Third, exclusion, where the patient clings to one ego state and excludes the other two. The patient is, for example, unable to use the Child for play, recreation or creativity, or unable to use the Adult for rational decision making and *reality testing*. The therapist helps the patient to move flexibly from one ego state to another by the process of stabilisation. The stabilised individual can use the ego state which is appropriate to the situation. Structural analysis further involves the construction of the patient's *egogram*.

BERNE, E. (1961), *Transactional Analysis in Psychotherapy* (Grove Press, New York).

Structural analysis of social behaviour (SASB)

An interpersonal diagnostic system developed by Lorna Benjamin (1982). The SASB is used by therapists of the *interpersonal school* of *psychoanalysis* and others for examining the behaviour of significant persons in the patient's life and the social and self-directed behaviour of the patient. In each of these areas there are two orthogonal dimensions: positive (affiliation) – negative (rejection and anger); and freedom – control. Benjamin has developed an interview, a questionnaire and a computerised interpretation of her system.

BENJAMIN, L. (1982), 'The structural analysis of social behaviour' (in Anchin, J. C. and Kiesler, D. J. (eds), *Handbook of Interpersonal Psychotherapy*, Pergamon, New York).

STRUCTURAL FAMILY THERAPY

Structural family therapy

An approach to *family therapy* developed from work with poor families by Minuchin and his colleagues and subsequently expanded for use with the whole socio-economic spectrum. Structural family therapists have also specialised in work with psychosomatic families (Minuchin *et al.* 1978). Based upon the structural viewpoints of Piaget (1970) and Lane (1970) and of *systems theory*, structural family therapy seeks to understand the structure of the *dysfunctional* family, to *restructure* its relationships and, where necessary, those of the family's ecosystem. The structural dimensions of *transactions* that are most often identified in structural family therapy are those of *boundary*, *alignment* and power. Other concepts that have been developed or used by this school to describe family structure include *enmeshed* and *disengaged*, the *parental child*, *coalition*, *triangulation* and *detouring* and the therapeutic processes of *joining*, *accommodation*, *mimesis*, *tracking* and *maintenance*.

Structural family therapists frequently work with family *sub-systems* and as Gorell-Barnes (1979) points out, intervention into one part of the system is regarded as bringing about change in the system as a whole. Structural family therapists have been influenced by *behaviour therapy*, and *tasks* and *homework assignments* play an important part in treatment. Therapy is here and now and future-oriented, and although an examination of the place of the family in its life cycle is considered to be important, past material is not usually investigated to any great extent. Length of treatment is relatively short-term, often between six and ten sessions, although Minuchin *et al.* (1978) report that about seven months is average in their work with psychosomatic families. Because of the involvement of Haley in both approaches, there is some overlap between the structural and *strategic* schools of family therapy.

APONTE, H. J. and VANDEUSEN, J. M. (1981), 'Structural family therapy' (in Gurman, A. S. and Kniskern, D. P. (eds), *Handbook of Family Therapy*, Brunner/Mazel, New York).

GORELL-BARNES, G. (1979), 'Family bits and pieces: creating a workable reality' (in Walrond-Skinner, S. (ed.), *Family and Marital Psychotherapy*, Routledge & Kegan Paul, London).

HALEY, J. (1976), *Problem Solving Therapy* (Harper & Row, New York).

LANE, M. (1970), *Introduction to Structuralism* (Basic Books, New York).

MINUCHIN, S. (1974), *Families and Family Therapy* (Tavistock, London).

MINUCHIN, S. and FISHMAN, H. C. (1981), *Family Therapy Techniques* (Harvard University Press, Cambridge, Mass.).

MINUCHIN, S. *et al.* (1978), *Psychosomatic Families* (Harvard University Press, Cambridge, Mass.).

PIAGET, J. (1970), *Structuralism* (Basic Books, New York).

Structural integration

A variety of *body therapy* developed by Ida Rolf (and thus often called 'Rolfing') during the 1930s and 1940s. It is directed entirely to the body but it can have important beneficial effects on the patient's self-esteem, body image and general sense of well-being. The therapist uses a form of massage to work on the tissue surrounding the muscles, stretching and realigning muscle groups to restore proper balance and allow freedom of movement. Balanced movement and correct breathing are also taught. By integrating and improving the co-ordination of the body, the method aims to make the patient's natural energy more available to him. Treatment is usually completed in the course of ten one-hour sessions. During the treatment, there may be a considerable release of feeling, encouraged but not made the primary focus by the practitioner. The combination of systematic work on the body, the increased energy level which results and what may be a strong emotional *catharsis* can combine to produce a powerful therapeutic method.

JOHNSON, D. (1977), *The Protean Body* (Harper & Row, New York).

ROLF, I. (1975), *Structural Integration* (Viking, New York).

ROLF, I. (1977), *Rolfing* (Denis Landman, Santa Monica, Calif.).

Structural model
In this model Freud views the mind as a structure of three 'agencies', the *id*, the *superego* and the *ego*, in relationship with each other. The id represents the animal instincts and supplies the mental energy, and the superego contains an accumulation of *introjected* social and moral standards and images of parents and other significant persons from the past, as well as a capacity for self-regard which measures the actual performance against these standards and ideals with consequent emotional satisfaction or pain. The ego consists of the sense of identity or self which has available the problem solving functions of the mind which are put to use to enable as much satisfaction of the id instincts as is allowed within the constraints of the superego, and taking account of the features of the current external reality.

FREUD, S. (1923), 'The ego and the id' (*Standard Edition*, vol. 19, Hogarth Press, London).

See also *Economic model, Metapsychology, Topographical model*

Structure
A relatively enduring pattern of organisation, pertaining to an individual, relationship or group. The composition of a family or group in terms of its individual members, *sub-systems*, role relationships, and the formation of an individual in terms of his body build, *mental apparatus, psychological type, character armour*, genetic inheritance, etc. The term is used in contrast to the terms function and *process*, a transitory state of motion which occurs within the structure and which brings about change in the structure. An interaction between static structure and changing process enables a group to remain stable but also to develop and adapt. In psychoanalytic theory, mental structure refers to the three aspects of the *psyche*, the *id*, ego, and *superego*, although the relation of structure and process in conceptualising these entities is more fluid than is sometimes

imagined, each of them being defined operationally in terms of their functions.

In therapeutic work, *diagnosis* of the structure of individual, family or group takes the form of *genotypic* assessment. Structure also refers to the *boundaries* created by the therapist around the therapeutic work, including the formation of a *contract*, established *goals* and the terms of the therapeutic activity. The therapist's creation of the structure for a *stranger group*, in terms of its composition, is an important part of all forms of group work. It allows the creation of an *ambience* which will promote the learning and growth of individual members and provides the material (in the form of interaction and learning from other members) that they need to overcome problems. Likewise in *family therapy*, the concept of the *minimum sufficient network* refers to the need for the therapist to ensure that the family *system* he involves in treatment is structurally sufficient for systemic work to take place.

See also *Group composition, Group process, Group structure, Structured exercises, Structured interview*.

Structured exercises
Exercises used in therapy and in the *training* of therapists to promote *communication*, develop interpersonal and/or therapeutic skills and (where appropriate) to effect group *cohesion*. Some methods of psychotherapy make particular use of structured exercises in their therapy and/or training programmes, for example, *microskills* training (Ivey and Authier 1978), *client-centred therapy* (Carkhuff 1969), group work training (Johnson and Johnson 1975), *social skills training* (Trower *et al.* 1978), and communication training (Bandler and Grinder 1975). Structured exercises include ice-breaker exercises for 'warming up' groups, relaxing, developing sensory and bodily awareness, developing self-identity, analysing and improving communication, discharging emotions and promoting *catharsis*, exploring fantasy, and developing creativity.

BANDLER, R. and GRINDER, J. (1975), *The Structure of Magic* (Science and Behavior

Books, Palo Alto, Calif.).
BROWN, G. (1975), *Micro Teaching: A Programme of Teaching Skills* (Methuen, London).
CARKHUFF, R. R. (1969), *Helping and Human Relations* (Holt, Rinehart & Winston, New York).
IVEY, A. E. and AUTHIER, J. (1978), *Counseling* (Charles C. Thomas, Springfield. Ill.).
JOHNSON, D. W. and JOHNSON, F. P. (1975), *Joining Together: Group Theory and Group Skills* (Prentice-Hall, Englewood Cliffs, New Jersey).
PFEIFFER, J. *et al.* (eds) (1969-1975), *Handbook of Structured Experiences for Human Relations Training* (University Associates, La Jolla, Calif.).
PHILLIPS, H. and BRANDES, D. (1978), *Gamesters' Handbook* (Hutchinson, London).
PRIESTLEY, P. and MCGUIRE, J. (1983), *Learning to Help* (Tavistock, London).
RABIN, C. (1983), 'Towards the use and development of games for social work practice' (*Brit. J. of Social Work*, vol. 13, pp. 175-96).
STREITFIELD, H. and LEWIS, H. (1970), *Growth Games* (Harcourt Brace Jovanovich, New York).
TROWER, P. *et al.* (1978), *Social Skills and Mental Health* (Methuen, London).

See also *Action techniques, Diagrams, Non-verbal communication.*

Structured interview

A diagnostic or therapeutic interview which is structured by an orderly series of questions that encourage the patient to provide specific information or which enable a specific *task* or *goal* to be achieved during the session. The aim of a structured interview is predetermined by the therapist. As well as using groups of questions in a pre-arranged way, it may involve the use of *personality tests* or a specific technique such as *family sculpting, genograms, sociograms* or other *action techniques,* and *structured exercises.* Structured interviews are frequently used in the course of *outcome* research.

See also *Interview.*

Study group

See *Tavistock group training.*

Style

A facet of the therapist's interaction with the patient that partly derives from his personality and characteristics that are personal to him such as his age, sex, class, etc., and partly from his theoretical orientation. Therapist style describes the manner in which he executes the therapeutic task as contrasted with the matter of his theoretical framework, treatment techniques or therapeutic *goals.* Pope (1977) points out that it is an elusive and ambiguous variable and yet appears to be an important aspect of the therapeutic *process.* Ingredients of therapeutic style that have been identified and studied include the therapist level of directiveness/non-directiveness; his level of activity/passivity; his tendency towards ambiguity or specificity; towards being opaque or *self-disclosing;* his domineering or egalitarian manner of relating; and his level of expressiveness of emotions and attitudes such as warmth, anger, criticism, hostility or acceptance. In *family therapy,* Beels and Feber (1969) identified two contrasting styles which could be summarised as the conductor versus the reactor style, and other terms such as facilitator, enabler, catalyst and director have been used to indicate an overall stylistic orientation in both group and family work.

Therapist style is expressed both verbally and non-verbally and a considerable amount of research has been undertaken on the linguistic aspects of the therapist's interventions. Duncan *et al.* (1968) explored the voice quality of the therapist in peak compared with poor therapy sessions, as rated by the therapist. They found that in good sessions, the therapist sounded serious, warm and relaxed compared with poor sessions where the therapist's voice was dull and flat and, when it took on more energy, the therapist seemed to be speaking for effect. Much work has also been done on trying to link style with theoretical orientation and discovering the relative weight that should be placed on therapy 'school' compared with *experience* in determining therapist style

(Fiedler 1950a, 1950b; Strupp 1958, 1960; Sunderland and Barker 1962). While Fiedler found that style remained more or less constant across orientations, Strupp, and Sunderland and Barker, found that theoretical orientation was an important influencing factor. But these differences largely depend on what stylistic factors are being used in the comparisons and style is more likely to vary according to the personal qualities of the therapist than in relation to his theoretical or professional orientation. Gender difference has also been found to influence style. Rice *et al.* (1974) found that female therapists described themselves as more variable in their psychotherapeutic behaviour, less anonymous and more judgmental. Whilst earlier multidimensional studies were interested in relating aspects of style to theoretical orientation, more recent ones such as the work of Duncan *et al.* (1968) have looked at the stylistic dimension itself, the way in which it is expressed and communicated and the way in which it affects different clients in different ways. Pope (1977) concludes that 'stylistic variables are not decorative embellishments on the process of therapy; they are the components of process'.

BEELS, C. and FERBER, A. (1969), 'Family therapy – a view' (*Family Process*, vol. 8, pp. 280-318).

DUNCAN, S. *et al.* (1968), 'Therapists' paralanguage in peak and poor psychotherapy interviews' (*J. of Abnormal Psychology*, vol. 73, pp. 566-70).

FIEDLER, F. E. (1950a), 'A comparison of therapeutic relationships in psychoanalytic, non-directive and Adlerian therapy' (*J. of Consulting Psychology*, vol. 14, pp. 435-6).

FIEDLER, F. E. (1950b), 'The concept of an ideal therapeutic relationship' (*J. of Consulting Psychology*, vol. 14, pp. 239-45).

POPE, B. (1977), 'Research on psychoanalytic style' (in Gurman, A. S. and Razin, A. M., *Effective Psychotherapy*, Pergamon Press, New York).

RICE, D. G. *et al.* (1974), 'Therapist sex, "style" and theoretical orientation' (*J. of Nervous and Mental Diseases*, vol. 159, pp. 413-21).

STRUPP, H. H. (1958), 'The psychotherapist's contribution to the treatment process' (*Behavioral Science*, vol. 3, pp. 34-67).

STRUPP, H. H. (1960), *Psychotherapists in Action* (Grune & Stratton, New York).

SUNDERLAND, D. M. and BARKER, E. N. (1962), 'The orientation of psychotherapists' (*J. of Consulting Psychology*, vol. 26, pp. 201-12).

See also *Relationship factors, Therapist variables.*

Sublimation

A quasi *defence mechanism* whereby the *ego* transforms the aim of a *drive* irrevocably on to socially desirable or creative activities. Freud did not develop the concept in a complete form and the dividing line with other concepts, such as *reaction formation*, is its absence of involvement in psychopathology. Sublimation is the means whereby the ego provides a channel for drives (whether aggressive or sexual) to be directed towards other forms of activity, for example, art, intellectual activity and religion. It can be distinguished from substitution (for example, a childless woman caring for foster children) because it involves a complete change in the activity engaged in (for example the entry of a woman into a convent, a total devotion to art, etc.). The term can however be used for the reversal of an instinct, for example, someone who has the urge to commit arson becomes a fireman. The notion is required within the terms of Freudian theory to explain other forms of apparently non-sexual creativity, in a scheme which postulates the ubiquity of the sexual instinct. Once this concept is modified or discarded, the need for a concept of sublimation diminishes. Sublimation is a particular kind of *displacement* on to a socially approved activity perceived by the individual as a higher life goal than the sexual gratification for which it is a replacement.

Submergence

See *Pole.*

Sub-system

The component parts of a *system*. As applied to

families, couples and other natural groups, a sub-system can be defined in one of two ways. First, all the individual members of the system can be designated as sub-systems. This approach calls attention to the constant *change* and variety that exists in all but the almost *closed system*, since the membership of the system in an average family changes frequently throughout the day and changes fairly regularly (though at a much slower rate) throughout a year, decade or longer time span. The fluctuation in the number of sub-systems when reckoned as individuals creates corresponding fluctuation in the number of reciprocal relationships operating at any one time. Broderick and Smith (1979) suggest that the number can be arrived at by the formula $R = \frac{M(M-1)}{2}$ where R stands for the relationships and M for the family members.

Second, the sub-groupings can be designated as sub-systems. This approach uses the concept of family role and examines the interlocking family roles which go to make up sub-groupings. Hence the marital dyad; the sibling group (further sub-divided into adolescent and young children's group and female and male sibling groups); the sexual *alliances* (father, male children and other male relatives, etc.); and generational sub-groups (grandparents, parents, children) – all these form interweaving sub-systems within the family system. This approach draws attention to the relative stability of family structure with different individuals able to exchange places in the sub-systems if one dies or leaves. The *parental child*, for example, moves into the parental dyad when a vacancy occurs.

Some theorists use concepts such as the decider sub-system (Miller 1965) or the executive sub-system (Minuchin 1974), drawing attention to the need for organisation, *hierarchy* and control within a system. The concept of sub-system is important for those using *family therapy* and *marital therapy* and their derivatives and it enables the therapist to consider choices regarding the type and timing of his intervention in relation to different parts of the system.

BRODERICK, C. and SMITH, J. (1979), 'The general systems approach to the family' (in Burr, W. R. *et al.*, *Contemporary Theories about the Family*, vol. 2, Free Press/Collier Macmillan, London).
MILLER, J. G. (1965), 'Living systems: basic concepts' (*Behavioral Science*, vol. 10, pp. 193-245).
MINUCHIN, S. (1974), *Families and Family Therapy* (Tavistock, London).

See also *Holon*.

Successive approximation

A series of responses of increasing difficulty which move nearer each time to the final response required. Each response which shows a greater likeness to the final response is reinforced to encourage further responses to be made.

See also *Operant conditioning, Reinforcement, Shaping, Token economy*.

Sud

Subjective unit of disturbance. A measurement used by Wolpe (1973) to gauge the level of anxiety experienced by the client when facing the anxiety-evoking *stimulus*. Wolpe constructs a subjective anxiety scale, ranging from 0 to 100, which allows the measurement of the client's suds. Items in the anxiety *hierarchy* can then be rated prior to the commencement of *systematic desensitisation*.

WOLPE, J. (1973), *The Practice of Behavior Therapy* (Pergamon, New York).

Sullivan, Harry Stack (1892-1949)

Sullivan, the chief exponent of the *interpersonal school* of *psychoanalysis*, was born in Norwich, New York State, in 1892. He was the only surviving child of Irish immigrant parents. His childhood was lonely and, ironically considering his clinical and professional interests in interpersonal relationships, he grew into a shy, withdrawn, though gentle person. He studied medicine at Chicago College, graduating in 1917. After several clinical posts, he became associate professor in psychiatry at the

University of Maryland and at the same time he did intensive work with schizophrenics. In 1930 he moved to New York and began formal analytic training with Clara Thompson. He began to develop contacts with social scientists and was greatly influenced by the work of Charles Cooley, George Mead and Ruth Benedict. He became increasingly interested in social and political issues and after the Second World War became involved with UNESCO and the World Health Organisation. He continued to lecture, see patients and write, although it was left to his students and colleagues to publish most of his written work after his death. For Sullivan, it was only through interpersonal relationships and the relationship of self with the cultural environment that the personality could develop, and he did much to help move psychoanalysis away from its almost total preoccupation with the *internal world*. He was responsible for the often repeated axiom, 'We are all more human than otherwise.' His ideas are best set out in *The Interpersonal Theory of Psychiatry* (1953), *Clinical Studies in Psychiatry* (1956) and *The Fusion of Psychiatry and Social Science* (1964).

Superconscious
A concept introduced by Assagioli as part of his theory of *psychosynthesis*. Assagioli suggests that the superconscious exists alongside the *conscious* and the *unconscious*. According to Assagioli, the superconscious is the region of the *psyche* from which 'we receive our higher intuitions and aspirations – artistic, philosophical or scientific, ethical "imperatives" and urges to humanitarian and heroic action. It is the source of higher feelings, such as altruistic love; of genius and of the states of contemplation, illumination and ecstasy.'

ASSAGIOLI, R. (1965), *Psychosynthesis: A Manual of Principles and Techniques* (Penguin, Harmondsworth).

Superego
One of the three *agencies* which between them, compose the structure of the *psyche*, according to psychoanalytic theory. The function of the superego is to act as a monitor and critic of the activities of the *ego*. Freud (1923) introduced the term and described the superego as part of the ego which becomes differentiated from it and able to function independently of it. The ideas expressed in Freud's (1923) paper marks the beginning of the development of what came to be called Freud's *structural model* of the psyche. The superego is viewed as having *conscious* functions, such as observation and evaluation, and in this sense it can be equated with conscience. But it also functions unconsciously to exert a prohibition and *censorship* upon the activity of the ego.

The superego is seen to emerge as a result of the resolution of the *Oedipus complex* whereby the individual renounces his parents as love objects and internalises them instead, along with their values, wishes and demands. This *internalisation* forms the superego. More specifically, Freud suggested that the superego was constructed on the model of the parents' own superego, rather than on the parents themselves. Since the superego emerges out of the resolution of the Oedipus complex, which, for Freud, occurs differently for boys than for girls, he suggested (Freud 1925) that the superego is therefore qualitatively different in men and women – in other words, that women are somehow less moral than men. Schafer (1974) challenges the assumptions and cultural limitations of Freud's reasoning on this point.

Klein departed from Freud in suggesting that the superego existed in embryonic form from the beginning of life. Feelings of guilt, she believed, are present as early as the fifth or sixth month, and emerge out of the destructive impulses of the *paranoid-schizoid position*. Within this conceptual framework the ego is regarded as a battleground fought over by the *id* and the superego which are always in conflict. The internalisation of the parents' superego and, later, the demands of other authority figures do not necessarily result in a replication of these models in the individual's own superego. His own superego may develop into a far more primitive agency, producing irrational guilt and stunting the development of the ego by its prohibitions; or, alternatively, being very lax, with major *lacunae* resulting in little restraint on the urgency of the id.

FREUD, S. (1923), 'The ego and the id' (*Standard Edition*, vol. 19, Hogarth Press, London).
FREUD, S. (1925), 'Some psychical consequences of the anatomical distinction between the sexes' (*Standard Edition*, vol. 19, Hogarth Press, London).
KLEIN, M. (1960), *Our Adult World and its Roots in Infancy* (Tavistock, London).
SCHAFER, R. (1974), 'Problems in Freud's psychology of women' (*J. of the Am. Psychoan. Assoc.*, vol. 22, pp. 459-85).

Superiority complex

Term introduced by Adler to describe a style of life which strives to gain power over others through a fictional view of the individual's own potentials and capabilities. His need to gain superiority over his environment arises out of a perception of his own fundamental powerlessness and inferiority. The superiority complex is thus a means of overcompensating for the individual's experience of insignificance and his effort to keep at bay an *inferiority complex*.

ADLER, A. (1956), *The Individual Psychology of Alfred Adler* (edited by Ansbacher, H. L. and Ansbacher, R. R., Basic Books, New York).

See also *Individual psychology*.

Supportive psychotherapy

Literally from the Latin 'sub-portare', meaning 'to carry'. A form of psychotherapeutic help offered to patients who are so disabled by their psycho-social problems that change is not regarded as a realistic *goal*. Wolberg (1967) contrasts supportive therapy with two other main sub-groups of psychotherapy – re-educative therapy and reconstructive therapy. Bloch (1979) defines supportive psychotherapy as 'that form of treatment which a therapist offers to a patient in order to sustain him when he is unable to manage his life independently'. It involves the frank recognition that some patients will require continuous, perhaps lifelong support. It should therefore be distinguished from those methods of psychotherapy which contain supportive elements *alongside* but not instead of techniques for enabling the patient to change.

Supportive psychotherapy aims to restore as many of the patient's abilities and resources as possible; enhance his self-esteem; increase his sense of reality regarding what treatment can achieve; prevent the deterioration of his condition; enable him to function with the minimum amount of support; and transfer as much of the support as possible to the patient's *network* of available friends or relatives. Apart from chronic situations where other treatments have been attempted and failed, supportive therapy is often temporarily indicated for normal or mildly disturbed individuals as part of *crisis intervention*.

Techniques used in supportive psychotherapy include reassurance, explanation, guidance, suggestion, encouragement and environmental changes to increase, for example, his social contacts, reduce frustration, improve his living conditions and financial benefits and give *advice* to members of his supportive network. The patient may also be encouraged to participate in *social skills training, assertiveness training, relaxation training*, etc., where appropriate.

Supportive psychotherapy may be offered in the community or as part of some form of institutional care. It may also include day hospital treatment. Supportive psychotherapy may demand a long-term commitment of love from the therapist, offered to perhaps the most neglected and chronically unhappy people who may be experiencing the effects of severe loneliness (Peplau and Perlman 1982). The chief dangers of supportive psychotherapy are, first, that the therapist gives up trying to help the patient to change; second, that he induces a chronic state of dependency; and third, that supportive psychotherapy is viewed as a 'Cinderella' method and relegated to the most inexperienced therapists with no proper training in how to apply the method effectively.

Positive *outcome* has been measured against

the criterion of a reduced rate of hospitalisation (Brandwin *et al.* 1976). Re-evaluating the criteria for successful psychotherapeutic outcome to include, for example, increased quality of life for the aged and the terminally ill might be accelerated by a better appreciation of the potential of supportive psychotherapy.

BLOCH, S. (1977), 'Supportive psychotherapy' (*Brit. J. of Hospital Medicine*, vol. 18, pp. 63-7).

BLOCH, S. (1979), *Introduction to the Psychotherapies* (Oxford University Press, Oxford).

BRANDWIN, M. A. *et al.* (1976), 'The continuing care clinic: outpatient treatment of the chronically ill' (*Psychiatry*, vol. 39, pp. 103-17).

MACLEOD, J. and MIDDLEMAN, F. (1962), 'Wednesday afternoon clinic: a supportive care program' (*Archives of General Psychiatry*, vol. 6, pp. 56-65).

MENDEL, V. M. (1975), *Supportive Care* (Mara Books, Santa Monica, Calif.).

NEKI, J. S. (1976), 'An examination of the cultural relativism of dependence as a dynamic of social and therapeutic relationships' (*Brit. J. of Med. Psychol.*, vol. 49, pp. 11-22).

PEPLAU, L. A. and PERLMAN, D. (eds) (1982), *Loneliness: A Source Book of Current Theory, Research and Therapy* (Wiley, New York).

WOLBERG, L. R. (1967), *The Technique of Psychotherapy* (2nd edn, vol. 1, Grune & Stratton, New York).

See also *Network intervention, Social therapy.*

Suppression

The relegation of disturbing ideas, feelings or memories from the *conscious* to the *preconscious.* It is distinguishable from *repression* by being relatively less total and more easily available to consciousness. It may be said to operate between the conscious and the preconscious and not in relation to the *unconscious.*

Supra-system

The environment of a *system.* When *systems theory* is applied to the family, marital pair or other natural grouping, the supra-system is viewed as being the whole interpersonal, material and physical environment. The term is used interchangeably with the term ecosystem. Since systems and *sub-systems* interlock, the supra-system of a sub-system is the system in which it is embedded. For example, a child viewed as a sub-system has as his immediate supra-system the family system itself and he also, as a sub-system, interacts with the *family's* supra-system, the neighbourhood, school, workplace, racial mixture, religious sub-grouping, etc. All these in turn form systems in their own right alongside the family system; and the family system in *its* turn becomes part of the supra-system of other systems. Some forms of systems therapy make more use of the supra-system than others. For example, *multiple family therapy* and *multiple couples therapy* both intervene in the family and couple's supra-system although the other couples/families in the group may or may not be those who naturally interact together. *Network intervention* is most centrally concerned with intervening in the family supra-system, although the overlap between the concepts implies that at this point the *network* has itself become the system. The relationships between system, sub-system and supra-system constitute differences in level of observation and analysis. The choice of intervention level is arbitrary in terms of the theory and is based on the pragmatic needs of the goals of therapy.

MESAROVIC, M. D. (1970), *Theory of Hierarchical Multilevel Systems* (Academic Press, New York).

MILLER, J. G. (1965), 'Living systems: basic concepts' (*Behavioral Science*, vol. 10, pp. 193-245).

WILDEN, A. (1972), *System and Structure* (Tavistock, London).

Symbiosis

Literal Greek 'sumbiosis', meaning 'a living together'. The close, interdependent attachment of two people. The term is derived from biology and implies a parasitic attachment between two organisms which is to their mutual advantage at some stage in their life cycles. Likewise, in psychological use, the symbiotic bond between the young infant and its mother is essential for the emotional well-being of both. It is a state described by Mahler *et al.* (1975) as the 'symbiotic orbit' and she places it as following the very early 'autistic' phase and preceding the next phase of *differentiation*. It becomes pathological when the need for differentiation, precipitated by the infant's development, is resisted by one or other of the parties. Beyond this functional symbiosis of early infancy, such a bond is detrimental to psychological growth. Scheflen (1980) comments that one or both members of symbiotic relationships 'feels totally as a part and has inadequate experience as a whole'. Such interdependency blocks the emotional development of each and renders both parties extremely vulnerable to the *crisis* of separation through death or accident. The relationship between symbiosis and separation anxiety is discussed by Weiland (1966) who suggests that it is a 'primitive means of coping with anxiety in addition to the more common assumption that it is the persistence of a normal developmental phenomenon'.

MAHLER, M. S. *et al.* (1975), *The Psychological Birth of the Human Infant* (Basic Books, New York).
SCHEFLEN, A. (1980), *Levels of Schizophrenia* (Brunner/Mazel, New York).
WEILAND, I. H. (1966), 'Considerations on the development of symbiosis, symbiotic psychosis and the nature of separation anxiety' (*Int. J. of Psychoan.*, vol. 47, pp. 1-5).

See also *Attachment theory, Double bind, Schizophrenogenic mother, Undifferentiated ego mass.*

Symbolic-experiential family therapy
See *Experiential family therapy.*

Symbolism
The representation of an *unconscious* idea, wish or conflict by something which possesses analogous qualities or which, because of its consistent associations with that which is symbolised, comes to stand for it. Jones (1916) clarified the particular nature of symbolism within psychoanalytic theory: 'it arises as the result of *intrapsychic* conflict between the repressing tendencies and the repressed. . . . The two cardinal characteristics of symbolism in this strict sense are (1) that the process is completely unconscious and (2) that the affect investing the symbolised idea has not, in so far as the symbolism is concerned, proved capable of that modification in quality denoted by the term "*sublimation*".' The notion of symbolism is central to psychoanalytic theory and psychoanalytic writers view *symptoms*, the *manifest content* of *dreams*, children's play, *phantasies* and *myths* as symbolic, in the sense that they all conceal a latent meaning.

Psychoanalysis has suggested a large number of universal symbols which, by analogy, are consistently used to represent central concerns such as the individual's own body, the parents, birth, death, the sexual organs and the sexual act. It was the discovery of universal symbols used across generations and across cultures which led to Jung's theory of the *collective unconscious*. Other symbols are idiosyncratically coined by the individual and require *interpretation* in terms of his or her unique usage of them.

Freud (1900) discussed symbolism in relation to dream material and its importance as a process in concealing (through *displacement* and *condensation*) and revealing (through *interpretation*) the unconscious wish or conflict. Symbolism and symbol formation are viewed as vital processes in the English or *Kleinian* school of psychoanalysis. Klein (1930) discussed how symbol formation was an essential prerequisite of early normal development and her investigations into the symbolism of the young child's play led her to an understanding of the way in which the *internal world* is constructed at a very early age. Moreover, the transfer of interest from one thing to another – from that which is symbolised to the symbol – is the first step in the infant's transference of interest from his subjective world to the outside world of external reality. For the baby, *objects* are regarded as being equivalent in the sense that one can symbolise another if there is some resemblance between them. Thus, the baby's fingers symbolise the breast when the breast is not available and the symbol serves as a bridge to the actual object. The ability to symbolise develops alongside the baby's ability to relate to whole objects, acquired as he moves into the *depressive position* (Segal 1957).

For Jung, symbolism is the essence of the transcendent function, whereby the activities of the *conscious* and the *unconscious* are integrated and the *psychological functions* are brought into harmony. Moreover, only through the use of symbols can psychological growth be achieved: 'The unconscious can be reached and expressed only by symbols, which is the reason why the process of individuation can never do without the symbol' (Jung 1962).

Amongst *behaviour therapists*, the acknowledgment of symbolism distinguishes the radical objective theorist from those who view cognitions and imagery as mediating between the *stimulus* and *response* in the *behavioural sequence* that governs human behaviour. *Communication* theory also acknowledges the importance of symbolism, the *digital* mode using symbolic representations to convey the content of the message. The whole development of language presupposes the ability to make use of symbols and symbolisation is therefore a prerequisite for language acquisition and language use.

FREUD, S. (1900), 'The interpretation of dreams' (*Standard Edition*, vols 4 and 5, Hogarth Press, London).

JONES, E. (1916), 'The theory of symbolism' (in *Papers on Psychoanalysis*, Ballière, Tindall & Cox, London).

JUNG, C. G. (1962), *Commentary on the Secret of the Golden Flower* (Collins/Routledge & Kegan Paul, London).

JUNG, C. G. (1964), *Man and his Symbols* (Aldous Books, London).

KLEIN, M. (1930), 'The importance of symbol formation in the development of the ego' (in *Contributions to Psychoanalysis*, Hogarth Press, London).

MILNER, M. (1955), 'The role of illusion in symbol formation' (in Klein, M. *et al.*, *New Directions in Psychoanalysis*, Maresfield Reprints, Karnac, London).

SEGAL, H. (1957), 'Notes on symbol formation' (in *The Work of Hannah Segal*, Jason Aronson, New York).

Symmetrical

Term used to describe a type of interaction which is characterised by equality between the parties. The parties mirror each other's behaviour and difference between them is minimised. Used in contrast to *complementary*, *communication* theorists such as Watzlawick *et al.* (1968) assert that 'all communicational interchanges are either symmetrical or complementary, depending on whether they are based on equality or difference'. A symmetrical relationship can be *functional* or *dysfunctional*. A functional relationship is however likely to include both symmetrical *and* complementary aspects, even though the symmetrical predominates. Thus, a symmetrical relationship is likely to become dysfunctional, either when it excludes all complementarity and leads to competitiveness, or when it loses its stability and escalates into a *runaway*. Typical of the dysfunctional symmetrical relationship is its escalation into violent conflict, leading to physical damage or to the disintegration of the relationship.

WATZLAWICK, P. *et al.* (1968), *Pragmatics of Human Communication* (W. W. Norton, New York).

See also *Schism*.

Symptom

The perceptible sign of distress or dysfunction in an individual, couple or family. The term is often used interchangeably with *presenting problem*. It derives from medical terminology and hence is used most frequently by medically trained therapists and by those who espouse a psychoanalytic orientation to therapy. In psychoanalytic therapies, the understanding and interpretation of the meaning of the symptom is a crucial part of treatment (Freud 1917a). In developing his general theory of the neuroses, Freud (1917b) viewed symptoms as a substitute for something held back by *repression*. The function of a symptom is to call attention to internal conflict generated by the demands of the *superego* or external world upon the *ego* on the one hand, and a repressed wish on the other. Psycho-analytic therapists take the position that when the *intrapsychic* conflict has been resolved, the symptom will abate. By contrast, behaviour therapists and strategic therapists tend to use the term 'problem' to describe the presented behaviour or pain and it becomes the primary focus for behavioural interventions. Whether or not the symptom is seen as the focus for treatment depends on the theoretical orienta-tion of the therapist (for a fuller discussion, see *Presenting problem*). The main debate regard-ing the behaviourists' direct treatment and removal of symptoms is with psychoanalytic therapists who regard such work as dangerous and superficial and likely to lead to *symptom substitution*. However, Haley (1963) and Watzlawick *et al.* (1968) have pointed out how the *analyst's* non-attention to symptoms is nevertheless symptom-oriented in the sense that the therapist who directs less of his attention to the patient's complaints about his symptoms is indicating that, for the time being at least, it is all right to have them. It is a short step from this position to the technique of *symptom prescription* utilised by strategic therapists.

While psychoanalytic therapists' concern is to avoid the appearance of new symptoms in the individual patient, systems therapists would usually regard symptomatic relief as more likely to lead to a new problem arising in another family or systems member, unless the relationship system had also undergone change (see *Symptom transfer*). For them, a symptom is a *metaphor* and exercises a function within the patient's interpersonal *context*, often involving *secondary gain* for other family members. The interpersonal meaning of the symptom needs to be understood prior to developing a treatment strategy for the symptom itself. For the family therapist, 'the symptom is only the most visible aspect of a connected flow of behaviours and acts as a primary irritant that both monitors the options for change, lest too rapid movement imperil

someone in the family, but also keeps the necessity for change constantly alive' (Hoffman 1980). Solomon (1973) has explored the relationship of family *crises* and symptom eruptions and shows how psychiatric and medical symptoms tend to cluster around the times of developmental crisis in a family.

The display of symptoms in order to pro-duce secondary gain, either for the patient himself or on behalf of another, is usually an unconscious process. It is discussed by both psychoanalytic, interactional and systems-based theorists. Symptoms are sometimes described as being 'masked', for example, the masked symptoms of depression expressed through behaviour problems. Hannay (1979), in an epidemiological study, showed that although three-quarters of the population exhibited psychological symptoms of one sort or another, only a quarter present for help.

FREUD, S. (1917a), 'The sense of symptoms' (*Standard Edition*, vol. 16, Hogarth Press, London).

FREUD, S. (1917b), 'Resistance and repres-sion' (*Standard Edition*, vol. 16, Hogarth Press, London).

FREUD, S. (1926), 'Inhibitions, symptoms and anxieties' (*Standard Edition*, vol. 20, Hogarth Press, London).

HALEY, J. (1963), *Strategies of Psychotherapy* (Grune & Stratton, New York).

HANNAY, D. R. H. (1979), *The Symptom Iceberg* (Routledge & Kegan Paul, London).

HOFFMAN, L. (1980), 'The family life cycle and discontinuous change' (in Carter, E. A. and McGoldrick, M. (eds), *The Family Life Cycle: A Framework for Family Therapy*, Gardner Press, New York).

SOLOMON, M. (1973), 'A developmental premise for family therapy' (*Family Process*, vol. 12, pp. 179-88).

WATZLAWICK, P. *et al.* (1968), *Pragmatics of Human Communication* (W. W. Norton, New York).

Symptom prescription

A form of *paradox* used by *strategic therapists* in which the therapist directs the patient to continue and/or increase his symptomatic behaviour. Sometimes a slight alteration in the circumstances surrounding the symptom is introduced. Thus, a child might be invited to have his temper tantrum for as long as he likes, but always in the same, designated part of the house. An insomniac might be instructed to stay awake or to set his alarm to waken him every hour in case he falls asleep. Symptom prescription is a particular example of the *therapeutic double bind* and, as with the therapeutic double bind, the patient is put into an untenable position with regard to his pathology. The technique enables the patient to move outside the restricting frame of reference imposed by his attempts at *first order change* and achieve *second order change* instead. Its efficacy rests on the therapist taking control of what has previously controlled the patient so that, in performing his symptoms at the request of the therapist, he replaces the therapist's control for the control previously exercised by the symptoms. A frequent result of this intervention is a rapid cessation of symptomatic behaviour, since it is difficult to continue spontaneous (i.e. controllable) symptomatic behaviour to order. The patient's position *vis-à-vis* his symptoms is, however, *always* changed. Even if symptomatic behaviour continues for the time being, he is now having symptoms in order to concur with the therapist's demand, which is very different from having them because he 'cannot help it'.

HALEY, J. (1963), *Strategies of Psychotherapy* (Grune & Stratton, New York).
JACKSON, D. D. (1963), 'A suggestion for the technical handling of paranoid patients' (*Psychiatry*, vol. 26, pp. 306-7).
WATZLAWICK, P. *et al.* (1967), *Pragmatics of Human Communication* (W. W. Norton, New York).

See also *Direct analysis, Negative practice.*

Symptom substitution
The replacement of a *symptom* that has been successfully eradicated by therapy with another, often in a cruder form. The subject is a controversial one. Concern about symptom substitution has routinely been expressed by psychoanalytic and humanistic therapists and both groups have, for this reason, been critical of the direct focus on symptom removal adopted by behavioural and some strategic therapists. Because the psychoanalytic therapist assumes that the symptom indicates underlying psychological *dysfunction*, they argue that the direct removal of symptoms is likely to lead to symptom substitution. Wolberg (1967), however, writing from a psychoanalytic viewpoint, disagrees and comments that 'symptom relief or removal is an essential goal in any useful psychotherapeutic approach'. Behavioural therapists assert that it is perfectly possible to treat the symptom or *presenting problem* as the problem without hypothesising that it is only the 'tip of the iceberg'. The debate is discussed by Montgomery and Crowder (1972). Reasons for symptom substitution, where it has been shown to occur, are variously given. First, the shock and humiliation experienced by the patient when he is denuded of his symptom very quickly (Rabkin (1976) reports this occurring after successful hypnosis). Second, the loss of *primary* or *secondary gains* from having the symptom may encourage the patient to replace it in order to regain these lost advantages. Third, symptom substitution may be a function of time lag. Since the patient is bound to encounter new problems after treatment has terminated, the appearance later on of a new symptom may be unconnected to the old one and may simply represent a new problem that needs to be overcome. Fourth, symptom substitution may occur through the behavioural technique of *reciprocal inhibition*. If the incompatible behaviour used in reciprocal inhibition is in itself undesirable, a new symptom may be gained. Symptom substitution, used as a therapeutic strategy, is discussed by Rabkin (1976) who cites various examples of a severe symptom being replaced by a very much milder one as a result of therapeutic intervention.

MONTGOMERY, G. T. and CROWDER, E. (1972), 'The symptom substitution hypothesis

and the evidence' (*Psychotherapy: Theory, Research and Practice*, vol. 9, pp. 98-102).
RABKIN, R. (1976), *Strategic Psychotherapy: Brief and Symptomatic Treatment* (Basic Books, New York).
WOLBERG, L. R. (1967), *The Technique of Psychotherapy* (Heinemann, London).

See also *Ripple effect, Symptom transfer*.

Symptom transfer

The expression of *symptoms* by one individual on behalf of another or others. The observation that symptoms could be passed from one person to another within a group, family or marital pair led to the understanding of the arbitrary nature of the choice of symptom bearer. Instead of viewing symptoms as the expression of *intrapsychic* disturbance, the concept of symptom transfer leads to an understanding of symptoms as products of intrasystemic disturbance or tension. The symptom may be transferred from one individual to another, as in the case of a phobic child who expresses similar problems to his agoraphobic mother, or it may erupt, apparently in isolation, leaving other members of the group symptom-free. In the latter case, the symptom is said to be transferred on to one individual by the needs of the whole group to release tension, reduce threats to its *homeostasis* or divert psychic energy away from other aspects of the group's functioning. A symptom may be both transferred and substituted. For example, a woman whose agoraphobic symptoms have been successfully treated may find that her husband becomes depressed. As in the case of *symptom substitution*, the idea of symptom transfer is controversial and it is hard to establish how widespread an occurrence it is. It has certainly been noted as a phenomenon for centuries. For example, Petetin in 1785 published a study of a young woman who, on the recovery of her severely ill baby, became catatonic (quoted in Ellenberger 1970). Strategies for preventing symptom transfer include *conjoint* treatment of the whole family, marital or other operational *system*. This may involve the active treatment of all members of

the group as individuals as well as their relationship system. Speck (1965), for example, reports the treatment of *a-symptomatic* family members with tranquilisers in order to prevent symptom transfer.

ELLENBERGER, H. F. (1970), *The Discovery of the Unconscious* (Allen Lane/Penguin, Harmondsworth).
SPECK, R. V. (1965), 'The transfer of illness phenomenon in schizophrenic families' (in Friedman, A. S. *et al.*, *Psychotherapy for the Whole Family*, Springer, New York).

See also *Folie à deux, Regulator, Scapegoat*.

Syncronicity

A term coined by Jung to describe meaningful coincidences that cannot be explained by the laws of linear *causality* and appear to be independent of time and space. He described syncronicity as an 'acausal connecting principle'. Jung (1950) suggested that syncronicity implies 'a peculiar interdependence of objective events among themselves as well as with the subjective states of the observer'. The term is often used loosely to embrace ESP, déjà vu, clairvoyance and telepathy. Jung identified three categories of syncronistic happening: a *phantasy* that occurs simultaneously with an actual event; the concurrence of a psychic state with an objective fact; and the imagining of some future happening. Jung linked syncronistic events with the existence of *archetypes* in the *collective unconscious* which he believed provided an explanation for syncronicity. The concept of syncronicity may be compared with ideas developed by sub-atomic physicists such as 'action-at-a-distance' (cf. Capra 1975).

CAPRA, F. (1975), *The Tao of Physics* (Wildwood House, London).
JUNG, C. G. (1950), Foreword to the I Ching (in 'Psychology and religion', *Collected Works*, vol. 11, Routledge & Kegan Paul, London).
JUNG, C. G. (1952), 'Syncronicity: an a-causal connecting principle' (in 'The structure and dynamics of the psyche', *Collected Works*, vol. 8,

Routledge & Kegan Paul, London).

See also *Parapsychology, Transpersonal psychotherapy.*

Synergy

The energy of a *system* which derives from its *nonsummativity* rather than from its individual parts. Synergy is the unique characteristic of systems and of the holistic approach to them and is the energy which a *systemic* therapist attempts to mobilise when he intervenes in the whole family or other psychosocial system.

See also *Holism, Systems theory.*

Syntaxic

See *Referential processes.*

System

A group of interacting parts which together form a whole. The classic definition of a system is given by Hall and Fagan (1956) as follows: 'A system is a set of objects together with the relationships between the objects and between their attributes.' Originally used in the physical and biological sciences, the term, along with other concepts from *systems theory*, is used in the psychotherapeutic field to describe natural groups such as a family, a marital pair, or a *network*. There is no reason however why it should not also be used to describe an individual when that individual is being viewed as an interacting whole. Essential properties of a system include its *sub-systems* (individual family members *and* sub-groupings such as the marital dyad, the sibling group, etc.); its existence within the *supra-system* (the family's physical, economic and interpersonal environment); its *boundary*; its level of *homeostasis* and whether it is relatively *open* or *closed*; its *feedback loops*; and its pattern and rules of *communication* through which the relationships between the sub-systems and between the system and its supra-system is expressed. *Nonsummativity* is an essential perspective from which to view a system: the whole pattern of inter-relationships is always greater than the sum of sub-system inputs. Critical events for a system are, first, its

developmental *crises* occurring during the family or couple's life cycle, where a developmental stage in one sub-system is likely to interlock with that of another (adolescent development, for example, with parents' mid-life crisis). Second, the entry and exit of members through birth, adoption, death or separation when the system's boundaries are tested. Increases and decreases in system membership affect family interaction dramatically, for example, as Broderick and Smith (1979) point out, when a couple have their first child, the number of reciprocal interactions goes up 300 per cent from one (H-W) to three (H-W, H-C, W-C), and the complexity increases from dyadic to triadic interaction. Third, changes that occur within the supra-system to which the family is called upon to adapt or to defend itself against, for example unemployment, loss of neighbours or friends, a move of house, etc.

The application of the systems metaphor to families, couples and other groups that have some continuity in time and in structure makes possible the application of *systems theory* to the study and treatment of these groups.

BRODERICK, C. and SMITH, J. (1979), 'The general systems approach to the family' (in Burr, W. R. *et al.*, *Contemporary Theories About the Family*, vol. 2, Free Press/Collier Macmillan, London).

HALL, A. D. and FAGAN, R. E. (1956), 'Definition of systems' (in *General Systems*, vol. 1, pp.18-28).

LEWIS, J. M. *et al.* (1976), *No Single Thread: Psychological Health in Family Systems* (Brunner/Mazel, New York).

MILLER, J. G. (1965), 'Living systems: basic concepts' (*Behavioral Science*, vol. 10, pp. 193-245).

Systematic desensitisation

A *counter conditioning* technique introduced by Wolpe (1958). Using the principles of *reciprocal inhibition*, a physiological state inhibitory of anxiety is induced in the patient, usually through *relaxation* procedures. (Wolpe also suggested that sexual arousal and anger could be used, the latter being helpful with cases of social anxiety.) The patient is exposed to small amounts of the anxiety-inducing *stimulus* and the exposure is repeated in progressively larger amounts while the patient is in a relaxed state, until the stimulus no longer evokes anxiety. As Wolpe (1973) points out, the technique has its roots in the experimental laboratory. Wolpe demonstrated that caged cats made fearful by repeated electric shock could be gradually desensitised to this fear by the introduction of food in a mildly and then increasingly anxiety-provoking environment.

One of the essential principles behind systematic desensitisation is that to eliminate or change a habit of reaction to a stimulus, that stimulus must be present in the deconditioning situation. There are three components to the desensitisation process: the construction of an anxiety *hierarchy*, relaxation training and scene presentation during relaxation. In a variety of experiments, Wolpe and others have demonstrated that the most positive outcomes are achieved through this combination of techniques. Wolpe (1973) outlines his techniques of relaxation training, derived originally from Jacobson's (1938) work. The training takes about six interviews and patients are asked to practise at home for two fifteen-minute periods each day. Second, an anxiety hierarchy is constructed, consisting of a list of stimuli on a theme, ranked according to the amount of anxiety they provoke, with the stimulus evoking greatest anxiety at the top of the list. The hierarchy construction is undertaken alongside the relaxation training, but not when the patient is actually in a state of relaxation. The final phase of treatment is the desensitisation procedure itself, when the patient is presented with the anxiety hierarchy in a step-by-step progression while under relaxation. Wolpe begins by using a 'control' scene, to establish whether or not the patient is anxious about or finds difficulty with visualising any material. He then moves into the anxiety hierarchy. Wolpe may present themes and material of any one of the patient's anxiety hierarchies during a single session (generally there are no more than four) with intervals of

between ten and thirty seconds between each scene.

Problems may be encountered if the patient finds the relaxation difficult, if he provides irrelevant anxiety hierarchies or if he cannot use visual imagery appropriately. In a follow up study, Wolpe (1974) found that out of thirty-nine randomly selected cases, thirty-five had sustained major improvement. Paul (1969), in a major review of the *outcome* of systematic desensitisation, concluded that the findings were 'overwhelmingly positive'. Wolpe and his associates have experimented with a number of variations on the basic technique, including the use of a tape recorder so that patients can desensitise themselves at home; desensitisation in a group for patients with the same phobias; and '*in vivo*' desensitisation. Some workers have found that graded exposure without relaxation is as effective, though '*in vivo*' exposure is then significantly more effective than fantasy.

EYSENCK, H. J. and RACHMAN, S (1965), *The Causes and Cures of Neurosis* (Pergamon, London).

JACOBSON, E. (1938), *Progressive Relaxation* (University of Chicago Press, Chicago).

PAUL, G. L. (1969), 'Outcome of systematic desensitisation' (in Franks, C. M. (ed.), *Behavior Therapy: Appraisal and Status*, McGraw-Hill, New York).

RACHMAN, S. (1967), 'Systematic desensitisation' (*Psychological Bulletin*, vol. 67, pp. 93-103).

WOLPE, J. (1958), *Psychotherapy by Reciprocal Inhibition* (Stanford University Press, Stanford, Calif.).

WOLPE, J. (1962), 'Isolation of a conditioning procedure as the crucial psychotherapeutic factor' (*J. of Nervous and Mental Diseases*, vol. 134, p. 316).

WOLPE, J. (1974), *The Practice of Behavior Therapy* (2nd edn, Pergamon Press, New York).

Systemic therapies

All therapeutic approaches which have as their overall aim change in the transactional pattern of members of a *system*, rather than *intrapsychic* or *interpersonal* change or development. Thus, *family therapy*, *marital therapy* and *network intervention* are systemic therapies since the goal of intervention is to bring about an alteration in the functioning of the system. The term is sometimes used erroneously to describe a particular orientation to *family therapy* (the Milan school) within the *strategic* approach. Although this sub-group is undoubtedly systemic, the term should properly be retained for its generic use to embrace all types of therapies which are directed towards systems change.

Systems theory

A theoretical framework for understanding the function and interaction of *systems*. The term was introduced by the biologist Bertalanffy (1952, 1968) to describe 'the principles of wholeness, of organisation and of the dynamic conception of reality [that had] become apparent in all fields of science' (1952). Analogous developments occurring after the war, such as the pioneering work of Wiener in cybernetics and the development of information theory and game theory, fed into and was influenced by the development of general systems theory. The essential features of systems theory are its focus on the relationship between parts as distinct from the analysis of parts into discrete entities; its capacity for examining complex multivariate problems and its transcendence of disciplinary boundaries, enabling links to be formed between the social and psychological sciences and many other fields of enquiry. Transitional languages have enabled the field of systems theory and the fields of psychology, *psychoanalysis* and psychiatry to relate to each other. A particular value of systems theory for the psychotherapist is that it provides a further theoretical framework, alongside group theory, from which to approach the treatment of natural groups as wholes rather than as groups of individual members. The application of systems theory to interpersonal behaviour is more easily accomplished than the development of intra-*psychic* systems theories but this, as Gray *et al.*

(1982) point out, is of equal importance. The shift that is required for the psychotherapist to adopt fully the implications and tenets of systems theory has been described as an epistemological leap of the greatest magnitude.

There are two broad divisions in the field. First, between those who emphasise the concepts of *equifinality* and the dynamic interaction of *morphostasis* and *morphogenesis* as sources of change and stability, compared with those who emphasise information processing elements and the *feedback loop*. Second, within the field of psychotherapy, between a more mechanistic and a more humanistic systems theory. The more mechanistic trend, when applied to interpersonal behaviour, risks losing the individual in its concentration on the system's interacting parts. When applied to the individual, it risks losing the importance of intra-psychic process and individual meaning in its concentration on external behaviour. Gray *et al.* (1982) suggest that psychotherapy can be both systemic *and* humanistic if the following five principles are adhered to: an insistence on an organismic and anti-reductionist approach; a refusal to view the individual as some sort of robot; an emphasis on specifically human characteristics and abilities such as the capacity to use *symbolism*; an allowance for growth-enhancing processes; and the acceptance of values, ethics and morals as being necessary for the understanding of human beings *per se* and in their social interaction.

ACKOFF, R. L. (1960), 'Systems, organisations and interdisciplinary research' (*General Systems*, vol. 5, pp. 1-8).

APPELBAUM, S. A. (1973), 'An application of general systems concepts to psychoanalysis' (*Brit. J. of Med. Psychology*, vol. 46, pp. 115-22).

BERTALANFFY, L. VON (1952), *Problems of Life* (Wiley, New York).

BERTALANFFY, L. VON (1968), *General System Theory* (Allen Lane/Penguin, Harmondsworth).

BUCKLEY, W. (1967), *Sociology and Modern Systems Theory* (Prentice-Hall, Englewood

Cliffs, New Jersey).

CAPRA, F. (1982), *The Turning Point: Science, Society and the Rising Culture* (Wildwood House, London).

GRAY, W. *et al.* (eds) (1982), *General Systems Theory and the Psychological Sciences* (Intersystems Publications, Seaside, Calif.).

GUNTERN, G. (1981), 'System therapy: epistemology, paradigm and pragmatics' (*J. of Marital and Family Therapy*, vol. 7, pp. 265-72).

LASZLO, E. (1972), *Introduction to Systems Philosophy: Toward a New Paradigm of Contemporary Thought* (Gordon & Breach, New York).

MILLER, J. G. (1965), 'Living systems; basic concepts' (*Behavioral Science*, vol. 10, pp. 193-245).

WILDEN, A. (1972), *System and Structure* (Tavistock, London).

See also *Communication, Family therapy, Holism, Homeostasis, Sub-system, Supra-system.*

T

T-Group training

T (training)-Group training was developed by the National Training Laboratory in Group Development in 1947, primarily from the work of Kurt Lewin. Shaffer and Galinsky (1974) define a T-Group as 'an intensive effort at interpersonal self study, and an attempt to learn from the raw experience of member participation in a group, how to improve interpersonal skills and to understand the phenomena of group dynamics'. The method makes maximum use of *participant observation*, group members learning about *group process* and their own behaviour in the group both through observation and through receiving *feedback* regarding their own behaviour from other group members. T-Group training has always combined the dual emphasis on examining the interpersonal behaviour of individuals in small groups and examining

group dynamics in order to learn how to influence social change in institutions and in society. The main emphasis now tends to be the study of interpersonal behaviour within small groups.

Characteristic features of a T-Group are its removal from everyday life experience, often using a residential format, and its mixture of didactic sessions, *large group* meetings and small group experiences. Usually about fifty people attend and are divided into four small groups which interact with each other from time to time. There is no fixed agenda, no structure and no *leadership* in the usual sense. The task of the trainer is to function as a facilitator and create a vacuum to be filled by the work of group members' own behaviour and its scrutiny. The fact that group members' own behaviour and their efforts to understand that behaviour is to provide the main medium of learning is not evident to members at the outset, even though this fact is explained in an opening session. Members therefore normally experience considerable confusion and anxiety at the ambiguity and unusualness of the situation and they make abortive attempts at producing structure and leadership.

T-Group training emphasises the fact that learning can be generated by members' own interaction rather than handed down by experts; that increased self-knowledge increases effective interpersonal communication; that being more effective in groups also involves understanding how other people function; that learning about how to be an effective leader has an important effect on group process, and all this learning can be used to bring about changes in institutional and organisational life. Important elements of the T-Group experience include a here-and-now focus – members try to examine group process, inter-group process and inter-personal behaviour as it is happening; the creation of an atmosphere of trust and group support; helping individuals to behave differently from the dictates of their usual role and circumstances; the encouragement of *self-disclosure* and the building in of appropriate limits and safeguards; and the giving of feedback. The role of the T-Group trainer includes facilitating learning, protection of group members when necessary, providing a model of openness, concern for others and attention to group process as well as using his expertise on group dynamics when appropriate.

T-Group training is used by business organisations, for training people in the helping professions and in helping community groups understand more about group interaction. It has also been used to help members of the same organisation who are at different hierarchical levels to function better together. Developments in T-Group training include the introduction of *action techniques* and the use of the format to explore specific clinical issues such as marital interaction, family relationships, being a woman, etc. There is often a shading into *group psychotherapy* on the one hand and *encounter groups* on the other. More properly, however, the term is reserved for an educational and training approach to the normal processes of interpersonal behaviour, group process and inter-group relationships.

BENNE, K. D. *et al.* (1975), *The Laboratory Method of Changing and Learning* (Science and Behavior Books, Palo Alto, Calif.).
BRADFORD, L. P. *et al.* (1964), *T-Group Theory and Laboratory Method* (Wiley, New York).
SHAFFER, J. and GALINSKY, M. D. (1974), *Models of Group Therapy and Sensitivity Training* (Prentice-Hall, Englewood Cliffs, New Jersey).

See also *Tavistock group training.*

Task

A directive given by the therapist to the patient, family, couple or group, to be carried out in the session or after the session has finished. In the latter case, the task becomes a *homework assignment.* The two terms are often used interchangeably but the term task more properly describes *any* piece of structured therapeutic work suggested by the therapist which, because of its symbolic relationship to the problem or the treatment *goal* is designed to carry forward the therapy. The term is used

by strategic and structural *family therapists* with a particular emphasis on its symbolic nature. For example, Walrond-Skinner (1976) comments, 'A therapeutic task often has no intrinsic value in itself; its meaning lies in the symbolic restructuring of relationships which is attendant upon its performance.' However, tasks may simultaneously have a practical value; for example, suggesting that the individual or family visits the DHSS, reorganise its sleeping arrangements, replan the family budget or try out new ways of tackling access arrangements for the non-custodial parent – all of which are likely to have a practical as well as a symbolic effect for the individual or family.

A task that is to be performed after the session is usually discussed in detail and tried out in some way during the session. Thus, if the therapist is helping a marital pair to communicate more functionally without *detouring* their conflict through a child, he may suggest that they have an outing together without the children. This can then be 'practised' in the session first by discussion and second by *family sculpting* or *role play* so that each family member can experience the way in which his own role in the family interaction has to change. Haley (1976) notes that the best task is 'one that uses the presenting problem to make a structural change'. Tasks may be either straight or *paradoxical.*

HALEY, J. (1976), *Problem Solving Therapy* (Harper & Row, New York).
MINUCHIN, S. (1974), *Families and Family Therapy* (Tavistock, London).
WALROND-SKINNER, S. (1976), *Family Therapy: The Treatment of Natural Systems* (Routledge & Kegan Paul, London).

See also *Paradox, Symptom prescription.*

Tavistock group training

A model of group learning developed at the Tavistock Institute of Human Relations, London, based on psychoanalytic concepts and theories of *group process*, Like *T-Group training*, Tavistock group training is not a form of *group psychotherapy* but is directed instead towards relatively well-functioning individuals, often within organisations, who wish to learn more about *group dynamics*. The Tavistock approach originated with W. R. Bion whose work during the Second World War led to the formulation of a variety of theories of small group behaviour, particularly the idea that groups have two levels of functioning, *work group* activity and *basic assumption behaviour*. Out of these ideas, Bion and his associates, Rice and Rioch, developed a model for group learning, consisting of a small study group, of between eight to twelve members, whose task it is to study its own behaviour as it is occurring; and a *consultant* whose task it is to interpret the latent meaning and basic assumption behaviour of the group. Meetings of the small study group are embedded in a conference framework which stretches over several days. The conference begins with an opening plenary, bringing the whole membership together, where the task of the conference is announced. The small study group meets regularly throughout the conference, alongside large group events consisting of the total membership of the conference and whose task is similarly to study the processes of large group behaviour. In addition, inter-group relations are studied by the assignment of members to new, membership groups, whose task it is to interact with other groups and to study these interactions as they occur. Members can send emissaries to other groups including the staff group, with the status of observer, delegate or plenipotentiary and he or she has the task of observing or negotiating with other groups on behalf of his or her membership group. The conference draws to a close with a plenary review where members' learning and experiences during the conference are reviewed, processed and, to some extent, integrated. Finally, an application group helps members to apply their learning to their own work organisation or home situation.

Some characteristics of Tavistock group training can be summarised as follows: the role of the consultant, except in the application group, is to remain aloof from individual members and as in the psychoanalytic situation with individuals, this makes him very prone to group members' *projections*; members have particular opportunity to learn about their own capacity to project, to *scapegoat* and to engage in irrational basic assumption behaviour. A great deal of learning is focused around the way in which authority figures are handled in the form of the consultant and the staff group, and the political, community and organisational aspects of inter-group relations can be examined during the inter-group event.

Tavistock group training can be focused on the needs of particular organisations and the Grubb Institute, London, arranges specialist conferences of this type. It can be used to examine particular types of inter-group relationship, such as the relationship of different racial groups or the relationships between men and women. It is also used in the training of social work and mental health professionals. Since 1957, the Tavistock Institute has combined with the University of Leicester in running regular conferences and similar events take place in a large number of training institutions in Britain and the United States.

BION, W. R. (1961), *Experiences in Groups* (Tavistock, London).
FREUD, S. (1921), 'Group psychology and the analysis of the ego' (*Standard Edition*, vol. 18, Hogarth Press, London).
PINES, M. (ed.) (1984), *Bion and Group Psychotherapy* (Routledge & Kegan Paul, London)
RICE, A. K. (1965), *Learning for Leadership* (Tavistock, London).
RIOCH, M. J. (1970), 'The work of Wilfred Bion on groups' (*Psychiatry*, vol. 33, pp. 56-66).
SHAFFER, J. and GALINSKY, M. D. (1974), 'The Tavistock approach to groups' (in *Models of Group Therapy and Sensitivity Training*, Prentice-Hall, Englewood Cliffs, New Jersey).
TURQUET, P. (1975), 'Threats to identity in the large group' (in L. Kreeger (ed.), *The Large Group: Dynamics and Therapy*, Constable, London; reprinted Maresfield Reprints, Karnac, London, 1984).

Team

Several therapists who work together for the

purpose of treatment or *training*. When used as a training device it becomes *live supervision*. Often an interdisciplinary group, the therapists may work together in face-to-face contact with the individual, couple or family as in *co-therapy*; or in different combinations as in *multiple impact therapy*. Some members of the team may observe from behind a *one-way screen* while one works with the clients as in the *Greek chorus* technique. Therapy teams are used almost exclusively in the treatment of couples, families, and in *network intervention*, although some forms of group work such as *Tavistock group training* and *T-group training* also make use of therapy-training teams. The technique has a primary place in several forms of *strategic therapy*. Negative effects are discussed by Berkowitz and Leff (1984).

BERKOWITZ, R. and LEFF, J. (1984), 'Clinical teams reflect family dysfunction' (*J. of Family Therapy*, vol. 6, pp. 79-90).
SPEED, B. (1982), 'A team approach to therapy' (*J. of Family Therapy*, vol. 4, pp. 271-84).

Teleology

The belief that behaviour and action is purposive and is significantly influenced by its intended final end. The concept is rejected by radical behaviourists, orthodox psychotherapists and some systems theorists who view behaviour, respectively, as determined by innate *drives*, *stimulus-response* mechanisms or the needs and constraints of the psycho-social *system*. In contrast, humanistic and existential psychotherapists view the patient's understanding of his life purpose, goals and intentions as the crux of the therapeutic process. Telelogy is of limited value on its own since it does not help determine the *means* by which goal-directed action occurs. Most schools of psychotherapy accept the need to include both a concept of purposive action *and* an understanding of how purposive action occurs. Woodfield (1976) points out that current studies of teleology are more concerned with *how* different alternatives are represented and how selection between them is made.

WOODFIELD, A. (1976), *Teleology* (Cambridge University Press, Cambridge).

Telephone (therapeutic use of)

The use of the telephone for therapeutic purposes has been described by several writers. Initial contact with the patient may be perceived as more direct, personal and engaging when made by telephone rather than by letter and both the therapist and the potential patient have the opportunity of accumulating more data about the other from a telephone conversation. Apparently resistant members of the *unit of treatment* can be spoken to direct rather than being sent messages via a third party both during the initial phase of contact and later during treatment; and in individual, *family* or *marital therapy* the telephone can be used as a means of circumventing the worst effects of the *absent member manoeuvre*. The telephone can allow a patient access to the therapist at moments of *crisis* and use of the telephone in this way can be built into a treatment *contract*. Saul (1972), for example, describes the way in which a full analysis was conducted, using one face-to-face interview per week and regular, prolonged telephone calls. In some forms of *self-help* or *crisis intervention*, the telephone may be the primary means of *contact* between the therapist or *paraprofessional* and the person in need of help. It may also be used in *task* work during an ongoing treatment contract; for example, a depressed patient may be asked to telephone the therapist (or his office) each day at a certain time or a non-assertive patient may be asked to telephone a potential employer between therapy sessions, etc. The telephone may also be used as a tool in the evaluation of *outcome* when a large number of patients are being followed up and when a means of contact halfway between a face-to-face *interview* or a written questionnaire is required.

CHILES, J. A. (1974), 'A practical therapeutic use of the telephone' (*Am. J. of Psychiatry*, vol. 131, pp. 130-1).
MILLER, W. B. (1973), 'The telephone in outpatient psychiatry' (*Am. J. of Psychotherapy*, vol. 27, pp. 15-26).
ROSENBAUM, M. (1977), 'Premature interruption of psychotherapy: continuation of

contact by telephone and correspondence' (*Am. J. of Psychiatry*, vol. 134, pp. 200-2).
SAUL, L. (1951), 'A note on the telephone as a technical aid' (*Psychoan. Quarterly*, vol. 20, pp. 287-90).
SAUL, L. (1972), *Psychodynamically Based Psychotherapy* (Science House, New York).

See also *Audio visual equipment*.

Termination
The planned termination of therapy and how it is managed is highly dependent upon the method of therapy being used and the *style* and theoretical orientation of the therapist. Planned termination can be theoretically distinguished from premature termination when patient or therapist terminates therapy unilaterally before the other party, or some third party, feels that the therapeutic process has been completed. In practice, however, such a distinction is harder to make since either party may collude with the other in bringing therapy prematurely to a close. Deciding on the optimal moment for terminating treatment is made easier if a *contract* has been agreed upon and the *goals* of treatment defined and where these goals are primarily *symptom*-focused. This is more likely to occur in *behaviour therapy*, *brief therapy* and *crisis intervention*, and the decision to terminate then rests upon a mutual agreement between patient and therapist that the treatment goals have been fully or approximately reached, or are, for some reason, no longer relevant or attainable.

Termination in *psychoanalysis* and in all long-term treatments is more complex. It has to take account of the ending of a significant, established relationship between patient and therapist as well as an assessment of less specific treatment goals. Whilst most types of psychotherapy seek to distinguish between 'life' goals and 'treatment' goals, the distinction is less easy to make in those therapies that conceive of the restructuring of the patient's whole *psyche* or psycho-social *system* as the overall goal of treatment. Freud's often cited measure of psychological health as being the capacity for enjoyment and efficacy (or the ability to love and to work) is too all-encompassing to be useful as a termination criterion. Psychoanalysts typically make this broad yardstick more limited by specifying that the patient should have gained *insight*; *worked through* his conflicts; gained an improved capacity for *object relations*; an ability to relate to the therapist without the distortions of the *transference*; and his *symptoms* should have been eliminated or reduced to a more tolerable level.

Theorists disagree as to whether the patient should be 'weaned' by encouraging a more reality-based relationship, with less frequent sessions, etc., or whether therapy should stop abruptly. Likewise, there is disagreement among therapists using time-limited treatments as to whether therapy should end automatically when the sessions contracted for have been completed or whether further sessions should be offered if major problems remain unresolved. Parsons (1982) argues that the unilateral imposition of a termination date by the therapist may be the only way of forcing critical issues into the open.

Since many patients present for help because of 'separation' problems of one sort or another, the potential for using the terminal phase of treatment therapeutically should be maximised. The therapist may need to allow the patient to regress to an earlier phase in treatment, regaining his or her symptoms and re-experiencing his or her dependency on the therapist. Careful review of work that has been accomplished during treatment; an avoidance of all that may be construed by the patient as rejection, and a restoration and redirection of the therapeutic relationship to one between peers, offers the patient a second opportunity to re-integrate some of the emotional work that has been covered during the course of treatment. Alternatively, *strategic therapists* suggest prescribing a relapse to the previous symptomatic state as a means of enabling termination to be achieved without regression. Termination is discussed in relation to different models by a variety of writers. Firestein (1974) and Ticho (1972) discuss the particular issues pertaining to the termination of psychoanalysis, and successful non-premature termination of *client-centred therapy* is discussed by Kreps (1972).

FIRESTEIN, S. K. (1974), 'Termination of psychoanalysis of adults: a review of the literature' (*J. of the Am. Psychoan. Assoc.*, vol. 22, pp. 873-94).
KREPS, R. (1972), 'Client-centred therapy: when and how should it end?' (*Psychotherapy: Theory, Research and Practice*, vol. 9, pp. 259-361).
PARSONS, M. (1982), 'Imposed termination of psychotherapy' (*Brit. J. of Med. Psychol.*, vol. 55, pp. 35-40).
TICHO, E. (1972), 'Termination of psychoanalysis: treatment goals, life goals' (*Psychoan. Quarterly*, vol. 41, pp. 315-33).

Thanatos
See *Death instinct.*

Thematic Apperception Test
Developed by Murray and his co-workers in 1938, this projective *personality test* requires a subject to respond to a series of picture cards by telling a story with a beginning, middle and end. Essentially, each subject is given twenty pictures, desirably in two sessions on different days. Shortened versions are often used. The subject tends to project himself into each picture, identifying with one or more of the characters displayed. Thus, his responses are dictated by his former and present experiences, conflicts, values, goals and ideals and by the impact upon him of various environmental forces. The clinician usually interprets responses not only in terms of content but also to include a subject's style of response. *Hypotheses* derived from a subject's responses to one picture are checked against similar hypotheses from other pictures to see if common themes occur.

MURRAY, H. A. (1938), *Explorations in Personality* (Oxford University Press, New York).

Theory of types
The theory was introduced and developed by the English philosophers A. N. Whitehead and Bertrand Russell to resolve a problem identified by Russell in 1901 when working on 'the principles of mathematics', a problem which threatened the philosophical foundations of mathematics. Russell called it 'the contradiction' but it has become known as 'Russell's paradox' and is a problem of self-reference. Developments of the theory, by Quine (1961) and others, are too complex to review here, but the problem may be identified. In considering classes that are not members of themselves, Russell asked whether the class of all such classes is a member of itself? Russell demonstrated that it is a member of itself if, and only if, it is not. The theory of types, developed to resolve this paradox, asserts that no class can be a member of itself (i.e. the class of cats is not itself a cat). To confuse the class with its members is to commit an error of logical typing.

As Bar-Hillel (1967) explains, the *paradox* is resolved by treating classes as logically different in type from their members. 'In particular, classes of individuals are not themselves individuals and classes of individuals are not themselves classes of individuals.' Therefore, 'to ask whether a class is a member of itself is a meaningless question and each of the two grammatically possible answers is a pseudo-statement – a sentence which, despite its grammatical form, is neither true nor false.'

Bateson (1973) and Watzlawick *et al.* (1968, 1974) have been primarily responsible for applying the theory to problems of learning and *communication* and hence to the understanding and treatment of psychopathology. These workers have demonstrated the ubiquitous nature of errors of logical typing brought about by confusing one level of a *hierarchy* of types with another. As Bateson pointed out, a schizophrenic who eats the menu instead of the meal is committing an error of logical typing since the menu describing the meal is not itself a meal. Distinguishing between different levels in the hierarchy of types enables distinctions to be made between the 'what' and the 'how' of messages. For example, the *context* (and hence the meaning) of the report or detonative level of communication (level one) is explained by the *metacommunictive* level (level two); and further, the relationship between levels one and two is clarified only by an elaboration of the rules of communication theory (level three). Each level is meta or one step up, in the hierarchy of levels from the one below.

Watzlawick *et al.* (1974) draw two important conclusions from the theory of types for understanding human behaviour and how to bring about change: first, that logical levels must be kept strictly apart in order to prevent paradox and confusion, and second, that moving from one level of a hierarchy to the next (from member to class) entails a discontinuous change. Watzlawick *et al.* (1974) suggest that psychotherapeutic interventions that are directed towards class *membership* involve *first order change* and those that involve the relationship between *levels* involve *second order change*. *Strategic therapy* makes great use of the insights derived from an understanding of the theory of types.

BAR-HILLEL, Y. (1967), 'Types, theory of' (in Edwards, P. (ed.), *The Encyclopaedia of Philosophy*, Macmillan, London).
BATESON, G. (1973), 'The logical categories of learning and communication' (in *Steps to an Ecology of Mind*, Granada, London).
COPI, I. M. (1971), *The Theory of Logical Types* (Collier Macmillan, London).
QUINE, W. V. (1961), *From a Logical Point of View* (2nd edn, Harper & Row, New York).
WATZLAWICK, P. *et al.* (1968), *Pragmatics of Human Communication* (W. W. Norton, New York).
WATZLAWICK, P. *et al.* (1974), *Change: Principles of Problem Formation and Problem Resolution* (W. W. Norton, New York).
WHITEHEAD, A. N. and RUSSELL, B. (1910-13), *Principia Mathematica* (2nd edn, 3 vols, Cambridge University Press, Cambridge).

Therapeutic alliance

The creation of a working relationship between therapist and patient. Prior to engaging in any change interventions, the therapist needs to gain the co-operation of the patient and overcome his *resistance* to treatment. This process involves the therapist making an *accommodation* to the patient's or family's view of the problem, using *joining* techniques to enter into the patient's culture and establishing the *core conditions* of therapy. The term implies that each party is conscious of entering into a particular kind of relationship in order to achieve mutually agreed *goals* and that some sort of *contract* of work is either explicitly or implicitly made.

The concept is relevant to most treatment methods except for those which employ covert strategies or where the co-operation of the patient cannot be gained in any direct manner. The concept is not found in early psychoanalytic writing, although Freud called attention to the fact that even when the patient is highly disturbed, the therapist seeks to enter into a 'realistic' relationship with the healthy part of his personality. Moreover, from the outset, Freud stressed the need to develop friendliness and trust and to encourage a positive *transference*. This should lead to what he called an 'analytic pact' being made between *analyst* and patient (Freud 1937). Anna Freud (1927) referred to the need for creating a 'treatment alliance' and emphasised its importance in work with children. Greenson (1967) has emphasised the use of techniques to develop confidence in the psychoanalytic patient to help build up the therapeutic alliance, particularly the importance of the real personality of the analyst.

The nature of the therapeutic alliance in *psychoanalysis* has been discussed amongst others by Zetzel (1958), Friedman (1969) and Adler (1980), and they illuminate the sensitivity that is required to allow an alliance to develop at an appropriate point in the relationship rather than being overemphasised or forced because of the analyst's own needs. The same caveat holds good for other treatment approaches. The quality of the therapeutic alliance appears to be a highly significant indicator of good prognosis. Premature *termination* or severe dependency on the therapist are both indicators that a good therapeutic alliance has not been achieved.

ADLER, G. (1980), 'Transference, real relationship and alliance' (*Int. J. of Psychoan.*, vol. 61, pp. 547-57).

FREUD, A. (1927), *The Psychoanalytic Treatment of Children* (International Universities Press, New York).

FREUD, S. (1937), 'Analysis terminable and interminable' (*Standard Edition*, vol. 23, Hogarth Press, London).

FRIEDMAN, L. (1969), 'The therapeutic alliance' (*Int. J. of Psychoan.*, vol. 50, pp. 139-53).

GREENSON, R. (1967), *The Technique and Practice of Psychoanalysis* (International Universities Press, New York).

KANZER, M. (1981), 'Freud's "analytic pact": the standard therapeutic alliance' (*J. of the Am. Psychoan. Assoc.*, vol. 29, pp. 69-89).

ZETZEL, E. R. (1958), 'The therapeutic alliance in the analysis of hysteria' (in *The Capacity for Emotional Growth*, International Universities Press, New York).

See also *Corrective emotional experience, Relationship factors, Social influence.*

Therapeutic community

The idea of community offering a means of healing and wholeness to its members has deep roots in the Judeo-Christian tradition. The possibility of the disturbed or sick withdrawing into such a community is reflected in the early idea of asylums as places of refuge and care. The loss of this emphasis in the eighteenth and nineteenth centuries led in turn to a rediscovery of the concept of community in the late nineteenth century and paved the way for the specific adoption of the term as it has come to be used in current psychotherapeutic literature. The term is used in several different ways because of its separate British and American derivations. In Britain the term was first used by Main (1946) to describe a general approach to the institutional care of patients, which sought to replace the regimented, punitive pre-war conditions of many psychiatric hospitals by a more liberal, egalitarian regime. The seminal work of Maxwell Jones (1965) during the war and the post-war period at the Henderson Hospital produced the main theoretical concepts which distinguish the specific method from a general approach to treatment. The essential features of the therapeutic community developed by Jones, Main and their colleagues include the formation of a non-hierarchical, participatory community life, in which both staff and patients take a full and almost equal part in decision making, including decisions about treatment. Although the distinction between professional staff and patients is not abolished, its hierarchical manifestations are reduced as far as possible and an informal, home-like atmosphere is encouraged within the community.

Three basic tools are employed in running the therapeutic community: community meetings, staff review meetings and living-learning situations. The community meeting usually occurs daily and makes use of the *large group* situation to review the previous twenty-four hours, examine difficulties that may have arisen between patients or between patients and staff and engage in joint planning and decision making regarding the daily running of the community. The object of the community meeting is to engage every participant in the day-to-day life of the group, to build *cohesion*, to model ways of coping with disagreements and arriving at consensus, to provide an opportunity for members to give each other *feedback* and to learn how to do this constructively. Typically, the community meeting is followed by a staff review which enables the staff to analyse the events and processes of the community meeting and to clarify tasks and areas of responsibility. Because there is no traditional pattern of role relationships between doctors, nurses, social workers, etc. there is a need for everyone to find new ways of relating to each other within the staff group as well as between the staff and patient groups. Jones introduced the idea of the 'living-learning situation' which he describes (Jones 1968) as 'face to face confrontation and joint analysis of the current interpersonal difficulty' which has just occurred within the community. An emergency community meeting is called and the *crisis* is worked out by engaging the efforts of all those who are involved.

A range of psychotherapeutic treatments were also introduced including *family therapy*, *group psychotherapy* and *psychodrama*. The two best known therapeutic communities run on these lines in Britain were the Henderson and Cassel Hospitals. The latter, under the directorship of Tom Main, adopted various modifications in the approach; in particular a clear distinction was made between the roles of doctors and nurses, the latter being designated as psychosocial nurses whose task it is to enable the work of the community to be undertaken in as adult a way as possible. Many of the ideas which originated with Tom Main have been introduced into a wide variety of different settings in Britain and America and they have been influential in the development of new therapeutic approaches to prison communities (for instance at Chino in California and at Grendon Underwood in Britain), acute psychiatric wards and in day hospitals.

In America, a second major strand in the development of therapeutic communities has been the 'concept-based' approach of Synanon. Founded in 1958 by an ex-alcoholic, Chuck Dederich, it focused primarily on work with drug addicts, using the inculcation of a powerful belief system and a set of moral values to change the inner motivation and behaviour of its members. In contrast to the democratic models of the Henderson and Cassel Hospitals in England, Synanon relies on an autocratic structure, an attacking style of group life amongst the residents and a daily routine which includes work assignments, group meetings and daily discussions based on philosophical readings, through which the basic moral 'concepts' are learned. Derivatives of Synanon include Day-Top Village and Phoenix House (1968) in New York, and many other experiments outside America have taken place on the original Synanon model. The concept-based therapeutic community emphasises the addict's need to take responsibility for himself. He is given a simple explanation of the causes of his addiction, told how the treatment works and what he must do to overcome his addiction. Total abstinence from all drugs and alcohol is insisted upon and the work activities and group meetings are supplemented by a variety of educational and social inputs. *Encounter groups* and *social skills training* are also used. The Synanon type of therapeutic community has received ongoing criticism for what some regard as its degrading punishments, its dictatorial regime and its carefully designed programmes of indoctrination. Yet it has been used as a model for successfully confronting hard-core addiction and has been modified and adapted for use in a variety of different cultures with considerable success.

A third type of therapeutic community arose out of the 'anti-psychiatry' movement of the 1960s. In Britain, psychiatrists Laing and Cooper and in the United States, Szasz and Leary attacked the principles behind conventional psychiatry and questioned the nature of mental illness, the social role enforced upon the psychiatrist by society's needs rather than the patient's welfare, and the conventional wisdom which defined normal and abnormal behaviour. These criticisms led to an effort to put into practice an alternative treatment regime, based on small households providing a living environment of therapists and patients interacting together within as unstructured a community as possible. Mental illness as such is to be understood in these communities as a myth and is redefined as a positive growth-promoting experience leading to a wholly new development of the personality. Thus it is a journey to be encouraged and explored. Kingsley Hall was the first community which was founded to enable this to happen. No distinctions were made between patients and staff; no drug treatment was given and patients were encouraged to regress as fully as necessary to accomplish their journey through psychosis and into a new and fuller experience of personhood. One of the most celebrated members of Kingsley Hall was Mary Barnes whose experiences were published in a book written jointly by her and her psychiatrist

Joseph Berke (1971). Kingsley Hall closed in 1970 but the approach has been continued in the work of the Philadelphia Association and at the Arbours Crisis Centre.

Today therapeutic communities exist all over the world and the movement has been enormously influential.

BARNES, M. and BERKE, J. (1971), *Mary Barnes: Two Accounts of a Journey Through Madness* (Hart Davis, MacGibbon, London).

BERKE, J. (1979), *'I Haven't Had to Go Mad Here'* (Penguin, Harmondsworth).

COOPER, D. (1967), *Psychiatry and Antipsychiatry* (Tavistock, London).

ILLICH, I. *et al.* (1977), *Disabling Professions* (Marion Boyars, London).

JANSEN, E. (ed.) (1980), *The Therapeutic Community* (Croom Helm, London).

JONES, M. (1965), *Social Psychiatry in Practice* (Penguin, Harmondsworth).

JONES, M. (1968), *Beyond the Therapeutic Community: Social Learning and Social Psychiatry* (Yale University Press, New Haven, Conn.).

KENNARD, D. (1983), *An Introduction to Therapeutic Communities* (Routledge & Kegan Paul, London).

LAING, R. D. (1967), *The Politics of Experience* (Penguin, Harmondsworth).

MAIN, T. (1946), 'The hospital as a therapeutic institution' (*Bulletin of the Menninger Clinic*, vol. 10, pp. 66-70).

MAIN, T. (1977), 'The concept of the therapeutic community' (*Group Analysis*, vol. 10, no. 2).

SYNANON, B. (1974), *Day-Top Village – A Therapeutic Community* (Holt, Rinehart & Winston, New York).

YABLONSKY, L. (1965), *Synanon: The Tunnel Back* (Macmillan, New York).

Therapeutic double bind

A technique used in *strategic therapy* and *focused problem resolution*, whereby the therapist creates the mirror image of a pathogenic *double bind* in order to promote *second order change*. The technique is based on the principle of homeopathic medicine where a minute portion of the pathogenic substance is used as part of the cure. An essential condition for an effective therapeutic bind is the presence of an intense therapeutic relationship, holding survival value for the patient. The therapist imposes a *task* which unexpectedly reinforces the behaviour which the patient has sought help to change; implies that this *reinforcement* is the vehicle of change; and creates a *paradox* by suggesting that the patient must change by remaining unchanged. As Watzlawick *et al.* (1968) point out, the patient is then put into an untenable position with regard to his pathology, whereby he is changed if he follows the therapist's directive and changed if he does not.

WATZLAWICK, P. *et al.* (1968), *Pragmatics of Human Communication* (W. W. Norton, New York).

See also *Devil's pact, Strategic therapy, Symptom prescription.*

Therapist variable

The influence of the person of the therapist on the *outcome* of psychotherapy is generally agreed to be of considerable importance in almost all methods. *Behaviour therapists* too, who place considerable emphasis on technique, also acknowledge the importance of the therapist variable (Wilson and Evans 1977). Therapist characteristics such as age, sex, race and socio-economic status are all likely to interact either favourably or unfavourably with comparable characteristics in the patient and this has led to some research into therapist-patient matching (Berzins 1977). His personal qualities and his professional attributes are also factors to be taken into account. Amongst personal qualities, various researchers have identified the therapist's capacity to express *empathy, unconditional positive regard, genuineness, congruence* and *humour* as being important; and professional qualities such as *experience, credibility* and *expertness* have all been examined in terms of their relation to good prognosis. The effects of the therapist's personality conflicts and needs and his attitudes towards the patient have also been studied (Parloff *et al.* 1978). Two approaches to research appear to be most fruitful in trying to understand the effect of this elusive variable: first, the effort to discover which therapist, having what characteristics, is most effective with which client, and second, an appreciation of the interactive nature of the many dimensions of the therapist variable and the way they relate to the characteristics and symptomatology of the patient.

BERZINS, J. I. (1977), 'Therapist-patient matching' (in Gurman, A. S. and Razin, A. M. (eds), *Effective Psychotherapy*, Pergamon Press, New York).
LØVLIE, A.-L. (1982), *The Self of the Psychotherapist* (Universitetsforlaget, Oslo).
PARLOFF, M. B. *et al.* (1978), 'Research on therapist variables in relation to process and outcome' (in Garfield, S. L. and Bergin, A. E. (eds), *Handbook of Psychotherapy and Behavior Change*, Wiley, New York).
WILSON, G. T. and EVANS, I. (1977), 'The therapist-client relationship in behavior therapy' (in Gurman, A. S. and Razin, A. M. (eds), *Effective Psychotherapy*, Pergamon, New York).

See also *Counter transference, Deterioration, Non-specific factors, Relationship factors.*

Third force
A name given to those who have promoted *humanistic psychology*, particularly Abraham Maslow, Carl Rogers, Gordon Allport and Kurt Goldstein. The term is used to contrast the humanistic approach from the 'first force' of *psychoanalysis* and the 'second force' of *behaviour therapy*.

Thorndike, Edward Lee (1874-1949)
Thorndike was born in Williamsburg, Massachusetts in 1874. He gained his PhD in psychology from Columbia University, New York in 1898, studying under J. M. Cattell. After a year spent at Western Reserve University, the rest of his professional life was spent in research, writing and teaching at

Columbia University from 1899 to 1940. Thorndike was the first psychologist to study animal behaviour experimentally in the laboratory and out of these studies he developed what became known as Thorndike's Laws: the law of effect and the law of exercise. The law of effect states that if a *response* is followed by a satisfying consequence it will be repeated but if it is followed by an unpleasant consequence it will not. The law of exercise states that the more often a response is performed in a given situation the more likely it is to be repeated. Most *learning theory* has incorporated these laws in modified form. Thorndike's later research interest was turned to human learning, the measurement of intelligence and tables of word frequency counts in English language use. He was a prolific writer, his most important works including *Educational Psychology* (1903), *Elements of Psychology* (1905), *The Psychology of Learning* (1913) and *The Fundamentals of Learning* (1932).

Thought stopping
A technique originally developed by Bain (1928) but introduced into the clinical literature by Taylor (1963). A form of *reinforcement*, thought stopping is probably effective because it establishes an inhibitory habit by positive reinforcement. The therapist first asks the client to verbalise a typical nonproductive thought sequence. The therapist then calls out 'stop' loudly and points out that the client's thoughts will have stopped. He is then taught to use this technique on himself whenever he finds himself subject to unwanted thoughts. Wolpe and Lazarus (1966) outline the technique, and recently Parenteau and Lamontagne (1981) describe its use with phobias, smoking and sexual deviations. However, the technique is not widely used except to counter obsessional ruminations, and it is unlikely to be very effective except in rather straightforward situations.

BAIN, J. A. (1928), *Thought Control in Everyday Life* (Funk & Wagnalls, New York).
PARENTEAU, P. and LAMONTAGNE, Y.

(1981), 'The thought stopping technique: a treatment for different types of ruminations?' (*Canadian J. of Psychiatry*, vol. 26, pp. 192-5). TAYLOR, J. G. (1963), 'A behavioural interpretation of obsessive compulsive neurosis' (*Behavior Research and Therapy*, vol. 1, p. 237). WOLPE, J. and LAZARUS, A. (1966), *Behavior Therapy Techniques* (Pergamon Press, New York).

Tickling the defences

A method of *confrontation* described by N. W. Ackerman and used to undermine the shared *defence mechanisms* of the family group. Ackerman describes this technique as a tactic for catching family members by surprise and for exposing discrepancies in what they are saying between their verbal and *non-verbal communication* and in the ineffective solutions they are using to solve their problems. Although highly descriptive of a familiar therapeutic procedure, the term is seldom used outside the literature of *psychoanalytic family therapy*.

ACKERMAN, N. W. (1966), *Treating the Troubled Family* (Basic Books, New York).

Time-limited psychotherapy

Forms of *brief therapy* distinguished by their conscious *manipulation* of a time-limited *contract*. Schlein *et al.* (1962) discuss some of the ingredients and effects of this method. The term 'time-limited' has been used by other workers to describe forms of short-term therapy (for example, Swartz 1969) but the method is most fully worked out by Mann (1973) as a specific method, distinguishable from other methods of brief treatment. Time-limited psychotherapy is thought to be particularly useful with conflicts of late adolescence.

The two main ideas that are involved are an emphasis on the *conscious* and *unconscious* meaning and influence of time; and the way in which an understanding of the underlying problem (or central issue) is arrived at and used to guide the therapy from beginning to end. The method employs a specific, structured framework, a precise *goal* and a predetermined time limit, and the usual number of sessions is twelve. Time is conceived of as a continuous, reciprocal relationship between the individual's experience of his past, his present and his future. The meaning of the passage of time is linked with different presentations of distress. For example, depressed patients see time as being over and past; manic patients, as being oppressively present; and anxious patients, as holding the fear of the future. The structured way in which therapy is time-limited symbolises the importance placed by the therapist on the understanding and management of time in the patient's life. Unlike long-term treatment, where time may only become an important issue when *termination* is being considered, time is consciously used as the primary active element throughout this form of brief therapy. This emphasis on the time limits of therapy prevents the patient's *regression* and confronts him at the outset of treatment with the demands of the adult world and especially with the universal experience of loss and separation.

Mann (1973) views the unresolved conflict about the 'recurring life crisis of separation-individuation' as universal. Evaluation of the patient's past history provides the data from which the therapist defines the central issue. The formulation of the central issue (similar to the salient issue in *single session therapy* and the *focal hypothesis* in *focal psychotherapy*) does not directly include the *presenting problem* as the patient conceives of it. However because the central issue serves to produce or maintain this problem in being, the patient feels that some important and hidden aspect of the self has been revealed by the therapist's formulation. Thus, *symptom* relief is a by-product of therapy, not its goal.

The first phase of treatment involves a delineation of the central issue which serves to create optimism in the patient and also helps to build a *therapeutic alliance* with the therapist. The use of *empathy* is an important part of the therapist's work and interaction with the patient. The second phase produces feelings of disappointment in the patient and, as the mid-point of treatment is reached, the patient feels progressively more disillusioned and cheated. The third phase involves the therapist's effort to help the patient accept the loss of the therapeutic relationship without withdrawing prematurely from it. Active *interpretations* are made to help the patient distinguish his feelings about the therapist from past and current significant others. The therapist steadily offers an empathic relationship, while the patient expresses his negative feelings. The patient internalises this empathic figure and, in the process, his self-perception is changed into something positive and accepting and he is helped to grow in autonomy and independence.

Research studies into time-limited psychotherapy have been conducted by Gelso and Johnson (1983) and Strupp (1980).

GELSO, C. J. and JOHNSON, D. H. (1983), *Explorations in Time Limited Counseling and Psychotherapy* (Teachers College Press, Columbia University, New York).

MANN, J. (1973), *Time-Limited Psychotherapy* (Harvard University Press, Cambridge, Mass.).

MANN, J. (1981), *A Casebook of Time-Limited Psychotherapy* (McGraw-Hill, New York).

SCHLEIN, J. M. *et al.* (1962), 'Effects of time limits – a comparison of two psychotherapies' (*J. of Counseling Psychology*, vol. 9, pp. 31-4).

STRUPP, H. H. (1980), 'Success and failure in time-limited psychotherapy' (*Archives of General Psychiatry*, vol. 37, pp. 595-603 and 707-16).

SWARTZ, J. (1969), 'Time-limited brief psychotherapy' (in Barten, H. H., *Brief Therapies*, Behavioral Publications, New York).

See also *Brief focal family therapy, Brief psychoanalytic psychotherapy, Short-term anxiety-provoking therapy*.

Time out

A behavioural technique whereby the client (usually a child) is temporarily removed from opportunities of receiving positive *reinforcement*. As time out has the function of reducing the frequency of a response it is technically a form of *punishment*. It usually takes the form of removing the child for a brief period of time to his bedroom or other socially isolating environment. Most researchers conclude that brief periods of time out are more effective than long periods (Drabman and Spitalnik 1973). MacDonough and Forehand (1973) outline some of the issues that still need to be investigated. Sherman and Baer (1969) suggest that the use of time out may involve at least four components: *response cost* because of the deprivation of some desired *stimulus* or positive reinforcement; reinforcement of appropriate behaviour, since time out is terminated when the child is acting properly; *extinction*, since the time out environment withdraws the reinforcing effect of attention; and punishment, since the isolation experience may be aversive. Because of the number of other operations involved, Moharty (1981) has suggested that the concept is redundant and unparsimonious and that time out should instead be categorised within existing theoretical concepts.

Time out differs from the frequently used parental practice of sending the child to his room when the parent's patience is exhausted. First, time out is not imposed in anger but as an automatic consequence of the occurrence of particular behaviours. Second, time out is terminated when the behaviour stops so that appropriate behaviour is reinforced. Third, after the cessation of time out, there are no further consequences for the child such as recriminations or complaints about the behaviour which has caused the time out. Some therapists have combined the use of time out with a paradoxical intervention. For example, the child is told that she may have tantrums but only in the temper tantrum room. Each time she begins, she is taken to the room and invited to continue for as long as she likes. If treatment is successful, the child may, after several days of tantrum-free behaviour, be told of her parents' concern about the lack of tantrums and again be invited to visit the temper tantrum room. Such a procedure, described by Breunlin (1980), is a form of *symptom prescription.*

Time out is also used in a different sense to describe the procedure whereby the therapist leaves the session to consult with colleagues behind a *one-way screen* (see *Greek chorus, Live supervision, Team*).

BREUNLIN, D. (1980), 'The Gwent family' (in Breunlin, D. *et al.*, *Family Therapy or Family Therapies?*, Barnardo Social Work Papers, no. 9, Barkingside, Essex).

DRABMAN, R. and SPITALNIK, R. (1973), 'Social isolation as a punishment procedure' (*J. of Experimental Child Psychology*, vol. 16, pp. 236-49).

MACDONOUGH, T. S. and FOREHAND, R. (1973), 'Response-contingent time out' (*J. of Behavior Therapy and Experimental Psychiatry*, vol. 4, pp. 231-6).

MOHARTY, A. K. (1981), 'Time out from positive reinforcement' (*Indian Psychological Review*, vol. 20, pp. 24-34).

SHERMAN, J. A. and BAER, D. M. (1969), 'Appraisal of operant therapy techniques with children and adults' (in Franks, C. M. (ed.), *Behavior Therapy: Appraisal and Status*, McGraw-Hill, New York).

Token economy

An environment that is structured in such a way that appropriate behaviour receives *reinforcement* and inappropriate behaviour is extinguished. The tokens have no intrinsic value but can be accumulated to earn the back-up *reinforcer* after behaviour has reached the desired level. A token economy is usually operated within an institutional setting such as a hospital ward, prison or school, and it increases the motivation of the whole staff-patient community towards achieving the treatment goals. It has been shown to be effective in changing behaviour even with long-term, institutionalised patients. However, there are various practical, ethical and legal problems attached (Kazdin and Bootzin 1972). *Generalisation* to other situations tends to be poor; reinforcers may lose their efficacy; and extraneous influences such as gifts and unscheduled visits from relatives may upset the reinforcement regime. Ethical problems may arise from the difficulty of ensuring the informed consent of patients when the programme is being operated within an institutional setting.

AYLLON, T. and AZRIN, N. H. (1968), *The Token Economy: A Motivational System for Therapy and Rehabilitation* (Appleton-Century-Crofts, New York).

KAZDIN, A. E. and BOOTZIN, R. R. (1972), 'The token economy: an evaluative review' (*J. of Applied Behavior Analysis*, vol. 5, pp. 343-72).

Tolman, Edward Chace (1886-1961)

Tolman was born at West Newton, Massachusetts, in 1886. He gained his PhD in psychology from Harvard University in 1915, studying under E. B. Holt. After spending a short time at Northwestern University, he spent the rest of his professional life engaged in research, teaching and writing at the University of California, Berkeley, from 1918 to 1954. Tolman made major contributions to *learning theory*, being influenced both by the behaviourist concepts of Watson and the ideas of *Gestalt psychology*. His theory of purposive *behaviourism* is a blend of both these two strands. He distinguished between learning as acquisition and learning as performance, reward being necessary for the execution of the latter but not for the former. His major work is his *Purposive Behavior in Animals and Men* (1932).

Topographical model

Because of his neurological and neuro-physiological background, Freud was attracted to a view of the mind which was organised into spatially separate areas of functioning. In *The Interpretation of Dreams* (1900) he put forward a well worked out model whereby impulses which are derived from the *drives* produce mental representations in the deeper layers of the mind – the *unconscious*. These impulses cannot be openly expressed, because of their explicitly sexual nature and hence their social unacceptability. The more superficial layers of the mind, the *preconscious* and *conscious*, function to modify these impulses, converting them into a form that is capable of being expressed in thought or action. There is therefore a continuous conflict between the three levels or layers of the mind. Gradually, however, Freud came to recognise various inconsistencies in this model. For example, many drives within the unconscious are anti-instinctual and it is therefore illogical simply to differentiate mental contents according to the one criterion of how accessible they are to consciousness. The inconsistencies in this model could not be resolved and led Freud in *The Ego and the Id* (1923) and *Inhibitions, Symptoms and Anxiety* (1926) to reformulate the whole spatial metaphor into a 'new topography of the mind'. All three agencies – *id*, *ego* and *superego* – are now seen as having unconscious and conscious aspects, and mental functions are now grouped according to the role that they play in conflict. This view is known as the *structural model*.

Some *ego psychologists* have felt that the topographical model is inadequate as a general explanatory framework for all human functioning and behaviour (Arlow and Brenner 1964). Gill (1963), however, proposed its continuing revision rather than its abandonment and this process has been continued by others.

ARLOW, J. and BRENNER, C. (1964), 'Psycho-analytic concepts and the structural theory' (*J. of Am. Psychoan. Assoc.*, Monograph Series no. 3, International Universities Press, New York).
FREUD, S. (1900), 'The interpretation of dreams' (*Standard Edition*, vols 4 and 5, Hogarth Press, London).
FREUD, S. (1923), 'The ego and the id' (*Standard Edition*, vol. 19, Hogarth Press, London).
FREUD, S. (1926), 'Inhibitions, symptoms and anxiety' (*Standard Edition*, vol. 23, Hogarth Press, London).
FREUD, S. (1940), 'An outline of psycho-analysis' (*Standard Edition*, vol. 23, Hogarth Press, London).
GEDO, J. and GOLDBERG, A. (1973), *Models of the Mind* (University of Chicago Press, Chicago).
GILL, M. (1963), *Topography and Systems in Psychoanalytic Theory* (International Universities Press, New York).
SANDLER, J. *et al.* (1978), 'Frames of reference in psychoanalytic psychology XI: limitations of the topographical model' (*Brit. J. of Med. Psychology*, vol. 51, pp. 61-5).

Tracking

A *joining* technique described by Minuchin (1974) in relation to *family therapy* by which the content and process of family *communication* is followed, encouraged and assessed. The therapist joins the family 'as an active, neutral listener. He helps track their story' (Minuchin and Fishman 1981). Minuchin's use of the term comes from the idea of a record player's needle 'following' the groove in the record. Thus, the term implies a sort of 'active passivity' and alert attention on the part of the therapist. While *attending* to and encouraging the expression of the content of what a family member is saying, he will also be noting the *alliances*, *coalitions* and communication rules: who speaks for whom, who is the spokesperson for the whole group, who are verbally silent but non-verbally active, etc. He will also be noting his own reactions to family members and how they are responding to him. He will notice discrepancies, *behavioural sequences*, repetitions, redundancies, areas of disagreement and areas of convergence as well as the family's own formulation of the *presenting problem* and their understanding of what the treatment *goals* might be. The therapist encourages the family member or individual to continue communicating, by non-verbal phonations such as 'ah-ha's, 'uh-hum's, nods, smiles, eye contact, etc., all of which convey the fact that the therapist is attending.

MINUCHIN, S. (1974), 'Structural family therapy' (in Caplan, G. (ed.), *Am. Handbook of Psychiatry*, vol. 3, Basic Books, New York).
MINUCHIN, S. and FISHMAN, H. C. (1981), *Family Therapy Techniques* (Harvard University Press, Cambridge, Mass.).

See also *Maintenance, Mimesis*.

Trading of dissociations

Term introduced by Wynne (1965) to describe a pathological defensive *network* within a family whereby members have acute perceptions about others but dissociations regarding the self. Each person locates the whole of a particular difficulty or feeling state in another family member, whilst that member reciprocally does the same. Thus, the fixed view that each person has of the other is unconsciously exchanged for a fixed view of himself held by the other. The concept is used in *psychoanalytic family therapy* and describes a *systemic* phenomenon comparable to the process of *projective identification* between individuals. The process is deeply *unconscious* and enables each member to *keep out* of his awareness his most dreaded qualities and ideas whilst keeping these qualities *retained* at a safe distance, by fixing them in the other. Because each responds to the other in terms of qualities that the other cannot acknowledge, a high level of disqualification and *mystification* characterises the *communication* processes within the relationship.

WYNNE, L. C. (1965), 'Some indications and contra-indications for exploratory family therapy' (in Boszormenyi-Nagy, I. and Framo, J. L. (eds), *Intensive Family Therapy*, Harper & Row, New York).

See also *Family myth, Fit (marital), Folie à deux*.

Training

Although the definition of psychotherapy training and its ability to produce effective psychotherapists are both uncertain, most psychotherapeutic approaches and orientations adopt some form of training in order to prepare people to practise their particular method. How far this requirement is viewed as essential varies widely however: for example, it would be impossible to practise as a psychoanalyst without first receiving a form of recognised training but it would be perfectly possible to set up as a *psychotherapist*, offering certain skills to the public without first under-

going any form of training. Those involved with the issue of the *regulation* of psychotherapists remain much concerned with defining what form of training is valid for what type of psychotherapy and to what extent this should be accepted as a legal requirement.

The older methods of psychotherapy have all developed well-organised training programmes, specific to their needs. Many of them require preliminary training in one of the major mental health disciplines. In the United States almost all schools of *psychoanalysis*, for example, require the candidate to undergo medical training first, although this is not the case in Britain. Psychoanalytic training is generally organised from private institutes and, with the exception of the Scottish Institute of Human Relations, these are almost entirely confined to London. They are responsible for establishing standards, curricula, selection procedures and passing out requirements. All psychoanalytic institutes require the candidate to undergo a *training analysis* of varying lengths. In Britain, Freudian training is organised by the British Psychoanalytic Society; Jungian training by the Society of Analytical Psychology; Kleinian training at the British Society and the Tavistock Clinic; and *child analysis* and *child psychotherapy* at the Tavistock Clinic, the Hampstead Clinic and the Society of Analytical Psychology. Training in *group analysis* and *group psychotherapy* is offered at the Institute of Group Analysis. *Behaviour therapy* is taught primarily to clinical psychologists within academic programmes leading to a qualification in clinical psychology. *Client-centred therapy* and *microskills* training both have well-established training programmes supported by extensive research. Beyond this, almost every other type of psychotherapy is taught via the medium of part-time or short courses that are mainly uncontrolled and unsystematic.

They may however be none the worse for that, since the research into the effectiveness of formal psychotherapy training is embryonic and most of the questions as well as most of the answers are unknown. Few approaches have been adequately researched except client-centred therapy, researched by Truax, Carkhuff and associates, and microskills training by Ivey. Both of these have emphasised a mixed experiential-didactic training approach, though Ivey's microskills training is more highly specific and behavioural. Truax and Carkhuff's work suggests that quite brief training programmes can be effective so long as appropriate people are selected in the first place. In *family therapy*, as well as in other methods, there is a continuing debate between those who emphasise the development of *therapist variables* and those who stress skill training more or less exclusively. (See Walrond-Skinner (1979) for a summary of the debate).

Usual components in any training course include didactic teaching on the theoretical model; the psychopathology that may be encountered in the relevant patient population; laboratory skills training; development of the therapist's self through some form of personal therapy in a one-to-one or group situation; and supervised clinical practice. Psychotherapy training generally seems to pay insufficient attention to the well-researched learning principles set out by workers such as Gagne (1965) or Holden (1965). Such aspects of learning as the use of frequent *reinforcement*, early *feedback, knowledge of results* and the integration of didactic and experiential learning is as important in psychotherapy training as in any other form of training.

Very little research has been carried out into the effectiveness of traditional psychotherapy or academic training programmes that include psychotherapy training. Such that there is is summarised by Hogan (1979). He finds that 'in virtually all studies that bear upon it, the findings have been uniformly negative. Simply put, traditional academic training programs seldom increase the therapeutic effectiveness of the average student.' Schmidt and Strong (1970) show that when the effectiveness of training is measured by the patient's evaluation of the trainee's performance, the results are also negative. Many practitioners feel that what is required is a separate training in psychotherapy, allowing for appropriate

specialisation in one or more methods, incorporating the findings of relevant research into optimal learning conditions and free from any other professional base such as medicine or clinical psychology. Some of these possibilites are discussed by Henry *et al.* (1971) and Holt (1971).

BRUCH, H. (1974), *Learning Psychotherapy* (Harvard University Press, Cambridge, Mass.).

CARKHUFF, R. R. (1981), *The Skilled Teacher: A System Approach to Teaching Skills* (Human Resource Development Press, Amherst, Mass.).

GAGNE, R. M. (1965), *The Conditions of Learning* (Holt, Rinehart & Winston, New York).

HENRY, W. E. *et al.* (1971), *The Fifth Profession: Becoming a Psychotherapist* (Jossey-Bass, San Francisco).

HESS, A. K. (ed.) (1980), *Psychotherapy Supervision: Theory, Research and Practice* (Wiley, New York).

HOGAN, D. B. (1979), *The Regulation of Psychotherapists* (4 vols, Ballinger, Cambridge, Mass.).

HOLDEN, D. (1965), *Principles of Training* Pergamon, London).

HOLT, R. R. (ed.) (1971), *New Horizon for Psychotherapy: Autonomy as a Profession* (International Universities Press, New York).

KASLOW, F. (ed.) (1984), *Psychotherapy with Psychotherapists* (Haworth Press, New York).

SCHMIDT, L. D. and STRONG, S. R. (1970), ' "Expert" and "inexpert" counselors' (*J. of Counseling Psychology*, vol. 17, pp. 115-18).

STOVER, L. and GUERNEY, B. G. (1967), 'The efficacy of training procedures for mothers and filial therapy' (*Psychotherapy: Theory, Research and Practice*, vol. 4, pp. 110-15).

TRUAX, C. B. and CARKHUFF, R. R. (1967), *Toward Effective Counseling and Psychotherapy: Training and Practice* (Aldine Press, Chicago),

WALROND-SKINNER, S. (1979), 'Education or training for family therapy?' (in Walrond-Skinner, S. (ed.), *Family and Marital Psychotherapy*, Routledge & Kegan Paul, London).

See also *Credibility, Experience, Expertness, Live supervision.*

Training analysis

A psychoanalysis undergone by a psycho-analytic trainee as a major part of his or her training in *psychoanalysis*. Originally, Freud did not distinguish very clearly between the necessity for trainees to be analysed by some-one else and the requirement to undergo a *self-analysis*. However, he always stressed the necessity for the trainee to gain *insight* into his own *unconscious* process in order to mitigate the effects of the *counter transference* when engaged in the psychoanalysis of others. In 1922, a training analysis was made mandatory for every would-be analyst. Balint (1948) has discussed some of the dilemmas inherent in making the analysis of a trainee thus 'task-focused' on the acquisition of a qualification. The idea of personal therapy for the would-be therapist has been adopted by many other schools of psychotherapy, logically adapted to the particular modality where possible. For example, group analysts favour a *group analysis* and family therapists have experimented with *family therapy* of a modified kind for the family therapist within his family unit.

BABOCK, C. G. (ed.) (1969), *Training Analysis: Report of the First Three-Institute Conference on Psychoanalytic Education* (Pittsburg Psycho-analytic Institute, Pittsburg).

BALINT, M. (1948), 'On the psychoanalytic training system' (*Int. J. of Psychoan.*, vol. 29, pp. 163-73).

BENEDEK, T. (1969), 'Training analysis – past, present and future' (*Int. J. of Psychoan.*, vol. 50, p. 437).

FREUD, S. (1910), 'The future prospects of psychoanalytic therapy' (*Standard Edition*, vol. 11, Hogarth Press, London).

FREUD, S. (1937), 'Analysis terminable and interminable' (*Standard Edition*, vol. 23, Hogarth Press, London).

KOVACS, B. (1936), 'Training and control analysis' (*Int. J. of Psychoan.*, vol. 17, Hogarth Press, London).

SACHS, H. (1947), 'Observations of a training analyst' (*Psychoanalytic Quarterly*, vol. 16, pp. 157-68).

WALLASTEIN, R. S. (1972), 'The future of psychoanalytic education' (*J. of Am. Psychoan. Assoc.*, vol. 20, pp. 591-606).

Transaction

A unit of *communication* which takes place between two people. The term was adopted from the work of Dewey and Bentley (1949) and is used to denote the treatment of events as processes that occur in the *context* of time and the environment. Transaction differs from interaction in that the concept of interaction implies two discrete and independently exist-ing objects that remain unchanged by their discourse with each other. In a transaction, on the other hand, both parties are changed by the process. In communication theory and the *systemic therapies* the term is therefore used to denote an ongoing, circular communication process that occurs between two parties. The term is used with a special meaning in *trans-actional analysis* and is defined as a *stimulus* and a related *response* that occurs between two persons' *ego states*. There are two basic levels of transaction: the social level which is overt, and the psychological level which is covert. There are three kinds of transactions: complement-ary (occurring between the same ego states in the sender and the recipient of the message, with congruency between communication levels); crossed (occurring between several different ego states, with congruency between communication levels); and ulterior (occur-ring between several different ego states and with lack of congruency between communica-tion levels). Ulterior transactions can be angular or duplex. An angular transaction involves three ego states and occurs when a message is sent from one ego state in the sender to two different ego states in the recipient. A duplex transaction involves four ego states, two in each person. Ulterior trans-actions provide the basis for *games*. From this set of concepts, several rules of communica-tion are derived. Complementary transactions are smooth and functional and, theoretically, they can proceed indefinitely. Crossed transactions usually result in breakdown of communication at least temporarily and ulterior transactions lead to complex pathological situations such as the *double bind*.

DEWEY, J. and BENTLEY, A. (1949), *Knowing and the Known* (Beacon Press, Boston).

Transactional analysis

A theory of personality and a method of psychotherapy developed during the 1950s by Berne (1961, 1966, 1972). Berne's ideas emerged from his psychoanalytic training and from his early work on intuition but transactional analysis quickly acquired an identity, language and theory of its own, based on the concept of the individual's *ego states*, their *structural analysis* and the *games* and *scripts* which are used as a defence against the demands of external reality. The term transactional analysis, although usually employed as a generic term to describe a method of psychotherapy, is more properly reserved for the analysis of *transactions* which occur between two or more individuals. Used in this latter sense, it is a technique *within* the generic method, alongside script analysis, games analysis and the structural analysis of the ego states.

Berne was at pains to develop a method that was relevant to curing patients in the shortest possible time. His theoretical framework demonstrates a clarity and simplicity which was borne out of his desire to involve the patient as an active partner with the therapist in the therapeutic endeavour. However, this clarity and common sense of some of transactional analysis's ideas has led to some odd oversimplifications. Intimacy and autonomy are seen as fleeting and illusive experiences; the 'constancy hypothesis' of the ego states' energy level is potentially as deterministic as Freud's psychoanalytic theories and the concept of the life script again has a deterministic ring.

Barnes (1977) analyses the current status of transactional analysis and its sub-division into three main schools: the classical school; the cathexis school of Schiff; and the redecision school of Goulding. Originally conducted mainly in the one-to-one situation, the more usual medium for transactional analysis is now a therapeutic group.

BARNES, G. (1977), *Transactional Analysis after Eric Berne* (Harper & Row, New York).

BERNE, E. (1961), *Transactional Analysis in Psychotherapy* (Grove Press, New York).

BERNE, E. (1966), *Principles of Group Treatment* (Grove Press, New York).

BERNE, E. (1972), *What Do You Say After You've Said Hello?* (Penguin, Harmondsworth).

BLAKENEY, R. N. (ed.) (1977), *Current Issues in Transactional Analysis* (Brunner/Mazel, New York).

GOULDING, R. (1972), 'New dimensions in transactional analysis' (in Sager, C. J. and Kaplan, H. S. (eds), *Progress in Group and Family Therapy*, Brunner/Mazel, New York).

KLEIN, M. (1980), *Lives People Live* (Wiley, Chichester).

PITMAN, E. (1984), *Transactional Analysis for Social Workers and Counsellors* (Routledge & Kegan Paul, London).

SCHIFF, J. L. *et al.* (1975), *The Cathexis Reader* (Harper & Row, New York).

STEINER, C. (1974), *Scripts People Live* (Grove Press, New York).

WOOLLAMS, S. and BROWN, M. (1978), *Transactional Analysis* (Huron Valley Press, Michigan).

Transfer of effects
See *Generalisation*.

Transference
The process whereby the patient displaces on to the therapist feelings, attitudes and attributes which properly belong to a significant attachment figure of the past, usually a parent, and responds to the therapist accordingly. Transference also refers to everything that is experienced in relation to the treatment arising from the *unconscious* phantasies that develop within the patient-therapist relationship. More widely, the term refers to the tendency to transfer on to any current relationship feelings and emotions that properly belong to a relationship with the past. To a greater or lesser extent, transference colours the real relationships of the present.

In its specific sense, the understanding and

resolution of transference is an essential ingredient of all psychoanalytic therapies. Freud originally explained its nature and regarded it as a primary tool in healing the patient. For Freud, the importance of the transference 'could hardly be overestimated' for it allows 'new editions of old conflicts' to be brought to consciousness within the patient-therapist relationship. This allows them to be relived, understood and then *worked through* to a more satisfactory resolution. To enable a transference to develop, the *analyst* must take care to present himself as a 'screen' or 'container' and to limit the presentation of him or herself as a real person. This also means avoiding offering transference gratifications. The transference is resolved through appropriate *interpretations* of its meaning by the therapist, enabling the repetition to be transformed into a memory and leaving the way open for a real relationship between therapist and patient to be established.

Jung (1929) originally agreed with Freud regarding the importance of the transference, calling it 'the alpha and omega of the analytic method'. But later he suggested that its importance in treatment is relative. Transferences were originally divided into a positive and a negative form. The former shows itself in an affectionate attachment to the therapist, with or without sexual overtones, the latter, in hostile rejection, passive *resistance* or compliance. Freud initially described both positive and negative transference as a resistance to the treatment and introduced the term *transference neurosis* to describe this development when the symptomatic elements of the neurosis were transformed into a relationship pattern with the analyst. Freud always maintained that the transference feelings were developed as an outcome of the patient's perception of some real aspect of the analyst. The concept of transference has been modified (Sandler 1983), especially by the writing of Heinmann (1956), to include the transference into the external relationship with the analyst of unconscious *phantasy*.

Transference is also recognised and used in some forms of *family therapy*, in *group analysis* and in most forms of individual treatment whether or not they are strictly psychoanalytically based. *Social learning theory* and hence the *behavioural therapies* either ignore transference or regard it as a special type of generalisation of an intense emotional experience to the relationship with the therapist. *Existential* and *humanistic* therapists are critical of the way in which transference can be used to avoid direct confrontation between patient and therapist and they argue that nothing that occurs in therapy is ever reducible to 'just transference'.

Quantitative research on transference is slight, considering the centrality of the concept within the psychoanalytic paradigm, and, according to Luborsky and Spence (1978), what research there is is seriously limited by its tenuous relationship to the concept. Luborsky *et al.* (1973) and Lower *et al.* (1973) have examined the extent of the transference as revealed over the course of treatment, using tape recordings of sessions. Graff and Luborsky (1977) examined the relationship of transference and resistance and found that those patients showing greater improvement displayed a pattern of increasing transference, with resistance staying at the same level or decreasing. Such a finding calls into question the assumption that successful resolution of the transference involves its eradication and replacement by a 'real' relationship. Luborsky (1977) has defined and measured a core conflictual relationship theme which he believes to be closely allied to the clinical concept of transference. He has shown that this core relationship theme deepened during treatment for both improvers and non-improvers. Gill and Hoffman (1976) have suggested that, contrary to Freud's warnings against early transference interpretations, the transference can be effectively interpreted in the early stages of treatment. In *focal psychotherapy*, Malan (1976) has shown that appropriate transference interpretations are correlated with positive therapeutic outcome.

FREUD, S. (1905), 'Fragment of an analysis of a case of hysteria' (*Standard Edition*, vol. 7, Hogarth Press, London).

TRANSFERENCE NEUROSIS

FREUD, S. (1915), 'Observations on transference love' (*Standard Edition*, vol. 12, Hogarth Press, London).

GILL, M. (1982), *Analysis of Transference* (vols 1 and 2, International Universities Press, New York).

GILL, M. and HOFFMAN, I. (1976), 'Definitions and scoring of latent and related transference behaviors in psychoanalytic sessions' (paper delivered to the American Psychoanalytic Association, 1976).

GRAFF, H. and LUBORSKY, L. (1977), 'Long-term trends in transference and resistance' (*J. of the Am. Psychoan. Assoc.*, vol. 25, pp. 471-90).

HEINMANN, D. (1956), 'Dynamics of transference interpretations' (*International Journal of Psychoanalysis*, vol. 37, pp. 303-10).

JUNG, C. G. (1929), 'Problems of modern psychotherapy' (*Collected Works*, vol. 16, Routledge & Kegan Paul, London).

JUNG, C. G. (1946), 'The psychology of transference' (ibid.).

KLEIN, M. (1952), 'The origins of transference' (in *Envy and Gratitude and Other Works*, Hogarth Press, London).

LOWER, R. B. *et al.* (1973), 'An experimental examination of transference' (*Archives of General Psychiatry*, vol. 29, pp. 738-41).

LUBORSKY, L. (1977), 'Measuring a pervasive psychic structure in psychotherapy: the core conflictual relationship theme' (in Freedman, N. (ed.), *Communicative Structures and Psychic Structures*, Plenum Press, New York).

LUBORSKY, L. *et al.* (1973), 'A clinical quantitative examination of consensus on the concept of transference' (*Archives of General Psychiatry*, vol. 29, pp. 69-75).

LUBORSKY, L. and SPENCE, D. A. (1978), 'Quantitative research on psychoanalytic therapy' (in Bergin, A. E. and Garfield, S. L. (eds), *Handbook of Psychotherapy and Behavior Change*, Wiley, New York).

MALAN, D. H. (1976), *Toward the Validation of Dynamic Psychotherapy* (Plenum Press, London).

SANDLER, J. (1983), 'Reflections on some relations between psychoanalytic concepts and psychoanalytic practice' (*International Journal of Psychoanalysis*, vol. 64, pp. 35-46).

SANDLER, J. *et al.* (1970), 'Basic psychoanalytic concepts III: transference' (*Brit. J. of Psychiatry*, vol. 116, pp. 667-72).

Transference neurosis

The term is used in two senses. First, it was originally used by Freud to describe a cluster of disorders, anxiety hysteria, conversation hysteria and obsessional neurosis which were different from the so-called narcissistic neurosis, i.e. psychoses. In his lecture on *transference*, Freud (1917) explains the reason for the use of this term, by pointing out that in these three disorders, transference possesses an extraordinary degree of importance whereas he thought that in the narcissistic neuroses, transferences did not develop. The second definition is the one which is commonly meant by the term today: an artificial development arising within the psychoanalytic treatment, whereby all the features of the patient's *symptoms* are reproduced but within his relationship with the *analyst*. Thus, as Freud (1914) pointed out, the patient produces 'new editions of old conflicts' within the transference, where they become susceptible to treatment. The development of a transference neurosis is therefore considered to be an essential part of the curative process in psychoanalytic treatment.

Jung (1946) disagreed with Freud, believing that the neurosis now re-enacted within the transference is 'neither new, nor artificial, nor created: it is the same old neurosis', but it is now being worked out in relation to the analyst. In relation to *child analysis*, Anna Freud (1947) believed that, although a transference developed, no transference neurosis could occur, since the parents in reality were still the child's primary love objects. Klein (1932), however, disagreed, and concluded that a full transference does occur in children and in a manner that is analogous to that which occurs in adults.

FREUD, A. (1947), *The Psychoanalytic Treatment of Children* (Hogarth Press, London).

FREUD, S. (1914), 'Remembering, repeating and working through' (*Standard Edition*, vol. 12, Hogarth Press, London).
FREUD, S. (1917), 'Introductory lectures on psychoanalysis' (*Standard Edition*, vol. 16, Hogarth Press, London).
JUNG, C. G. (1946), 'The psychology of the transference' (*Collected Works*, vol. 16, Routledge & Kegan Paul, London).
KLEIN, M. (1932), *The Psychoanalysis of Children* (Hogarth Press, London).
LOEWALD, H. (1971), 'The transference neurosis: comments on the concept and the phenomenon' (*J. of the Am. Psychoan. Assoc.*, vol. 19, pp. 54-66).
WEINSHELL, E. M. (1971), 'The transference neurosis: a survey of the literature' (*J. of the Am. Psychoan. Assoc.*, vol. 19, pp. 67-88).

Transgenerational family therapy

Approaches to *family therapy* which emphasise the importance of including at least three generations as part of the *unit of treatment* for some or all of the treatment process. Advocates suggest that the most economical way of treating current dysfunction is to enable the *identified patient* or marital pair to *de-triangulate*, resolve or distance themselves from the problems that have occurred in earlier generations. Current problems are viewed as a thematic reflection of the past, inherited both through *conscious* repetition and through *unconscious* phenomena such as the *family transference* and the *family myth*. Parental loyalty and guilt in relation to their families of origin is transferred and *acted out* through the children. Different transgenerational family theorists suggest different approaches to treatment. For example, Bowen (1978) and Lieberman (1979) help individual family members to explore their position within their *family constellation* and gain *insight* into the antecedents of their difficulties through the use of a *genogram*. They also encourage them to make contact with and achieve *differentiation* from a wide range of family members through the process of *coaching*. Framo (1982) uses *multiple couples therapy* and also includes individual sessions with each

spouse and his/her family of origin. Boszormenyi-Nagy (Boszormenyi-Nagy 1981), who currently describes his approach as contextual family therapy, helps family members identify the multigenerational legacy, loosen the chains of invisible loyalty and explore new a-symptomatic behavioural options. Paul (Paul and Grosser 1965) uses *cross confrontation* to enable the family to mourn effectively for its past. Transgenerational family therapy draws on the *interpersonal school* of *psychoanalysis* as well as on psychoanalytic and *object relations* theory.

BOSZORMENYI-NAGY, I. and SPARK, G. (1973), *Invisible Loyalties: Reciprocity in International Family Therapy* (Harper & Row, New York).
BOSZORMENYI-NAGY, I. (1981), 'Contextual family therapy' (in Gurman, A. S. and Kniskern, D. P. (eds), *Handbook of Family Therapy*, Brunner/Mazel, New York).
BOWEN, M. (1978), *Family Therapy in Clinical Practice* (Jason Aronson, New York).
FRAMO, J. L. (1982), *Explorations in Marital and Family Therapy: Selected Papers of James L. Framo* (Springer, New York).
HALL, C. M. (1981) *The Bowen Family Theory: Its Uses* (Jason Aronson, New York).
LIEBERMAN, S. (1979), *Transgenerational Family Therapy* (Croom Helm, London).
PAUL, N. L. and GROSSER, G. H. (1965), 'Operational mourning and its role in conjoint family therapy' (*Community Mental Health J.*, vol. 1, pp. 339-45).

See also *Differentiation of self scale, Triangle, Triangulation, Undifferentiated ego mass*.

Transitional object

A term introduced by D. W. Winnicott to describe the infant's first possession and the way in which he or she uses it to develop in understanding from subjective experience based on infantile omnipotence to that which is objectively perceived through acknowledging a separate external world. Winnicott suggests that the baby negotiates the 'transitional' or intermediate phase between primary *narcissism* and *object relations* by becoming attached to a material possession such as a piece of blanket, rag or other soft object. The transitional object has in the child's possesson the paradoxical quality of being 'me' and 'not-me' at the same time. It acts as a defence against *annihilation* anxiety and is especially important to the child at bedtime, when lonely or during periods of *regression* to an earlier phase of development. Winnicott suggests that the transitional object starts to be used between four and twelve months and may continue during the first few years of life. The use of transitional objects is a normal part of psychic growth and development.

WINNICOTT, D. W. (1953), 'Transitional objects and transitional phenomena' (*Int. J. of Psychoan.*, vol. 34, pp. 77-89).
WINNICOTT, D. W. (1971), *Playing and Reality* (Penguin, Harmondsworth).

Transparency

The ability to be open, authentic and genuine in relationship with others. The term is used by writers within the *humanistic psychology* tradition, who stress the need for the therapist to be non-manipulative in his dealings with the patient and de-emphasising the use of technique in preference to *relationship factors*. Jourard (1971) describes the 'transparent self' as one who is sufficiently free of self-deception and defensive manoeuvres to be able to disclose himself fully to others. Like *congruence*, *genuineness* and *authenticity*, transparency on the part of the therapist is believed to promote *self-disclosure* on the part of the patient. In a factor analytic study of relationship variables, Lietaer (1974) found a 'transparency' factor which appears to be indistinguishable from Barrett-Leonard's (1962) congruency dimension.

BARRETT-LEONARD, G. T. (1962), 'Dimensions of therapist response as causal factors in therapeutic change' (*Psychological Monographs*, vol. 76, no. 562).
JOURARD, S. (1971), *The Transparent Self* (Van Nostrand Reinhold, New York).
LIETAER, G. (1974), 'The relationship as

experienced by clients and therapist in client-centred and psychoanalytically oriented therapy' (paper presented at fifth annual meeting of the Society for Psychotherapy Research, Denver).

Transpersonal psychology

Approaches to therapy which focus on spiritual, religious or mystical experiences, on altered states of consciousness and on questions relating to the value of life and the meaning of existence. Anthony Sutich (Tart 1975), the founder of the *Journal of Transpersonal Psychology*, identifies transpersonal psychology as the 'fourth force' in the field, following *psychoanalysis, behaviour therapy* and *humanistic psychology*. Eastern religions have provided much of the source material. But some precursors are also to be found in the West. Both Augustine and Thomas Aquinas can be considered as early thinkers who combined a psychological awareness with a spiritual and philosophical focus. More recently, William James (1958) anticipated the claims of current transpersonal psychology that altered states of consciousness can be induced and can give access to special knowledge which cannot be gained through ordinary *conscious* processes.

Jung developed many ideas that are centrally relevant to transpersonal psychology, including the *collective unconscious* and the *archetype*, and his whole approach to psychotherapy acknowledges the value and importance of the spiritual dimension of human existence. *Individuation*, for example, includes the re-integration of the spiritual as well as the psychic. Spiritual wholeness is also an aspect of some *client-centred therapy* and some *existential therapy*. Current approaches which can be included in transpersonal psychology are the humanistic approaches to *self-actualisation* which result in *peak experiences*; *psychosynthesis*; *meditation*; spiritual healing and *parapsychology*.

BOORSTEIN, S. and SPEETH, K. (eds) (1978), *Explorations in Transpersonal Psychotherapy* (Jason Aronson, New York).
FRANK, J. D. (1974), *Persuasion and Healing*

(Schocken Books, New York).

JAMES, W. (1958), *Varieties of Religious Experience* (New American Library, New York).

TART, C. T. (ed.) (1975), *Transpersonal Psychologies* (Harper & Row, New York).

WALSH, R. and BORN, E. (1980), *Beyond Ego: Transpersonal Dimensions in Psychology* (Tatcher, Los Angeles).

WATTS, A. (1973), *Psychotherapy, East and West* (Penguin, Harmondsworth).

See also *Synchronicity*.

Trauma

Literal Greek meaning wound. A term derived from physical medicine and applied to psychology. As in medicine, it implies the idea of violent shock, severe wounding and the consequences of both for the individual's psychic functioning. Freud introduced the concept of psychic trauma to describe real or imaginary incidents which occurred during childhood and whose effects crucially influence the individual's subsequent life and his predisposition for coping with stress. Freud (1940) believed that all neurotic illnesses are the result of early trauma. The degree of traumatic damage in adult life is dependent on the interaction between severity of the stimulus and the predisposition of the personality to withstand the shock of the external event. Although, like the term *crisis*, trauma is used rather loosely to indicate either the external event or its intrapersonal repercussions, it is best reserved for describing the inter-relationship of the first of these to the second. Thus, in the psychoanalytic sense, the term refers to the traumatic event and its intrapsychic repercussions, brought about when the psyche's protective barrier is immature or has been breached. As defined by Caplan, the term crisis is very close in meaning.

FREUD, S. (1940), 'An outline of psycho-analysis (*Standard Edition*, vol. 23, Hogarth Press, London).

FURST, S. (ed.) (1967), *Psychic Trauma* (Basic Books, New York).

Treatment barrier

Term introduced by Scott (1973) to describe the obstacles to treatment which are created by the cultural view of mental illness prevailing in Western society. Scott uses the term to include the use of the *medical model* for describing non-medical conditions and the process of *labelling* one member of a family, group, etc., as sick. This process gets in the way of redefining the problem in terms of interpersonal relationships rather than individual pathology, and thus becomes a barrier to treatment.

SCOTT, R. D. (1973), 'The treatment barrier', parts 1 and 2 (*Brit. J. of Med. Psychology*, vol. 46, pp. 45-67).

See also *Attribution theory, Identified patient, Praxis, Sick role*.

Triangle

Term used by Bowen (1966) to describe a threesome relationship within a *system*. Bowen uses it to describe the basic building block of any emotional system and asserts that the triangle is the smallest stable relationship system, a pair only being stable for a short time until some form of stress or *crisis* induces it to involve a third person. When tension in this triangle becomes too great, others become involved and become a series of interlocking triangles. Over time, the emotional forces within a system move from one interlocking triangle to another and they remain constantly in motion within and between the triangles. Bowen used the term triangle to distinguish his meaning from that of triad used in *communication* theory. Although there is much overlap between the concepts and the term triangle is used equally by Minuchin (1974) and sometimes by Haley too, Bowen tends to view the triangle as the inevitable lowest common denominator of system structure, whereas Haley and others view the triad as uncompromisingly pathogenic. Moreover, Bowen views triangles and the process of *triangulation* as a much more fluid process with a sense of constant motion and flux in the interlocking triangular forms. Bowen distinguishes between 'normal' *dysfunctional* triangles in terms of their fluidity/rigidity and not, as do the communication theorists, in terms of their presence or absence. Bowen views therapy as an effort to unlock individual family members from a rigid position within a triangle and since triangles interlock and are therefore reactive to one another, change that occurs in a person's position in a distant triangle from the past will have a positive effect on current triangular relationships.

BOWEN, M. (1966), 'The use of family therapy in clinical practice' (*Comprehensive Psychiatry*, vol 7, pp. 345–74).
FOGARTY, T. (1970), 'Triangles' (*The Family*, vol. 2, pp. 11–19).
MINUCHIN, S. (1974), *Families and Family Therapy* (Tavistock, London).

See also *De-triangulation, Homeostasis, Transgenerational family therapy, Undifferentiated ego mass.*

Triangulation
The process whereby a dyadic *sub-system* draws in a third party as a means of diffusing conflict between the pair. The process is described by Minuchin (1974), Minuchin *et al.* (1978) and by Bowen (1966), but is used widely by many writers on *systems* and *family therapy*. It occurs between family members such as the parental sub-system's triangulation of a child, parent or lover, and can be regarded as a systemic defence against conflict resolution. Where the third party is a child, one parent will side with the child against the other parent, so that both the triangled child and the excluded parent experience intense stress. Minuchin *et al.* (1978) regard triangulation, along with *detouring* and *coalition* as one of the three strategies used to create and maintain a rigid triad in being.

Triangulation also occurs between the family and an outside helper, whereby the therapist, for example, is triangulated into a marital sub-system and used as a homeostatic *regulator* instead of an agent of change. This type of triangulation is an ingredient in most systems therapy, although it is particularly potent and obvious in *conjoint marital therapy*

where the therapeutic system is literally a triangle.

BOWEN, M. (1966), 'The use of family theory in clinical practice' (*Comprehensive Psychiatry*, vol. 7, pp. 345-74).
MINUCHIN, S. (1974), *Families and Family Therapy* (Tavistock, London).
MINUCHIN, S. and FISHMAN, H. C. (1981), *Family Therapy Techniques* (Harvard University Press, Cambridge, Mass.).
MINUCHIN, S. *et al.* (1978), *Psychosomatic Families* (Harvard University Press, Cambridge, Mass.).
WOODWARD, J. B. and WEST, L. W. (1979), 'A model for observing and classifying triangulation phenomena in groups' (*Int. J. of Group Psychotherapy*, vol. 29, pp. 149-62).

True self
A term introduced by Winnicott (1960) to describe the optimal adaptation and development of early infancy attained by a baby who is nurtured by a good enough mother. If the environment is not sufficiently facilitative and impinges on the infant's omnipotence, the infant may develop a *false self* instead.

WINNICOTT, D. W. (1960), 'Ego distortion in terms of true and false self' (in *The Maturational Processes and the Facilitating Environment*, Hogarth Press, London, 1965).

U

Umwelt
Literal German meaning 'world around'. A term introduced into biology by von Vexkull (1909) to describe the subjective environment of an organism. Its use was later extended to the subjectively meaningful psycho-social environment of an individual or group. The term is used in social psychology and applied to *existential psychotherapy* by Binswanger, who viewed it as one mode of being-in-the-world.

HARROW, R. (1979), *Social Being: A Theory for*

Social Psychology (Blackwell, Oxford).
VON VEXKULL, J. (1909), *Umwelt und Inwelt der Tiere* (Springer, Berlin).

See also *Context, Dasein, Eigenwelt, Mitwelt.*

Unbalancing

An intervention technique in *systems* and *family therapy* the aim of which is described by Minuchin and Fishman (1981) as change in the hierarchical relationship of members of a *sub-system*. The therapist challenges the *dysfunctional* structure of the system by taking sides with individual members or with one sub-system against another and switching his allegiance in unpredictable ways. By doing so, he enables *scapegoated* and weaker members to negotiate for themselves a more favourable position in the system, all members to experiment with new role relationships, dysfunctional *coalitions* to dissolve and the rigid *homeostasis* of the system to give way and allow change and growth to occur. Unbalancing a system requires the therapist to work from a proximate, participatory and non-neutral position and makes great demands on his agility and on his ability to move in and out of relationships with apparently hostile and therefore threatening family members.

Minuchin and Fishman describe three categories of unbalancing techniques. First, *affiliation* with family members, whereby the therapist affiliates with a weaker member, strengthening his position in the group; or with a dominant member, to escalate to the point of absurdity his or her control of the system. This may involve reversing the family's view of *causality* and 'blaming' a family member who is considered to be the victim of someone else's actions. Second, alternating affiliation, whereby the therapist alternates his affiliation with conflicting sub-systems to diffuse their competition and promote a new type of cooperation between them (for example, the therapist might support the parent's right to make parental decisions and the adolescent's right to question them and negotiate new decision making rules). Third, ignoring family members, whereby the therapist refocuses

attention away from a dominant or demanding member. He does this either by a process akin to *extinction* techniques, i.e. by withdrawing the *reinforcement* of his interest and acceptance of that member; or by an active intervention in which the therapist discusses and/or criticises or supports the behaviour of the dominant person in his presence, in discussion with other members of the group. Both the passive and active forms of ignoring have the effect of realigning the coalitions in the group and temporarily or permanently excluding the target member.

MINUCHIN, S. and FISHMAN, H. D. (1981), *Family Therapy Techniques* (Harvard University Press, Cambridge, Mass.).

See also *Alliance, Collusion, Confrontation, Intensification, Neutrality, Symmetrical.*

Unconditional positive regard

One of the *core conditions* postulated by Rogers as a necessary and sufficient ingredient of therapy and used interchangeably with non-possessive warmth. According to Rogers, unconditional positive regard is manifest when a 'therapist communicates to his client a deep and geniune caring for him as a person with human potentialities, a caring uncontaminated by evaluations of his thoughts, feelings or behaviour' (Rogers 1967).

A major part of the training for *client-centred therapy* is the development of the capacity to convey unconditional positive regard for the client. The client is valued, accepted and 'prized' for himself regardless of his behaviour. This conceptual distinction between the client's 'self' and his behaviour lies at the centre of Rogers's thinking about therapy but Schmitt (1980) suggests that the ensuing assumption that the client's self and his behaviour be treated differently contains a paradox and is more problematic to adhere to than seems at first sight.

The central element in unconditional positive regard is its *unconditional* aspect and, unlike in some behavioural treatments, when the response is used to reinforce desired behaviour, unconditional positive regard is thought to be an unvarying necessary condition for a client-centred therapist to adopt. The research into its effectiveness and correlation with *outcome* is discussed by Mitchell *et al.* (1977) and by Gurman (1977).

GURMAN, A. (1977), 'The patient's perception of the therapeutic relationship' (in *Effective Psychotherapy*, Pergamon Press, New York).
MITCHELL, K. M. *et al.* (1977), 'A reappraisal of the therapeutic effectiveness of accurate empathy, non-possessive warmth and genuineness' (ibid.).
ROGERS, C. (1967), *The Therapeutic Relationship and its Impact* (Greenwood Press, Westport, Conn.).
SCHMITT, J. P. (1980), 'Unconditional positive regard: the hidden paradox' (*Psychotherapy: Theory, Research and Practice*, vol. 17, pp. 237-43).

Unconditioned response

A behavioural event which follows from an *unconditioned stimulus* independently and unconditional upon learning. In *classical conditioning* theory, the response is seen as autonomic, and derived from the innate sensory physiological processes that are not governed by learning. Thus, the hunger drive in Pavlov's dogs acted as the innate stimulus to produce the unconditioned response of salivation.

Unconditioned stimulus

A cue which provokes a *response* independently and unconditional upon learning. In *classical conditioning* Watson and Rayner (1920) showed that a young child's fear of loud noises could be *generalised* by conditioning to a white rat. In this example, the loud noise was the unconditioned stimulus because it existed independently of learning promoted by the experimenter.

WATSON, J. and RAYNER, R. (1920), 'Conditioned emotional reactions' (*J. of Experimental Psychology*, vol. 3, pp. 1-14).

Unconscious

The term is used both as an adjective and as a noun in psychoanalytic theory. Used adjectively, the term is a description applied to certain mental contents which are not currently within the individual's consciousness. These include both the contents of the *preconscious* and the system unconscious. Used as a noun, the term refers to the system unconscious, that region of the mind which remains unavailable to the individual, until it emerges into consciousness through certain products (*dreams*), processes (*word associations, free association* and *parapraxes*), or behaviours (*symptoms*).

As Ellenberger (1970) describes, the concept of the unconscious, which had for centuries found a place in both Eastern and Western mystical writing, became extremely popular as a research area amongst psychologists during the last decades of the nineteenth century. Schopenhauer and von Hartnan, amongst others, discussed it from a philosophical point of view. Others such as Leibniz drew close to a psychological view by suggesting that many small 'perceptions' lay beneath the threshold of consciousness, whilst Herbart developed a *dynamic* concept of interchange between the *conscious* and the perceptions and representations that he believed existed beneath consciousness. Experimental approaches to the study of the unconscious were introduced by Fechner and by Galton, who devised the *word association* test which Jung was to use in his early psychotherapeutic work, as a means of gaining access to the unconscious. With the work of these and many other researchers, the problem of the unconscious had been approached from several points of view before Freud's work began.

Building on this work by others, the empirical discovery of the clinical importance of the unconscious must nevertheless be ascribed to Freud, and it became the cornerstone of his whole theoretical structure and clinical practice. Freud used the term in two senses: first in a descriptive sense to mean whatever lay outside the field of consciousness; and second in a dynamic sense to 'designate not only latent ideas in general, but especially ideas with a certain dynamic character, ideas keeping apart from consciousness in spite of their intensity and activity' (Freud 1912). It is in the second sense that the unconscious is described by Freud as part of his *topographical model* of the *mental apparatus* and, as such, it exists at the deepest level of the *psyche* beneath the preconscious and the conscious. As elaborated by Freud in his *structural model*, each of the three psychic *agencies* lies partly within the realm of the unconscious, although only the *id* exists entirely within it. The contents of the unconscious are made up of *phantasies* and images or representations which make their way into consciousness through symbolic products, processes and behaviours. Some of these contents exist already in the unconscious and some of them are derived from conscious material that has been *repressed*. Its mode of operation is through *primary process* and the working out of the pleasure principle.

The enormous importance attributed by Freud to the role of the unconscious in determining the functioning of every aspect of the individual's life changes somewhat in Freud's later writings. The unconscious is viewed more as a quality of mental phenomena than as a major region of the mind and conscious and preconscious processes grow in importance and emphasis. The vital role of the unconscious is however preserved and is endorsed by Jung, Klein and all psychoanalytic writers, though in varying degrees. Adler, for example, while believing that early childhood events unconsciously determined the adult's style of life, did not accept the idea of continuous inner conflict generated between the contents of the unconscious and the conscious. Jung (1954) called the unconscious 'hypothetical' because, by definition, it is not amenable to direct observation and can therefore only be inferred. He expanded Freud's concept to include both a personal and a collective aspect. The personal unconscious is manifested in *complexes* and *imagos* and the *collective unconscious* is structured by *archetypes*.

The importance ascribed to the role of an unconscious aspect of the psyche is highly determinative of the view taken of symptoms and psychopathology in general. For psychoanalytic therapists, the root to understanding and treating psychological problems lies through the unconscious and symptoms are viewed as conscious manifestations of unconscious conflict. The term *depth psychology* is used to describe psychoanalytic processes because of their primary focus on the unconscious or deepest layer of the psyche. For behavioural, cognitive and strategic therapists, the unconscious may or may not exist but it is in any case largely redundant as an explanatory principle in the understanding of and treatment of psychological problems. Therapists from other schools and approaches are distinguishable in an important way by the view they take of the role of unconscious processes.

ELLENBERGER, H. F. (1970), *The Discovery of the Unconscious* (Allen Lane, London).

FREUD, S. (1900), 'The interpretation of dreams' (*Standard Edition*, vols 4 and 5, Hogarth Press, London).

FREUD, S. (1912), 'A note on the unconscious in psychoanalysis' (*Standard Edition*, vol. 12, Hogarth Press, London).

FREUD, S. (1915), 'The unconscious' (*Standard Edition*, vol. 14, Hogarth Press, London).

JUNG, C. (1954), 'The practice of psychotherapy' (*Collected Works*, vol. 16, Routledge & Kegan Paul, London).

WHYTE, L. L. (1962), *The Unconscious Before Freud* (Tavistock, London).

Undifferentiated ego mass

Term introduced by Bowen (1966) to describe the fusion of identity and *ego* functioning that is present in many *dysfunctional* families. Bowen describes it as 'a conglomerate emotional oneness that exists at all levels of intensity'. In severely undifferentiated *systems* or under high levels of stress, family members may feel that they 'know' each other's thoughts, experience each other's *phantasies*, and dream each other's *dreams*, etc. The discomfort of the fusion is expressed in marital conflict, generational conflict or in the production of *symptoms* in one or more members. The *goal* of treatment is reached through *coaching* individual family members in developing their *differentiation* from the ego fusion of the group.

BOWEN, M. (1966), 'The use of family theory in clinical practice' (*Comprehensive Psychiatry*, vol. 7, pp. 345-74).

See also *Folie à deux, Symbiosis*.

Unit of treatment
The target of therapeutic or consultative intervention. Prior to the introduction of group and systems treatments, the unit of treatment was, rather obviously, the individual patient. The differential use of other *modalities*, viz. *group psychotherapy, family therapy, marital therapy, network intervention* and *social therapy*, means that the unit of treatment may be a *stranger group*, the family *system*, the marital relationship, a *network*, a *therapeutic community*, a staff *team*, a community group, or a combination of any of these as well as, or instead of, one or more individuals.

In each treatment approach, a decision has to be made as to which unit of treatment is most appropriate in helping to achieve the *goals* of therapy. In *family therapy*, the unit of treatment may be the marital relationship or an individual family member; in marital therapy, it may be the husband and wife as individuals in *concurrent sessions*; in *child psychotherapy*, it may be the child and his parents in *conjoint* sessions, etc. In some methods, for example *network intervention, multiple impact therapy, conciliation* work, etc., there may be particularly complex problems involved in deciding which sub-groups are to be the primary target of therapeutic intervention and in what order of priority.

Several different yardsticks have been used for deciding upon the unit of treatment. Aponte (1976) has suggested the concept of *context* replication. When the dynamics in the family group are replicated in another adjacent system, for example the school, the unit of treatment should be the interface between these two social systems. Skynner (1971) has suggested the concept of the *minimum sufficient*

network as a means of deciding on the unit of treatment, and Palazzoli *et al.* (1980) have drawn attention to the fact that the referring person may need to be included in the unit of treatment in order to prevent him or her acting as a homeostatic force against change. When the unit of treatment has been agreed between therapist and client(s), it may be seen as part of the *contract*, and failure to maintain this unit as the target of intervention (except by mutual agreement and in response to the changing needs of the therapy) may indicate *resistance* by the client(s) and *collusion* with that resistance on the part of the therapist.

APONTE, H. (1976), 'The family-school interview: an eco-structural approach' (*Family Process*, vol. 15, pp. 303-11).
PALAZZOLI, M. S. *et al.* (1980), 'The problem of the referring person' (*J. of Marital and Family Therapy*, vol. 6, pp. 3-9).
SKYNNER, A. C. R. (1971), 'The minimum sufficient network' (*Social Work Today*, vol. 9, pp. 3-7).

See also *Absent member manoeuvre, Diagnosis*.

V

Valence
Term introduced by Lewin from chemistry into *field theory* and used by him to describe the power of an object to attract the individual (by exerting a positive valence) or repel him (by exerting a negative valence). If conflict is experienced when the individual is attracted by two mutually exclusive positive valences or if he has to choose between two negative ones, he may try to solve the dilemma by not choosing or by what Lewin describes as 'leaving the field'.

The term is also used by Bion to describe the capacity for instantaneous, involuntary combination between individuals in a group in order to act on a *basic assumption*.

BION, W. R. (1961), *Experiences in Groups* (Tavistock, London).
LEWIN, K. (1935), *A Dynamic Theory of Personality* (McGraw-Hill, New York).

See also *Approach-avoidance conflict*.

Vector

Term used by Lewin in *field theory* to describe the directed line of motivation between the individual and the object of his movement. A vector tends to produce movement toward or away from objects according to the *valence* of the object. The term is also used by Howells (1976) to describe an influence coming from the environment which impinges upon a family.

HOWELLS, J. G. (1976), *Principles of Family Psychiatry* (Pitman Medical, London).
LEWIN, K. (1935), *A Dynamic Theory of Personality* (McGraw-Hill, New York).

See also *Vector therapy*.

Vector therapy

A variety of *social therapy* described by Howells (1976) which is designed to re-adjust the pattern of emotional forces in the individual or family's lifespace to bring about a lessening of frustration and an increase in satisfaction and emotional well-being. This is achieved by the therapist bringing his influence to bear on the patient's environment. In so far as this involves the patient's immediate psycho-social environment, the family, the method is indistinguishable from *family therapy*. It may also, however, include such interventions as organising substitute care for a child or for a woman where physical violence is occurring; facilitating custody or access arrangements in families where there has been separation or divorce; intervening in the school situation where conflict between a teacher and child cannot be resolved; helping to organise job opportunities or intervening to support the patient at his place of work; and linking the patient with community resources such as playgroups, day care, financial benefits, welfare rights, holiday provisions, GP ancilliary services, family planning, etc., etc. Howells suggests that vector therapy, which takes place beyond the *interview* situation, should often go hand in hand with ordinary psychotherapy. Although Howells coined the term vector

therapy for this form of intervention, it is hard to see how it differs from good routine social work, community work or other forms of social *therapy* practised within the community by a range of professionally trained mental health workers.

HOWELLS, J. G. (1976), *Principles of Family Psychiatry* (Pitman Medical, London).

Vegetotherapy

See *Reichian therapy*.

Video tape

See *Audio visual equipment*.

W

Watson, John Broadus (1878-1958)

John Broadus Watson was born in Greenville, South Carolina. He gained his PhD in psychology from the University of Chicago in 1903, studying under J. R. Angell. After teaching for a period at the University of Chicago, he was appointed professor of psychology at Johns Hopkins University in 1908. The turning point in his career came in 1913 when he published a paper entitled 'Psychology as the behaviorist sees it' which marked the beginning of *behaviourism* and an entirely new approach to the understanding of human functioning. In 1919 he published *Psychology from the Standpoint of a Behaviorist* in which he further elaborated his views. In 1920 he was forced to resign his chair at Johns Hopkins because of his divorce. During the next twenty years he worked for private advertising firms and made important contributions to the psychological approach to advertising. He also devoted time to writing for popular journals and in 1928 his *Psychological Care of Infant and Child* became a best seller.

Whole object

See *Object*.

Wholeness
See *Holism, Nonsummativity.*

Will therapy
A method of psychotherapy introduced by Otto Rank (1936). Rank was greatly influenced by his original training in *psychoanalysis* and by his close association with Freud. However, he replaced the Freudian emphasis on the *Oedipus complex* as the source psychic conflict by his concept of *birth trauma.* Rank stresses creativity as a basic human need and views the task of therapy as a process of freeing the client from his separation anxiety and fears so that he can take responsibility for his own choices in life and for his own creative self-expression. He emphasises the individual's will as 'a positive guiding organisation and integration of the self, which utilises creativity as well as inhibits and controls the instinctual drives'.

Therapy consists in helping the client return to his initial birth trauma, accept his separateness and discover ways of taking risks and taking charge of his life. He focused more on the current events of the session than most therapists and set a definite time limit to treatment, which was of shorter duration than orthodox analysis. He believed that the client has to be helped to accept that 'there is no other equality possible than the equal right of every individual to become and to be himself, which actually means to accept his own difference and have it accepted by others'. Rankian will therapy does not have many adherents *per se*, but Rank's ideas have been influential in social work practice as well as within the different approaches to *humanistic psychology.*

KARPF, F. B. (1953), *The Psychology and Psychotherapy of Otto Rank* (Greenwood Press, Westport. Conn.).
RANK, OTTO (1936) *Will Therapy* (Knopf, New York).

See also *Primal therapy, Rebirthing.*

Winnicott, Donald, W. (1896-1971)
Paediatrician and psychoanalyst, Donald Winnicott was the elder son of Sir Frederick Winnicott, Lord Mayor of Plymouth. After medical training, Winnicott worked as an assistant physician at Paddington Green Children's Hospital from 1923, remaining there for forty years. During the early 1930s, he moved into *psychoanalysis*, undertaking his *training analysis* with James Strachey and Joan Rivière. He qualified in the mid 1930s and for the remainder of his life he concentrated on the integration of his original paediatric discipline with his psychoanalytic work. Some of the concepts he introduced into psychoanalytic theory included an understanding of the child's *transitional object*; the need for a *good enough mother*, an understanding of the individual's *true* and *false self* and the importance of maternal holding and mirroring of the infant's emotional states. Although he worked with adults, and in particular with analysts in training, most of Winnicott's major contributions were made in relation to his work with children. His introduction of the *squiggle game* became an important tool in gaining an understanding of the child's *internal world.* Although greatly influenced by the work of Melanie *Klein*, Winnicott is usually considered to be a part of the *British school* of psychoanalysis. However, it might be more accurate to consider him as an original and independent thinker, unattached to any of the main subgroupings. He married his second wife Clare, a social worker, in 1951 and this broadened his influence into the field of social work and related disciplines. He was twice president of the British Psychoanalytic Society and made considerable contributions to the literature of psychoanalysis and *child analysis*. His most important works include *Collected Papers: Through Paediatrics to Psychoanalysis* (1948), *The Maturational Processes and the Facilitating Environment* (1965), *The Child, the Family and the Outside World* (1964), and *Playing and Reality* (1971).

Word association
A technique used in various *personality tests* whereby diagnostic conclusions are drawn from the subject's associative response to particular *stimulus* words provided by the

therapist. The experimental use of word association goes back to Galton's work in 1879 and Wundt's in 1880. Jung made use of the technique for the elucidation of *unconscious* processes and his theoretical work on the unconscious was in part derived from this early experimental work. Jung also used these 'complex indicators' as he called them to confirm his clinical findings. Freud acknowledged the value of this empirical validification of the concept of the unconscious. The word association technique is no longer used clinically.

JUNG, C. G. (ed.) (1969), *Studies in Word-association* (Routledge & Kegan Paul, London).

See also *Analytical psychology, Complex.*

Work group

A term introduced by W. R. Bion to describe one aspect of any small group which functions alongside its second aspect, called by Bion *basic assumption behaviour.* The work group aspect involves rational focus on the task to be accomplished. As Bion (1955) points out, the work group's activity is 'geared to a task, it is related to reality, its methods are rational and, therefore, in however embryonic form, scientific'. Its characteristics are therefore similar to those displayed by the *ego* in the individual and are congruent with the operation of the *reality principle* and of *secondary process.* Bion suggested that no small group can operate entirely in terms of its work group aspect and that, as with the individual, a group will be subject to regressive basic assumption behaviour to varying degrees. A group is most likely to be able to mobilise its work group aspect if its task is limited and clearly defined, if each member has a clear role to perform and if there are clear boundaries around time and resources.

BION, W. R. (1955), 'Group dynamics: a review' (in Klein, M. *et al., New Contributions to Psychoanalysis*, Maresfield Reprints, Karnac, London).
BION, W. R. (1961), *Experiences in Groups* (Tavistock, London).

See also *Tavistock group training.*

Working alliance
See *Therapeutic alliance.*

Working through
The process whereby the patient's *resistance* is overcome and he moves towards the experience of *insight* following a correct *interpretation* by the *therapist.* The term was introduced by Freud (1914) and is a central feature of, although not restricted to, the analytic therapies. The process of working through enables the patient to move from rejection of the interpretation or mere intellectual acceptance of it to an emotionally meaningful insight, the experience of which frees him to move towards change and development. It is the analytic activity 'par excellence' which leads to permanent change. Working through thus describes the period of time which elapses between the interpretation and its acceptance and further indicates the nature of the work involved, which is essentially that of the 'repetitive, progressive and elaborate explorations of the resistances which prevent an insight from leading to change' (Greenson 1967). The term is also used more widely to describe the efforts to develop a gradual acceptance of loss as in the process of *mourning.*

FREUD, S. (1914), 'Remembering, repeating and working through' (*Standard Edition*, vol. 12, Hogarth Press, London).
GREENSON, R. R. (1967), *The Technique and Practice of Psychoanalysis* (vol. 1, International Univ. Press, New York).
NOVERY, S. (1962), 'The principle of working through in psychoanalysis' (*J. of the Am. Psychoan. Assoc.*, vol. 10, pp. 658-76).

Wounded healer
Term used by Jung (1951) to describe the therapeutic potential of the therapist's own psychic pain and the way in which his vulnerability can be used in the service of the patient. The wounded physician is part healer and part sufferer. The patient is part sufferer and part

healer. By tacitly acknowledging his own vulnerability (the part of him which is potential patient), the physician allows the patient to mobilise the patient's own potential for healing and so be an active participant in the healing process and not merely a passive receiver. This two-way communication is referred to as the 'dialectical process', i.e. a form of dialogue. Jung's whole approach is opposed to the use of the detached authority of the therapist as expert. Instead, he emphasised that it is the therapist's 'own hurt that gives the measure of his power to heal'. The image of the wounded healer suggests too the inherent cost to the therapist of the practice of psychotherapy.

GUGGENBUHL-CRAIG, A. (1971), *Power in the Helping Professions* (Spring Publications, New York).

JUNG, C. G. (1951), 'Fundamental questions of psychotherapy' (*Collected Works*, vol. 15, Routledge & Kegan Paul, London).

KERENYI, C. (1959), *Askelepios: Archetypal Image of the Physician's Existence* (Bollingen, New York).

MEIER, C. A. (1967), *Ancient Incubation and Modern Psychotherapy* (North Western University Press, Evanston).

Y

Yavis

An acronym for the ideal patient: someone who is young, attractive, verbal, intelligent and successful. Schofield (1964) criticises the way in which psychotherapists tend to expend a disproportionate amount of time and energy on patients of this description rather than on those who are suffering from major psychopathology and who come from a low socio-economic grouping.

SCHOFIELD, W. (1964), *Psychotherapy: The Purchase of Friendship* (Prentice-Hall, Englewood Cliffs, New Jersey).

Z

Z-process attachment therapy

A therapeutic method introduced by Zaslow (1970, 1981) which uses a combination of *confrontation*, prolonged holding and verbal interviews to convert the patient's rage and frustration into constructive energy. Zaslow developed the approach for children and parents who have experienced bonding problems and where appropriate attachment and separation have not been achieved. Zaslow views all psychopathology as a disturbance of attachment which requires active methods rather than interpretative psychotherapy to overcome. Much of his thinking is based on Bowlby's *attachment theory*.

Zaslow suggests that the rage and grief of the detachment experience must be brought to an active state of protest to develop sufficient energy for attachment bonds to form. It is by holding a person in a state of face-to-face protest and resistance that positive attachments can be made and broken attachments repaired. The face is felt to be the major symbol for the creation of bonding and the need for close eye contact between therapist and patient is emphasised. Therapy consists in one or two preparatory interviews during which a history is taken and the therapy process described. Holding sessions involve one therapist for a small child and several for an adolescent or adult, holding different parts of the body. Tactile stimulation or tickling may be used to stimulate protest and resistance. During the holding process, the primary therapist asks the patient a series of questions regarding his age-appropriate behaviour, autonomy and identity. Each holding session is followed by a series of family or individual interviews to *work through* the issues that have been raised. The method is relatively new and has been used with behavioural and psychosomatic disorders and with psychosis.

ZASLOW, R. W. (1970), *Resistances to Growth and Attachment* (San Jose State University

Press, San Jose, Calif.).
ZASLOW, R. W. (1981), 'Z-process attachment therapy' (in Corsini R. J., *Handbook of Innovative Therapies*, Wiley, New York).
ZASLOW, R. W. and MENTA, M. (1977), *Rage, Resistance and Holding: Z-Process Approach* (San Jose State University Press, San Jose, Calif.).

Zen telegram
Free form designs combined with a few words which serve as spontaneous expressions of a patient's mood and feelings. The patient is asked to close his eyes and make some marks or design on a large sheet of paper. He is then asked to open his eyes and write down whatever words occur to him about the drawing. If used in group work, members are encouraged

to share their drawings with each other, talk about them and allow thoughts and associations to occur spontaneously. The technique can be used as a warm-up procedure in *group psychotherapy*.

REPS, P. (1959), *Zen Telegrams* (Tuttle, Rutland, Vermont).

See also *Squiggle game*.

Zootherapy
See *Pets (therapeutic use of)*.

Zurich school
Name given to the followers of C. G. Jung.

See also *Analytical psychology*, *Psychoanalysis*.